Using E
for Wi...
Special Edition

RON PERSON

Publisher: Lloyd J. Short

Acquisitions Manager: Rick Ranucci

Managing Editor: Paul Boger

Product Development Manager: Thomas H. Bennett

Book Designers: Scott Cook and Michele Laseau

Production Team: Claudia Bell, Scott Boucher, Michelle Cleary, Brook Farling, Denny Hager, Audra Hershman, Carrie Keesling, Betty Kish, Laurie Lee, Jay Lesandrini, Anne Owen, Juli Pavey, Joe Ramon, Caroline Roop, Kevin Spear, Johnna VanHoose, Lisa Wilson, Allan Wimmer, Phil Worthington, Christine Young

CREDITS

Product Director
Shelley O'Hara

Production Editor
H. Leigh Davis

Editors
Jo Anna Arnott
Tracy L. Barr
Fran Blauw
Kellie Currie
Kelly D. Dobbs
Donald R. Eamon
Jeannine Freudenberger
Frances R. Huber
Lori L. Lyons
Susan M. Shaw
Colleen Totz

Editorial Assistant
Melissa Keegan

Technical Editors
Reed Jacobson, a Microsoft Consulting Partner
Donald A. Buchanan, a Microsoft Consulting Partner

Composed in Cheltenham and MCPdigital by Que Corporation

Ron Person has written more than 12 books for Que Corporation, including *Using Windows 3.1*, Special Edition; *Using Word for Windows 2*, Special Edition; and *Windows 3.1 QuickStart*. Ron is the principal consultant for Ron Person & Co. He is a Microsoft Consulting Partner and has an M.S. in physics from The Ohio State University and an M.B.A. from Hardin-Simmons University.

Ron Person & Co., based in San Francisco, has attained Microsoft's highest rating for Microsoft Excel and Word for Windows consultants: Microsoft Consulting Partner. The firm helps corporations nationwide develop in-house programming and support expertise in the embedded macro languages found in Microsoft Excel, Word for Windows, and other major Windows applications. The firm's macro developer's courses have enabled many corporations to develop their own financial, marketing, and business-analysis systems in a minimum amount of time. If your company plans to develop applications using Microsoft's embedded macro languages, you will gain significantly from the courses taught by Ron Person & Co. For information on course content, on-site corporate classes, or consulting, contact Ron Person & Co. at the following address:

Ron Person & Co.
P.O. Box 5647
3 Quixote Court
Santa Rosa, CA 95409

(415) 989-7508   Voice
(707) 539-1525   Voice
(707) 538-1485   FAX

ACKNOWLEDGMENTS

The expertise, knowledge, and production that go into a book like *Using Excel 4 for Windows*, Special Edition, requires teams of talented people. I'd like to thank the people that made Microsoft Excel the most powerful Windows application available and thank the consultants and editors who helped communicate that power in this book.

Thanks to Microsoft Excel's development teams and marketing managers. Excel is an amazing combination of power, flexibility, and accessibility. Your energy and insight have redefined what a worksheet can do. Thanks also to Christie Gersiche, Matthew Crinklaw, and Kelli West for keeping us in touch and informed.

Thanks to the consultants and trainers who assisted in drafting and writing portions of *Using Excel 4 for Windows*, Special Edition. Their knowledge and assistance added to the value and timeliness of this book.

Reed Jacobson is a Microsoft Consulting Partner in Excel from Arlington, Washington. Reed does corporate consulting and training on Excel in the Pacific Northwest. Reed is an amazing source of tips and useful Excel knowledge. He wrote the section on the Analysis ToolPak and took on the Herculean effort of the technical edit of the book. Reed's scrutiny and tips from the frontlines of consulting added to the value of this book.

Steve Wexler, president of WexTech Systems, Inc., in New York, is a Microsoft Consulting Partner in Excel and Word for Windows. Steve's company does corporate consulting and training in Excel and Word for Windows. Steve drafted the ChartWizard Quick Start and portions of the section on customizing the toolbar.

Ricardo Dobson, an experienced Que author from Louisville, Kentucky, drafted sections of the book dealing with the Report Manager and Scenario Manager and wrote the section on running Lotus 1-2-3 macros in Excel. Ricardo is a highly qualified 1-2-3 consultant who is developing expertise in Excel.

Donald Buchanan, a Microsoft Consulting Partner in Excel from Burbank, California, did the technical edit on the chapter on the Solver and Analysis ToolPak.

Thanks to all of these consultants for their technical expertise. Although their technical prowess and scrutiny give this book a high level of confidence, the responsibility for any errors lies solely with me.

The skillful pens of our editors ensure that our books are consistent and easy to read. That they succeed in their jobs is evident by the comments of our corporate clients on the quality and value of Que books.

Shelley O'Hara, a Que best-selling author, also was the product development manager for this book. Shelley has been a valuable guide in writing and organizing *Using Excel 4 for Windows*, Special Edition. Her questions always point the book in a direction that makes it more valuable to the reader.

H. Leigh Davis, production editor, brought her editing talents to the high-pressure job of updating this book. She was quick, professional, and graceful under pressure. And thanks to Kelly Dobbs and Fran Huber for their art in words and their long hours over weekends.

Karen Rose, Bob Voss, and Wilma Thompson of Ron Person & Co. are gratefully acknowledged for their assistance during the author reviews.

TRADEMARK ACKNOWLEDGMENTS

Que Corporation has made every effort to supply trademark information about company names, products, and services mentioned in this book. Trademarks indicated below were derived from various sources. Que Corporation cannot attest to the accuracy of this information.

1-2-3, Lotus, Symphony, and VisiCalc are registered trademarks of Lotus Development Corporation.

Adobe Type Manager is a trademark and PostScript is a registered trademark of Adobe Systems, Inc.

Ami Professional is a trademark of SAMNA Corporation.

BrainCel is a registered trademark of Promised Land Technologies, Inc.

CompuServe is a registered trademark of H&R Block.

CorelDRAW! is a trademark of Corel Systems, Inc.

dBASE is a registered trademark and dBASE IV is a trademark of Ashton-Tate Corporation.

Hewlett-Packard, DeskJet, and LaserJet are registered trademarks of Hewlett-Packard Company.

IBM, PC, and PC DOS are registered trademarks and SQL is a trademark of International Business Machines Corporation.

Linotronic is a registered trademark and Helvetica, Times, and Palatino are registered trademarks of Linotype-Hell Co.

Microsoft, Microsoft Excel, Microsoft Mouse, MS-DOS, Microsoft Word, and PowerPoint are registered trademarks and Windows is a trademark of Microsoft Corporation.

Microsoft Paintbrush is a trademark of ZSoft Corporation.

Microsoft TrueType is a registered trademark of Apple Computer Corporation.

PageMaker is a registered trademark of Aldus Corporation.

Q+E is a trademark of Pioneer Software.

Quicken is a registered trademark of Intuit.

WordPerfect is a registered trademark of WordPerfect Corporation.

Trademarks of other products mentioned in this book are held by the companies producing them.

CONTENTS AT A GLANCE

IV Excel Databases

V Excel Macros

VI Advanced Techniques

Introduction

On May 22, 1990, a revolution occurred in the world of personal computers—Windows 3 was introduced. This new version of Windows created almost as much change in the use of computers as the introduction of IBM's first personal computer. By the introduction of Microsoft Excel 4, approximately 2 years later, more than 10 million copies of Windows have been sold.

During this time, major magazines and consultants have proclaimed Microsoft Excel as the easiest worksheet to use and yet the most powerful. With the introduction of Excel 4, no doubt remains that worksheets have a new standard: Microsoft Excel.

The eventual release of other Windows-based worksheets made Microsoft Excel's power and ease more obvious. Many corporations and professionals who had been safely inert by sticking with their old standards found that moving to a new standard was not only worthwhile but also demanded by many users. MIS departments were unable to meet the goals of downsizing applications and offloading responsibilities to user departments until they switched to more capable software, such as Windows, Excel, and Word for Windows. Users who saw the difference between old and new systems began to lobby within their departments for transition.

The new software, like Excel 4, enables decisive companies to make quantum leaps over competitors. The positive effects of leaping over competitors through innovation was documented in many industries. Now that Windows technology has passed the leading edge, companies that adapt quickly force their competitors into a never-ending race of catch-up.

The *bleeding edge* of the revolution has passed. Decisions based on the safety of inertia, by sticking with old standards, are without foundation. Consider the following points:

■ Every business computer sold now runs Windows and Windows software.

■ Windows programs, such as Microsoft Excel, Word for Windows, Ami Pro, Aldus PageMaker, and WordPerfect 5.1 for Windows, are compatible with older software and coexist with existing software found in your office.

■ Excel is fully compatible with Lotus 1-2-3, so offices don't need to worry about having a double-standard. Older systems can run 1-2-3 while systems purchased in the past few years gain the power of Windows and Excel. Excel's capability to read and write 1-2-3 files and formats, run 1-2-3 macros, and use 1-2-3 commands and navigation keys enables your company to make an easy transition to more power.

Reviewing Excel Features

The following sections present Excel's major strengths and capabilities. Features new to Excel 4.0 are indicated by the Version 4 icon in the margin.

Lotus 1-2-3 Capability

You don't need to worry about converting from 1-2-3 to Excel—the task is easy. Excel reads and writes all versions of 1-2-3 worksheets, including the formats. Excel even runs 1-2-3 Release 2.01 macros, so you can continue to use 1-2-3 macros. Excel also loads 1-2-3 charts and 3-D worksheets; you don't lose productivity, and you gain significantly more.

You can set up Excel to accept 1-2-3 navigation keys, database methods, or menu choices. When you use the 1-2-3 command demonstrator, Excel accepts 1-2-3 and then demonstrates how to perform the equivalent process in Excel. As you watch the Excel demonstration, you learn how to use the program. By using your 1-2-3 knowledge with new Excel worksheets, you can continue to perform productive work and learn Excel simultaneously.

Operating Ease

Excel is distinguished as the easiest-to-use and the most capable worksheet. This paradox is possible because of Excel's toolbar and shortcut menus.

Drag and drop is a concept so beneficial that, when you see it work, you wonder why it didn't become a standard many years ago. With drag and drop technology, you can select a group of cells, then use the mouse to drag the cells (or a copy of the cells) to a new location. When you release the mouse button, the cells drop onto the cells below the mouse pointer.

A concept similar to drag and drop is the *fill handle*. By dragging the fill handle, you can copy formulas into adjacent cells. The fill handle reduces a multiple-step process to a quick drag with the mouse.

Toolbars are strips or rectangles of tools (buttons). Each button represents a familiar command. By just clicking on a button, you can shortcut many keystrokes. When you use a mouse with the toolbars, you have quick access to the most frequently used commands in a worksheet. Microsoft Excel comes with nine toolbars, but you can add or remove additional tools from the toolbars and even create toolbars to which you can add tools you create.

Shortcut menus enable you to click the right mouse button on a worksheet or chart item; the most relevant commands appear immediately under the mouse pointer; and the commands you use most frequently are immediately accessible.

Worksheet Publishing

Excel is easily the leader in worksheet publishing capabilities. Besides having all the formatting capability of desktop publishing software, Excel is the first worksheet to include a built-in spelling checker. By using the spelling checker, you can feel confident that the quality of your analysis isn't impugned by poor spelling.

Layout and worksheet design also are easy in Excel, because Excel now includes a zoom feature. Zooming enables you to reduce or magnify the view of the worksheet so that you can see a close-up view to adjust formats or a compressed view to see the big picture. If you frequently view different areas of the document by using different display settings or print different areas with various print settings, you also may be interested in the new View Manager, which enables you to give different names to each view or printing setup.

The templates and cell styles available in Excel can help you greatly if you need to create a frequently used worksheet or a worksheet that presents a standardized appearance. Templates act as master documents that contain worksheet layouts, text, formulas, cell styles, custom menus, and macros. When opened, a template gives you a new worksheet that contains everything in the original template. You must save the document to a new name, which preserves the template as a master.

Styles are a powerful feature found in professional-level word processors. By using a style, you can name a collection of formatting commands and apply all the formats by selecting this style name. A style named Total, for example, may contain the formats Arial 12 point, bold, right align, currency with two decimal places, and a double-line upper border. Changing the definition of a style changes all cells formatted with this style.

Excel enables you to use the full capability of your printer. On a laser printer, for example, Excel can print up to 256 different fonts on a worksheet or chart, use up to 18 shades of gray, use a custom palette of 16 colors, and use numerous line and underline combinations.

If you need a numeric or date format that isn't on the list of formats, you can design custom formats. You also can add text in a format so that numbers include abbreviations, such as 5.678 Kph. You also can design formats so that numbers or dates within ranges appear in different colors.

Excel's printing preview capabilities show you how print is positioned on the page. You can zoom in to see the detail of character and drawing positions. While in the preview, you also can drag column and margin markers to reposition columns and change print margins.

Analytical Tools

Although Excel has always been known for offering more analytical tools than other worksheets, the additional analysis tools in Excel 4 make analysis easier for novice users and expand the upper limits for scientists, engineers, and financial analysts.

 Anyone who occasionally tests many different inputs and their results can easily appreciate the Scenario Manager. By using the Scenario Manager, you can name a set of input variables. After you have multiple names of inputs you want tested, you can run the Scenario Manager, which generates a report that shows all the different inputs and their results.

Some problems must be solved for an optimum solution. For these problems, Excel includes the Solver. The Solver is a free Excel add-in that uses linear and non-linear programming techniques to find the best solution to a problem.

Excel's hundreds of built-in functions, which are predefined formulas, have been expanded with the addition of the Analysis ToolPak. The Analysis ToolPak is another of Excel's free add-in programs. If your job requires extensive statistical or financial and investment analysis, install the Analysis ToolPak when you install Excel.

Graphics Features

You can perform many kinds of drawing on Excel worksheets. By using the drawing tools on the toolbars, you can draw lines, arrows, rectangles, ovals, circles, and arcs. You also can draw freehand and then reshape the freehand drawing by dragging lines and corners into new locations. You can create text boxes that you can position anywhere on the page. All the colors in the custom color palette and many shades of gray are available for emphasis. The graphic features are like getting a high-level drawing program as a free part of Excel.

You can embed charts or cell pictures in a worksheet. The cell pictures or charts can be taken from the same or a different worksheet. When you change data, the embedded charts or cell pictures update, which enables you to position pieces of worksheet or charts in any arrangement on a worksheet. You can arrange these pieces in the same way that a desktop publisher builds newsletters or annual reports.

With Object Linking and Embedding, OLE, which is now built into Excel, you can embed drawings and graphics from dedicated graphics programs. Embedded graphics are more than images in the worksheet; these images include the actual data necessary to recreate the graphic. Double-click on an embedded graphic, and a graphic program that can edit that graphic format opens and then loads the graphic. Many Windows programs now ship with free *applets*, which are miniature applications designed to work with embedded objects. One such applet, Microsoft Draw, comes free with some Windows programs from Microsoft and gives you extensive drawing capability from within Excel.

Linking and Consolidating Features

Excel is flexible enough to adapt to many business situations. Within Excel, you can link worksheets to fit the way you work. You can link cells or ranges of cells between open worksheets or worksheets on disk.

When you need to gather data from multiple divisions or different times into a single worksheet, use Excel's consolidation feature. Excel can consolidate data from Excel or 1-2-3 worksheets. By using one method, you can link worksheets according to the contents of cells in a specific location. All cells at the top-left corner of a range, for example, move together. One competing worksheet uses this method, but the feature is not flexible because all worksheets must be designed in exactly the same manner—a rare occurrence in the real world.

Excel's more flexible method uses the row and column labels to the left of and above the areas you want to consolidate. Excel examines the row and column name of each item in all the worksheets and works with the items that are identical. Items that are unique are given a unique position in the consolidation. This flexibility is helpful when some divisions or departments have different budget line times or different products.

When you work with collections of worksheets, macros, and charts, you begin to appreciate Excel's workbook feature. Workbooks are collections of files that you can bind together into a single file or leave as a collection of individual files. Workbooks include an actual table of contents to make moving between documents easy. While you work in a workbook, you can click on a page icon to turn to the next or previous document; or you can click in the table of contents to immediately display a document in the workbook.

Charting Capabilities

Excel has approximately one hundred chart formats from which to choose, but building a chart is extremely simple when you use Excel's ChartWizard. The ChartWizard guides you through the process of building charts. As you select alternatives, you can see the affect of the choices you make. At any time, you can back up and make an alternative selection. The ChartWizard doesn't limit your capability; Excel's nearly one hundred chart formats are available.

After you create a chart by using one of the available Excel formats, you can use all of Excel's charting tools. You can drag the legend to any position on the chart, orient text sideways, use up to 256 different fonts, and link numbers and text back to worksheet cells. Excel's charting capability rivals the capability of dedicated charting programs.

By using a chart as the data-entry device, Excel even enables you to solve worksheet problems. In line, bar, and column charts, you can drag a *chart marker* (line symbol or top of bar or column) to a new location. If the marker reflects the result of a formula in a worksheet, Excel asks you for the cell that you want to manipulate to accomplish the chart result you want. This feature provides a way to back into solutions and uses the chart to specify the final answer.

Database Capabilities

A database is like a card-file system that stores information. Because so many worksheet problems involve a collection of historical sales, marketing, engineering, or scientific information, Excel has built-in database capabilities. To enter and find information in a database, you only need to know the two commands, **D**ata Set Data**b**ase and **D**ata **F**orm.

If you need more database features or the capability of analyzing database contents, Excel still can help you. Excel enables you to statistically analyze database contents; you can find the average amount owed in all accounts receivable, for example, that are more than 30 days but less than 90 days overdue.

When you need to work with extremely large databases or databases stored on a mainframe computer or a local area network server, you may want to use Q+E, a program that comes with Excel. Q+E adds commands to Excel that enable you to link worksheets to large databases external to the worksheet.

Worksheet Outlines

Excel contains an outline, which is a feature valuable to anyone who must create extensive reports. The outline enables you to quickly expand and collapse databases and worksheets so that you see only the level of information you need to print or display on-screen.

Outlining also enables you to *drill down*. When you build a summary report by consolidating other worksheets, you have the choice of maintaining links from the source worksheets to the summary. When you double-click on a summary number in the consolidation worksheet, Excel drills down and opens the source worksheet.

Macro and Programming Language

You can easily customize Excel by recording commands and procedures and then assigning these commands and procedures to a shortcut key combination or to tool on a toolbar that you can select. You also can go far beyond the easy-to-use macro recorder, however.

Excel has an extensive built-in programming language so that experienced users can customize Excel's menus and dialog boxes, link Excel to other Windows programs, automate processes, control other Windows programs, and upload or download mainframe data by default.

If you are inexperienced with programming, you can use Excel's macro recorder to create automated procedures to save time. To run these procedures, you press a shortcut key, choose the macro name from a list, or click on a *hot-button* on the worksheet.

Although many other add-ins are available, Excel comes with Solver and Q+E, which are two powerful add-in products for more advanced users. Solver enables you to find the optimal solution to linear and nonlinear problems. To link Excel to databases on disk or on a mainframe, you may want to use Q+E. Q+E is a database query and edit program that runs as a stand-alone Windows program or as an intermediary that passes data-base information to Excel worksheets.

Because Excel is a Windows application, Excel works smoothly with many other Windows programs, You can manually copy data, charts, and graphics between Excel and other Windows applications, or you can link programs so that data is passed by default when you make changes.

Using This Book

Using Excel 4 for Windows, Special Edition, contains six parts. Parts II and III begin with Quick Starts, which are short but important tutorials that guide you through the most important concepts for creating a worksheet and creating a chart. Using the Quick Starts to learn the fundamentals is the quickest way to become productive. The following list presents an overview of the major parts in *Using Excel 4 for Windows*, Special Edition:

Part I, "Excel Installation," shows you how to install and run Excel. The chapters in this section introduce concepts that apply to all Windows programs.

Part II, "Excel Worksheets," shows you how to create, edit, format, and print worksheets. The chapters in this section include beginning topics, such as data entry, and also intermediate chapters on the many features and functions available in Excel. Chapter 5 tells 1-2-3 users how to learn Excel.

Part III, "Excel Charts," shows you how to create, format, and manipulate charts. The chapters in this section cover topics that range from basic charts, to charts embedded in worksheets, to advanced charting tricks.

Part IV, "Excel Databases," shows you how to create and maintain a data-base. The chapters in this section teach you how to enter, edit, sort, find, and extract information from a database. An advanced chapter also discusses how to analyze database contents.

Part V, "Excel Macros," shows you how to record and then modify simple macros to accept dialog box entries, ask for input, and check for validity. Other chapters explain how to build custom menus and dialog boxes and how to perform more advanced programming. A chapter of sample macros lists examples you can use and from which you can learn.

Part VI, "Advanced Techniques," shows you how to use Excel with other software, both DOS programs and Windows applications. The final chapter describes how to customize many Windows and Excel features.

The Appendix, "Support Services," shows you how to find other products that work well with Excel. The Appendix lists telephone hot-line support numbers, on-line public databases that give Windows and Excel support, and training and consulting companies.

Conventions Used in This Book

Certain conventions are used in *Using Excel 4 for Windows*, Special Edition, to help you more easily use this book and understand Excel's concepts.

Typefaces and Keystrokes

Words in all capital letters are used to distinguish DOS commands and file names from Excel features.

Shift+End indicates that you press the Shift key and hold it down while you also press the End key.

Italic type indicates text that the user must type.

Keyboard shortcuts for Excel commands are indicated in boldface by the letter(s) you must press, such as the Fo**r**mula **D**efine Name command.

A `special typeface` indicates on-screen prompts or directions you must follow or respond to.

Version 4 Icon

This book uses a special margin icon to indicate new Excel 4.0 features or tasks you can perform only in the current version. If the icon appears next to a section head, all the information in the following section is new.

Cross-References

Using Excel 4 for Windows, Special Edition, uses cross-references to help you access other parts of the book for related information. At the end of major topic sections, related tasks you may need to perform are listed by section name and page number.

From Here...

Consider this book a resource that you can consult when you need to look up advanced features, solve a unique situation, or troubleshoot a problem. Most of the learning, however, takes place at the computer. Your first step should be to find the worksheet and chart Quick Starts in the book, then reach for the mouse and keyboard.

To quickly become an adept user of Excel, set aside a few hours to work through each Quick Start. Although working your way through these Quick Starts probably won't take this long, you may become caught up in interesting experiments and side trips. The Quick Starts, which are like built-in tutors, have been used to train many students. Readers have praised the Quick Starts for efficiently presenting the most important Excel concepts.

Excel Installation

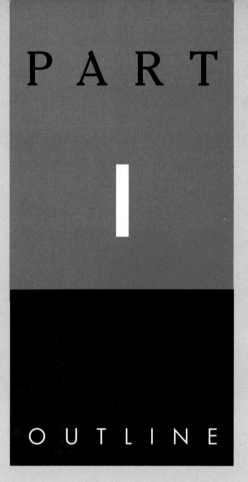

P A R T

1

O U T L I N E

Installing Excel

Learning Windows and Excel Basics

Installing Excel

E xcel is a leader in the new generation of software running under Windows. In this chapter, you learn to install and run Excel in Windows. In addition, you discover how to create special icons that start Excel by opening specific worksheets. The last section of this chapter helps you decide how to use the rest of this book the most effectively, as you learn about Excel's features.

Reviewing Hardware Requirements

To provide optimum performance for Excel, your computer should meet or exceed the following requirements:

- An Industry Standard Architecture (ISA) or Micro Channel Architecture (MCA) compatible computer with an 80286, 80386, or 80486 processor.

- IBM VGA, Extended Graphics Adapter, or other graphics cards and monitors that are compatible with Windows 3 or later version. The quality of display and the performance of Excel may vary significantly with the graphics card.

- A minimum of 2M of random-access memory for Excel for Windows. Performance will be significantly better with at least 4M of memory.

■ A hard disk with at least 5M of available storage. To install all options, a minimum of 10M is required.

■ At least one 360K, 1.2M, or 1.44M floppy-disk drive.

■ DOS 3.1 or later version with Windows 3 or later version.

In addition, Excel supports the following configurations:

■ A wide range of printers and plotters, including the Hewlett-Packard LaserJet and PostScript-compatible laser printers.

■ A mouse.

■ Extended memory, for increased memory and performance.

■ Math coprocessors (Intel 80287 and 80387), to decrease math recalculation time.

■ Personal computer networks supported by Windows 3 or later version.

If you are unfamiliar with the equipment you have, check your equipment manuals or the sales receipt. You also can consult the dealer or your corporate MIS hotline.

Installing Excel

Before you install Excel, you should have Windows 3.0 or later version installed and running. To learn how to install, operate, and enhance Windows 3.1, refer to the Que book, *Using Windows 3.1*, Special Edition.

To install Excel, perform the following steps:

1. Protect your original disks from accidental change. On 5 1/4-inch disks, place a write-protect tab over the square-cut notch on the edge. On 3 1/2-inch disks, slide the write-protect notch so that it is open.

2. Start Windows by typing *win* at the DOS prompt.

3. Insert the Setup disk into drive A, and close the drive door.

4. Open the Program Manager window, if it is not already open. (The Program Manager window contains program icons.) If the Program Manager is an *icon*, a small picture, at the bottom of the screen, move the tip of the mouse pointer onto the icon and double-click so that the icon expands into a window (see fig. 1.1).

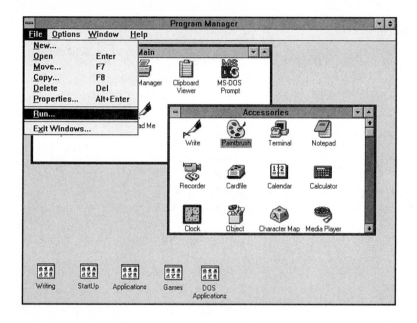

FIG. 1.1

The Program Manager window showing the File menu.

5. Choose the **File Run** command by clicking on the File menu and then selecting the Run command with the mouse pointer, or press Alt, F, and then R.

6. When the Run dialog box appears (see fig. 1.2), type the following command:

    a:setup

FIG. 1.2

The Run dialog box.

7. Press Enter.

8. Read and follow the directions that appear on-screen.

As you complete the installation process, you have the opportunity to make corrections or to quit and begin again. You can choose to install Excel and its associated programs and add-ins or only those files absolutely necessary for running Excel.

The installation program asks you to enter the path (disk and directory) in which you want Excel installed. The default is C:\Excel.*. Upgrading and file management will be easier if you install Excel in a directory directly off the hard-disk root. Installing Excel as a subdirectory under the Windows directory causes additional file management work. If you are upgrading an earlier version of Excel, the program asks whether the earlier version should be deleted.

You have the following four different options for installation:

- If you choose *Complete setup*, Excel and its additional programs are installed. Complete setup requires 10M of disk space.

- If you choose *Custom setup*, you have the opportunity to select which of the additional programs and sample files are installed. When you use a Custom setup, you can see how much free storage is available and what the storage requirements will be for each additional item you install.

- If you choose *Minimum setup*, only files necessary to run Excel are installed. Minimum setup requires 4.5M of memory.

- If you choose *Network Admin. setup*, the program helps you install Excel on a network server. Excel can be installed so that other users can run the program from the copy on the server or install their own copies from the server copy.

T I P You can install add-in programs and options at any time. If your requirements or available disk space changes, you can run the Excel setup program at any time by repeating this same process and choosing the Custom setup button. This flexibility enables you to install add-ins or options that you did not initially install.

During Custom installation, you can choose the Excel and ancillary programs that you want to install. Following is a list of the programs you can choose to install:

Excel and Ancillary Programs

Microsoft Excel	Worksheet, database, charts, macros, and add-in programs. Click on the Excel button and select the optional add-ins you need.
Microsoft Excel Tutorial	Guided Excel tutorial.
Dialog Editor	Custom dialog box drawing program used for macro programming.

Macro Translator	Converts Lotus 1-2-3 macros into Excel macros.
Example Files	Sample worksheets, charts, and macros helpful in learning.
Macro Library Files	Sample files and macros put into a LIBRARY directory.
Microsoft Excel Solver	Linear and nonlinear programming application that finds the optimal solution to worksheet problems.
Microsoft Analysis ToolPak	Additional business, statistical, and engineering functions.
Q+E	Enables Excel worksheets to link to disk-based network database and some mainframe database files.

Before you install Excel and ancillary programs by using Custom setup, be certain that you have enough available disk space for the selected programs. Look at the bottom of the dialog box for the required disk space; compare that space to the reported disk space. If enough space is not available, you have several options: select fewer ancillary programs to install, change the Excel directory to a disk with more space, or exit the installation process and erase files from the current disk. If you are installing Excel on the same disk as the Windows directory, be certain that a few megabytes are free after the Excel installation to be used by the Windows temporary swap files and the Print Manager.

During installation, you can enable 1-2-3 navigation keys and formula evaluations (Alternate Expression Evaluation). Enable this option only if you are a very experienced 1-2-3 user who must immediately be productive in Excel. If you are an average 1-2-3 user, you can learn Excel faster by turning on only the 1-2-3 command demonstration help described in Chapter 5. This option can be turned on from within the worksheet.

When installation is complete, you have the option of running Excel immediately or returning to Windows. When you return to windows, you will see a new group window in the Program Manager. This new window contains Excel and its related programs, as shown in figure 1.3. Chapter 2 describes how to start and exit Excel after it is installed.

If you choose to install Q+E, you can *hot-link* Excel worksheets to data on disk-based files or you can query databases from within Excel by using SQL (Structured Query Language). You can choose to link Excel with disk-based Excel databases; an SQL Server (Microsoft Server/ORACLE); dBASE II, III, IV; and ASCII files. You also can elect to start Q+E when Excel starts and limit Q+E so that it can query and extract from files but not update files.

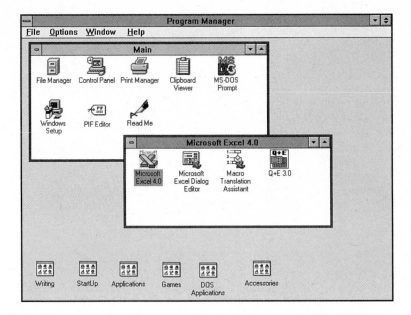

FIG. 1.3

The Microsoft Excel
group window.

Creating an Excel Work Group

You can create your own group window in which to place an icon that
starts Excel. In fact, you also can create an icon that starts Excel and
immediately loads a worksheet, chart, or macro sheet. This feature
enables you to have icons that match the specific jobs that you do.

If you are unfamiliar with how to choose commands and select options
from dialog boxes, read Chapter 2 before creating your own group
windows and program item icons.

To create a new group window in the Program Manager, perform the
following steps:

1. Activate the Program Manager window by clicking on it or by
   pressing Alt+Tab until it is the topmost window.

2. Choose the File menu and select the New command.

3. Select the Program Group option.

4. Choose OK or press Enter. The Program Group Properties dialog
   box appears (see fig. 1.4).

5. Select the Description box, and type the title you want for this
   group window: *Month End Tasks*, for example. The title appears in
   the bar at the top of the window. Do not type in the Group box.

6. Choose OK or press Enter.

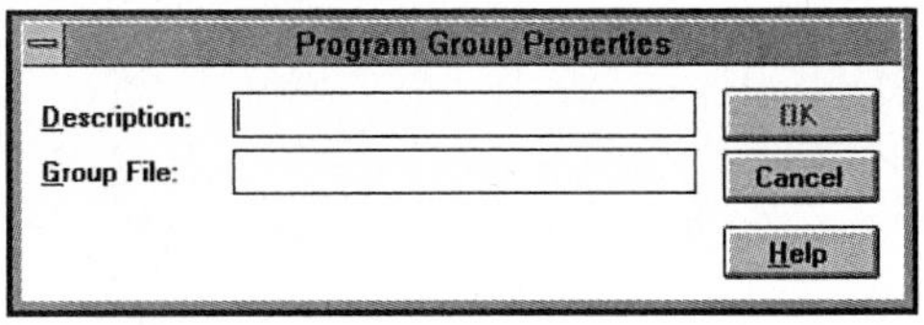

FIG. 1.4

The Program Group
Properties dialog box.

You do not need to create a new program item icon if you have one
for the same program in another group window. Consider copying
existing program icons. In the Program Manager, open the group window that contains the icon and the group window in which you want a
copy. Hold down the Ctrl key and drag the icon from one window into
the other, then release the mouse button. Change names or icon properties on the copied icon by selecting it and choosing the **File Properties** command.

T I P

To add a program item icon to the group window in Windows 3.1 that
starts Excel or another program of your choice, follow these steps:

1. Activate the group window in which you want to add the icon by
   clicking on it or by pressing Ctrl+F6 or Ctrl+Tab.

2. Choose the File menu and select the **New** command.

3. Select the Program **I**tem option from the New Program Object
   dialog box.

4. Choose OK or press Enter. The Program Item Properties dialog box
   appears (see fig. 1.5).

5. Select the **D**escription text box, and type the title you want to
   appear under the program item icon.

6. Select the **C**ommand Line text box.

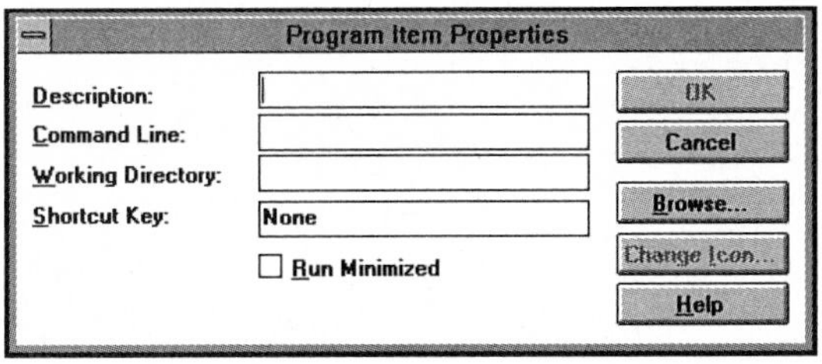

FIG. 1.5

The Program Item
Properties dialog box.

7. Choose the **B**rowse button to display the Browse dialog box (see fig. 1.6), from which you can choose a program name.

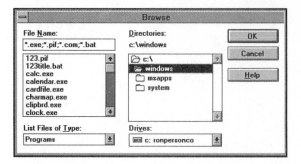

FIG. 1.6

The Browse
dialog box.

8. From the **D**irectories list, select the drive and directory in which the program is located, and then choose OK or press Enter.

9. Select from the File **N**ame list the file name of the program that you want the icon to start. Choose OK or press Enter.

   The program name and its directory appear in the **C**ommand Line of the Program Item Properties dialog box.

10. Modify the **C**ommand Line box of the Program Item Properties dialog box to start with a special file, without a startup worksheet, or with a read-only worksheet. These modifiers are listed later in this section.

11. Enter a startup directory in the **W**orking Directory edit box. This is the directory you will be in when Excel starts.

12. Choose OK or press Enter.

You can modify the **C**ommand Line to start Excel a specific way by using the following options:

Command Line	Result
C:\EXCEL\EXCEL.EXE C:\FINANCE\BDGT.XLS	Excel starts and loads the worksheet file BDGT.XLS.
C:\EXCEL\EXCEL.EXE /r C:\FINANCE\BDGT.XLS	Excel starts and loads the worksheet file BDGT.XLS as a read-only file.
C:\EXCEL\EXCEL.EXE /e	Excel starts but does not open the blank worksheet Sheet1.XLS.

If you want Excel to start when you start Windows 3.1, then hold down the Ctrl key and drag a copy of the Microsoft Excel 4.0 icon into the group window named StartUp.

T I P

Learning Excel

If you want to learn Excel as quickly as possible, use the following steps for using this book:

1. If you are a former Lotus 1-2-3 user, review Chapter 5 and learn how to use Excel's 1-2-3 help facility. By using this feature, you can use your 1-2-3 keystroke and command knowledge to work in Excel and learn Excel at the same time.

2. Work through the worksheet and chart Quick Starts in Chapters 3 and 17.

3. Skim through the chapters so that you are familiar with the available features.

4. Glance through the Table of Contents and the Index. Use the Index if you know the specific word that describes what you want. Use the Table of Contents to find general ideas.

For Related Information:

▶▶ "Getting Help with 1-2-3," p. 118.

▶▶ "Installing Q+E," p. 865.

FROM HERE...

Chapter Summary

After you install Excel, you may want to read Chapter 2 to learn techniques for operating Windows and then complete the worksheet Quick Start in Chapter 3. If you are a 1-2-3 user, you definitely should read Chapter 5, "Making the Switch from 1-2-3 to Excel." From there, you can skip to the worksheet and chart Quick Starts.

After you complete the Quick Starts, you will have a good foundation for understanding the other chapters in the book.

Learning Windows and Excel Basics

T his chapter is the place to start if you are not familiar with Microsoft Windows or Microsoft Excel. You will use the ideas and concepts that you learn here in all your Excel operations. In fact, what you learn in your first Windows application will carry over to other Windows applications.

You learn to control Excel's menus and dialog boxes and the windows that contain Excel and its worksheets, charts, and macro documents. By the end of this chapter, you should be able to choose commands from menus, select options from dialog boxes, and manipulate windows on-screen. You need to know how to choose from menus and to select options in dialog boxes to run the application. Beyond these basic tasks, you should be able to organize windows so that you can access and use multiple worksheets at once or to clear off your desktop so that you can concentrate on one job.

Starting Windows and Excel

To activate Excel, follow these steps:

1. Start Windows by typing *win* and pressing Enter.

2. Activate the group window that contains Excel. This will be the Microsoft Excel 4 group or a group in which an Excel application item icon has been created. Figure 2.1 shows the Microsoft Excel group window and the Microsoft Excel application item icon within.

Activate the group window by clicking on the window or double-clicking the window's icon. From the keyboard, press Ctrl+Tab until the desired group window is active or until the title of the group icon is highlighted. Press Enter to restore the selected icon into a window.

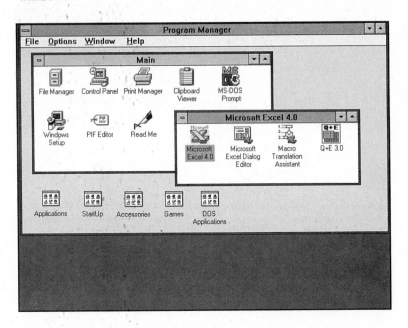

To start the Excel application, perform the following steps:

1. Double-click the Excel application item icon.

2. Press the arrow keys until the title of the Excel application item icon is highlighted, and then press Enter.

You also can start Excel by choosing a worksheet, chart, or macro file from the File Manager. To start Excel and load the document, double-click on the file name for an Excel document, or select the file name and press Enter. If this procedure does not work, check to see whether the PATH command in the AUTOEXEC.BAT file gives the directory where the EXCEL.EXE file is located. If this procedure still does not work, you may need to *associate* Excel files with Excel. The **File Associate** command in the File Manager associates a data file extension with a specific application. The association process is described in the Windows manual and in *Using Windows 3.1,* Special Edition, from Que.

Understanding a Windows Screen

One advantage of Windows applications is the capability to run several applications and display them on-screen simultaneously. Chapters 31 and 32 describe how to run Excel and other Windows or DOS applications together and transfer on-screen information among them. This capability can save you time when you transfer numbers into or out of Excel, transfer charts to graphics programs for further enhancements, create automatically updated links between Excel worksheets and Windows applications, or embed Excel data into other Window application documents.

Each Windows application, such as Excel, runs in its own application window. Because some application windows can contain multiple document windows, you can work simultaneously with more than one worksheet, chart, or macro sheet. Figure 2.2 shows the Excel application window with a worksheet and a chart document window inside.

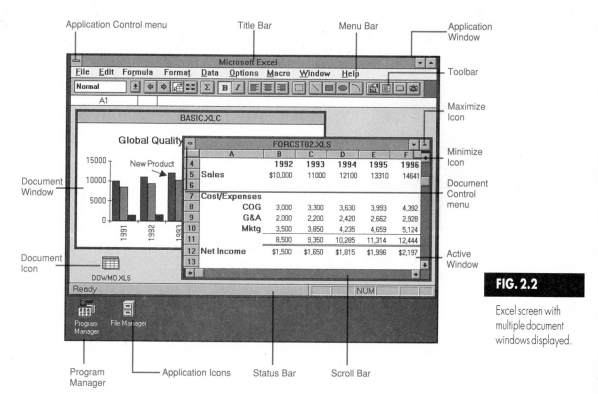

FIG. 2.2

Excel screen with multiple document windows displayed.

Table 2.1 lists and describes the parts of an Excel screen.

Table 2.1. Parts of an Excel Screen

Part	Description
Application window	The window within which Excel runs.
Application icon	The icon of a running application.
Document window	The window within which worksheets, macro sheets, and charts are displayed.
Document icon	The icon of a worksheet within the application window.
Application Control menu	The menu that enables you to manipulate the application window.
Document Control menu	The menu that enables you to manipulate the active (top) document window.
Active window	The window that accepts entries and commands; this window is shown with a solid title bar and is normally the top window.
Mouse pointer	The on-screen arrow, cross, or I-beam that indicates the current location affected by your mouse actions.
Title bar	The bar at the top of an application or document window.
Toolbar	A bar containing tools (buttons) that, when chosen with the mouse pointer, produce a function or action.
Menu bar	A list of menu names displayed below the title bar of an application.
Menu	A pull-down list of commands.
Command	A function or action chosen from a pull-down menu.
Minimize icon	A down arrowhead at the right of a title bar that stores an application as an application icon at the bottom of the screen; equivalent to the application Control Minimize command.

Part	Description
Maximize icon	An up arrowhead at the right of a title bar that fills available space with the document or application; equivalent to the Control Maximize command.
Restore icon	A double arrowhead at the right of a title bar that restores an application or document into a sizable window; equivalent to the Control **R**estore command.
Scroll bar	A gray horizontal and vertical bar that enables the mouse to scroll the screen; a scroll box in the bar shows the current display's position relative to the entire document.
Split window icons	Dark bars at the end of the scroll bar that you can drag across the scroll bar to split a window into two views of the same document.
Status Bar	A bar at the bottom of the screen that explains the selected command or that prompts you with guidance.

Using the Mouse

The mouse is an optional piece of hardware that attaches to your PC and enables you to move the on-screen pointer as you move the mouse with your hand. In Excel, you can control the program with mouse movements or with keystrokes. Some Excel actions, such as drawing graphical objects, require the use of a mouse; other actions, such as manipulating charts, are significantly easier when you use a mouse. Basic worksheet and database features are all accessible through the use of the keyboard. You will find that combining mouse actions, touch-typing, and shortcut keys is the most productive way to work.

Moving the Mouse

The mouse, shown in figure 2.3, is a small hand-held device that lies on your desktop and fits comfortably under your palm. As you move the mouse across your desk, the *mouse pointer*, a shape on-screen, moves in the same relative direction across the screen. You will find that using the mouse to *point* at an item on the screen with the mouse pointer becomes a natural process. The mouse is especially useful for selecting large cell areas, copying and pasting cells, exploring menus, changing the sizes and locations of windows, moving objects on charts, and drawing.

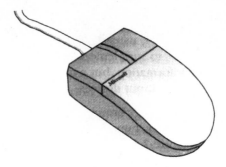

FIG. 2.3

A Microsoft mouse.

Hold the mouse so that the wire projects forward, away from your arm, and the buttons are under your fingers. A mouse can have two or three buttons; Excel, however, uses only the left and right buttons.

T I P   If you are left-handed, you can run the Mouse program and switch the left and right mouse button controls. To find the Mouse program, start the Control Panel from the Main group window of the Program Manager.

As you move the mouse pointer on-screen, the mouse may run out of clear space on your desk. This does not mean that you need a larger desk or that you need to shovel away the work that has stacked up. Instead, when the mouse collides with something, pick up the mouse, move it to a clear area, put it down, and continue the motion. Usually, about one square foot of clear desk space gives you enough room to control the mouse.

Understanding the Mouse Pointer

The mouse pointer changes appearance depending on its location. You usually see the mouse pointer as an arrow when it is in the menus or as a thick cross when it is in the worksheet. When located over an area of text that can be edited, the pointer appears as an I-beam. When you use the mouse pointer for drawing graphical objects or embedding objects on a worksheet, its shape changes to a cross hair (a thin cross). Each shape signals to you what action you can perform at that location. Table 2.2 shows and explains the different shapes of the pointer.

Table 2.2. Mouse Pointer Shapes

Pointer Shape	Locations	Use
▱	Menu, scroll bar, toolbar	Select by moving the tip of the arrow onto a name or icon and then clicking the mouse button.
I	Text boxes, Formula Bar	Repositions the flashing cursor (insertion point) within editable text. To move the insertion point location, move the I-beam to the location in the text and then click.
+	Appears during placement, resizing, or drawing of objects	Choose object placement command and drag across sheet, or move to square handle on object and drag to resize.
↔	Appears between column headings or on window edge	Drag to change column width or position of window edge.
↕	Appears between row headings or on window edge	Drag to change row height or position of window edge.
◪	Window corners	Drag to reposition two window edges at one time.
✛	Inside worksheet	Click to select cells in worksheet.
⬌	Split bar at ends of scroll bar	Drag to split window into two views.
Q	Print Preview	Select document area for closer view.
☝	Help window, macro buttons	Click for help or to run macro.
⊠	Any screen	Means "Please wait."

Understanding Windows and Excel Terms

All Windows applications, including Excel, require the same keyboard and mouse actions to select what is changed on-screen or to give commands. By learning the actions named in table 2.3, you will learn how to operate menus and to select items within any Windows application.

Table 2.3. Windows and Excel Actions	
Action	**Description**
Select	Highlight or mark a menu name, command, dialog box option, cell location, or graphical object with the keyboard or with mouse actions.
Choose	Execute and complete a command.

Mouse Actions

Mouse techniques are simple to learn and to remember. These techniques make using Excel much easier. In fact, for such work as charting, drawing, and embedding objects, the mouse is nearly indispensable. Table 2.4 describes the mouse actions that you use in carrying out Excel operations.

T I P Some mouse actions have a different effect when you hold down the Shift or Ctrl key as you click, double-click, or drag with the mouse. As a general rule, holding down the Shift key as you click selects text or cells between the current location and the location where you Shift+click. Holding down the Ctrl key as you drag across nonadjacent areas enables you to select areas that are not contiguous. With this method, you can format multiple areas with one command.

Table 2.4. Mouse Actions

Action	Description
Click	Place the tip of the mouse pointer or the lower portion of the I-beam pointer at the desired location and then quickly press the left mouse button *once*. This action selects a menu, command, cell, or graphical object so that you can work with it; this action also places the insertion point in text boxes and formula bars.
Right Click	Position the tip of the mouse pointer in the desired location on a worksheet, chart, or toolbar and then click the right mouse button. This action displays a menu appropriate to the item on which you clicked.
Double-click	Position the tip of the mouse pointer or the lower portion of the I-beam pointer at the desired location and then quickly press the left mouse button *twice*. This action is usually a shortcut for selecting and changing the item you click.
Drag	Position the tip of the mouse pointer, center of the cross hair, or the lower portion of the I-beam on an item; then hold down the left mouse button as you move the mouse pointer. This action selects multiple items, cells, or text characters or moves graphical objects.

Keyboard Actions

The keyboard is most useful for entering text and numbers, performing fast operations with shortcut keys, and operating with portable or laptop computers that don't have a mouse. Don't forget, however, that the best way of operating Excel and other Windows applications is through the combined use of mouse and keyboard. Table 2.5 lists and describes the keyboard actions that you will use in Excel.

Table 2.5. Keyboard Actions

Action	Description
Type	Type, but do not press the Enter key.
Enter	Type and then press the Enter key.
Alt	Press the Alt key.
Alt, letter	Press the Alt key, release it, and then press the underlined letter or number shown. The active letters that appear underlined on-screen appear in bold print in this book.
Letter	Press only the underlined letter shown in the menu, command, or option.
Alt+letter	Hold down the Alt key as you press the under-lined letter.
Alt, hyphen	Press the Alt key, release it, and then press the hyphen key.
Alt, space bar	Press the Alt key, release it, and then press the space bar.
Tab	Press the Tab key.
Esc	Press the Esc key

Throughout this book, you see combinations of keys indicated with a plus sign (+), such as Alt+**F**. This combination means that you must hold down the Alt key while you press **F**. After pressing **F**, release both keys. (This book shows capital letters, as with the F, but you don't need to hold down the Shift key unless indicated.)

Keystrokes that appear separated by commas should be pressed in sequence. Alt, space bar, for example, is accomplished by pressing and releasing Alt and then pressing the space bar.

If you have a mouse, try using both mouse actions and keystrokes to perform commands and tasks. The exercises in the Quick Starts in this book provide instructions for using both methods. You soon will find that the keyboard works well for some commands and features and that the mouse works well for others. A combination of mouse and keyboard usually is the most efficient. The Quick Reference card bound inside the back cover of this book shows both keyboard and mouse shortcut methods.

The keyboard also is useful for many shortcut keys. These shortcut keys are listed in the appropriate areas throughout this book.

The 12 function keys give you a shortcut method of choosing commands that you normally choose from a menu. Some function keys use other keys in combination. When two or more keys are listed with a plus sign, hold down the first key(s) as you press the second key. Table 2.6 lists the function keys and their equivalent menu commands.

Table 2.6. Function Keys and Menu Command Equivalents

Excel Application Window Function Keys	Menu Command
Alt+F4	Close

Excel Document Window Function Keys	Menu Command
Ctrl+F4	Close
Ctrl+F5	Restore
Ctrl+F6	Next Document Window
Ctrl+F7	Move
Ctrl+F8	Size
Ctrl+F9	Minimize
Ctrl+F10	Maximize

Excel Menu Commands Function Keys	Menu Command
F1	Help
Shift+F1	Context Choosing Help
F2	Activate Formula Bar
Shift+F2	Formula Note
Ctrl+F2	Window Show Info
F3	Formula Paste Name
Shift+F3	Formula Paste Function
Ctrl+F3	Formula Define Name
Ctrl+Shift+F3	Formula Create Names
F4	Formula Reference
Ctrl+F4	Control Close (document window)
Alt+F4	File Exit

continues

Table 2.6. Continued

Excel Menu Commands Function Keys	Menu Command
F5	Formula Goto
Shift+F5	Formula Find (cell contents)
Ctrl+F5	Control Restore (document window)
F6	Next Pane
Shift+F6	Previous Pane
Ctrl+F6	Control Next Window
Ctrl+Shift+F6	Previous Document Window
F7	Formula Find (next cell)
Shift+F7	Formula Find (preceding cell)
Ctrl+F7	Control Move (document window)
F8	Extend Mode (toggles on/off)
Shift+F8	Add Mode (toggles on/off)
Ctrl+F8	Control Size (document window)
F9	Options Calculate Now
Shift+F9	Options Calculate Document
F10	Activate Menu Bar
Shift+F10	Display Shortcut Menu
Ctrl+F10	Control Maximize (document window)
F11	File New (chart)
Shift+F11	File New (worksheet)
Ctrl+F11	File New (macro sheet)
F12	File Save As
Shift+F12	File Save
Ctrl+F12	File Open
Ctrl+Shift+F12	File Print

Notice that key combinations are listed on the right side of some pull-down menus. These key combinations execute the command immediately, without going through the menu and menu item. Instead of choosing the **E**dit **C**lear command, for example, you can press Del to clear a cell or group of cells.

If you are working in Excel and forget a function key or shortcut key combination, choose the **H**elp **C**ontents command, and then, under the Reference section, choose the Keyboard Guide topic for keyboard listings and shortcuts.

For Related Information:

▶▶ "Customizing the Mouse," p. 1076.

FROM HERE...

Choosing Commands

Excel uses the same menu-selection methods used by all Windows applications. The various methods you can use to choose commands from Excel menus illustrate the application's versatility. You can control commands with the mouse, keystrokes, directional keys, or shortcut keys. With Excel, you can learn easier methods first and then graduate to methods that best fit your work style and the function you want to perform. You often can mix your methods of menu selection by starting with one method and finishing with another.

> You cannot use a shortcut key while a menu is pulled down or a dialog box is displayed.
>
> **T I P**

When choosing a command by mouse or keyboard, you first pull down the menu and then choose the command. Figure 2.4 shows a menu pulled down.

Notice that some commands in a menu may be gray. These commands are unavailable at that current point in Excel operation. Commands that are grayed may be inappropriate for the current situation or may require that another procedure be accomplished first; for example, you need to perform **E**dit Cu**t** or **E**dit **C**opy before **E**dit **P**aste becomes available.

Commands in the menu that are followed by an ellipsis (...) need more information from you before they execute. These commands display dialog boxes that ask you for more information.

NOTE In some applications, you cannot explore new territory and then escape easily when you need to. In Excel, however, you can. You can back out of any pull-down menu or dialog box by pressing Esc. If you are using a mouse, you can back out of a menu by clicking on the menu name a second time or by clicking on the Cancel button in a dialog box.

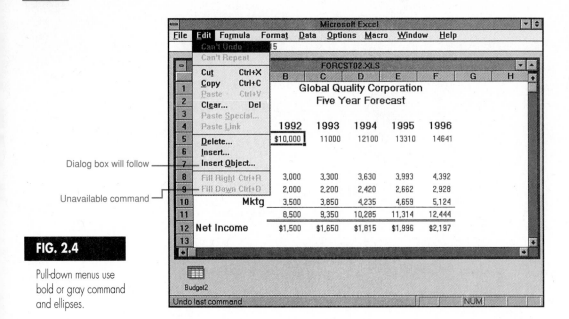

Dialog box will follow

Unavailable command

FIG. 2.4

Pull-down menus use bold or gray command and ellipses.

Choosing Commands with the Mouse

Most people prefer to learn Windows applications with the mouse. As your familiarity and confidence increase, you can add or replace mouse operations with keyboard operations.

Follow these two steps if you know the command that you want to execute:

1. Click on the menu name.

   You do not need to hold down the mouse button to keep the menu pulled down. It stays down by itself.

2. Click on the command name.

If you are unfamiliar with a menu or command, you can see a prompt that describes the action the command performs. To see a description of a command, follow these steps:

1. Click on the menu name.

2. Hold down the mouse button.

3. Continue holding down the button as you drag down to a command.

4. Continue holding down the button as you read the command's description in the Status Bar at the bottom of the screen.

5. To complete the command, release the mouse button while the pointer tip is on the command. If you do not want to use the command, slide the pointer off the menu and then release the mouse button.

If you need to find a command, but do not know in which menu it is located, you can read adjacent menus without selecting a command. Click on one menu name, hold down the mouse button, and drag across to other menu names. Click a second time on a menu name to remove the pull-down menu.

Choosing Commands from Shortcut Menus

You can save yourself time by using shortcut menus. Shortcut menus display the most frequently used commands that relate to a selected item or object.

To display a shortcut menu, click with the right mouse button on the item or object for which you need a shortcut menu. If you are using a keyboard, select the item and then press Shift+F10.

Some areas on the toolbar do not respond to a right click. A right-click on a drop-down list in a toolbar, such as the Style or Fonts list, will not display the toolbar shortcut menu. To display the toolbar shortcut menu, use a right-click over a tool's button or over the toolbar background.

T I P

Shortcut menus appear under the mouse pointer or at the top left, if activated by keyboard. Select a command by clicking on it or by pressing the up-or down-arrow key and then pressing Enter. To remove a shortcut menu, click outside the menu or press the Esc key.

The following figures show a few shortcut menus, and the captions indicate the items with which the menus appear.

FIG. 2.5

Cell or range
shortcut menu.

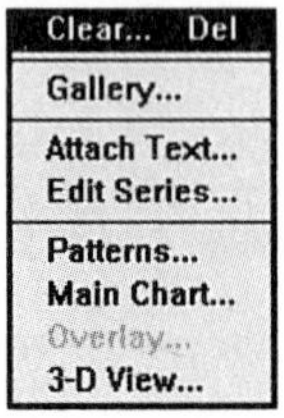

FIG. 2.6

Chart marker
shortcut menu.

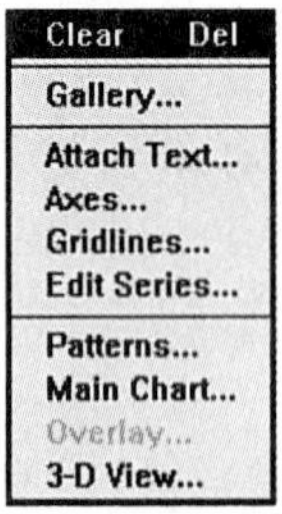

FIG. 2.7

Chart axis
shortcut menu.

FIG. 2.8

Toolbar shortcut menu.

Choosing Commands with the Keyboard

When you are familiar with the Excel menus, you can perform the following steps to touch-type commands:

1. Press Alt to select the menu bar.

2. Press the underlined letter in the menu name; for example, press **F** for **F**ile. The menu pulls down.

3. Press the underlined letter in the command name; for example, press **O** for **O**pen.

You do not need to wait for the menu to appear when you touch-type commands.

If you are not familiar with the Excel menu structure, you can choose commands by looking for them and reading an explanation about them. Perform the following steps:

1. Press Alt to select the menu bar.

2. Press the right- or left-arrow key to highlight the menu name. Notice that the Status Bar at the bottom of the screen explains the menu's function.

3. Press Enter to display the selected menu.

4. Press the up- or down-arrow key to select (highlight) a command. Read the Status Bar at the bottom of the screen for an explanation of each command.

5. Press the right- or left-arrow key to move from one menu to another.

6. Select the command that you want and then press Enter; or you can press Esc to back out without selecting.

While a command is selected in step 6, notice that you can read a description of the command's action from the Status Bar at the bottom of the Excel window.

Choosing Alternative Commands with Shift

You can choose alternative commands from some menus and with a few tools on toolbars. To display these additional commands, hold down the Shift key while you choose the menu or toolbar. The following table lists normal commands and shifted commands:

Normal Command	Shift Command
File Close	File Close All
Edit Copy	Edit Copy Picture
Edit Paste	Edit Paste Picture
Edit Paste Link	Edit Paste Picture Link
Edit Fill Right	Edit Fill Left (h)
Edit Fill Down	Edit Fill Up (w)

Selecting Options from Dialog Boxes

One reason that Windows applications are easier to operate than most DOS programs is that Windows applications do not have the 10 or 12 layers of menus that some DOS programs have. Menus are one layer deep. If more information is needed after a command is chosen, a dialog box appears. Dialog boxes enable you to select options, enter data, and control how a command operates.

A dialog box displays all available options in one view. Both beginners and advanced users have an opportunity to see all the features available.

In the pull-down menus, commands that require additional information are followed by an ellipsis (...). Choosing one of these commands displays a dialog box in which you enter needed information. The Format Alignment... command, for example, results in the dialog box shown in figure 2.9.

FIG. 2.9

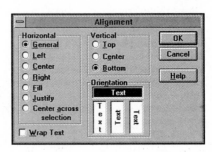

The Format Alignment dialog box.

Dialog boxes contain different types of items. These items are described in more detail in the sections immediately following. To familiarize yourself with Excel dialog box items, read the following list:

- *Text box.* A box in which you can type and edit text or numbers.

- *Option button.* A button that gives you one choice from a group of options.

- *Check box.* A square box that can be turned on or off.

- *List boxes.* A list or pull-down list that scrolls to display available alternatives.

- *Command buttons.* Buttons that complete or cancel the command; some buttons give you access to additional options.

To select options in a dialog box, perform the following steps:

With a mouse, move the pointer tip onto the option button, check box, text box, or item in a scrolling list; then click.

From the keyboard, press Alt+*letter*, where *letter* is the underlined letter in the name of the edit box, check box, or group of options you want. Move to the selection in a list or move between option buttons by pressing an arrow key.

To complete a command from a dialog box, perform the following steps:

Click on the OK command button, or double-click on the desired item in a list box.

Press Enter to select the default button (with the heavy border); or Tab until a dashed line appears around OK, and then press the space bar.

To back out of a dialog box, perform the following steps:

Click on the Cancel button.

Press the Esc key.

Some dialog boxes include command buttons in addition to OK or Cancel. To choose command buttons, click on the button or press the Tab key until the button is selected and then press Enter or space bar.

Selecting Option Buttons and Check Boxes

Figure 2.10 shows check boxes and a group of option buttons. You can select only one option button from within a group, but you can select one or more check boxes.

FIG. 2.10

A dialog box with
option buttons and
check boxes.

To select an option button with the mouse, click on the button. To clear
an option button, you must click on another in the same group. A dot
within the option indicates that the option is on. Remember that you can
select only one button in a group.

To select an option button from the keyboard, hold down the Alt key and
then press the underlined letter of the option group you want. Alternatively, press Tab until an option in the group is enclosed by dashed
lines. After you select the group, press the arrow keys to select the option button that you want from within the group.

Check boxes are square boxes that you can turn on or off and use in
combination with other check boxes. A check box is on when an X appears in the box.

To select or deselect a check box, click on the check box that you want
to change. From the keyboard, press Alt+*letter* where *letter* is the underlined letter in the name of the check box.

T I P   When you are making a succession of changes in a dialog box, pressing the Tab key is probably the easiest way to move between items in
the box. (Shift+Tab moves in the reverse direction.) The active item is
enclosed in a dashed line or contains the flashing insertion point for
text editing. To change a check box that is enclosed by the dashed
line, press the space bar. To change an option button in a group enclosed by the dashed line, press the arrow keys.

Editing Text Boxes

You use text boxes to type information, such as file names and numbers, into a dialog box. You can edit the text within a text box the same way you edit text elsewhere in Excel.

When the mouse pointer is over a text box, it appears in the shape of a capital I, which is known as an I-beam. The actual location where typing will appear is indicated by a flashing vertical bar, as shown in figure 2.11.

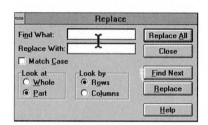

FIG. 2.11

The Formula Replace text box.

The following instructions explain how to select a text box:

> Move the mouse pointer over the box. Notice that the pointer changes to an I-beam. Position the I-beam where you want the insertion point (cursor) to appear in the text and then click. Move the I-beam away to see the insertion point in the text.

> Press the Alt+*letter* combination for the text box or press Tab until the text box is selected. Type to replace all the selected (highlighted) text. You also can press the left- or right-arrow keys to move the flashing insertion point and then type the text you want to insert.

Delete characters to the right of the flashing insertion point by pressing the Del key. Delete characters to the left of the insertion point by pressing the Backspace key.

To select multiple characters so that you can delete or replace them by typing, perform these actions:

Select	Keyboard Action
Multiple letters	Shift+arrow
Words	Shift+Ctrl+arrow
To the beginning of current line	Shift+Home

Select	Keyboard Action
To the end of current line	Shift+End
Active cell to A1	Shift+Ctrl+Home
Active cell to last document cell	Shift+Ctrl+End

Select	Mouse Action
Multiple letters	Drag across letters
Word	Double-click on word
Words or formula terms	Double-click on word; then drag

Selecting from List Boxes

In some cases, Excel has multiple alternatives from which to choose. The Format **F**ont dialog box, for example, shows you lists of fonts and sizes (see fig. 2.12).

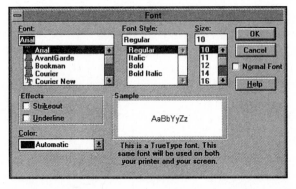

FIG. 2.12

Forma**t F**ont list boxes.

Some list boxes show only the current selection in what appears to be a text box. To see the entire list of alternatives, you must pull down the list. Figures 2.13 and 2.14 show the Forma**t P**atterns dialog box before and after the Patterns list has been pulled down.

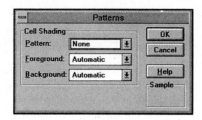

FIG. 2.13

The Patterns dialog box with the **P**attern list up.

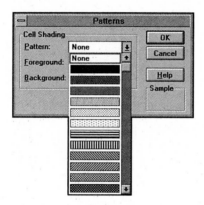

FIG. 2.14

The Patterns dialog box with the **P**attern list down.

Perform the following steps to select an item from a list box:

1. If the list is not displayed, click on the down arrow to the side of the list or activate the list box by pressing Alt+*underlined letter*. If you are using the keyboard and the box is a pull-down list box, press Alt+down-arrow key.

2. When the list is displayed, click on the arrowheads in the scroll bar to scroll to the name you want. Alternatively, scroll to the name you want by pressing the up-arrow key, down-arrow key, Home key, End key, or the first letter of the name.

3. Click on the name in the list that you want.

4. Click on OK if you are in a dialog box or press Enter to complete the command.

In most dialog boxes, you can double-click on a name in a list box to select the name and choose OK in one operation. (You cannot double-click on a name in a pull-down list box.)

 NOTE   Before you select a command button such as OK, make sure that the name you want to select from the list box is selected (highlighted), not just surrounded by a dashed line.

T   I   P You can find names in a list box quickly because they appear in alphabetical order. Select the box by clicking in it once or by pressing Alt+down-arrow key. Then press the first letter of the name for which you are searching. The list will scroll to the first name beginning with that letter. You also can scroll with the up- and down-arrow keys and with the Home, End, or PgUp and PgDn keys.

Choosing Command Buttons

Command buttons usually appear at the upper-right corner or down the right side of dialog boxes. You usually use these buttons to execute or cancel a command. Occasionally, as figure 2.15 shows, command buttons give you other options for executing a command, such as expanding a dialog box, *tunneling through* to another dialog box, or executing the command but keeping the dialog box open. Choosing the **Gallery** 3-**D** **Co**lumn command, for example, displays a dialog box that shows predefined 3-D column charts. The box also contains buttons that you can use to tunnel through to other types of predefined charts.

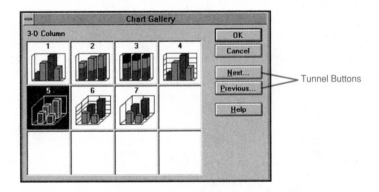

FIG. 2.15

The Gallery 3-D dialog box.

The right side of the dialog box in figure 2.15 contains the command buttons OK, Cancel, **Next**, and **Previous**. OK always executes the command and closes the dialog box. Cancel removes the dialog box without executing the command.

With the mouse, you can choose a command button by clicking on it. From the keyboard, you can choose a command button in three different ways. If the command button contains an underlined letter, press

Alt+*underlined letter*. If a button is bold, press Enter to choose the button. Choose Cancel by pressing Esc. You can select any command button by pressing Tab until the button name is enclosed in dashed lines and then pressing Enter.

Using the Toolbars

The toolbars in Excel give you quick access to frequently used commands and procedures. To use a tool on a toolbar, click on the tool that represents the command or procedure you need. You decide which toolbars are displayed and where they appear on-screen. Toolbars are always accessible because they float above worksheets.

In Excel, you can display and work with more than one toolbar at a time. Excel has nine predefined toolbars, described in the following list.

- *Standard toolbar*. The Standard toolbar contains the tools most frequently used for formatting, file handling and printing (see fig. 2.16).

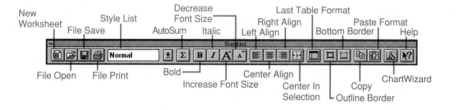

FIG. 2.16

The Standard toolbar.

- *Formatting toolbar*. The formatting toolbar contains tools used for formatting fonts, setting alignment, applying numeric formats, formatting borders, and applying shading (see fig. 2.17).

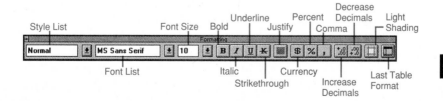

FIG. 2.17

The Formatting toolbar.

■ *Utility toolbar.* The Utility toolbar contains tools used for a variety of jobs, including copying and pasting, sorting, working with outlines, checking spelling, and performing calculations (see fig. 2.18).

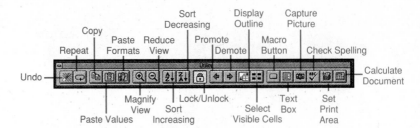

FIG. 2.18

The Utility toolbar.

■ *Chart toolbar.* The Chart toolbar contains the tools used to set the chart gallery type and to add or remove the legend, arrows, or text boxes (see fig. 2.19).

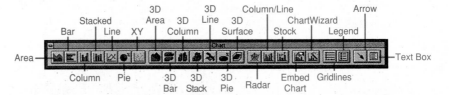

FIG. 2.19

The Chart toolbar.

■ *Drawing toolbar.* The Drawing toolbar contains tools for drawing, filling, reshaping and grouping objects in the worksheet (see fig. 2.20).

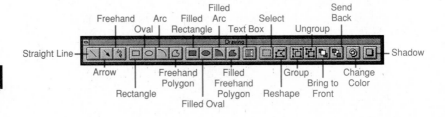

FIG. 2.20

The Drawing toolbar.

■ *The Microsoft Excel 3.0 toolbar.* This toolbar contains tools that match the standard set designed for Excel 3.0 (see fig. 2.21).

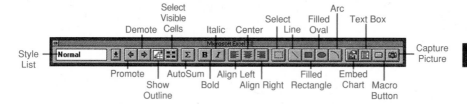

FIG. 2.21

The Microsoft Excel 3.0 toolbar.

■ *Macro toolbar.* The Macro toolbar contains tools for recording and debugging macros (see fig. 2.22).

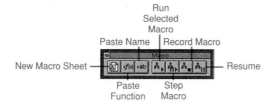

FIG. 2.22

The Macro toolbar.

■ *Macro Recording toolbar.* The Macro Recording toolbar contains a tool to stop macro recording (see fig. 2.23).

FIG. 2.23

The Macro Recording toolbar.

■ *Macro Paused toolbar.* The Macro Paused toolbar contains a tool that enables you to resume macro operation when a macro pauses (see fig. 2.24).

FIG. 2.24

The Macro Paused toolbar.

T I P Excel comes with many tools that are not on the predefined toolbars. To customize predefined toolbars, you can drag off the tools that you do not need and drag on the tools that you do need. See Chapter 33 to learn how to customize your toolbars.

You can use libraries of additional tools to customize predefined toolbars or to create your own toolbars. You can create your own toolbars by modifying predefined toolbars, adding predefined tools to a new blank toolbar, or drawing and adding your own tools and macros to any toolbar.

Customizing a toolbar is not difficult. Chapter 33 describes the tools you can add to existing toolbars and how to modify or build your own toolbars.

T I P If someone has used Excel before you, the predefined toolbars may be modified. Additional custom toolbars may be available to you that previous users have created or that have been created to assist you with specific tasks.

Using Tools

Excel has more than 100 tools and each tool is accompanied by a small drawing to represent its function. You quickly will learn which tools you need, however. This section gives you some tips for learning about the tools and their uses.

Tools execute commands or macros that are assigned to the tool. Many tools work in the same way as Windows commands: you select text or an object and then perform an action. Select text and then click on the Bold tool, for example, to toggle the text between boldface or plain. Select a list and then click on the Sort tool to sort the list, using the active cell as the primary sort key. Select a range and click on the Copy tool to copy the range into the Clipboard. The use of specific tools is described in the appropriate sections throughout the book.

Getting Help on Tools

To see the name of a toolbar, click and hold in the gray area of the toolbar background. While you hold the mouse button, the toolbar name appears in the Status Bar at the bottom of the screen.

To see the name of a specific tool, click and hold on the tool. The tool's name appears in the Status Bar at the bottom of the screen. If you do not want to execute the tool, drag the pointer off the tool before you release the mouse button.

By holding down the Shift key while you click on some tools, you can use the tools to perform two different tasks. By clicking on the Rectangle tool in the Drawing toolbar, for example, you can drag and draw an empty rectangle. When you press Shift and click on the Rectangle tool, however, you can drag and draw a filled rectangle. Because the Shift-click combination may duplicate the action of another tool, you may be able to replace the duplicated tools on the toolbar with tools you use more frequently.

When you need help using a tool, click on the Question Mark (**?**) tool, if available, and then click on the tool. If the **?** tool is not visible, press Shift+F1 and click on a tool. A help window appears to show you how to use the tool. Press Alt+F4 or choose **F**ile E**x**it to close the Help window.

Displaying or Hiding Toolbars

You can use the **O**ptions T**o**olbars command or the toolbar shortcut menu to display and hide toolbars. To use the **O**ptions T**o**olbars command to display additional toolbars, perform the following steps:

1. Choose the **O**ptions T**o**olbars command to display the Toolbars dialog box shown in figure 2.25.

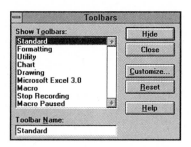

FIG. 2.25

The Toolbars dialog box.

2. Select the toolbar that you want to display. For this example, select the Formatting toolbar.

3. Choose the Show button. Excel displays the toolbar you selected across the top part of the screen, as shown in figure 2.26. The toolbar may display in a position different than shown.

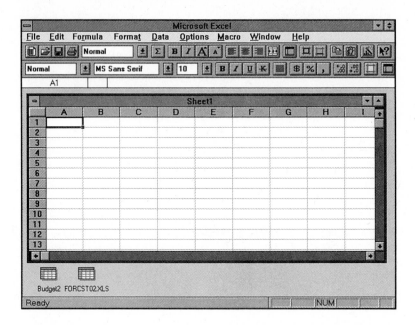

FIG. 2.26

The Standard toolbar and the Formatting toolbar.

The Show button appears only if your selection is not already on-screen. If the toolbar you select is already on-screen, the Hide button appears.

The easiest way to display a toolbar, if another toolbar already appears on-screen, is to click with the right mouse button anywhere on a toolbar except over a pull-down list box. This action displays the toolbar short-cut menu. Click on the toolbar you want to display. Toolbars that are displayed appear with a check mark.

You can hide a toolbar in three ways. You can click on the toolbar with the right mouse button to display the toolbar shortcut menu. In the shortcut menu, click on the name of the toolbar that you want hidden. If a toolbar is in a floating window, you can close it by clicking once on the window's Control menu icon at the upper-left corner of the window toolbar. Finally, you can close a toolbar by choosing the Options Tool-bar command. When the Toolbars dialog box appears, double-click on the toolbar name, or select the toolbar you want to hide and then choose the Hide button.

Excel records the toolbars and their locations. When you restart Excel, the toolbars you last used will be available to you. Chapter 33 describes how to create custom toolbars and how to save a file of different toolbar combinations.

Moving and Reshaping Toolbars

The Standard toolbar is the default toolbar that appears directly below the Excel menu bar after you initially start Excel. You can move or re-shape toolbars to fit the way you want to work.

Toolbars can be *docked* in a position along an edge of the window or they can *float* free in their own window. Docked toolbars are one tool wide or high. You can reshape toolbars that float in a window and drag them wherever they are most convenient to use. Figure 2.27 shows float-ing and docked toolbars.

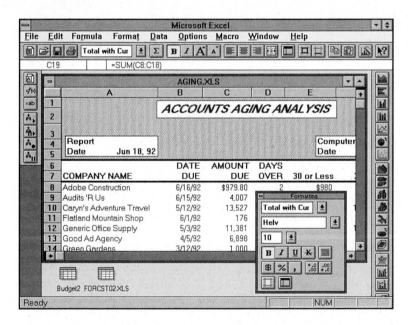

FIG. 2.27

Docked and floating toolbars.

To move a toolbar, click in the gray area outside a tool and drag. If you drag the toolbar to the bottom of the Excel window, the toolbar docks against the edge. A toolbar is ready to dock when its gray outline be-comes thinner. Toolbars that contain pull-down lists, such as the Style toolbar, cannot dock against a left or right edge because the list will not fit in the width of the toolbar.

Toolbars also can float free in a window. To move a floating toolbar, drag
its wide edge. You can resize a floating toolbar window by clicking on its
border and dragging, as shown in figure 2.28. To return the toolbar to a
dock, drag the floating toolbar's title bar to an edge of the screen and
then release. To dock a floating toolbar in the last place it docked before
becoming a floating toolbar, double-click on the toolbar's title bar.

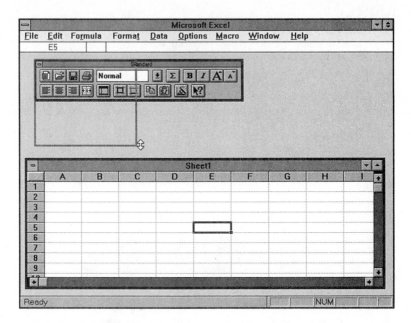

FIG. 2.28

Resizing a floating
toolbar.

FROM HERE...

For Related Information:

▶▶ "Customizing Toolbars," p. 1060.

Getting Help

Windows and Excel have Help information to guide you through new
commands and procedures. Excel's Help files are extensive and explain
topics that range from parts of the screen to commands, dialog boxes,
and business procedures.

To get help in Excel or a Windows application, choose a command from the **H**elp menu, press F1, or choose the **H**elp button that appears in many dialog boxes. The **H**elp **C**ontents command or F1 will display the window shown in figure 2.29. From this window, you can learn how to use Help or you can see the contents of all Help topics. Notice that you can access or control Help information in different ways. You can use the menus at the top of the Help window or you can use the buttons under the menus to **S**earch for a topic or to see a **H**istory of all the previous topics you have viewed.

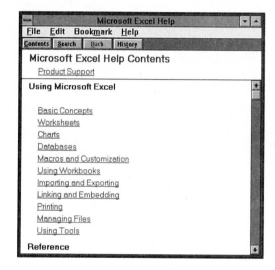

FIG. 2.29

The **H**elp **C**ontents window.

The following list describes the menu commands available in Help:

Command	Action
File Open	Opens a Help file to another application.
File Print Topic	Prints the current Help topic to the current printer.
File Printer Setup	Sets up a printer.
File Exit	Exits the Help program.
Edit Copy	Copies the active Help window's text contents into the Clipboard so that you can paste this information into a work-sheet or macro sheet. You can select function examples from Help, copy them into the Clipboard, then paste them into a worksheet to test.

Command	Action
Edit Annotate	Displays a notepad in which you can type your own notes to attach to the current Help topic. Topics with custom notes show a paper-clip icon at the top to remind you that these topics have annotations.
Bookmark **D**efine	Creates a bookmark name that attaches to the current Help topic. You can quickly return to this topic by selecting the name from the list in the Bookmark Define list or by choosing the name from under the Bookmark menu. (Bookmarks are like range names in Excel.)
Book**m**ark # *name*	Lists the available bookmarks so that you can choose one and quickly go to the topic where that bookmark is located. (# *name* is not a visible command until bookmarks have been created.)
How to Use **H**elp	Shows you information about how to use Help.
Always on **T**op	Keeps the Help window on top of the application so you can read Help information as you work.
About Help	Shows the copyright and version of your Help file.

T   I   P By marking the location of interesting topics and annotating those topics with notes, you can customize Help to fit your work. Bookmark enables you to mark a location in the help contents with a name. That name will then appear on the Bookmark menu so you can quickly jump to the marked location. The Annotate command enables you to add your own comments and references to the end of a Help topic.

Command buttons are located under the menu and help you move through the Help topics. Choose a button by clicking on it or by pressing Alt+*letter*. The following command buttons help you move through information:

Button	Action
Contents	Shows the index or contents of Help at the highest level.
Back	Returns to the preceding Help topic. With this button, you can retrace the topics you have viewed back to the initial Help Index.
History	Shows a list of the previously selected topics. Double-click on a topic to return to it or press the up- or down-arrow keys to select the topic, and then press Enter.
Search	Displays a list of key words. Choosing a key word displays a list of Help topics related to that keyword. Choosing from the topics displays the help for that topic.

Searching for Help

The Search dialog box enables you to find topics related to the subject you need help with. To use Search, choose the **Help** **S**earch command. If the Help window is already displayed, choose the **S**earch button. The dialog box shown in figure 2.30 appears.

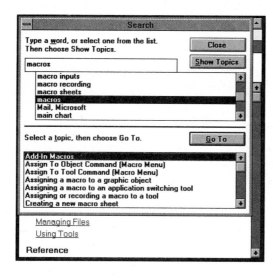

FIG. 2.30

The Search dialog box.

If you are using a mouse, click on the **S**earch button to display the Search dialog box. Type a word in the top box or select a topic from the top list and then choose the **S**how Topic button. The bottom list will display topics related to the word. Select a topic from the bottom list and choose the **G**o To button.

If you are using the keyboard, press Alt+S to activate the Search mode, and then press Alt+W to choose the top list. Type a topic in the text box. As you type, the list scrolls to topics that start with the letters you type. To scroll through the list, press Tab so that a topic in the list is enclosed with dashes, and then press the up- or down-arrow key. Press Enter to choose the **S**how Topic button, and the Go To list will fill with related topics. Press the up- or down-arrow key to select a topic and then press Enter to choose the **G**o To button.

Jumping between Help Topics

Hot words or phrases appear within the actual Help text. These words or phrases have a solid or dashed underline, meaning that the word or phrase is linked to additional information. Words or phrases with definitions appear with a dashed underline.

To jump to the topic related to a solid underlined word, click on the word or press Tab until the word is selected; then press Enter.

To display the definition of a word that appears with a dashed underline, click on the word or tab to the word and press Enter. Click again or press Enter to remove the definition.

Getting Dialog Box Help

You can get help for any dialog box or error message that appears in Excel. Figure 2.31 shows the error box that appears when you attempt to enter a formula containing an error. When any dialog box from a command or from an error message appears, press F1 to get help. Figure 2.32 shows the Help message that appears when you have an error in the Formula Bar and after you press F1.

FIG. 2.31

The Error dialog box for a formula that contains an error.

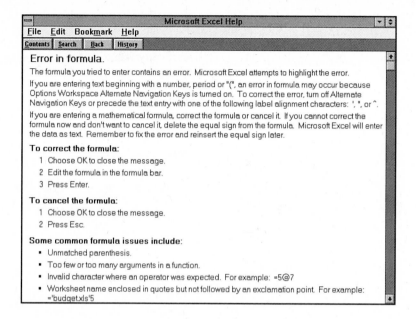

FIG. 2.32

The Help box for
an error in the
Formula Bar.

To learn what action a command performs or how a portion of the screen works, press Shift+F1 and then click on the command or portion of the screen. Notice that the mouse pointer changes to a question mark that overlays the pointer. You can press Shift+F1 to ask a question about the item you click.

Because Help is an actual application, you need to close its window when you are done. To remove the Help window, double-click on the Control menu icon to the left of the Help title bar; or press Alt, space bar, and then C for Close (Alt+F4).

Manipulating Windows

When you use Excel with Windows, you can display and run more than one application in Windows or use multiple worksheets, charts, and macros in Excel. See that much information on your screen can be confusing unless you keep your windows organized. Just as you organize folders and papers on your desk, you can organize your Windows applications and Excel documents.

You will see two types of windows on-screen. An application window contains an application, such as the File Manager, Excel, or Microsoft Word for Windows. A document window contains an Excel document. You can open multiple document windows within the Excel window.

Switching between Windows

You can work in an application or document only when its window is active. The active window has a solid title bar. Notice the difference between the title bars in figure 2.33. In most cases, the active window is also the top window. In a few instances, however, such as during the process of linking worksheets together, the active window may not be on top.

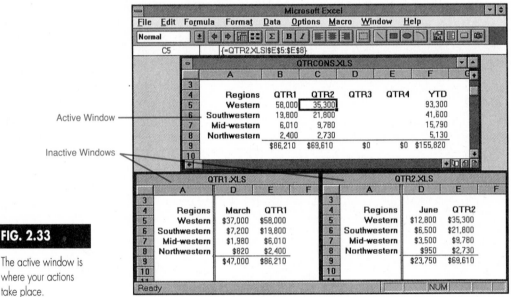

Active Window

Inactive Windows

FIG. 2.33

The active window is where your actions take place.

If you are running Excel with other Windows or non-Windows applications, you can switch between application windows by activating the application whose window you want. Press Ctrl+Esc to display the Task List. To choose an application from the Task List, double-click on its name or press the up- or down-arrow key to select the application, and then press Enter.

You also can cycle between applications by holding down the Alt key and pressing Tab. A dialog box or a title bar shows which application will be activated. Release all keys when you see the title of the application that you want to activate.

Because Excel makes working with several worksheets and charts easy, you frequently have more than one document window on-screen. You can affect only the active document, however. From within the Excel window, if you can see the document, you can make it active by clicking on the document with the mouse pointer. If you cannot see the document, move the other windows so that you can see it.

To switch to another window from the keyboard, choose the **W**indow menu and then press the number of the document window that you want to activate. The name of each document appears in the menu. You can cycle between documents by pressing Ctrl+F6.

Shrinking, Expanding, and Restoring Windows

You soon will find that your computer desktop can become as cluttered as your real desktop. To gain more space, you can store applications by minimizing them so that they become small symbols (icons) at the bottom of the screen.

When you need one of the applications or documents that has been minimized, you can restore the icon to its former window at the original location and size. When you want a window to fill the entire available area, you can maximize it. The icons for minimizing and maximizing space are shown in figure 2.34.

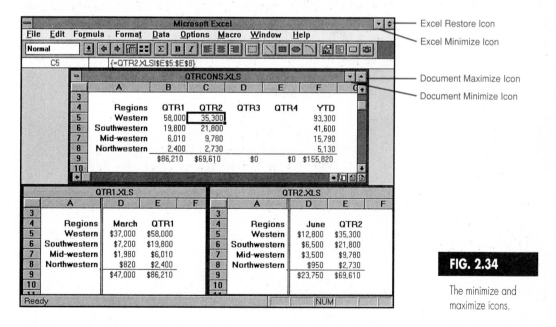

FIG. 2.34

The minimize and maximize icons.

To maximize an application or document window with the mouse, click on the maximize icon for the active window or double-click in the title bar of the window. To maximize an application or document window from the keyboard, press Alt, hyphen to display the document Control menu, or press Alt, space bar to display the application Control menu. Press **X** for the Maximize command.

You can minimize application or document windows so that they are stored temporarily at the bottom of the screen. To use the mouse to minimize a window, click on the minimize icon. From the keyboard, press Alt, hyphen to display the document Control menu or press Alt, space bar to display the application Control menu. Press **N** to choose Minimize. You can minimize the active document window by pressing Ctrl+F9.

You can restore Excel and document windows from their maximized or minimized sizes into their preceding window size. If Excel or a document is an icon at the bottom of the screen, double-click on it. If Excel or a document window is maximized, click on the double-headed icon to the right of the Excel or document title bar to restore it to a window. With the keyboard, press Alt, space bar to select the Excel Control menu or press Alt, hyphen to select the document Control menu, and then choose **R**estore (see fig. 2.35).

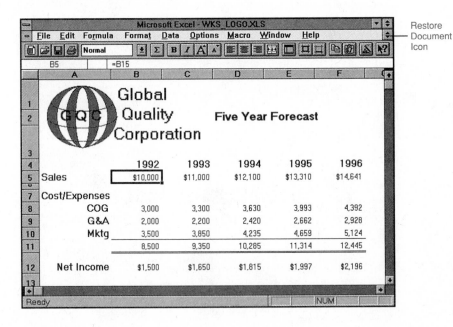

FIG. 2.35

The restore document icon.

Moving a Window

With multiple applications or multiple Excel documents on-screen, you will want to move windows for the same reason that you shuffle papers on your desk. You can move a window with the mouse or the keyboard by following these steps:

> If you are using a mouse, activate the window that you want to move. Drag the title bar until the shadow border is where you want the window to be located. Release the mouse button to fix the window in its new location.

> From the keyboard, select the application or document Control menu by pressing Alt, space bar for the application Control menu or Alt, hyphen for the document Control menu. Press **M** to select **M**ove. A four-headed arrow appears in the title bar. Press an arrow key to move the shadowed outline of the window. Press Enter to fix the window in its new location, or press Esc to retain the original location.

Sizing a Window

You often want to see only part of an application or document window. The following steps show you how to change the size of the window by using the mouse or the keyboard.

Perform the following steps to resize a window with the mouse:

1. Click on the window to activate it.

2. Move the pointer over the edge or corner that you want to resize; the pointer changes to a two-headed arrow.

3. Drag the two-headed arrow in the direction that you want that edge or corner to move.

4. When the shadow edge is in the correct location, release the mouse button.

Perform the following steps to resize a window from the keyboard:

1. Activate the window and move it so that you can see the edge you want to resize. Press Alt+Tab until Excel is active or press Ctrl+F6 until the document you want is active.

2. Choose the Control menu by pressing Alt, space bar for the application Control menu or Alt, hyphen for the document Control menu.

3. Press **M** for **M**ove.

4. Press the arrow key that points to the edge you want to move.

5. Press the arrow keys to move that edge.

6. Press Enter to fix the edge in its new location or press Esc to cancel.

Closing a Document Window

When you finish with the application, worksheet, or chart, you should close the window to remove it from the screen and to free memory. If you made a change since the last time you saved the document, Excel displays an alert dialog box, as shown in figure 2.36, asking whether you want to save your work before closing.

FIG. 2.36

The Save dialog box.

To close the active document window, perform the following steps:

1. Close the window by double-clicking on the document Control menu icon on the left side of the document's title bar. If you are using the keyboard, press Alt, - (hyphen) to choose the document Control menu and press C for **C**lose. The window closes if no changes were made.

   If you have more than one window opened onto the same file, you can close the file and all of its windows by choosing **F**ile **C**lose. The window closes if no changes were made.

2. If you made changes to the document, a dialog box appears, asking you to confirm whether you want to save your changes.

   In the dialog box, choose the **N**o command button if you don't want to save the changed version of the file or choose the **Y**es command button to save your changes.

3. If you chose Yes, and the file has not been saved before, a Save As dialog box will appear. Enter a new file name.

4. To close all visible documents, hold down the Shift key as you choose the **F**ile menu. The **C**lose All command will be available in place of **C**lose. Choose **C**lose All to close all visible documents.

5. Enter the new name in the Save Worksheet dialog box that appears, and then choose OK or press Enter.

> **T I P**
>
> You can avoid frustration and lost work if you save different versions of your work. When you save your document using the same file name, your previous work is replaced by the current work, and you cannot go back to old files.
>
> Instead of using the same file name over and over, reserve two characters at the end of each file name for a version number—for example, BUDGET07, BUDGET08, and so on. By saving different versions of your file under different version names, you can return to your previous work. (Don't retype the entire name; press the left-arrow key or Backspace to edit the old name.) When you have too many files of the same type, erase the old ones with the **File Delete** command.

For Related Information:

FROM HERE...

▸▸ "Saving and Magnifying Worksheet Displays," p. 408.

▸▸ "Viewing a Window through Multiple Panes," p. 414.

▸▸ "Viewing One Document through Multiple Windows," p. 418.

▸▸ "Grouping Documents into Workbooks," p. 426.

Quitting Excel

Close or quit Excel when you are finished working for the day or when you need to free memory for other applications. To quit Excel, perform the following steps:

1. Double-click on the application Control menu icon, which is on the left of the Excel title bar. Alternatively, press Alt, space bar to display the application Control menu and press **C** to choose the **Close** command; or press Alt+F4. Excel quits immediately if you made no changes since the last time you saved your documents.

2. Confirm whether you want to save your changes.

   If you made changes to any document, Excel displays an alert box asking whether you want to save your current work. Choose the **Yes** command button or press Enter to save your work, or choose the **No** command button to quit without saving.

3. Repeat step 2 for each document name displayed in an alert box. The alert box appears for each document you have on-screen that has been changed.

T I P To save all the documents and their current window arrangements, use the **File Save Workbook** command, described in Chapter 11.

FROM HERE...

For Related Information:

▶▶ "Managing Files," p. 158.

Chapter Summary

Work through the Worksheet Quick Start in Chapter 3. This Quick Start will take you step-by-step through a small practice worksheet. If you are familiar with Lotus 1-2-3, read Chapter 5, "Making the Switch from 1-2-3 to Excel," to learn about Excel's improvements over Lotus 1-2-3 and the differences between Excel and Lotus 1-2-3.

After you go through the Worksheet Quick Start in Chapter 3, you may want to skim through the worksheet chapters and look for features or examples that relate to your work. Experiment with a few small test worksheets and basic features, such as formatting and editing, before you attempt to build a large worksheet.

PART II

Excel Worksheets

OUTLINE

Worksheet Quick Start

Whether you are new to electronic worksheets or you are an experienced user, you will find the Quick Start for worksheets a good introduction to Excel. Even if you are familiar with Excel, you should work through this Quick Start. You will discover some new features and shortcuts available in Excel. The Quick Start is an introduction; the chapters that follow discuss details and include many practical examples.

This Quick Start gives you enough information to begin building simple worksheets on your own. Because you may not have enough time to work through the entire Quick Start at one sitting, a midway section describes how to save your work so you can restart later.

Creating a Forecasting Worksheet

The two most frequent uses for worksheets are budgeting and forecasting. The following example prepares a simple forecast of sales and expenses as a percentage of sales. In the example, the Global Quality Corporation has a single source of revenue and only three expense items. The three cost and expense items are entered as a percentage of each year's sales.

Figures 3.1 and 3.2 represent the kind of forecast worksheet you might create. The upper rows of the worksheet, in figure 3.1, show the calculated results of the forecast. These rows contain only text and formulas. The lower rows, in figure 3.2, contain an area to enter data. When you change the numbers in the lower rows, you immediately see the recalculated results in the upper rows. The two portions are kept separate to reduce the chance of typing a number over a formula, which is the single largest cause of errors in worksheets.

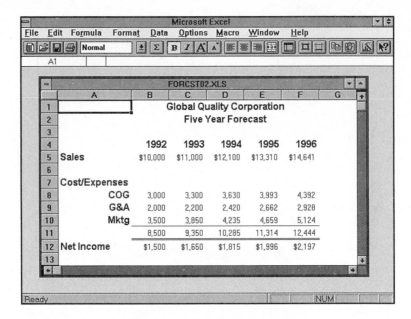

FIG. 3.1

The calculated forecast portion of the worksheet.

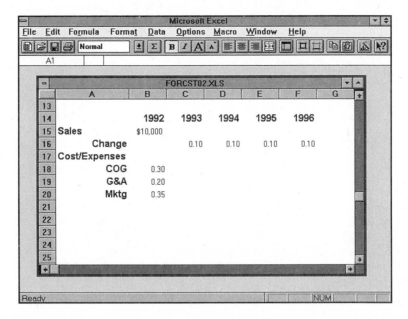

FIG. 3.2

The data-entry portion of the worksheet.

If you haven't yet started Excel, do so before you continue. For instructions on starting the program, see Chapter 1, "Installing Excel." If you are not familiar with working in a Windows environment or operating menus and dialog boxes, you will want to experiment with Windows as you read Chapter 2, "Learning Windows and Excel Basics."

Reviewing the Worksheet

Excel opens with a blank worksheet entitled *Sheet1*. Sheet1 appears in its own document window. Figure 3.3 points out important parts of the Excel and document window.

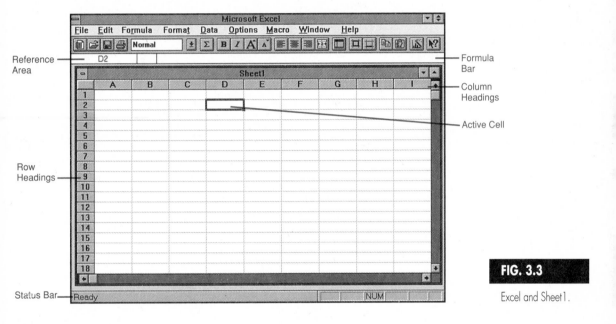

FIG. 3.3

Excel and Sheet1.

The worksheet contains 256 columns with alphabetic headings and 16,384 numbered rows. Each intersection of row and column is a unique cell that can be referenced by its row and column; for example, the cell where row D intersects with column 1 is named cell D1. In each cell, you can type a number, text, or a formula.

In figure 3.3, cell D2 is the active cell. The active cell has a border around it. This is the cell affected if you type or give a command. Even if you cannot see the active cell, its cell reference shows in the Reference Area. Other information also shows in the Reference Area, such as the active record in a database or the number of a graphic object.

Preparing the Worksheet

Before beginning the Quick Start, you will want to customize some of Excel's features. You can, for example, turn off the gridlines that display on the worksheet.

To choose a menu by using a mouse, move the mouse pointer to the menu name and click the left mouse button. When the menu appears, click the command name. When a dialog box appears, click the button or check box for the option you want to select (turn on).

Selected options appear with a darkened dot (round option buttons) or an X (check boxes). Only one option button (round circle) can be selected in a group at a time. Click a check box to select or clear the X in a check box.

When you are ready to execute the command choose (click) the OK button. You back out of a command by choosing the Cancel button.

To choose a menu by using the keyboard, press the Alt key, release it, and then press the letter underlined in the name of the menu you want. The Quick Start shows these keystrokes as Alt, letter. Choose the command from the pull-down menu by pressing the letter underlined in the command. If a dialog box appears, select or clear option buttons or check boxes by holding down the Alt key as you press the underlined letter. The Quick Start shows these keystrokes as Alt+letter. Selected options display a darkened center (buttons) or an X (check boxes). Select an option button by selecting the group of buttons and then pressing an arrow key to move between options in the group. Clear a check box by selecting it a second time. When you are ready to execute the command press Enter or back out by pressing Esc.

To turn off the gridlines, perform the following steps:

1. Click **O**ptions **D**isplay; or press Alt, O, and then D.

2. Clear the **G**ridlines check box so that the feature is turned off by clicking the **G**ridlines check box or by pressing Alt+G.

3. Choose OK or press Enter.

If you are using a mouse with Excel, you can save time by using toolbars. Toolbars give you quick access with a mouse to frequently used commands. There are eight predefined toolbars, and you can create custom toolbars. If the Standard toolbar shown in figure 3.3 is not shown on your screen, display it by following these steps:

1. Click **O**ptions **T**oolbars or press Alt, O, then O.

    The Toolbars dialog box shown in figure 3.4 appears.

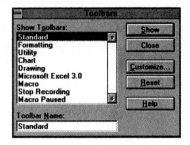

FIG. 3.4

The Toolbars dialog box enables you to display or hide toolbars.

2. Choose the Standard toolbar from the Show **T**oolbars list. With a mouse, click Standard. From the keyboard, press the up- or down-arrow key to choose Standard.

3. Choose the **S**how button or press Enter (Enter chooses the bold command button).

For Related Information:

◄◄ "Choosing Commands," p. 35.

◄◄ "Using the Toolbars," p. 47.

▶▶ "Setting Preferences," p. 142.

FROM HERE...

Building a Text Skeleton

Worksheets are much easier to build when you have a text skeleton, or outline, as a guide for entering data and formulas. To build a text skeleton, move the active cell to the cell you want to enter data in and then type.

Entering Text

To change a cell or its contents, you must select the cell first. Follow these steps to select cells for the text entries in your sample worksheet:

1. Select cell A1 or press Ctrl+Home to make cell A1 active.

2. Select cell D1 by clicking it or by pressing the right-arrow key to move the active cell to D1.

Notice that the reference for the active cell, D1, appears in the Reference Area to the left of the Formula Bar.

3. Type the following title: *Global Quality Corporation*. Your text appears in the Formula Bar, as shown in figure 3.5.

4. Enter the title into cell D1 by clicking the check box to the left of the Formula Bar or by pressing Enter.

   Clicking the Cancel box or pressing Esc cancels your text.

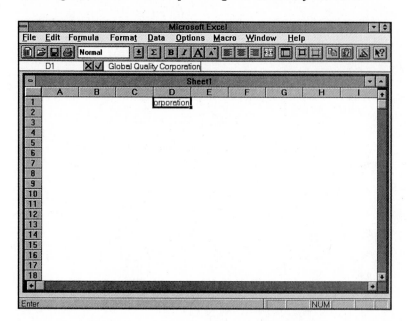

FIG. 3.5

Text appears in the Formula Bar before it is entered into a cell.

5. Select cell D2 and type the title *Five Year Forecast*; then press Enter.

6. Next, you highlight cells D1 and D2 so that the worksheet looks like figure 3.6. You can either click and drag the mouse to highlight both cells, or from the keyboard, move to cell D1 and press Shift+down-arrow key to highlight both cells.

   Notice that cell D1 is still active (it has the bold border), but cell D2 is also selected and appears darkened. Selected cells are the cells affected by commands. To return to having a single cell active, select any cell outside the selected cells.

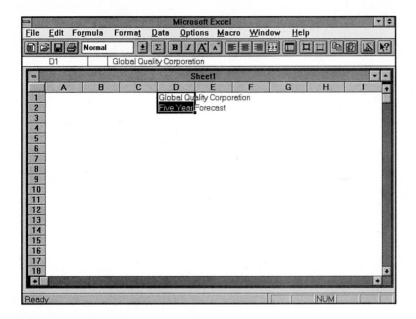

FIG. 3.6

You can select and change more than one cell at a time.

Correcting Mistakes

If you make a mistake or enter something incorrectly during the Quick Start, you can erase a cell's format or contents easily. Select the cell(s) you want to correct, and then press the Delete (Del) key. A dialog box with option buttons appears. Press the arrow keys to select whether you want to erase formulas (contents), formats, or everything in the cell, and then press Enter. To bring back what you have just erased, choose the **Edit U**ndo command. Most commands in Excel can be undone.

To edit the contents of a cell, select the cell, and then press the Edit key, F2. The contents of the cell are displayed in the Formula Bar. You can use the left- or right-arrow keys to move, the Delete and Backspace keys to erase, and the typing keys to insert characters. Press Enter to reenter the cell contents.

Centering Text

You now can use the following steps to change the text alignment of the selected cells, D1 and D2, at the same time. If you are using a mouse, the toolbar, shown in figure 3.7, makes the most frequently used commands readily available.

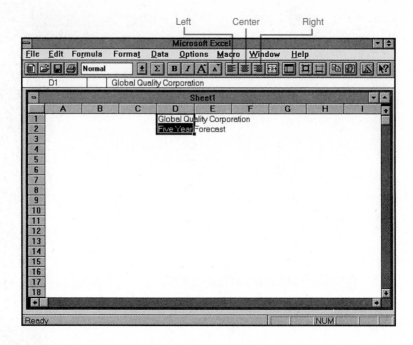

FIG. 3.7

The Alignment tools align contents left, center, or right in a cell.

 To use the mouse and toolbar to center cell contents, perform the following steps:

1. Be certain that cells D1 and D2 are selected.

2. Click the Center Alignment tool to center the selected text. Figure 3.7 shows some of the tools on the Standard toolbar.

If you are using a keyboard or the toolbar is not visible, follow these steps:

1. Be certain that cells D1 and D2 are selected.

2. Click on Format, or Press Alt, T.

The Format menu, shown in figure 3.8, appears below **Format.**

NOTE Notice that an ellipsis (...) follows the **Alignment** command on the menu. Ellipses indicate that a dialog box requesting more information will be displayed when you select that command.

3. Click the **Alignment** command or press A.

The Alignment dialog box appears, displaying an option button for each alignment or orientation (see fig. 3.9).

FIG. 3.8

The Format menu.

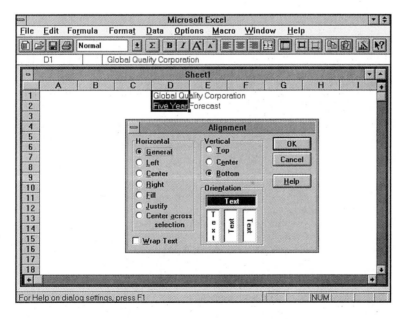

FIG. 3.9

The Alignment
dialog box.

4. Click the **C**enter button, or press Alt+C.

5. Choose the OK button, or press Enter.

6. Do not move or select other cells. You will continue formatting cells D1 and D2.

Now, both titles center on column D and the cells containing the text.

Changing the Font

Because both cells remain selected, you can continue to choose commands to change the appearance of the text.

To change the font and style of the headings by using a mouse, click the Bold tool, **B**, to make the selected text bold.

If you are using a keyboard or you are using a mouse and the toolbar is not visible, follow these steps:

1. Choose the Forma**t** **F**ont command or press Alt, T, then F.

    Figure 3.10 shows the Font dialog box.

    The fonts you have available in your printer, shown in the Font list with a printer icon, may be different than the ones shown in the figure.

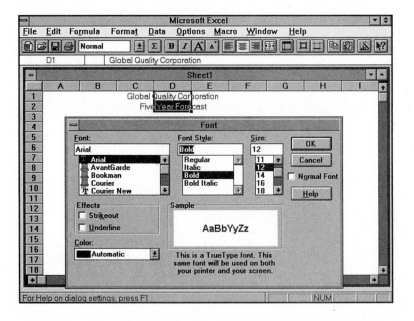

FIG. 3.10

The Font dialog box.

> If you are using Windows 3.1 or later version, you may have TrueType **T I P**
> fonts available. If you are using Windows 3.1 and you cannot see fonts
> that show a TT icon in the list, you should run the Font program from
> the Windows Control Panel and enable TrueType fonts. If you do not
> have the Arial font (TrueType) shown in the figures, use a sans serif
> font, such as Helv or Helvetica.

2. Select the Arial font from the Font list. With a mouse, click the
   scroll arrows to the right of the Font list until you see Arial; then
   click Arial. From the keyboard, press Alt+F; then press the up- or
   down-arrow key until Arial is selected.

3. Select 12 point from the Size list.

4. Select Bold from the Font Style list.

5. Choose OK or press Enter.

Finishing the Text Skeleton

Complete the text skeleton as shown in figures 3.11 and 3.12. To enter
the text, select the cell you want to enter text in, type the entry, and then
press Enter. *Do not* put spaces in front of the entries COG, G&A, or Mktg.
This text will be aligned later. Type the years as numbers.

After entering the text, you may want to format the cells containing
headings so that the headings appear as shown in figures 3.11 and 3.12.
Use 12-point Arial or Helv font in bold or italic style. If you are using the
Standard toolbar, you can make a font bold by selecting the cell, and
then clicking the Bold tool. Increase or decrease the font size by clicking
the Increase or Decrease font size tool that appears as two tools containing the letter A.

Right-Aligning Text

To make the worksheet clearer, you can align the three expense
items—COG, G&A, and Mktg—against the right column edge. Follow
these steps to align the contents:

1. Select the cells containing COG, G&A, and Mktg.

2. If the toolbar is visible, click the Right Alignment tool in the toolbar.
   Alignment is completed.

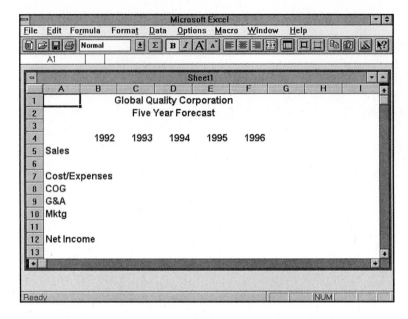

FIG. 3.11

The upper half of the worksheet.

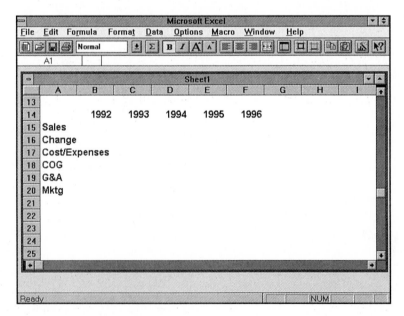

FIG. 3.12

The lower half of the worksheet.

If you are not using the toolbar, click the Format Alignment command; or press Alt, T, then A.

3. Click the **R**ight option button, or press Alt+R.

4. Choose the OK button or press Enter.

Align cells A16 and A18 through A20 by using the same method. In Excel, a selection of multiple cells is called a range. The range in which A18 is one corner and A20 is the opposite corner is noted as range A18:A20.

Adjusting a Column Width

After entering the text, you probably noticed that some of the text is wider than the default column width. To widen column A with a mouse, follow these steps:

1. Move the cell pointer over the line that separates the A and B headings at the top of the column.

2. When the pointer changes to a two-headed arrow, drag the pointer to the right.

3. Release the mouse button.

> Automatically adjust a column to the best fitting width by double-clicking the line that separates A and B in the headings.
>
> **T I P**

To widen column A from the keyboard or to widen the column so that the widest contents fit well, follow these steps:

1. Select cell A7, the cell containing the widest contents.

2. Click the Forma**t C**olumn Width command, or press Alt, T, then C.

   In the dialog box that appears, notice that the **C**olumn Width text box is selected. Although you can type a number for the width of the column, there is a faster method.

3. Choose the **B**est Fit button so that Excel widens the column to fit the contents of cell A7.

After column A is widened, you can see that Excel normally aligns text against the left edge of the column. Numbers and dates align against the right edge. Either numbers, dates, or text can be aligned left, right, or center within a cell.

Saving Your Worksheet

As you work, you should save your file, especially before taking breaks. Saving your work enables you to come back at a later time and open your work at the point where you left it. Worksheets that are not saved are lost when the worksheet is closed, Excel is closed, or the power is lost.

To save your partially completed worksheet, follow these steps:

1. Click the **File Save As** command (see fig. 3.13), or press Alt, F, and A.

2. Select the new drive to save the file to by clicking the arrow to the right of the **Drives** drop-down list, selecting the drive letter, and choosing OK. Or, press Alt+V, use the up- or down-arrow key to select the drive, and then press Enter.

3. Select the new directory by scrolling through the **Directories** list and selecting an upper or lower directory to which you want to move, and choosing OK. Or, press Alt+D, use the up- or down-arrow key to select the directory into which you want to move, and press Enter.

4. Type the name *FORCST01* in the File **Name** text box.

5. Choose OK or press Enter.

Notice that the worksheet name in the worksheet title bar has changed from Sheet1 to FORCST01.XLS, the name you specified. XLS is the DOS file extension for an Excel worksheet.

If you decide to exit Excel at this point, follow the instructions for exiting provided at the end of this Quick Start. When you want to return to the Quick Start, start Excel again and begin with the following topic on opening saved worksheets.

FROM HERE...

For Related Information:

▶▶ "Managing Files," p. 158.

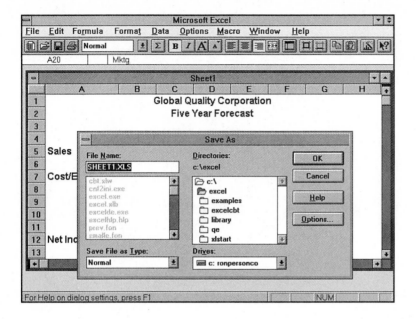

Opening a Worksheet

You can reopen worksheets that are on a disk or diskette. If you saved
the FORCST01 worksheet and exited Excel, you can reopen the worksheet with the following steps:

1. Choose the **F**ile **O**pen command (see fig. 3.14).

2. To open a file from a different drive, click the arrow to the right of
   the **D**rives drop-down list, select the drive letter, and choose OK.
   Or, press Alt+V, select the drive, and press Enter.

3. To open a file from a different directory, scroll through the **D**irectories list and select an upper or lower directory to which you want
   to move, and then choose OK. Or, press Alt+D, select the directory
   into which you want to move, and press Enter.

4. In the File **N**ame list box, select or type *FORCST01.XLS*.

5. Choose OK or press Enter.

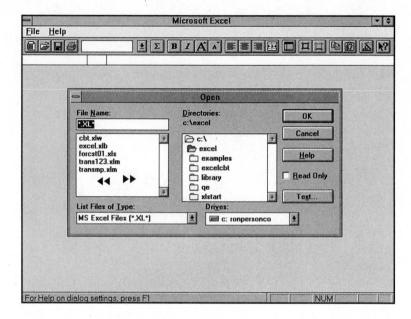

FIG. 3.14

The Open dialog box.

Entering Simple Data

Use simple data for sample inputs when you are creating a text skeleton. If you enter simple data before entering formulas, you will be able to see the results of a formula as soon as you enter the formula. This technique can help you pinpoint problems. If you use simple data, you can immediately tell whether a solution is realistic.

Whenever Excel recognizes a numeric, date, or time format, Excel stores the corresponding numbers and automatically formats the cell so that any number entered in that cell will appear with that numeric, date, or time format.

Follow these steps to enter an item with a numeric format:

1. Select cell B15.

2. Type *$10,000* and press Enter.

Notice that Excel accepts the number and retains the currency format with no decimal places. Only the number without formatting appears in the Formula Bar.

To enter a number, select the cell, type the number, and then press Enter or Tab. You can change Excel so that the active cell automatically moves down or stays on the same cell after you enter data. You also can make the numeric pad automatically enter a decimal point like a ten-key machine. Excel has a number of data-entry and data-formatting shortcuts described in Chapter 7, "Entering and Editing Worksheet Data," and in Chapter 22, "Entering and Sorting Data."

Enter the following data:

Label	Cell	Data
1991 Sales	B15	$10,000
Change	C16	0.1
Change	D16	0.1
Change	E16	0.1
Change	F16	0.1
COG	B18	0.3
G&A	B19	0.2
Mktg	B20	0.35

Sometimes Excel doesn't recognize how you want a number or date formatted. To use one of Excel's predefined formats to format numbers with two decimal places, follow these steps:

1. Select the change data cells, C16:F16.

2. Choose the Format Number command. The Number Format dialog box appears (see fig. 3.15).

3. Click on the 0.00 format, or press Alt+F to select the Format Codes List; then press the up- or down-arrow key to select 0.00.

4. Choose OK or press Enter.

Change numbers now show a leading zero with two decimal places. Repeat this procedure, but select cells B18:B20 and format them with 0.00.

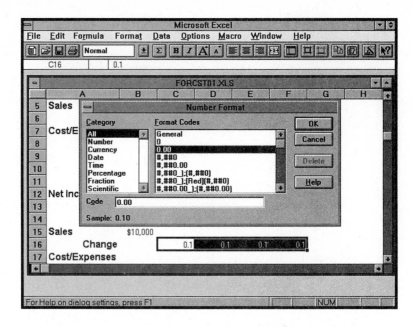

FIG. 3.15

The Number Format
dialog box.

T I P   The Style list in the Standard and Formatting toolbar enables you to
apply currency and comma styles with the mouse. In addition, the
Formatting toolbar has numeric formatting tools.

The simple data portion of your worksheet should now look like
figure 3.2 near the beginning of this chapter.

For Related Information:

FROM HERE...

▶▶ "Selecting Cells," p. 147.

▶▶ "Entering Data," p. 169.

▶▶ "Editing Text and Formulas," p. 195.

▶▶ "Changing Character Fonts, Sizes, Styles, and Colors," p. 257.

▶▶ "Aligning Text and Numbers," p. 264.

Entering and Copying Formulas

Electronic worksheets are useful because of the formulas entered in worksheet cells. These formulas produce new answers whenever the data used by the formulas changes.

Cells may contain simple formulas that refer only to the value stored in another cell, or they may contain complex formulas that include text manipulation, built-in formulas called *functions*, and array mathematics. All formulas begin with an equals sign (=).

Entering Formulas by Typing

A text skeleton and simple sample data help you see which cells are involved in a formula. To enter a formula, you will select a cell, enter the formula, and then press Enter or click the Enter box in the Formula Bar.

One way to enter a formula is to type it. Use the following steps to enter a simple formula that reads the value $10,000 from cell B15 to cell B5:

1. Select B5.

2. Type the formula *=B15*.

3. Choose the Enter box in the Formula Bar or press Enter.

The number 10000 from cell B15 and the formatting from cell B15 will appear in B5. As long as the cell in which you are entering a formula has the General (default) format, then the format is brought with the result.

Entering Formulas by Pointing

In addition to typing a formula, you can enter it by *pointing* to the cells used in the formula. The pointing method reduces typographical errors, and you can use the method with either a mouse or keyboard.

The formula you enter into cell C5 adds to the value in cell B5 the amount of sales increase according to the percentage in cell C16. The formula is =B5+B5*C16.

Follow these steps to enter the formula by using the pointing method:

1. Select cell C5.

2. Type an equals sign (=) to let Excel know that you are entering a formula.

3. Select cell B5 to add B5 to the formula (see fig. 3.16).

4. Type the next operator, which is the plus sign (+).

   The formula now should look like =B5+. Entering a math operator tells Excel to freeze the cell you pointed at (B5) so that you can point to the next cell reference to include in the formula.

5. Select B5 again by clicking it or pressing the left-arrow key. The formula should look like =B5+B5.

6. Type the multiplication operator (*).

7. Select cell C16 (the last cell reference in the formula).

8. If the Formula Bar displays =B5+B5*C16, enter the formula by pressing Enter or clicking the Enter box. If the formula is not displayed correctly, press Esc or click the X box, and then recreate the formula.

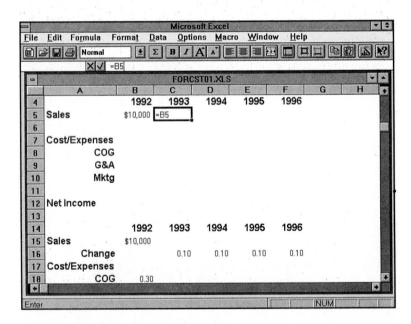

You can see that the result of the formula in cell C5 is 11000. Because you expected a 10 percent increase over 1990's value of 10000, the result appears to be correct.

Copying and Pasting Formulas

If you had to go through the process of typing or pointing to enter every formula, building a worksheet would take a long time. Instead, you can copy formulas into other cells. The cell references in the formulas automatically adjust to their new locations. To copy a formula, follow these steps:

1. Select C5, the cell containing the formula you want to copy.

2. Choose the **Edit Copy** command by clicking the Copy tool in the toolbar (it looks like two overlapping sheets of paper) or by pressing Alt, E, then C.

    Notice that the Status Bar at the bottom of the screen gives you hints on what to do next. The Status Bar will guide you or give you hints with many commands. When you hold the mouse on a tool, the Status Bar shows you the name and function of the tool.

3. Select cells D5:F5 (see fig. 3.17) as the location for the copied formula.

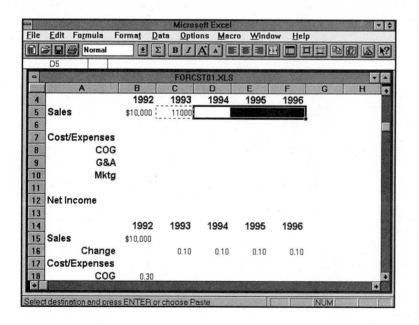

FIG. 3.17

Selected cells in which you will paste the copied formula.

4. Choose the **Edit Paste** command, or press Enter if you only want to paste one time.

The **Edit C**opy command copies the contents of cell C5 into temporary memory called the *Clipboard*. The **Edit P**aste command transfers the contents of the Clipboard into the selected cells, D5 through F5. A copy of the contents remains in the Clipboard.

Press Esc to remove the dashed marquee encircling C5, if you want.

Formatting the Formula Results

The formula result in cell C5 and all of its copies need to be formatted with a currency format with no decimal places. To format these cells, follow these steps:

1. Select the range C5:F5. Drag from C5 to F5 by using the mouse; or move to C5, then hold down the Shift key as you press the right-arrow key and move to F5.

2. Choose the Forma**t N**umber command.

3. Select Currency from the **C**ategory list.

4. Select the $#,##0_);($#,##0) format from the **F**ormat Codes list, as shown in figure 3.18.

5. Choose OK or press Enter.

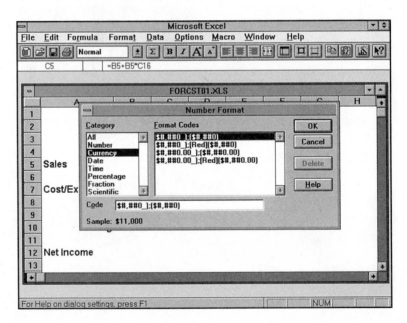

FIG. 3.18

Numeric and date formats are easier to find when you look in a category.

Using Absolute and Relative Cell References

When Excel pastes a formula from one cell into a new location, each formula adjusts to fit its new location. Move to each of the copied formulas in cells C5 through F5 and notice the difference between the original formula and the copies.

C5	=B5+B5*C16	Original Formula
D5	=C5+C5*D16	Duplicate Formula
E5	=D5+D5*E16	Duplicate Formula
F5	=E5+E5*F16	Duplicate Formula

Cell references that adjust to their new location when copied are known as *relative references*. Excel normally enters cell references in a formula using a relative reference. The formula actually refers to a cell's location by its position *relative* to the formula, such as two rows up and one column left.

In some cases, you will *not* want Excel to change a cell reference when the formula is copied and pasted into a new location. This is the case for the formula you will enter in cell B8 for the Cost of Goods (COG), =B5*B18. Copying this formula from B8 and pasting it into C8 results in the adjusted formula =C5*C18; this formula is incorrect because no number exists in cell C18. If Excel adjusts the relative reference, the formula no longer will be valid.

Instead, you want the B18 cell reference to stay the same no matter where the formula is copied. References that stay the same are known as *absolute references*. (The reference stays *absolutely* the same wherever it is copied.) To copy the contents of B18 as an absolute reference, put a dollar sign in front of the row and column address: $B$18.

The following Excel shortcut enters a formula using both relative and absolute references:

1. Select cell B8.

2. Create the formula =B5*B18 using either pointing or typing. *Do not press Enter.*

3. While the flashing insertion point is touching B18 in the Formula Bar, press F4 (the Reference key) so that B18 changes to $B$18.

4. Press Enter or click the check mark to enter the formula =B5*$B$18.

The result, 3000, in cell B8 appears reasonable because COG was 30 percent of the 10,000 in first year sales.

Use the previous steps to enter the following formulas and check for a reasonable answer:

Cell	Formula	Result
B8	=B5*$B$18	3000
B9	=B5*$B$19	2000
B10	=B5*$B$20	3500

Do not enter other formulas across these rows. You can fill the rows later with a single command.

Summing a Column of Numbers

The sample worksheet needs to display in cell B11 a total of the expenses in cells B8:B10. You could enter a formula in B11, such as =B8+B9+B10, but then the total would not include new expense items inserted into new rows. A much better method for writing this formula uses Excel's SUM( ) function. Functions are predefined formulas built into Excel. SUM( ) totals all the values that are within the range of cells you specify. To enter the formula for the total in cell B11, follow these steps:

1. Select cell B11.

2. If you are using a mouse and the Standard toolbar, quickly click the AutoSum tool twice. The AutoSum tool is to the left of the Bold (**B**) tool. This automatically enters the AutoSum formula and totals the range B8:B10.

   Or, press Alt+ equals sign (=).

   Or, type the formula =*SUM(B8:B11)*, and then press Enter.

The result, 8500, appears to be the correct total. You also can enter the SUM( ) formula with the pointing method by typing =*SUM(*, then selecting the cells from B8 to B10, typing the closing parenthesis, *)*, and then pressing Enter.

Finish the calculations for column B by typing the formula for Net Income, which is Sales minus the total Cost/Expenses. Type the formula =*B5-B11* in cell B12. The result should be 1500.

Excel includes more than 100 mathematical, financial, logical, and text functions like SUM( ). If you are unsure of the function you need, you can paste a function into the toolbar by using the Formula Paste Function command.

Using Borders

You can make your worksheets look more professional by using under-lines to set off columns of numbers from their subtotals or totals. Use a solid single line for subtotals and a double line for final totals. To draw a line at the bottom of cells, follow these steps:

1. Select cell B10.

2. Click on the Bottom Border tool; or choose the Forma**t B**order com-mand. The Border dialog box appears (see fig. 3.19).

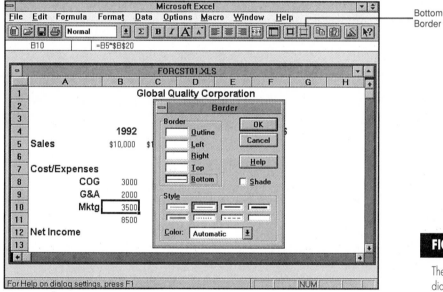

Bottom
Border

FIG. 3.19

The Border
dialog box.

3. Select the **B**ottom check box.

4. Click the single-underline box, or press Alt+E, then use the arrow keys to select the single-underline box.

5. Choose OK or press Enter.

The underline in the cell may not be visible until you select another cell.

Add a double underline to the bottom of cell B11 by selecting cell B11 and repeating the preceding steps. In step 4, select the double-underline box. The result of your nearly completed worksheet appears in figure 3.20.

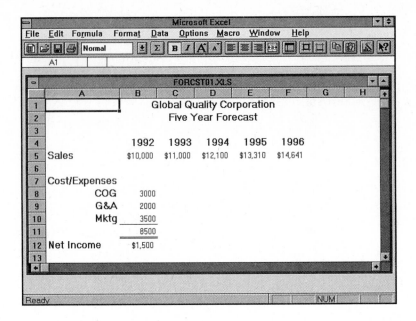

FIG. 3.20

The worksheet after
underlines are added.

Formatting Formula Results

Formulas in cells that have the default numeric format of General do not
display the number in a format. Cells B5 and B12 received the currency
format from cell B15, which you formatted with a dollar sign and comma.

However, the cells in B8 to B11 should appear with a comma and no
decimal values. You will need to apply a new format to cells B8:B11.

To format cells B8:B11 with commas, you need to apply a format using
the Format Number command. To format the cells, follow these steps:

1. Select the range B8:B11.

2. Choose the Format Number command.

3. Select the format #,##0_);(#,##0).

4. Choose OK or press Enter.

Figure 3.21 shows the format selected. The positive part of this format,
before the semicolon, ends with the characters _). The underscore character, _, marks the next character as invisible. Because the negative
number is enclosed in parentheses, you will need to use this invisible)
at the end of a positive number so that positive and negative numbers
will line up evenly when right aligned. Using the symbols you see in the
Format Codes list, you can enter your own custom formats into the Code
edit box to create the numeric, date, or time format you need.

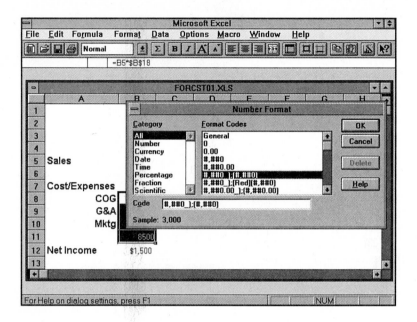

Filling Adjacent Cells
with Formulas and Formats

Another useful method of duplicating formulas, besides copying and
pasting, is filling a formula into an adjacent area. The following procedure fills the remainder of the worksheet with the formulas and formats
in column B.

To fill cells B8:B12 across to column F by using the mouse:

1. Select the range B8:B12.

2. Drag the fill handle to the right so that the gray outline of the area
   to be filled stretches from B8 to F12. Figure 3.22 shows the fill
   handle. Figure 3.23 shows the area after the Ctrl+drag.

3. Continue holding the Ctrl key as you release the mouse button, and
   then release the Ctrl key.

If you are using commands or the keyboard, you fill formulas by following these steps:

1. Select cells B8:F12.

   The cells to be copied, B8:B12, are on the left edge of the range into
   which they will be copied, as shown in figure 3.24.

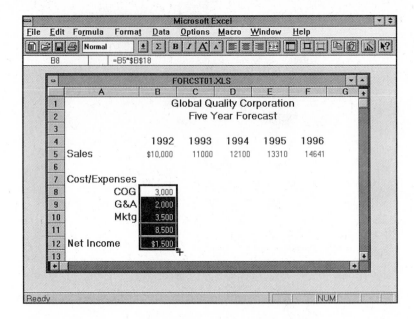

FIG. 3.22

Drag a fill handle
to create a series or
fill in a formula.

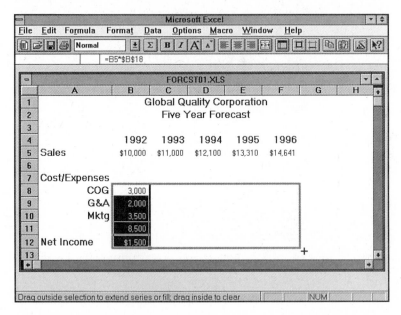

FIG. 3.23

Drag across to enclose
the area that you want
to fill.

2. Choose the **E**dit Fill Ri**g**ht command.

The formulas and formats from the left column fill the cells to the right,
as shown in figure 3.25.

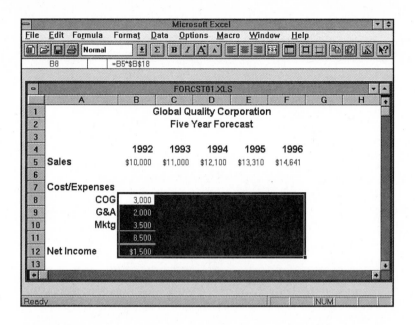

FIG. 3.24

Fill formulas
from one edge
into adjacent cells.

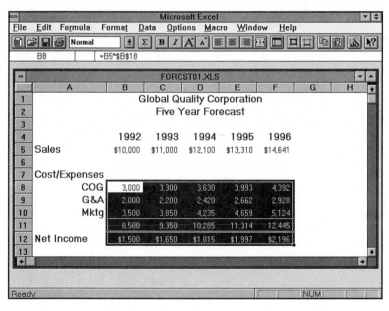

FIG. 3.25

Filling in remaining
formulas and formats
quickly completes the
worksheet.

Whether you use the fill handles or the **E**dit Fill Rig**ht** command, formulas fill into the range you selected just as though they were copied. Formulas adjust relative references the same as if they were copied. Use a copy technique if the source and target cells are separate; use a fill technique if source and target cells are adjacent. You also can fill up, fill down, or fill left by using commands, shortcut keys, or tools.

Making Calculations by Using Formatted Numbers

Notice that the numbers in cells F8, F9, and F10 do not appear to total the result in cell F11. The displayed numbers have been rounded by formatting; however, calculated results use the full number. In other electronic spreadsheets, this discrepancy is difficult to fix; in Excel, the discrepancy is resolved with one command. Figure 3.26 shows the finished worksheet with this discrepancy resolved.

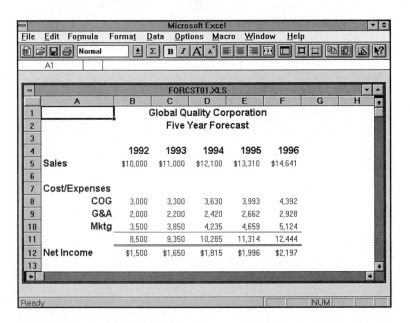

FIG. 3.26

Be certain that calculated results match formatted numbers.

Choose the **O**ptions **C**alculation command. When the dialog box appears, select the **P**recision as Displayed check box and press Enter. When the alert appears, choose OK. The alert warns you that Excel will round constant numbers that have more decimal places than their formatting allows. The forecast worksheet now uses the numbers displayed to perform its calculations.

For Related Information:

▶▶ "Entering Formulas," p. 175.

▶▶ "Filling or Copying Cell Contents," p. 234.

▶▶ "Formatting Numbers," p. 272.

▶▶ "Adding Color, Patterns, and Borders," p. 293.

FROM HERE...

Saving Your Worksheet

You should save your worksheet. You will use it again in the Quick Start for charting. Follow these steps to save the worksheet:

1. Choose the **F**ile Save **A**s command so that you can rename the file. (Use **F**ile **S**ave to save with the same name.)

2. Type the file name *FORCST02*.

3. Choose OK or press Enter.

These steps save your worksheet to the hard-disk directory shown in the dialog box.

For Related Information:

▶▶ "Managing Files," p. 158.

FROM HERE...

Exiting Excel

To exit Excel, follow these steps:

1. Choose the **F**ile E**x**it command.

   If you have made changes to the worksheet since the last time you saved it, an alert box asks whether you want to save the worksheet (see fig. 3.27).

2. Choose **Y**es if you want to save the worksheet or **N**o if you do not.

3. If you choose **Yes** in step 2, Excel saves the file with its current name.

You return to the Windows desktop.

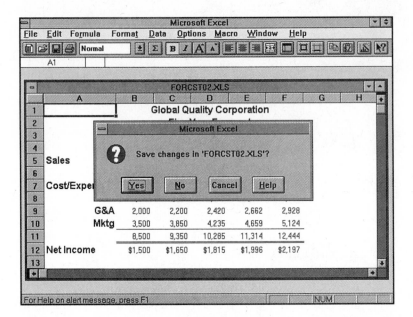

FIG. 3.27

You are asked to save any changed worksheets before closing Excel.

FROM HERE...

For Related Information:

▶▶ "Exiting Excel," p.167.

Chapter Summary

This Quick Start covers only a few of Excel's basic capabilities. Excel has many more features and functions. Other chapters show you how to import graphics and draw on the worksheet, how to use multiple worksheets or split a single worksheet into multiple views, how to link and consolidate data between worksheets, and how to use the many add-in programs that come free with Excel.

As you read through the following chapters, you may want to experiment with the worksheet you have created. Experimenting will give you more hands-on experience. Save an unchanged copy of this worksheet for use with the "Chart Quick Start," Chapter 17.

Designing Worksheets

Y ou have two options when you start a new worksheet. You can spend a little time planning ahead in the beginning, or you can spend a great amount of time repairing and restructuring the worksheet methods later. For small, one- or two-screen worksheets, planning and design are helpful. For anything larger, planning and building the worksheet in the correct order is essential for saving you time and effort. Planning also increases the flexibility of your system if you need to change it.

Designing a good worksheet involves at least 14 steps.

Although the following steps are not a checklist, they should be part of your general philosophy concerning using worksheets. These steps save time, reduce the work of maintenance and changes, and reduce the likelihood of errors. To design a good worksheet, complete the following steps:

1. Understand the problem and the desired solution.

2. Make thumbnail sketches or feasibility studies.

3. Build a text skeleton.

4. Enter simple sample data.

5. Enter formulas.

6. Check for reasonable results.

7. Apply formatting and styles.

8. Cross-check for accurate results.

9. Add graphics and explanatory text boxes.

10. Link the worksheet to other sheets in the system.

11. Automate the system.

12. Cross-check your system.

13. Document the worksheets and system.

14. Archive your system and documentation.

This chapter discusses these steps. To read more about a specific step, find its section heading.

Understanding the Problem and Desired Solution

You must understand the problem and the desired solution before you start to create a worksheet or larger system. Regardless of whether you are creating a worksheet for yourself or for someone else, you must know what the finished system needs to accomplish and how users expect to use it. One way to prevent miscommunication is to create prototype data-entry screens and reports. You can create sample data-entry screens and report output in Excel. From these examples, the users can tell you what changes are needed before you get too far into the project.

The following questions need to be answered before you design a worksheet:

■ What solution are you seeking?

■ What input do you need in order to find that solution?

■ What is the best design for entering data?

■ How do you want the output to look?

■ Should you build the system on one worksheet or on many worksheets linked together?

Making Thumbnail Sketches

Every great artist from Michelangelo and Leonardo da Vinci to Pablo Picasso has made thumbnail sketches, which are small practice exercises, and sample drawings before starting a major work. When you create a worksheet or system of worksheets, you may want to do more than just use thumbnail sketches of the layout.

Drawing charts of the data flow and maps of the worksheet layout, such as the one shown in figure 4.1, can be very helpful. These flowcharts and maps often pinpoint problems before you have committed yourself to a specific design. You can even draw the flowchart on an Excel worksheet.

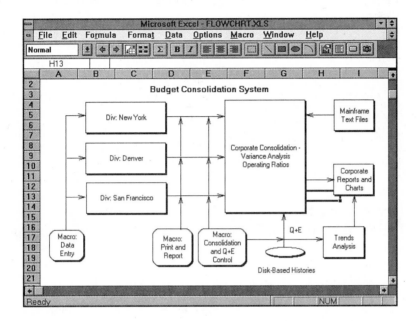

When creating a worksheet or collection of worksheets that solve a problem new to you, you should do a feasibility study. Can the problem be solved by using the method you propose? Make a simplified model of the problem; then create a small worksheet by using the commands, functions, and macros that you think will work. If you are facing a new type of problem, you may find that working on three or four small feasibility studies will save you time and embarrassment from wasted work on a large system that must be redesigned before its completion.

Remember to design the layout so that you can modify it easily in the future. Few worksheets ever remain the same. Before laying out a worksheet, read through the discussions in this book concerning conserving memory, linking multiple worksheets, creating workbooks, and improving performance. Your worksheet map should show blocks that indicate the data-entry areas, calculation areas, report formats and embedded charts, the database, the database extract areas for printed reports, and other major parts of the worksheet.

Keep data-entry cells separate from calculation areas. This practice reduces the chance of errors and allows room for instructions and entry-checking formulas. You should try to make the data-entry screen look like a paper form. Keep values that might change, such as growth rates, outside of the formulas in cells. When you keep data that is likely to change in a cell, updating the data is easy. Putting changeable data in a formula requires you to find and edit formulas if you want to change data.

Building a Text Skeleton

One of the easiest ways to design a worksheet is to create a framework on which you can build (see fig. 4.2). Your framework is the text that shows where data will be entered, where formula results will appear, and so on. Text skeletons enable you to easily enter sample data in the correct locations and to select the correct cells for use in a formula. If you later decide that you don't like your original layout, Excel's editing commands make moving cell contents easy. When you move the cells used in formulas, Excel automatically adjusts the formulas so that they continue to work correctly.

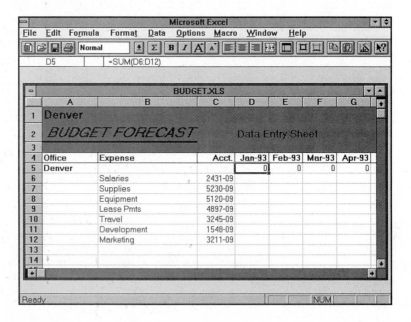

FIG. 4.2

A data-entry text skeleton for the Denver office.

Entering Simple Sample Data

The text skeleton will show you where to enter simple data that you use as sample data. Use simple data, such as .1 and 200, so that you can immediately recognize whether the results of formulas are correct. Figure 4.3 shows the simple data used to build a budget worksheet. If you enter this type of data before entering formulas, you can tell as soon as you enter the formula whether the result is reasonable and correct. Using complicated sample data, such as .8765 and 198.7, increases the difficulty in determining whether the results are correct. Using easily understood sample data increases the odds that you will immediately detect an error.

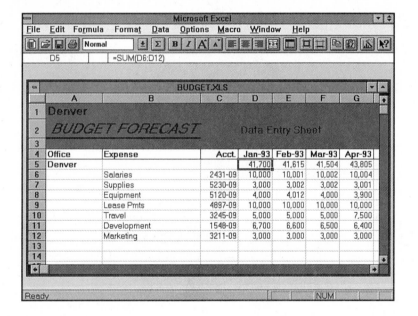

FIG. 4.3

Simple data in a worksheet entered as a sample.

Entering Formulas

When you enter formulas, start with the simple ones and work toward the more complex formulas that depend on the results of other formulas. Never enter numbers that can change, such as an interest rate, directly in a formula. Enter such numbers in a cell, and then use the cell address in the formula. By keeping variables out of the formulas, you increase the reliability of your worksheet and reduce the need for corrections later. In this way, you can update variables by typing a new number in one cell, rather than editing formulas throughout the worksheet. Entering and editing formulas is described in Chapter 7, "Entering and Editing Worksheet Data."

Checking for Reasonable Results

Because you entered sample data first, most of your formulas produce a result as soon as you enter them. And because the data is simple, you should be able to judge whether the formula is correct. Ask yourself whether the answer seems reasonable so that you can catch obvious mistakes as soon as you enter the formula.

Applying Formatting and Styles

One of Excel's powerful features is its capability to create a polished printed or on-screen result. At this point, you should apply formatting that you have not already used. You can save time by selecting all the cells and ranges requiring the same format and formatting them with one command. The selected cells do not need to be adjacent. Define styles for formats that you use repeatedly. Styles contain a combination of formats that you define. When you change the definition of a style, all cells using the style change to reflect the new definition.

If you need a numeric or date format that doesn't exist, create the format by using custom numeric or date formatting. Keep in mind that formatting rounds off the displayed number but not the number used in Excel's internal calculations. To make the calculated numbers match the display, choose the **Options Calculations** command, and select the **Precision as Displayed** option.

Use borders, shading, and color formats to create a pleasant and more readable screen. Change the worksheet and window display appearance with the **Options Display** and **Options Workspace** commands. Formatting and styles are covered in Chapter 8.

Cross-Checking for Accurate Results

Use real data and compare the worksheet results against more than one hand-calculated answer from previously solved problems. Never trust a new worksheet. Add data-entry checking formulas, such as those described in Chapter 13.

Adding Graphics and Text

You can create worksheets that include your company's logo, include explanatory text boxes, display charts next to the worksheet, and add graphics to make your worksheet look polished and professional. You can use the drawing and text tools in Excel, or you can paste or embed graphics and charts drawn in other programs. Your Excel charts can even use pictures or logos as markers where bars or columns would normally appear. Chapter 9 describes how to draw on your worksheet, add text boxes, and import or embed graphics from other Windows programs.

Linking or Consolidating Worksheets

After verifying that individual worksheets work correctly, you may need to link multiple worksheets together to form a larger system. Or you may want to group worksheets together into workbooks. The power of linking, consolidating or embedding data is described in Chapter 12. Remember that you also must verify that your worksheet works correctly as part of a larger system.

If the worksheet you created will be used as a master from which other sheets will be created, you may want to save the worksheet as a template. Templates act as partially completed worksheets from which other worksheets can be built and include all the data, text, formulas, styles, outlines, and macros of the original. Building systems involving multiple worksheets or templates is covered in Chapter 11.

Automating the System

Consider adding features to the system that make operation easier or automated. You may want to add workbooks, macros, custom toolbars, named printing ranges, custom menus, custom dialog boxes, and even custom help files. Building systems is covered in Chapter 11. Automating systems by using macros is treated in Chapters 27-30.

Cross-Checking Your System

Just as editing your own writing is difficult, so is verifying your own worksheets. Run your system, just as the actual operators would, by using real numbers, and compare the results against manual calculations. Ask operators to run the completed system during a trial period to check for errors in calculations and operating procedures. Ask these operators to keep log books of errors and how they occurred. If the system is critical to your business, operate parallel business functions by operating manual *and* Excel systems until you are sure that the Excel system works correctly. Solve problems or verify operations with the worksheet audit and macro-debugging features built into Excel or included free in the LIBRARY directory.

Documenting the System

Enter a date and version number in a corner of the completed worksheets along with the creator's initials and the initials of the audit team. Document macros by using the three-column method of writing macros, which is described in Chapters 27-30.

Use the **F**ormula **N**ote command to attach notes to cells. In these notes, you can explain formulas and assumptions and add instructions (see fig. 4.4). Notes can help you and others remember how your worksheet works, why you used certain numbers, or how a formula was derived.

Archiving Your System

To coin a new computer maxim: *There are those who back up their work and those who wish they had backed up their work.* Save copies of your worksheets about every 15 minutes as you build them. Use different version numbers for each worksheet so that you can refer to previous versions, such as the sequence FORCST12, FORCST13, and FORCST14. You later can erase outdated versions by using the **F**ile **D**elete command.

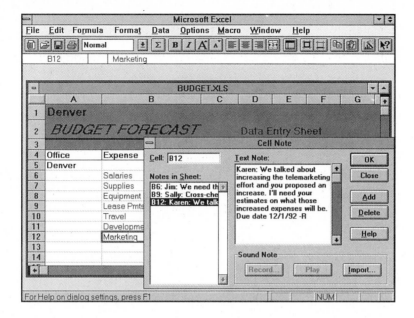

FIG. 4.4

A note window used
for documentation.

If your worksheets and data are important, store copies in physically separate locations. If the building burns or if a thief steals the computer and disks, you will not lose your original *and* backup disks.

Chapter Summary

This short chapter gave you a general philosophy for building worksheets and databases. If you haven't followed the worksheet Quick Start in Chapter 3, you should do so before you explore Chapters 5-16. The Quick Start will give you a working overview of the steps required for building a worksheet. The following chapters describe in detail the many features available in Excel worksheets.

Making the Switch from 1-2-3 to Excel

If you used Lotus 1-2-3 in the past, you can make the transition to Excel smoothly, continue to use your 1-2-3 knowledge, and gain the increased power available from Excel and the other Windows applications Excel works with so well.

Excel's new Help features enable you to enter the 1-2-3 keystrokes and commands you are familiar with. Excel then demonstrates in your worksheet how to perform the same commands by using Excel. This approach enables you to use your 1-2-3 experience to learn Excel. Within a few weeks, you will progress beyond the best level you achieved with 1-2-3. Although Excel is more flexible and powerful than other spreadsheets, you will find that it is more accessible, so you can use more of its features with less effort.

When you open your 1-2-3 worksheets in Excel, you can enter formulas in the way that you entered them in 1-2-3. Formulas and database queries work the same in Excel as in 1-2-3, and you can turn on navigation keys that enable you to use the keystrokes you've memorized. Excel also loads the 1-2-3 FMT and FM3 formatting files so that the new Excel worksheet has the same formatting as 1-2-3. If you have many 1-2-3 macros, you will appreciate Excel's capability to run 1-2-3 macros located in the Excel worksheet without translation.

Reviewing Excel Features

If you are unfamiliar with Excel's features, you may want to review the following list.

Entering Data

■ Automatically format cells when Excel recognizes a numeric or date/time format in the entered data. For example:

Entering	*Displays*
Sep 9, 91	9-Sep-91
$3,500	$3,500

■ Automatically enter a decimal just as you would with a ten-key calculator through the **O**ptions **W**orkspace command and **F**ixed Decimal option.

■ Move the active cell down when you press Enter. (This option can be turned off.)

■ Enter multiple numbers simultaneously by selecting the cells before typing, entering the number, and then pressing Ctrl+Enter.

Editing Formulas or Text

■ Enter cell references or ranges by clicking or dragging with the mouse during formula creation or editing.

■ Paste worksheet functions and their arguments into formulas with the **F**ormula Paste Function, so you do not have to remember the correct syntax.

■ Paste names into formulas with **F**ormula **P**aste Names.

■ Undo typing, editing mistakes, and commands with **E**dit **U**ndo.

■ Search and replace values or parts of formulas with **F**ormula Replace.

■ Check the spelling in worksheets, databases, or charts.

Calculating

■ Calculate partial results within a formula to aid you in troubleshooting.

■ Recalculate tables automatically or on command.

■ Create multiple data tables per worksheet.

■ Calculate large worksheets in the background as you continue to work in the worksheet, on other worksheets, or in other Windows applications.

Formatting

- Use tools on movable toolbars to reformat or reorganize worksheets or charts with a single click.

- Create custom numeric and date/time formats that include special characters, symbols, decimal precision, and colors.

- Create worksheets, text boxes, graphics, pictures and charts on the same page.

- Draw on the worksheet by using Excel's drawing tools.

- Paste high-quality drawings, logos, or artwork on worksheets from other applications.

- Format a cell's contents with a font, size, style, and color.

- Use up to 256 fonts per worksheet.

- Add color formats, shades of grey, and patterns to the worksheet.

- Create your own color palettes.

- Add eight different types of cell borders including double-underlining.

- Change row height or column width.

- Wrap words within a cell so that they display and print as a paragraph.

- Double-click on column-heading border to adjust column width to best fit.

- Hide worksheets, rows, columns, or cells.

- Align numbers, dates, or text.

- Switch number, currency, and date formats to many international styles.

Worksheet Functions

- Use Excel's built-in functions for math, finance, statistics, and science. Add-in functions that come free with Excel give you advanced statistical and financial functions, such as Fourier analysis and bond and financial analysis.

- Create custom functions for frequently used formulas so that your functions appear in the built-in functions list.

Printing

- Preview documents on-screen to see exactly how they will appear on paper.

■ Change margins by dragging them to new locations within the preview document.

■ Print named collections of worksheet ranges and charts.

■ Print vertically or horizontally.

■ Print worksheet ranges, text boxes, graphics, and pictures and charts on the same page.

Database

■ Automatically generate a data-entry, edit, and search form for a database by using the **Data Form** command.

■ Develop impressive cross-tabulation reports from databases with the guidance of the Crosstab Wizard.

■ Link worksheets to disk-based databases or to selected SQL query databases by using the Q+E application that comes with Excel.

Charts

■ Create any predefined chart with guidance from the ChartWizard.

■ Modify data ranges used in existing charts with the ChartWizard.

■ Choose from eight types of two-dimensional charts, combination charts, and six types of three-dimensional charts.

■ Select from many predefined chart formats.

■ Customize charts with colors, patterns, shading, fonts, overlay charts, hi-lo points, floating text, scaling, arrows, and more.

■ Create picture charts by using pictures in place of bars or columns.

■ Move a bar or column in a chart and cause the corresponding worksheet value to change.

■ Rotate and change the perspective on 3-D charts by dragging the chart axis.

Linked and Consolidated Worksheets

■ Link worksheets, databases, and charts so that data changed in one passes to another.

■ Link sheets on-screen or on disk.

■ Consolidate data between worksheets by range or by row and column heading titles.

■ Link Excel with other Windows applications by using Dynamic Data Exchange (DDE).

■ Embed data or graphics in Excel worksheets so that the data becomes an integral part of the Excel worksheet file.

Worksheet Add-In Applications

■ Use the Solver to find optimal solutions for worksheet problems.

■ Use the What-If add-in to find the data-entry value needed to solve for a specific solution.

■ Use the Scenario Manager to store and analyze different sets of input data and the resulting outcomes.

■ Use the Analysis ToolPak to solve statistical, engineering, and scientific problems that require advanced mathematical formulas.

■ Use the many free add-ins included with Excel, such as a worksheet auditor for troubleshooting, a macro debugger, an autosaver, a slide show application, and many other features.

Debugging and Documenting

■ Use the free Audit and Debug add-in applications to find and troubleshoot errors in worksheets and macros.

■ Tag notes on cells with the Formula Note command.

■ Add voice messages to cells that others can play back.

■ Find formulas, terms, or errors with Formula Find or Formula Select Special.

■ Find cells that feed into or out of a formula with Formula Select Special.

■ More easily resolve errors with more specific error types: #N/A, #VALUE!, #DIV/0!, #NAME?, #NULL!, #NUM!, and #REF!.

Windowing

■ Save named views of worksheets so that you can return to the same layout.

■ Group worksheets, charts, and macro sheets into workbooks.

■ Edit and enter data and formats into groups of worksheets.

■ Display multiple applications and multiple data documents on one screen.

■ Split windows into up to four panes showing different views of the same sheet.

■ Open multiple windows onto the same sheet.

Macros

■ Record macros by using keystrokes, shortcut keys, or mouse actions.

■ Keep macros independent of documents so that you can use them with other documents.

■ Create buttons that run macros.

■ Link macros to pictures so that selecting a picture runs a macro.

■ Create custom menus and full-featured dialog boxes.

■ Operate other Windows applications under Excel control. For example, an Excel macro can control the time when a communication application begins printing.

■ Customize the menus, commands, toolbars, and dialog boxes of Excel to completely reflect your own application.

Windows Environment

■ Copy and paste data with standard DOS or Windows applications.

■ Link data to other Windows applications.

■ Embed data from other Windows applications.

Making the Transition Smoothly

When you change from 1-2-3 to Excel, consider the following important concepts:

■ **Learning a new skill.** Sometimes learning a new skill that is similar to an old skill can be difficult. An old skill can interfere with a new, but similar skill. If you understand that this happens, you will find that Excel and its related Windows applications are well worth the transition.

■ **Command/Range or Range/Command.** Make changes to an Excel sheet or chart by first selecting the cells or graphics you want to change, and then choosing the command to affect the cells or graphics.

1-2-3 works the opposite way. In 1-2-3, you choose a command and then select the cells to be affected. The advantage of Excel's method is that after an Excel command is completed, the range remains selected, so you can make additional changes to the same selected cells or graphical item.

■ **Use Alt for Excel menus; use / for 1-2-3 menus.** Although you can choose to activate Excel menus by pressing the / (slash) key, this procedure is not a good idea. Use the Alt key.

If you are an experienced 1-2-3 user, pressing the / key cues your mind that you will begin typing a string of 1-2-3 commands. When instead you begin typing Excel commands, you must slow down and you may create errors. To prevent this, use the Alt key to activate Excel menus. The Alt key is the standard menu key used by all Windows applications. You can continue to use the / key to run 1-2-3 menus through Excel's 1-2-3 Help system described in a later section.

■ **Use your 1-2-3 knowledge to learn Excel.** Use Excel's Help Lotus 1-2-3 commands to learn Excel while you continue working with Lotus keystrokes or commands. (See the following section.)

The Help Lotus 1-2-3 feature accepts your 1-2-3 keystrokes and menu selections. The feature then demonstrates how to accomplish the same command by using Excel's commands. This feature actually demonstrates the Excel command on your worksheet by using the range of cells you select. The result is that you can continue to work and learn at the same time.

■ **Help is always available.** Press F1 whenever Excel displays a dialog box that you aren't familiar with. When a dialog box or error box is displayed, press F1 to see an explanation of what each option does. Press Alt+F4 to close the Help window. If you do not want to complete the dialog box, press Esc.

■ **Don't think that you are restricted to using a mouse.** You can operate Excel with the mouse, arrow keys, function keys, shortcut keys, or by touch-typing. Excel and many Windows applications are designed to be flexible. You aren't limited to one mode of operation. Use a combination of the methods that make you the most productive. After becoming proficient, most people find that a combination of mouse and shortcut keys gives them the greatest speed. The easiest way to learn and remember is by using the mouse.

Understanding Excel Procedures and Terms

Excel follows a standard procedure for changing a worksheet, chart, or macro. You perform the following steps for nearly all commands:

1. Select the cell, range, or graphical object to be affected.

2. Choose a command, press a shortcut key, or click on a tool in a toolbar.

3. Select options from a dialog box, if necessary; then choose OK or press Enter.

The *active* cell is the cell surrounded by a darker border. Your data entry or pasted data goes into the selected cell.

Selected cells are darkened. *Selected objects* are enclosed in black or white *handles* that look like small squares. Commands affect the selected cells or objects. Objects enclosed in black handles can be moved to new locations or reshaped by dragging them with a mouse.

A *range* of cells is a rectangular group of selected cells. In Excel, you can select a discontiguous range (nonadjacent cells) so that a single command affects multiple areas simultaneously. You also can select multiple nonadjacent rows and columns and with one command change their contents. Within a selected range, the active cell is white surrounded by a dark border.

Excel can use the A1 or R1C1 methods of *cell referencing.* The A1 method is used most commonly in worksheets. The R1C1, row number/column number, method is used in recorded macros.

Getting Help with 1-2-3

To get Help information on switching from 1-2-3 to Excel, choose the **H**elp **C**ontents command by pressing Alt, H, then C. Press the Tab key to select Switching from Lotus 1-2-3 at the bottom of the list; then press Enter.

Press Tab to select the topic you want; then press Enter. You can jump between locations in Help files, search for topics, and print the Help information you see. Close the Help window by holding down Alt and pressing F4 (Alt+F4).

Excel contains hundreds of pages of help information that is available through the **H**elp menu or by pressing F1. The Help feature is described in more detail in Chapter 2, "Learning Windows and Excel Basics."

If you are familiar with 1-2-3, you can learn Excel quickly with the new Excel Help features. You can use your 1-2-3 knowledge and skills to do the same work you did in 1-2-3. As you learn Excel, you can use its more accessible and greater power to do even more than you could in 1-2-3.

Using 1-2-3 Commands To Learn and Operate Excel

Excel will accept your 1-2-3 commands and paste a temporary list of instructions on your worksheet or show you how to perform the equivalent operation in Excel. As Excel demonstrates the equivalent operation, it acts on your worksheet to produce the result you wanted; you can work and learn simultaneously. As you gain more knowledge of Excel, you can use its accessible features and enhancements directly from Excel menus.

To configure Excel to paste instructions or to demonstrate 1-2-3-equivalent procedures, perform the following steps:

1. Choose the **O**ptions **W**orkspace command to display the following dialog box (see fig. 5.1).

2. Select the **Alternate** Menu or Help Key by pressing Alt+A and typing the / (slash), if a slash is not already there.

3. Select the **Lotus** 1-2-3 Help option by pressing Alt+L. The option is selected when the circle is darkened.

4. Press Enter to choose the OK button.

Now when you press the / (slash) key, the Lotus 1-2-3 Help dialog box is displayed.

If you want to temporarily paste instructions on your worksheet, perform the following steps:

1. Press the / (slash) key. The Help for Lotus 1-2-3 Users dialog box, shown in figure 5.2, is displayed.

2. Check to be certain that the **I**nstructions option is selected (darkened). Press Alt+I if you need to select the **I**nstructions option.

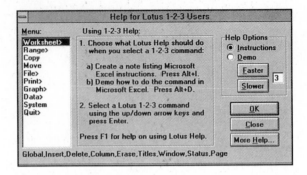

FIG. 5.2

Select the Instructions option to temporarily paste Help on your worksheet.

3. Select 1-2-3 commands from the **M**enu list by pressing the same keystrokes you use in 1-2-3. Touch-type with the first letters or press arrow keys to select a 1-2-3 command; then press Enter. With a mouse, double-click on a command. Press Esc to back up to previous menu options.

Excel pastes a list of instructions over your worksheet, as shown in the lower-right corner of the worksheet in figure 5.3. You can move this list by dragging it to a new location with a mouse as you would drag any graphical object on an Excel worksheet. You can select and copy the list to make a permanent copy. To remove the temporary instruction list when you are done, press Esc.

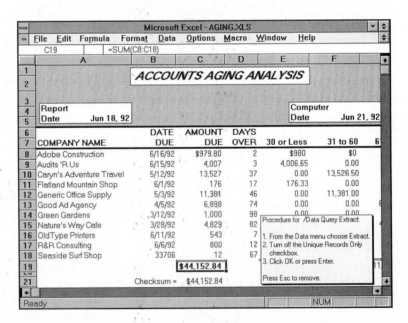

FIG. 5.3

Excel temporarily pastes instructions over the worksheet.

If you want Excel to accept your 1-2-3 keystrokes and demonstrate how to perform the equivalent Excel keystrokes, complete the following steps:

1. Press the / (slash) key. The Help for Lotus 1-2-3 Users dialog box shown in figure 5.4 is displayed.

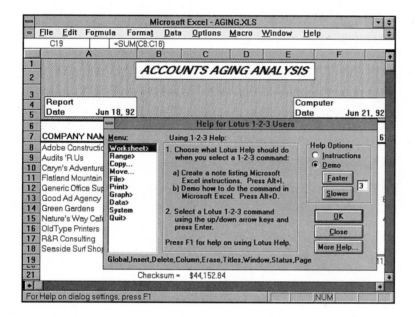

FIG. 5.4

Select the Demo option for Excel to demonstrate the equivalent of your 1-2-3 commands.

2. Check to be certain that the **D**emo option is selected (darkened). Press Alt+D if you need to select the **D**emo option.

3. Choose the **F**aster (Alt+F) or **S**lower (Alt+S) buttons to change the speed of the demonstration or change the speed number to any number 1-5.

4. Select 1-2-3 commands from the **M**enu list by pressing the same keystrokes you use in 1-2-3. Touch-type with the first letters or press arrow keys to select a 1-2-3 command; then press Enter. With a mouse, click on a command. Press Esc to move back through the 1-2-3 menu.

   If more information is required, Excel displays a 1-2-3 Help bar across the top of the screen after you select a 1-2-3 command, as shown in figure 5.5. The bar in the figure is for the Lotus /Copy command. In your 1-2-3 Help bar, enter the necessary cell ranges or data required to complete the command.

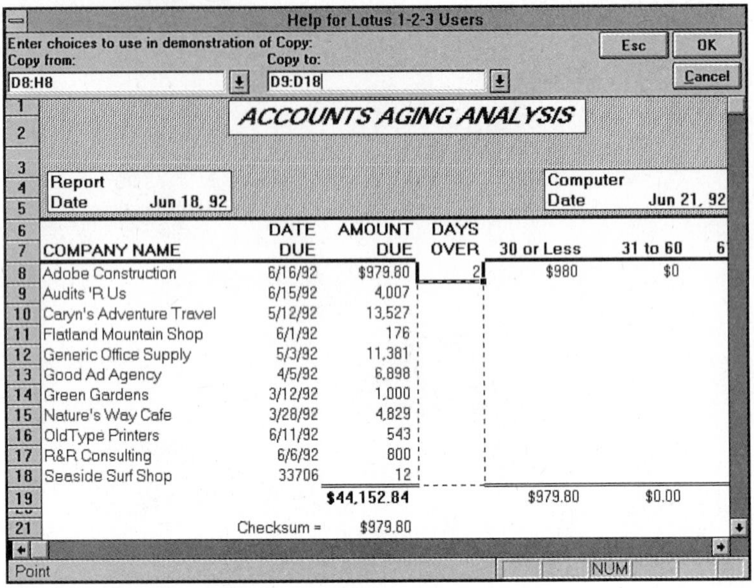

FIG. 5.5

Excel displays 1-2-3 range prompts that work the same as in 1-2-3.

5. Press Enter to move between text boxes and buttons in the 1-2-3 Help bar. Enter data, such as the number of decimals in a format, by selecting the text box and typing. Select a range of cells to be affected, by using 1-2-3 or Excel techniques.

To select a cell range by using 1-2-3 techniques, use the same methods of specifying the range that you would use in 1-2-3. Type the range or use arrow keys to point to a cell. Press Enter to move to a second text or cell reference box, if required. Press the period (.) key to fix one cell reference as the corner of a range. Press Esc to remove the period and unanchor a cell reference or to move back to the previous text or cell reference.

To select a range by using Excel techniques, drag across the range with a mouse or move to one corner of the range; then hold down the Shift key as you move by keyboard to the opposite corner.

Press the Esc key to undo a mistake.

6. When the 1-2-3 Help bar is filled, press Enter or click on the OK button to see the demonstration using the commands and worksheet range you selected.

Using Functions Keys

Many of the Excel function keys are the same as those in 1-2-3. Excel has many additional function and shortcut keys available. You hold down Shift, Ctrl, or Alt as you press the function key. Additional Excel function keys are listed in the pull-out Quick Reference card at the back of the book. Table 5.1 lists compatible Excel and 1-2-3 function keys.

Table 5.1. Compatible Excel and 1-2-3 Function Keys

Function Key	1-2-3	Excel
F1	Help	Help
F2	Edit	Edit
F4	Absolute Reference	Absolute Reference
F5	Goto	Goto
F6	Window	Next Pane
F9	Calc	Calculate Now (all worksheets)
Shift+F9	N/A	Calculate Document (active document only)

Excel recalculates data tables automatically, so there is no need for the F8 key to calculate tables. (You can toggle automatic table calculation on or off through the menu.) The Graph key, F10, is unnecessary in Excel because you can display graphs simultaneously with their supporting worksheets.

Moving and Selecting Cells and Ranges

You can move and select cells in Excel by using 1-2-3 or Excel navigation keys. If you are not familiar with 1-2-3, you should use Excel navigation keys.

Moving and Selecting with 1-2-3 Navigation Keys

While you are learning Excel, you may want to use 1-2-3 keystrokes to move and select cells. Excel has many more shortcut keys, function keys, and movement and selection keys than are available in 1-2-3. You will be more productive if you learn the Excel keys listed in the following sections and in the following chapters. While you learn Excel, you may want to use these alternate navigation keys. To use alternate navigation keys in Excel, perform the following steps:

1. Choose the **O**ptions **W**orkspace command by pressing Alt, O, and then W.

2. Select the Alternate Navigation **K**eys check box by holding down the Alt key as you press K (Alt+K).

3. Choose OK or press Enter.

Return to the normal Excel navigation keys by following the same procedure and deselecting the Alternate **K**eystrokes check box. (A check box is selected when an X appears in it.)

The alternate navigation keys are listed in table 5.2. The table shows the major differences between Excel and alternate navigation keys. Those keystrokes that are not listed are the same for both methods.

Table 5.2. Alternate Navigation Keys

Keystroke(s)	Excel	Alternate
Ctrl+left arrow	Move left to edge of filled data cells	Move left one screen
Ctrl+right arrow	Move right to edge of filled data cells	Move right one screen
Home	Move to first cell in row	Move to cell A1
Ctrl+PgUp	Move left one window	Next worksheet in Workbook (like movements in 3-D worksheets)
Ctrl+PgDn	Move right one window	Previous worksheet in Workbook (like movements in 3-D worksheets)
Tab	Move right one cell	Move right one page
Shift+Tab	Move left one cell	Move left one page

To select cells as you move across them, hold down the Shift key and press a movement key. To select a range of cells from the active cell to the edge of a data block, move to the first cell, press End, and then hold down the Shift key as you press the arrow in the direction you want to select. To select a range of cells with the Goto key, press F5, enter the range you want by using a colon (:) to separate cell references, such as B5:C12, and then press Shift+Enter.

While the Alternate Navigation **K**eys option is selected, you also can enter text, functions, and formulas. You can use methods that are similar to those in 1-2-3 (see table 5.3).

Table 5.3. Alternate Data-Entry Keys	
Keystroke	**Result**
'	Left align following text in cell (also available when Alt Nav keys are off)
"	Right align following text in cell
^	Center following text in cell
\	Fill cell with following characters
@	Precede a function or formula (optional)
+ - (1 to 9)	Start a formula or use Excel's = (equals sign)

Moving and Selecting with Excel Navigation Keys

To move the active cell, use the arrow keys, page keys, or Ctrl+arrow. An alternate method is pressing the Goto key, F5, type a location or select a location's name, and press Enter.

For such tasks as formatting, editing, and entering data, you must *select* the cell or range of cells to be affected. To select a cell range by keyboard, complete the following steps:

1. Move to one corner of the rectangular range you want selected.

2. Hold down the Shift key, and move to the opposite corner of the range by pressing the movement keys.

3. Make your menu selection.

If you are using a mouse, complete the following steps:

1. Click on a cell at one corner of the range.

2. Hold down the mouse button, and drag the mouse pointer to the opposite corner.

3. Release the mouse pointer.

Chapter 6, "Creating Worksheets," lists numerous shortcuts for selecting ranges and for accelerating movements by key or by mouse.

Entering Formulas by Using 1-2-3's Method

You can enter formulas in Excel worksheets in two ways: by typing them as you would in 1-2-3 or by typing them in Excel's method. To change between the two methods of entering formulas, choose the **Options Cal**culation command. In the Calculation Options dialog box, shown in figure 5.6, select the Alternate **F**ormula Entry check box if you want to use the 1-2-3 method of formula entry.

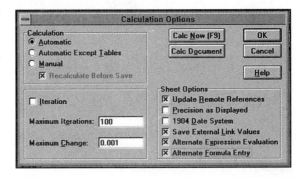

FIG. 5.6

The Calculation Options dialog box.

T I P	Excel automatically recognizes the following characters:

Character	Use
'	Precede text for left alignment
..	Range operator, as in B36..B42
@	Precede Excel function name
+	Begin formula

Formulas and database criteria are evaluated differently in 1-2-3 and Excel. To change between the two methods of evaluating formulas and criteria, choose the **O**ptions **C**alculation command. In the Calculation dialog box that appears, select the Alternate E**x**pression Evaluation check box if you want to use the 1-2-3 method of evaluating formulas and criteria.

> **NOTE** Alternate **F**ormula Entry and Alternate E**x**pression Evaluation are included in Excel for compatibility with your existing 1-2-3 worksheets. You will find that learning Excel is easier and that your worksheets will be more compatible with worksheets from other applications if you use these formulas only when necessary for 1-2-3 compatibility.

Opening a 1-2-3 worksheet automatically turns on Alternate E**x**pression Evaluation. If the worksheet contains a 1-2-3 macro, Excel turns on Alternate **F**ormula Entry to aid macro operation. Even if you save the 1-2-3 worksheet to disk with an Excel format, these two check boxes remain on. You must manually turn these check boxes off to revert to the Excel method.

> **CAUTION:** Do not indiscriminately turn off the Alternate Formula Entry and Alternate Expression Evaluation check boxes on worksheets that originated in 1-2-3. Due to differences in formula calculation and criteria evaluation, the worksheet may no longer give valid results. If you turn off these options, be certain that you validate the worksheet before using it.

When Alternate Formula Entry is on, you perform tasks in the following methods:

- Enter a formula by using a reference and the reference immediately converts to the appropriate range name on entry, if that range name is defined. In Excel, range names do not automatically replace cell references.

- Edit a range name in a formula to a reference. When you enter the formula, bar range names automatically convert to their reference equivalent.

- Delete a range name, and all the formulas using that range name convert to the equivalent reference. In Excel deleted names produce a #NAME? error.

Entering Formulas by Using Excel's Method

Enter formulas by selecting a cell, then beginning the formula with a plus sign (+) or an equals sign (=). After you start a formula, you can enter cell references by typing, by moving to a cell by using keys, or by clicking on the cell. You can use the Goto key, F5, during formula entry. Press the Enter key to enter a formula or press Esc to back out.

Functions do not begin with an @ sign unless the alternative formula entry option is on. You can paste functions and their arguments into worksheet or macro sheet cells by choosing Formula Paste Function and selecting the Paste **A**rguments check box. This technique is useful when you forget what the arguments are or the order in which they should be typed. (An *argument* is the information enclosed by the parentheses that follow a function.)

Press the Edit key, F2, to edit the formula in the active cell. Press the Absolute Reference key, F4, to cycle between absolute and relative references while entering or editing a cell reference.

Retrieving and Saving 1-2-3 Files

You do not need to run a conversion application to open or save 1-2-3 files with Excel. Excel does this automatically. When you save a 1-2-3 file into Excel format, be certain that you follow the directions that follow later. You must select a conversion alternative from a list; you cannot convert a file by changing only its file extension.

Opening 1-2-3 Worksheets and Charts

To load a 1-2-3 worksheet file, perform the following steps:

1. Choose the **File O**pen command.

2. Select the File **N**ame text box, and type a new file pattern of *.WK?*, then choose OK.

   Or, select the List Files of **T**ype drop-down list and select the Lotus 1-2-3 File (*.WK*) option.

   Figure 5.7 shows the File Open dialog box with the File **N**ame text box changed to display 1-2-3 files.

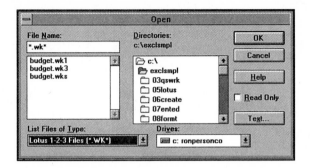

FIG. 5.7

Change the File Name text box to see a list of 1-2-3 files.

3. Select the File Name list box by pressing Alt+N, then Tab, or by clicking in the list. Click on the file name you want, or press the up- or down-arrow key to highlight the name of the file you want to open.

4. Choose the OK button or press Enter.

NOTE If Excel encounters a formula it cannot translate, Excel displays an alert box containing the reference for that formula. The value of the 1-2-3 formula is put in the corresponding cell of the Excel worksheet. Excel will then open the file as Read Only so that you must give it a new name when you save it and not lose information in the original 1-2-3 file.

The 1-2-3 file you selected is opened and automatically converted. When Excel opens a 1-2-3 file, Excel changes its default settings so that it can be more compatible with the 1-2-3 file. When you open a 1-2-3 worksheet, the following changes occur:

- Alternative Formula Entry check box is turned on if a 1-2-3 macro is on the sheet.

- Alternative Expression Evaluation check box is turned on.

- Alternate Navigation Keys check box is turned on.

- FMT and FM3 formatting files are read if they are in the same directory as the 1-2-3 worksheet file. Their formatting is applied to give the Excel worksheet the same formatting as that in 1-2-3.

- 3-D WK3 files are loaded into Excel Workbooks.

- Unprotected cells are formatted with blue font.

- Normal font for sheet is set to 10-point Courier.

Notice that the document's title bar still shows that the file has a 1-2-3 extension. If you save the file without setting file type to Normal, Excel will save as the file as a 1-2-3 file, and you will lose any Excel enhancement or charts you add.

While 1-2-3 files are on-screen, you can treat them as you would any Excel file. You can link them, and you can enhance them with Excel formulas and features. Saving the file back in its 1-2-3 format loses all the Excel enhancements. Links or consolidations are preserved where a 1-2-3 worksheet supplies an Excel worksheet with data.

Saving 1-2-3 Worksheets with Excel Formats

If you open a 1-2-3 file into Excel and save it by using the **File S**ave or **F**ile Save **A**s command without changing the Save File as **T**ype to Normal, you will save the file in its original 1-2-3 format and lose any Excel enhancements you have added. To preserve the enhancements, you must save the 1-2-3 file in an Excel format.

To save a 1-2-3 file in an Excel file format, complete the following steps:

1. Choose the File Save **A**s command.

   The Save As dialog box appears.

2. Type the file name in the File **N**ame text box.

3. Select the Normal format from the Save File as **T**ype list (see fig. 5.8).

4. Choose OK or press Enter to save the file.

FIG. 5.8

Save to a different file format with the Save File as **T**ype list.

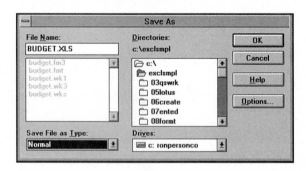

Saving Excel Worksheets as 1-2-3 Files

To save Excel worksheets as 1-2-3 files, complete the following steps:

1. Choose the **File** Save **As** command. The Save As dialog box appears.

2. Type the file name in the File **Name** text box. Do not type a file extension.

3. Select a WKS, WK1, or WK3 format from the Save File as **Type** list.

4. Choose OK or press Enter to save the file.

Excel saves formatting you have applied to an FMT or FM3 file in the same directory as the worksheet.

NOTE If your worksheet used Excel functions or features that cannot be converted into 1-2-3 functions, Excel displays an alert box asking whether you want cells reported that cannot be converted. Tell Excel that you want these cells reported so that you can write a list of which cells to check later. Formulas that cannot be converted are placed in the 1-2-3 worksheet with the value found in the Excel sheet. Figure 5.9 shows the alert box referencing a cell that could not be converted.

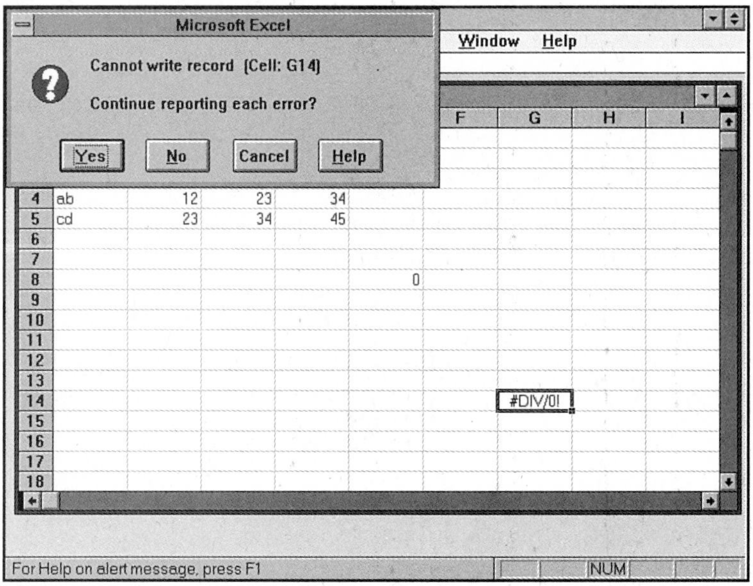

FIG. 5.9

Excel references cells that cannot be converted to 1-2-3.

Noting Translation Differences

Excel automatically converts 1-2-3 worksheets into Excel and saves them back in 1-2-3 format. Some worksheet characteristics do not convert between the two applications.

Excel thoroughly converts formats, cell protection, formulas, names, and 1-2-3 graphs. However, some characteristics, such as windowing, cannot be converted because of their functional differences.

If any 1-2-3 function or formula does not translate into Excel, a dialog box appears and shows the cell location of the errant formula. The 1-2-3 file is opened as a read-only file so that you cannot accidentally save the converted worksheet over the original 1-2-3 file. Choose the Yes button if you want to continue seeing these messages in an alert box. Choose the No button if you want to convert the 1-2-3 worksheet without the messages. Cells containing formulas that do not convert will contain the value of the original formula.

Data tables do not translate between either application. Formulas and values in the left column and top row of the tables remain in their original cells; however, you must reapply the Data Table commands for both applications. Excel data tables constantly recalculate and are actually formulas, whereas 1-2-3 tables are generated with the /Data Table command and must be recalculated by pressing a key.

Excel's seven error values translate into ERR and NA values in 1-2-3 as appropriate.

You can create larger worksheets with Excel than you can with 1-2-3. When Excel rows exceed the limit of a 1-2-3 worksheet, the extra rows wrap around from the top. Some versions of 1-2-3 can contain only 8,192 rows. If you save an Excel worksheet that contains 8,193 rows to 1-2-3 Release 2.x, Excel's bottom row becomes row 1. If you think this might happen, rearrange your Excel worksheets or make them into multiple linked worksheets.

1-2-3 cannot handle multiple simultaneous ranges, range operators (intersect, range, and union), or array formulas, so these features are not converted from Excel. The formula result is stored in 1-2-3 as a value.

Excel loads 1-2-3 graphs that are active in the worksheet or are named with the /Graph Name command. Each named graph appears in its own window. Excel does not save Excel charts as 1-2-3 graphs because Excel's charts have more features and formats. Excel cannot read or translate 1-2-3 print graph files, which are PIC files that have been saved for printing with PGRAPH.

Running the 1-2-3 Macro Interpreter

The 1-2-3 Macro Interpreter enables Excel to run 1-2-3 macros originally developed in 1-2-3 worksheets. This gives you the capability to make a smoother transition from using 1-2-3 for your work to using Excel.

NOTE Although Excel reads WK3 files and WYSIWYG formatting, the Macro Interpreter functions exclusively with 1-2-3 menu commands, functions, and advanced macro commands compatible with 1-2-3 Release 2.01.

Therefore, macros with WYSIWYG menu commands must be rewritten prior to using them with the 1-2-3 Macro Interpreter.

Macro libraries designed for the Lotus Macro Manager Add-in must be transferred from off-sheet to on-sheet memory before being used with the Excel 1-2-3 Macro Interpreter. To prepare such a macro library for Excel, complete the following steps:

1. In 1-2-3, use the 1-2-3 Macro Manager Add-in commands to copy the macro library from off-sheet memory to worksheet memory.

2. While you are in 1-2-3, save the worksheet as a file.

3. Start Excel.

4. In Excel, open the 1-2-3 worksheet file to which you saved the macro library.

Opening a 1-2-3 Macro File

Figure 5.10 shows a pair of simple macros in a 1-2-3 worksheet. These macros were created in 1-2-3 Release 2.2. The \a macro enables a user to enter numbers down a column until a label value, text such as the letter "a," is entered. As long as numbers are entered, the macro accepts the input, puts it in the current cell, and moves the active cell down one row. Next, the macro branches back to begin the cycle again. When a label value is typed, the macro erases the cell's contents. Then, the macro quits.

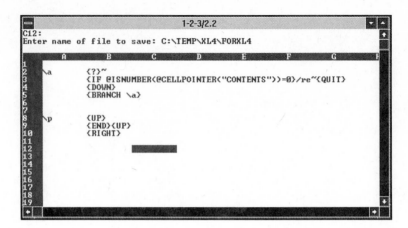

FIG. 5.10

A pair of 1-2-3 macros to simplify entering numbers down several columns.

The \p macro in figure 5.10 picks up where \a leaves off at positioning the active cell for the next column of numbers. First, the macro moves the cell pointer up one row to move to the last entry in the column of numbers. Second, an <END><UP> navigation command sequence moves the cell pointer to the first entry in the column. Third, the <RIGHT> navigation command moves the cell pointer one column to the right so that a new column of numbers can be entered.

This pair of macros was saved as a worksheet file in the C:\TEMP\XL4 directory. The file name used for the worksheet is FORXL4.WK1.

Open the FORXL4.WK1 worksheet file as described earlier. Figure 5.11 shows the File Open dialog box with the File Name box set to show all 1-2-3 worksheet files in the default directory, C:\TEMP\XL4.

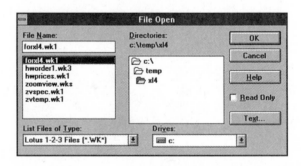

FIG. 5.11

A File Open dialog box with all WK* file types set to show.

NOTE Autoexec macros, named \Ø, are started automatically unless the Shift key is held down when choosing OK or pressing Enter. If an Excel worksheet contains both an Excel Auto_Open and a 1-2-3 \Ø autoexec macro, the Excel Auto_Open macro runs first when the file opens then the 1-2-3 autoexec macro runs.

Running a 1-2-3 Macro

To run the \a macro, press Ctrl+A. Figure 5.12 shows the opened worksheet after the \a macro was started. Notice that the Status Bar shows MI during a macro pause to indicate that the 1-2-3 macro interpreter is running. The Pause indicator after MI reflects the macro's pause for user input. This pause is caused by the {?} command that starts \a.

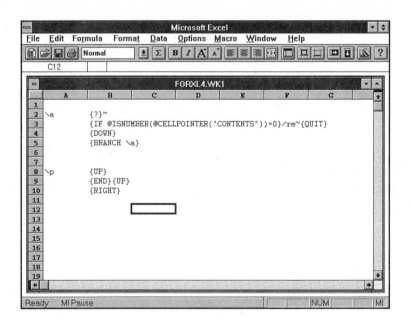

FIG. 5.12

The 1-2-3 worksheet file after the \a macro is started in Excel.

To start a 1-2-3 macro in Excel by using a shortcut key, press Ctrl plus the letter instead of Alt plus the letter.

NOTE

You can modify but not create 1-2-3 macros while in Excel. Excel reads from 1-2-3 worksheets the \name that indicates a 1-2-3 macro. But you cannot create a new name in Excel that starts with a \; \ is an illegal character when creating an Excel name. You can, however, modify the keystroke and commands in the 1-2-3 macro that follow the macro name. This capability enables you to modify your 1-2-3 macro while it is in Excel. Chapters 27 through 30 describe macro programming in Excel.

Using Macros that Prompt or Display Menus

Macros that use the GETLABEL, GETNUMBER, /XN, or /XI commands display a dialog box when run in Excel. The Status Bar displays a message about obtaining help. When custom 1-2-3 menus are displayed with /XM, MENUBRANCH, and MENUCALL commands, a custom menu dialog box is presented.

Figure 5.13 shows a macro in operation with a dialog box displayed from the {GETLABEL} command in the first line of \l. This line prompts the user to type an item name. The user replied by entering *Screws*. When the Enter key is pressed, the Item Name? dialog box will be replaced by the Quantity ordered? dialog box. Figure 5.14 shows the worksheet after \l is run.

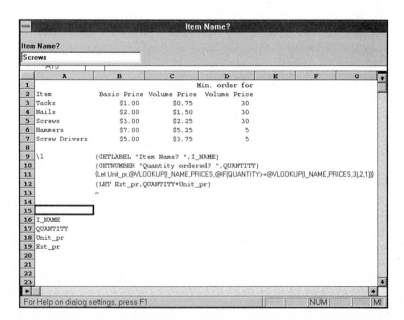

FIG. 5.13

The {GETLABEL} command displays a dialog box at the top of the window.

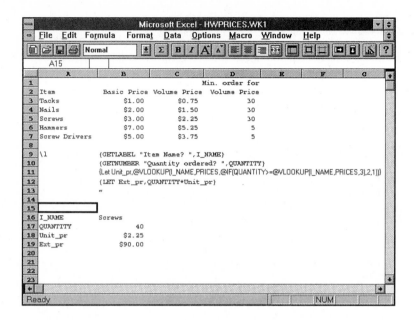

FIG. 5.14

The \l macro updates the I_NAME, QUANTITY, Unit_pr, and Ext_pr ranges from user input.

When your 1-2-3 macro uses a /XM, MENUBRANCH, and MENUCALL command to display a custom menu, Excel also displays a custom menu. Figure 5.15 shows a custom menu macro and the menu it displays.

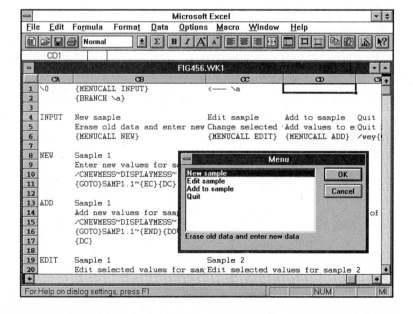

FIG. 5.15

Excel's Macro Interpreter also displays custom menus written in 1-2-3 macros.

Adding an Excel Subroutine

You may need to modify a 1-2-3 macro to include Excel features or add an Excel portion to an existing 1-2-3 macro to include Excel features, such as printing. To modify your 1-2-3 macro so that it runs an Excel macro as a subroutine, use the following command:

{XLMACRO *excel_macro_name*}

The Excel macro acts like a subroutine and returns to the 1-2-3 macro that called it when it is finished. The macro sheet containing the Excel macro sheet must be open. Remember to include the macro sheet name in the *excel_macro_name* argument, as in the following example:

{XLMACRO PRINTLB.XLM!Print.Preview}

Chapter Summary

If you are an experienced 1-2-3 user, you may find some initial difficulty in using Excel. Learning dysfunctions commonly occur when you learn new skills that are similar to old skills. You probably remember the steep learning curve involved in initially learning 1-2-3. It was tough for many people. Learning Excel will again require a learning period. But the transition is worth it.

If you are a power user of 1-2-3, your skills are not lost; instead, these skills are enhanced. Excel shifts everyone up the productivity curve. Excel beginners perform the equivalent of intermediate 1-2-3 work; and Excel intermediates perform the equivalent of advanced 1-2-3 work. For 1-2-3 power users, Excel opens new horizons. The extensive macro language, array math, the Solver, Q+E, and Object Linking and Embedding give you access to more power by using the same problem-solving knowledge you already have.

If you have read this chapter before other chapters in the book, you should work through the worksheet and chart Quick Start tutorials to develop a foundation in Excel. After you work through the Quick Starts, try the **Help Lotus** 1-2-3 command. It's a quick way to continue being productive while you learn Excel.

Creating Worksheets

This chapter teaches the basics of using Excel. In this chapter, you learn how to move and scroll across a worksheet, how to select areas in a worksheet to change them, and how to save and open the worksheet, chart, and macro files that you create.

If you need to learn about the parts of an Excel screen and how to operate the menus and dialog boxes, how to move and size windows, and how to use Help, read Chapter 2, "Learning Windows and Excel Basics."

Before you continue with this chapter, take a moment to review the concepts that apply to all Windows programs.

To affect any portion of a worksheet, follow these steps:

1. Select the cells, text, or graphic element you want to change.

2. Choose the command from the menu that makes the change.

3. Select options from the dialog box if one appears.

4. Choose OK or press Enter.

5. Choose another command if necessary to further affect the item that you selected in step 1.

As a shortcut for those tasks you perform frequently you also can perform the following steps:

1. Select the cells, text, or graphic element you want to change.

2. Press a shortcut key, or click a button in the toolbar.

All these steps condense into the most important concept you will use
for all Windows programs: Select, then do.

Learning the Parts
of the Excel Screen

When Excel appears, you may see a screen like the one shown in figure 6.1. In this figure, the Excel program window fills the entire screen,
and a smaller document window displays a blank worksheet. Depending on how Excel is configured or was last used, the program window
may not fill the entire screen. Chapter 2 describes how to maximize
the program so that it fills the screen.

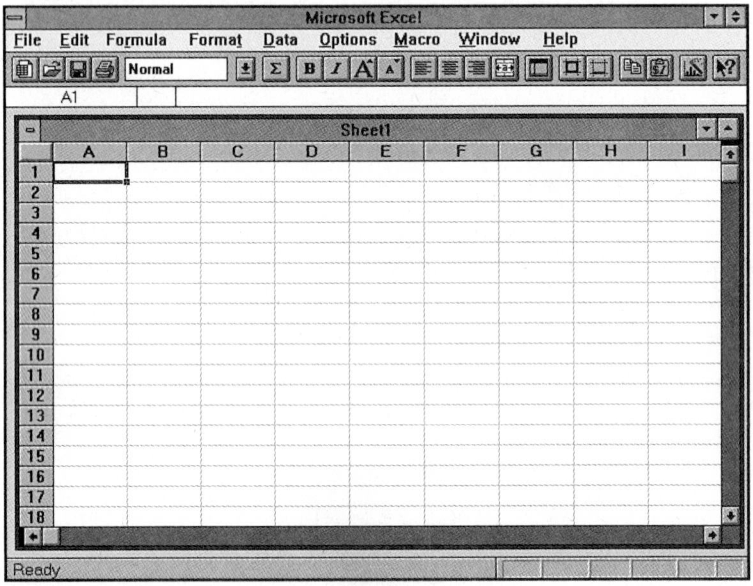

FIG. 6.1

The Excel screen.

The document window, Sheet1, has a solid title bar, indicating that it is
the active document window. You can have multiple worksheets, charts,
or macro sheets open at the same time, but you enter data and commands only into the active document window. Inactive windows are normally behind the active window and have a lighter colored or cross-
hatched title bar. Figure 6.2 shows the Excel program window with a
worksheet, macro sheet, and a chart document. Notice the differences in
the title bars.

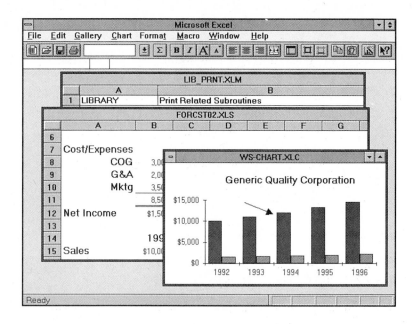

FIG. 6.2

Excel screen with a
worksheet, macro
sheet, and chart
document displayed.

The components in an Excel screen are described in table 6.1.

Table 6.1. Parts of the Excel Screen

Part	Description
Document window	The window within the program window, where worksheets, macro sheets, and charts are displayed.
Active window	The document window that accepts entries and commands; this window has a solid title bar and is normally the top window.
Inactive window	These windows contain documents that are loaded, but are not affected by commands; these windows have a grayed title bar and are normally behind the active window.
Toolbar	A bar containing buttons that gives quick access to commands and tools, such as bold, italic, create chart, styles, and drawing tools. A toolbar can be moved to different locations and reshaped to a different orientation.

continues

Table 6.1. Continued

Part	Description
Formula Bar	The area of the screen where you enter text, numbers, or formulas. The Formula Bar is below the menu bar or toolbar.
Status Bar	A bar at the bottom of the screen that shows what Excel is prepared to do next; watch the Status Bar for prompts, explanations of the current command, or guidance.
Indicators	These display modes of operation, such as NUM when the numeric pad is on, SCRL when the Scroll Lock has been pressed, or EXT when the Extend mode is on.

FROM HERE...

For Related Information:

◀◀ "Understanding a Windows Screen," p. 25.

◀◀ "Using the Toolbars," p. 47.

Setting Preferences

Excel contains a number of features that enable you to customize Excel for your own work preferences. The choices that you make immediately are described here. These preferences enable you to change such options as enabling Lotus 1-2-3 movement keys or changing the mouse buttons and speed. Other preferences, such as setting the numeric keypad for automatic decimal placement (as in a 10-key calculator) or changing worksheet grid colors, are described in later chapters. Customizing worksheet features, such as the toolbars, is described in Chapter 33.

Operating with 1-2-3 Keys

If you are familiar with Lotus 1-2-3, you can use your knowledge to learn Excel. In fact, you can modify Excel to aid you in your switch from 1-2-3. Chapter 5 describes how to make the transition from 1-2-3 to Excel.

If you want to use operating methods similar to 1-2-3 as you learn Excel, choose the **O**ptions **W**orkspace command and enter a slash (/) character into the **A**lternate Menu or Help Key text box. Next, select the 1-2-3 Help option. These choices will display Excel's help for users whenever you press the slash key. While in a worksheet, you can press the keys that you would use for a 1-2-3 process, and Excel will demonstrate the equivalent Excel keystrokes. This method, described in Chapter 5, enables you to use 1-2-3 knowledge while you continue to work productively and learn Excel.

> If you are only casually familiar with 1-2-3 techniques, you should learn Excel directly rather than using the 1-2-3 navigation and command keys.
>
> **T I P**

If you select the Alternate Navigation **K**eys check box after choosing the **O**ptions **W**orkspace command, you can use many of the 1-2-3 cell movement methods, such as End, arrow. However, Excel has all the equivalent navigation keys compared to 1-2-3, so unless you are intimately familiar with 1-2-3 keystrokes, you should learn the Excel navigation keystrokes.

Moving the Active Cell After Entering Data

When you type data, Excel keeps the active cell in place or moves it to the next lower cell after you press the Enter key. If you want the active cell to stay in place, choose the **O**ptions **W**orkspace command and clear the **M**ove Selection After Enter check box.

Customizing the Mouse

You can customize the mouse to operate more slowly, and you can switch the button actions between left and right sides. To customize the mouse, follow these steps:

1. Choose the Excel Control Menu by clicking it or by pressing Alt, space bar.

2. Choose the **R**un command.

3. From the dialog box that appears, select the Control **P**anel option.

4. Choose OK or press Enter.

The Control Panel appears. This is the same Control Panel that you can open from the Main group window within the Program Manager.

Next, you open the Mouse program and change the settings. Follow these steps:

1. To open the Mouse program, double-click the icon; or press the arrow keys until the icon is selected, and then press Enter. The Mouse dialog box appears (see fig. 6.3).

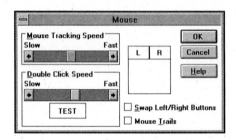

FIG. 6.3

The Mouse dialog box.

2. You can change any of the following options:

   Mouse Tracking Speed: The speed the on-screen pointer moves with respect to your movement of the hand-held mouse. Use slow while learning.

   Double Click Speed: The speed with which you must double-click for a double-click to be accepted. Use slow while learning.

   Swap Left/Right Buttons: Swaps the active mouse button to the opposite side. Use for operating the mouse from the opposite hand.

   Mouse **T**rails: Produces a shadowed trail of mouse pointers that makes the pointer easier to see on LCD panel displays (used in laptop computers). This option is available in Windows 3.1 only.

3. Choose OK or press Enter.

4. To close the Control Panel, double-click its program Control menu; or press the program close shortcut key, Alt+F4.

FROM HERE...

For Related Information:

◀◀ "Getting Help with 1-2-3," p. 118.

◀◀ "Moving and Selecting with 1-2-3 Navigation Keys," p. 123.

Moving around the Worksheet

The Excel worksheet can be very large. If the worksheet were a piece of paper, the entire sheet would measure as wide as two cars and stand as tall as a 30-story building. If you are going to find things on a worksheet, you will need to know how to get around efficiently.

Scrolling with the Mouse

When you scroll a window, imagine that the worksheet is staying still and you are moving the window over the top of the worksheet. To scroll the window with the mouse, use the scroll bars located at the right side and bottom of each worksheet (see fig. 6.4). The arrows in the scroll bars show the direction the window moves over the worksheet.

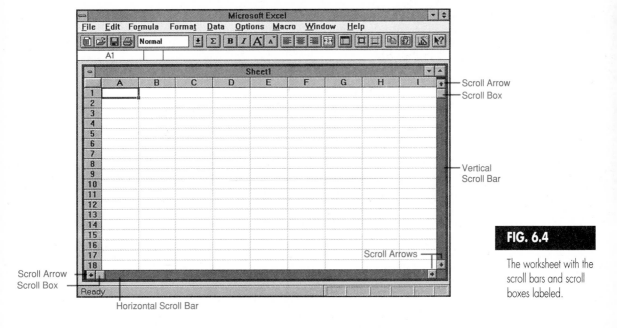

FIG. 6.4

The worksheet with the scroll bars and scroll boxes labeled.

To scroll the worksheet in single-row or column increments, click the arrowhead in either the horizontal or vertical scroll bar. The arrowheads point in the direction the window moves over the worksheet. To scroll continuously, put the pointer's tip on a scroll arrow and hold down the mouse button.

The position of the scroll box in the scroll bar shows the relative position of the window on the area where data has been entered into the worksheet. Note the vertical and horizontal scroll boxes to see where you are on the worksheet.

To scroll through the worksheet in increments of a full window, click the mouse pointer in the gray area on either side of the scroll box. For example, clicking in the gray scroll bar below the scroll box moves the window down by the span of one window.

To scroll large expanses, click the scroll box and drag the box to a new position on the scroll bar. As you drag the box, notice that the row or column position for the new location is shown in the Reference Area at the top of the screen to the left of the Formula Bar. When you see the row or column that you want, release the mouse button. The window will show the new location.

T   I   P

If your work suddenly disappears from the screen, do not panic. You may have accidentally scrolled to a new location. Check the row and column headings to move back to your original work area. If you cannot see the active cell where you were working last, press Ctrl+Backspace to move the window back so that the active cell is displayed.

Scrolling with the Keyboard

From the keyboard, you can scroll the window over the worksheet by using normal movement keys, but you must press the Scroll Lock key first. When Scroll Lock is on, you see SCRL at the bottom of the screen. This indicator means that if you press the arrow or movement keys, the screen will scroll without moving the cells you have selected. On many keyboards, a light appears on the key or keyboard when Scroll Lock is enabled. After you are finished scrolling, do not forget to press the Scroll Lock key a second time to return the movement keys to their normal function.

The keys that scroll the window are listed in table 6.2.

FROM HERE...

For Related Information:

◄◄ "Using the Mouse," p. 27.

Table 6.2. Keys that Scroll the Window

Press Scroll Lock until the SCRL indicator appears at the bottom of the screen and then press one of the following keys.

Key	Movement
Up arrow	Scrolls up one row
Down arrow	Scrolls down one row
Right arrow	Scrolls right one column
Left arrow	Scrolls left one column
PgUp	Scrolls up one window
PgDn	Scrolls down one window
Ctrl+PgUp	Scrolls right one window
Ctrl+PgDn	Scrolls left one window
Home	Moves to the top left cell in the window
Ctrl+Home	Moves to cell A1

Selecting Cells

Before you can enter, edit, or modify the contents of a cell, you must select the cell or cells you want to change. The single cell that receives the data or formula you enter is the *active cell*. A selection of multiple cells is referred to as a *range*.

The cell defined by a bold border and white background is the active cell. Commands affect all selected cells; data and formulas are entered in the active cell.

Selected cells are highlighted or reversed from the rest of the worksheet. If you select a range of cells, all the cells will be highlighted, but one cell will have a bold border and white background.

If you want to see the active cell, but it is not visible in the window, press Ctrl+Backspace. The window scrolls to show the active cell. Selected ranges remain selected.

Selecting a Single Cell

Use either the mouse or the arrow keys to select cells. Selecting a cell with the mouse is easy; just move the mouse pointer over the cell and click the mouse button.

To select a single cell from the keyboard, press the appropriate movement key to move the active cell. Table 6.3 shows the keys that move the active cell. To issue key combinations, such as Ctrl+PgUp, hold down the first key (Ctrl) as you press the second key (PgUp).

Table 6.3. Keys that Move the Active Cell

Key	Movement
Up arrow	Moves the active cell up one cell
Down arrow	Moves the active cell down one cell
Right arrow	Moves the active cell right one cell
Left arrow	Moves the active cell left one cell
Tab	Enters data and moves the active cell right
Shift+Tab	Enters data and moves the active cell left
Enter	Enters data and moves the active cell down (when a range is selected or when the **M**ove Selection After Enter option is selected from the **O**ptions **W**orkspace command)
Shift+Enter	Enters data and moves the active cell up in the selected range
Ctrl+arrow End+arrow	Moves the active cell in the direction indicated until the edge of a block of data is reached
Home	Moves the active cell to column A of the current row
Ctrl+Home	Moves the active cell to the first cell in the worksheet (A1)
Ctrl+End	Moves the active cell to the last cell in the used portion of the worksheet
PgUp	Moves the active cell up one full window
PgDn	Moves the active cell down one full window
Ctrl+PgUp	Moves the active cell one screen left
Ctrl+PgDn	Moves the active cell one screen right

Moving to the End of a Block of Cells

If you have a large worksheet or database, you need a way to accelerate your moves across blocks of data. Using Excel's accelerator techniques, you can use the mouse or keyboard to move the active cell quickly across a filled row or up or down a filled column.

When using a mouse, double-click the side of a cell in the direction you want to move. If the current cell is filled, the active cell moves to the edge of the filled area on the side you double-clicked. If the current cell is empty, the active cell moves to the first blank cell at the edge of the next filled cell in the direction you click. Just double-click the side of a cell in the direction you want to go. You may find this technique easier if you turn the gridlines on by using the **O**ptions **D**isplay command and select the **G**ridlines check box.

The Ctrl or End keys can save you time when you need to move across a filled row in a worksheet or when you need to move up or down a filled column. The Ctrl+arrow or End, arrow key combinations act as express keys that move the active cell as if the cell were on an expressway or an elevator. These key combinations move the active cell in the direction of the arrow until the active cell reaches the edge of a block.

To use these keys, select a cell, and then hold down the Ctrl key as you press an arrow key in the direction you want to move. To use the End key, press the End key, then release it, then press the arrow key in the direction you want to move.

If the current cell is filled, the active cell moves in the direction of the arrow key to the edge of the filled area. If the current cell is empty, the active cell moves in the direction of the arrow to the first blank cell at the edge of the next filled area.

Using Goto

The **F**ormula **G**oto command moves the active cell to any address you request. To use the Goto command, follow these steps:

1. Choose the **F**ormula **G**oto command or press F5 to display the Goto dialog box (see fig. 6.5).

2. Type the cell address or range you want to go to, or select from the list box the named location you want to go to.

3. Choose OK or press Enter.

If you choose a named cell or range with the **G**oto command, the entire range is selected. (Named ranges are cells or ranges that are given a text name, such as *Revenue*; ranges are discussed in detail in Chapter 7, "Entering and Editing Worksheet Data.")

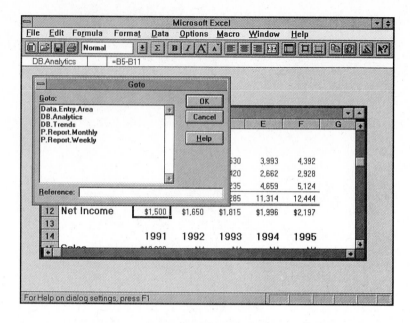

FIG. 6.5

The Goto dialog box.

T I P Use the **G**oto command to select frequently used ranges quickly. Name the cells or ranges you use frequently with the **Fo**rmula **D**efine Names command. After you have named the cells, you can go to and select those cells or ranges by pressing F5, selecting the name, and choosing OK. For a shortcut, press F5 and double-click the name.

T I P If you go to a location by pressing F5, entering an address or name, and then choosing OK, you can quickly return to your original location. To return to the previous location, press F5 and choose OK or press Enter without selecting a named range or entering a reference. The Formula Goto command remembers the previous location. In fact, the Formula Goto command remembers the four most recent locations and lists them at the top of the **G**oto list box. You can return to any of these locations by selecting the location name and choosing OK or by double-clicking on the location name.

When you know the text, number, or formula you are looking for but don't know the location, use the Formula Find command. Formula Find locates numeric or text values, partial or whole formulas, or the contents of a note attached to a cell. Chapter 7, "Entering and Editing Worksheet Data," contains more information about the Find command.

Selecting a Range

Select a range of cells when you want to apply a command to all the selected cells or enter data into the cells in the range.

To select a range of cells with the mouse, click the cell at one corner of the range, and drag to the opposite corner of the range. Release the mouse button. A rectangular range of cells is selected, as shown in figure 6.6. The pointer can wander on the screen as it moves to the opposite corner; just make sure that the pointer is on the correct cell when you release the mouse button.

If a corner of the range is off the screen, drag the mouse pointer against the document window's edge in the direction you want to move. The window will scroll over the worksheet.

To select cells by using the keyboard, hold down the Shift key as you press movement keys. Or press F8, press movement keys, and then press F8 again to turn off Extend mode.

If the opposite corner is outside the edge of the window, continue to hold down the Shift key and press the movement keys. The window will scroll to let you see the direction you are selecting.

The Reference Area, at the left end of the Formula bar, shows you how many rows and columns you are selecting as you drag the mouse or press the arrow keys (see fig. 6.6).

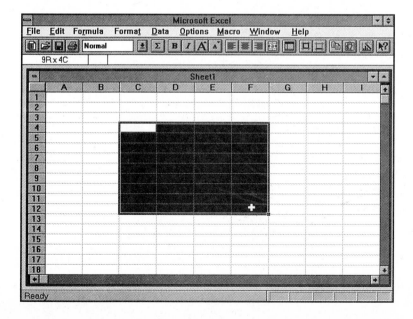

FIG. 6.6

A selected range of cells.

Selecting a Large Range

In some cases, a range is so large that dragging or pressing keys from one corner to another takes a long time. You can use quicker methods for selecting large areas. To select a large area, follow these steps:

1. Select one corner of the range.

2. Scroll the window so that the opposite corner is displayed. (Do not click in the worksheet. The original corner must remain active.)

3. Hold down the Shift key as you click the opposite corner. All cells between the two corners will be selected.

If you have a range to select that is too large to scroll or move to, follow these steps:

1. Select one corner of the range.

2. Choose the Formula **G**oto command or press F5.

3. Type the cell reference of the opposite corner in the **R**eference text box.

4. Hold down the Shift key as you choose the OK button, or press Enter. To select a range different from where you are located, choose the Formula **G**oto command, or press F5 and type a range address in the **R**eference box, such as A5:F12. Choose OK or press Enter. In this case, the active cell is A5 and the range selected is from A5 to F12.

You also can select ranges using the F8 function key to turn on Extend mode. Extend mode produces the same result as continuously holding down the Shift key.

To select a range by using Extend mode, follow these steps:

1. Select a corner of the range by using the mouse or keyboard.

2. Press F8 to enter the Extend mode. Extend mode acts the same as holding down the Shift key as you move. Notice the EXT indicator at the bottom of the window.

3. Select the opposite corner of the range by clicking it or moving to it with the movement keys.

4. Press F8 again to turn off Extend mode.

As long as EXT is displayed in the Status Bar, the first corner selected remains anchored.

Keep in mind that you can use all the mouse actions or movement keys combined with the Shift or F8 key to select a range with the keyboard. Table 6.4 lists shortcut keys for selecting ranges.

Table 6.4. Shortcut Keys for Selecting Ranges

Key	Extend selection from active cell to
F8	Next cell selected
Shift+arrow	Next cell selected
Shift+Home	Beginning of row
Shift+Ctrl+Home	Beginning of worksheet (A1)
Shift+Ctrl+End	End of worksheet
Shift+End	Lowest right cell used in worksheet
Shift+space bar	Entire row of active cell
Ctrl+space bar	Entire column of active cell
Shift+Ctrl+space bar	Entire worksheet
Shift+PgUp	Cell in same column one window up
Shift+PgDn	Cell in same column one window down
Shift+Ctrl+PgUp	Cell in same row one window right
Shift+Ctrl+PgDn	Cell in same row one window left
Shift+Ctrl+arrow	Edge of the next block of data in the direction of the arrow key

T I P

To keep a range selected and move the selected area of any corner in the range, perform the following steps:

1. Press Ctrl+. (period) until the active cell is in the corner opposite from the one you want moved. Each press of Ctrl+. moves the active cell to the next corner.

2. Hold down the Shift key and press a movement key. The window changes to show you the corner being moved.

Selecting Multiple Ranges

Excel has the capability to select multiple nonadjacent (non-contiguous) ranges simultaneously. This capability enables you to format multiple ranges with a single command, print different parts of the worksheet with a single command, or erase multiple data-entry cells with a keystroke. To select multiple ranges by using the mouse, follow these steps:

1. Select the first range.

2. Hold down the Ctrl key as you select each additional range.

3. Release the Ctrl key.

To select multiple ranges by using the keyboard, perform the following steps:

1. Select the first cell.

2. Press F8 to enter Extend mode (EXT) and select a range.

3. Press Shift+F8 to enter Add mode (ADD) so that you can move while keeping the current selection.

4. Move to a corner of the next range.

5. Repeat steps 2, 3, and 4 until you have selected all the ranges you need.

Remember that pressing F8 enables you to select multiple adjacent cells. Pressing Shift+F8 enables you to keep the current selections while you move to a nonadjacent cell to start a new range.

Selecting Blocks of Adjacent Cells

Often, the data that you want to copy or format lies in a contiguous block of cells, such as the rows in a filled budget sheet or the filled columns in a database. Selecting all the cells in such a row or selecting a column can be easy with the following mouse shortcuts or shortcut keys. For these shortcuts, you should remember that holding down the Shift key as you move selects the cells you move across.

With the mouse, you can select contiguous cells by holding down the Shift key as you double-click the edge of the cell in the direction you want to select. In figure 6.7, for example, the active cell is cell A5. To select cells A5:F5, hold down the Shift key and double-click the vertical cell edge between A5 and B5.

With the keyboard, you can select contiguous cells by holding down the Shift key and then pressing either the Ctrl+arrow or End, arrow combination to move to the opposite edge of a block of filled cells.

Consider one caveat in using these selection techniques. If you are on a filled cell and you select a row or a column with this technique, the selection stops as soon as a blank cell is reached. This limitation can cause problems in a database where one or more blank cells may be in a column. You think you have selected the entire column, but the selection was stopped part way by a blank cell.

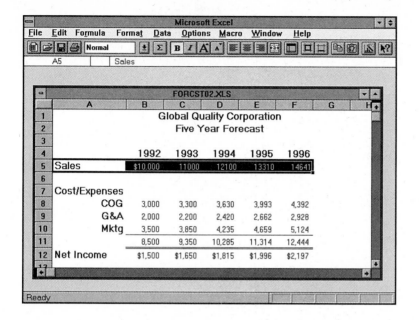

FIG. 6.7

Select a filled row or
column with mouse or
key shortcuts.

Another method for selecting a rectangular block around all touching
filled cells is to select one of the filled cells, and then press Ctrl+*
(Shift+8). This is the shortcut key for choosing the Formula Select
Special command and selecting the Current Region option.

Selecting Rows and Columns

Some operations are quicker if you select an entire row or column at one
time. Formatting is also more memory efficient if you select and format
an entire row or column instead of formatting each cell in the row or
column.

To select an entire row or entire column with the mouse, click the row or
column heading. Click the number 5 at the left edge of the document, for
example, to select row 5. You can select adjacent rows or columns by
dragging across the headings or by clicking the first and Shift+clicking
the last. Select multiple nonadjacent rows or columns by holding down
the Ctrl key as you click each heading.

To select the row containing the active cell with the keyboard, press
Shift+space bar. Press Ctrl+space bar to select the column containing the
active cell. After you have a row or column selected, you can select additional adjacent rows or columns by holding down the Shift key as you
press the arrow movement keys.

Figure 6.8 shows how you can select multiple rows and columns before you give a single bold command or click the bold button in the toolbar. These rows and columns were selected by holding down the Ctrl key and clicking each row or column heading.

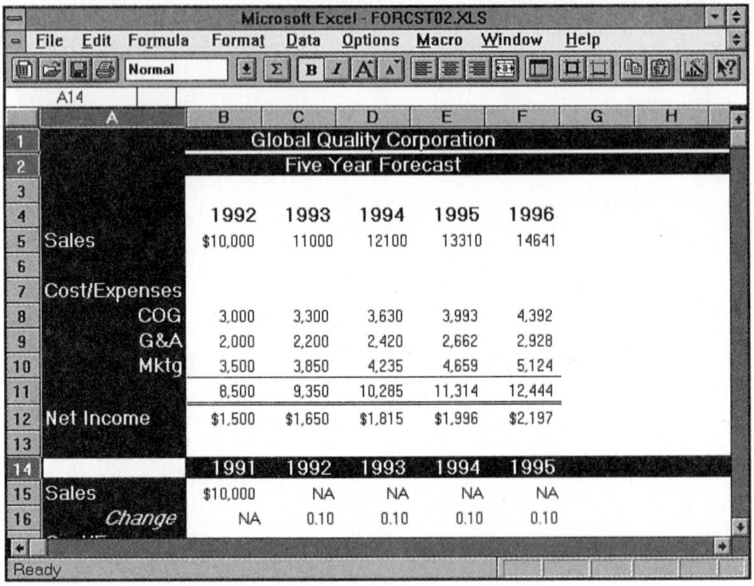

FIG. 6.8

Selected rows and formatting.

Selecting Cells by Their Type of Content

Excel contains a valuable command that enables you to select cells by their content or by their relationship to formulas. You will find this command useful when you check a worksheet for the location of notes. Cells can contain hidden notes. You also will find this command valuable when you want to locate errors in a worksheet.

To select cells according to their content, perform the following steps:

1. Select a single cell if you want to check the entire worksheet for a specific cell content, or select a range of cells if you want to check cells in a range.

2. Choose the Formula Select Special command. The Select Special dialog box appears (see fig. 6.9).

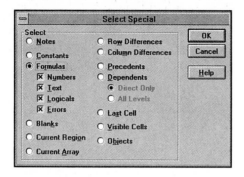

FIG. 6.9

The Select Special
dialog box.

3. Select one of the following options:

   Notes: Selects cells containing notes. (Shortcut: Ctrl+?).

   Constants: Selects cells containing constants of the type specified in the check boxes below.

   Formulas: Selects cells containing formulas that produce a result of the type specified in the check boxes below.

   Numbers: Selects cells containing numbers.

   Text: Selects cells containing text.

   Logicals: Selects cells containing logical values.

   Errors: Selects cells containing errors.

   Blanks: Selects blank cells.

   Current Region: Selects a rectangular block of cells that includes all touching non-blank cells. (Shortcut: Ctrl+*).

   Current Array: Selects the array containing the active cell. (Shortcut: Ctrl+/).

   Last Cell: Selects the lowest, rightmost cell used by the active worksheet.

   Visible Cells Only: Selects the visible cells; prevents changes to collapsed outline data or hidden rows or columns.

   Objects: Selects all graphical objects.

4. Choose OK or press Enter.

For Related Information:

◄◄ "Using the Mouse," p. 27.

FROM HERE...

T I P   Other options in the Formula Select Special command are discussed in Chapter 13's discussions on troubleshooting worksheets. Many of the options in Formula Select Special are valuable aids in finding and resolving worksheet problems.

After you select cells with the Formula Select Special command, you can maintain the selections and move between the cells by pressing Tab, Shift+Tab, Enter, or Shift+Enter. This technique enables you to move the active cell between selected cells and see the contents, such as formulas, in the Formula Bar while maintaining the selected range.

Managing Files

In the text that follows, you learn how to save, open, clear, and delete Excel documents. You find out how to save your work in progress so that you can restore it.

T I P   If you work with many related files and open and close files as a group, or you work with files that you need open together, then you should learn about workgroups. Workgroups are described in Chapter 11, "Building Systems and Managing Multiple Windows."

Creating a New File

When you start Excel, the program opens with a blank worksheet titled Sheet1, but you can open new worksheets, templates, charts, or macro sheets at any time. If you open a template, you open a worksheet that has been already constructed and is ready for operations. Templates make it easy for you to find and open master documents used to create other documents. Templates are covered in Chapter 11. If you work with groups of worksheets, be sure to read the section on workbooks described in Chapter 11.

To open new documents, perform the following steps:

1. Choose the File New command.

2. Select a worksheet, chart, macro, workbook, or the name of a template from the New list box in the File New dialog box (see fig. 6.10).

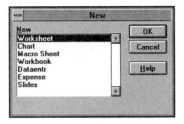

FIG. 6.10

The New dialog box.

Your dialog box may show available templates that are different from those in the figure. The templates DATAENTR, EXPENSE, and SLIDES have been added to this list as templates.

3. Choose OK or press Enter.

You can open a new worksheet with the toolbar by clicking on the new Worksheet tool, which is the farthest to the left on the toolbar. Each additional open document reduces the memory available to your computer. Depending on your computer and its memory, the reduced memory can limit the size of files you can later open; the reduced memory also may lower performance. When you close nonessential document windows, you free memory and improve performance.

Opening an Existing Document

To open an existing document, follow these steps:

1. Click the Open File tool, which is a picture of an open file folder in the toolbar, or choose the **File O**pen command. The File Open dialog box appears (see fig. 6.11).

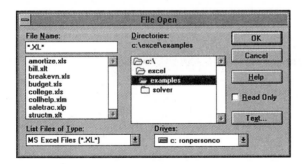

FIG. 6.11

The File Open dialog box.

2. Open, if necessary, the disk and directory that contain the file you want.

With a mouse, click the down arrow on the Drives pull-down list, and then click a drive letter. Open a new directory by double-clicking the directory folder in the **D**irectory list.

From the keyboard, press Alt+V to select the Drives list, and then press the up or down arrows to select the driver. Press Enter. Select the **D**irectories list box by pressing Alt+D. Move to the directory folder by pressing the up- or down-arrow key, and then press Enter.

3. Select the type of file you want to open by changing the file extension.

With a mouse, click the down arrow by the List Files of **T**ype pull-down list, and then click the file type you want displayed in the File Names list.

From the keyboard, press Alt+T to select the List File of **T**ype list, press the up- or down-arrow key to select the type of files you want, and then press Enter.

4. Select the file that you want from the File **N**ame list box.

or

Type the name of the file you want into the File **N**ame text box.

5. Choose OK or press Enter.

T I P   Excel keeps the names of the four most recently opened documents at the bottom of the **F**ile menu. If you want to open one of these files, click the filename at the bottom of the menu. This action opens the file, but does not change the directory.

T I P   You can open multiple documents simultaneously. To open files whose names are adjacent, select the first file name, and then hold the Shift key as you click the last. With the keyboard, hold down the Shift key as you move to the last file name. To open files whose names are not together, hold down the Ctrl key as you click each name. Nonadjacent files cannot be opened by keyboard.

When you open Excel files on the network, others cannot open the
same file. To allow others to open the same file, select the **R**ead Only
check box before opening. You must save your changes to the file
under a different name, but while you work on the file others will also
be able to open it.

T I P

Worksheets can have two types of password protection. The password
can protect the worksheet against unauthorized opening, and the password can protect against changes saved back to the original name. If the
file that you want to open is protected, you are prompted for the password. Type the password, using the exact upper- and lowercase letters
as the original password, and then choose OK or press Enter.

If the worksheet has been saved with the read-only option recommended, you are asked whether you really need to make changes.
Choose Yes to open the file as read only; choose No to open the file so
that you can make changes; or Cancel if you decide not to open the file.

To quickly change directories and open files, press Ctrl+F12 or click
the File Open button. This displays the File Open dialog box. After the
dialog box is open, double-click the directory you want to change to,
and then double-click the file you want to open. Double-clicking selects the name and chooses OK.

T I P

Listing Other File Types

The file extension can help you find the file you want. Excel files use
different file extensions for each type of file. Changing the file extension
in the File **N**ame text box or in the List Files of **T**ype list and choosing OK
displays files that match the extension you want. To see chart files, for
example, use *.XLC; to see Lotus 1-2-3 files, use *.WK*; to see all files,
use *.*. Some of the more frequently used file extensions that Excel
reads are described in table 6.5.

Changing Disks and Directories

Excel displays files, directories, and drives in the File **O**pen and File **S**ave
dialog boxes. With these dialog boxes, you can change the directory and
drive that Excel uses for saving and retrieving. The current drive and
directory appear as text in the middle of these boxes.

Table 6.5. File Extensions Read by Excel

Extension	File Type
.	All Files
.XLS	Excel worksheet
.XLC	Excel chart
.XLM	Excel macro sheet
.XLW	Workbook
.CSV	Comma-separated values
.TXT	Tab-delimited text
.WKS	1-2-3 Release 1A
.WK1	1-2-3 Release 2
.WK3	1-2-3 Release 3
.DBF	dBASE

Use the Drives list box to select a new drive. This procedure is discussed in the preceding section. You do not have to select a file to change directories or disk drives. When you reach the step to select a file, you can choose Cancel or press Esc and remain in the new disk or directory that you selected.

Use the **Directories** list box to select a new directory. Daughter directories are indented to the right from the parent directory in which they reside.

Saving Documents

You should save your documents every 15 to 20 minutes. You may also want to use version numbers in file names, such as FORCST03.XLS and FORCST04.XLS, each time you save. In this way, you always can return to previous versions of your work. If you save to the same file name each time, the previous work is replaced. (Delete old versions of work with the **File Delete** command or with the File Manager from Windows.)

The **File Save As** command also is the easiest method of saving your worksheet data into formats readable by other Windows and DOS programs. Figure 6.12 shows the Save As dialog box. Chapters 31 and 32 explain how to save Excel files in formats that you can use with other programs, such as 1-2-3, dBASE, or many forms of text files. To learn how to save a worksheet as a template or as part of a workbook, see Chapter 11, "Building Systems and Managing Multiple Windows."

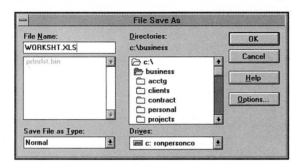

FIG. 6.12

The File Save As dialog box.

To save the active worksheet, chart, or macro sheet, follow these steps:

1. Activate the document that you want to save. (The document window on top is the file that will be saved.)

2. Choose the **File Save As** command, or press F12 or Alt+F2.

3. If you want to save to a different drive or directory, select the drive from the Drive list or the directory from the **Directories** list box and choose OK.

4. Enter a new name or edit the existing name in the File **Name** box. Do not type a file extension, because Excel adds the extension automatically.

5. If you want to make a backup copy of the file or add read-only or file-protection status, select the **O**ptions button. Select the option you want and type any passwords required. The backup file has the same name with a BAK extension.

6. Choose OK or press Enter.

Use DOS file names with one to eight characters. File names can include letters, numbers, and some symbols. Because only some symbols can be used, the best practice is to use only the underline (_) and the hyphen (-).

To save a file to the same file name and directory to which it has been saved previously, click the File Save tool (picture of a diskette) or press Shift+F12.

File names can never include spaces. Spaces confuse DOS's capability to store the file with the name you want. Also, don't use periods in file names, other than the period before the extension.

T I P

For safety, you may want to use the Save **As** command instead of the **S**ave command. The Save **As** command shows you the directory and gives you a chance to change the file name for each save. The **F**ile **S**ave command or File Save tool saves the document under the name last used.

Password-Protecting Your File

You can protect your documents against unauthorized opening or unauthorized changes by saving them with different types of passwords. To add protection to a file, choose the **O**ptions button from the Save As dialog box. The dialog box shown in figure 6.13 appears.

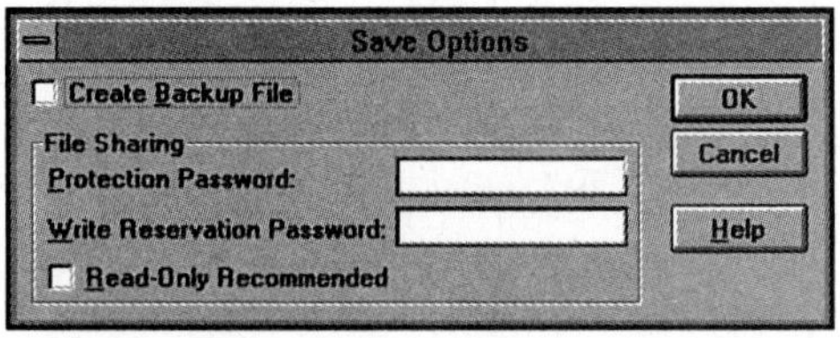

FIG. 6.13

The Save Options dialog box.

To protect a file so that a password is requested before the file can be opened, type a password of up to 15 characters into the **P**rotection Password text box. The password can contain text, numbers, spaces, and symbols. Remember to note upper- and lowercase letters. You will be asked for the exact upper- and lowercase letters that you used originally. Because asterisks show on-screen in place of the password, you will be asked to reenter the Protection password to ensure that you typed it correctly. You can use passwords to protect templates, documents, and charts.

If you want to ensure that only authorized users can change a file, type a password in the **W**rite Reservation Password text box. When the file is opened, operators are prompted for the Write Reservation password. Without the password, operators can open the file only as a Read-Only file. This restriction forces operators to save the file with a new file name and preserves the original file. If operators know the Write Reservation password, they can make changes to the file and save the file over the original file.

If you want to recommend that operators open a file as Read-Only, but not force them to, select the **R**ead-Only Recommended check box. This selection enables operators to make changes to the original without a password, but reminds them to check the **R**ead-Only check box for normal work. This option is best when you want to protect files against accidental changes, but you want all operators to have open access to the files.

Saving to Old Excel File Formats

Microsoft Excel 4 opens worksheets, macros, and charts from earlier versions of Excel. When you save one of these older files from Excel 4, it is saved with the new Excel 4 format unless you specify otherwise.

To save an Excel file in a previous Excel format, choose the **F**ile Save **A**s command, select the **O**ption button, and select the format you want from the Save File as **T**ype list box.

If you use a worksheet feature that is not supported by the earlier version of Excel, the value result of that feature is calculated and used in the worksheet. Chart characteristics that are found only in Excel 4 are not saved. A chart format that does not exist in earlier versions of Excel is changed to a format that does exist.

Saving All Open Files

Excel can save all your open files and remember their sizes and locations. They are saved together as a *workbook*. Workbooks are useful for many reasons. A few of the most important are that you can group together related files that are worked on in the same tasks and save them as a single workbook. This capability enables you to easily open the files together, pass a complete set of files to work associates, and protect the entire workbook with the same security.

Workbooks also aid you if you need to develop a packaged book containing worksheets, databases, macro sheets, and charts. By including them all in one workbook, you ensure that windows open in the correct location, no files are lost, and the appropriate macros always stay with the worksheets and charts that need them.

To learn how to save, create and maintain your own workbooks, read Chapter 11, which discusses working with multiple files.

Deleting Files

You can delete individual files from within Excel with the **File Delete** command. Choose the **File Delete** command, select the file you want to delete from the list box, and choose OK or press Enter. An alert box appears asking you to confirm the deletion; choose **Yes** to delete.

To delete multiple files at one time, use the File Manager in the Main group of the Program Manager. The book *Using Windows 3.1,* Special Edition, published by Que Corporation, explains how to use the File Manager and lists many shortcuts.

After you delete files, you cannot use the **Edit Undo** or Esc commands to restore them.

Closing Documents

You can close the active document window by choosing the **File Close** command. The mouse shortcut for closing a window is to double-click the document Control menu to the left of the document's title bar. Be certain that you double-click the Control menu to the left of the document's title (to the left of the File menu name when the document is maximized), not to the left of the Excel title. By keyboard, you can press Ctrl+F4.

If you made changes since the last time you saved the document, an alert box appears (see fig. 6.14). If you want to save the document before closing, choose **Yes**.

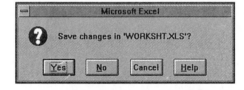

FIG. 6.14

The Close and Save alert box.

T I P   To close all the document windows with a single command, hold down the Shift key as you select the **File** menu. The command Close All appears. Choosing **Close** All closes all worksheets; you can confirm whether you want to save worksheets that you have changed.

Exiting Excel

To exit Excel, choose the File Exit command or press Alt+F4. With a mouse, double-click the program Control menu to the left of the Excel title bar. If you made changes to documents since they were last saved, you are asked whether you want to save the changes.

For Related Information:

▶▶ "Grouping Documents into Workbooks," p. 426.

FROM HERE...

Chapter Summary

You can operate Excel in any way that fits your style and the task at hand. You can use the mouse, Alt+letter menu selections, Alt+arrow key menu selections, shortcut menus, toolbar tools, or shortcut keys. You should, however, avoid using the same commands over and over, year after year, without considering Excel's additional capabilities. Occasionally, take the time to learn a few shortcuts or learn about Excel features you don't use all the time. You will find many ways you can save time and make your work more productive.

Remember that the Help menu contains a great deal of information. You also can get help by pressing F1 when a dialog box is open or by pressing Shift+F1 and then clicking a menu, command, or toolbar.

The next chapter deals with data entry and editing. If you are familiar with Lotus 1-2-3, you are familiar with Excel's basic data-entry and editing concepts. Nonetheless, you will want to read these chapters; Excel has many timesaving techniques and powerful features.

Entering and Editing Worksheet Data

E xcel's value lies in storing, manipulating, and displaying data. But before you can use data in Excel, you must enter it. This chapter discusses the types of data a cell can contain and explains how to enter text, numbers, and dates. You also learn how to create formulas that manipulate data and how to create and use English names, such as *Revenue*, for cell references instead of using inscrutable references like *B37*.

In addition to telling you how to enter data, this chapter describes how to edit the contents of a cell and how to move and rearrange the layout of the worksheet. You can save considerable time building worksheets after you learn how to move or copy text or formulas.

Entering Data

Excel worksheet cells can contain values or formulas. The constant values that cells can contain are numbers, text, dates, times, logical values, and errors. A logical value, such as TRUE or FALSE, is the result displayed after a condition is tested. Error values, such as #NUM!, occur when Excel cannot properly evaluate a formula in a cell.

When you type a value or formula in the active cell, your entry appears at the insertion point, or cursor, in the Formula Bar near the top of the screen (see fig. 7.1). The entry appears in the long text box on the right side of the Formula Bar. The insertion point, a flashing vertical line in the Formula Bar, indicates where characters you type will appear. When you type or edit in the Formula Bar, two boxes appear to the left of the Formula Bar. If you are using a mouse, clicking the Cancel box cancels an entry; clicking the Enter box enters the Formula Bar contents into the active cell.

Formula Bar

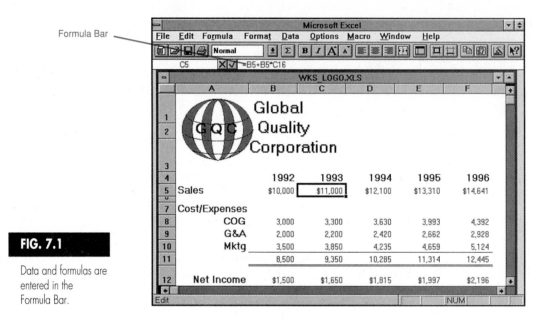

FIG. 7.1

Data and formulas are entered in the Formula Bar.

To enter data in a worksheet, perform the following steps:

1. Select the cell in which you want to enter data.

2. Type the entry.

   The entry appears in the Formula Bar as you type. If you decide that you want to cancel the entry in the Formula Bar, click the Cancel box in the Formula Bar or press Esc.

3. Enter what you have typed by clicking the Enter box in the Formula Bar or by pressing Enter.

If you want to back out before the value or formula is entered in a cell, press Esc or click the Cancel box in the Formula Bar.

This is the basic procedure; in the following sections, you learn many shortcuts for entering data and formulas.

Undoing and Repeating Changes

When you want to undo your last entry or last executed command, choose the **E**dit **U**ndo command. The **U**ndo command changes to show you the last command it can undo. After you have chosen the **U**ndo command, you can choose it again to undo the undo. To use the **U**ndo command, you must choose it immediately after the action you want to undo. If you want to repeat the last command, choose the **E**dit **R**epeat command. Not all commands can be repeated.

Entering Text

Text can include alphabetical characters, numbers, and symbols. To enter text in a cell, select the cell, type the text entry, and then enter the text by clicking the Enter box or pressing Enter.

You can type as many as 255 characters in a cell. (Note that all the characters may not show in the worksheet if the cell is not wide enough and if the cell to the right contains data.) When you enter text in a cell that still has the original General format, the text automatically aligns on the left side of the cell.

You can make Excel accept numbers as text by placing an equal sign in front of the numbers and enclosing the numbers in quotation marks. Suppose, for example, that you enter 45,000, which Excel normally considers a number, as *="45,000"*.

Entering this number as text enables the number display to exceed the cell's width. If you enter a number in the normal way and the cell is not wide enough to display it, the cell fills with # signs. Entering a number as text also is useful if you need to create a text heading, for example ($000), that Excel would normally treat as a number. If you use this method, Excel can convert the text number into a number if it is needed in a numeric formula.

If you need to display quotation marks on-screen within a formula involving text, you must enclose the quotation marks you want within quotation marks. Enclosing the quotation marks rather than the text results in three quotation marks on either side of the text, as in the following example:

="""The Absolute Best"""&" the worst"

Excel enables you to type phrases that begin with a number directly into the worksheet. For example, the following address is accepted by Excel as text because it contains letters:

45 Oak Ridge Trail

Entering Numbers

Numbers are constant values containing only the following characters:

1 2 3 4 5 6 7 8 9 0 _ + / . E e

To enter a number, you select the cell, type the number, and then press Enter or click the Enter box. You can enter integers, such as 135 or 327; decimal fractions, such as 135.437 or 327.65; integer fractions, such as 1 1/2 or 2/3; or scientific notation, such as 1.35437E+2.

As you create worksheets, Excel may display newly entered numbers or formulas in scientific notation, for example, 2.67E+9, or as ######### (see fig. 7.2). Scientific notation is another way of representing the same number, for example, 2.67E+9 represents 2.67 times 10^9 (1 with 9 zeroes behind it.)

A cell filled with # signs indicates that the column is not wide enough to display the number correctly. In this case, you need to change the numeric format or widen the column. Formatting worksheets is described in Chapter 8.

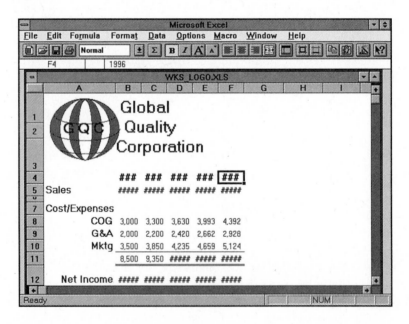

FIG. 7.2

Scientific format or the signs ##### appear when a column is not wide enough to display a number or date.

You may need to convert a numeric or date result into text. To do so, use the TEXT() function. The TEXT() function also formats numeric or date results using any of the predefined or custom numeric and date formats.

T I P

Electronic worksheets like Excel store both the number typed into a cell and the format or appearance in which the number should be displayed. When you enter a number into a cell, Excel tries to establish how the number should be formatted. For example, Excel accepts and displays the entries listed in table 7.1 with the formats indicated.

Table 7.1. Excel's Automatic Formats

Typed Entry	Excel's Automatically Chosen Format	Displayed Result
897	Number, General	897
7999 Knue Rd.	Text, left aligned	7999 Knue Rd.
$450.09	Number, dollar format	$450.09
54.6%	Number, percent format	54.60%
2 3/4	Number, fraction	2 3/4
0 3/4	Number, fraction	3/4
45,600	Number, comma format	45,600
-678	Number, negative	-678
(678)	Number, negative	-678
1/5/93	Date, m/d/yy	1/5/93
4/5	Date, m/d/yy (current year assumed)	5-Apr

The second example, 7999 Knue Rd., illustrates that if an entry is not a number or date, then Excel stores it as text. This feature is convenient when you are entering database information, such as inventory codes or street addresses.

To enter a fraction, you must type an integer, a space, and then the fraction. If you are entering only the fractional part, type a zero, a space, and then the fraction; otherwise Excel will interpret the entry as a date. The result is a number that can be used in calculations.

Entering Dates and Times

Excel recognizes dates and times typed in most common ways. When you type a date or time, Excel converts your entry to a *serial* number. The serial number represents the number of days from the beginning of the century until the date you type. Time is recorded as a decimal fraction of a 24-hour day.

If Excel recognizes your entry as a valid date or time format, you see the date or time on-screen. Correctly entered dates appear in the Formula Bar with the format m/d/yy, regardless of how the cell is formatted.

A valid date entry typed into an unformatted cell is aligned as a number, to the right. A valid date entry typed into a cell that has been previously formatted with a numeric format appears as a serial number. If, for example, you type *5 Nov 93* in a cell formatted to show numbers with a comma and two decimal places (#,##0.00), you will see that date as 34,278.00.

If Excel does not recognize your entry as a valid date or time format and you type a text date, such as *Sept 5 92*, Excel treats the entry as text and, in an unformatted cell, aligns it to the left.

To enter a date, type the date into the cell with any of these formats:

> 7/8/93
>
> 8-Jul-93
>
> 8-Jul (The year from the system date is used.)
>
> Jul-93 (Only the month and year show.)
>
> 6/8/93 09:45

In any of these date formats, you can use either a /, -, or space to separate elements.

Enter times in any of these formats:

13:32

13:32:45

1:32 PM

1:32:45 PM

6/8/93 13:32

The first two examples are from a 24-hour clock. If you use a 12-hour clock, follow the time with a space and A, AM, P, or PM (in either upper- or lowercase). Be sure that you leave a space before the AM or PM. Do not mix a 24-hour clock time with an AM or PM. As the last format shows, you can combine the date and time during entry.

For information about formatting or changing the formats of dates and times, refer to Chapter 8, "Formatting Worksheets."

> In some cases when you enter a correctly formatted date or time, the displayed result appears as a number, not in a date or time format. This occurs when the cell's format has been previously changed from the default, General. To reformat for the correct display, select the cell, choose Format Number, or click the right mouse button on the cell and select Number, select the date or time format from the list box, and choose OK or press Enter.

T I P

For Related Information:

FROM HERE...

▸▸ "Changing Character Fonts, Sizes, Styles, and Colors," p. 257.

▸▸ "Formatting Numbers," p. 272.

▸▸ "Formatting Dates and Times," p. 285.

Entering Formulas

Formulas perform calculations, which is the reason for Excel's existence. Formulas automatically recalculate and produce current results when you update data used by the formulas. Formulas refer to the contents of a cell by its cell reference, such as B12. In formulas, you can use math operators, such as + or -, as well as built-in formulas, called functions, like SUM() or PMT() (payment).

A simple formula might appear in the Formula Bar under the menu as the following:

=B12*D15

This formula multiplies the contents of cell B12 by the contents of cell D15.

Normally, the worksheet displays the results of formulas rather than the formulas themselves. The formula in the active cell is displayed in the Formula Bar. Figure 7.3 shows the active cell as C11, and its formula is displayed in the Formula Bar.

Figure 7.4 shows the formulas in the worksheet. The formulas are displayed in the worksheet when you choose the **O**ptions **D**isplay command and select the Formulas check box.

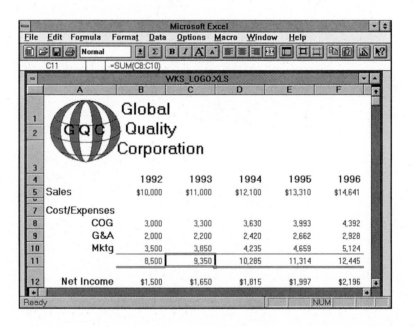

FIG. 7.3

The Formula Bar displays the formula in the active cell.

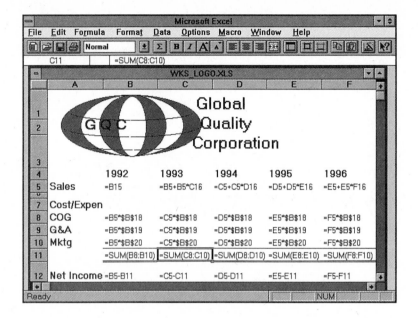

FIG. 7.4

Formulas also can be displayed in the worksheet.

To enter a formula, perform the following steps:

1. Select the cell that will contain the formula.

2. Type an equals sign (=).

3. Type a value, cell reference, function, or name.

4. If the formula is complete, press Enter or click the Enter box (a check mark) in the Formula Bar. If the formula is not complete, continue to step 5.

5. Type an operator. Operators can be of many types. The most common are math symbols, such as + and -.

6. Return to step 3.

Always separate terms in a formula with operators or parentheses. Do not leave any spaces in the formula.

Before a formula has been entered, you can clear it from the Formula Bar by clicking the Cancel box, an X, to the left of the Formula Bar. From the keyboard, press Esc.

T   I   P   If you know you want to enter a formula and copy it into adjacent cells, you can perform the entry and copy simultaneously with the following shortcut:

1. Select the range of cells to contain the formulas or data.

2. Enter the value or formula that is appropriate for the active cell.

3. Press Ctrl+Enter or hold Ctrl and click the Enter box.

The Ctrl+Enter combination both enters your value or formula in the active cell and copies it into other cells in the selection. Any formulas you enter with Ctrl+Enter adjust their relative cell references to their new locations just as though you had copied them or filled them into the selected cells. (Relative cell references are described in the section "Using Cell References in Formulas.")

Entering Cell References by Pointing

The least error prone method of entering cell references in a formula is by pointing to the cell you want to include in a formula. Although you can type an entire formula, it is often easy to make a typing error or misread the row or column headings and end up with D52 in a formula when it should be E53. When you point to a cell to include in a formula, you actually move the pointer to the cell you want in the formula. It is obvious when you have selected the correct cells.

To enter a cell reference into a formula by pointing, perform the following steps:

1. Select the cell for the formula.

2. Type an equals sign (=).

3. Point to the cell you want in the formula and click it, or press the movement keys to move the dashed *marquee* around the cell you want to include in the formula.

   The address of the cell you point to appears at the cursor location in the Formula Bar. The cell pointed to is enclosed by a dashed line.

   You also can enter ranges into formulas by pointing. Instead of clicking, drag across the range you want in the formula. Instead of moving with arrow keys, move to one corner of the range, and then hold down the Shift key as you move to the opposite corner.

4. Enter an operator, such as the + symbol.

5. Point to the next cell.

6. Repeat from step 4 to continue the formula, or enter the formula by clicking the Enter box or pressing Enter.

You do not have to type the last parenthesis if you are creating a formula composed of a function that encloses all other terms.

T I P

Entering Cell References in Existing Formulas

Using the same techniques you used to create formulas, you can edit formulas to change or add new cell references. You can enter new cell references by typing them, pointing to them and clicking them, or moving to them with the movement keys.

To insert a new cell reference or range into an existing formula, perform the following steps:

1. Position the insertion point in the Formula Bar where you want the new cell reference or range. Select a cell reference or range you want to replace completely. (Drag across it with the pointer or use Shift+arrow keys.)

2. Type or click the new cell reference. If your new reference is a range, click one corner and drag to the opposite corner. Or, from the keyboard, type the new cell reference or press the movement keys to move to the cell you want as the new reference. To include a range in the formula, press F2 to change to Entry mode, use the movement keys to move to one corner of the range, hold down Shift, and move to the opposite corner of the range. Press F2 again to return to Edit mode.

   Watch the Formula Bar as you perform step 2. The new cell reference replaces the old.

3. Add cell references, or choose OK or press Enter. Press Esc to back out of your changes.

T I P   If you are adding cell references to a formula by pointing to them, you can go to the distant location by pressing the F5 key. Once there, you can select that cell or another close by. If the cell or range you want to add is in the Goto dialog box that appears after pressing F5, choose the name from the list box and choose OK. The name appears in the formula, and a marquee appears around the named cells.

Using Cell References in Formulas

You can refer to a cell's location in Excel with a *relative reference* or an *absolute reference*. Be careful to use the correct type of cell reference in each formula you create. If you understand the difference between the two types of cell references used in Excel, you can avoid creating formulas that change incorrectly when copied to new locations.

You use relative and absolute references in your daily life. Suppose, for example, that you are in your office and you want someone to take a letter to the mailbox. Using a relative reference, you would tell the person: "Go out the front door; turn left and go two blocks; turn right and go one block." These directions are *relative to* your office location at the time you give the instructions. If you move to a different location, these directions do not work anymore.

To make sure that your letter gets to the mailbox no matter where you are when you give the directions, you must say something like this: "Take this letter to the mailbox at 2700 Mendocino Ave." No matter where you are when you speak, the mailbox will be at one absolute location: 2700 Mendocino Ave. The address *absolutely* will not change.

Using Relative References

Unless you specify otherwise, Excel uses relative referencing for cell addresses when you enter a formula. This means that cell references in a formula change when you copy the formula to a new location or when you fill a range with a formula. You most often will want formulas to use relative cell references.

In figure 7.5, the formula in cell C5 is =B5+B5*C16. All these references are relative. The formula, translated into English, would read as follows:

> In cell C5, multiply the number in the cell one column to the left in same row (cell B5 in this example) and the number in the cell 11 rows down in same column (cell C16). Add the number contained in the cell one column to the left in the same row (cell B5).

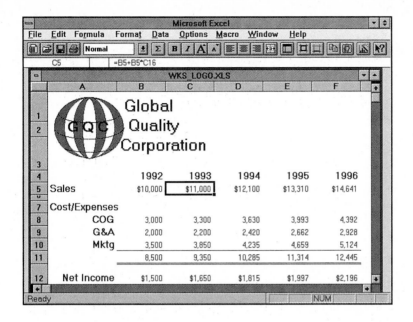

FIG. 7.5

The relative reference formula in C5 shown in the Formula Bar.

You can see the equivalent formula in R1C1, row-column format, by choosing the **O**ptions **W**orkspace command and selecting the R1C1 option. If you change the formula display to R1C1 format, the formula in the same cell, R5C3, is =RC[-1]+RC[-1]*R[11]C. The R1C1 format makes relative references more obvious because the cell references are presented as the relative change from the current cell. For example, C[-1] means one column left, and R[11] means 11 rows down from the active cell.

When you copy either formula across row 5, the formulas automatically adjust their cell references to their new positions. The copied formulas are as follows:

Cell Containing Formula	A1 Format	R1C1 Format
D5 or R5C4	=C5+C5*D16	=RC[-1]+RC[-1]*R[11]C
E5 or R5C5	=D5+D5*E16	=RC[-1]+RC[-1]*R[11]C
F5 or R5C6	=E5+E5*F16	=RC[-1]+RC[-1]*R[11]C

Notice how the formula using A1 format changed to give its cell references the same relative position from the cell containing the formula. Formulas using R1C1 format do not change when copied because the formula always shows the relative position of the cell being used.

Most of the time, you will want cell references to change when they are copied. In some cases, however, these changes can cause problems. What would happen if the worksheet didn't have a row of values all the way across row 16? What if row 16 had a single value that each copied formula had to use? What if your worksheet had only a single change number in row 20 to be used for each year's revenue increase? Each of the copied formulas in these cases would have been wrong. When you need to copy a formula and you want to make sure that some terms in the formula do not adjust to their new locations, you should designate those terms as absolute references.

Using Absolute References

To keep cell references from changing when you copy or fill a formula to new locations, use absolute references. If you use the A1 formula format, indicate absolute references by putting a dollar sign ($) in front of the column letter or row number that you want to freeze. In R1C1 format, indicate an absolute cell reference by typing a specific row or column number; do not enclose the number in square brackets.

In figure 7.6, the COG factor is referred to by using an absolute reference address of $B$18 in A1 format or R18C2 in R1C1 format. In A1 format, the dollar sign in front of each part of the address, *B* and *18*, prevents the cell reference from changing during a copy or fill; in R1C1 format, the specific row and column numbers without brackets prevent the cell reference from changing during a copy or fill operation.

The formula in B8, for example, was copied into cells C8, D8, E8, and F8. Cell B8's formula is =B5*$B$18 in A1 format or =R[-3]C*R18C2 in R1C1 format. When copied, only the first term changes in each new cell that the formula is copied into. The second term remains *absolutely* the same. This was necessary because there was a value in B18, but no corresponding values in C18, D18, E18, and F18. Had the formula used B18 instead of $B$18, all the copied formulas would have referenced the blank cells C18, D18, E18, and F18.

You can enter an absolute reference in any of three ways:

■ As you enter the formula, type the dollar sign in front of the row or column that you want to remain the same. In R1C1 format, delete the square brackets.

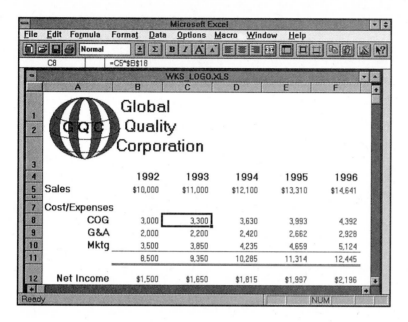

FIG. 7.6

Absolute reference
formulas use a $ to
freeze a row or
column reference.

- Choose the Formula **R**eference command after typing a cell address.

- Move the flashing insertion point in the Formula Bar so that it is inside or touching the cell reference, and press F4, the reference key. (If the formula already has been entered, select its cell and press F2 to edit it.) Each time you press F4, the type of reference changes.

To enter an absolute reference by using the Formula **R**eference command or F4 key, perform the following steps:

1. Type an equals sign (=) and the cell reference you want to be absolute.

2. Choose the Formula **R**eference command or press F4, the absolute reference key, until the correct combination of dollar signs appears. For R1C1 format, type the specific row or column number without brackets, or use the Formula **R**eference command or press F4.

3. Type the next operator and continue to enter the formula.

You can use the Formula **R**eference command or F4 key when editing an existing formula.

Using Mixed References

On some occasions, you will want only the row to stay fixed when copied or only the column to stay fixed. In these cases, you need to use a mixed reference, one that contains both absolute and relative references. For example, the reference $B5 prevents the column from changing, but the row changes relative to a new copied location; the dollar sign keeps the column from changing. In B$5, just the opposite occurs. The column adjusts to a new location but the row always stays fixed at 5; the dollar sign keeps the row from changing.

A mixed reference in R1C1 style might look like R[1]C2, where the R[1] means one row down from the formula and C2 means the absolute second column. R2C[–1] means the absolute second row and the column one left of the formula.

You can create mixed references in the same ways you can create absolute references. Type the dollar signs or specific row and column numbers without brackets, choose the Formula **R**eference command, or press F4. Each choice of Formula **R**eference or each press of F4 cycles the cell reference to a new combination.

Each time you select the Formula **R**eference command or F4, Excel cycles through all combinations of relative and absolute references. Press F4 four times, for example, and you cycle from B22 through $B$22, B$22, $B22, and B22.

Changing Cell Reference Style

An Excel worksheet is composed of 256 columns and 16,384 rows. The intersection of each row and column creates a cell. Within a cell, you can place text, a number, or a formula.

You can refer to a specific cell in the current worksheet using one of two styles: A1 or R1C1. The A1 style of reference indicates a cell by its column letter and row number—B4, for example. This style is used in Lotus 1-2-3 and is familiar to many people. The worksheet's 256 columns are designated A through IV. You can locate or refer to any cell's contents by the address of the cell's column and row.

You can refer to ranges, or rectangular groups of cells, with the notation D7:F10. The opposite corners of the range (D7 and F10) are separated by a colon (:). In Excel, you can select multiple ranges at one time. You use ranges when you want a command to affect multiple cells or when you use a formula involving the contents of multiple cells.

The R1C1 style indicates a cell by its row number, R1, and its column number, C1. You also can designate a range in R1C1 style. This style is familiar to users of Multiplan and is easier to use in complex formulas involving relative positions and in macro programming.

You can switch the worksheet's row and column headings between the A1 and R1C1 styles by choosing the **O**ptions **W**orkspace command and selecting or clearing the R1C1 check box. When you change the reference style, formulas throughout the worksheet change to reflect the new style. This book uses the A1 style of references, except where indicated in complex formulas or in macros.

You can switch from the A1 to R1C1 style of displaying cell references by choosing the **O**ptions **W**orkspace command, selecting the R1C1 check box, and then choosing OK. Figure 7.7 shows a formula in the bar in R1C1 style. To switch from R1C1 style back to A1 style, clear the R1C1 check box and choose OK.

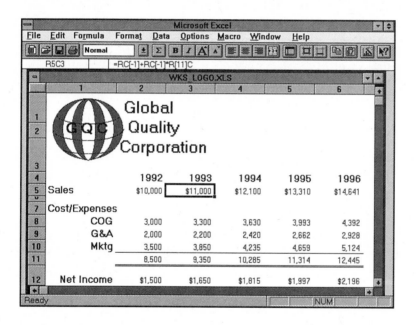

FIG. 7.7

The R1C1 reference style can be easier to use in complex formulas and macros.

Editing Absolute and Relative References

To change an absolute or relative cell reference that is already entered in a formula, perform the following steps:

1. Select the formula.

2. Move the insertion point so it touches the cell reference you want to change.

3. Press F4 to cycle through combinations of absolute and relative cell references.

4. When the formula is displayed correctly, press Enter.

Figure 7.8 shows a Formula Bar with the insertion point in a cell reference before F4 was pressed. Figure 7.9 shows the effect of pressing F4 one time.

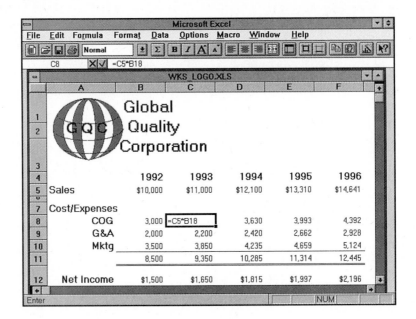

FIG. 7.8

Move the insertion point next to the cell reference you want to change.

Using Operators in Formulas

Operators tell formulas what operations to perform. Excel uses four types of operators:

Operators	Signs
Arithmetic	+, -, *, /, %, ^
Text	&
Comparative	=, <, <=, >, >=, <>
Reference	colon (:), comma (,), space ( )

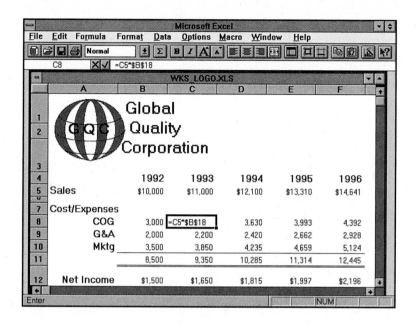

FIG. 7.9

Each press of the F4
key changes the mix of
absolute and relative
references.

Table 7.2 illustrates how you can use each of the arithmetic operators in formulas.

Table 7.2. Arithmetic Operators

Operator	Formula	Result	Type of Operation
+	=5+2	7	Addition
-	=5-2	3	Subtraction
-	-5	-5	Negation (negative of the number)
*	=5*2	10	Multiplication
/	=5/2	2.5	Division
%	5%	.05	Percentage
^	=5^2	25	Exponentiation (to the power of)

Excel can work with more than just arithmetic formulas. Excel also can manipulate text, perform comparisons, and relate different ranges and cells on the worksheet. The ampersand (&) operator, for example, joins text within quotation marks or text contained in referenced cells. Joining text is known as *concatenation*. Table 7.3 illustrates how you can use text operators.

Table 7.3. Text Operators

Operator	Formula	Result	Type of Operation
&	="Ms. "&"Gibbs"	Ms. Gibbs	Text is joined.
&	=A12&" "&B36	Ms. Gibbs	Text is joined when A12 contains Ms. and B36 contains Gibbs.

When you need to compare results, you can create formulas using comparative operators. These operators return a TRUE or FALSE result, depending on how the formula evaluates the condition. Table 7.4 lists the comparative operators.

Table 7.4. Comparative Operators

Operator	Type
=	Equal to
<	Less than
<=	Less than or equal to
>	Greater than
>=	Greater than or equal to
<>	Not equal to

The following are examples of comparative operators in formulas:

Formula	Result
=A12<15	TRUE if the content of A12 is less than 15; FALSE if the content of A12 is 15 or more.
=B36>=15	TRUE if the content of B36 is 15 or more; FALSE if the content of B36 is less than 15.

Another type of operator is the reference operator (see table 7.5). Reference operators do not make changes to constants or cell contents. Instead, they control how a formula groups cells and ranges of cells when the formula calculates. Reference operators enable you to combine absolute and relative references and named ranges. Reference operators are valuable for joining cells together (union) or referring to a common area shared between different ranges (intersect).

> Use the range operator (:) to reduce your work in formulas. If, for example, you want a formula to refer to all cells in column B, type *B:B*. Similarly, the range that includes all cells in rows 5 through 12 is entered as 5:12.
>
> **T   I   P**

Table 7.5. Reference Operators

Operator	Example	Type	Result
:	SUM(A12:A24)	Range	Evaluates as a single reference the cells in the rectangular area between the two "corners."
,	SUM(A12:A24,B36)	Union	Evaluates two references as a single reference.
space	SUM(A12:A24 A16:B20)	Intersect	Evaluates the cells common to both references (if no cells are common to both, then #NULL results).
space	=Yr92 Sales	Intersect	Cell contents at the intersect of the column named Yr92 and the row named Sales.

T I P   Excel uses a colon (B12:C36) to designate a range in the same way that 1-2-3 uses two periods (B12..C36). You can use a comma to select multiple ranges (B12:C36,F14:H26) for many functions.

Excel follows a consistent set of rules when applying operators in a formula. Working from the first calculation to the last, Excel evaluates operators in the order shown in table 7.6.

Table 7.6. The Order in which Excel Evaluates Operators

Operator	Definition
:	Range
space	Intersect
,	Union
-	Negation
%	Percentage
^	Exponentiation
* and /	Multiplication and division
+ and -	Addition and subtraction
&	Text joining
=, <, <= >, >=, <>	Comparisons

You can change the order in which calculations are performed by enclosing in parentheses the terms you want Excel to calculate first. Notice, for instance, the difference between these results:

Formula	Result
=6+21/3	13
=(6+21)/3	9

Pasting Names and Functions into Formulas

You can use English *names* in formulas to reference cells or ranges. You also can reduce the size of formulas and make them operate faster and with less change of typographical error by using the built-in formulas, called *functions*, that are part of Excel. Names and functions can be pasted into formulas. Excel enables you to choose the name or function you want from a list, and then paste it into a formula. This process is easier and more accurate than typing. Naming cells, ranges, formulas, and values is described later in this chapter. For a detailed discussion of functions, see Chapter 10, "Using Functions."

To paste a name into an existing formula, perform the following steps:

1. Move the insertion point in the Formula Bar to where you want the name.

2. Choose the Formula **P**aste Name command to display the Paste Name dialog box (see fig. 7.10).

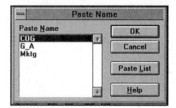

FIG. 7.10

The Paste Name dialog box.

3. Select the name you want to paste.

    If you have not named any cells, ranges, formulas, or values, no names will appear in the list.

4. Choose OK or press Enter.

To paste a function into the Formula Bar, perform the following steps:

1. Move the insertion point in the Formula Bar to where you want the function.

2. Choose the Formula Paste Function command to display the Paste Function dialog box (see fig. 7.11).

3. Select the type of function you want to paste from the Function **C**ategory list. Selections other than All limit the Paste **F**unctions list to specific types of functions.

4. Select the function you want to paste from the Paste **F**unctions list.

5. Select the Paste **A**rguments check box if you want to see prompts for arguments. This check box is very helpful and normally should be selected.

6. Choose OK or press Enter.

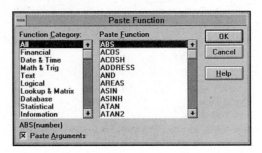

T I P You can select from most list boxes and choose the OK button simultaneously by double-clicking your selection in the list.

Entering Text, Dates, and Time in Formulas

Enter text, dates, and time in formulas by including the data in quotes:

="Yosemite National Park"

If you want to perform date math on explicit dates, which are dates that are not in cells, use a formula such as

="5/14/93"-"5/14/48"

or

="5 May, 93"-"5 May, 48"

These formulas produce the number of days between the two dates.

When you need numeric or date results from a formula or reference to appear as text, use the TEXT() function with a predefined or custom format. For example, use

="Today is" & TEXT(A13,"mmm dd, yy")

to produce a text date from the contents of cell A13.

Entering Array Formulas

Using array formulas is a way of saving memory and time. When you find yourself entering one formula and then copying or filling it into adjacent rows or columns, you may be able to use an array formula.

An array formula is entered into Excel's memory as a single formula, but this one formula is used in all the cell's that are part of the array. To learn more about array formulas and the special power of array formulas when used for analysis see Chapter 13 on the topics of array math and array formulas.

Changing Formulas to Values

In some situations, you may want to freeze a formula's results so it changes into a value. To *freeze* a formula into its resulting value, perform the following steps:

1. Select the cell of an existing formula and press F2 (the Edit key), or click in the Formula Bar.

2. Choose the **O**ptions Calculate **N**ow command, or press F9.

   The formula in the Formula Bar is replaced by its calculated value.

3. Choose OK or press Enter.

Troubleshooting Formulas

The following small techniques, if developed as habits, will help reduce errors you may have when entering formulas:

- Type functions, names, and cell references in lowercase characters in the Formula Bar. If Excel recognizes them, they change case when you enter the formula. Functions and cells references convert to uppercase. Names convert to match the upper- and lowercase characters used to create the name. If a function, name or cell reference stays in lowercase, then you probably have mistyped or forgotten to create the name.

- One of the most common problems when entering formulas is having mismatched parentheses: the number of left and right parentheses are not equal. To check how parentheses pair up and to see whether the pairings enclose the correct terms, move the insertion point next to a parenthesis, and then press the arrow key to move the insertion point across the parenthesis. As the insertion point moves across, the matching parenthesis of the pair is highlighted.

■ A single term in a formula with many parts may be causing the problem. To check a partial result or term in a formula, you can change part of the formula into a value or calculate part of the formula.

In the Formula Bar, select the part of the formula you want to see the result of, and then press F9. If, for example, you type the formula =*B12*C36+(D12/D35)*, select the cell references B12*C36 and press F9. You will see what the result is for that part of the formula. The portion you select must be a valid formula in its own right. Press Alt+Backspace (**E**dit **U**ndo) to return to the formula or press Esc when you are finished to ensure that the calculated terms do not replace the formula. (This method also works to evaluate part of a long or nested macro function.)

■ Use the error values returned by Excel to help find the problem. Excel returns the following error values:

Value	Meaning
#DIV/0!	The formula is dividing by zero. Look for a reference to a blank cell. The AUDIT.XLA add-in can help find references to blanks. Or select terms in the formula and press F9.
#N/A	The formula returns a Not Available result. Some functions such as the lookup functions return #N/A when the function is used incorrectly or cannot find a valid result. Array formulas entered into a range larger than the array result will show #N/A in cells where no result is returned (the selection has more cells than the answer).
#NAME?	Formulas that return this result contain a name that Excel does not recognize. Either you have not yet created the name or the name is mistyped. A mistyped function may return #NAME? because Excel does not recognize it is a function and thinks it is a name that has not been created.
#NULL!	The null value is returned from an intersect operation between two areas that do not intersect. Because no intersect exists, there was nothing to return.
#NUM!	A number in the equation is causing a problem. The number may be used incorrectly as an argument or may be too large or small for the function in which it is being used.

#REF!	The formula contains an incorrect reference. This can occur if you delete cells, rows, or columns that a formula referenced. Function macros that reference a function on a macro sheet that is not open return #REF!.
#VALUE!	The value error occurs when you use an incorrect argument in a function. For example, an argument should be a number and you enter text. Some macro functions result in #VALUE! if they fail.

For Related Information:

▶▶ "Entering Worksheet Functions," p. 356.

▶▶ "Using Formulas To Make Decisions," p. 492.

▶▶ "Adding a Worksheet Auditor and Troubleshooter," p. 613.

FROM HERE...

Editing Text and Formulas

Whether you are editing a text box in a dialog box or a formula in the Formula Bar, you use the same editing principles used in all Windows applications. Before you can edit text, you must put the cell's contents in the Formula Bar. To do this, perform the following steps:

1. Select the cell containing the formula.

2. Move the insertion point into the text.

   Move the pointer over the text until it changes into an I-beam. Position the pointer in the text you want to edit, then click. A flashing insertion point indicates where typing and editing take place.

   If you have selected a cell, press the Edit key, F2. Press the movement keys to move the insertion point to the point in the text where you want to edit.

3. Edit the formula.

T I P   The time may come when you know that a formula contains an error, but you cannot find it. Because of the error, you cannot enter the formula. If you press Esc, the Formula Bar will clear and you will lose the formula. To preserve your formula so that you can return to it later, delete the equals sign at the front and press Enter. The formula becomes text in the cell. When you have the time or the insight to fix the formula, reselect that cell, reenter the equals sign, and fix the formula.

Table 7.7 lists shortcut keys and mouse actions you can use for editing.

Table 7.7. Shortcut Keys and Mouse Actions for Editing Formulas

Key	Mouse	Action
F2	Click Formula Bar	Moves the cursor into the Formula Bar for editing.
F4	Formula **R**eference	Cycles the cell reference touching the insertion point through all combinations of absolute and relative references.
F9	N/A	Calculates the select part of a formula.
Ins	N/A	Toggles between Insert and Typeover modes.
Del	N/A	Clears the selected characters or character to the right of the insertion point.
Backspace	N/A	Clears the selected characters or character to the left of the insertion point.
Ctrl+Del	N/A	Clears all characters from the insertion point to the end of the line.
Ctrl+X	N/A	Cuts the character or selection to the right of the insertion point.
Ctrl+C	**E**dit **C**opy	Copies the selection to the Clipboard.

Key	Mouse	Action
Ctrl+V	**Edit P**aste	Pastes the text at the insertion point, or replaces the selected characters.
Ctrl+2	**Edit U**ndo	Reverses many editing actions.
Home	N/A	Moves the insertion point to the front of the Formula Bar.
End	N/A	Moves the insertion point to the end of the Formula Bar's contents.
Shift+Home	Drag up and left	Selects all characters from the insertion point to the front of the current line of the Formula Bar.
Shift+End	Drag down and right	Selects all characters from the insertion point to the end of the current line of the Formula Bar.
Shift+Ctrl+Home	Drag up and left	Selects all characters from insertion point to beginning of formula (even in multiline formulas).
Shift+Ctrl+End	Drag down and right	Selects all characters from insertion point to end of formula (even in multiline formulas).
Shift+arrow	Drag across	Selects characters the insertion point crosses over.
Ctrl+left/right arrow	N/A	Moves a word or formula a term at a time.
Shift+Ctrl+ left/right arrow	Double click, Double-click+drag	Select a word or formula a term at a time.

When you need to insert the same text in several places, select the text and copy it with the **Edit C**opy command. Then move the insertion point to each spot where you want to place the text and choose **Edit P**aste.

Excel normally is in Insert mode, so what you type inserts itself at the insertion point. If you want to type over existing text, press Ins (Insert), and then type. Pressing Ins a second time toggles back to Insert mode.

You can delete single characters to the left of the cursor by pressing Backspace. Delete single characters to the right of the cursor by pressing Del.

 NOTE   When Excel beeps and prohibits you from editing a cell's contents, the cell may be protected against changes. Protection is described in Chapter 8, "Formatting Worksheets."

Increasing Data-Entry Efficiency

Data entry usually is tedious, but it must be done correctly. The following sections show you how to speed up the data-entry process.

You can make editing easier by dragging editing tools to the toolbars with which you work. Customizing toolbars is described in Chapter 33. The editing tools are available by choosing the **O**ptions T**o**olbar command, and then selecting the **C**ustomize button. Select Edit from the **C**ategories list. Following are the edit tools you can drag onto toolbars:

Undo Last Command	Repeat Last Command
Cut	Copy
Paste	Clear Formulas
Clear Formats	Paste Formats
Paste Values	Edit Delete
Delete Rows	Delete Columns
Insert	Insert Rows
Insert Columns	Fill Right
Fill Down	

Entering Numbers with a 10-Key Keypad

If you are accustomed to using a 10-key keypad that enters decimal points automatically, you will appreciate the fixed decimal feature of Excel. You can make Excel automatically enter the decimal by choosing the **O**ptions **W**orkspace command. When the Workspace dialog box appears, select the **F**ixed Decimal check box. In the **P**laces text box, enter the number of decimal places you want (two is normal). Choose OK or press Enter.

To enter the number 345.67, for example, you can type *34567*. When you press Enter, Excel enters the number and inserts the decimal point. You can override the automatic decimal placement by typing the decimal in the number you enter.

The feature continues to work until you turn it off by clearing the **F**ixed Decimal check box.

Moving the Active Cell

To quicken the data-entry process, select the range in which you want to enter data; the active cell will move automatically after pressing a data-entry key. This feature is especially convenient for data-entry forms and databases. Figure 7.12 shows a selected data-entry area.

To enter data in a selected area, press the appropriate key:

Key	Action
Tab	Enters data and moves right in the selected area; at the right edge of the selected area, wraps to the left.
Shift+Tab	Enters data and moves left in the selected area; at the left edge of the selected area, wraps to the right.
Enter	Enters data and moves down in the selected area; at the bottom of the selected area, wraps to the top.
Shift+Enter	Enters data and moves up in the selected area; at the top of the selected area, wraps to the bottom.

When the active cell reaches the edge of the selected area, it automatically wraps around to the next appropriate cell. If, for example, you press Tab repeatedly, the active cell reaches the right edge, and then jumps to the first cell in the next row of the left edge.

Using Data-Entry Shortcut Keys

As you enter data in a database, you may want to copy information from the cell above the active cell or insert the current date and time. Excel has shortcut keys that make these tasks easy and convenient to do.

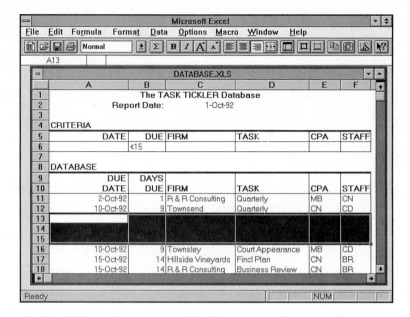

FIG. 7.12

Selecting data-entry cells before typing automatically moves the active cell to the correct location.

Key	Action
Ctrl+' (apostrophe)	Copies the formula from the cell above (cell references are not adjusted to the new location).
Ctrl+" (quotation mark)	Copies the value from the cell above.
Ctrl+; (semicolon)	Inserts the date.
Ctrl+: (colon)	Inserts the time.

Entering a Series of Data

Much of the work in worksheets consists of series or sequences of dates, times or numbers. For example, the headings across a budget usually consist of dates at evenly spaced intervals. As another example, you may need a sequence of numbers down the left column of a list—numbers running from 1 to 100 in steps of 2. Both of these are examples of data series.

Excel easily can take date or numeric series and extend them for you—filling in the cells you select with the rest of a series. To learn about how to use the fill handle on a selection or the **Data Series** command, see Chapter 13.

Working While Excel Recalculates

When Excel recalculates, it calculates only those formulas involved with the data that has changed. Your worksheet recalculates faster, and you spend less time waiting.

When it recalculates, Excel incorporates two additional features that can increase your productivity. First, you can continue entering data, changing formulas, or giving commands as the worksheet recalculates. Excel incorporates the changes you make as it recalculates. Second, you can start a recalculation on a worksheet, activate other Windows applications, and work in them as Excel continues recalculating the worksheet.

Finding Formulas

The Formula Find command finds whatever you want in the worksheet (or database), including text or formulas. You can use the Formula Find command to locate formulas that contain a unique term, a specific text label, a cell note containing a specific word, or error values. The Formula Find command is especially helpful when you are correcting a worksheet you may not be familiar with.

To find text or a value with Formula Find, perform the following steps:

1. Select the cells you want to search. Select a single cell to search the entire worksheet.

2. Choose the Formula Find command or press Shift+F5 to display the Find dialog box (see fig. 7.13).

3. Type what you are searching for in the Find What box.

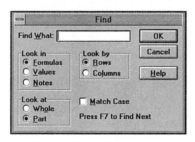

FIG. 7.13

Use Formula Find to look for values, text in notes, or terms in a formula.

4. From among the Look In options, select the option that describes the items you want to search through:

Formulas	Search through formulas in the cells indicated.
Values	Search through values in the cells indicated.
Notes	Search through notes attached to the cells indicated. (Notes are hidden descriptive text that can be attached to cells.) See the "Saving Notes and Voice Messages" section in this chapter.

5. Select one Look At option to define how much of the cell contents must match:

Whole	The entire cell contents must match.
Part	A part of the cell contents must match.

6. Select the Look By option that describes the direction in which you want the search to proceed:

Rows	Search across rows starting at the current cell.
Columns	Search down columns starting at the current cell.

7. Select the **M**atch Case check box if you want to exactly match upper- and lowercase.

8. Choose OK to find the next match, or press Shift and choose OK to find the previous match. Choose Cancel to stop finding items.

After you have completed step 7 and find the item, edit the formula with normal editing procedures.

To quickly find the next cell that satisfies the same conditions, press F7 to find the next occurrence, or press Shift+F7 to find a previous occurrence.

Formula **F**ind cannot be used with comparative operators, such as =, <, and >=. Entering <12 in Cell Find, for example, creates a search for the text <12 rather than for numbers less than 12. If your data is properly laid out, you can search on many different criteria using the techniques described in the database chapters.

You can search for "near misses" by using wild cards. You can use an * in the Find What box to search for any group of characters, numbers, or cell references, and use a ? to search for any single character or part of a cell reference. If, for example, you type =B12~*(C3+*) in the Find What box, Excel looks for formulas that have anything as the last term in the parentheses. If you type =B?, Excel finds formulas with first terms that are relative references in the B column. Note that the first asterisk is preceded by a tilde. This tilde tells Excel to treat the asterisk as normal text, not as a wildcard.

> Find cells linked to other cells, worksheets, or Windows applications
> by searching for occurrences of an exclamation mark. Use the Look in
> Formulas and the Look at **P**art options.
>
> To find cells that feed into the current formula or cells that depend on
> the current formula, use the Formula **S**elect Special command and
> select the **P**recedents or **D**ependents options. The **D**irect Only and All
> Levels options indicate how many levels of precedents or dependents
> should be selected.

T I P

Using Formula Replace

The Formula **R**eplace command is a big help when you overhaul a
worksheet. The command works the same way as a search-and-replace
command does in a word processing application. You tell Excel what the
new text will be and what text it will replace. You can replace selectively
or replace throughout the entire worksheet.

Formula **R**eplace can save you from financial mistakes. If you must make
major changes to a term or formula used throughout a worksheet, missing a single formula can have dire consequences. With Formula **R**eplace,
you can be sure that you have found and replaced all the incorrect formulas or terms.

To search and replace, perform the following steps:

1. Select the cells you want to search. Select a single cell to search the
   entire worksheet.

2. Choose the Formula **R**eplace command to display the Replace dialog box (see fig. 7.14).

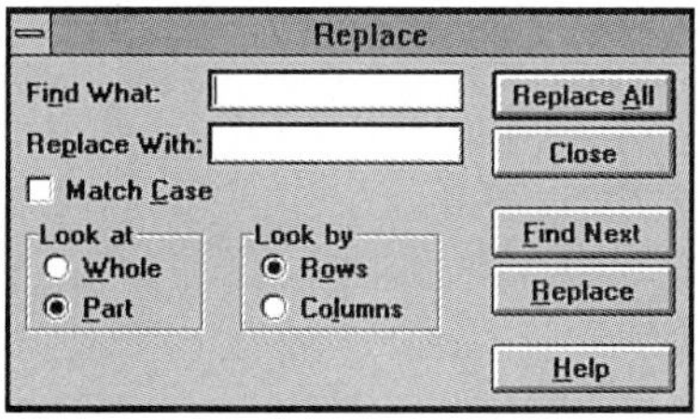

FIG. 7.14

The Formula Replace
command is valuable
for making changes
quickly throughout
your worksheet or
database.

3. Select the Fi**n**d What box and type the text, cell reference, or formula term to be replaced.

4. Select the Replace **W**ith box and type the replacement text.

5. Select the Look At option:

    Whole   The text in the Find What box must match the entire cell contents.

    Part   The text in the Find What box can match any part of the cell contents.

6. Select the Look By option:

    Rows   Search across each row.

    Columns   Search down each column.

7. Select the Match **C**ase check box if you want to find and replace only those words that exactly match upper- and lowercase.

8. Choose the Replace **A**ll button to find and replace all matches, **F**ind Next to find the next match, or **R**eplace to replace the current found item. Choose Close to stop the **R**eplace command and put away the dialog box. Choosing Close does not undo replacements that already have occurred.

If you need to undo changes you have made, choose the **U**ndo Replace command.

To search for items to replace, you can use the * and ? wild cards as described in the previous section on the Formula **F**ind command. This method can be a very efficient way to change formulas or database contents in a portion or in the entire worksheet.

T   I   P   To recalculate only selected cells on a worksheet, select all the cells you want to recalculate, and then use the Formula **R**eplace command to replace the equal signs (=) with equal signs (=). This causes each formula to recalculate as though it were reentered. However, the results of this method may be inaccurate if you do not include all cells involved in the calculations.

FROM HERE...

For Related Information:

▶▶ "Entering a Series of Numbers or Dates," p. 482.

Checking Spelling

Excel has a built-in spelling checker that can give you the confidence
your spelling matches the accuracy of your numbers. With Excel's dictionary you can check one word, the entire worksheet, or even a chart. You
even can check against a custom dictionary that contain abbreviations
or words specific to your clients or industry.

Using the Standard Dictionary

When Excel checks the spelling on a worksheet, it checks more than just
cell contents. It checks embedded charts, text boxes, and buttons. To
spell check a document, perform the following steps:

1. Select a single cell if you want to spell check the entire contents of
   a document. Select a range, embedded chart or object to limit the
   check to the selected item. Select a single word or phrase in the
   Formula Bar to check individual words.

2. Choose the **O**ptions **S**pelling command.

   If a word cannot be found in the standard or custom dictionary, the
   Spelling dialog box, shown in figure 7.15, appears. The word appears at the top-left corner after the `"Not in Dictionary:"`
   phrase. Depending on the setting of the **A**lways Suggest check box,
   the suggested alternate spelling may show in the Suggestions list.

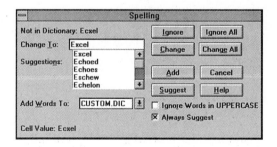

FIG. 7.15

The Spelling dialog
box appears when a
misspelled word is
found.

If no misspelled words are found, the Spelling dialog box never
appears. A dialog box appears and tells you the word in the Formula Bar or the document has no misspelled words.

3. Accept or edit the word in the Change To edit box; then choose the **C**hange button. Choose the Chang**e** All button to change this word throughout the document.

Or

Select one of the alternatives from the Suggestions list, and then choose the **C**hange button. Choose the Chang**e** All button to change this word throughout the document.

Or

Choose one of these alternatives:

Ignore	Ignore this word and continue.
I**g**nore All	Ignore this word throughout the document.
Add	Add this word to the current custom dictionary.
Cancel	Stop the spelling check.
Suggest	Suggest some alternatives from the dictionary.
Help	Display a window of help on how to use spell checking.

If Excel did not spell check the contents above the starting point, you are asked whether you want to continue the check from the top of the document.

4. Choose **Y**es to continue from the top of the document. You can choose Cancel at any time to stop spell checking.

5. When an alert box tells that the entire worksheet has been checked, choose OK to complete the spell check.

If you prefer to see possible correct words in the Suggestion list, select the **A**lways Suggest check box. Spell checking may take longer when you request suggestions. If you want to skip over words that are capitalized, such as part numbers, account codes, and IDs, select the Ignore Words in UPPERCASE check box.

 NOTE To use Excel's built-in spelling checker you must have installed the spell checking utility. If you did not install spell checking during initial installation, you can repeat the installation and select to install only spell checking.

Creating Custom Dictionaries

You may need a custom dictionary with your worksheets so that you are not frequently prompted to verify the spelling of client names, abbreviations, product codes, industry terms, and so on. When Excel checks spelling, it looks first at the standard dictionary. If a word is not found there, Excel checks the custom dictionary. You can have multiple custom dictionaries, but only one can be selected for each spell check.

Unless you specify otherwise, words you add go into the dictionary named CUSTOM.DIC. This name appears in the **A**dd Words To pull-down list. You can build your own custom dictionaries and select them from the list. You can have as many custom dictionaries as you like, but only one can operate at a time with the standard dictionary.

To create a new dictionary, perform the following steps:

1. Choose the **O**ptions **S**pelling command.

2. Type the dictionary name in the Add **W**ords To edit box.

3. Choose the **A**dd or Cancel button. Choosing **A**dd adds the current word to the dictionary.

A dialog box appears asking whether you want to create a new custom dictionary. Choose **Y**es to create a new dictionary.

At any time when the Spell dialog box is open, you can change to a different custom dictionary by selecting the dictionary from the Add **W**ords To list.

To add words to your custom dictionary, start the spell check. When you want to add a word to a custom dictionary, select the dictionary from the Add **W**ords To list and choose the **A**dd button.

Custom dictionary files are stored in a spelling directory specified in the WIN.INI file. The default for this directory is WINDOWS\MSAPPS\PROOF.

T   I   P

Controlling Calculations

Excel normally recalculates each time data changes. This process can slow down data entry if a worksheet is large and requires a long calculation time. In that case, you may want to disable automatic recalculation.

Controlling When Calculation Occurs

To disable automatic recalculation, perform the following steps:

1. Choose the **O**ptions **C**alculation command to display the Calculation dialog box, shown in figure 7.16.

2. Select the **M**anual option if you want to determine when the worksheet recalculates, or select Automatic Except **T**ables to recalculate the worksheet without recalculating data tables.

3. Choose OK or press Enter.

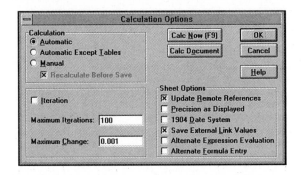

FIG. 7.16

Control when and how Excel recalculates with the Calculation Options dialog box.

When manual calculation is selected, a calculate message appears in the status bar whenever you make a change to the sheet. This message indicates that the worksheet must be recalculated before the results will be correct.

When manual recalculation is turned on, the worksheet does not automatically recalculate. What you see on the screen or print could be wrong. If the calculate message appears at the bottom of the screen, make sure that you choose the **O**ptions **C**alculation **N**ow command or press F9 to recalculate documents before printing or using the results. If you want to calculate only the active document, choose the **O**ptions Calculation command and select the Calc Document command in the Calculation Options dialog box or press Shift+F9. Reselecting the **A**utomatic calculation option also calculates the document.

Calculating by Using the Displayed Value

In some instances, an equation's result may appear to be incorrect because the number used in calculations may be slightly different than the number displayed. Excel stores numbers with 15-decimal precision. You can change the format to display fewer digits, but the full number is still used in calculations. Formatted numbers can cause problems if you are not aware of the difference between the formatted display and the number used in calculation.

To solve this problem, review the **O**ptions **C**alculation command with the **P**recision as Displayed check box selected and the ROUND() function, both discussed in the first part of Chapter 8, "Formatting Worksheets."

Saving without Calculating

Some large worksheets, tables, or databases can take a long time to recalculate. Because Excel normally recalculates before saving a file, the recalculation time can be bothersome. To turn off recalculation before saving, choose the **O**ptions **C**alculation command, select the **M**anual option, and clear the Recalculate Before **S**ave check box.

To save without calculating, perform the following steps:

1. Choose the **O**ptions **C**alculation command.

2. Select the **M**anual option.

3. Clear the Recalculate before **S**ave check box.

4. Choose OK or press Enter.

After you reopen this file, you need to press F9 or reselect the Recalculate Before **S**ave check box for your worksheet to recalculate.

Files that are sources for linked data always should be recalculated before being saved. This practice ensures that linked data will be correct.

NOTE Another method of stopping the recalculation during a save is to press the Esc key. Excel displays a dialog box asking whether you want to recalculate before completing the save. Be careful, however; if you press Esc during a save and the disk is nearly full, you may lose the file you are saving to.

For Related Information:

◄◄ "Managing Files," p. 158.

FROM HERE...

Naming Cells

If you get tired of trying to decipher the meaning of B36 or F13:W54 in a formula, you should use names. If you get tired of selecting the same ranges over and over for reports that you need to print each day or each week, you should use names.

You can, for example, give an area to be totalled the name Sales_Total. You can give the print range F19:L65 an easily recognizable name, such as Sales_Report. Named cells and ranges in Excel are similar to range names in Lotus 1-2-3, but in Excel, you can paste names into formulas, create compound names, and even assign frequently used formulas and constants to names.

Using names in worksheets has the following advantages:

■ Names reduce the chance for errors in formulas and commands. You are likely to notice that you mistyped Sales.Report when you meant to type Sales_Report, but you might not notice an error when you type F19:L65. When you enter an unrecognizable or unde-fined name, Excel displays a #NAME? error.

■ You can name any frequently used constant or formula and use the name in formulas. (The named constant or formula does not have to reside in a cell.) You can, for example, enter a name, such as RATE, into a formula, and then at any later time use the Formula Define Name command to assign a new value to the name RATE. The new assignment changes the value of RATE throughout the worksheet. Nowhere in the worksheet does the value of RATE have to be typed. This technique enables you to create predefined con-stants and formulas that others using the worksheet can use by name.

■ Named ranges expand and contract automatically to adjust to in-serted or deleted rows and columns. This feature is important for creating print ranges, charts, databases, macros, and linked worksheets that continue to work no matter how a named range is expanded or contracted.

■ Names make finding your way around the worksheet easy. You can choose the Formula Goto command, or press F5 and select the name of the location you want to go to. Choosing the Formula Goto command and then selecting Data.Entry or Report.Monthly is a time saver.

■ Using names in macros when referring to specific locations on worksheets helps make your macros more versatile. The macros continue to work on rearranged worksheets.

■ Names make formulas easy to recognize and maintain. For example, the following formula

> =Revenue–Cost

is much easier to understand than the following formula

> =A12–C13.

■ Names make typing references to other worksheets easy. You do not need to know the cell reference in the other worksheet. If the other worksheet has a named cell reference, then you can type a formula such as

> =YTDCONS.XLS!Sales

This formula brings the information from the Sales cell in the worksheet with the file name YTDCONS.XLS into the cell in your active worksheet.

■ Names are easier to remember than cell references. After you name cells or ranges, you can look at a list of names and paste the names you want into formulas with the Formula Paste Name command (see this chapter's earlier section "Pasting Names and Functions into Formulas").

The CHANGE.XLA add-in macro can be found in the LIBRARY subdirectory under the directory containing Excel. CHANGE.XLA adds additional naming commands and features to Excel. For more information on CHANGE.XLA and other add-ins, refer to Chapter 15.

T I P

Creating Names

When the time comes to create names, you must remember a few rules. Names must start with a letter, but you can use any character after the initial letter except a space or a hyphen. Do not use a space in a name; instead, use an underline (_) or a period (.).

Incorrect Names	Correct Names
SALES EXPENSES	SALES_EXPENSES
SALES-EXPENSES	SALES_EXPENSES
Region West	Region.West

Incorrect Names	Correct Names
1993	YR1993
%	Rate

Although names can be as long as 255 characters, you will want to make them shorter. Because formulas also are limited to 255 characters, long names in a formula leave you less room for the rest of the formula, and the full name will not show in a dialog box. Names of up to 15 characters will display in most scrolling list boxes.

Names can be typed in either upper- or lowercase letters. Excel recognizes and continues to use the capitalization used to create the name.

T   I   P   Names are more compact if you use a period (.) to separate multipart names rather than an underscore. If you create names with leading uppercase letters, such as MktgFrance.DivA, you can find problems easier. If you type these names as all lowercase letters in formulas, and the leading letter does not capitalize when you enter the formula, then you know there is a typing error or the name has not been created yet. Excel converts the capitalization to match the way the name was created.

Do not use names that look like cell references, such as B13 or R13C2.

To name a cell, range of cells, or multiple range, perform the following steps:

1. Select the cell, range, or multiple ranges you want to name.

2. Choose the Formula Define Name command.

3. If Excel proposes an acceptable name, leave the name or type the name you want in the **N**ame box.

4. Leave the cell reference in the **R**efers to box, if it is acceptable, or type an equals sign (=) followed by the correct reference. (This procedure is described later.)

5. Choose OK or press Enter.

You can see in figure 7.17 that Excel often proposes a name for the cells you select. Excel looks at the left edge for a text name of a row or looks above for a text name of a column. If you select a range, Excel checks for a name in the upper-left corner of the range. If the text contains a blank space, as in the figure, Excel automatically replaces the blank with an underscore to make the name legal. Excel has done this in the figure.

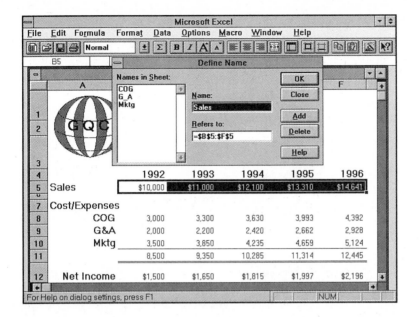

FIG. 7.17

Formula Define
Name attempts to
propose names for
the cell or range
you select.

Excel does not immediately replace existing cell references in formulas with range names. You have the advantage of specifying the areas of the worksheet where formulas show the range names. This procedure is described in the "Applying Names" section later in this chapter.

T I P

Creating Names from Worksheet Text

If you have built a text skeleton for your worksheet (as described in Chapter 4, "Designing Worksheets"), you can use the text on the worksheet to assign names to adjacent cells. Moreover, by selecting a range of cells, you can assign a number of names at the same time. This technique of creating multiple names from text labels is important to creating well-written macros.

To assign a number of names at the same time, use the Formula **C**reate Names command. You can choose whether Excel uses as names the existing text along one or more edges of the selected area.

To create names using text in the worksheet, perform the following steps:

1. Select the range of cells you want to name. Be sure to include the row or column of text cells that will be used as names (see fig. 7.18).

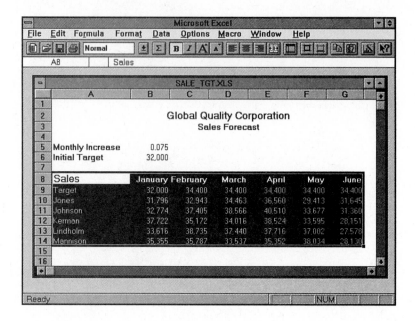

FIG. 7.18

Include text you want as names in the range you select.

2. Choose the Formula Create Names command. The Create Names dialog box appears (see fig. 7.19).

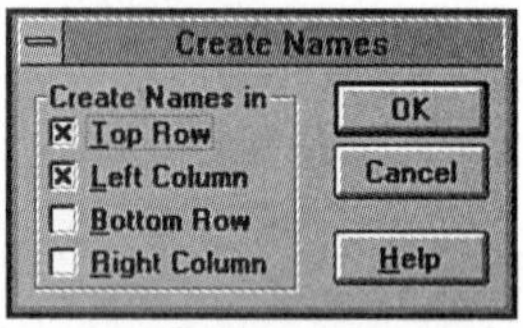

FIG. 7.19

The Create Names dialog box enables you to choose the location of text that will be used as names.

3. Select the **T**op Row check box to use text in the top row of the selection as names for the columns. Similarly, the **B**ottom Row check box uses the bottom row of text as names for the columns. The **L**eft Column check box uses text in the left column to name the rows to the right of the text; and the **R**ight Column check box uses the text in the right column to name the rows to the left of the text.

4. Choose OK or press Enter.

In figure 7.20, the range under the columns is selected. The names at the top of the column can be assigned by selecting the Top Row check box. In figure 7.21, the rows are selected. The names at the left edge of the selection can be assigned to the rows by selecting the Left Column check box.

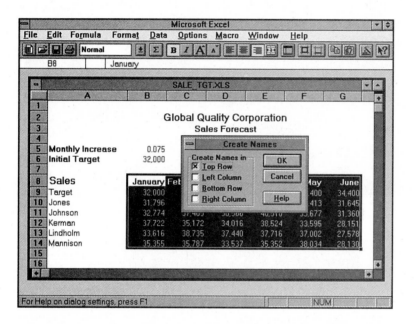

FIG. 7.20

Use names at the top of these columns to name the cells going down.

If you attempt to assign a duplicate name, a dialog box appears, warning you that the name is already in use. Choose the **Yes** button to update the name to the new references; choose the **No** button to retain the old name and references; or choose the Cancel button to retain the old name and back out of creating new names.

Text in cells used as names can include spaces. Excel automatically replaces the space with an underscore mark in the created name. For example, SALES RATE in a cell becomes the name SALES_RATE. You can fit longer names in a tighter space if you use a period as a separator rather than an underscore.

If you use Formula Create Names to name cells, try to use names that do not violate the rules for names. Remember that names cannot begin with numbers. Illegal characters are replaced with underscores, so a text label such as North %Margin will result in the name North__Margin, substituting underscores for the blank and the illegal %.

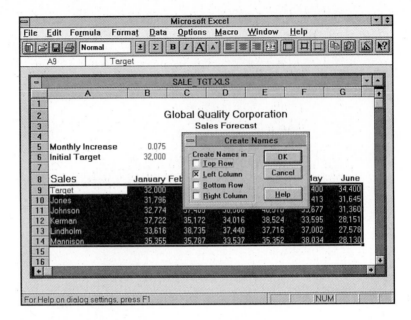

FIG. 7.21

Use names at the left of rows to name the selected cells in the rows.

> **T I P**   You can create both row and column names at the same time in the selection shown in figure 7.22. Just select both the Top Row and Left Column check boxes. Both row and columns names will be created. The entire range of data, not including the names, will be named with the name at the top-left corner.

You can select more than one box from the Create Names dialog box. As a result, you can name cells in different orientations with different names. If you select two options that overlap, then any text in the cell at the overlap is used as the name for the entire range. If, for example, you select both the **Top Row** and **Left Column** options, then the text in the cell at the top left of the selected range is the name for the entire range. In figure 7.22, the name SALES applies to the range B9:H14, the names on the left apply to the rows, and the names at the top apply to the columns.

You can create intersecting names using row or column headings. For example if you select a range with text labels along the top and down the left edge you can select the **Top Row** check box and the **Left Column** check box. This uses the names along the top row to name each column in the selected range. The names down the left column name each row in the selected range. For example, assigning names using the names in the top row and left column in figure 7.22 would enable you to use the following formula to see January's sales amount for Jones:

=Jones January

The blank between the names Jones and January acts as the intersect operator. This formula selects the cell that is common to both the row named Jones and the column named January. The result in the cell containing the formula is 31,796.

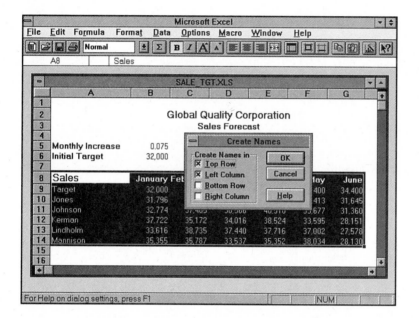

Pasting a List of Names

As part of your worksheet documentation, you should include a list of the names used. Excel can paste into your worksheet a complete list of names and the cells they name. Move the active cell to a clear area; be careful to select an area without data, or the list will overwrite any existing data. Choose the Formula **P**aste Name command and the Paste **L**ist button. A list of all the names and corresponding cell addresses appears in your worksheet.

Changing or Deleting Names

Sometimes you will want to change a name or the cells that the name refers to. Also, from time to time, you may want to delete names that no longer are needed. Deleting unneeded names keeps your list of names free of clutter.

To change a name or the cells that the name references, perform the following steps:

1. Choose the Formula **D**efine Name command. This is the same command you use to name a cell or range of cells manually.

2. Select from the list box the name you want to change.

3. Select the **N**ame box or the **R**efers to box.

4. Edit the name or cell reference in the appropriate text box. Use the arrow keys, Backspace, and Delete keys to edit in the text box.

5. Choose OK or press Enter.

To delete a name, select the name you want to delete and choose the Delete button.

When you change a name, formulas that used the old name are not updated to reflect the new name. For a more extensive name change, use the Change Name add-in.

The CHANGER.XLA file found in the LIBRARY directory under Excel adds the command Formula Change Name. For a complete description of this additional command see Chapter 15's discussion of Excel add-ins.

 After you have deleted a name, selecting Cancel does not undelete it.

Using Names in Formulas and Commands

Names can be used wherever you use cell or range references. In formulas, you can type a name. You also can paste a name into a formula by moving the insertion point in the Formula Bar where you want the name to appear, and then choosing the Formula **P**aste Name command or pressing F3. Select the name from the Paste **N**ame list and choose OK.

Names also can be used in dialog boxes to indicate a cell reference or range. Just type the name in the edit box requiring the reference.

Applying Names

When you create or define names, they do not automatically appear in existing formulas in the worksheet. If you create formulas before names, you need to apply the names to the formulas. With the Formula **A**pply Names command, Excel gives you the capability to select where you want names applied (see fig. 7.23).

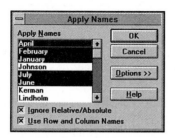

FIG. 7.23

To apply names to existing formulas, use the Formula Apply Names command.

To apply existing names to formulas containing named cell references, perform the following steps:

1. Select a single cell if you want to apply names to the entire worksheet, or select a range to apply names to formulas in the range.

2. Choose the Formula **A**pply Names command.

   The most recently created name(s) will be selected in the Apply **N**ames list box, but you can choose whatever names you want to apply.

3. You select the names you want applied from the Apply **N**ames list box by clicking each name you want to apply. To select a range of adjacent names, click the first name, press the Shift key, and click the last name. To select multiple non-adjacent names, press the Ctrl key as you click on the names. To select adjacent names with the keyboard, press the Shift key and use the arrow keys to select names.

   To select multiple non-adjacent names, press space to select or unselect a name, and hold down Ctrl to keep from deselecting the selected names as you use the arrow keys to move through the list.

4. Select the **I**gnore Relative/Absolute check box if you want names to replace absolute and relative references. Normally this box should be selected. Clearing this box applies absolute names to absolute references and relative names to relative references.

5. Select the **U**se Row and Column Names check box if you want Excel to rename cell references that can be described as the intersect of a named row and a named column. In figure 7.23, for example, cell G10 can be referenced as *Jones June*. (A space character is the intersect operator.) Clear this box if you want only individual cell names to apply to cell references.

6. Select the **O**ptions button to omit row or column names when the cell containing the formula is in the same row or column as the name. The following options are available:

   Omit **C**olumn Name if Same Column

   Omit **R**ow Name if Same Row

   After selecting **O**ptions, you also can select the order in which you want row and column names to appear. Simply select or clear the options for Name Order: Ro**w** Column and Co**l**umn Row.

7. Choose OK or press Enter.

Naming Formulas and Values

Your worksheets are much more readable and understandable if you create names for commonly used constants or frequently used formulas. You can name any number or formula, and then use that name in a cell or formula. The number or formula does not have to be in a cell.

Named formulas and values (constants) differ from named cells and ranges. In named cells and ranges, the name references a worksheet location. In named formulas and values, the name references a formula or value that doesn't exist on the worksheet.

To name a value or formula you enter, perform the following steps:

1. Choose the Fo**r**mula **D**efine Name command.

2. Select the **N**ame text box and enter the name.

3. Select the **R**efers to box.

4. Type the constant number or the formula. Enter the formula or constant as you would in the Formula Bar. You can edit in the **R**efers to box as you edit in the Formula Bar.

   If you need to use the arrow keys to move around within the formula, press F2 to change to Edit mode. Otherwise, arrow keys point to cells on the worksheet.

5. Choose OK or press Enter.

Figure 7.24 illustrates how a formula is assigned a name. Because the formula or constant stored in the name does not have to be stored in a cell, your worksheets stay neater and are easier for inexperienced users to work with.

```
 ═                    Define Name
Names in Sheet:                        ┌──────────┐
April                    ▲             │    OK    │
February                               └──────────┘
January          Name:                 ┌──────────┐
Johnson          │Sales.Increase    │  │  Close   │
July                                   └──────────┘
June             Refers to:            ┌──────────┐
Kerman           │=Sales*(.05*$B$5)│   │   Add    │
Lindholm                               └──────────┘
Mannison                               ┌──────────┐
March                    ▼             │  Delete  │
                                       └──────────┘
                                       ┌──────────┐
                                       │   Help   │
                                       └──────────┘
```

FIG. 7.24

Assign frequently used
formulas or constant
values to a name.

If you build formulas in the **R**efers to box by pointing to cell references
(clicking them or moving to them), Excel supplies only absolute references, such as $D$15. These references are absolute because a name
usually applies to one specific location on a worksheet. You can type
relative references or edit out the dollar signs to create names that act
like relative references. (Named relative reference formulas can be confusing to use, so be careful.) If, for example, the active cell is C6, you
might type the formula =C12 in the **R**efers to box. You could give the
formula the name RIGHT6. You then can use the name RIGHT6 in a formula or cell to indicate the contents of the cell six cells to the right of
the cell containing =RIGHT6. You can move the Define Name dialog box if
it is in the way of the cell you need in a formula.

T I P

Deleting all the rows or columns that make up a named range does not
delete the name. These names simply refer to cell references that no
longer exist. In the Define Name dialog box, selecting an invalid name
like this displays a #REF! error in the **R**efers To box.

To find invalid names, use the Fo**r**mula **W**orksheet Auditor command
to generate a list of bad names. The **W**orksheet Auditor command is
added to the Formula menu when you open the AUDIT.XLA add-in
macro located in the LIBRARY directory underneath the Excel directory. The AUDIT.XLA is a worksheet troubleshooting tool that is described in Chapter 15.

For Related Information:

▶▶ "Pasting Functions and Arguments," p. 357.

▶▶ "Linking Cells with Copy and Paste Link Commands," p. 456.

▶▶ "Adding a Name Changer," p. 609.

FROM HERE...

Changing Worksheet Layout

After you have drafted and tested your worksheet, you may find that you need to reorganize or restructure the layout of the worksheet. This need is especially true if you inherit old worksheets or need to convert old 1-2-3 spreadsheets. When you restructure, you may need to insert or delete cells, rows, or columns.

Shortcut keys that are very helpful to reorganizing the worksheet layout are shown in table 7.8.

Table 7.8. Shortcut Keys for Changing the Worksheet Layout	
Key	**Action**
Del	Clears selected cells; same as **Edit Clear**. Select whether to clear **A**ll, **F**ormats, **F**ormulas, or **N**otes.
Ctrl+Del	Clears selected formulas; same as **E**dit **C**lear with **F**ormulas selected.
Backspace	Clears the Formula Bar; activates and clears Formula Bar.
Ctrl+C	Copies the selection so that it can be pasted; same as **E**dit **C**opy.
Ctrl+X	Cuts the selection so it can be pasted; same as **E**dit Cut.
Ctrl+V	Pastes at the selected cell; same as **E**dit **P**aste.
Ctrl+Z	Undoes last command from **E**dit menu.
Ctrl+2	Repositions the worksheet so that the active cell is in view.

Clearing Cell Contents

Excel gives you alternatives when clearing or erasing cells. You can clear or erase everything in a cell or range, erase the format only, erase the formulas only, or erase the notes only.

NOTE When many people first use Excel, they make the mistake of choosing the **E**dit **D**elete command to remove the contents of a cell. They should use the **E**dit **C**lear command. The **E**dit **D**elete command removes the actual cell from the worksheet, like pulling a brick out of a wall. The **E**dit **C**lear command leaves the cell in place, but erases the cell's contents.

CAUTION: Novice worksheet users commonly think they can type a blank space, and then press Enter to erase a cell's contents. *Cells with spaces create problems.* For example, in most worksheet functions and database commands, Excel does not see that cell as blank, but as a cell containing a space character. Uncovering this problem can be difficult.

To clear the contents of a cell, perform the following steps:

1. Select the cell or range of cells you want to clear.

2. Choose **E**dit **C**lear or press the Del key to display the Clear dialog box (see fig. 7.25).

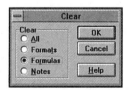

FIG. 7.25

Pressing the Delete (Del) key enables you to clear different characteristics of a cell.

3. Select the button that describes what you want cleared:

All	Clears cell contents and notes; returns the format to General format.
Formats	Returns the format to General format.
Formulas	Clears formulas but does not change formats or notes.
Notes	Clears notes but does not change formulas or formats.

4. Choose OK or press Enter.

If you want to clear other cells immediately after this, you can save steps by choosing **E**dit **R**epeat Clear.

If you accidentally clear a cell's contents, immediately choose the **E**dit **U**ndo command (or press Ctrl+2). This command undoes your most recent edit.

Cells that have been cleared appear as zeros to formulas. Clearing cells may cause formulas that depend on those cells to produce errors. To find formulas with errors, select a single cell so that search will apply to the whole document, choose the For**m**ula **S**elect Special command and select the For**m**ula option. Turn off all the check boxes, but leave the **E**rrors check box selected; then choose OK or press Enter. All cells containing error values (such as #NAME?) are selected. Press Tab to move among the selected cells.

Inserting or Deleting Cells, Rows, and Columns

With Excel, you can delete or insert entire rows or columns. You also can easily delete or insert cells, leaving the surrounding rows or columns unaffected. This technique enables you to add or remove cells without having to change entire rows or columns.

Deleting Cells, Rows, and Columns

The **E**dit **D**elete command removes cells, rows, or columns from the worksheet. This command is useful when rearranging your worksheet to give it a more suitable layout.

Edit **D**elete is different than the **E**dit Cl**e**ar command. The **E**dit Cl**e**ar command clears a cell's contents or format, but it leaves the cell intact. **E**dit **D**elete completely removes cells, rows, or columns; it doesn't just remove their contents.

When **E**dit **D**elete deletes cells, it completely removes the selected cells and *slides in* other cells to fill the gap. You can choose the direction in which the remaining cells move. Figures 7.26 and 7.27 show a worksheet before and after cells were deleted. The lower cells were moved up to fill the gap. Notice that the worksheet area to the right of the deleted cells was not affected. **E**dit **D**elete is an excellent command for sliding rows or columns into a new location without affecting adjacent cells.

When you need to remove cells, rows, or columns from the worksheet, perform the following steps:

1. Select the cells or range to be deleted, or select cells in the rows or columns to be deleted.

2. Choose the **E**dit **D**elete command, or press Ctrl+ - (minus). The Delete dialog box appears (see fig. 7.28).

   If you selected a whole row or column, the dialog box does not appear.

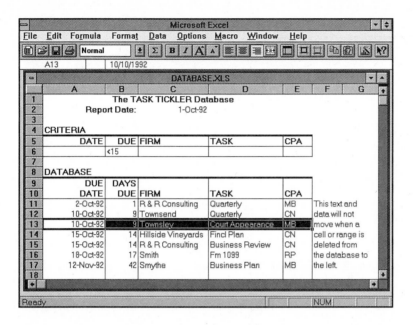

FIG. 7.26

A worksheet before cells are deleted.

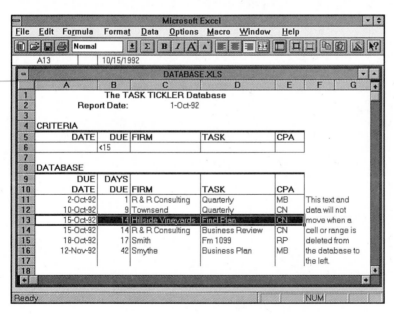

FIG. 7.27

Surrounding cells fill in the gap after cells have been deleted.

FIG. 7.28

The Delete dialog box.

3. If you want to delete cells, select the direction in which you want remaining cells to move:

Shift Cells **Left**   Cells to the right of the deleted cells move left.

Shift Cells **Up**   Cells below the deleted cells move up.

If you want to delete the row(s) or column(s) containing the selected cells, select one of the options:

Entire **Row**   Deletes each row containing a selected cell.

Entire **Column** Deletes each column containing a selected cell.

4. Choose OK or press Enter.

To undo an incorrect deletion, choose **Edit** **U**ndo Delete (or press Ctrl+Z) immediately.

You can delete rows or columns quickly by selecting the entire row or column, and then using the **Edit** **D**elete command or pressing Ctrl+ - (minus). Click row or column headings to select the entire row or column, or press Shift+space bar to select a row and Ctrl+space bar to select a column.

Depending on the design and layout of the worksheet, deleting cells, rows, or columns that contain information used by formulas can cause errors. Because the cell and its contents no longer exist, formulas that used that cell cannot find a cell to reference. These cells produce a #REF! error. To make sure that you do not delete rows or columns containing formulas or values, first select the cells, rows, or columns that you want to delete, and then choose the **Fo**rmula **S**elect Special command. Select the Dependents Direct Only option, and choose OK. If you are presented with the No cells found message, you can safely delete the cells.

T I P

In 1-2-3, if you delete a row or column that contains a range boundary, formulas and functions that depend on that range are lost. If you delete a row or column on a range boundary in Excel, Excel reduces the range to compensate. In other words, with Excel, you can delete the last row of a database or SUM() column without producing errors and destroying your worksheet.

Inserting Cells, Rows, or Columns

Sometimes you must insert cells, rows, or columns to make room for new formulas or data. You can insert cells, rows, or columns as easily as you can delete them.

To insert cells, rows, or columns, perform the following steps:

1. Select a cell or range of cells where you need new cells inserted. Or select cells in the rows or columns where you want to insert new rows or columns.

2. Choose the **E**dit **I**nsert command, or press Ctrl+ + (plus). The Insert dialog box appears (see fig. 7.29).

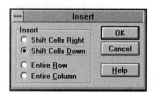

FIG. 7.29

The Insert dialog box.

3. If you want to insert cells, select the direction you want selected cells to move when blank cells are inserted:

    Shift Cells **R**ight   Selected cells move right.

    Shift Cells **D**own   Selected cells move down.

    If you want to insert rows or columns, select the option button desired:

    Entire **R**ow   Insert a row at each selected cell.

    Entire **C**olumn   Insert a column at each selected cell.

4. Choose OK or press Enter.

In figure 7.30, a range of cells has been selected where blank cells will be inserted. Figure 7.31 shows the results after insertion. Notice that the data in the cells to the right of the inserted area has not moved. Only the cells below the insertion move down to make room for the inserted cells.

Excel takes some of the work out of inserting. In most cases, when you insert a row or group of cells, you want each inserted cell to have the same format as the cell above. Excel automatically formats the inserted row or cells with the format above. If you don't want this format, use the method described in Chapter 8 to format the new cells.

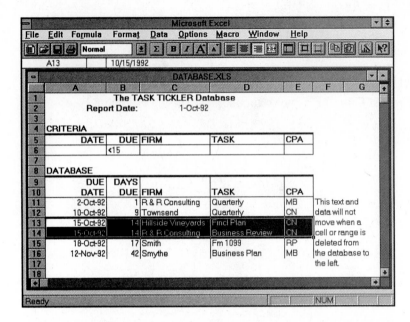

FIG. 7.30

Cells will be inserted
in the selected range.

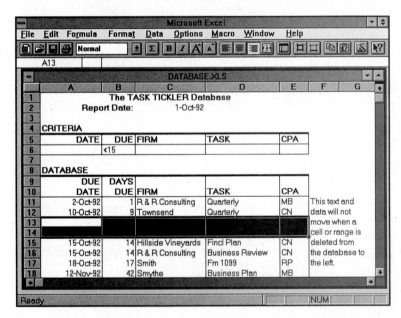

FIG. 7.31

Existing cells move to
make room for inserted
cells.

> **For Related Information:**
>
> ◄◄ "Entering and Copying Formulas," p. 87.
>
> ◄◄ "Selecting Cells," p. 147.
>
> ►► "Linking Pictures of Worksheet Cells," p. 448.

FROM HERE...

Moving Cell Contents

Cutting and pasting is a valuable function for reorganizing your worksheet. You *cut out* a range of cells and *paste* them elsewhere. This operation moves cell contents, the format, and any note attached to the moved cells.

Formulas remain the same when you move them by cutting and pasting. You do not need to worry about relative and absolute cell references.

Moving by Dragging

If you have a mouse, the easiest and most intuitive way to move a cell or range is to drag it to its new location and drop it. Excel moves the cell contents and formats. To drag cells to a new location, perform the following steps:

VERSION

1. Select the cell or range you want moved.

2. Move the mouse pointer over the selection's border. The pointer changes to an arrow when over a border.

3. Drag the pointer and the gray outline of your selection to its new location. Drag past the edge of a window to make the window scroll.

   Figure 7.32 shows the wide gray border enclosing the area to be pasted.

4. Release the mouse button when the gray outline is where you want the pasted copy.

The cell contents you selected in step 1 will paste over the contents of the receiving cells. Choose **E**dit **U**ndo (or press Ctrl+Z) if you need to undo the command.

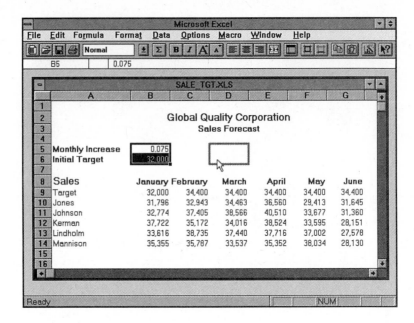

FIG. 7.32

Drag the outline of your selection to its new location.

> **NOTE** If the printer does not change to an arrow when you move it to the selections border, choose the Options Workspace command and select the Cell Drag and Drop option. Choose OK or press Enter.

Moving with Commands

Although the drag and drop technique is useful, you cannot use it to move data between different worksheets, between panes in a split worksheet, or to another application. You can make these moves with menu commands or shortcut keys. To move a cell or a range to a new location, perform the following steps:

1. Select the cell or range you want to move.

2. Choose **Edit Cut**, or press Ctrl+X. The cells you have selected appear surrounded by a *marquee*, a moving dashed line.

3. Select the cell at the upper-left corner of where you want the pasted cells.

4. Choose **Edit Paste**, or press Ctrl+V.

The cells you selected in the first step are cut out and moved to the location you indicated. The area from which they were cut is blank and has a General format. If you accidentally paste over existing data or formulas, choose the **Edit Undo** command. (Pasting over existing cells replaces the cell's previous content and format with the pasted content and format.)

You need to select only the upper-left corner of the new location. The move procedure is similar to moving a picture from one place on a wall to another. You do not need to describe where all four corners of the picture go; you need to specify only the upper left corner.

As you select the range to cut, notice the Reference Area at the left of the Formula Bar; it shows you the size of the range you are cutting (for example, 8R X 4C). This helps you determine whether you can move the data without pasting over existing cells and replacing their contents.

Dragging and Inserting Cells

You also can drag a cell or range and insert it so that existing cells move aside. This procedure replaces having to insert cells to make room for new data, and then moving in the new data. This is an excellent way to rearrange a list or move individual records in a database.

To move data and insert it so that existing data moves aside, perform the following steps:

1. Select the cell or range you want moved.

2. Move the mouse pointer over the selection's border. The pointer changes to an arrow when over a border.

3. Hold down the Shift key and drag the pointer to where you want the data inserted. The location where the data will be inserted appears as a grayed partial cell boundary, as shown in figure 7.33.

4. Continue holding the Shift key as you release the mouse button.

5. Release the Shift key.

The cells you drag are inserted at the location of the grayed boundary. Other cells move down or right.

Moving and Inserting with Commands

In some cases, you can move cells to a new location and move existing cells aside. This technique uses the **Insert Paste** command. To insert pasted cells, perform the following steps:

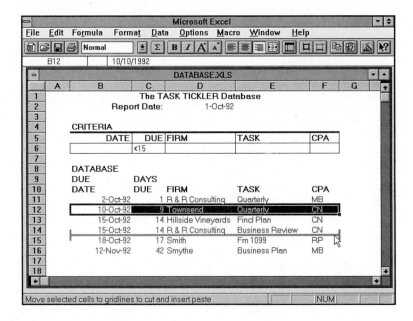

FIG. 7.33

The grayed cell
boundary shows
where the moved data
will insert.

1. Select the cells you want to move.

2. Choose the **Edit Cut** command, or press Ctrl+X.

3. Select a cell in which to insert the cut cells.

   You cannot place an insert into a cell that would cause the source range of the copy to shift.

   Figure 7.34 shows a cut range and where it will be inserted.

4. Choose the **Insert Paste** command.

   The Insert Paste dialog box, shown in figure 7.35 appears if Excel needs information about which direction to shift existing cells.

5. If the Insert Paste dialog box appears, select the Shift Cells **R**ight option to shift existing cells right. Select the Shift Cells **D**own option to shift existing cells down. Choose OK or press Enter.

   The cut range is inserted into the worksheet, shifting cells down or to the right. Figure 7.36 shows the database record from figure 7.34 after it has been inserted. Notice that the other cells have been shifted down.

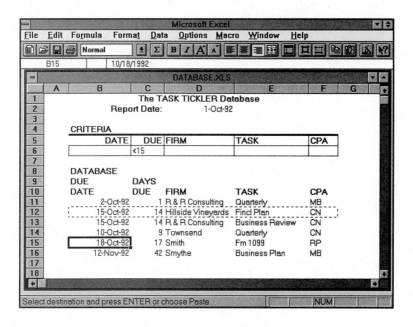

The marquee encloses
cells to be cut out.

The Insert Paste dialog
box appears if Excel is
unsure which direction
to shift cells.

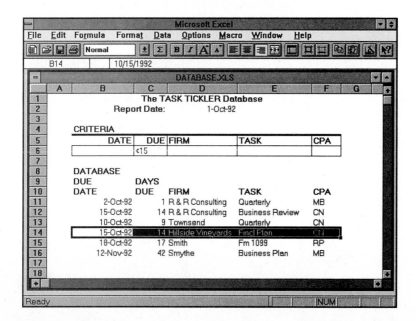

Existing cells are
shifted down or to
the right.

Filling or Copying Cell Contents

You can save yourself a lot of data-entry time with Excel's copy and fill commands and the many shortcuts that copy or fill. Instead of typing each formula in a worksheet, you can type a few formulas and copy or fill them into other cells. You even can copy the formula and format at the same time.

> **NOTE** Some formulas do not produce the correct results when copied because cell references in the formulas change relative to their new cell locations. Always cross-check copied or filled formulas to ensure that they produce reasonable results. If you suspect an error, review the descriptions of relative and absolute cell references in the "Using Cell References in Formulas," section earlier in this chapter.

Using the Fill Handle

If you use a mouse and need to fill data or formulas into adjacent cells, you will want to learn how to use the *fill handle*. The fill handle is a black square at the lower-right corner of the selected cell or range. Dragging the fill handle across cells can fill the cells with copies or a data series. A data series is a series of data that continues some pattern. To learn more about creating a math or date series, see Chapter 13, "Using Power Worksheet Features."

To fill adjacent cells, perform the following steps:

1. Select the cell or range containing the data or formulas.

2. Drag the fill handle so that the wide gray border encloses all cells to be filled. Figure 7.37 shows an area being filled by the mouse. Notice the shape of the pointer.

3. Release the mouse button, and then the Ctrl key.

Filling formulas into an area produces the same result as copying and pasting. Relative reference formulas adjust as though they were copied.

If you select two cells and then drag the fill handle, Excel uses the values in the two cells as seeds to create a series of data that fills your selection. A series is a sequence of data that has a mathematical, date, or text pattern. Series are useful for filling in a sequence of dates or a list of numbers. Series are described in Chapter 13.

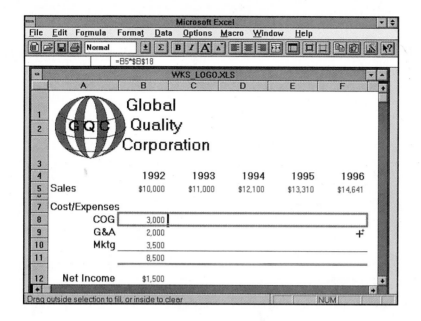

FIG. 7.37

Drag on the fill handle
to copy formulas into
selected cells.

If you want to fill multiple rows or columns at one time, select all the
original cells; then use the Ctrl+drag procedure or a shortcut tool to
fill all the cells at one time.

T I P

Using Ctrl+Enter to Fill Cells

You can fill cells as you enter data or formulas if you first select the
adjacent cells or ranges to be filled. Next, type the formula or value in
the active cell. Instead of pressing Enter, press Ctrl+Enter. Formulas and
values fill into all selected cells just as though you used a fill or copy and
paste command. This method also works with non-adjacent multiple
selections.

Using the Fill Commands

If you do not have a mouse, you need to use the fill commands on the
Edit menu to fill formulas or data into adjacent cells. You can fill cells
left or right across a row and up or down a column. To use the menu fill
commands, perform the following steps:

1. Select the row or column you want to fill. The cell containing the formula or value used to fill other cells must be on the outside edge. Figure 7.38 shows cells in the worksheet selected before filling.

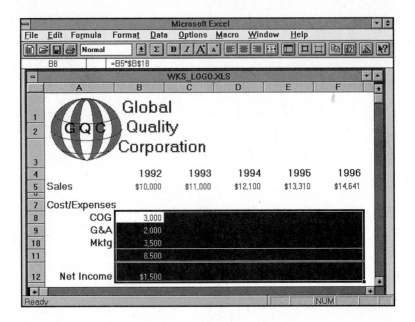

2. Choose **Edit Fill Right** to fill right, or choose **Edit Fill Down** to fill down from the dialog box. To fill up or left, hold down the Shift key as you choose the **Edit** command and select **Edit Fill Left** (**h**) or **Edit Fill Up** (**w**). Figure 7.39 shows the resulting filled cells.

3. Check to see that the filled formulas have produced reasonable answers.

The result of an **Edit Fill** command is the same as copying. Relative references adjust to their new locations. Duplicated formulas or values replace any cell contents they cover. The formatting of the original cells also is copied to the filled cells.

Shortcut keys for filling are Ctrl+R to fill right and Ctrl+D to fill down.

If you are filling an area involving hidden rows or columns or outlines, you may want to fill visible areas only. To avoid filling these hidden areas, choose the **Fo**rmula **S**elect Special command with the **Visible Cells** option.

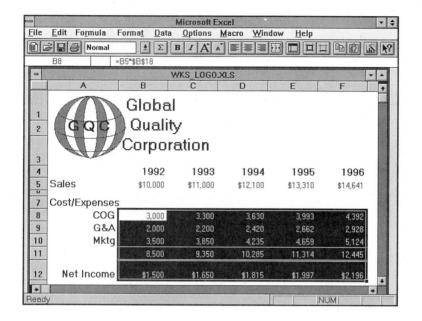

FIG. 7.39

The Fill commands fill the original formula or value into the rest of the range.

Copying by Dragging and Dropping

Using the mouse, you can copy just by making a selection and dragging the selection to where you want it. To copy formulas or data with the mouse, perform the following steps:

1. Select the range of cells you want to copy.

2. Hold the Ctrl key and move the pointer over an edge of the selection. The pointer becomes an arrow with a + (plus) sign.

3. Continue holding Ctrl as you drag the edge of the selection to where you want the copy. The copy's location appears enclosed by a wide gray border as shown in figure 7.40.

4. When the gray border is where you want the copy, release the mouse button, and then the Ctrl key.

Using the drag and drop method, you can make only a single copy. You cannot copy to multiple locations or fill a range. See some of the preceding mouse shortcuts if you need to do this.

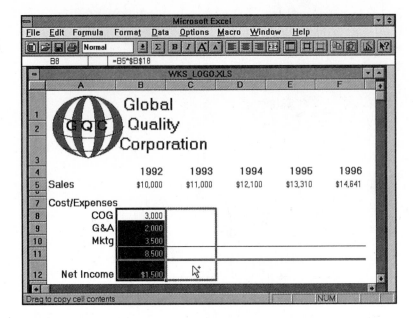

FIG. 7.40

Ctrl+drag enables you to drag copies to new locations.

T I P If you release the Ctrl key before you release the mouse button, the copy operation becomes a move operation; the plus sign next to the arrow disappears. You can press Ctrl again to switch back to a copy operation. As long as you don't release the mouse button, you can change your mind about whether you want to copy or move the selection.

Copying with Commands

Copying works well for duplicating values or formulas to cells that are not adjacent to the original. Copying adjusts formulas to their new locations. Other chapters in the book describe how copying also is used to transfer information to other Windows applications (see Chapter 31), link worksheets together (see Chapter 12), and link worksheets and charts (see Chapters 18 and 20).

To copy a cell or range to a new location, perform the following steps:

1. Select the cell or range of cells you want to copy. As you copy, check the size of the range you are copying by watching the Reference Area to the left of the Formula Bar.

2. Choose the **E**dit **C**opy command, or press Ctrl+C. The cells to be copied appear surrounded by a marquee, a moving dashed line.

3. Select the cell at the top-left corner of where you want the duplicate to appear. Check to see whether other cell contents will be written over. If needed cells will be overwritten, see the following section on inserting copied cells.

4. Choose the **E**dit **P**aste command or press Ctrl+V to paste and retain the copy in memory. Press Enter to paste one time.

Because the size and shape of the copied area is already established, you need to indicate only the upper-left corner of the paste location. Selecting the wrong size area to paste into prevents Excel from pasting and displays an alert box.

To remove the marquee or cancel the copy once it has been started, press the Esc key.

Pasting Multiple Copies

You can make multiple copies of a range with a single command. Remember to select only the top-left corners of where you want each of the duplicate ranges to go. Figure 7.41 shows the marquee around a copied column of formulas and the top of each column where the original column will be pasted. Notice that pasting in multiple columns is like hanging wallpaper; you need to indicate only where the tops of each roll of wallpaper will go; the wallpaper hangs down correctly by itself. Figure 7.42 shows the pasted columns.

Figures 7.43 and 7.44 show how to copy an original row into multiple rows. Notice that only the left cell is selected where each duplicated row will be pasted.

Pasting Non-Adjacent Multiple Copies

Well-formatted worksheets may interfere with some of the previous methods of copying or filling formulas into a range, because worksheets may need blank rows or columns as separators for appearance. However, these blank rows and columns prevent filling data with a single command.

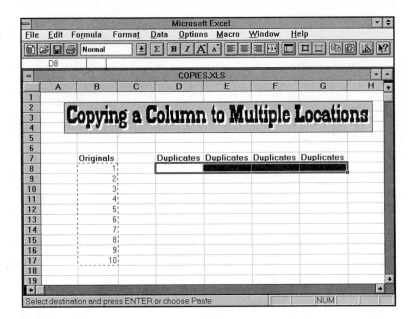

FIG. 7.41

Select the top cell where you want duplicated columns to appear.

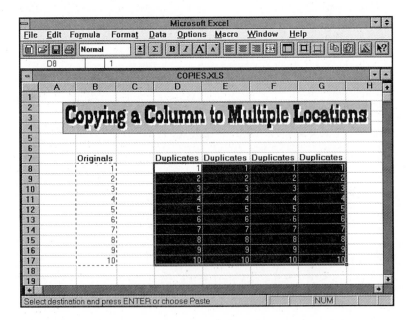

FIG. 7.42

Columns after pasting.

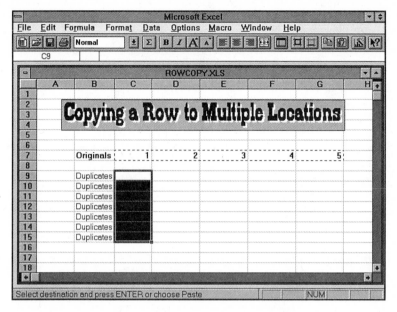

FIG. 7.43

Select the left cells where you want duplicated rows to appear.

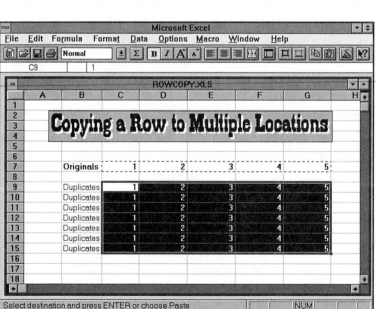

FIG. 7.44

Rows after pasting.

Using non-contiguous selections, like those shown in figure 7.45, you can paste multiple copies even if the areas into which you are pasting are not adjacent.

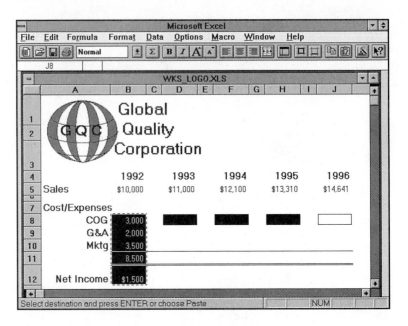

FIG. 7.45

You can paste into multiple areas even if they are separated.

To paste into non-adjacent areas, perform the following steps:

1. Select the cells or ranges to copy.

2. Choose the **Edit C**opy command, or press Ctrl+C.

3. Select the top-left corner where you want each copy to paste.

    With the mouse, hold down the Ctrl key as you click each cell to receive a pasted copy.

    With the keyboard, move to the first cell to receive a copy and press Shift+F8 so that the ADD indicator appears in the Status Bar. Move to the next cell to receive data and press Shift+F8 until ADD disappears, then reappears. Move to the next cell and so on.

4. Choose the **Edit P**aste command.

Notice that the target cells are separated by blank columns. Figure 7.46 shows the result of the paste operation.

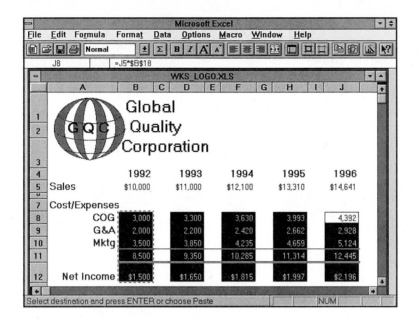

FIG. 7.46

Pasted data enters the
worksheet in non-
adjacent ranges.

Inserting Copied Cells with Commands

Normally, pasted cell contents replace the cell contents they paste over.
In some cases, you may want to copy and paste to insert the copied ma-
terial into the worksheet so that existing cell contents are moved aside.
You can do this with the **Edit I**nsert Paste command.

To copy cells or a range of cells and insert them into another location,
perform the following steps:

1. Select the cells or range of cells you want to copy.

2. Choose the **Edit C**opy command.

3. Select the cell at the top left of where you want to insert your
   copies.

4. Choose the **Edit I**nsert Paste command.

5. Select the Shift Cells **R**ight option if you want cells being pasted
   over to move right. Select the Shift Cells **D**own option if you want
   cells being pasted over to move up.

You must recopy the original data each time before you do an insert paste.

You cannot perform an insert paste over the original data. You also cannot perform an insert paste so that the original data is forced to move. If you attempt an illegal paste, Excel displays an alert box.

Pasting Formats, Values, or Transposed Data

The Edit Paste Special command is handy when you want to copy and paste part of a cell's attributes, such as its format or value, but not both. With this command you can reorient database layouts into worksheet layouts and vice versa. The command also enables you to combine the attributes of cells by pasting them together. This feature is useful when you need to combine or consolidate different parts of a worksheet. Consolidation is covered extensively in Chapter 12, "Linking and Consolidating Worksheets."

T I P   You can paste just the formatting from a copied cell using the toolbar. After issuing the Edit Copy command and selecting the destination, click on the Paste Format button (a picture of a Clipboard with a $ and *I* on it).

To use the Edit Paste Special command for any of its many operations, perform the following steps:

1. Select the cell or range of cells.

2. Choose the Edit Copy command.

3. Select the upper-left corner of where you want to paste.

   If you are transposing (flipping) rows and columns, be sure to consider which cells will be covered when the pasted area is rotated 90 degrees.

4. Choose the Edit Paste Special command to display the Edit Paste Special dialog box, shown in figure 7.47.

   If a Paste Special dialog box showing a Data Type list displays, the last copy you completed was from an application other than Excel. Return to step 1 to copy and paste within Excel.

FIG. 7.47

The Paste Special
dialog box.

5. Select the characteristics you want transferred:

All	Transfer all of the original's contents and characteristics.
For**m**ulas	Transfer only the formulas.
Values	Transfer only the values and formula results. This option converts formulas to values.
For**m**ats	Transfer only the cell format.
Notes	Transfer only note contents.

6. Select from the dialog box how you want the transferred characteristics or information combined with the cells being pasted into:

None	Replace the receiving cell.
Add	Add to the receiving cell.
Subtract	Subtract from the receiving cell.
Multiply	Multiply by the receiving cell.
D**i**vide	Divide into the receiving cell.

7. Select the Skip **B**lank check box if you do not want to paste blank cells on top of existing cell contents.

8. Select the Transpos**e** check box if you want rows changed to columns or columns changed to rows.

9. Choose OK or press Enter.

By copying the range of formulas you want to freeze, you can convert formulas into their results so that they do not change. After copying, without moving the active cell, use **P**aste **S**pecial with the **V**alues and **N**one check boxes checked to paste the values over the original formulas.

T I P

The Transpose option in the **P**aste **S**pecial dialog box can save you time and work if you use database information in your worksheets or worksheet data in your database.

The Transpose option rotates a range of cells between row orientation and column orientation. This option is useful for switching between a database's row layout and a worksheet's column layout. You cannot transpose over the range containing the original data. Figure 7.48 shows an original range on the left and its transposition on the right.

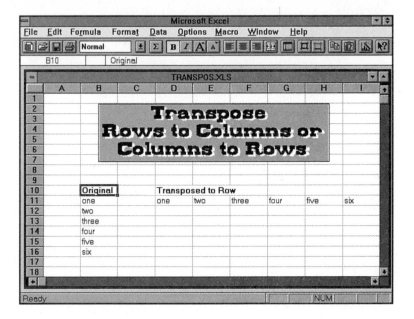

FIG. 7.48

Transposing changes rows to columns or vice versa.

For Related Information:

◄◄ "Entering and Copying Formulas," p. 87.

◄◄ "Selecting Cells," p. 147.

►► "Linking Pictures of Worksheet Cells," p. 448.

Saving Notes and Voice Messages

Notes and voice messages can be attached to cells in a worksheet or database. Notes appear in special dialog boxes or are printed when you request. You attach notes to cells for two reasons: to preserve your sanity and to preserve your business.

Voice messages can be attached to cells and played back for the same purpose as text notes. They help you give more information than what is shown on the worksheet. Voice messages can add more emphasis and personality to a message. They also are the first of many ways in which Windows applications like Excel will be able to enhance documents with voice and video.

Using Text Notes

Include in notes any information that is helpful to the next person using the worksheet. That next person might even be you in two months, after you have forgotten how and why the worksheet operates.

You can put many things in a note. For example, in cell A1, you can put the following:

- The author's name.
- The auditors' names.
- The date the last time the worksheet was audited.

In data-entry cells, you can put the following:

- The worksheet's assumptions.
- Any data-entry limits.
- The historical significance of a value (such as the high sale of the year).

In formula cells, you can put the following:

- The origin or verification of a formula.
- Any analytical comments about a result.

Creating Text Notes

To create a text note, perform the following steps:

1. Select the cell you want to contain the note.
2. Choose the Formula Note command or press Shift+F2 to display the Cell Note dialog box (see fig. 7.49).

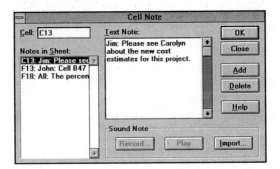

FIG. 7.49

Cell Note dialog box.

3. Enter text in the **N**ote area.

   If you need to move to a new line, press Alt+Enter.

4. Press Enter or choose OK when the note is completed.

T I P A small red dot at the upper-right corner of a cell indicates the cell contains a note. To turn these indicator dots on or off in the display, choose the **O**ptions **W**orkspace command and select or clear the **N**ote Indicator option.

The Notes in **S**heet box lists all the notes in the worksheet preceded by their cell references. When you select a note from the list, the text appears in the **T**ext Note box, and the cell reference appears in the **C**ell box. You can view another note by selecting it from the Notes in **S**heet list.

The **A**dd button adds information from the **N**ote box to the cell shown in the **C**ell box. This method enables you to add new notes to cells without having to return to the worksheet. You can enter cell references in the **C**ell box by typing them, or by clicking the **C**ell box, and then clicking the cell in the worksheet.

T I P To quickly view the note attached to a cell, double-click on the cell. The Cell Note dialog box opens.

Displaying and Finding Notes

If the Note Indicator option is selected, a red dot appears in the top right of cells containing notes. To display the note behind a cell, double-click the cell, or select the cell and press Shift+F2. Select all the cells containing notes by choosing the Formula Select Special command and selecting the Notes option or by pressing Ctrl+?. Move between the cells containing notes with Tab or Shift+Tab, and press Shift+F2 to read the note behind the cell.

Use the Formula Find command to search quickly through cells and find a note that contains a pertinent word. Select the Look in Notes option in the Find dialog box, and choose the Look at Part option to find any occurrence of the word in context.

You can print the notes in a worksheet by selecting either the Notes or Both option in the File Print dialog box.

Editing a Text Note

To edit a note, select the cell and choose the Formula Note command. Edit the note as you normally edit text in Excel. To delete a note, select it from the Notes in Sheet box, and then choose the Delete button.

Using Sound Messages

Sound messages can carry greater emphasis than text notes. Leaving a voice explanation in Excel is one of the first examples of how personal computers can incorporate different media within a frequently used business application.

 To record sound messages, you need a Windows-compatible sound board installed in your computer and a microphone matched to that sound board. You also must be using Excel and Windows 3.0 with Microsoft's Multimedia Extensions 1.0 or later or Windows 3.1 or later. The Que book, *Using Windows 3.1*, Special Edition, describes how to install the drivers and use embedded voice messages in many Windows applications.

Recording Sound Messages

If your system is capable of recording sound, follow these steps to leave a message in a cell:

1. Select the cell to which you want to add a voice message.

2. Choose the Formula Note command.

3. Choose the **R**ecord button.

   The **R**ecord dialog box appears. You can record for up to 2 minutes. The scale shows you the length of your recording. The graph shows you your voice modulation.

4. Begin recording your message.

5. Choose the appropriate VCR type button to replay, pause, rewind, or rerecord your message.

6. Choose the **S**top button to stop the recording.

   You can replay your recorded message by choosing the rewind control, and then choosing the Replay button.

7. Choose OK or press Enter to enter the voice message.

Importing a Sound Message

If you have used the Windows Sound Recorder accessory or another Windows multimedia software to record a voice or other sound message, you can import the .WAV file containing the sound. To import a sound file into a note, choose the **I**mport button from the Note dialog box. When the Open file dialog box displays, select the sound file you want to import. Choose OK or press Enter.

Playing Sound Messages

Cells that have a voice message contain the usual note indicator at the top right of the cell. You can turn this indicator on or off by choosing the **O**ptions **W**orkspace command and selecting or clearing the **N**ote Indicator check box.

Before you can play back a voice message, your computer must have a Windows-compatible sound board installed and have the sound board drivers correctly installed for Windows 3.0 with Multimedia Extensions or Windows 3.1 or later.

To play back a voice message, perform the following steps:

1. Double-click the cell.

   If there is no text note, the voice message immediately replays. If there is a text message and voice message, the Note dialog box appears.

2. Select the note from the Notes in **S**heet list. Sound messages display an * (asterisk).

3. Choose the Play button.

Deleting Sound Messages

To erase a voice message, choose the Fo**r**mula **N**otes command. Select the note you want to delete the voice message from, and then choose the **E**rase button. When you erase a voice message, the **E**rase button changes to **R**ecord so that you can record another message in the cell. The **I**mport button also becomes available.

Chapter Summary

You can use the worksheet you created in Chapter 3 to experiment further with different methods of entering formulas and data. If you already have worked through the Quick Start, reopen the worksheet and try some of the data-entry and editing techniques described in this chapter. Chapter 22, "Entering and Sorting Data," describes additional data-entry methods useful with databases.

When you begin editing, you probably will use the Edit menu primarily, but do not stop with the menus. As you gain confidence, try the shortcut keys listed in table 7.8 and the toolbar tools. You will find that they save you time and effort.

Chapter 8, "Formatting Worksheets," shows you how to dress up your worksheets. After you have experimented with some of the ideas the chapter contains, you should be ready to build and format your own worksheets.

Formatting Worksheets

Appearance isn't everything, but it counts for a great deal when you need to communicate with confidence. Your work may be excellent, but it may make a poor impression if important information is obscured or has a slipshod appearance.

Excel has formatting features that make worksheets and databases easier to read and understand. One of these powerful features is the capability to use TrueType fonts. With these fonts, you can see on-screen how a font will look when printed. Another useful formatting feature is AutoFormatting, which enables you to format tables and reports in one step with predesigned combinations of numeric formats, alignments, borders, and shading.

In addition to changing column widths or selecting predefined numeric and date formats, you can create your own numeric and date formats; change the height of rows; change the font, size, color, and style of characters; control the placement of text within cells; hide columns, rows, and grid lines; and shade, color, and border ranges. You also can use styles to simplify your formatting tasks and can protect portions of your document that you don't want changed. With Excel, your printed worksheet or database can look as though it just came from the typesetter. You can drive your point across with emphasis and elegance.

Formatting with AutoFormats

Even if you are a first-time Excel user, you can create beautifully formatted database reports, tables, and lists with Excel's AutoFormat feature. If you are an advanced Excel user, you also will appreciate this feature because it can save you so much time.

With AutoFormat, which is predefined by Excel, you can apply predesigned formats to the labels, backgrounds, lines, and numbers in Excel tables. These formats are designed for tables of information in which labels run down the left column and across the top rows. SUM() functions or totals are expected in the bottom row or right column. These predesigned formats include formatting for numbers, borders, font, pattern, alignment, column width, and row height. You have the option of selecting which of these formatting elements are used when you format with Format AutoFormat.

Figures 8.1, 8.2, and 8.3 show a few of the 14 formats available through the use of a single Format AutoFormat selection.

FIG. 8.1

This spreadsheet illustrates the Classic 3 format.

	AUTOFRMT.XLS						
	B	C	D	E	F	G	H
1							
2	**Sales**			*Sales Forecast*			
3		*January*	*February*	*March*	*April*	*May*	*June*
4	**Target**	$32,000.00	$34,400.00	$34,400.00	$34,400.00	$34,400.00	$34,400.00
5	**Jones**	31,796.24	32,942.71	34,463.13	36,559.95	29,413.25	31,644.73
6	**Johnson**	32,774.02	37,404.78	38,565.76	40,509.87	33,677.34	31,360.42
7	**Kerman**	37,721.97	35,172.15	34,015.90	38,524.11	33,595.34	28,151.34
8	**Lindholm**	33,616.44	38,735.06	37,439.90	37,715.77	37,002.05	27,577.77
9	**Mannison**	35,354.91	35,786.68	33,536.58	35,352.35	38,034.37	28,130.04
10		$203,263.59	$214,441.37	$212,421.28	$223,062.05	$206,122.35	$181,264.30
11							

FIG. 8.2

This spreadsheet illustrates the Financial 3 format.

	AUTOFRMT.XLS						
	B	C	D	E	F	G	H
1							
2	*Sales*	*Sales Forecast*					
3		*January*	*February*	*March*	*April*	*May*	*June*
4	*Target*	$32,000.00	$34,400.00	$34,400.00	$34,400.00	$34,400.00	$34,400.00
5	*Jones*	31,796.24	32,942.71	34,463.13	36,559.95	29,413.25	31,644.73
6	*Johnson*	32,774.02	37,404.78	38,565.76	40,509.87	33,677.34	31,360.42
7	*Kerman*	37,721.97	35,172.15	34,015.90	38,524.11	33,595.34	28,151.34
8	*Lindholm*	33,616.44	38,735.06	37,439.90	37,715.77	37,002.05	27,577.77
9	*Mannison*	35,354.91	35,786.68	33,536.58	35,352.35	38,034.37	28,130.04
10		$203,263.59	$214,441.37	$212,421.28	$223,062.05	$206,122.35	$181,264.30
11							
12							

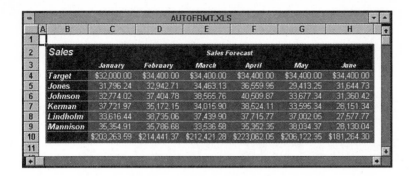

FIG. 8.3

This spreadsheet illustrates the Colorful 1 format.

Formatting a Table Automatically

To apply one of the predesigned formats to a table, complete the following steps:

1. Select the range containing the table. If the table is a block of contiguous cells surrounded by clear rows and columns, select a single cell within the table.

2. Choose the Format AutoFormat command. The AutoFormat dialog box appears, as shown in figure 8.4.

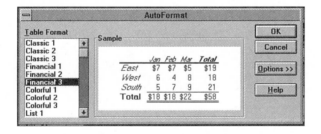

FIG. 8.4

Select a table format from the AutoFormat dialog box.

3. Select the format you want from the Table Format list.

4. Review the Sample box to see whether this table format is the one you want. If not, return to step 3 and select a different table format.

5. Choose OK or press Enter after you have found the appropriate format.

If the format does not appear as you expected, immediately choose the **Edit Undo** AutoFormat command to restore the table to its previous format.

After you have formatted a table with AutoFormat, the formatting in the cells is the same as if you had applied normal formatting. Use the techniques described throughout this chapter to change cell formatting to enhance or remove the formatting applied by AutoFormat.

T I P   Click the Last Table Format tool on the Standard toolbar to apply to your current selection the last table format that you set with the Format AutoFormat command.

AutoFormat works well for tables or databases of data. If you include wide titles within the formatted area, however, their width may cause automatic column-width adjustments to make columns too wide. To create wide titles that do not affect automatic column-width adjustments, center the title across selected cells, as described in this chapter's section on "Centering Text across Cells." You also can use the technique described to turn off automatic column-width and row-height formatting in the "Changing AutoFormatting" section.

AutoFormat may reduce major headings to a font that is too small. If this problem occurs, use the Increase Font Size tool or the Decrease Font Size tool on the Standard toolbar to adjust heading size. Each of these tools appears as a capital A with an up or down arrowhead.

Changing AutoFormatting

You don't need to accept the AutoFormat formats exactly as they are. You can decide which parts of the AutoFormats are applied to your selection. This capability can be useful, for example, if you have formatted with different colors or have applied custom numeric or date formats that you do not want AutoFormatting to change.

To accept or reject different parts of AutoFormatting, complete the following steps:

1. Select the table's range.

2. Choose the Format AutoFormat command.

3. Select the table format you want applied.

4. Choose the Options button. The dialog box expands to include a Formats to Apply group of options.

5. Clear formats in the Formats to Apply group that you do not want applied. Figure 8.5 shows the AutoFormat dialog box with the borders format turned off.

NOTE When you deselect an option, that particular option cannot be changed. If you use one AutoFormat design and then change to another and turn off formats, you may get undesirable results.

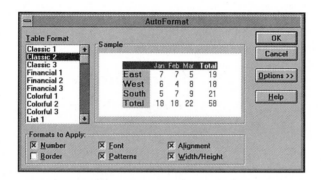

FIG. 8.5

You can turn off the border format or any of the other formats applied by an AutoFormat.

6. Review your changes in the Sample box.

7. Choose OK or press Enter.

Changing Character Fonts, Sizes, Styles, and Colors

You see different character fonts and styles every day. Fonts are the various typefaces used in printed materials. Font heights are measured in points, with 72 points per inch. Fonts also appear in different styles: plain, bold, italic, underline, and strikeout. With Excel, you also can change font colors, which appear on-screen and can be printed if you have a color printer. Figure 8.6 shows examples of different fonts with various point sizes and styles.

Excel can use up to 256 different fonts on a worksheet. If you use more than a few fonts per worksheet, however, your worksheet may look like a ransom note made from assorted magazine clippings.

You can use one of three methods to change the appearance of your data: a tool on a toolbar, a menu command, or a shortcut key.

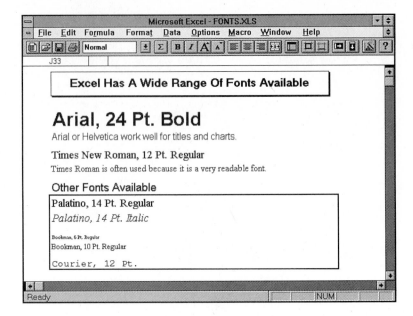

FIG. 8.6

Excel enables you to easily use the fonts available to your printer.

T I P You can save time when formatting by first creating a *style*. A style *associates,* or ties, a group of format preferences to an assigned name. The style name applies the formats collectively. Applying the style name to a cell or range applies all the formats associated with that style name. Changing the definition of a style name changes the format in all cells that have that style. Styles are described near the end of this chapter in the section on "Using Styles."

T I P If you use a mouse, you quickly can access the Font menu by clicking the cell or selected cells you want to format with the right mouse button to display the shortcut menu. Then choose Font.

Using the Toolbars

The toolbars give you quick access to frequently used formatting commands. To use a formatting tool, select the cell or range you want to format, or select the text in a text box or button. Then click the appropriate formatting tool. Operating steps for using the tools are inserted in the appropriate sections of this chapter.

If you are unsure what a tool does, click and hold the mouse on the tool. Look in the Status Bar at the bottom of the screen to see the tool's name. Drag off the tool before releasing the button if that tool is not the one you want. For help with a tool, press Shift+F1 and then click the tool to open a help screen for that tool.

T I P

Figure 8.7 shows the Standard and Formatting toolbars and their formatting tools. Normally, the Standard toolbar is displayed. To display the Formatting toolbar, choose the **O**ptions **T**oolbars command, select Formatting from the Show T**o**olbars list, and choose **S**how.

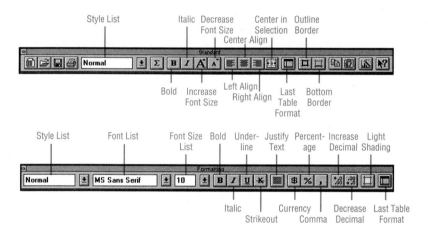

FIG. 8.7

The Standard and Formatting toolbars help you format worksheets.

Additional formatting tools that you can add to any toolbar are available. To see these additional formatting tools, complete the following steps:

1. Click any tool on a toolbar with the right mouse button.

2. Choose the Customize command.

3. In the Customize dialog box, choose Formatting from the **Cate**gories list. The tools you can add to the toolbar appear in the Tools box.

You can add these and other tools to any toolbar. Read Chapter 33 for information on how to customize a toolbar.

Formatting Characters with the Menu

To change the font, size, or font style of characters with a command, complete the following steps:

1. Select the cell, range, or multiple ranges.

2. Choose the Format Font command. The Font dialog box shown in figure 8.8 appears.

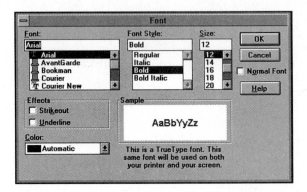

3. From the Font list, select the font to which you want to change. Check the Sample box to see how that font appears.

4. From the Font Style list, select the font style.

5. From the Size list, select the point size. Remember that approximately 72 points equal one inch of height.

6. If you prefer, select the Strikeout or Underline check box from the Effects group.

7. From the Color list, select a color. Use Automatic for black-and-white printers.

8. Choose OK or press Enter.

If you want to return the selected cells to the default font style and size, use the same procedure and select the Normal Font check box.

Using Shortcut Keys

To format cells quickly with shortcut keys, select the cell, range, or text. Then press the appropriate shortcut key combination. The following chart explains which shortcut key combination applies which format.

Format	Shortcut Keys
Normal style	Ctrl+1
Bold (toggle on/off)	Ctrl+2 or Ctrl+B
Italic (toggle on/off)	Ctrl+3 or Ctrl+I
Underline (toggle on/off)	Ctrl+4 or Ctrl+U
Strikeout (toggle on/off)	Ctrl+5

Using TrueType Fonts

You can use TrueType fonts with Excel when it's operating under Windows 3.1 or later. A type of built-in font-generation software, TrueType generates screen and printer fonts so that what you see on-screen is exactly the same as what prints, whether you have a laser or a dot-matrix printer.

Understanding Screen, Printer, and TrueType Fonts

Windows applications use screen fonts and printer fonts. In Windows 3.1 you have the choice of using several different types of screen and printer fonts.

Screen fonts are used to display characters on-screen. *Printer fonts* are used to print your spreadsheets. Some laser and dot-matrix printers come with built-in sets of printer fonts, which may be stored in permanent memory in the printer. You also may be able to plug in cartridges containing printer fonts. Some printers contain PostScript, an application that generates fonts of different styles and sizes. And some printers, usually network printers, have sets of fonts downloaded to them from a computer.

Although you may be using a built-in printer font to print your spreadsheets, a separate screen font is used to display the characters on-screen. When you installed your printer in Windows, a set of screen fonts to match your printer should have been installed. These screen fonts represent your printer fonts so that what you see on-screen is close to what prints. Screen fonts are limited to certain styles and sizes, however, so not all screen representations match the printed results.

T I P   Using one of the screen fonts built for your printer gives you the best speed, but the screen display may not be exactly the same as what prints. Make sure that when you install your printer you specify any font cartridges, additional memory, or soft fonts available for your printer.

When you choose Forma**t F**ont to display the Font dialog box, printer fonts available with your printer are listed in the Font list with printer icons next to them (see fig. 8.9).

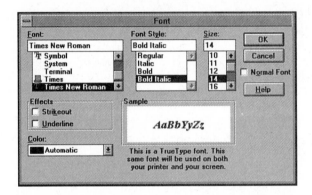

FIG. 8.9

Icons in the Font list show the type of fonts you have available.

T I P   After you select a new font from the Font list, read the description in the Sample box. It describes the type of font you have selected and how it affects printing.

Screen fonts that do not match any font in your printer also can be used in your worksheets or charts. Because the printer does not have a matching font, however, Windows selects a similar type and size of font when you print. In some cases, the printer font may be close; in others, it may be very different. Screen fonts that do not match a printer font appear in the **F**ont list without an icon.

TrueType fonts are fonts generated by Windows 3.1 or later. The character shapes, sizes, and styles for both the screen and the printer are generated as they are needed. Because they are generated by the same application and because Windows knows the type of screen and printer you are using, what you see on-screen is the same as what prints. TrueType fonts appear in the **F**ont list of the Font dialog box preceded by a TT icon. TrueType fonts give you a wide range of sizes and styles, and you can purchase additional typefaces designed for TrueType. The disadvantage is that the generation time needed to create the screen fonts and download the characters used slows system performance slightly.

Enabling TrueType Fonts

TrueType fonts are installed automatically for you during the installation of Windows 3.1 or later. But to make sure that you have them available for applications like Excel, you need to enable the fonts. If the Font list in the Font dialog box shows the TT icons with the font names Arial, Courier New, Symbol, and Times New Roman, you have TrueType fonts enabled. If the list does not show these fonts, you need to enable TrueType.

To enable TrueType fonts, complete the following steps:

1. Open the Control Panel from the Main group window in the Program Manager.

2. Start the Fonts application by double-clicking the Fonts icon or selecting the icon with the arrow keys and pressing Enter.

3. Choose the TrueType button. The TrueType dialog box shown in figure 8.10 appears.

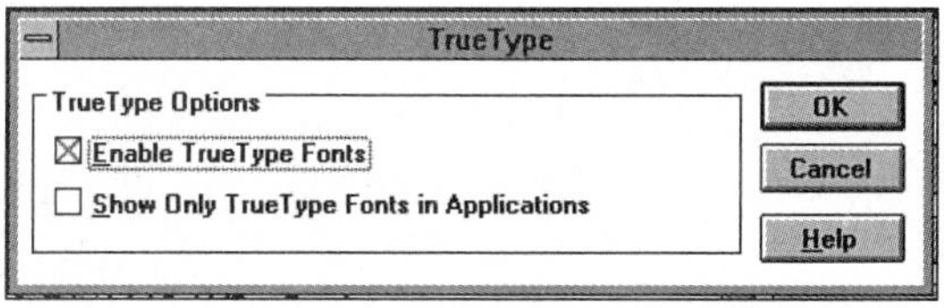

FIG. 8.10

Enable TrueType fonts from the Fonts application in the Control Panel.

4. Select the Enable TrueType Fonts check box if you want to use TrueType.

5. Select the Show Only TrueType Fonts in Application check box if you want to see only TrueType fonts and not screen or printer fonts in Font lists.

6. Choose OK or press Enter.

7. If you changed the setting for the Enable TrueType Fonts check box, another dialog box appears. Choose the Don't Restart Now button if you want to return to your Windows applications to finish work and save documents. Choose the Restart Now button if you want to restart Windows immediately. (Excel asks whether you

want to save any changed worksheets.) Keep in mind that changing the **E**nable TrueType Fonts check box does not take effect until you exit and restart Windows.

Aligning Text and Numbers

In an unformatted cell, text aligns against the left edge of the column, and numbers align against the right edge. To enhance your worksheet, you can align values or formula results so that they are left, right, or centered in a cell. You also can align a title across a selection of cells, which enables you easily to center a heading over a table or report. You can fill cells with a character that you specify, such as a dash or an equal sign, to create lines across your worksheet. You can rotate text within a cell. Excel also wraps words within a cell so that you can put a readable paragraph within one cell.

T I P   You quickly can display the Alignment dialog box by clicking the cell or selected cells you want to align with the *right* mouse button. The shortcut menu, from which you choose Alignment, appears.

Aligning Cell Entries

By using the three alignment icons on the Standard toolbar, you can align text or numbers quickly within a cell. (As shown in figure 8.11, these icons appear as small pages with lines that are aligned left, right, or center.) To use the toolbar to align cell contents, complete the following steps:

1. Select the cell(s) containing the contents you want to align.

2. Click the Left, Center, or Right Align icon in the toolbar.

You also can use the menu to change the alignment of cell contents. Complete the following steps:

1. Select the cell(s) that you want to format.

2. Choose the Forma**t A**lignment command to display the Alignment dialog box (see fig. 8.12).

3. Select one of the following alignment buttons in the Horizontal group:

Select **G**eneral, the default setting, to align text to the left and numbers to the right.

Select **L**eft to align cell contents at the left edge.

Select **C**enter to center the cell contents within the cell. Characters may extend outside the cell.

Select **R**ight to align cell contents at the right edge.

Select **F**ill to repeat the text to fill the cell.

Select **J**ustify to align cell contents to both edges.

Select Center **a**cross selection to align cell contents in the center of a selected group of cells (see the following section for details).

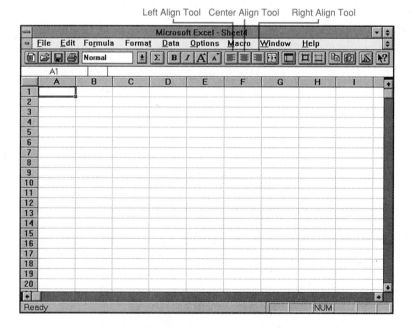

FIG. 8.11

The Standard toolbar contains alignment icons.

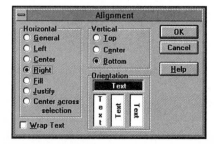

FIG. 8.12

Use the buttons in the Alignment dialog box to align cell contents.

4. Choose OK or press Enter.

Centering Text across Cells

One problem you may have faced when building worksheets and databases in other software applications is not being able to center titles
within or at the top of tables or databases. With Excel's Center across
selection option or Center text in selection tool, centering titles becomes
easy.

To center a title across multiple cells with the Center text in selection
tool, do the following:

1. Type and format the title in the left cell of the range in which you
   want the title centered.

2. Select the range.

3. Click the Center text in selection tool.

To center a title across multiple cells with the Center across selection
tool, follow these steps:

1. Type and format the title in the left cell of the range in which you
   want the title centered. Figure 8.13, for example, shows the new
   title *Sales Forecast* entered in cell C7.

2. Select the cells across which you want the text centered.

3. Choose the Format Alignment command.

4. Select the Center across selection option.

5. Choose OK or press Enter. The text centers between the cell where
   the text is entered and the final cell you selected.

Figure 8.14 shows the results.

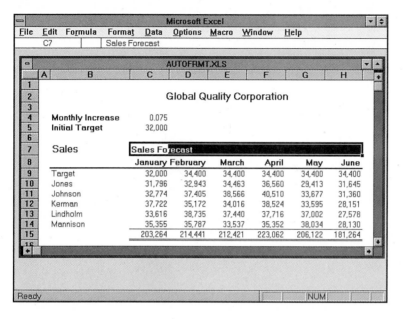

FIG. 8.13

Select the title and cells you want it centered across.

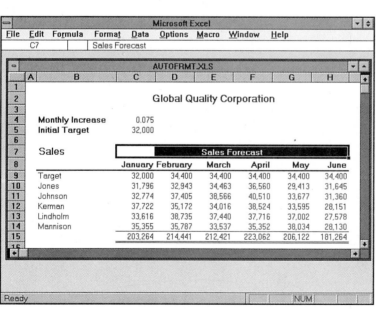

FIG. 8.14

You easily can center titles over tables and databases.

You also can center text across a selection by choosing the Center in Selection tool on the Standard toolbar.

T I P

Wrapping and Concatenating Text

If you have made a lengthy text entry in a cell, you can have Excel wrap the text so that it forms a paragraph that fits in a cell. The cell's height increases to contain multiple lines. Figure 8.15 illustrates how the **Wrap** Text option works. Notice that the text in cell B4 extends outside the cell. The text in cell B7, however, where the **Wrap** Text option has been selected, wraps within the cell to form a single paragraph.

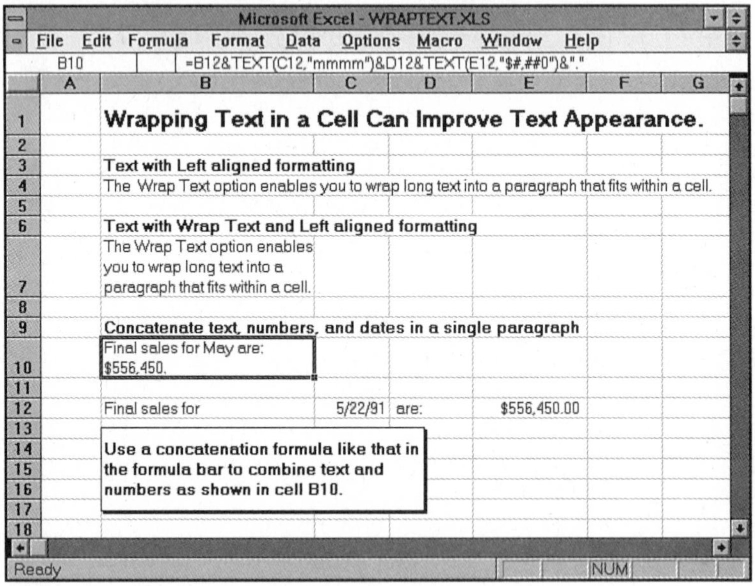

FIG. 8.15

Use **W**rap Text to fit paragraphs into a cell.

To have Excel wrap text within cells, complete the following steps:

1. Select the cell or range containing the text you want to wrap.

2. Choose the Forma**t** **A**lignment command.

3. In the Alignment dialog box, select **Wrap** Text.

T I P Reformatting wrapped text to a new size does not automatically readjust the height of the cell. You could use the Forma**t** **R**ow Height command to adjust the height, but double-clicking the bottom line under the wrapped text is quicker. Excel then adjusts the row height to best fit the paragraph the row contains. You can select the entire work-sheet and double-click the bottom of any row heading to adjust all the rows at the same time.

Figure 8.15 also shows you an example of concatenation, the combining of text, numbers, and dates within a single cell. The formula in the Formula Bar illustrates how to combine the text, numbers, and dates from cells B12, C12, and D12 into the single cell B10. The formula is:

=B12&TEXT(C12,"mmmm")&D12&Text(E12,"$#,##0")&"."

The & is a concatenation operator that joins text, numbers, and dates into one long text string. The contents of B12 and D12 are text. The TEXT() functions format the contents of C12 to appear as a month and E12 to appear as currency. The TEXT( ) function can use any of the custom numeric formats that Excel recognizes. These formats are described in the section "Designing Custom Numeric Formats."

Tabbing and Breaking Lines

Long formulas or text wrapped within a cell as a paragraph can be difficult to read. But inserting tabs and line breaks, also called carriage returns, can give lengthy text entries and formulas a structure that makes them easier to read and understand.

To enter a line break, hold down the Alt key as you press Enter. To enter a tab, hold down the Ctrl key as you press the Tab key. Delete the tab and carriage-return characters as you would any character.

Justifying Text Lines

Excel has elementary word processing capability with its Format Justify command. This command takes long strings of text, divides them into lengths that you specify, and reenters each length in its own cell. The result appears as a paragraph with each line starting in the next lower cell. You can use Format Justify to join and wrap strings of text that are not in the same cell. Cell heights do not change as they do with the Wrap Text option of the Format Alignment command.

NOTE If you want to create a box of text that uses more sophisticated formatting options than are available with Format Justify, examine the text boxes described in Chapter 9, "Drawing and Placing Graphics in Worksheets," or use an application such as WordArt or Microsoft Draw to embed a text box.

The worksheet shown in figure 8.16 contains strings of text in cells A2, A3, A4, A6, and A7 that would look better if they were of similar length. To justify such strings of text, complete the following steps:

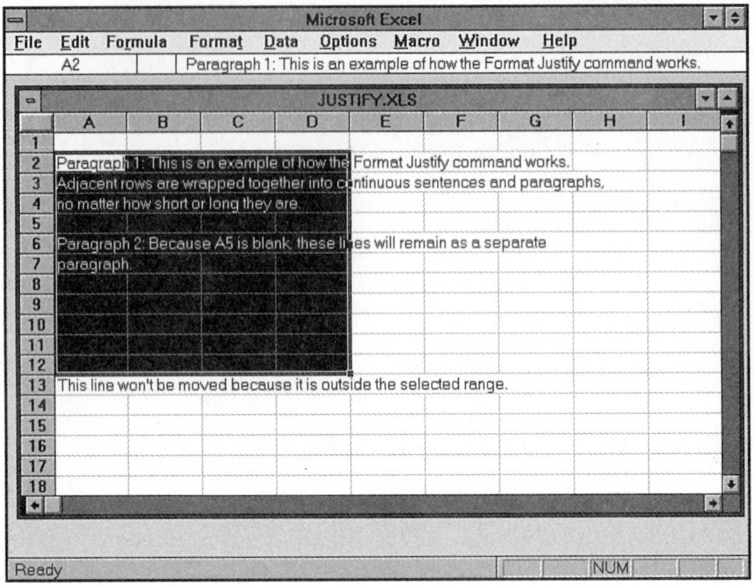

FIG. 8.16

You can justify text to
fit within a selected
range.

1. Select the range that contains the cell entries you want to justify. Extend the range to define how much space the text can occupy after justification. In the example, the range A2 through D12 is selected.

2. Choose the Format Justify command.

Figure 8.17 shows the results of the justification. Notice that blank lines occurring in the text remain blank after justification. This feature keeps paragraphs separated as they were before justification. Text in adjacent rows, no matter how short a line, merges to form continuous sentences and paragraphs. Data outside the range that you specify does not move when you choose the Format Justify command.

If the text cannot justify and fit within the range you specify, Excel displays an alert box. If you choose OK rather than Cancel, the text justifies even though it will not fit into the specified area. The Format Justify command does not move numbers or formulas down to make way for text, so existing numbers or formulas may be overwritten.

If you accidentally cover information with justified text, immediately choose the Edit Undo Justify command. When you have insufficient space to justify text, either select a larger area in which to justify the text or move the obstructing information.

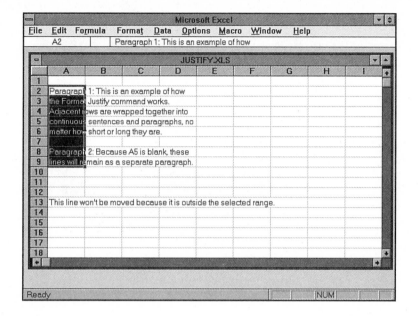

FIG. 8.17

After justification, the
text wraps for a
smoother appearance.

Rotating Numbers and Text

When you need vertical titles for reports or to label the sides of drawings or embedded charts, use Excel's Format Alignment command to
rotate the text or numbers. Figure 8.18 shows an example of how you can
use rotated text.

To rotate text or numbers, complete the following steps:

1. Select the cells containing the title or label to be rotated.

   Until you are familiar with this feature, you may want to do one cell
   at a time so that you can see what happens step by step.

2. Choose the Format Alignment command.

3. In the Alignment dialog box, select a text orientation from the
   Orientation group (see fig. 8.19).

   The default Text orientation is horizontal, reading left to right. You
   also can align text so that the letters are stacked, reading top to
   bottom; rotated 90 degrees counter-clockwise, reading top to bottom; or rotated clockwise, reading top to bottom.

4. Choose OK or press Enter.

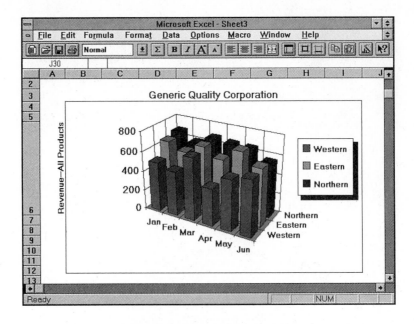

FIG. 8.18

Rotated text used in a
graph.

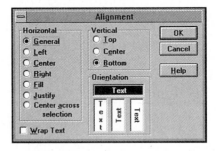

FIG. 8.19

Change the orientation
of text with the
Alignment dialog box.

Only a few characters of vertically rotated text display in a normal cell.
If some characters are missing, display the entire rotated text entry by
double-clicking the bottom line under the row heading number or by
using the Forma**t R**ow Height command to change the row height to best
fit the row's contents.

Formatting Numbers

Excel has many numeric and date/time formats that already are defined.
In addition, you can design your own custom formats. These custom
formats can contain characters and symbols that you specify, designate
the precision you want, and use 16 different colors. The format and color
can even change according to the range of values in the cell.

Cells that have not been used or that have been cut or cleared have the General numeric format, which means that Excel displays a number to the greatest precision possible. If the number is too large or small, the display appears in scientific format, such as 5.367 E+05. If a number or date is still too large to fit in the specified format, the cell fills with # symbols.

> You can display the Number Format dialog box by using the *right* mouse button to click the cell or selected cells whose numbers you want to format. The shortcut menu appears. Choose Number.

T I P

Applying Predefined Numeric Formats

Numbers, dates, and times are stored in cells as pure numbers without formatting. Excel examines the format of the number you enter, however, to determine whether the application can format a cell for you. If you enter the number $12.95 into a General format cell, which is the default setting, for example, Excel formats the cell for currency ($X,XX0.00). Enter a percentage, such as 15%, and you see it in the worksheet as 15%, although it appears in the Formula Bar as .15.

> If a cell fills with # characters, the column is not wide enough for the number in its current format. To correct this problem, widen the columns. If widening the columns causes formatting problems elsewhere in the worksheet, use the TEXT( ) function to change the number to text. The number or date then can exceed cell width and can have any format, including custom formats.

T I P

Understanding Format Codes

Excel's predefined formats and the custom formats you create have four parts, as shown in the following syntax example:

> *positive format*;*negative format*;*zero format*;*text format*

Notice that each of the parts is separated from the next by a semicolon. The first position specifies the format for positive numbers in the cell, the second for negative numbers, and so on. Although not all these for-mat positions are used in the predefined formats, they are useful with custom formats.

The symbols used in the predefined numeric formats act as placeholders or format specifiers. Notice that the 0 acts as a placeholder and displays a 0 in that position when no number is in the position.

The symbols _) following a positive format ensure that positive numbers leave a space on the right that is the same width as the right parenthe-sis,), that is included with negative numbers. Positive and negative num-bers then align evenly along the right edge of each column.

Table 8.1 shows how three sample entered numbers, 2500, -2500, and .5, display in the different predefined numeric formats Excel provides.

Table 8.1. Using Predefined Number Formats

Format Code	Display Results		
Entered Number:	*2500*	*-2500*	*0.5*
General	2500	-2500	0.5
Number			
0	2500	-2500	1
0.00	2500.00	-2500.00	0.50
#,##0	2,500	-2500	1
#,##0.00	2,500.00	-2500.00	0.50
Currency			
$#,##0_);($#,##0)	$2,500	($2,500)	$1
$#,##0_);[RED]($#,##0)	$2,500	($2,500)*	$1
$#,##0.00_);($#,##0.00)	$2,500.00	($2,500.00)	$0.50
$#,##0.00_); [RED]($#,##0.00)	$2,500.00	($2,500.00)*	$0.50
Percentage			
0%	250000%	-250000%	50%
0.00%	250000.00%	-250000.00%	50.00%

Format Code	Display Results		
Scientific			
0.00E+00	2.50E+03	-2.50E+03	5.00E-01
Fraction			
# ?/?	2500	-2500	1/2
*This negative number displays in red.			

Formatting Numbers with the Toolbar

The Formatting toolbar contains tools to help you quickly format cells for numeric display (see fig. 8.20). To use a tool, just select the cells you want to format and click the appropriate tool. The toolbar offers tools for currency, percentage, or comma format. Also, if you want to increase or decrease the decimals displayed, click one of the tools that looks like a decimal and zeros. One increases and the other decreases the number of decimal places.

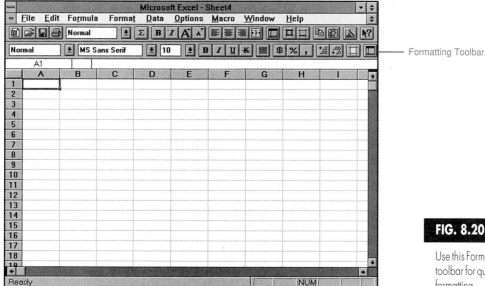

Formatting Toolbar

FIG. 8.20

Use this Formatting toolbar for quick formatting.

The Style list in some toolbars includes predefined styles for some numeric formats. Choose Comma for comma format with two decimals, Currency for dollar format with two decimals, and Percentage for the percent format with a percent sign. For more information on style, see "Using Styles" in this chapter.

Formatting Numbers with the Menu

To use menu commands to format cells for a specific numeric appearance, complete the following steps:

1. Select the cells you want to format.

2. Choose the Format Number command to display the Number Format dialog box (see fig. 8.21).

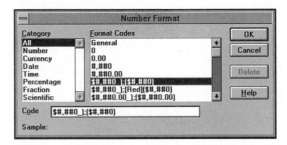

3. Select the type of number you want to format from the Category list. This selection limits what appears in the Format Codes list.

4. Select the format you want from the Format Codes list. Custom formats that you have created appear at the bottom of the list.

5. Choose OK or press Enter.

Formatting Numbers with Shortcut Keys

Shortcut keys that bypass the Format Number command and immediately format the selected cell are described in table 8.2.

Table 8.2. Formatting Numbers with Shortcut Keys

Format	Shortcut Key
General	Shift+Ctrl+~
#,##0.00	Shift+Ctrl+!
$#,##0.00_);($#,##0.00)	Shift+Ctrl+$
0%	Shift+Ctrl+%
0.00E+00	Shift+Ctrl+^

Designing Custom Numeric Formats

You can design your own numeric formats for financial or scientific tasks and create formats for catalog numbers, telephone numbers, international currency, and so forth. Any time you need to display a number in a special way, consider using a custom numeric format.

To create custom formats you can use anywhere on the worksheet, complete the following steps:

1. Select the cells for which you want to use the custom format.

2. Choose the Format Number command.

3. If an existing format is close to the custom format you want to create, select that format by choosing the appropriate category from the Category list and choosing the closest code from the Format Codes list.

4. In the Code text box, edit the custom format's pattern, as shown in figure 8.22.

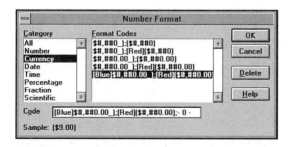

FIG. 8.22

Type custom formats in the Code text box.

5. Choose OK or press Enter.

To test the custom format in the selected cell, enter positive, negative, and zero values in the cell and watch the displayed result.

You can reuse this custom format on any cell in the worksheet by selecting the same category as when you created the format, scrolling to the bottom of the Format Code list, and selecting the custom format as you would any predefined format.

Excel uses a semicolon (;) to separate the formats for positive, negative, and zero formats, in this form:

positive format;negative format;zero format;text format

To understand how these parts work, examine this sample custom format:

$#,##0_);($#,##0); "Zero"

It displays a positive number in the $#,##0 format, a negative number in the ($#,##0) format, and the text Zero for a zero.

Symbols that you can use when creating custom formats are described in table 8.3.

Table 8.3. Formatting Symbols for Custom Formats

Formatting Symbol	Function
General	Uses the default format for unformatted cells. Displays numbers as precisely as possible for column width. Displays in scientific format for large or small numbers.
#	Acts as a placeholder for digits. 0 is not displayed if a number is absent. Decimal fractions round up to the number of #s to the right of the decimal. The value 3.5 with format $#,###.##, for example, is displayed as $3.5, and the number .245 as $.25.
0	Acts as a placeholder for digits. Used to display a 0 if no number is entered. Decimal fractions round up to the number of 0s to the right of the decimal. The value 3.5 with a format $#,##0.00, for example, is displayed as $3.50, and the number .245 appears as $0.25.
?	Acts as a placeholder for digits in the same way the 0 does. Insignificant 0s are removed and spaces inserted so that numbers still align correctly. Use this symbol as the integer portion with fractional custom formats so that a number does not appear if you type a fraction such as 0 3/4.

Formatting Symbol	Function
_ (underscore)	Skips the width of the character following the underscore. Typing _) at the end of a positive format, for example, inserts a blank space that is the width of the). This feature enables you to align a positive number correctly with a negative number enclosed in parentheses. Without the _), the character at the far right of the positive number would align with the closing) of a negative number.
. (decimal)	Marks the location of the decimal point. Use a 0 to the left of the . (decimal) to indicate a leading 0.
, (comma)	Marks the position of thousands. You need to mark only the location of the first thousand.

TIP: You can use a comma to divide the number by 1000. This is useful for displaying thousands or millions of dollars. 123456789 formatted as $#,##0.OO,,"M" displays as $123.45M.

%	Multiplies the entry by 100 and displays the number as a percentage with a % sign. A decimal number appears in the Formula Bar.
E_E+e_e+	Displays the number in scientific notation. One or more 0s or #s to the right of the E or e indicate the power of the exponent.
: $ _ + ( )	Displays this character in the same position in the formatted number.
/ (slash)	Serves as a separator in fractions. Type a decimal fraction, such as 1.667, into the cell; or type a leading integer followed by a fraction, as in 1 2/3, to produce a fractional display of 1 2/3.
\ (backslash)	Indicates a single text character or symbol when it precedes an entry.
"text"	Displays the specified text within quotation marks.
* character	Fills the remaining column width with the character following the asterisk (one asterisk per format).

Table 8.3. Continued

Formatting Symbol	Function
@	Acts as a format code to indicate where user-input text will appear in the format.
[*color*]	Formats cell content with the color specified. For more information, see this chapter's section on "Formatting Data with Color."
[*condition value*]	Uses conditional statements within the number format to specify when a format will be used. Conditions can be <, >, =, >=, <=, and <>. Values can be any number. For more information, see this chapter's section on "Formatting Conditionally."

Figure 8.23 shows examples of custom formats and how they can be used. The format shown in column C was entered in the Number Format dialog box as a custom format. This format then was used to format the number in column D so that the number appears as shown in column E.

Figure 8.24 shows uses for custom numeric formats beyond just formatting numbers.

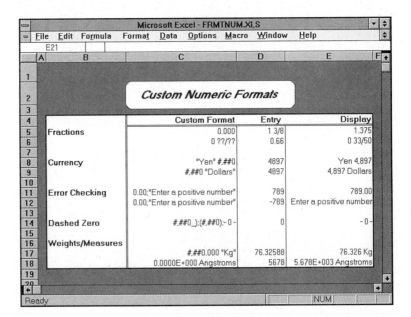

FIG. 8.23

Use custom formats to design your own numeric formats.

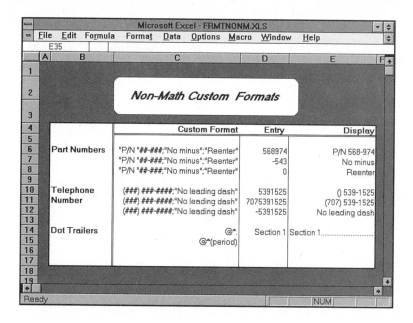

FIG. 8.24

You can use custom formats for more than just numbers.

Display text by enclosing the text in quotation marks and inserting these text elements at appropriate locations between semicolons. If you want a part number always to be preceded by P/N and to show a hyphen before the last three numbers, for example, create a custom format such as the following:

"P/N "####-###;"Use Positive";"Enter Number"

With this format, the number 5768953 is displayed as P/N 5768-953. Entering a negative number displays the text Use Positive, and entering a zero produces the text Enter Number.

To hide numbers in your custom format, don't put a format code between semicolons where Excel expects one. Table 8.4 gives some examples of ways you can use text and the semicolon to your advantage. In the second example in table 8.4, negative numbers and zeros are hidden.

Table 8.4. Custom Formats that Hide Values

Custom Format	Positive	Negative	Zero
$#,###_);($#,###);	$2,500	($2,500)	
$#,###_);;	$2,500		
$#,### ;($#,###);"Zero"	$2,500	($2,500)	Zero
;;	All values hidden but used in calculation		

As you can see in the table, a double semicolon hides all numbers. Hidden numbers are still in the worksheet and can be used by other formulas. You can see these numbers in the Formula Bar if you select a cell containing one of them. Select and reformat cells to redisplay hidden numbers.

T   I   P   Set the numeric, date, and time formats throughout your worksheet from the Control Panel. Choose the Program Control menu (press Alt and then the space bar) and choose the **Run** command. Select the Control **P**anel option from the displayed box and then choose OK. When the Control Panel appears, open the International application. Change formats by selecting a different country from the **C**ountry list or by choosing **D**ate, **T**ime, **C**urrency, or **N**umber format and selecting different options in the dialog box that appears.

Formatting Data with Color

Colored text or numbers can help you pick up discrepancies in data entry or flag numbers that are out of tolerance. The color format works on a cell along with the numeric or date formats.

You must type the color symbol in the custom format within the portion of the format in which you want to use the color, in the positive, negative, zero, or text portion. Color formats in the text format position, for example, change the color of text. And if you want the positive format to be blue and the negative format to be red, use a format such as this one:

    [BLUE]$#,##0.00_0;[RED]($#,##0.00)

Colors that you can use include the eight named colors and any of the custom colors. Specify the color with one of the following color symbols:

    [BLACK]
    [WHITE]
    [RED]
    [GREEN]
    [BLUE]
    [YELLOW]
    [MAGENTA]
    [CYAN]
    [COLOR#] (where # is a color numbered from 1 to 16 on the
    color   palette)

Colors on the palette are numbered from top to bottom and from left to right. (The top left is 1; the lower right is 16.) Mix custom colors with the **O**ptions Color Palette command.

Formatting Conditionally

When you use the [*condition value*] formatting symbol in your custom format, you can format a cell so that numbers appear in different formats or colors, depending on the value of the number. This technique is especially valuable for error checking on data entry, for exception reporting from analysis, and for executive information systems.

The following format, for example, makes all numbers in the cell use the 0.00 numeric format, but the numbers appear black when greater than or equal to 1,000, red when less than or equal to 500, and blue for any number in between these values:

    [BLACK][>=1000]0.00;[RED][<=500]0.00;[BLUE]0.00

Deleting Custom Formats

To remove a custom format, complete the following steps:

1. Choose the Format Number command.

2. Select the custom format from the Format Codes list.

3. Choose the Delete button.

You cannot delete predefined formats.

Hiding Zeros

Hiding zeros often makes worksheets easier to read. In Excel, you have three options for hiding zeros: hiding them throughout the worksheet, creating a custom format, or using an IF() function.

To hide zeros throughout the entire worksheet, choose the Options Display command and clear the Zero Values box. Reselect the Zero Values box when you want to see the zeros again.

To hide zeros by using a custom format, use the semicolon in the appropriate position to indicate that a zero format follows, but do not enter a format for zero numbers, as in the following format:

    $#,###_);($#,###);

In formulas, use an IF() function to hide a zero, as in the following example:

    =IF(A12+B12=0,"",A12+B12)

This formula says that if A12+B12 equals zero, Excel displays what is between the quotation marks, which is nothing. (Beware of using a space to indicate zeros; a space causes problems in some databases or numeric and text functions.) If A12+B12 does not equal zero, Excel displays the result of the formula.

Understanding the Danger in Formatted Numbers

The formatted values that appear on-screen may not be the same values used in calculations. This discrepancy can cause the displayed or printed results to be different from manually calculated answers.

Figure 8.25 illustrates this problem. Worksheet columns C and D contain the numeric values. Columns E and G contain the same formula that multiplies the adjacent cells in C and D. Cells E15 and G15 contain SUM( ) functions that sum their respective columns. Notice that the totals for columns E and G do not agree. Column G has been formatted to appear with two decimal places, but the numbers used in calculation have three decimal places. That third decimal place causes the displayed and actual results to appear differently.

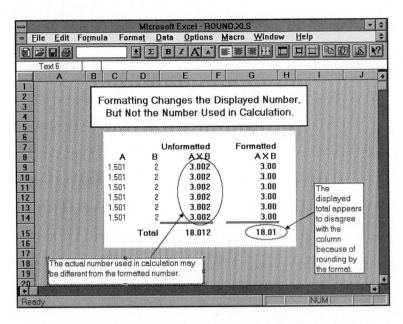

FIG. 8.25

Formatting rounds the displayed number but not the calculated number.

You can resolve the problem either for the entire worksheet or for individual cells. To resolve the problem for the entire worksheet so that the numbers displayed match those used in the calculation, choose the **Op**tions **C**alculation command and select the **P**recision as Displayed check box. When you choose OK or press Enter, you are warned that constant numbers throughout the worksheet will be rounded permanently to match cell formatting.

A second method enables you to round individual cells. This method uses the ROUND( ) function. For the example in figure 8.25, you can use the formula =ROUND(C9*D9,2) in cell E9. This formula rounds the multiplied value before it is summed. Always round before doing further calculations. Rounding the SUM( ) results in E15 (the "Total" row) does not solve the problem.

Formatting Dates and Times

Type dates and times in cells the way you are accustomed to reading or writing them. Excel recognizes dates and times entered in any of the formats shown in table 8.5. If you type the date 1/12/92 into a cell with the default General format and then press Enter, for example, Excel formats the cell in the m/d/yy date format.

Table 8.5. Predefined Excel Date and Time Formats

Format	Example
m/d/yy	12/24/91
d-mmm-yy	24-Dec-91
d-mmm	24-Dec
mmm-yy	Dec-91
h:mm AM/PM	9:45 PM (12-hour clock)
h:mm:ss AM/PM	9:45:15 PM (12-hour clock)
h:mm	21:45 (24-hour clock)
h:mm:ss	21:45:15 (24-hour clock)
m/d/yy h:mm	12/24/88 21:45 (24-hour clock)

If the cell is in the default General format, you do not need to format the cell. Excel changes the General format to agree with the date and time format that you first enter. You can change this format or create a custom format at any time.

If you enter a date or time and see it appear on the left side of the cell, Excel did not interpret your entry as a date or time but instead accepted the entry as text. Check to see whether the Formula Bar shows the date in the pattern m/d/yy. If so, the entry was accepted as a date.

When Excel accepts a date or time, the application calculates the serial number, which is the number of days from the beginning of this century to the date you enter. You can use this serial number to perform date arithmetic, such as calculating the days between dates. Time is calculated as the decimal portion of 24 hours. To see the serial date number in a date/time cell, reformat the cell to General format.

The following shortcut keys can save you time when entering and formatting dates and times:

Shortcut Key	Format Result
Ctrl+;	Inserts current date
Ctrl+: (Shift+;)	Inserts current time
Shift+Ctrl+@	Formats in h:mm AM/PM
Shift+Ctrl+#	Formats in d-mmm-yy

Using Predefined Date and Time Formats

Regardless of how you enter or calculate the date and time, you can display the date and time in any of Excel's predefined formats. You also can select a different color for the cell's contents or set a format for dates and times within a range.

To change the date and time format of a cell, use the same process you use to format a number. Select the cells or range of cells you want to format. Choose the Format Number command, select Date or Time from the Category list, select a format from the Format Code list, and choose OK or press Enter.

Creating Custom Date and Time Formats

If you cannot find the date or time format you want, you can create it with the same process you use to create custom numeric formats. The only difference is that you use different formatting symbols for date and time formatting. The custom formatting characters you can use for date and time formats are described in table 8.6.

Table 8.6. Date and Time Symbols for Custom Formats

Type/Symbols	Display Result
General	Serial date number of days from the beginning of the century. Dec 24, 1991, for example, is 33596. Times appear as decimal portions of 24 hours.
Days	
d	Day number from 1 to 31; no leading zero.
dd	Day number from 01 to 31; leading zero.
Months *	
m	Month number from 1 to 12; no leading zero.
mm	Month number from 01 to 12; leading zero.
mmm	Three-letter month abbreviation from Jan to Dec.
mmmm	Full name of month from January to December.
Years	
yy	Two-digit year number from 00 to 99.
yyyy	Full year number from 1900 to 2078.
Hours	
h	Hour number from 0 to 24; no leading zero.
hh	Hour number from 00 to 24; leading zero.
Minutes	
m	Minute number from 0 to 59; no leading zero.
mm	Minute number from 00 to 59; leading zero.
Seconds	
s	Second number from 0 to 59; no leading zero.
ss	Second number from 00 to 59; leading zero.

continues

Table 8.6. Continued

Type/Symbols	Display Result
AM/PM	am/pm
A/P	Displays the hour, using the 12-hour clock.
Separators	
_	Places dash divider between parts.
/	Places slash divider between parts.
:	Places colon divider between parts.
*Excel interprets m characters that follow an h as minutes.	

Some examples of custom date formats are shown in table 8.7.

Table 8.7. Sample Custom Date and Time Formats

Format	Display
mmmm d, yyyy	April 1, 1992
d mmm, yy	1 Apr, 93
yy/mm/dd	92/12/01
[BLUE] d mmm, yy	1 Apr, 92 (in blue)
[RED][>=33596] d mmm, yy;d mmm, yy	24 Dec, 92 (in red)
	23 Dec, 92 (in black)
	(The number 33596 is the serial date number for 24 Dec, 91.)

To find the serial date number for a date to use in a conditional format, enter the date in a cell and then change the format to General. The serial date number appears.

Formatting Rows and Columns

You can improve the appearance of your worksheet or database by adjusting column widths and row heights. Appropriate adjustments also help you fit more data on a page. You even can hide confidential data in a row or column. The following paragraphs describe these tasks.

Adjusting Column Width

You can adjust one or more columns in Excel to get the best appearance in your worksheet or to fit the maximum data on-screen or in a printout. If a column is not wide enough to display a number, date, or time, Excel lets you know by displaying # characters in the cell. The standard width for a column is 8.43 characters, based on the font defined for Normal style. This width may vary in practice, however, with the varying width of characters and fonts.

> Double-clicking the column heading separator on the right side adjusts a column to fit its widest contents. The width of the column is based on the screen fonts. If you are using TrueType fonts, the column width also should be correct for printing.
>
> **T I P**

To change one or more column widths, complete the following steps:

1. Select multiple columns by dragging the pointer across the column headers. You do not need to select the column to change a single column. Select nonadjacent columns with Ctrl+Click (see fig. 8.26).

2. Move the pointer onto the vertical line to the right of the heading of the column you want to change. To change the width of column B, for example, move onto the line between the B and C headers. The pointer changes to a two-headed horizontal arrow.

3. Drag the column left or right until the shadow is where you want it; then release the mouse button. All selected columns drag to the same width.

You also can use the keyboard to change column widths by following these steps:

1. Select cells in the columns that you want to change. Change multiple columns by selecting a cell in each column. Chapter 6 describes how to select adjacent or nonadjacent cells.

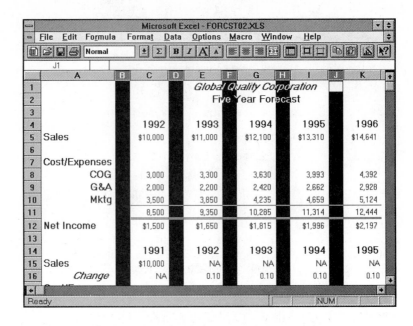

FIG. 8.26

Select nonadjacent
columns with a
Ctrl+Click on each
column heading.

2. Choose the Forma**t** **C**olumn Width command to display the Column Width dialog box shown in figure 8.27.

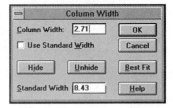

FIG. 8.27

View the Column Width dialog box by choosing Format Column Width.

3. Use one of the following techniques to adjust column widths:

Adjust columns to a specific width by typing the column width as the number of Normal style characters in the **C**olumn Width edit box.

Adjust columns widths to best fit the longest character string they contain by choosing the **B**est Fit button.

Adjust all columns that have not had the width formatted by typing the column width to be used as the standard width in the Standard **W**idth edit box.

4. Choose OK or press Enter.

To return column widths of the selected cells to the default setting, select the Use Standard Width check box.

Hiding Columns

When you generate a database or worksheet for multiple users, you may not want to print all the information that you enter. You can hide columns temporarily so that they do not appear on-screen or print.

To hide selected columns, choose Format Column Width and select the Hide button in the Column Width dialog box. Reveal hidden columns by selecting cells that span the hidden column; then choose the Format Column Width command and select the Unhide check box.

Adjusting Row Height

You may want to change row heights to create more space for titles or more space between subtotals and grand totals. The procedure for changing the height of rows is similar to that for changing column widths. Row heights change automatically to accommodate the tallest font in the row. Before making a row height smaller, you may want to make sure that you will not be cutting off the tops of large characters.

To adjust a row height to the best fit for the tallest characters in the row, double-click the separator line underneath the row's number in the row headings.

To change the height of one or more rows, complete the following steps:

1. Select one or more rows. Drag across row headings or use Ctrl+Click to select nonadjacent rows (see fig. 8.28).

2. Move the mouse pointer onto the line below the heading of the row you want to change. When correctly positioned, the mouse pointer changes to a two-headed vertical arrow.

3. Drag the two-headed arrow up or down until the shadow of the row bottom is where you want it. Then release the mouse button. You also can double-click the bottom of one of the row headers.

To change row height by using the keyboard, follow these steps:

1. Select a cell in each row you want to change.

2. Choose the Format Row Height command to display the Row Height dialog box shown in figure 8.29.

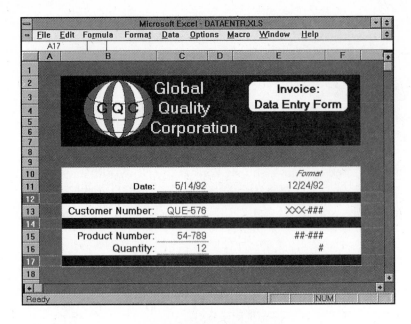

FIG. 8.28

Select nonadjacent
rows with a Ctrl+Click
on each row heading.

FIG. 8.29

Use the Row Height
dialog box to change
the height of selected
rows.

3. Enter the height in the **R**ow Height text box.

4. Choose OK or press Enter.

If you want to return the row to normal height, open the Row Height
dialog box and select the Use **S**tandard Height check box.

Hiding Rows

To hide rows of information, use steps similar to the ones you use to
change the row height. Select the rows you want to hide, choose the
Forma**t** Row Height command, and select the **Hi**de button. Reveal hidden
rows by selecting cells that span the hidden row; then choose the Forma**t** **R**ow Height command and select the **U**nhide check box.

Adding Colors, Patterns, and Borders

Shading, borders, and even colors can dress up your worksheet or reports to make important information stand out. These features create an impression of high-quality, polished work. This section explains the color and pattern changes you can make.

You can add emphasis and polish to your worksheets by using different shadings and patterns as backgrounds for tables of numbers, as shown in the examples throughout this book. Figure 8.30 shows the 18 black-and-white patterns available. The number shown in each shaded cell is used by the PATTERNS( ) macro function to specify a shade.

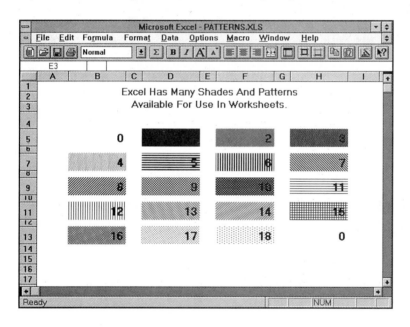

FIG. 8.30

You can choose from these 18 patterns.

You also can create these shadings by using foreground and background colors within a pattern. Colors can emphasize screen display, output printed to any color-capable Windows-compatible printer, and output projected on-screen with a color screen projector.

Another way to add shading is with the Light Shading and Dark Shading tools. These tools can be found in the Customize dialog box for the Formatting toolbar and added to any toolbar. (By default, the Light Shading tool is included on the Formatting toolbar.) To use a shading tool, just select the cells you want shaded and then click the tool.

Adding a Pattern or Color

To add a pattern in black and white or color to your worksheet, complete the following steps:

1. Select the cell(s) to which you want to add color or a pattern.

2. Choose the Format **P**atterns command. The Patterns dialog box appears, as shown in figure 8.31.

FIG. 8.31

You can choose 16 foreground and background patterns from the Patterns dialog box.

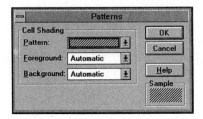

3. Select a pattern from the **P**attern pull-down list.

4. If you want a colored pattern, select a foreground and a background color from the **F**oreground and **B**ackground pull-down lists. Check the Sample area in the lower-right corner of the dialog box to see the color and pattern.

> **NOTE**   You can use as many as 16 colors for the foreground or background. The 16 colors available are specified on the color palette. Use the **O**ptions Color Pal**e**tte command to change the available colors. This command is described in Chapter 33, "Customizing Excel."

5. Choose OK or press Enter.

If you use a particular color or shade frequently, assign a color numeric format to a style name. For more information on styles, see "Using Styles" in this chapter.

> **T I P**   Add the Color Cell tool to one of your toolbars, and you can color cell backgrounds quickly and easily. Each time you click the tool, the selected range cycles to the next color in Excel's 16-color palette.

TIP

Change the color of cell contents by specifying a color in a custom numeric format or by changing the color of the font.

TIP

You can display the Patterns dialog box by clicking the right mouse button on the cell or selected cells you want to format. The shortcut menu, from which you choose Patterns, appears.

Adding Borders and Lines

You can place borders around cells or use borders as lines and double lines under cells to add emphasis, to define data-entry areas, or to mark totals and subtotals. When combined with shading, borders make your documents easier to read and give them flair.

TIP

Borders are displayed better if you turn off the grid lines in a worksheet. Use the **O**ptions **D**isplay command and clear the Grid lines check box to turn off grid lines.

Figure 8.32 shows examples of vertical and horizontal lines used as borders.

Use border tools on the Standard and Formatting toolbars to border selected cells. Additional border tools are available by dragging tools from the Customize dialog box onto your toolbar. To format with the tools, select the cells you want to border; then click the appropriate tool. (See Chapter 2 for more information about toolbars.)

TIP

Many 1-2-3 users are accustomed to creating lines or double underlines by filling cells with dashes or equal signs. Although you can continue to use this technique in Excel, a more effective method is to use Excel's Format **B**order command and select one of the many underline alternatives.

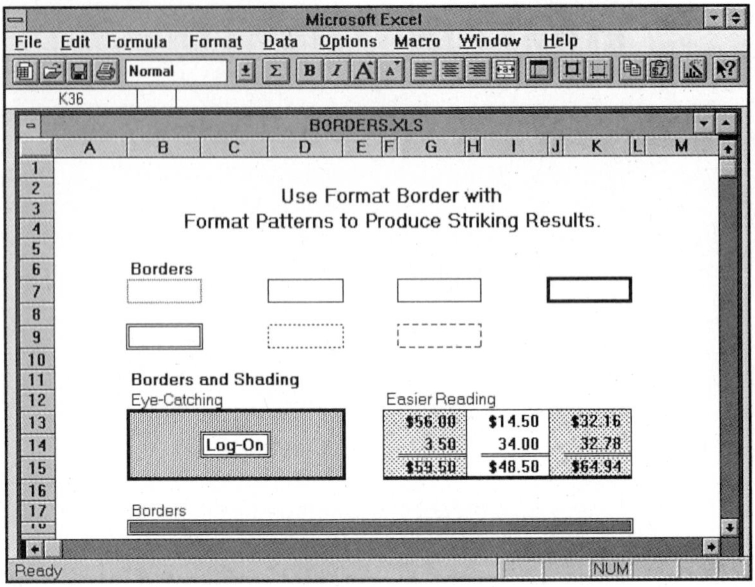

FIG. 8.32

The Format Border command draws many types and weights of lines.

To add borders (or borders to use as lines) to selected cells, complete the following steps:

1. Select the cell, range, or multiple ranges.

2. Choose the Format Border command to display the Border dialog box shown in figure 8.33.

FIG. 8.33

Use the Border dialog box to choose your borders.

3. In the Border group, select the parts of the cell or range that you want bordered. You can choose Outline, Left, Right, Top, or Bottom. Outline puts a border around the outside of the selected cells. To put lines inside a range, select one or more of the other edges.

4. In the Style group, select the style of line you want for the border. Press Alt+E, and then use the arrow keys to move between the different styles. Use the double-underline style for totals.

5. Select the color you want for the border from the Color drop-down list box. Click the down arrow or press Alt+C, and then Alt+down arrow. Use the arrow keys to move to the color you want.

6. Choose OK or press Enter.

Although the Border dialog box includes a Shade check box, use the Format Patterns command to shade with greater variety. This command offers colors and more levels of shading.

T I P

To create an underline that breaks between cells, put narrow columns between columns with borders, or format left and right borders with thick, white borders.

T I P

You can display the Border dialog box by clicking the right mouse button on the cell or selected cells to which you want to add a border. The shortcut menu, from which you choose Border, appears.

T I P

Creating Styles

Styles are a powerful formatting feature in Excel that can save you time and help you apply a group of formats consistently. By giving a set of combined formats a style name, you can apply that combination to one or more cells by choosing the style name instead of all the individual formats. If you later change the definition of formats associated with that style, all cells having that style immediately change to the new definition.

Styles are helpful because they eliminate the need to choose multiple commands for repetitive formats, and they reduce the need to reformat worksheets. If you work in a company in which a standard appearance for proposals and presentations is important, styles can ensure that everyone uses consistent formatting. The company can create preferred styles for titles, headings, bodies of financial reports, and totals. Everyone then can use these styles to reduce the workload and produce a consistent corporate image.

A style can contain all the formatting you use for numbers, font, alignment, borders, patterns, and cell protection. You can even specify whether any of these format types should not be used in a style so that an existing format in a cell remains after the style is applied. A style, for example, can specify a numeric format and font but leave the existing color unchanged.

Using Styles

You can use styles in worksheets, templates, and macro sheets. The default Excel worksheet comes with a few predefined styles: Comma, Currency, Normal, and Percent. Normal is the default style for the entire worksheet. Redefining the formats associated with the Normal style changes the format used throughout a worksheet in those cells not affected by special formatting.

You can apply a style in two ways. Both ways require that you first select the cell(s) to which you want the style's formats applied. Then you choose the style from the Style list on the toolbar or from the Style dialog box.

If you are using a mouse and a toolbar containing a Style list, you can choose a style quickly. To apply a style with this method, complete the following steps:

1. Select the cell(s) you want to format.

2. Select the Style list in the toolbar by clicking the down arrow (see fig. 8.34).

3. Click the name of the style that defines the formats you want to apply.

T I P   If you have a large number of style names in the worksheet, you may find that selecting the Style list in the toolbar, typing a style name, and pressing Enter is quicker than scrolling through the list to find the right style.

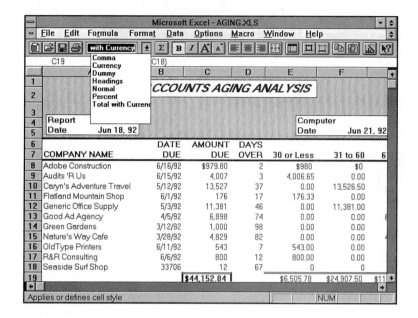

FIG. 8.34

The Style list is displayed on the left side of the Standard toolbar.

To apply a style by using the Style dialog box, complete the following steps:

1. Select the cell(s) to which you want the style applied.

2. Choose the Format Style command to display the Style dialog box (see fig. 8.35).

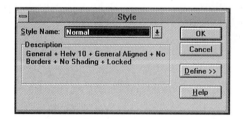

FIG. 8.35

You can use the Style dialog box to apply styles.

3. Select the style name from the Style Name list box (see fig. 8.36) and then select the style name from the list. Alternatively, you can type the name in the box. When you select or type the name, the Description box shows the formats that are contained in that style.

4. Choose OK or press Enter.

Whether a style's formats overwrite existing formats in a cell depends on whether check boxes in the Style Includes group were selected to override conflicting styles. The Style Includes group of options drops down when you choose the **D**efine button. If you cleared the **P**attern check box in the Style Includes group when you created the style, for example, you can use the style on any cell without changing the existing pattern in the cell. The following section describes how to define a style.

T I P   You can see quickly which style has been applied to a selected cell by looking at the style listed in the toolbar's Style box.

Creating Styles

You can create styles in three different ways. You can create them by using the existing format in a cell as an example; you can create them by choosing formats from dialog boxes; or you can *merge* styles that exist on another worksheet.

Creating a Style by Example

If a cell on the worksheet or macro sheet already has the formats you want associated with a style, you can use the formats in that cell to define a new style. You can use this method of *style by example* to create styles with either the toolbar and mouse or with the Format **S**tyle command. If you have multiple cells selected, the style includes only formatting attributes that are common to all of the cells.

To use the toolbar to create a style by example, complete the following steps:

1. Select the cell that contains the formats you want to include in a style.

2. Type the new style name in the Style box on the toolbar.

3. Press Enter to create the new style, or press Esc to back out.

To use menu commands to create a style by example, complete the following steps:

1. Select a cell containing the formats you want to include in a style.

2. Select the Format **S**tyle command.

3. Select Style Name and type the new style name in the **S**tyle Name text box.

4. Choose OK or press Enter.

Notice that you can read a description of what the current cell's formatting contains, and what the new style will contain, in the Description box within the Style dialog box.

Creating a Style by Command

If you do not have a mouse or if an example of your style does not exist in the document, you can define a style by selecting formats just as you select formats from the Format commands.

To define a style by using the Format **S**tyle command, complete the following steps:

1. Choose the Format **S**tyle command.

2. Select the **S**tyle Name list box, and type a new name. Excel does not warn you if you are about to change an existing style. To make sure that you are not using an existing name, click the down arrow and scroll through the list; or press Alt+S, then Alt+down arrow and scroll down.

3. Choose the **D**efine >> button to expand the dialog box (see fig. 8.37).

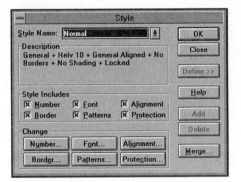

FIG. 8.37

The expanded Style dialog box enables you to define styles.

4. Select the formats you want to associate with this style by selecting the appropriate check boxes in the Style Includes group. Any formats with the check box cleared are not used in the style.

5. Select a formatting button from the Change box. (Only the buttons for selected options in the Style Includes group are available; others are dimmed.)

   When you select a Change button, the dialog box that corresponds to that button's Format command appears. If you choose the Number button, for example, the Number Format dialog box is displayed (see fig. 8.38).

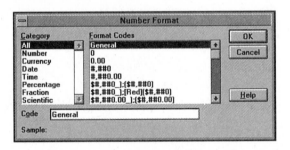

FIG. 8.38

Change buttons display the same formatting dialog boxes as the Format commands.

6. In the dialog box that appears, select the formatting options you want to associate with the style; then choose OK or press Enter to get back to the Style dialog box.

7. Repeat steps 5 and 6 until the style contains all the formatting you want, as defined in the Description box.

8. If you want to keep this style and define additional styles, choose the Add button. If you want to keep this style and apply it to the selected cells, choose OK or press Enter. If you want to keep this style but not apply it to the selected cells, choose Add and then Close.

Clearing a format check box in the Style Includes group does two things. While the Style dialog box is open, Excel grays the corresponding button in the Change box so that this format cannot be changed. Also, after the style is defined and you apply it to a cell already containing formats, the cell keeps its original formatting for those formats that were cleared in the Style Includes group.

Merging Styles

You may have worksheets or macro sheets that contain the styles you want to use on other worksheets and macro sheets. You can copy styles between documents through a process called *merging*. But you must take into consideration the fact that *all* styles from the source document are merged in; unless you specify otherwise, these replace styles in the target document having the same name.

To copy styles from a source document to a target document, complete the following steps:

1. Open both documents and activate the document that will receive the styles.

2. Choose the Format **S**tyle command.

3. Choose the **D**efine >> button.

4. Choose the **M**erge button. The Merge Styles dialog box shown in figure 8.39 appears.

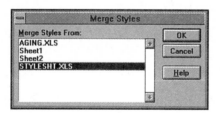

FIG. 8.39

Use the Merge Styles dialog box to designate from which document you want to merge styles.

5. Select from the **M**erge Styles From list the source document that contains the styles you want to copy.

6. Choose OK. You see an alert box (see fig. 8.40).

   You only get the alert box if the source sheet has different definitions for styles that are on the target sheet. If all the styles are the same or new, Excel goes ahead with the merge.

FIG. 8.40

Excel asks whether you want to replace existing style names with merging styles that have the same name.

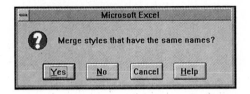

7. If the source document contains styles with the same name as styles in the target document, select one of these alternatives:

Select **Yes** if you want the source styles to replace styles with the same name in the target document.

Select **No** if you want to merge all styles except those with the same name.

Select Cancel if you don't want to merge styles after all.

Excel returns you to the Style dialog box.

8. Choose the Close button in the Style dialog box to close the dialog box without applying a style to the current selection.

Redefining Styles

In addition to saving time used in applying multiple formats, styles also save you time when you need to reformat a document. If your document uses styles, you need only to redefine the style, and all cells using that style immediately reformat to match the style's new definition.

If you decide that you need a format different from the one used in an existing style, you have two choices: create a new style for use with new formatting, or redefine an existing style. The advantage to redefining an existing style is that all cells currently assigned to that style update to use the new formats in the redefined style. This feature makes reformatting all the headings, titles, dates, or totals in a document an easy task. If you redefine the formats associated with a style named Headings, for example, all cells that use the Headings style take on the new format definition.

T I P The capability of redefining styles combined with the merge capability can be very useful in formatting sheets for both screen display and printing. You can have two source documents, one with Printer Styles, and switch back and forth as needed.

Redefining a Style by Example

To redefine a style by using an example, complete the following steps:

1. Select a cell that is formatted with the style you want to redefine.

2. Format the cell so that it has the new formats you want for the style's definition.

3. Apply the style name to the cell as you did when you first applied the style. See "Creating a Style by Example" to review the instructions, and use either the toolbar or the Format Style command.

4. When a dialog box similar to the one in figure 8.41 appears, choose one of these alternatives:

    Select Yes to redefine the existing style.

    Select No to keep the existing style and apply it again to the cell.

    Select Cancel to make no changes to the style or cell.

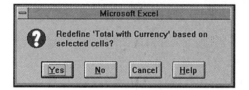

FIG. 8.41

This dialog box appears when you redefine a style by example.

Redefining a Style by Command

If a style is complicated or if you know exactly how you want to redefine the style, you probably want to redefine the style through dialog boxes. To redefine a style through dialog boxes, complete the following steps:

1. Choose the Format Style command.

2. Choose the Define >> button to expand the Style dialog box.

3. Select the style you want to redine from the Style Name box.

4. In the Style Includes group, clear check boxes that you do not want the style to have.

5. Select the appropriate Change buttons, making the changes you want to the formats defined for the style.

6. Choose OK to redefine the style and apply it to the current cell. Choose Add to redefine the style and keep the dialog box open for more definitions.

7. Choose Close to close the dialog box without applying the style to the selected cell, or choose OK to close the dialog box and apply the redefined style to the selected cell(s).

Redefining the Default (Normal) Style

The default, or global, format is stored in Excel's Normal style format. If you type an unformatted cell, Excel uses the Normal style. If you redefine the Normal style, all the cells that you did not format separately change to match the new Normal definition. If you delete formats from a cell, the cell is reset to the Normal style. Normal style is also used for the column and row headings fonts and as the default font for print headers and footers.

To redefine the Normal style, redefine the formats associated with that style by using either the style by example or the dialog box method.

Deleting Styles

If you no longer use a style, delete it to prevent clutter and make other styles more accessible. To delete a style, complete the following steps:

1. Choose the Format Style command.

2. From the Style Name list, select the style you want to delete. You cannot delete Excel's predefined styles.

3. Choose the Define >> button.

4. Choose the Delete button.

5. If you want the cell to return to Normal style, choose OK or Close. If you want to apply a new style, select the style and choose OK.

Controlling the Worksheet Display

You can change many characteristics of Excel's worksheet display so that worksheets and databases are displayed in a custom-designed appearance. By removing grid lines, row and column headings, and scroll bars, you can create windows that appear to be custom programmed.

Formatting the Entire Worksheet

Set formats when you begin your worksheet. After planning your worksheet and drawing thumbnail sketches, set the entire worksheet to the most common formats you plan to use. If you know that you want your entire worksheet to use a particular font and size or if you want all numbers formatted in a certain way, for example, you can make these choices before you begin building your worksheet. To set formats for the entire worksheet *before* you make any other entries, complete the following steps:

1. Select the entire worksheet by clicking to the left of the column A header or by pressing Shift+Ctrl+space bar.

2. Choose the appropriate commands from the Format menu; then select the formatting options that you want to apply to your entire worksheet.

3. Use the worksheet or save it as a template or in a workbook if you want to preserve these formats and workspace settings for future use.

Hiding Row and Column Headings

You can create special displays in Excel for data-entry forms, on-screen information, and help screens. These displays appear as they would in an uncluttered paper printout when you remove row and column headings. Choose the **O**ptions **D**isplay command and clear the **R**ow & Column Headings check box. This action does not affect the row and column headings for printing.

Displaying Formulas

You need to display formulas on-screen or in your printout at the following particular times: when debugging your worksheet (finding and correcting problems), when reviewing an unfamiliar worksheet, or when printing a documentation copy of the worksheet for future reference. To show the formulas in a worksheet, choose the **O**ptions **D**isplay command and select the **F**ormulas check box.

When printing a worksheet to show formulas, make sure that the Row & Column Headings check box is selected from the Page Setup dialog boxes.

Turning Off Grid Lines and Changing Grid Color

Turning off the grid lines displayed on-screen gives a better appearance to final results. But you may want the grid lines on while you build formulas or place text boxes and objects. To turn the screen grid lines on or off, choose the **Options Display** command, and select or clear the Grid lines check box.

Figure 8.42 illustrates how a corporate information system front-end can be displayed without grid lines. This same procedure also makes data-entry worksheets look more like paper forms. In figure 8.42, the row and column headings, Status Bar, and scroll bars also have been turned off with the **Options Workspace** command. (To turn off these options on your screen, clear the **S**tatus Bar, **S**croll Bars, and Fo**r**mula Bar options.)

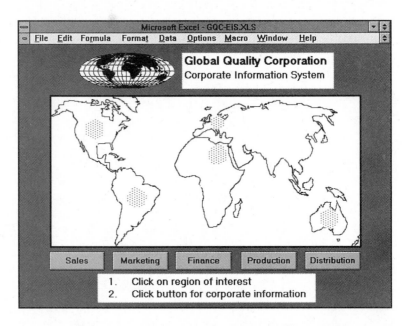

FIG. 8.42

Turning off grid lines enhances graphic menu systems and data-entry forms.

You also can change the color of your grid lines and headings. Complete the following steps:

1. Choose the **Options Display** command.

2. Select Gridline & Heading **C**olor by clicking the down arrow or by pressing Alt+C, and then Alt+down arrow.

3. Select the color you want to apply.

4. Choose OK or press Enter.

If you want to color individual cell or range contents, use the Format Patterns command or the Cell Color tool described earlier in this chapter.

Protecting Worksheets

If you develop Excel worksheets for use by inexperienced operators, if you create worksheets for sale, or if you work in the mistake-filled hours after midnight, you will find this section helpful. With Excel, you can protect cells, graphical objects, and windows. If you need to protect confidential or proprietary information, you also can hide formulas so that they do not appear in the Formula Bar. And you can use a password to prevent unauthorized people from changing the protection status or the display of hidden information.

The procedure for protecting a worksheet and its contents involves two commands. The first command formats the cells or objects that you want to be unprotected. The second command turns on protection for all the cells or objects that have not been unprotected.

Unprotecting and Hiding Formulas

Cell protection is a valuable feature that prevents someone from accidentally entering data on top of a formula and prevents unauthorized users from changing your formulas. You also can specify whether a cell's contents are visible in the Formula Bar. Even when the cell contents are hidden from the Formula Bar, the cell's value or formula results still appear in the worksheet.

The default format for all cells is protected and visible. Using the following steps, you can change cell formats to be unprotected or hidden. Protection and hiding do not take effect until you choose the Options Protect Document command.

To unprotect or hide a cell's contents, complete the following steps:

1. Select the cell or range that you want to unprotect or whose contents you want to hide from the Formula Bar.

2. Choose the Format Cell Protection command to display the Cell Protection dialog box shown in figure 8.43.

FIG. 8.43

Use the Cell Protection
dialog box to remove
cell protection and
hide cells.

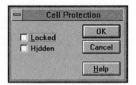

3. Clear the **L**ocked check box to mark the cell or range as one that can be changed.

4. Select the **H**idden check box to mark the cell or range as one whose contents do not show in the Formula Bar. You can continue to change all cells on the worksheet and see any cell contents until you turn on protection for the worksheet.

5. Choose OK or press Enter.

Turning On Protection

To turn on protection, complete the following steps:

1. Choose the **O**ptions **P**rotect Document command. The Protect Document dialog box appears.

2. Select what you want to protect: **C**ells, **W**indows, or **O**bjects.

3. If you prefer, enter a password in the **P**assword text box. You can include numbers, spaces, and upper- and lowercase characters.

4. Choose OK or press Enter.

Protected windows, cells, and objects cannot be moved, sized, or formatted. Protect objects that you want to lock into place on a worksheet, and protect windows that are prepositioned for novice users.

Whether or not you enter a password in the Protect Document dialog box, worksheet protection is turned on when you select protection options. Excel then does not ask for a password. To turn it off, choose the **O**ptions Un**p**rotect Document command.

To unprotect your worksheet, choose the **O**ptions Un**p**rotect Document command, type the password in the **P**assword text box, and choose OK.

After you protect the worksheet, look through some of the menus. Notice that most of the commands are grayed and unusable.

Don't forget your password. If you do, you cannot get back in and change the worksheet. Here are a few helpful hints for choosing passwords:

- Remember the characters that you capitalize in a password. Excel passwords differentiate between upper- and lowercase letters.

- Avoid using passwords that are easy to figure out, such as the following commonly used choices: your mother's maiden name, your spouse's maiden or middle name, your birthdate, or your employee number.

- Don't stick your password to the computer with a piece of tape. (Some people do.)

- Use symbols or uncommon capitalization that you will not forget.

- Have a senior officer in the company keep a confidential list of passwords to ensure that a password is accessible if the original guardian isn't.

- Change passwords whenever you doubt security.

Chapter Summary

Many people who use spreadsheets learn only the basic procedures for entering, editing, formatting, and printing. After you read Chapter 16, "Printing Worksheets," you will know enough to start creating and using Excel worksheets. By exploring Excel's numerous other worksheet capabilities, however, you will be able to use your knowledge to improve your work.

If you plan to learn more about Excel at this time, congratulations. From here, you probably should scan Chapter 10, "Using Functions," and then read Chapter 11, "Building Systems and Managing Multiple Windows," and Chapter 12, "Linking and Consolidating Worksheets." These chapters are useful in nearly all business and engineering situations.

Drawing and Placing Graphics in Worksheets

With Excel, you have the power to communicate with emphasis and polish. Your Excel worksheets can contain more than just numbers; the layouts can include any of the following elements that add information and value to your reports:

- Drawings composed of lines, arrows, ovals, circles, rectangles, and squares.

- Text boxes containing titles or paragraphs of word-wrapped text.

- Embedded charts and text from other Windows applications.

- Pictures of charts or worksheet ranges that are updated automatically when you update the charts or ranges.

- Professional graphics, illustrations, or logos from Windows drawing programs or scanned artwork.

- Macros linked to graphic objects so that selecting an object runs a macro.

Excel's information and analysis systems now can carry out more functions, in less time and at a fraction of the cost, than many high-end executive or management information systems. Excel's analytical and charting power, combined with worksheet graphics and macros, provides the publishing and design capability of systems costing more than $100,000.

Figures 9.1, 9.2, 9.3, and 9.4 show how you can enhance information displays, program controls, and printed reports by using the tools described in this chapter and in the charting sections.

Figure 9.1 shows an Excel worksheet that is the front-end to a management information system. This system enables users to retrieve business information from global divisions. Users click a shaded area of the world map, and then click one of the macro buttons at the bottom of the screen. The shaded pattern sets off areas where the business is involved. The shaded pattern actually is a shaded oval with no border; each oval has a macro assigned to it. The buttons at the bottom of the screen are macro buttons, described in Chapters 27 through 30. Two graphics have been imported from other Windows applications: the globe and the world map. Text boxes create the title at the top and the instructions at the bottom. **O**ptions **D**isplay and **O**ptions **W**orkspace settings have been changed to remove gridlines, row and column headings, scroll bars, and so on.

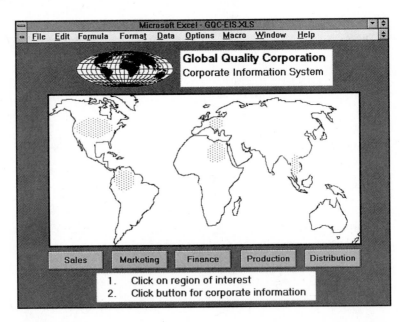

Figure 9.2 shows the use of charts, linked cell pictures, text boxes, ovals, and arrows. Shading sets off screen areas. The chart titles and analysis box are created with text boxes. The arrow and oval are drawn with

tools from the Drawing toolbar. The two charts are embedded charts. The small bar chart in the lower-right corner was drawn on top of the larger chart. For better positioning, text boxes with invisible (None) borders and fills are used for chart titles. The numeric table at the top-right corner shows stock details for the last three months. This chart was created by using a picture of cells from the stock data worksheet and embedding and expanding the cell picture on the worksheet. Later in this chapter, you learn how double-clicking embedded cells displays the worksheet area from which the picture came.

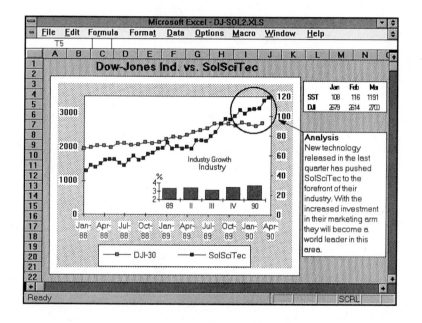

FIG. 9.2

Combine embedded and overlapped charts and cell pictures for a concise display of much information.

Figure 9.3 shows how Excel's graphic capabilities can enhance even simple worksheet information. Shading and thick underlines delineate information. Text boxes aligned with row and column grids create the column titles. You can perform this technique by holding down the Alt key as you draw the text boxes. Each text box is text-center aligned and has a shadow border.

Figure 9.4 shows an accounts receivable database. The worksheet is set up so that all the aging analysis is in one screen. Light shading helps differentiate parts of the screen. A database below the screen contains accounts receivable information. By typing into cell D6 a criteria for the number of days overdue, a list of overdue accounts is generated in the table at the lower left. Clicking the macro button at the top-left corner extracts data from the database to fill out the table. Chapter 24 explains how to extract a list of information from a database; Chapters 27 through 30 explain how to create a macro and assign it to a button to automate the process.

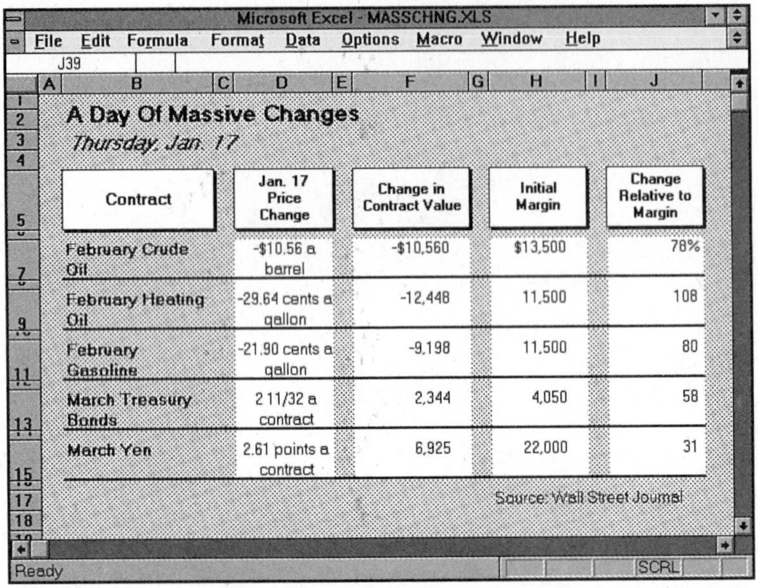

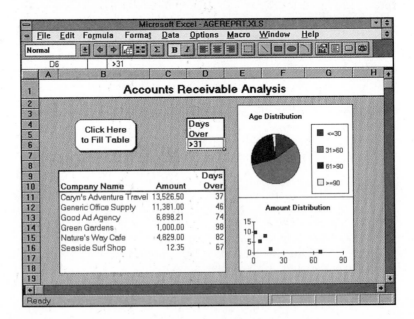

FIG. 9.3

Shading and borders make even simple tables attractive and easy to read.

FIG. 9.4

Get the big picture quickly by combining different views of the same information.

The two charts are linked to the same data to display aged receivables in two different ways. The information to create the charts comes from a database analysis that uses the **D**ata **T**able command and DSUM( ) function. Chapter 13 describes the **D**ata **T**able command. Chapter 26 describes how to analyze a database using a data table combined with DSUM( ) functions.

For Related Information:

FROM HERE...

◄◄ "Controlling the Worksheet Display," p. 306.

►► "Using the ChartWizard," p. 651.

►► "Embedding a Chart Document," p. 689.

Creating Graphic Objects

Excel worksheets can contain graphic objects that appear on-screen and print on the worksheet printout. These objects reside in layers that cover the worksheet.

 Nearly all work with worksheet graphics requires a mouse. Few features are available for graphic objects without the mouse. One of the few tasks you can perform with a keyboard is take a picture of a worksheet range or chart and paste it onto the worksheet.

Using the Drawing Tools

The Excel toolbars come with a collection of drawing tools to help you produce an attractive worksheet. The toolbars enable you to click a tool, and then immediately draw, shade, or outline on the worksheet. The section "Using the Toolbar" in Chapter 2 describes how to use toolbars. You can customize toolbars as described in Chapter 33.

T   I   P   Some drawing tools perform two functions. If you Shift+click a tool, you will see the alternate function for the tool in the Status Bar at the bottom of the window. You may want to save toolbar space by removing those tools that are duplicated with Shift+click.

T   I   P   You cannot draw directly on an Excel chart, but you can create floating text that *wraps* in text boxes. You also can paste graphic objects (for example, drawings of cars or trains) into charts, creating a picture chart in which objects replace column, bar, or line markers. This Excel feature is covered in detail in Chapter 19, "Formatting Charts."

Two toolbars contain drawing tools: the Drawing toolbar and the Microsoft Excel 3.0 toolbar. The Microsoft Excel 3.0 toolbar is a good compromise of a combination of general tools. The Drawing toolbar (see fig. 9.5) is dedicated to many drawing tools (see table 9.1). Some tools on other toolbars, such as font formatting and alignment tools, also are helpful. If you need a specialized collection of drawing tools, see Chapter 33 to learn how to drag the tools you need onto your own custom toolbar.

If no toolbar is displayed, choose the Toolbar command, select the toolbar, and choose OK. If a toolbar is displayed, click with the right mouse button on the toolbar, and select the toolbar you want from the shortcut menu.

FIG. 9.5

Tools give you instant access to make drawing easier.

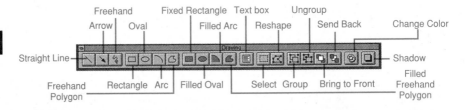

Table 9.1. Drawing Tools

Drawing Tool	Function
Arc tool	Draws an arc.
Arrow tool	Draws an arrow.
Bring to front tool	Brings a selected object above other objects.
Change color tool	Changes selected cell foreground or object color. Each click cycles to next color in palette. Shift-click to cycle backwards.

Drawing Tool	Function
Filled arc tool	Draws a filled arc.
Filled oval tool	Draws a filled oval or circle.
Filled freehand polygon	Draws a polygon or freehand shape that closes end points.
Filled rectangle tool	Draws a filled rectangle or square.
Freehand polygon tool	Draws a polygon or freehand shape.
Freehand tool	Draws smooth curves.
Group object tool	Groups together selected objects.
Line tool	Draws lines.
Oval tool	Draws ovals or circles.
Rectangle tool	Draws rectangles or squares.
Reshape tool	Reshapes a freehand line by dragging at points along the line.
Select object tool	Selects groups of objects by dragging a rectangular marquee around them.
Send to back tool	Sends selected object behind other objects.
Shadow tool	Draws a shadow behind text boxes and buttons most shapes.
Lines tool	Draws straight lines.
Text box tool	Draws boxes for word-wrapped text.
Ungroup object tool	Separates the selected group into individual objects.

To use most of the drawing tools, you click the desired tool and drag the mouse pointer across the worksheet to create the object. After you create the object, the easiest way to change borders, colors, and thicknesses is to click the object with the right mouse button to display a shortcut menu.

Using Drawing Shortcut Menus

You can save much time when you are drawing and formatting in Excel with the use of shortcut menus. To display a menu applicable to any changeable item—the worksheet background, an object you are drawing, or even the toolbar—use the right mouse button to click the item. A shortcut menu, like the one in figure 9.6, appears under the pointer. Click the command you want with left or right button.

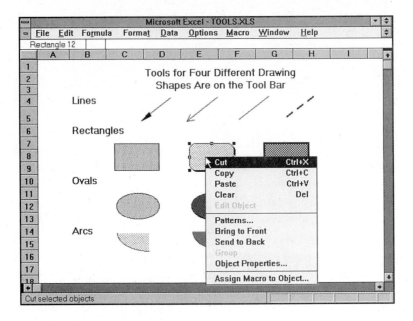

FIG. 9.6

Click with the right
mouse button to
display shortcut menus.

Drawing Lines, Ovals, Rectangles, and Arcs

With the drawing tools available in the toolbar, you can add enhancements to your worksheet. These enhancements include boxes and arrows that pinpoint specific data, shadow box frames, simple logos, and special macro buttons.

You use the lines, ovals, rectangles, and arcs as basic drawing elements in Excel. After formatting your worksheets with patterns and line widths, you can layer and combine these simple shapes to create more complex drawings. If the Excel drawing tools don't produce the result you need, you can paste in drawings created with Windows applications programs, such as Windows Paintbrush, CorelDRAW!, or Micrografx Designer. Or you can use the free applets, such as Microsoft Draw and WordArt, that come with many Microsoft applications.

The process of pasting drawings from other applications into Excel is explained in Chapter 31, "Using Excel with Windows Applications," and later in this chapter under the heading "Importing Graphics." Embedding drawings from applets is explained later in this chapter and in Chapter 12.

To draw a line, oval, rectangle, or arc, complete the following steps:

1. Select the drawing tool you want by clicking it. The mouse pointer symbol is replaced with a cross hair symbol.

2. Move the cross hair to where you want to start the drawing.

3. Follow these procedures if you want to constrain drawing to certain positions:

   Hold down the Shift key to keep lines vertical, horizontal, or at 45 degrees; ovals and arcs circular; and rectangles square.

   Or, hold down the Alt key to align the corner of the object with cell gridlines.

4. Drag the cross hair until the object has the size and orientation you want.

5. Release the mouse button to complete the object.

Figure 9.7 shows only a few of the shapes, patterns, borders, and shadows you can draw with Excel tools.

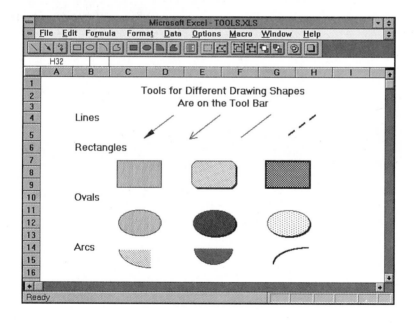

FIG. 9.7

Drawing tools produce many different shapes.

The object is selected when you finish. Selected objects display black handles at the edges and corners of an invisible rectangular frame enclosing the object. Objects must be selected before you can format or change them. You can use functions explained later in this chapter to change the lines, borders, and patterns used in an object.

To deselect a tool after you have clicked it, click it again or press Esc. To remove a graphic object, you must delete it. The procedure for deleting is explained later in this chapter.

If you want to draw multiple objects using the same tool, double-click the tool. The tool stays selected when you finish drawing an object. To return to normal pointer, click the same tool again or press Esc.

T I P

If you find that objects print in a slightly different location than they appear on the displayed worksheet, preview the worksheet by using the File Print Preview command. Make sure that you have the printer selected that you will be printing to. Choose the Zoom option to see the location of printed objects.

Drawing and Reshaping Freehand Objects

Excel has freehand drawing tools that enable even the non-artist to produce good work. The program offers three freehand drawing tools and one tool that enables you to reshape a freehand drawing after it's completed. The three freehand drawing tools enable you to draw smooth freehand shapes or polygons, which are shapes with many straight sides. Either type of freehand can be filled. The following table explains how you can use the freehand tools:

Freehand Tool	Function
Drawing tool	Draws smooth freehand lines.
Freehand polygon tool	Draws straight lines between clicks; draws smooth lines with drags.
Filled freehand polygon tool	Draws like the freehand polygon tool, but the end points automatically close and white fills the figure.

The Reshape tool enables you to drag an existing line end point in a freehand shape to a new position.

Figure 9.8 shows freehand drawing with each of the three tools. Notice that you can draw smooth curves with either of the polygon tools as well as the drawing tool. You can draw smooth curves by dragging the tool rather than clicking at end points.

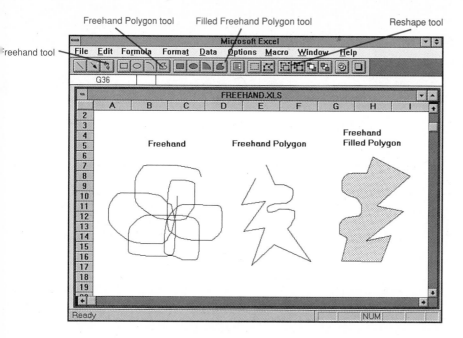

FIG. 9.8

You can draw
freehand or polygon
shapes.

To draw with one of the freehand tools, complete the following steps:

1. Click one of the freehand tools.

   The pointer changes to a cross hair.

2. Move the cross hair to where you want to begin drawing.

3. Draw with one of these techniques.

Drawing tool	Hold down the mouse button and move the pointer to draw any shaped line.
Freehand Polygon tool	Click to set a line end, move to where you want the next end, and click. Click another end and so on. Excel draws a straight line between each click. Draw smooth lines by holding down the mouse and dragging the cross hairs.
Filled Freehand Polygon tool	Follow the same technique as used for drawing a freehand polygon.

4. End the drawing by double-clicking at the last point.

Reshaping a freehand line is amazing the first time you see it done. After you draw a shape and then click the Reshape tool, you find that the shape is composed of small lines connected by movable handles called *nodes*. You can drag any one of these nodes to change the shape.

To reshape a freehand or polygon object, complete the following steps:

1. Select the freehand or polygon object.

   If it is an unfilled object, move the pointer so that it changes to an arrowhead with its tip on the line, and then click. If you have trouble clicking a line, use the Select tool to enclose the object you want to select. (The Select tool is described elsewhere in this chapter.)

2. Click the Reshape tool. The tool appears as a polygon with handles at each corner.

3. Move the pointer to a handle, and drag the handle to a new location.

4. Click in the background when you are done.

Figure 9.9 shows the previous figure's shapes selected with the Reshape tool. Figure 9.10 shows one of these shapes with it's corner being *stretched* to a new location.

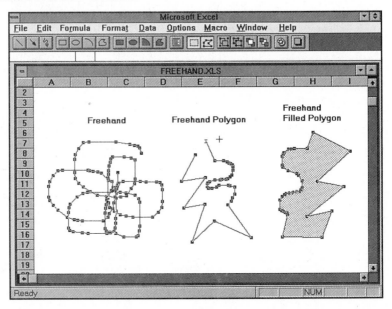

FIG. 9.9

Freehand objects selected with the Reshape tool show handles that can be moved.

Drawing Text Boxes

Excel enables you to place text boxes of word-wrapped text anywhere on the worksheet. You can edit and format the text in these miniature pages just as you edit and format text in most Windows word processing software. Figures 9.1 through 9.4 show how you can enhance a worksheet or chart with text.

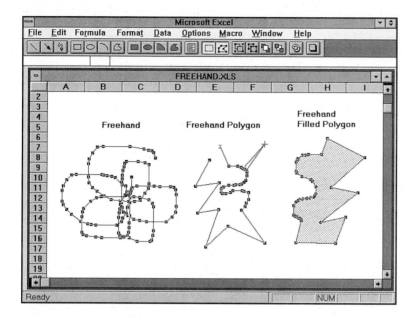

FIG. 9.10

Handles can be dragged to new locations with the Reshape tool.

When positioned over worksheet tables, text boxes make excellent titles. Because text boxes *float* in a layer over the worksheet, you can position a title of any size anywhere without affecting worksheet row or column positions.

The Forma**t A**lignment command also can help you center a title across selected cells. Select the cells in which you want the text centered, type the title, press Enter, click the Center selection tool or choose the Forma**t A**lignment command, and select the Center **A**cross Selection option.

T I P

To draw a text box, complete the following steps:

1. Click the Text box tool. The mouse pointer becomes a cross hair.

   Hold down the Shift key if you want a square text box.

   Hold down the Alt key if you want the text box aligned with the cell grid.

2. Drag from one corner to the opposite corner where you want the text box.

3. Release the mouse button.

When you release the mouse button, a flashing insertion point appears in the text box, indicating that you can begin typing text. Type continuously (as you would with word processing software); the text wraps when you reach the margin. If you type more text than will fit in the box, the box contents scrolls so that you can see what you are typing; the full contents may not be visible. If you later decide to change the size or shape of the text box, the text inside wraps to fit the new shape.

To edit material in the text box, use the arrow keys to move the insertion point in the text. Press Ctrl+left arrow or right arrow to move by whole words. Use Del or Backspace to delete a character or selected characters. To insert new material, begin typing at the insertion point. To replace existing text, select the section to be replaced and type the new text. To select with the keyboard, hold down Shift as you move with the arrow keys. Select entire words by double-clicking the word or by pressing Shift+Ctrl+left arrow or right arrow.

Text in a text box is different from text in a cell. In a cell, all the words and characters must have the same format. In a text box, formats can vary. To change the format of text in a text box, select the text to be changed, and then format it by clicking the box with the right mouse to display a shortcut menu, or by choosing the Format menu and selecting Text, Font, or Patterns commands. Selecting the Automatic Size check box on the Format Text command menu makes the text box fit tightly around the text. You also can click the Bold and Italic icons in the toolbar to change characters, or click the Left, Right, or Center icons to change alignment of all text in the box.

T I P When you want to frame worksheet contents and include text, use a text box that has its pattern formatted with a fill of None.

Notice in figure 9.11 that you can rotate text in a text box. Figure 9.12 shows the Format Text dialog box used to rotate text and align it vertically or horizontally in the box. When you click a rotated text box to edit the text, the text box positions itself so that it can be read while you edit. Click outside the text box when you are finished editing.

FROM HERE...

For Related Information:

◄◄ "Choosing Commands from Shortcut Menus," p. 37.

◄◄ "Using the Toolbars," p. 47.

◄◄ "Changing Character Fonts, Sizes, Styles, and Colors," p. 257.

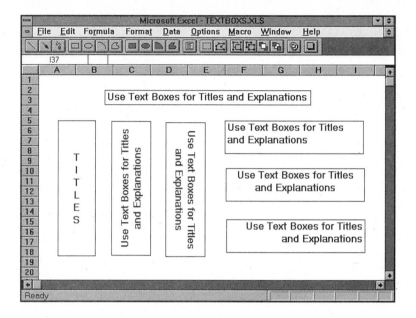

FIG. 9.11

Format, align, and rotate text boxes as needed.

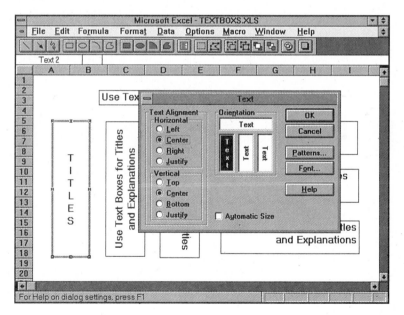

FIG. 9.12

Use the Format Text dialog box to rotate the contents of text boxes.

Combining Data and Charts on the Same Page

You can make worksheet information easier to understand by presenting related data and charts on the same page. With numeric forecasts, for example, you may need to show a table of census data and a chart of those forecasts; these related items can appear on the worksheet. You also probably have faced the problem of wanting to print multiple areas on the same page. With the following techniques, you learn how to take *pictures* of worksheet ranges, and then arrange them however you want on a printed page—much like a desktop publishing program.

You can combine worksheet ranges and charts on the same page in two ways. You can create a picture of a worksheet range or chart and paste it in the appropriate spot on a worksheet, or you can embed the picture in a worksheet. Pasted pictures are not updated when the original changes. Embedded pictures can be reformatted and updated when the original worksheet range or chart changes. Chapter 12 goes into more detail about embedding data from other Windows applications.

Displaying or printing charts and worksheets together on the same page is an important Excel feature. This feature enables you to create printouts that illustrate your point with a chart, along with presenting details in a worksheet. You even can add a text box on the same page to give written explanation. Figure 9.4 illustrates the use of charts on a worksheet.

Deciding between Pasting and Embedding Charts

You can put two types of chart pictures on an Excel worksheet: an *unlinked* picture of a chart and an *embedded* picture of a chart. Use unlinked pictures when you do not want the chart picture to change, even when the data changes. Because worksheets with unlinked charts load and recalculate faster, consider using an unlinked chart picture if your worksheet needs frequent recalculating, or if the chart will not require updating.

Embedded charts contain external references linking the embedded chart to the worksheet cells it was created from. When the data changes on the worksheet, the embedded picture changes. You can double-click an embedded chart to open the chart into a window, where you can use normal charting techniques to reformat the chart. Activating and formatting embedded charts is described in more detail in the chapters on charting.

To format or change an embedded chart, you double-click the chart to put it in a window. While it is in a window, you may be tempted to maximize the window during your formatting. You can, but don't. With the window maximized, you might use larger fonts and add arrows, legends, and gridlines that will not display well in the smaller size of the embedded chart.

T I P

Embedding Linked Pictures of Charts in a Worksheet

You can create embedded charts directly on the worksheet by using the ChartWizard and the procedures described in Chapters 17 and 18. If you already have an embedded chart you want to reuse or you have a chart in its own window that you want to embed, complete the following steps:

1. Select the chart by activating the chart document and choosing the **Chart Select Chart** command (if it is a chart document in its own window) or by clicking on an embedded chart.

2. Choose the **Edit Copy** command.

3. Activate the worksheet in which you want to paste the chart.

4. Select a cell that will be the upper-left corner for the picture.

5. Choose the **Edit Paste** command.

The picture appears on the worksheet, selected and ready for formatting. Figure 9.13 shows two charts pasted into a worksheet.

Embedded charts remain linked to the worksheet data they use. Even if you create an embedded chart by copying a chart from a document window, the embedded chart is linked to the worksheet that supplied the original data. Refer to the chapters on charting to learn how to activate and reformat embedded charts.

Pasting Unlinked Pictures of Charts in a Worksheet

If you want a picture of a chart that will not change when data changes and that is not linked to a worksheet, paste a chart picture. To paste pictures of charts to a worksheet, complete the following steps:

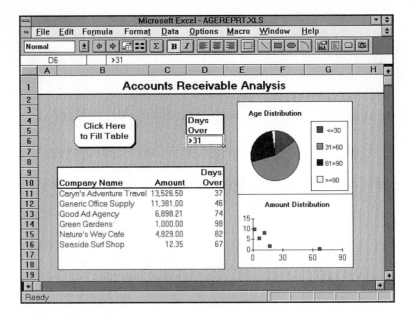

FIG. 9.13

Charts can be embedded on a worksheet so that they display and print on the same page.

1. Select the chart by activating the chart document and choosing the **C**hart Select **C**hart command (if it is a chart document in its own window) or by double-clicking an embedded chart.

2. Hold down the Shift key and choose the **E**dit **C**opy Picture command. The Copy Picture dialog box asks which picture you want (see fig. 9.14).

FIG. 9.14

You can copy a chart picture as it appears on-screen or as it appears when printed.

3. Select the copy options you want, depending on which picture appears better when pasted:

>   *Appearance*   As Shown on **S**creen copies the picture as it appears on-screen.

As Shown when **P**rinted copies the picture
with the resolution and formatting used
when printing.

Size   As Shown on **S**creen copies the size shown
on-screen.

As Shown when **P**rinted copies the printed
size.

4. If you select Appearance As Shown on **S**creen, you have the choice
   of selecting Format Picture or Format **B**itmap.

   You can edit a bitmap image by copying it into Paintbrush. A
   bitmap image has lower resolution when printed and loses quality
   when resized. You can edit a picture image in programs by using
   the Windows Metafile format through the Clipboard. You can edit a
   picture image by copying it into the Microsoft Draw applet that
   comes with many Microsoft applications. Editing and modifying
   embedded objects, such as these charts, is explained in Chapter 12.

5. Choose OK or press Enter.

6. Activate the worksheet in which you want to paste the chart.

7. Select a cell that will be the upper-left corner for the picture.

8. Choose the **E**dit **P**aste command.

The picture appears on the worksheet, selected and ready for formatting. Finding the best choice of these copy options, so that text and
charts appear accurately positioned, may depend on your printer and
the fonts available.

Embedding Pictures of Cells in a Worksheet

Linked or unlinked pictures of cells can help you get past layout or formatting obstacles you may face when building reports or displays. By
using embedded cell pictures, you can put different parts of one or more
worksheets next to each other on the same screen or the same printed
page.

Pictures of cells are like snapshots of a selected worksheet or macro
range. You can put those snapshots anywhere on the same or a different
worksheet or macro sheet. Figure 9.15 shows a picture of cells at the top-
right corner of the background worksheet. The smaller window shows
the area of the worksheet the cell picture came from. Each picture appears in its own box and can be formatted, sized, or moved separately.

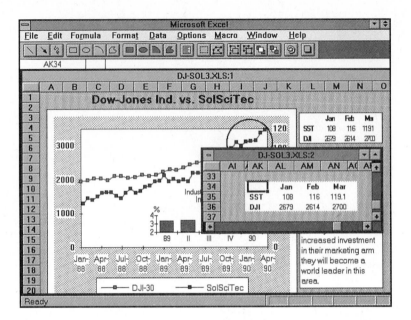

Pictures of cells link to original data even if the data is on a different worksheet.

Cell pictures give you the flexibility to organize your macro sheet or worksheet in the best way for data entry, analysis, or programming. You can copy reporting and print areas as pictures and arrange them on pages alongside text boxes and charts. You can have separate print areas all printed on the same page. If the cell pictures are linked, they will be updated when the source cells are changed.

Deciding between Linked or Unlinked

Pictures can be linked or unlinked. Linked cell pictures are updated when their original data is changed.

An advantage of linked cell pictures is that you can use them to create tables or boxes containing information from another area of the worksheet or macro. You can size the linked picture into a small box and double-click the box to display the source worksheet. It's like having a telescopic window to other parts of the worksheet.

T I P If you double-click an embedded cell picture, you are taken to the source of that picture, even if it is on another worksheet. To return to the last active cell before you double-clicked, press the Goto key, F5, and choose OK. Excel remembers the preceding location.

Embedded (linked) cell pictures are useful for data that changes frequently. However, worksheets with embedded cell pictures take longer to load and to recalculate. If your data does not change frequently, or if speed is critical, you might choose to use unlinked cell pictures.

Copying Linked Cell Pictures

To copy linked pictures of cells by using the Camera tool, complete the following steps:

1. Select the cells you want to use for the picture.

2. Click the Camera tool in the Utility or Microsoft Excel 3.0 toolbars. The mouse pointer becomes a cross hair.

3. Activate the worksheet or macro sheet in which you want the picture to appear.

4. Click the upper-left corner of the area where you want the cell picture to appear.

    The linked picture of cells is pasted into place with its upper-left corner at the cross hair.

To copy linked pictures of cells by using commands, complete the following steps:

1. Select the cells you want to use for the picture.

2. Choose the **Edit Copy** command.

3. Activate the worksheet or macro sheet and select the cell where you want the upper-left corner of the picture to appear.

4. Hold down the Shift key and choose the **Edit Paste Picture Link** command.

Pasted cell pictures are updated when data changes or when you change the worksheet display of the source cells. For example, Excel will update pasted picture cells when you change the display of the source cells by turning gridlines on or off.

To update cell pictures or change the formats in source cells, double-click the embedded cell picture. If the source macro sheet or worksheet for the cell picture is open, Excel activates and selects the range of the linked cells. If the source sheet is not open, Excel opens the sheet and selects the range. When the range is selected, change the data, formulas, or formats as desired. The cell pictures are updated automatically.

To return to your original location, press the Goto key, F5, then immediately press Enter. Goto remembers the preceding location.

Copying Unlinked Cell Pictures

To copy unlinked pictures of cells, complete the following steps:

1. Select the cells you want to use for the picture.

2. Hold down the Shift key and choose the **Edit C**opy Picture command.

3. Select the copy options you want, depending on which picture appears better when pasted:

    Appearance   As Shown on **S**creen copies the picture as it appears on-screen.

    As Shown when **P**rinted copies the picture as it appears when printed.

4. If you select Appearance As Shown on **S**creen, you have the choice of selecting Format Picture or Format **B**itmap.

    You can edit a bitmap image by copying it into Paintbrush. A bitmap image has lower resolution when printed. You can edit a picture image with programs using the Windows Metafile format through the Clipboard. You can edit a picture image by copying it into the Microsoft Draw applet that comes with many Microsoft applications. Editing and modifying embedded objects, such as these charts, is explained in Chapter 12.

5. Choose OK or press Enter.

6. Activate the worksheet or macro sheet and select the cell or object where you want the picture to appear.

7. Choose the **Edit P**aste command.

T I P   Unlinked pictures can display gridlines as well as row and column headings. If you do not want row and column headings or gridlines to appear on pictures of a worksheet, use the **O**ptions **D**isplay command to clear the **G**ridlines and Row & Column **H**eadings options in the original document.

Importing Graphics

If you aspire to produce worksheets that any graphic artist would be proud of, you aren't limited to the drawing tools in the Excel toolbar.

You can create drawings in almost any Windows graphics program, copy the drawings, and then paste them into your worksheet where you can resize and move them. You also can add pictures, photos, or hand drawings to your worksheet by scanning them with a digital scanner, copying the image, and pasting the image into the worksheet. Excel accepts any graphic that can be copied into the Clipboard in the Windows Metafile or bitmap format.

NOTE Many Windows applications come with applets, small window applications designed to enhance a major application. These applications are available by choosing the **E**dit Insert **O**bject command and selecting the applet you want to run. Chapters 12 and 31 describe some applets and their use with Excel.

Putting graphics in your worksheets can do more than just make the worksheets more attractive. Now you can put your company logo on worksheets; add architectural or engineering symbols to specifications, plans, or bids; add schematics or drawings that explain proposals; or create graphic *push-buttons* that run macros when clicked.

TIP If you frequently use the same graphics or pictures, you can save time by collecting them in an Excel worksheet. You can, for example, draw graphics and pictures with programs like Windows Paintbrush, Windows Draw, or CorelDRAW!, and then copy the graphics and paste them into a worksheet that acts as a scrapbook. Paintbrush and Windows Draw will insert embedded objects on your worksheet that can be edited by double-clicking. Chapters 12 and 31 explain more about these applets. Be sure to give the worksheet/scrapbook a descriptive name, such as TRNSPORT.XLS, BUSINESS.XLS, ENGNEER.XLS, SYMBOLS.XLS, and so on.

Storing your graphics and pictures in a worksheet makes it easy to find the graphic you want, copy it, and paste it into the worksheet you are working on. There's no need to start the Windows graphics program. Figure 9.16 shows part of an Excel worksheet serving as a scrapbook. You can store images like these in reduced size in a worksheet and resize the images after you paste them into the worksheet.

To copy graphics from another Windows program for use in Excel worksheets or macro sheets, complete the following steps:

1. Activate the drawing program and select the graphic you want to copy.

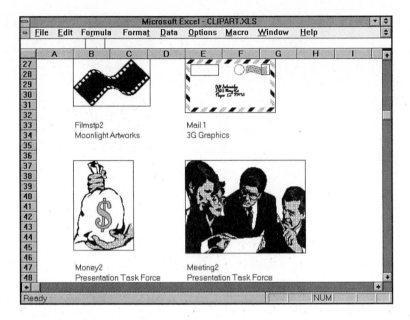

FIG. 9.16

Use a worksheet as a
scrapbook to store
frequently used
graphics or symbols.

2. Choose the **Edit Copy** command or the appropriate program procedure to copy the selected graphic to the Clipboard.

3. Activate Excel and select the cell or object where you want the
graphic to appear.

4. Choose the **Edit Paste** command.

After the graphic is on the Excel worksheet or macro sheet, you can treat
it like any other graphic object. You can link a macro to it, resize or
move it, or change its borders.

T I P   Clip art is artwork that professional artists have drawn and sold for
reuse by non-artists. Clip art usually comes in collections by subject
matter, such as transportation (trucks, cars, planes), business (dollar
symbols, people, computers), and so on. Clip art works with most
major graphics programs. A few programs, such as Microsoft Draw,
CorelDRAW!, Microsoft Publisher, and Word for Windows 2.0, include
collections of clip art.

For Related Information:

▶▶ "Linking Pictures of Worksheet Cells," p. 448.

▶▶ "Linking Worksheet Cells and Ranges," p. 453.

▶▶ "Embedding Data from Other Applications into Worksheets,"
   p. 1023.

▶▶ "Embedding Data in a Worksheet," p. 1034.

FROM HERE...

Working with Graphic Objects

You can format the graphics you draw or paste into Excel with different borders, patterns, and colors. You also can group multiple drawings into a single graphic, fix graphics to a cell location, change the order in which graphics overlap, and protect graphics from change.

Selecting Graphic Objects

In all Windows programs, you must select an item before you can change it. Graphic objects that have been selected are enclosed in an invisible rectangular *frame*. The corners and edges of the frame display black squares, or *handles*, that you use to move the object. Figure 9.17 shows a graphic object with frame and handles.

Each graphic object is identified by its type and a number that indicates the order in which it was created. The identifier of the selected object is displayed in the Reference Area to the left of the Formula Bar. Examples of identifiers include Rectangle 1, Arc 2, Oval 5, and Picture 8.

When you move the mouse to select an object, watch the mouse pointer. It must be shaped like an arrow to select the object. The pointer changes to an arrow over the inside of a filled object or picture and on the border of transparent objects, pictures, or text boxes.

To select a single object, move the mouse pointer over the object's border or center, then click. To select multiple objects, click the first object, and then hold down the Shift key as you click additional objects.

Using the keyboard, select all objects by choosing the Formula Select Special command then selecting the Objects option and pressing Enter. After all objects are selected, you can move the selection between them by pressing Tab or Shift+Tab.

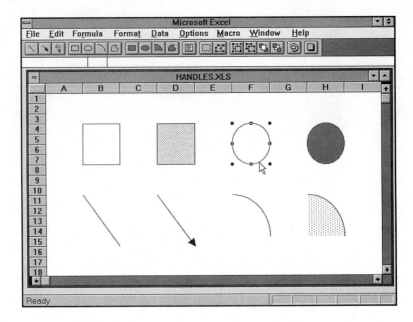

FIG. 9.17

You can move
selected objects
enclosed by black
handles.

Figure 9.18 shows a group of selected objects. If multiple objects are grouped closely together, you can select them by enclosing them with the Selection tool (see fig. 9.19). To use this method, click the Selection tool in the toolbar and drag the cross hair across all the objects. As you drag, a rectangular marquee encloses the objects. You must completely enclose an object to include it in the selection. When you release the mouse button, all enclosed objects are displayed with black handles and the marquee disappears.

To enlarge the area enclosed with the Selection tool, click again on the Selection tool and hold down the Shift key as you drag across additional objects. To select all graphic objects in a worksheet, choose the Formula Select Special command, select the Objects option, and choose OK.

If you want to exclude a few objects from a large group you have already selected, hold down the Shift or Ctrl key and click the individual objects you want to deselect. You can exclude a group of objects by clicking the Selection tool, holding down the Shift key, and dragging the mouse pointer across the group. To deselect all objects, press the Esc key or click a cell in the worksheet.

Graphic objects can have macros assigned to them. Clicking such an object causes the macro assigned to it to run. To select an object without running its assigned macro, press and hold the Ctrl key when you click the object.

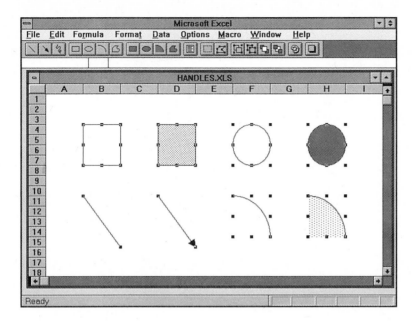

FIG. 9.18

Select a group of
objects with
Shift+click, Ctrl+click,
or with the Selection
tool.

FIG. 9.19

The Selection tool.

Deleting Graphic Objects

Deleting graphic objects is straightforward. Click the object to select it;
then press Del or Backspace or choose the Edit Clear command. When
deleting text boxes, make sure that you have the box selected and not
the text. Select a text box by clicking its edge.

If you accidentally delete an object that you want to keep, immediately
choose the Edit Undo command, or press Ctrl+Z.

Formatting Graphic Objects

Excel gives you a wide array of colors, patterns, and line styles to use for
formatting objects. You can change lines to arrows with heads of different weight and size. You also can change the thickness, style, color of
borders, and the fill pattern and color used in objects. Some objects
even can use rounded corners or shadow box options.

T I P The quickest way to display a formatting menu is to click an object with the right mouse button. Although you can release the button and the menu will stay under the pointer, it's more convenient to continue holding down the right mouse button and drag down to the command you want to choose.

Formatting Lines and Arrows

You can format lines for thickness, line style, and color. You also can put arrowheads on your lines. To format a line, complete the following steps:

1. Select the line you want to format.

2. Click the line with the right mouse button, choose Patterns from a shortcut menu, or choose the Forma**t P**atterns command. Figure 9.20 shows the Line Patterns dialog box.

T I P Click on the Arrow tool in the Drawing toolbar, drag from where you want the foot of the arrow to the tip, then release.

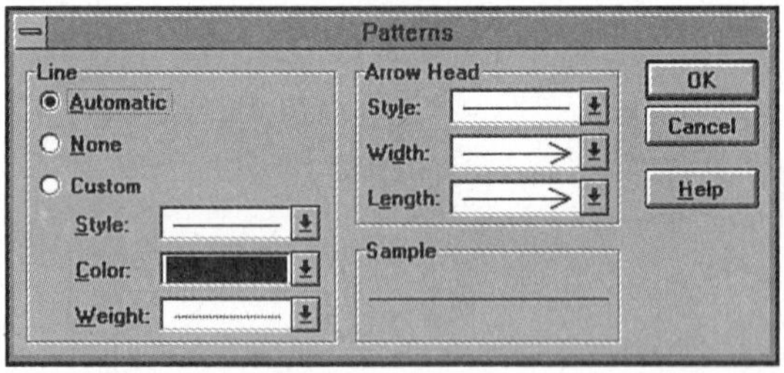

FIG. 9.20

Select lines and arrowhead styles from the Line Patterns dialog box.

3. Select from the Line options. To use the default line format, select **A**utomatic. Select **N**one for an invisible line. Select **C**ustom to select **S**tyle, **C**olor, and **W**eight of line from the pull-down list.

4. Select from the Arrowhead options if you want an arrow. Select from the St**y**le, Wi**d**th, and **L**ength pull-down lists to choose the type of arrowhead. You must choose an arrowhead from St**y**le, or Wi**d**th and **L**ength will not affect the line. Figure 9.21 shows the list for different arrowhead lengths.

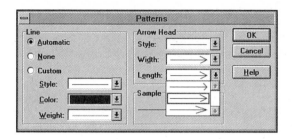

FIG. 9.21

Select the style, width, and length of arrow-head you prefer.

5. Check your selection in the Sample box at the lower-right corner of the line Patterns dialog box. Change your selections if necessary.

6. Choose OK or press Enter.

Figure 9.22 shows examples of different lines, weights, and arrowheads.

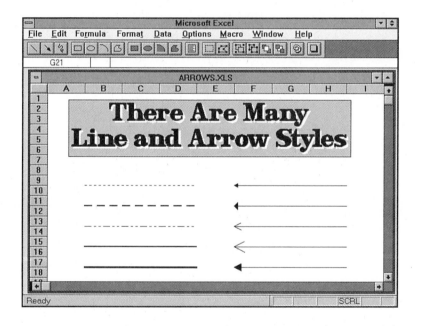

FIG. 9.22

You can create lines with different weights, colors, and arrowhead styles.

Formatting Borders and Patterns

All the graphic objects you draw in Excel can be formatted with different colors, patterns, and line styles or weights.

To change the fill pattern or border of an object, complete the following steps:

1. Select the object or objects.

2. Click the object with right mouse button, then choose Patterns from the shortcut menu; or double-click the object to display the Patterns dialog box; or choose the Format **P**atterns command if the object is an embedded chart or linked picture. Hold down the Ctrl key while clicking if the object has an assigned macro. Figure 9.23 shows the Patterns dialog box for a pattern that has been selected previously.

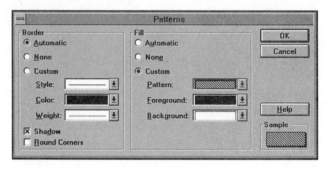

3. Select from the Border group the style, weight, and color of border. Click the down arrow to the right of a pull-down box to see the full list of selections.

4. Select the S**h**adow check box if the object needs a shadow.

5. Select from the Fill group the pattern and colors for the fill. Fill patterns use two colors. Select different colors from the **F**oreground or **B**ackground pull-down list to see how the color patterns appear. Select the Non**e** option if you want an invisible fill that lets the background show through.

6. Review your selection in the Sample box at the lower-right corner of the Patterns dialog box. Change your selections if necessary.

7. Choose OK or press Enter.

Figure 9.24 shows examples of patterns you can use to fill objects.

If you are unsure of which colors, weights, or patterns to use, or if you want to return to default colors, select the **A**utomatic option for these commands.

To format the internal portion of objects that are pictures linked to other documents, you must reformat the source document for the link. Open the source document by double-clicking the object. Then reformat the source document as you like. Use normal object formatting to format a picture's border or shadow.

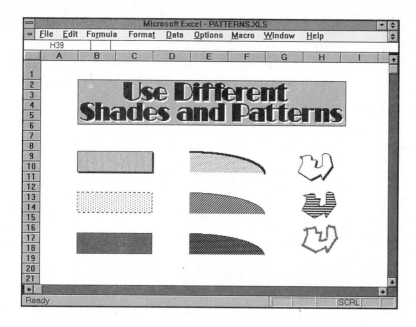

FIG. 9.24

Patterns use foreground and background colors.

To highlight important results, draw rectangles or ovals around cells. Then use the None option to fill the rectangle or oval, letting the worksheet data show through the rectangular or oval border.

T I P

Sizing, Moving, and Copying Graphic Objects

You can size and move graphic objects just as you would in other Windows programs.

To resize an object, select it so that you can see the black handles. Move the mouse pointer over a handle until the pointer becomes a cross hair. To change the size in one dimension (height or width), drag a handle in the middle of one side. To resize two sides, drag a corner handle.

To resize an object while keeping its proportions, hold down the Shift key and drag a corner handle. To see the proportions of an imported graphic or embedded chart that you are resizing, watch the Reference Area to the left of the Formula Bar. This area shows proportions as a percentage of the original object size.

To move an object, select it and drag the object to its new location. Be sure to drag objects that have an invisible (None) fill and all text boxes by their edges. If you drag an object by its black handle, you will resize it. If you need to move an object a long distance, cut the object to the Clipboard, move to the new location, and paste the object in place.

Move multiple objects by selecting them together, and then dragging them to the new location.

 To constrain movements to vertical or horizontal, hold down the Shift key while dragging. If you want the object to align on underlying cells, hold down the Alt key as you drag an object.

To cut or copy objects, select them and choose the Edit Cut or Copy command. Select the new location for the object, and choose the Edit Paste command.

Grouping Graphic Objects

Grouping objects together fuses them into a single object. When related objects are fused, they are easier to move and size. You can ungroup objects if you later need to separate them.

To group objects together, select the objects you want to group by using one of the multiple-selection techniques, and then choose the Format Group command. To separate a group into its individual elements, select the group and choose the Format Ungroup command.

Reordering Layers of Graphic Objects

Objects in Excel overlap each other in layers. Because objects overlap in the order in which they were created, the most recently drawn or pasted object appears in front. Figure 9.25 shows a text box that was created before the shaded box that partially covers it.

To reorder the layers so that the shaded box appears behind the text box as a shadow, move the shaded box to be slightly offset from the text box and choose the Format Send to Back command. Figure 9.26 shows the text box in front with a shadow box background. To bring an object to the front, select it and choose the Format Bring to Front command. To preserve these two as one object, use grouping, which is described in the previous section.

You can hide all graphics so that you can see the worksheet underneath the graphic objects. Hide all objects by choosing the Options Display command and selecting the Hide All option. Deselect the Hide All option to redisplay objects. Pressing Ctrl+6 toggles between normal object display, displaying placeholders and hidden objects.

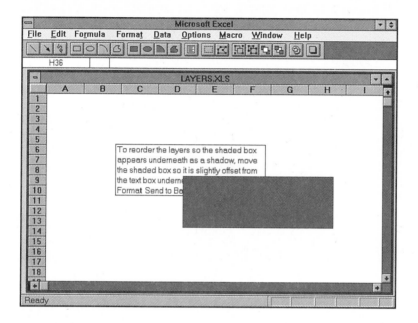

FIG. 9.25

The most recently created objects appear in front.

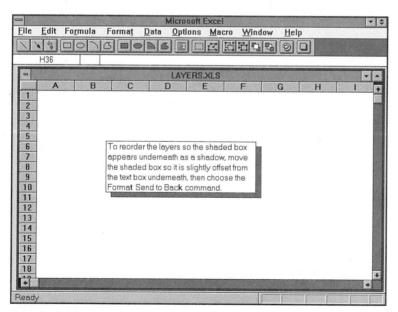

FIG. 9.26

Reorder layers of objects by bringing one to the front or sending one to the back.

Fixing Object Positions

You can position objects relative to their underlying cells in three ways. These three ways enable you to specify how an object behaves when you insert, delete, or change the dimensions of underlying rows and columns.

Drawn objects, such as text boxes, rectangles, and ovals, are attached to underlying cells; when you affect the underlying cells, the objects move and change shape. The Move and Size with Cells option is automatically selected with drawn objects; this option attaches the object to the cells under the object's top-left and lower-right corners. The Move and Size option is useful when you draw rectangles or ovals around specific data on the worksheet, or when you use lines or arrows drawn between two points. As the underlying sheet changes, the end-points of the object remain fixed, enclosing the data if the object is a rectangle or oval, and pointing to the correct items if the object is a line or arrow.

When first created, an embedded chart or pasted graphic is attached to the underlying cell at the upper-left corner of the object. An object moves with the cell during insertions, deletions, or dimension changes, but the size and proportion of the object remain the same. During cell changes, pictures and charts stay proportional, and they continue to look the way you want them to look.

Use the Move and Size with Cells option if you want an object to change size and shape relative to the worksheet cells it covers.

To change how an object is attached to underlying cells, complete the following steps:

1. Select the object.

2. Choose the Format Object Properties command, or click the object with the right mouse button and choose Object Properties. Figure 9.27 shows the Object Properties dialog box.

3. Select one of the following attachment options.

Move and Size with Cells	Attaches an object to the cells under the object's top-left and lower-right corners. The object moves or changes size with the underlying cells, rows, or columns. This is the normal attachment when objects are first drawn.
Move but Don't Size with Cells	Attaches the object to only the cell underlying the top-left corner of the object. The object moves with the cell during insertions or deletions, but it keeps

its original size and proportions. This is the normal attachment when graphics are pasted or charts are embedded.

Don't Move or Size with Cells
Objects are not attached to the underlying worksheet. They must be moved and sized by themselves.

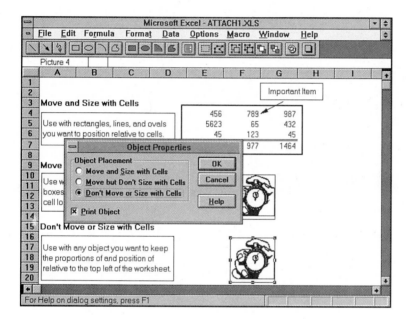

Object Properties controls how worksheet changes affect objects.

4. Choose OK or press Enter.

Use the **M**ove but Don't Size with Cells option for charts, pasted graphics, groups of lines, and rectangles and ovals you have created a logo or design with. This option keeps the graphics in position but prevents them from stretching.

If you don't want objects to change shape or move, use the **D**on't Move or Size with Cells option. This option preserves an object's shape and keeps it fixed in position relative to the top-left corner of the worksheet.

Figure 9.28 shows objects with different object properties. Figure 9.29 shows the same worksheet after a column is inserted.

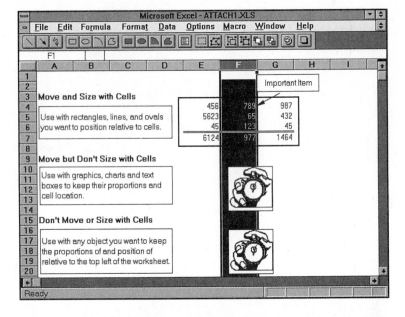

You can use three methods of attaching objects to the underlying worksheet.

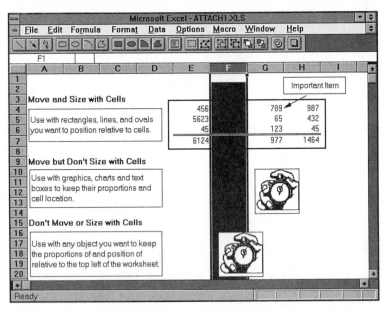

Attachment methods work differently when the underlying worksheet changes shape.

Protecting Graphic Objects

You can protect objects to keep other people from changing them. You protect objects just as you protect cells. Mark the objects you want to remain unprotected by choosing the Format Object Protection command and deselecting the Locked check box. To activate protection for the worksheet, choose the Option Protect Document command, select the Objects check box, and enter a password if desired. Choose OK. Those objects that were unlocked prior to document protection can be changed when the document protection is turned on.

Printing Graphic Objects

In most cases when you print, you want graphic objects to display, but you don't want macro buttons on worksheets to display. And that's exactly how Excel sets its defaults. All graphic objects print, except macro buttons.

If you want to change whether a graphic object or macro button prints, select the object and choose the Format Object Properties command. Select or clear the Print Object check box.

Hiding Objects

When you scroll windows or recalculate a worksheet that contains graphic objects, Excel redraws the objects. Because redrawing objects requires extra computer power, Excel's performance may slow down. Remember that Excel can show all objects, show placeholders for better performance, or hide all objects so that you can see the underlying worksheet. To speed up Excel's performance, change the display of objects. Choose the Options Display command, and select the Hide All option or Show Placeholders. Toggle between these display modes by pressing Ctrl+6. Behind the Display dialog box, you can see the shaded placeholders that take the place of graphic objects. Figure 9.30 illustrates the display options.

For Related Information:

▶▶ "Previewing the Document," p. 637.

FROM HERE...

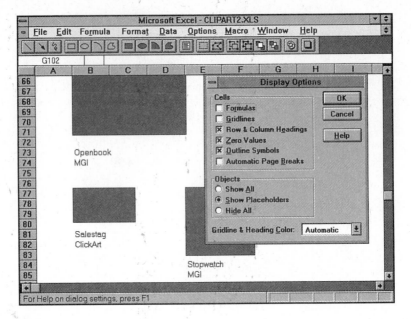

FIG. 9.30

For increased performance, choose to display object placeholders or hide objects.

Chapter Summary

Graphic elements, artwork, shading, and embedded charts all make your worksheets and screens more attractive. But they do much more. By using these elements properly, you can add emphasis to important points, lead the eye to critical data, and make information more accessible.

Many business people, engineers, and scientists like to see the overall picture, and then focus on the details of specific areas. By combining embedded charts, pictures of tables from the worksheet, and text boxes, you give these readers the opportunity to absorb information in several ways. They can scan a chart quickly for trends, examine the adjacent backup table for specific numbers, and read the text box for explanation.

Now that you are familiar with graphics, you can add a new dimension to your worksheet by assigning macros to graphic objects. When the operator clicks an object, the macro assigned to that object runs. This feature enables you to put icons on worksheets to perform specific operations. Clicking a small picture of a printer could, for example, print the selected area, or clicking a map section could display reports for offices in that area.

One form of graphics mentioned in this section is embedded charts. For more information on using charts, see the charting section, Chapters 17-20. If you want to learn more about working with graphics that are brought in from programs, such as Windows Paintbrush, CorelDRAW!, or Microsoft Draw, read Chapter 31, "Using Excel with Windows Applications."

Using Functions

E xcel uses prebuilt worksheet functions to perform math, text, or logical calculations or to find information about the worksheet. Whenever possible, you should use functions rather than writing your own formulas. Functions are fast, take up less space in the Formula Bar, and reduce the chance for typographical errors.

Functions act on data in much the same way that equations act on numbers. Functions accept information, referred to as *arguments*, and return a result. In most cases, the result is a math calculation, but functions also return results that are text, references, logical values, arrays, or information about the worksheet. The functions listed in this chapter can be used in worksheets and in macro sheets. Your macros can have all the analytical capability of worksheets.

In the first part of the chapter, you learn what functions are and how to use them. The latter part of the chapter is a directory of the majority of Excel's approximately 200 worksheet functions with descriptions of the arguments that the functions use. The directory is segmented by types of functions and includes examples for many of the functions.

Understanding Functions

Functions accept data through arguments. You enter arguments, enclosed in parentheses, after the function name. Each function takes specific types of arguments, such as numbers, references, text, or logical values. Functions use these arguments in the same way that equations use variables.

If, for example, you want to write an equation to determine a mortgage or loan payment, you need the following information:

Argument	Description
rate	Interest rate per period
nper	Number of periods
pv	Present value (starting value of loan)
fv	Future value (ending value at loan completion)

Because the equation for an amortized loan payment requires many complex terms, you are more likely to make typographical errors. In addition, Excel solves an equation you enter more slowly than it solves a built-in function for the same operation.

Instead of manually entering a long equation to calculate the loan payment, you can use one of Excel's worksheet functions, PMT(). In parentheses, you enter the values or references for the information needed to do the calculation. The PMT() function is entered in this form:

=PMT(*rate,nper,pv,fv,type*)

The arguments here give the same information as just described, but with the addition of the argument *type*. Some functions return different answers depending on the value of *type*. In the case of PMT(), Excel can calculate payments for different types of loans depending on the value used for *type*. An actual PMT() function might look like this:

=PMT(Mo.Int,A12,B36)

Here, Mo.Int is the name of the cell that contains the monthly interest rate (*rate*), A12 contains the number of months (*nper*), and B36 contains the present value (*pv*). The arguments *fv* and *type* are optional and were not used in this calculation of a simple mortgage payment.

Excel uses various types of arguments for different types of information. As shown in table 10.1, you often can tell the required types of arguments by the names of the arguments. The argument names appear in the parentheses in this chapter's directory, in the Microsoft reference manual, in the on-line Excel Help file, and in the Formula Bar when functions are pasted into formulas with the Formula Paste Function command.

Table 10.1. Types of Arguments

Argument	Type	Sample Function and Argument Names
text	text	**LEFT(*text*,*num_chars*)** (in quotation marks or a reference)
value	value	**LOOKUP(*lookup_value*,*array*)** (text in quotation marks, a number, or a reference)
num	numeric	**RIGHT(*text*,*num_chars*)** (a number or a reference)
reference	cell reference	**COLUMN(*reference*)**
serial_number	date/time number	**DAY(*serial_number*)** (or a reference)
logical	logical	**OR(*logical1*,*logical2*,...)** (or a reference)
array	array	**TRANSPOSE(*array*)** (or a reference)

The function names and their arguments never contain a space, unless it is in quoted text. Instead, some argument names include an underscore, as in *num_chars*. Each argument is separated by a comma. You can enter carriage returns (Alt+Enter) and tabs (Ctrl+Tab) in long formulas and functions to make them more readable.

Some functions can have as many as 14 arguments. These functions, such as the OR() function, show the additional arguments with ellipses (...).

Some functions have optional arguments, which are shown in the directory in *italic type*. Mandatory arguments are shown in ***bold italic type***. If you leave out all the optional arguments, you do not need to enter their preceding commas. If you use some of the optional arguments, you must enter the commas that would have preceded the omitted optional arguments. These commas act as place holders so that Excel understands the position of the optional arguments that you do enter. For example, the following is the format of the PMT() function with all its arguments:

PMT(*rate*,*nper*,*pv*,*fv*,*type*)

If you omit the *fv* optional argument, but use the *type* argument, you would enter the function as

PMT(*rate*,*nper*,*pv*,,*type*)

Be certain that you enclose text in quotation marks (""). Text contained in a cell and referenced by the cell address does not have to be in quotation marks. Do not enclose range names in quotation marks. If your text includes a quotation, use two quotation marks to begin and end each internal quotation. For example, to find the length of the following phrase:

She said, "So!"

You must use

=LEN("She said,""So!""")

Do not type spaces between the quotes. Text values in a cell, including the quotation marks, can be up to 255 characters long.

T I P   To produce a blank cell display, use two quotation marks with nothing between them, as in the following example:

=IF(A12>15,"","Entry must be greater than 15!")

When A12 is greater than 15, nothing is displayed in the cell, because the TRUE portion of the IF() function returns "". When A12 is 15 or less, the following message is displayed:

Entry must be larger than 15!

Entering Worksheet Functions

You can enter worksheet functions as a single entry in the Formula Bar, such as this:

=PMT(A12,B36,J54)

Or, worksheet functions can be part of a much larger formula, including nested functions that are within other functions, as in this example:

=IF(LEFT(A12,4)="VDT",SUM(B36:B54),SUM(C36:C54))

You can enter functions by manually typing the function or by pasting the function into the formula bar. One function, SUM(), also can be pasted from the toolbar.

Typing Functions

You can type any function into the Formula Bar just as you would type in a formula. If you remember the function and its arguments, typing may be the fastest method. If you are unsure of the function's spelling or its arguments, paste in the function.

Using the AutoSum Tool

The most frequently used function is SUM(). This function totals the numeric value of all cells in the ranges it references. For example, SUM() can total all the cells between two endpoints in a column or row. Because SUM() is used so frequently, an AutoSum tool, which you can use to total adjacent columns or rows automatically, appears on the Standard and Excel 3.0 toolbars. As well as entering the SUM() function, the AutoSum tool selects the cells in the column above the SUM() or in the row to the left of the SUM(). SUM() is useful for totaling columns of expenses or rows of sales by region.

Before using the AutoSum tool, turn on the Standard toolbar by choosing the **O**ptions **T**oolbar command and selecting the Standard toolbar. If a toolbar already is displayed, you can right click it anywhere except a list box to display a shortcut menu from which you can choose Standard. Figure 10.1 shows how to enter a SUM() function in cell B11 by using a mouse. Select cell B11, below the column you want to total, and then click the AutoSum tool. Excel inserts the SUM() function and enters that column's range between parentheses, as shown in the figure. You can continue the formula by adding more terms, or you can enter the SUM() function into the cell by clicking the SUM() tool a second time.

You can enter multiple SUM() functions at one time by clicking, just as though they were filled into adjacent cells. In figure 10.1 for example, select cells B11:F11, and then double-click the AutoSum tool. The SUM() function is entered in the active cell and filled into the adjacent selected cells.

T I P

Pasting Functions and Arguments

A good way to enter functions is to paste them into the worksheet by selecting them from a scrolling list. You also can choose to have Excel paste in prompts to remind you of the arguments and their correct order. To paste a function and its arguments into the worksheet, click the Paste function tool (if you have added it to a toolbar), or complete the following steps:

1. Select the cell where you want to enter the function.

2. Choose the Formula Paste Function command to display the dialog box shown in figure 10.2.

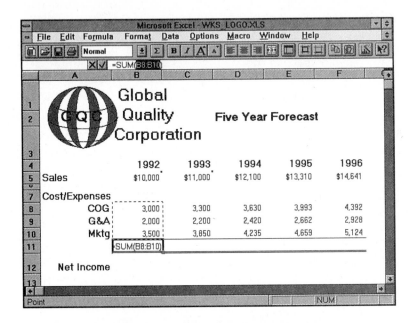

FIG. 10.1

The AutoSum tool enters a SUM( ) function in the selected cell.

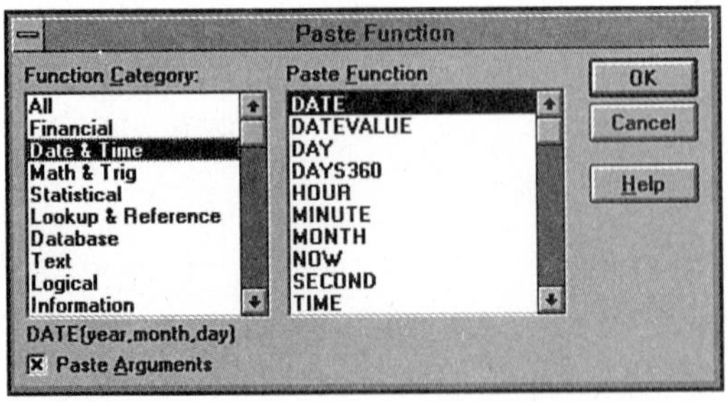

FIG. 10.2

The Paste Function dialog box.

3. Select the type of function you want from the Function Category list. These categories segment the large number of functions into smaller lists. If you are unsure of the category, use All.

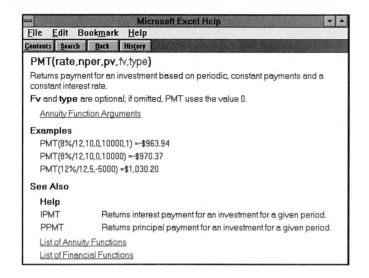

FIG. 10.4

Extensive function help is available.

Excel Function Dictionary

In the function directory that follows, each Excel function is listed with its arguments. The directory also includes explanations, limitations, examples, and tips. Function definitions are grouped by type and are listed in alphabetical order within each group. The function groups include the following:

- Database
- Date and Time
- Financial
- Information
- Logical
- Lookup and Reference
- Mathematical
- Matrix
- Statistical
- Text
- Trigonometric

T I P If you don't find the worksheet function you need but do know the formula or equation to find an answer, you can create your own worksheet functions and even add them to the list shown in the Paste Functions dialog box. To create your own functions, see Chapter 27 to learn to build function macros. Chapter 30 contains examples of function macros.

Database Functions

Each of Excel's database functions uses the same arguments: *database*, *field*, and *criteria*. The descriptions of these arguments in the discussion of DAVERAGE() apply to all the database functions. Examples of database functions and tips to help you analyze your database contents are provided in Chapter 26, "Building Extensive Databases."

The *criteria*, *field*, and *database* arguments used in D*functions* do not have to be the same as those used in **D**ata Set Data**b**ase or **D**ata Set **C**riteria. You can have several D*functions* working at the same time on different ranges of data, and each function can have its own criteria range.

DAVERAGE(*database, field,criteria*)

This function averages the numbers in the *field* of the *database* for records that match the query in *criteria*.

For the *database* argument, you can specify a range (such as B36:D54), a range name (such as INVENTORY), or the name DATABASE (which you create with the **D**ata Set Data**b**ase command). The *criteria* argument can be a reference (such as B12:D13), a name (such as Crit.Sales), or the name CRITERIA (which you create with the **D**ata Set **C**riteria command). The *field* argument specifies the column to average. You can specify the *field* by its field name in quotation marks ("Sales"), by a reference to a cell containing the field name, or by a number (1 is the first field [column], 2 the second, and so on).

The *database*, *field*, and *criteria* arguments do not have to be the same as those used for the **D**ata **F**ind and **D**ata **E**xtract commands. This means that you can analyze multiple databases on the same worksheet. If you want to analyze multiple databases with range names, give each database and criteria a unique name, such as Crit.Sales.1 and Crit.Sales.2.

The following examples are valid DAVERAGE() functions:

    =DAVERAGE(Database,2,Criteria)

where Database and Criteria are set with the **D**ata Set Data**b**ase and **D**ata Set **C**riteria commands, and the second field will be averaged.

=DAVERAGE(B12:H534,"Days",Crit.Sales)

where the *database* being analyzed is in B12:H534, the *field* being averaged has the heading Days, and the *criteria* is in a range with the name Crit.Sales. Notice that when the name of a field heading is used, it is enclosed in quotation marks.

DCOUNT(*database, field,criteria*)

Counts the numeric records in the *database field* that satisfy the *criteria*.

> Limits: If the *field* argument is omitted, DCOUNT() counts all records in the *database* that satisfy the *criteria*.

DCOUNTA(*database, field,criteria*)

Counts the number of nonblank cells in the *field* of the *database* for those records that satisfy the *criteria*.

> Limits: If the *field* argument is omitted, DCOUNTA() counts all nonblank records in the *database* that satisfy the *criteria*.

DGET(*database, field,criteria*)

Extracts from the *database* the single record that matches the *criteria*. If no records match the *criteria*, #VALUE! is returned. If more than one record matches the *criteria*, #NUM! is returned.

DMAX(*database, field,criteria*)

Finds the largest number in the *database field* for records that satisfy the *criteria*.

DMIN(*database, field,criteria*)

Finds the smallest number in the *database field* for records that satisfy the *criteria*.

DPRODUCT(*database, field,criteria*)

Multiplies all values in the *field* of the *database* for records that satisfy the *criteria*. This function is similar to DSUM(), but the values are multiplied rather than added.

DSTDEV(*database, field,criteria*)

Calculates the standard deviation of a sample population, based on the numbers in the *field* of the *database* for records that satisfy the *criteria*.

DSTDEVP(*database, field,criteria*)

Calculates the standard deviation of the entire population, based on the numbers in the *field* of the *database* for records that satisfy the *criteria*.

DSUM(*database, field,criteria*)

Totals all numbers in the *field* of the *database* for records that satisfy the *criteria*.

DVAR(*database, field,criteria*)

Calculates the estimated variance of a sample population, based on the numbers in the *field* of the *database* for records that satisfy the *criteria*.

DVARP(*database, field,criteria*)

Calculates the variance of an entire population, based on the numbers in the *field* of the *database* for records that satisfy the *criteria*.

Date and Time Functions

Excel records dates and times as serial numbers. A date is the number of days from January 1, 1900, to the date you specify; a time is a decimal fraction of 24 hours. Serial numbers provide the capability to calculate elapsed days, future times, and so on. For example, the serial number for January 1, 1992, 6:30 PM, is 32142.7708333, where 32142 is the number of days from the beginning of the century and .7708333 is the decimal fraction of 24 hours representing 6:30 PM.

Windows Excel normally counts dates from the beginning of the year 1900. (On the Macintosh, Excel uses a date system based on 1904.) If, however, the 1904 **D**ate System option is selected in the **O**ptions **C**alculation dialog box, the first day for serial dates is January 1, 1904. You may need to select this option when you are reading Excel worksheets created on the Macintosh. The following definitions and examples assume that the 1904 **D**ate System is not selected.

T I P The same date and time formats that you type into a worksheet, such as *10/12/91* or *9-Sep-92*, can be used with worksheet functions. When a function's argument is *serial_number*, you can use the serial date number or a reference to a cell containing a date or time, or you can enter a date as text in the argument, such as *"24-Dec-92"*. Remember to enclose the text date in quotation marks because it is treated as text.

DATE(*year,month,day*)

Produces the serial number for a specific date. Use the DATE() function to calculate a serial number from formulas that produce a numeric year, month, or day. Enter numbers for the *year*, *month*, and *day* or reference cells that contain numeric values or formulas.

Limits: Excel returns serial numbers for dates between January 1, 1900, and December 31, 2078. Enter years between 1900 and 2078 (or 00 and 178), months from 1 to 12, and days from 1 to 31.

Example: DATE(1988,7,B11) produces the serial number 32336 if B11 contains the day number 12.

Calculate the last day of a month by using =DATE(year,month=1,0). Calculate the last day of the previous month by using =DATE(year,month,0).

T I P

DATE(1992,CHOOSE(*QTR*,1,4,7,10),1) produces serial numbers for the first day of each quarter when *QTR* refers to a cell that contains a number between 1 and 4. Use Format Number to format the cell containing a serial number so that it appears as a date.

T I P

Do not use Excel's DATE() and DATEVALUE() functions to enter dates as you would with the @DATE and @DATEVALUE functions in 1-2-3. Cells in Excel directly accept dates in the format used by the country set in the International Program in the Control Panel.

T I P

DATEVALUE(*date_text*)

Converts a date written as text into a serial number. The *date_text* can be in any of Excel's predefined date formats. These formats are found in the list box of the Format Number command's dialog box. Excel accepts text dates entered in formulas or directly into cells.

Limits: Excel returns serial numbers for dates between January 1, 1900, and December 31, 2078. Enter years between 00 and 178, months from 1 to 12, and days from 1 to 31.

Example: DATEVALUE("24-Dec-92") produces 33962.

If you need to combine (concatenate) dates, numbers, and text into a single text line, or you want to format a date so that it can exceed the width of a cell use the TEXT() function. It changes numbers and dates into text.

T I P

DAY(*serial_number*)

Converts a *serial_number* to the number of the day of the month between 1 and 31. Format the cell as a number.

Limits: The serial number must be in the 0 to 65380 range.

Examples: DAY(32501) produces 24.

DAY("24-Dec-91") produces 24.

DAY(B11) produces 24 when B11 contains 24-Dec-91.

DAYS360(*start_date,end_date*)

Produces the number of days between the *start_date* and the *end_date* in a 360-day year. These calculations are necessary for accounting and finance systems based on 12 30-day months.

Limits: If the *end_date* occurs before the *start_date*, Excel returns a negative number.

Example: DAYS360("4/1/91",B12) produces 90 when B12 contains the date 7/1/91.

HOUR(*serial_number*)

Hours are the fractional part of a day in a serial number. HOUR() returns the number of hours (based on a 24-hour clock) for the fractional day in the *serial_number*. Format the cell as a number.

Examples: HOUR(32501.75) produces 18.

HOUR("24-Dec-92 18:00") produces 18.

MINUTE(*serial_number*)

Returns the number of minutes from a *serial_number*. The fractional part of a day is based on a 24-hour clock. The number of minutes returned is between 0 and 59. Format the cell as a number.

Example: MINUTE(32501.75456) produces 6 minutes.

MONTH(*serial_number*)

Converts the *serial_number* to the number of the month (from 1 to 12). Format the cell as a number.

Examples: MONTH(32501.7546) produces 12.

MONTH(B14) produces 12 if B14 contains "24-Dec-92".

NOW()

Calculates the serial number of the date and time in the computer's clock. Excel updates the date and time only when the worksheet is opened or recalculated.

Limits: You must include the empty parentheses when entering this function. NOW() does not use an argument.

> Use the NOW() function to stamp a worksheet with the date and time of printing. Enter NOW() in a cell formatted with the Format Number command as a date/time format. Each time you retrieve the worksheet or recalculate, the cell contents are updated. Use Edit Paste Special with Values selected to freeze a date or time. Do not use NOW() in a header or footer; use the codes &D and &T for date and time.

T I P

SECOND(*serial_number*)

Returns the number of seconds (between 0 and 59) in the fractional part of the *serial_number*.

Examples: SECOND(32501.753) produces 19.

SECOND("24-Dec-92 18:04:19") produces 19.

TIME(*hour,minute,second*)

Calculates the serial number when given the *hour*, *minute*, and *second* of time on a 24-hour clock.

Example: TIME(18,4,19) produces .752998.

TIMEVALUE(*time_text*)

Converts a time written as text into a serial number. The *time_text* must be enclosed in quotation marks and must use one of Excel's predefined date or time formats.

Limits: You must enclose the text in quotation marks and use one of Excel's predefined date or time formats. The date is not converted.

Examples: TIMEVALUE("18:04:19") produces .752998.

TIMEVALUE("12:00 PM") produces .5.

TODAY()

Calculates the serial number of the computer's current date. This acts the same as the NOW() function but does not return the time portion of the serial number. Excel updates the serial number when the worksheet is opened or recalculated.

WEEKDAY(*serial_number*)

Converts the *serial_number* to the day of the week. The result is a number from 1 (Sunday) to 7 (Saturday).

Examples: WEEKDAY("24-Dec-92") produces 5 (Thursday).

WEEKDAY(B12) produces 5 when cell B12 contains 24-Dec-92.

YEAR(*serial_number*)

Converts the *serial_number* into the year.

Example: YEAR(33962) produces 1992.

Financial Functions

Instead of typing financial formulas, you can use Excel's financial functions. Excel functions operate faster and with less chance of error than typed formulas.

Excel provides a family of functions that solve annuity problems. An annuity is a series of even cash flows over a period of time. For example, cash flows may be rent payments coming in according to a regular time period or payments that you make to a retirement fund. A few of the functions that involve annuities include the following:

FV(*rate,nper,pmt*,*pv,type*)

NPER(*rate,pmt,pv,fv,type*)

PMT(*rate,nper,pv,fv,type*)

RATE(*nper,pmt,pv,fv,type,guess*)

The *rate* is the periodic interest. The interest period must have the same unit as *nper*—the number of periods (such as months) in the life of the cash flow. For example, the annual interest rate should be divided by 12 if payments or receipts are monthly.

The *pmt* (payment) is the constant amount paid or received in each period on an investment or amortized loan such as a mortgage. Normally, *pmt* contains both principal and interest. Enter cash you pay out, a negative *pmt* (payment), as a negative amount in the function. The worth of something at the end of the last period is the *fv* (future value), and *pv* (present value) is the worth of something at the beginning of the period.

Some functions perform different tasks depending on the number you enter as the *type* argument. When *type* equals zero, cash flow is assumed to be at the end of the period. If *type* equals 1, cash flow is assumed to be at the beginning of the period. If no value is entered for *pv* or *type*, each is assumed to be zero.

guess is your best estimate of the final rate. Usually, a *guess* between 0 and 1 will produce an answer. If *guess* is not entered, a *guess* of 10 percent (.1) is assumed. If your *guess* is too far off, Excel cannot find an answer and #NUM! error is returned.

NOTE If #NUM! appears after you enter one of the financial functions, you may have incorrectly entered the positive or negative signs for pmt, pv, or fv. Remember that money you are paying out should appear as a negative number.

Excel also includes functions to analyze uneven cash flows and to calculate depreciation. A few of these functions follow:

IRR(*values,guess*)

MIRR(*values,finance_rate,reinvest_rate*)

If you do work with any form of financial analysis, make sure that you review the additional financial analysis tools that can be added to Excel with the Analysis ToolPak. The Analysis ToolPak comes free with Excel and is described in Chapter 14.

T I P

The financial functions include the following:

DB(*cost,salvage,life,period,month*)

DDB(*cost,salvage,life,period,factor*)

VDB(*cost,salvage,life,start_period,end_period,factor,no_switch*)

These calculate the depreciation for the *period* you indicate, using the double-declining balance depreciation method. You must indicate the initial *cost*, the *salvage* value at the end of depreciation, and the *life* of the item. *factor* is how quickly the balance declines. If omitted, *factor* is assumed to be 2 for double-declining depreciation. In DB(), declining balance, *month* is the number of months in the first year. The default for *month* if it is not used is 12.

Limits: The *period* and economic *life* must be in the same units. Check with your CPA or accountant to determine the appropriate economic life.

The function uses the following equation in its calculations:

DDB=((*cost*−prior total depreciation)*factor)/*life*

Example: The lathe in your factory cost $130,000 and will be worth $4,800 at the end of its economic life in 15 years. What is the depreciation amount at different points in the life?

DDB(130000,4800,15,12)

results in $3,591.33 for year 12.

DDB(130000,4800,15*12,12)

results in $1,277.39 for the month 12 in the first year.

FV(*rate,nper,pmt*,pv,type)

Calculates the future value of a series of cash flows of equal *pmt* amounts made at even periods for *nper* periods at the constant interest *rate*. A lump sum, *pv*, can be invested at the beginning of the term.

Limits:	If no values are entered for *pv* and *type*, they are considered to be zero.
Example:	You invest $2,000 as a lump sum, and you add $100 at the beginning of each month for 5 years (60 months) at an interest rate of 8 percent compounded monthly. Use the following function to find the worth of the investment at the end of the term:

FV(.08/12,60,–100,–2000,1)

The result is $10,376.36. Notice that amounts you pay out are negative, and amounts you receive are positive.

IPMT(*rate,per,nper*,pv,fv,type)

Calculates the interest portion of a payment on an annuity. You can use this function to calculate the interest paid on a mortgage at some period, *per*, within the term of the mortgage, *nper*.

Limits:	The value of *per* must be in the range 1 to *nper*. If no values are entered for *fv* and *type*, they are considered to be zero.
Example:	A flat-rate mortgage of $150,000 is made at 10 percent interest for 30 years. How much was paid toward interest in the 14th month? Use this function to calculate the answer:

IPMT(.10/12,14,360,150000,0,0)

The result is $–1242.44. The result rate is negative because it is the amount you paid out.

IRR(*values*,guess)

Produces the internal rate of return for the series of periodic cash flows found in *values*. The function uses your *guess* as to the rate of return as a starting point for estimation. The result is the rate of return for a single period.

The *values* can be positive and negative cash flows of uneven amounts contained in a range or array of referenced cells. The cash flows must be in the order received. The array or range of values must include at least one sign change or Excel returns a #NUM! error. If you paid money out at time zero in the investment, the initial value should be a negative number.

guess is your best estimate of the final rate. Usually, a *guess* between 0 and 1 will produce an answer. If *guess* is not entered, a *guess* of 10 percent is assumed. If your *guess* is too far off, Excel cannot find an answer and a #NUM! error is returned.

The IRR() function makes continuous estimates of the rate of return until two estimates differ by no more than .00001%. If this resolution cannot be reached after 20 tries, IRR() produces the error value #NUM!. If this occurs, change the *guess* and recalculate.

Limits:	The IRR() method used by all spreadsheets can produce a different solution for each change of sign in the cash flow. You must try different guesses to find the most accurate solution. The IRR() method does not allow you to reinvest positive cash flows or save for negative cash flows at realistic rates. The MIRR() function produces more realistic results.
Example:	Figure 10.5 shows the forecasted cash flows from an apartment complex. Year 0 is the purchase price plus rehabilitation costs. The internal rate of return function in cell G6 is

      IRR(D5:D15,0.1)

      The result of the function is 0.1111655, or 11 percent return. (Cell G6 shows a text version of the function used in cell G5.)

MIRR(*values,finance_rate,reinvest_rate*)

Calculates the modified internal rate of return from a series of positive and negative cash flows in the range *values*. The *finance_rate* specifies the cost of the investment funding. The *reinvest_rate* is the safe rate at which positive cash flows can be reinvested.

Limits:	At least one positive and one negative cash flow must be specified.
Example:	Consider the same forecasted cash flows from an apartment complex as those used for the IRR() function in figure 10.5. For this example, a finance rate of 12 percent and a reinvestment rate of 7 percent are used to make the calculation more realistic. (Finance rate is the rate charged to you on money that you borrow for the investment; reinvestment rate is the rate at which you can

reinvest positive cash flows in a safe instrument, such as a CD.) The function in cell G10 is

MIRR(D5:D15,G8,G9)

The result is .104732. This result is a half percent less than it was with the IRR() method. On projects with different cash flows or with large amounts, the difference between the IRR() method and MIRR() method can be substantial. The MIRR() method is more realistic.

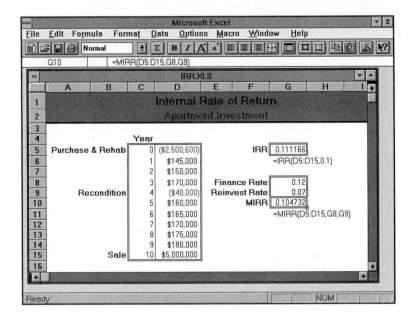

FIG. 10.5

Although IRR( ) is commonly used to analyze cash flows, MIRR( ) returns a more accurate result.

NPER(*rate,pmt,pv, fv,type*)

Calculates the number of periods required to create the annuity specified by the given arguments.

Limits:	If no values are entered for *fv* and *type*, they are considered to be zero.
Example:	NPER(0.10/12,–500,10000) produces 21.969, or 22 payments.

NPV(*rate,value1,value2,...*)

Calculates the net present value of a series of cash flows found in the range or array of *value1*, *value2*, and so on, given a discount rate equal to *rate*. The net present value of a series of cash flows is the value that a future stream of cash represents in terms of cash today, given the fact that future cash can be invested to earn the *rate* percentage.

Limits: The cash flows are considered to be at the end of each period. Cash flows do not have to be equal amounts. The rate must be the rate per period. You can have a maximum of 13 values.

Example: You purchased a piece of equipment for $40,000 cash. You could have invested the cash at 8 percent. At the end of each year for the next five years, the equipment will have saved you $9,000, $6,000, $6,000, $5,000, and $5,000, respectively. At the end of the sixth year, the equipment saves you $5,000, and you sell the equipment for $20,000. Is the purchase worth making?

The net present value of the purchase is

NPV(0.08,9000,6000,6000,5000,5000,25000).

If the values were entered in an array or range of cells the formula also could be

NPV(.08,C15:H15)

The result is $41,072.67. The purchase saved you $1,072.67 over what an equivalent amount invested at 8 percent would earn.

PMT(*rate,nper,pv,fv,type*)

Calculates the periodic payment for different *type*s and future values (*fv*) of investments given the investment's *rate*, term (*nper*), and present value (*pv*).

Limits: If no values are entered for *fv* and *type*, they are considered to be zero.

Example: Suppose that you want to purchase a one-room bungalow in California with a mortgage amount of $190,000 and a flat-rate mortgage of 30 years at 10 percent. If the annual interest is in B12, the annual term in B13, and the mortgage amount in B14, the function would appear in this form:

PMT(B12/12,B13*12,B14)

The result is $-1667.39. The amount is negative because you will be paying out the mortgage. Make sure that the interest rate and term are in the same units as your payment frequency—for example, term in months, interest per month, and one payment per month.

PPMT(*rate,per,nper,pv,fv,type*)

Calculates the principal portion of a payment made on an amortized investment. This portion is the part of the PMT() function that reduces a loan balance.

Limits: If no values are entered for *fv* and *type*, they are considered to be zero.

Example: Consider the mortgage described in the PMT() function example. The payment toward principal in the 12th month will be

PPMT(B12/12,12,B13*12,B14)

The result is $-92.09, which is negative because you are paying out the money.

PV(*rate,nper,pmt,fv,type*)

Calculates the present value of a series of future cash flows of equal *pmt* amounts made at even periods for *nper* periods at the constant interest *rate*. PV() is the amount in current dollars that equals an even cash flow in the future. If the amounts of the cash flow are uneven, use the NPV() function.

Limits: If no values are entered for *fv* and *type*, they are considered to be zero.

Example: You know that you can afford a car payment of $220 per month for the next four years. Current loans are at 9 percent. How large a loan can you afford? The function you need for the calculation is

PV(0.09/12,48,220)

The result is $8,840.65.

RATE(*nper,pmt,pv, fv,type,guess*)

Calculates the interest rate for the annuity that you define with the arguments.

Limits: If no values are entered for *fv* and *type*, they are considered to be zero. If you do not enter an estimated interest rate for *guess*, Excel uses 10 percent (.1). RATE() may return more than one solution, depending on the value used for guess. If *guess* is too far from the correct value, Excel may not be able to make an estimate and may return #NUM!.

Example: RATE(12,–800,9000) results in an interest rate of 1.007 percent per month (12.09 percent per year).

SLN(*cost,salvage,life*)

Returns the annual amount of straight-line depreciation when given the initial *cost* of an item, the *salvage* value at the end of the item's economic life, and the economic *life* of the item.

> Example: SLN(40000,12000,5) produces $5,600 per year depreciation.

SYD(*cost,salvage,life,per*)

Calculates the depreciation for the period, *per*, using the sum-of-the-years depreciation method. You must indicate the initial *cost*, the *salvage* value at the end of the economic life, and the *life* of the item.

> Examples: SLN(40000,12000,5,1) produces $9,333 depreciation for the first year.
>
> SLN(40000,12000,5,2) produces $7,467 depreciation for the second year.

VDB(*cost,salvage,life,start_period,end_period*, *factor,no_switch*)

The variable declining-balance depreciation function returns the depreciation on an asset for the period you indicate. The *cost*, *salvage*, and *life* arguments have the same definitions as described in earlier functions.

Start_period is the period at which you want to start calculating depreciation and *end_period* is the ending period for the calculation. Both must be in the same units as the *life*.

Factor is the rate at which the balance declines. If *factor* is omitted, it is assumed to be 2 (for double-declining balance).

No_switch is a logical argument indicating whether VDB should switch to straight-line depreciation when it is greater than the declining-balance depreciation. Using TRUE for *no_switch* prevents the switch to straight-line method. FALSE, or omitting the *no_switch* argument, enables the switch to straight-line method. All arguments must be positive.

Information Functions

The information functions listed here are primarily for compatibility with worksheets from other vendors. Excel's macro functions contain extensive information gathering capabilities giving you the ability to test for conditions ranging from which worksheets or open, to whether a cell is formatted with Helv bold, to whether the worksheet is running on a Mac or PC and how much memory is available.

CELL(*info_type*,*reference*)

Returns information about the cell contents of the active cell, or the *reference* cell. The *info_type* determines what the cell contents are checked for. The possible values of *info_type* and the result returned by the function are listed in table 10.2.

This function is primarily included for compatibility with other worksheets. Refer to the IS.*functions* for more commonly accepted Excel functions. In macros, use Excel's GET.*functions*.

Table 10.2. Results Returned by the CELL Function

info_type	Returned value
"width"	The column width in integer numbers, measured in terms of the currently selected font.
"row"	The row number of the reference.
"col"	The column number of the reference.
"protect"	0 if the cell is not locked; 1 if it is locked.
"address"	The first cell in the reference, given in text form; for example, $B$2.
"contents"	The value in the reference.
"format"	The text value showing the cell format; examples:

Format	Text Value
General	G
0	F0
#,##0	,0
0.00	F2
#,##0.00	,2
$#,##0_);($#,##0)	C0
$#,##0_);[Red]($#,##0)	C0–
$#,##0.00_);($#,##0.00)	C2
$#,##0.00_);[Red]($#,##0.00)	C2–
0%	P0
0.00%	P2

info_type	Returned value	
	Format	**Text Value**
	0.00E+00	S2
	#?/? or #??/??	G
	m/d/yy or m/d/yy h:mm	D4
	d-mmm-yy	D1
	d-mmm	D2
	mmm-yy	D3
	h:mm AM/PM	D7
	h:mm:ss AM/PM	D6
	h:mm	D9
	h:mm:ss	D8

In addition, – is returned for negative formats that use color and () is returned for negative formats that use parentheses.

"prefix"   The label prefix for alignments:

    '   Left alignment

    "   Right alignment

    ^   Center alignment

    ""   All other alignments

"type"   The text value showing the cell format:

    b   Blank

    l   Text constant (label)

    v   Value (all other values)

"color"   1 if cell is formatted for color with negative number; 0 if it is not.

"filename"   The path and file name of the file that contains the reference; nothing is returned if the sheet has not been saved.

"parentheses"   1 is returned if the cell is formatted so that positive numbers display in parentheses; 0 if positive numbers are displayed without parentheses.

Limits: The CELL() function is used primarily with macros trans-
            lated from Lotus 1-2-3. For greater capabilities with Excel
            macros, use the GET.CELL macro.

Example: CELL("type",B36) results in b if B36 is blank.

T I P   IF(CELL("type",B12)="b","Enter a name here","") results in the text
                Enter a name here whenever cell B12 is blank. This text prompts
                you for data entry.

ERROR.TYPE(*error_val*)

Produces a number depending upon the type of error in the cell referenced by *error_val*. Use ISERROR() or ISERR() to firsst detect an error.
Then, use an IF() function with ERROR.TYPE() to handle diferent types
of errors differently. The values returned by different errors are as
follows:

Error	Value Returned
#NULL!	1
#DIV/0!	2
#VALUE!	3
#REF!	4
#NAME?	5
#NUM!	6
#N/A	7
Other values	#N/A

Other functions that evaluate errors are ISERROR() and ISERR().

INFO(*type_num*)

Determines information about the operating system and environment. *type_num* indicates what information you want to learn,
as in the following list. If you are using a macro, use GET.*functions*,
DOCUMENTS(), and other functions to examine the worksheet and
environment. The following table indicates specific arguments.

type_num	Returned Value
"directory"	Current directory
"memavail"	Memory available
"numfile"	Number of active worksheets
"osversion"	Operating system version
"recalc"	Recalculation mode: Automatic or Manual
"release"	Microsoft Excel version
"system"	Operating system name: Windows = pcdos; OS/2 = pcos2; Macintosh = Mac
"totmem"	Memory available, in bytes; includes memory in use
"memused"	Memory used for data, in bytes

IS*function(value)*

Excel has nine worksheet functions that determine whether a cell meets certain conditions, such as whether it is blank or contains an error value. Depending on the status of the cell, the IS*function* produces either a TRUE or FALSE *value*.

The IS*functions* can be entered into worksheet cells—adjacent to a data-entry cell, for example—or used in a macro to control macro flow.

IS*functions* are most useful when used with the IF() function to test whether a cell or range is blank or contains numbers, text, or errors. For example, you might want to prevent the division by zero error, #DIV/0!. Consider the following formula entered in a cell next to C13:

=IF(ISERROR(B12/C13),"C13 must not be zero",B12/C13)

This formula determines whether B12/C13 produces an error. If an error is produced, the formula prints the message C13 must not be zero. If an error is not produced, the division result appears.

You also can use IS*functions* to test for the proper type of entry. This example tests to make sure that B36 contains a number:

=IF(ISNUMBER(B36),"Good entry","Entry not a number")

The IS*functions* and their results are listed in table 10.3.

Table 10.3. Excel IS*functions*

Function	Result
ISBLANK(*value*)	TRUE if *value* is a blank reference; FALSE if *value* is nonblank.
ISERR(*value*)	TRUE if *value* is any error other than #N/A; FALSE for any other *value*.
ISERROR(*value*)	TRUE if *value* is any error value; FALSE if *value* is not an error value.
ISLOGICAL(*value*)	TRUE if *value* is a logical value; FALSE if *value* is not a logical value.
ISNA(*value*)	TRUE if *value* is the #N/A error value; FALSE if *value* is not #N/A.
ISNONTEXT(*value*)	TRUE if *value* is not text; FALSE if *value* is text.
ISNUMBER(*value*)	TRUE if *value* is a number; FALSE if *value* is not a number.
ISREF(*value*)	TRUE if *value* is a reference; FALSE if *value* is not a reference.
ISTEXT(*value*)	TRUE if *value* is text; FALSE if *value* is not text.

N(*value*)

Translates *value* into a number. N() translates numbers or numbers as text ("9") into numbers, and logical TRUE into 1. Any other value becomes 0. The N() function is used primarily to provide compatibility when converting other worksheets. A related function is VALUE().

Examples: N("9 nine") produces 0.

N(A12) produces 1 if A12 is TRUE.

T I P   Numbers entered into 1-2-3 worksheets preceded by a ', ", or ^ are actually text. When the worksheets are opened in Excel, these *numbers* may not be evaluated as numbers. Use the VALUE() or N() function to convert the text numbers into numbers that Excel can evaluate.

NA()

Always produces the error value #N/A, which means "No value Available." NA() does not take an argument. You can type *#N/A* directly into a cell for the same result. Include the parentheses after NA().

> Enter *#N/A* into blank data-entry cells. If a data-entry cell is not filled, the formulas that depend on this cell result in #N/A.   **T I P**

TYPE(*value*)

Determines the type of a cell's contents and produces a corresponding code, as shown in table 10.4.

Table 10.4. Results of the TYPE Function

Value	Result
Number	1
Text	2
Logical value	4
Error value	16
Array	64

Examples: TYPE(B36) results in 1 if B36 contains a number.

TYPE(B36) results in 16 if B36 contains #N/A.

Logical Functions

The logical functions are powerful worksheet functions that enable you to add decision-making and logical preferences to your worksheets results. The IF() statement is useful for testing conditions and making decisions. AND() and OR() functions can test multiple *criteria* or test conditions for use in IF functions.

AND(*logical1*,*logical2*,...)

Joins test conditions: Returns TRUE if all *logical* arguments are TRUE; FALSE if any *logical* argument is FALSE.

Limits: Arguments must be single logical values or arrays that contain logical values. AND() cannot contain more than 14 *logical* values. The #VALUE! error results if there are no logical values in the arguments.

Example: AND(B36,C12>20) is TRUE only when B36 is not zero and C12 is greater than 20.

FALSE()

Always produces a logical FALSE. Type the parentheses without an argument. Excel also recognizes FALSE without parentheses.

IF(*logical_test,value_if_true*,*value_if_false*)

Produces the *value_if_true* when the *logical_test* evaluates as TRUE; produces the *value_if_false* when the *logical_test* evaluates as FALSE. If *value_if_false* is omitted, the value FALSE is returned when *logical_test* evaluates as FALSE.

IF() is one of the most valuable functions in Excel; this function can test cells and make decisions based on the cell contents.

> **T I P**   Use the AND(), OR(), and NOT() functions with the IF() function to make complex decisions. Examples of AND() and OR() can be found in Chapter 13, "Using Power Worksheet Features," and in the macro examples in Chapters 27-30.

In macros, *value_if_true* and *value_if_false* can be GOTO() functions or action functions, as in this example:

IF(Counter>10,GOTO(End),GOTO(Loop))

Limits:	Up to seven IF() functions can be nested.
Example:	IF(Invent.Qnty<Invent.Order,"Reorder","") results in the message Reorder whenever the inventory quantity falls below the order quantity.

NOT(*logical*)

Reverses the result of the *logical* argument from TRUE to FALSE or from FALSE to TRUE. Use this function to return the opposite condition of the logical_test in an IF() statement.

Example:	IF(NOT(OR(B36=12,B36=20)),"Not a 12 or 20","Is a 12 or 20"). This statement determines whether B36 contains a 12 or 20 and produces the message Not a 12 or 20 when the cell does not.

OR(*logical1*,*logical2*,...)

Joins test conditions: Returns TRUE if one or more *logical* argument is TRUE; FALSE only when all *logical* arguments are FALSE.

Limits:	OR() is limited to 14 or fewer arguments. Arguments cannot be blank cells, error values, or text. Use IS*functions* in OR() functions to test for blank cells, error values, or text.

Example: IF(OR(B36=12,B36=20),"Is a 12 or 20","Not a 12 or 20").
This statement checks whether B36 contains either 12 or
20 and produces the message Is a 12 or 20 when it
does. If B36 contains anything else, the message Not a
12 or 20 appears.

TRUE()

Always produces TRUE. Type the parentheses without an argument.
Excel also recognizes TRUE without parentheses.

Lookup and Reference Functions

The LOOKUP() and MATCH() functions enable your worksheets to retrieve a value from within a table. Examples of many of these functions
are found in Chapter 13, "Using Power Worksheet Features." INDEX()
functions enable you to extract specific values from within an array. The
OFFSET() function, listed later with Reference Functions, enables you
to retrieve information that is offset a specified distance from a base
reference.

Reference functions are necessary when you need to determine cell contents, ranges, or selected areas. Some of them, such as OFFSET() also
are used in macro sheets and are a necessity for more advance macros.

ADDRESS(*row_num,column_num*,*abs_num,a1,sheet_text*)

Produces a cell reference in text form for the cell indicated by the
row_num and *col_num*. Use one of four values in *abs_num* to specify the
type of reference:

1   Absolute reference (default)

2   Absolute row, relative column

3   Relative row, absolute column

4   Relative reference

If the *a1* argument is TRUE, or omitted, Excel returns A1 style references.
FALSE returns the R1C1 style reference. *sheet_text* is the name of the
worksheet or macro sheet used by the reference.

Other functions related to ADDRESS() are CELL(), ACTIVE.CELL(),
OFFSET(), INDEX(), ROW(), COLUMN(), and SELECTION().

Examples: ADDRESS(15,4,2,TRUE) returns D$15.

ADDRESS(Counter.Row,4,4,FALSE,"ASSETS.XLS") returns
ASSETS.XLS!R[25]C[4] where Counter.Row is a name
containing the value 25.

AREAS(*reference*)

Returns the number of areas in *reference*. Use the AREAS() function to find how many selections are within an area.

Example: AREAS(PRINTOUT) results in 2 when the range named PRINTOUT is defined as the two ranges A1:F55 and G56:O210.

CHOOSE(*index_num,value1,value2,...*)

Chooses from the list of *values* a value that corresponds to the *index_num*. For example, when the *index_num* is 2, the function chooses *value2*. When used in a macro, the CHOOSE() function can have values that are GOTO() or action functions.

Limits: CHOOSE() displays #VALUE when the *index_num* is less than one or greater than the number of items in the list.

Examples: CHOOSE(B12,5,12,32,14) produces 32 when B12 contains 3.

DATE(1992,CHOOSE(*QTR*,1,4,7,10),1) produces the serial number for the first day of each quarter when *QTR* refers to a cell containing a number from 1 to 4.

COLUMN(*reference*)

Produces the column number of the *reference* cell. If *reference* is an array or a range, then the column numbers of each column in the range return as an horizontal array. If the *reference* argument is not specified, COLUMN() produces the column number of the cell that contains the function. *Reference* cannot contain multiple areas. Use the INDEX() function to read values from an array.

Examples: COLUMN(C15) returns 3.

If Print is the range name of the range C5:E20, COLUMN(Print) returns the array {3,4,5}.

COLUMNS(*array*)

Returns the number of columns in *array*.

Example: COLUMNS(E4:G6) produces 3.

HLOOKUP(*lookup_value,table_array,row_index_num*)

Looks across the top row of the range defined by *table_array* until the *lookup_value* is met; then looks down that column to the row specified by *row_index_num*.

Limits: Values in the first row of *table_array* must be in ascending order, both alphabetically (A-Z) and numerically

(0-9). The *lookup_value* and the values in the first row of the *table_array* can be text, numbers, or logical values.

If the *lookup_value* is not found, HLOOKUP() uses the largest value that is less than or equal to the *lookup_value*. This results in the return of a value even though an exact match for the *lookup_value* is not found. If you want to find an exact match in a table, use the MATCH() and INDEX() functions in combination, as described in Chapter 13, "Building Extensive Worksheets."

row_index_num begins with 1. To return a value from the first row, use 1, and from the second row, use 2, and so on. If *row_index_num* is less than 1, HLOOKUP() produces the #VALUE! error. If *row_index_num* is greater than the number of rows in the table, #REF! is displayed.

Examples: Refer to Chapter 13, "Building Extensive Worksheets," for examples using the HLOOKUP() function.

INDEX(*array*,*row_num*,*column_num*)

In the array form of INDEX(), *row_num* and *col_num* return the value of a cell in the array. The definitions of *row_num* and *col_num* are the same as described in the reference version of INDEX().

Examples: INDEX({3,4,5;8,9,10},2,3) produces 10.

INDEX({3,4,5;8,9,10},0,3) produces the single-column matrix {5;10} when the INDEX() function is entered as an array formula by using Shift+Ctrl+Enter.

INDEX(*reference*,*row_num*,*column_num*,*area_num*)

In the reference form, INDEX() produces a cell reference from within the *reference* specified and at the intersection of the *row_num* and *column_num*. If *reference* is a singlerow or column, then the column_num or row_num argument can be omitted: =INDEX(A1:A10,5), for example. Other functions convert the value returned by INDEX() to a cell reference or value as needed.

The referenced area is *reference*. If this area contains multiple ranges, enclose the reference in parentheses, as in (B36:D45,G56:H62). If *reference* contains more than one area, *area_num* can choose between areas. In the preceding example, an *area_num* of 2 will choose G56:H62. If you do not include an *area_num*, Excel assumes that it is 1.

The arguments *row_num* and *column_num* choose a cell in the area specified. The first row or column is 1. Omitting the *row_num* or *column_num* or using 0 returns a reference for the entire row or column. A second form of the INDEX() function is used with arrays.

Limits:	If either *row_num* or *column_num* is outside the specified area, INDEX() results in the message #REF!.
Example:	INDEX((B2:C5,E7:G9),1,2,2) produces the reference or value in F7, the second area, first row, second column.

INDIRECT(*ref_text,a1*)

Returns the contents of the cell whose reference is in the cell indicated by *ref_text*. The *ref_text* argument must be an A1 or R1C1 reference or a cell name; otherwise, an error is returned. Ref_text can be a string formulas, =INDIRECT("range" & B5), and even an external reference, =INDIRECT(sheet&"!Range"). When *a1* is TRUE, 1, or omitted, INDIRECT() expects *ref_text* to be A1 style. When *ref_text* is FALSE, or 0, INDIRECT() expects R1C1 style.

Example:	INDIRECT(A20) results in 5 if A20 contains the cell reference B35 (without quotation marks) and cell B35 contains 5.

LOOKUP(*lookup_value,lookup_vector,result_vector*)

LOOKUP() can be either a vector or an array function. This description applies to the vector function. This function is useful for looking up values from a table with incremental numbers, such as discount schedules and tax tables. A *lookup_vector* contains a single row or column. This function searches through the *lookup_vector* until the *lookup_value* is found. The function then produces the value that is in the same location in the *result_vector*. If the *lookup_value* cannot be found, LOOKUP() returns a value corresponding to the largest value less than or equal to the *lookup_value*. If the *lookup_value* is smaller than any value in *lookup_vector*, the message #NA is returned.

Limits:	Values in *lookup_vector* can be text, numbers, or logical values. They must be sorted in ascending order to give the correct return.

LOOKUP(*lookup_value,array*)

The array form of LOOKUP() is similar to HLOOKUP() and VLOOKUP(). LOOKUP() searches for a match to *lookup_value* in the first row or the first column of the *array*, depending on the shape of the array. If the array is square, or wider than tall, LOOKUP() searches across the first row for the *lookup_value*. If the array is taller than it is wide, the search proceeds down the first column.

If LOOKUP() cannot find the *lookup_value*, it finds the largest value less than the *lookup_value*. If *lookup_value* is smaller than the smallest value in the row or column being examined, the message #N/A is returned.

The value returned is taken from the last row or column in the *array* that matches the *lookup_value*.

Limits: The row or column being examined for the *lookup_value* must be sorted in ascending order.

MATCH(*lookup_value,lookup_array*,*match_type*)

MATCH() returns the position of the match for *lookup_value* in the *lookup_array*. The type of match is determined by *match_type*. The *lookup_value* can be a number, text, logical value, or cell reference.

When combined with the INDEX() function, as shown in Chapter 13, the MATCH() function enables you to find exact matches to a *lookup_value* or return an error. This prevents the possible use of an incorrect value returned by VLOOKUP(), HLOOKUP(), or LOOKUP().

The types of match are given here with a description of what each match type finds:

match_type	Finds
1, or omitted	Largest value less than or equal to *lookup_value*. The *lookup_array* must be in sorted order. The default is 1 if *match_type* is omitted.
0	First value that is an exact match.
–1	Smallest value greater than or equal to *lookup_value*. The *lookup_array* must be in sorted order.

See Chapter 15, "Using Excel's Add-In Macros," to learn how to add the FASTMATCH() function to your worksheets. Chapter 13, "Using Power Worksheet Features," contains examples of how to use MATCH() and INDEX() to look up exact matches from a list.

Limits: MATCH() returns the row or column position in the array of the found item, not its value or cell reference.

OFFSET(*reference,rows,cols*,*height,width*)

Returns the cell reference "offset" from a reference by a number of rows and a number of columns. The reference used is the *reference* argument. The reference may be a single cell or a range. The height and width of an offset range can be controlled by the *height* and *width* values. If *height* and *width* are omitted, OFFSET() uses the height and width of the *reference*.

In a worksheet, OFFSET() is an excellent way to retrieve data from a historical table of information. The second example shows how this function can be used to retrieve data from a table of sales histories.

T I P OFFSET() used in a FORMULA() macro function is an extremely powerful way of retrieving data from one worksheet location and putting the data into another worksheet location. Because the row and column location from the "base point" can be calculated, you can use FOR-NEXT loops or calculations to determine exactly where data should come from and where it should go to. The combination of FORMULA() and OFFSET() in macros is much, much faster than COPY() and PASTE() when used to move data from one location to another. Chapters 27 through 30 describe macros and show examples.

Use OFFSET() with the SELECTION() and FORMULA() functions in macros to select ranges or to enter values on worksheets. Using OFFSET() to specify the cell to act on is much faster than concatenating text references. For more information on how OFFSET() is used in macros, refer to OFFSET() examples in Chapters 27-30.

Limits: If the offset extends beyond the edge of the worksheet, or if the row or height is less than one, the function returns the #REF! error.

Examples: OFFSET(C3,1,2) entered in a worksheet results in the value stored in E4.

OFFSET(Sales.History,A3,B3) entered in a worksheet returns the value stored in the cell that is offset from the cell named Sales.History by the number of rows in cell A3 and the number of columns in cell B3.

OFFSET(C3,1,2,3,4) returns an array of values three rows high and four columns wide. These values are returned from a range of cells of the same size and whose upper left corner is specified as offset from C3 by one row and two columns, or E4. When OFFSET() is used in this manner it returns more results than fit in one cell—in this case 12 results (3 x 4). An *array formula* like this must be entered as an array into a range that is the same size (3 rows by 4 columns). Enter array formulas by selecting the cells on the worksheet (3 rows by 4 columns), typing the formula and pressing Shift+Ctrl+Enter instead of just Enter. If you select a cell range larger than the three-by-four range in which to enter the array, unneeded cells return the #N/A error.

You also can retrieve information from the array returned by an offset by putting the OFFSET() function inside of an INDEX() function. The INDEX() function retrieves data from one result out of the three-by-four array.

ROW(*reference*)

Results in the row number of the *reference* cell. If *reference* is a range, ROW() produces a vertical array of the row numbers. If you don't specify the *reference* argument, ROW() produces the row number of the cell in which the function is entered. Use the INDEX() function to extract a row number as a specific element within ROW().

Examples: ROW(D5) results in 5.

ROW(D5:F7) results in {5;6;7}. When entered into a single cell, the result displays as 5. When entered by selecting three cells in a column and pressing Shift+Ctrl+Enter, the result displays each row number.

The formula =INDEX(ROW(D5:F7),3,1) entered in a single cell finds the row number in the third row of the first column of the array. The array {5;6;7} has only one column and three rows, so the value returned is 7.

ROWS(*array*)

Produces the number of rows in *array*.

Example: ROWS(B12:D35) results in 24.

VLOOKUP(*lookup_value,table_array,col_index_num*)

Looks down the left column of *table_array* until the *lookup_value* is met, and then looks across that row to the column specified by *col_index_num*. Values in the first column can be text, numbers, or logical values in ascending order. Upper- and lowercase text are considered the same.

Limits: If VLOOKUP() cannot find the *lookup_value*, the function searches for the next largest value in the first column. Other limits are the same as described in the discussion of the HLOOKUP() function.

Examples: Refer to Chapter 13, "Using Power Worksheet Features," for examples using the lookup functions.

Mathematical Functions

Mathematical functions provide the foundation for the majority of worksheet calculations. Most scientific and engineering functions are found under mathematical functions. If you do not find the function you need, you can create your own by referring to Chapter 27, the section "Building Function Macros."

T I P   For additional mathematical tools, such as Fourier transforms, review the Analysis ToolPak described in Chapter 14. It adds additional analysis tools into Excel. The Analysis ToolPak comes free with Excel.

ABS(*number*)

Returns the absolute (positive) value of the *number*.

Examples: ABS(–5) produces 5.

ABS(5) produces 5.

CEILING(*number,significance*)

Produces a number that has been rounded up to the level of significance you specify. If you want to round down, use the FLOOR() function.

Examples: CEILING(A12,.10) rounds the number in cell A12 up to the nearest dime.

CEILING(145321,100) rounds the number 145321 up to 145400.

COMBIN(*number,number_chosen*)

Produces the combination of items without regard to order. For example, if there are 23 socks in a drawer and you pull out two socks, there are COMBIN(23,2) different combinations you could choose from. The answer is 253.

EVEN(*number*)

Rounds a number up to an even number.

Examples: EVEN(4.6) produces 6.

EXP(*number*)

Returns e raised to the power of *number*. EXP() is the inverse of the LN() function.

Limits: The value of e is 2.71828182845904.

Examples: EXP(0) produces 1.

EXP(LN(10)) produces 10.

FACT(*number*)

Returns the factorial of the *number*. A noninteger *number* is truncated.

Example: FACT(4) produces 24 (4*3*2*1).

FLOOR(*number,significance*)

Rounds a number down to the level of significance that you specify.

Example: FLOOR(5432,100) produces 5400.

INT(*number*)

Rounds the *number* down to the nearest integer.

Examples: INT(7.6) produces 7.

                INT(–7.6) produces –8.

Use INT() to round a number down to the nearest integer. Use TRUNC() to truncate a number by removing the decimal portion. Use ROUND() to round a number to a specific number of places to the left or right of the decimal.

T I P

LN(*number*)

Returns the natural log of the *number* in base e. LN() is the inverse of EXP().

Limits: The value of the *number* must be positive.

Example: LN(3) produces 1.098612289.

LOG(*number,base*)

Returns the logarithm of the *number* in the *base* specified.

Limits: The value of the *number* must be positive. LOG() uses base 10 if the *base* argument is omitted.

Examples: LOG(10) produces 1.

                LOG(64,2) produces 6.

LOG10(*number*)

Returns the logarithm of the *number* in base 10.

Examples: LOG10(10) produces 1.

                LOG10(100) produces 2.

MOD(*number,divisor*)

Produces the remainder (modulus), of the *number* divided by the *divisor*.

Limits: The #DIV/0! error appears if the *divisor* is zero.

Examples: MOD(7,6) produces 1.

                MOD(32,15) produces 2.

ODD(*number*)

Produces a number rounded up to the closest odd number.

    Example: ODD(455.5) produces 457.

PI()

Returns the value of π.

    Limits: An estimate of π, 3.14159265358979, is used. The parentheses must be included even though the function does not take an argument.

PRODUCT(*number1*,*number2*,...)

Multiplies *number1* by *number2* by the rest of the arguments.

    Limits: You can specify up to 14 arguments. Arguments that are blank cells, logical values, error values, or text are ignored. Text that can be converted into a numeric value is converted.

    Example: PRODUCT(B12:C14) produces 24 when cells B12 through C14 contain the numbers 1, 2, 3, and 4.

RAND()

Produces a random decimal number from 0 to 1. The function does not take an argument between the parentheses. Press F9, choose **O**ptions Calculate **N**ow, or hold down Shift and choose **O**ptions Calculate Docume**n**t to produce new random numbers. Freeze random numbers by copying them with **E**dit **C**opy and pasting them on top of themselves. For this operation, choose **E**dit Paste **S**pecial and select the Paste **V**alues and Operations N**o**ne options.

See Chapter 15, "Using Excel's Add-In Macros," to learn how to add the RANDBETWEEN() function to your worksheets. Chapter 14's discussion of the Analysis ToolPak explains how to use a more statistically accurate random number generator.

ROUND(*number*,*num_digits*)

Rounds the *number* to the number of digits, *num_digits*, specified. If *num_digits* is positive, the number rounds to the specified decimal places to the right of the decimal point. If *num_digits* is zero, the number rounds to an integer. If *num_digits* is negative, the number rounds upward to the left of the decimal point.

    Examples: ROUND(456.345,2) produces 456.35.

                          ROUND(546789,–3) produces 547000.

> If you need to round up or down to a given number of decimals, use the CEILING() or FLOOR() functions.
>
> **T I P**

SIGN(*number*)

Produces 1 when the *number* is positive, 0 when it is 0, and –1 when it is negative.

Example: SIGN(B12) produces 1 when B12 contains 5, and –1 when B12 contains –23.

SQRT(*number*)

Returns the square root of the *number*.

Limits: The value of the *number* must be positive.

Example: SQRT(25) produces 5.

SUM(*number1,number2,...*)

Calculates the sum of the arguments. Arguments can be individual values or ranges and are limited to 14 arguments. Arguments that cannot be converted from text to numbers or error values are ignored.

Example: SUM(B36:B40) produces 25 if the range includes the numbers 3, 4, 5, 6, and 7.

SUMPRODUCT(*array1,array2,...*)

Results in the sum of the product of the arrays. All the arrays must have the same size and shape. You can specify 2 to 14 arguments.

Example: SUMPRODUCT(B8:B10,C8:C10) results in 32 where B8:B10 contains 1, 2, and 3 and C8:C10 contains 4, 5, and 6.

SUMSQ(*array*)

Produces the sum of the squares for all numbers in the range ***array***. This was an add-in macro in Excel 3.0 using the name SUMSQUARES().

TRUNC(*number,num_digits*)

Changes the *number* to an integer by cutting off, or *truncating*, the decimal fraction portion. If *num_digits* is omitted, it is assumed to be zero.

Example: TRUNC(5.6) produces 5.

Matrix Functions

MDETERM(*array*)

Produces the determinant of *array*. The array can be a reference, such as B36:C37, or an array constant, such as {1,2,3;5,6,7;8,9,10}.

MINVERSE(*array*)

Produces the inverse of *array*. The array can be a reference, such as B36:C37, or an array constant, such as {1,2,3;5,6,7;8,9,10}.

Because the MINVERSE() function produces an array as a result, you must enter this function as an array formula by selecting a square range of cells of equivalent size, typing the formula, and then pressing Shift+Ctrl+Enter.

MMULT(*array1,array2*)

Produces the product of *array1* and *array2*. The number of columns in *array1* must be the same as the number of rows in *array2*. The arrays must contain only numbers.

Because the MMULT() function produces an array as a result, you must enter the MMULT() function as an array formula, as described under MINVERSE().

SUMX2MY2(*array_x,array_y*)

Produces the sum of the difference of squares of values in two arrays.

Limits: The values in arrays must be numbers, blanks, or #N/A! values. Other values produce #VALUE! errors. Arrays that do not have the same number of elements produce #N/A! errors.

SUMX2PY2(*array_x,array_y*)

Produces the sum of the squares of values in two arrays.

Limits: The values in arrays must be numbers, blanks, or #N/A! values. Other values produce #VALUE! errors. Arrays that do not have the same number of elements produce #N/A! errors.

SUMXMY2(*array_x,array_y*)

Produces the sum of the squared differences from values in two arrays.

Limits: The values in arrays must be numbers, blanks, or #N/A! values. Other values produce #VALUE! errors. Arrays that do not have the same number of elements produce #N/A! errors.

TRANSPOSE(*array*)

Transposes the current *array* so that the first row in the current *array* becomes the first column of the new array, the second row of the current *array* becomes the second column of the new array, and so on.

Because the TRANSPOSE() function produces an array as a result, you must enter the TRANSPOSE() function as an array formula. Entering the TRANSPOSE() function is described in Chapter 13, "Building Extensive Worksheets."

Statistical Functions

Statistical functions can help you with simple problems, such as finding an average or counting items. Statistical functions also can do simple statistical analysis, such as biased or nonbiased standard deviation. Not all of the worksheet statistical functions are explained in the listings in this section. Table 10.5 lists the additional statistical functions that are not explained. You can learn more about these functions from the Help files and from the Microsoft function reference manual.

> In addition to the worksheet statistical function, make sure that you examine the Analysis ToolPak, described in Chapter 14. The Analysis ToolPak contains many more statistical and analytical tools. The Analysis ToolPak comes free with Excel.

T I P

Explanations for some of the more commonly used statistical functions are listed here.

AVERAGE(*number1*,*number2*,...)

Returns the average (mean) of the arguments. Arguments may be single values or ranges. The ranges can contain numbers, cell references, or arrays that contain numbers. Text, logical values, errors, and blank cells are ignored.

Limits: AVERAGE() can take from 1 to 14 arguments.

Examples: AVERAGE(B12:B15) produces 3.5 when B12:B15 contains the numbers 2, 3, 4, and 5.

AVERAGE(B12:B15,20) produces 6.8 when B12:B15 contains the numbers 2, 3, 4, and 5.

Table 10.5. Additional Statistical Functions

AVEDEV()	GAMMADIST()	PEARSON()
BETADIST()	GAMMAINV()	PERCENTILE()
BETAINV()	GAMMALN()	PERCENTRANK()
BINOMDIST()	GEOMEAN()	PERMUT()
CHIDIST()	HARMEAN()	POISSON()
CHITEST()	HYPGEOMDIST()	PROB()
CONFIDENCE()	INTERCEPT()	QUARTILE()
CORREL()	KURT()	RANK()
COVAR()	LARGE()	RSQ()
CRITBINOM()	LOGINV()	SKEW()
DEVSQ()	LOGNORMDIST()	SLOPE()
EXPONDIST()	MEDIAN()	SMALL()
FDIST()	MODE()	STANDARDIZE()
FINV()	NEGMINOMDIST()	TINV()
FISHER()	NORMDIST()	TRIMMEAN()
FISHERINV()	NORMINV()	TTEST()
FORECAST()	NORMSDIST()	WEIBULL()
FREQUENCY()	NORMSINV()	ZTEST()
FTEST()		

COUNT(*value1*,*value2*,...)

Produces a count of the numbers in the arguments. The *value* arguments can be numbers, cell references, or arrays that contain numbers. Text, logical values, errors, and blank cells are not counted.

Limits: You can include from 1 to 14 arguments in COUNT().

Example: COUNT(B12:B15) produces 4 when B12 to B15 contains the numbers 2, 3, 4, and 5. The statement produces 3 if B12 is blank instead of containing 2.

COUNTA(*value1*,*value2*,...)

Produces a count of the values in the arguments. This function counts text values as well as numbers. Empty cells in arrays or references are ignored. COUNTA() determines the number of nonblank cells.

Limits: You can include from 1 to 14 arguments in COUNTA().

Example: COUNTA(A12:A20) produces 8 if cell A13 is the only blank cell.

COUNTA(B12:B15) produces 4 when B12:B15 contains the values 2, "Tree", 4, and "Pine".

GROWTH(*known_y's,*known_x's,new_x's,const*)

Calculates the exponential growth curve that best fits the test data contained in the ranges *known_y's* and *known_x's*. GROWTH() then uses the *new_x's* values to calculate new *y* values along the calculated curve. If *const* is TRUE or omitted, the constant term is calculated. If *const* is FALSE, 1 is used for the constant term.

Because the GROWTH() function produces an array, you must enter the GROWTH() function as an array formula. See Chapter 13 for examples on entering similar trend analysis functions.

LINEST(*known_y's,*known_x's,const,stats*)

LINEST() calculates the straight line equation that best fits the data and produces an array of values that define the equation of that line. If *known_x's* is omitted, an array equal in size to *known_y's* is used with values of {1,2,3,...}.

The line has the equation

$$y = b + m_1 * x_1 + m_2 * x_2 + ...$$

Excel uses a least-squares fit to find the best straight-line fit to the data. The array returned is of the form $\{m_1, m_2, ..., b\}$. The constants within that array can be used to calculate *y* values on the line for any given set of x_1, x_2, and so on.

If *const* is TRUE or omitted, the constant term is calculated; if FALSE, the constant is zero. If *stats* is FALSE or omitted, the slope and y-intercept are returned. If *stats* is TRUE, the following statistics are returned:

- Standard error for each coefficient
- Standard error for the constant b
- Coefficient of determination (r-squared)
- Standard error for the y-estimate
- F-statistic
- Degrees of freedom
- Regression sum of squares
- Residual sum of squares

Examples of the trend analysis functions are included in Chapter 13, "Using Power Worksheet Features."

LOGEST(*known_y's,known_x's,const,stats*)

Calculates the exponential curve of the form

$$y=b*(m_1{}^{\wedge}x_1)*(M_2{}_{\_}{}^{\wedge}x_2)*....$$

that best fits the data. When given the data *known_y's* and *known_x's*, the values for *b* and *m* are returned in a horizontal array of the form $\{m_1,m_2,...,b\}$.

If *const* is TRUE or omitted, the constant term is calculated. If *const* is FALSE, the constant is 1. If *stats* is FALSE or omitted, only the slope and y-intercept are returned. If *stats* is TRUE, the function returns the following statistics in an array:

- Standard error for each coefficient

- Standard error for the constant b

- Coefficient of determination (r-squared)

- Standard error for the y-estimate

- F-statistic

- Degrees of freedom

- Regression sum of squares

- Residual sum of squares

MAX(*number1,number2,...*)

Produces the largest value among the arguments.

Limits:	MAX() can take up to 14 arguments. Arguments that are error values or text that cannot be interpreted as a number are ignored. Within a referenced array or range, any empty cells, logical values, text, or error values are ignored.
Example:	MAX(C2:D4) produces 32 if the numbers in these cells are –2, 4, 32, and 30.

MEDIAN(*number1,number2,...*)

Returns the median value of the arguments.

MIN(*number1,number2,...*) ·

Produces the smallest value among the arguments.

Limits:	MIN() can take up to 14 arguments. Arguments that are not numbers are ignored. If the arguments contain no numbers, MIN() produces 0.

Example: MIN(C2:D4) produces -2 if the numbers in these cells are
            -2, 4, 32, and 30.

STDEV(*number1*,*number2*,...)

Calculates an estimate of the standard deviation of a population from a
sample of the population.

Limits: STDEV() can take up to 14 arguments. If the arguments
            include the entire population, use STDEVP.

Example: STDEV(B2:B12) produces 12.12 when the range from
            B2 to B12 contains 98, 67, 89, 76, 76, 54, 87, 78, 85, 83,
            and 90.

STDEVP(*number1*,*number2*,...)

Calculates the standard deviation of a population, where the entire
population is listed in the arguments.

Limits: STDEV() can take up to 14 arguments. If the arguments
            do not include the entire population, use STDEV.

Example: STDEVP(B2:B12) produces 11.55 when the range from
            B2 to B12 contains 98, 67, 89, 76, 76, 54, 87, 78, 85, 83,
            and 90.

TREND(*known_y's*,*known_x's*,*new_x's*,*const*)

Returns the values along a straight line that best fit the data in the arrays
known_y's. If a *known_x's* array is omitted, an array of the same size is
used that contains the values {1,2,3,...}. For each value in the *new_x's*
array, the TREND function produces an array of corresponding y values.
If *const* is TRUE or omitted, the constant term is calculated. If FALSE, the
constant term is zero.

Examples of the trend analysis functions are included in Chapter 13,
"Using Power Worksheet Features."

VAR(*number1*,*number2*,...)

Calculates an estimate of the variance in a population from a sample
given in the arguments.

Limits: Use VARP() if the arguments contain the entire
            population.

VARP(*number1*,*number2*,...)

Calculates the variance when given the entire population as arguments.

Limits: Use VAR() if the arguments contain only a sample of the
            population.

Text Functions

Text functions enable you to manipulate text. You can parse text to pull-out portions you need from long strings of text. Or you can change numbers and dates to text so that they can exceed a cell's width without producing a cell filled with #####. Numbers or dates converted to text can be concatenated (joined) to text in titles, sentences, and labels. Text functions are also very important for manipulating text that will be converted to ASCII files to be loaded onto mainframe computers.

CHAR(*number*)

Produces the character corresponding to the ASCII code *number* between 1 and 255.

Example: CHAR(65) is A.

CLEAN(*text*)

Removes from the specified *text* argument any characters that are lower than ASCII 32 or above ASCII 127. These characters are not printed. This function is useful for removing control codes, bells, and non-ASCII characters from imported text.

CODE(*text*)

Produces the ASCII code of the first letter in the specified *text*.

Example: CODE("Excel") produces 69.

DOLLAR(*number*,*decimals*)

Rounds the *number* to the specified number of *decimals* to the right of the decimal point and converts the number to text in a currency format. This text can be concatenated with other text phrases.

Use the DOLLAR() function to incorporate numbers in text. For example, consider the following statement:

="Your reimbursement is "&DOLLAR(A12,2)&"."

When A12 contains the number 2456.78, this is the result:

    Your reimbursement is $2,456.78.

If you specify a negative number for the *decimal* argument, the function rounds the *number* to the left of the decimal point. If you omit the *decimal* argument, the function assumes two decimal places.

Examples: DOLLAR(32.45,2) results in $32.45.

DOLLAR(5432.45,_3) results in $5,000.

EXACT(*text1,text2*)

Compares *text1* and *text2*: if they are exactly the same, returns the logical TRUE; if they are not the same, returns FALSE. Upper- and lowercase text are considered to be different.

Example: EXACT("Glass tumbler", A12) produces TRUE when A12 contains the text "Glass tumbler", but produces FALSE when A12 contains "glass tumbler".

FIND(*find_text,within_text,start_num*)

Beginning at *start_num*, FIND() searches the text specified by *within_text* to locate *find_text*. If *find_text* is found, the FIND() function produces the character location where *find_text* starts. If *start_num* is out of limits or a match is not found, the #VALUE! error value is displayed. If *start_num* is not specified, it is assumed to be 1.

Example: FIND(B12,"ABCDEFGHIJKLMNOPQRSTUVWXYZ") produces 3 if B12 contains "C".

FIXED(*number,decimals,no_commas*)

Rounds the *number* to the specified *decimals* and displays it as text in fixed decimal format with commas. If you omit *decimals*, the *number* is rounded to two decimal places. If you specify a negative number of *decimals*, the function rounds the *number* to the left of the decimal point. When no_commas is TRUE, commas are removed from the result.

Examples: FIXED(9876.543) produces 9,876.54.

FIXED(9876.543,–3) produces 10,000.

LEFT(*text,num_chars*)

Produces the leftmost number of characters from *text*.

Limits: The value of *num_chars* must be greater than zero. If the value is omitted, it is assumed to be 1.

Example: LEFT(A17,3) produces Que if A17 contains "Que Corporation".

LEN(*text*)

Produces the number of characters in *text*. The LEN() function is particularly useful when paired with the LEFT(), MID(), and RIGHT() functions so that portions of long text can be separated.

LOWER(*text*)

Changes *text* to all lowercase.

Example: LOWER("Look OUT!") produces look out!.

MID(*text,start_num,num_chars*)

Produces characters from the specified *text*, beginning at the character in the *start_num* position and extending the specified *num_chars*.

Example: MID("Excel is the worksheet",10,3) produces the.

PROPER(*text*)

Changes *text* to lowercase with leading capitals.

Example: PROPER("excel, the worksheet") produces
Excel, The Worksheet.

REPLACE(*old_text,start_num,num_chars,new_text*)

Replaces the characters in *old_text* with *new_text*, starting with the character at *start_num* and continuing for the specified *num_chars*. The first character in *old_text* is character 1.

Example: REPLACE(A12,8,11,"one") takes the phrase in cell A12

We are many people on an island in space.

and changes it to

We are one on an island in space.

REPT(*text,num_times*)

Repeats the *text* for *num_times*.

Limits: The value of *num_times* must be positive and nonzero. The maximum number of resulting characters is 255.

Example: REPT("__..",3) produces __ . . __ . . __ . .

RIGHT(*text,num_chars*)

Results in as many characters as specified by *num_chars* from the right end of *text*. The value of *num_chars* defaults to 1 when omitted.

Examples: RIGHT("San Francisco, CA",2) produces CA.

RIGHT(B12,2) produces 02 when B12 contains the numeric ZIP code 95402.

SEARCH(*find_text,within_text,start_num*)

Begins at *start_num* in the specified *within_text*, searches through it for the *find_text*, and produces the character number where *find_text* begins. The first character position in *within_text* is 1. If *start_num* is omitted, it is assumed to be 1. SEARCH() ignores case differences. If *find_text* is not found or if *start_num* is out of limits, #VALUE! is returned.

The wild card ? can be used in *find_text* to specify any single character at that location within the text being found. The wild card * can be used in *find_text* to specify any group of characters at that location within the text being found.

Examples: SEARCH("an","Marathoners run long distances",14) produces 26.

SEARCH("l*g","Marathoners run long distances") produces 17.

SUBSTITUTE(*text,old_text,new_text,*instance_num)

Substitutes *new_text* for *old_text* within the specified *text*. If *old_text* occurs more than once, *instance_num* specifies which occurrence to replace. If *instance_num* is not specified, every occurrence of *old_text* is replaced.

Example: SUBSTITUTE("The stone age","stone","information") produces `The information age`.

T(*value*)

Returns text when *value* is text; returns blank when *value* is not text.

Examples: T(B12) produces `Top` if B12 contains "Top".

T(57) produces blank.

TEXT(*value, format_text*)

Converts the numeric *value* to text and displays it with the format specified by *format_text*. The result appears to be a formatted number, but actually is text. Use one of the predefined or custom numeric or date formats to specify the format for the *value*. These formats and custom formats are described in Chapter 8, "Formatting Worksheets." The format cannot contain an asterisk (*) or be in the General format.

Example: TEXT(4567.89,"$#,##0.00") produces `$4,567.89`.

Enter a title with date or number in a cell narrower than the width that would normally display the date or number by using a formula such as the following:

"Today's date is "&TEXT(NOW( ),"mmm d, yyyy")

TRIM(*text*)

Deletes all spaces from *text* so that only one space remains between words. This can be useful for *cleaning* text used in databases or imported to or exported from Excel.

Example: TRIM("this is the breathy look") produces `this is the breathy look`.

UPPER(*text*)

Changes *text* to all uppercase.

    Example: UPPER(B2) produces ENOUGH! when B2 contains
                      "enough!".

VALUE(*text*)

Converts text numbers or dates in one of Excel's predefined formats into
numbers that are usable in formulas. Because Excel normally converts
numeric text into numbers when necessary, this function is used primarily to ensure compatibility with other spreadsheets.

    Limits: The text number must be in one of the predefined nu-
              meric formats available in Excel.

    Example: VALUE(B2) produces 52 when B2 contains the text
                      "$52.00".

Trigonometric Functions

T I P   If you work with Excel doing scientific or engineering analysis, make
sure that you review Chapter 14's description of the additional features and functions available in the Analysis ToolPak. The Analysis
ToolPak comes free with Excel.

Trigonometric functions use angles measured in radians. Convert between radians and degrees with these equations:

    Radians = Degrees*π/180

    Degrees = Radians*180/π

The add-in functions described in Chapter 15, "Using Excel's Add-In Macros," include a function that converts between degrees and radians.

ACOS(*number*)

Produces the arc cosine of the *number* in radians. ACOS() is the inverse
of the COS() function. The *number* must be in the range –1 to 1. The resulting angle will be in the range 0 to π radians (0 to 180 degrees).

    Example: ACOS(.2) produces 1.369438406 radians.

ACOSH(*number*)

Produces the inverse hyperbolic cosine of the *number*. The *number* must be greater than or equal to 1.

ASIN(*number*)

Produces the arc sine of the *number* in radians. When given a *number*, the result of a sine function, ASIN() produces the original angle measured in radians. The *number* must be in the range –1 to 1. The resulting angle will be in the range –π/2 to π/2 radians (–90 to 90 degrees).

   Example: ASIN(.2) produces `.201357921` radians.

ASINH(*number*)

Produces the inverse hyperbolic sine of the *number*.

ATAN(*number*)

Produces the arc tangent of the *number* as a radian angle. ATAN() is the inverse of the TAN() function. The resulting angle will be in the range –π/2 to π/2 radians (–90 to 90 degrees).

ATAN2(*x_number,y_number*)

Produces the arc tangent for coordinate values of *x_number* and *y_number*. The resulting angle is in the range –π to π radians (–180 to 180 degrees) excluding –π (–180 degrees). If *x_number* and *y_number* are both 0, the function produces the message `#DIV/0!`.

ATANH(*number*)

Produces the inverse hyperbolic tangent of the *number*. The *number* must be between, but not including, –1 and 1.

COS(*number*)

Produces the cosine of the radian angle *number*.

COSH(*number*)

Produces the hyperbolic cosine of the *number*.

SIN(*number*)

Produces the sine of the radian angle *number*.

   Example: SIN(.5) produces `.479425539`.

SINH(*number*)

Produces the hyperbolic sine of the *number*.

TAN(*number*)

Produces the tangent of the radian angle *number*.

TANH(*number*)

Produces the hyperbolic tangent of the *number*.

FROM HERE...

For Related Information:

▶▶ "Using Formulas To Make Decisions," p. 492.

▶▶ "Using Formulas To Look Up Data in Tables," p. 495.

▶▶ "Using the Analysis ToolPak," p. 573.

▶▶ "Adding Functions," p. 606.

▶▶ "Using Basic Database Functions," p. 897.

▶▶ "Building Function Macros," p. 926.

Chapter Summary

Use this chapter as a reference guide. Remember that Excel contains a great deal of worksheet help. It is almost a necessity to paste functions with their argument prompts. Not only will it save you from typographical errors, it will save brain cells because you won't have to memorize needless trivia.

To understand what the arguments represent and for additional information about the limits or use of a function, choose the **Help Contents** command and select the topic *Worksheet Functions* or choose the Help button from the Paste Functions dialog box. From the list that appears, select the exact function that you need help with, or select the type of function group you are interested in.

Examples of worksheet functions and arrays are in Chapter 13, "Using Power Worksheet Features." Examples of database analysis using D*functions* appear in Chapter 26, "Building Extensive Databases."

If you do financial analysis, statistical or trends analysis, or work in science and engineering, make sure that you review the Analysis ToolPak that adds features to Excel. It and other advanced analysis tools are described in Chapter 14.

Building Systems and Managing Multiple Windows

E xcel is more than just a worksheet. It is an environment in which you can develop systems for business, science, and engineering. Excel can be a base for developing systems because of its capability to open and link multiple documents. Excel has an extensive set of features and enables you to customize its menus and dialog boxes for your own purposes. In this chapter, you learn how Excel can open and manage the multiple documents that usually are required for larger systems.

After reading and experimenting your way through this chapter, you may see worksheets in a new way. You learn how to start Excel and automatically load the documents you want to use. If you have large worksheets, you will want to learn how to zoom so that you can see more of your worksheet at one time. You also learn how to open multiple windows in a single worksheet or divide one window into as many as four panes through which you can see different worksheet areas. You learn about workbooks, which help you when you need to collect multiple worksheets into a single group.

Saving and Magnifying Worksheet Displays

Large worksheets or worksheets that present many different displays and print areas could cause you extra work. They might require searching for the correct worksheet area, changing of display and print settings, and other tasks that slow you down. However, Excel has two commands that enable you to easily view large areas or to print the same areas with the settings you use frequently.

The **Windows Zoom** command gives you the capability to magnify or reduce the worksheet's display so that you can reduce or magnify the worksheet characters. This command doesn't change the printed result, but it does enable you to reduce a worksheet so that you can see more of it or magnify one part to make formatting easier. Magnifying the worksheet by zooming also makes a screen easier to read when it is projected with an LCD projection panel.

By using **Windows View**, you have the capability to store the range and the display and print settings for worksheet areas you frequently view or print. You can set up the areas with the display or print settings, position the worksheet on-screen as you want to view it, then save the view and settings to a name. The next time you want to see that view with the same settings, you can choose its name from the Views dialog box.

If you want to print an area with a view name you have saved, then use Excel's Report Manager to select the name of the view you want to print. The named view stores the print settings saved with each view, so you don't need to change print settings with each view. You also can print views in sequence and include sequential page numbers to create a large report.

Magnifying and Reducing the View

When you need to magnify a portion of the worksheet or see a larger area, you should use Excel's zoom feature. Zoom enables you to get a close-up view of a selected part of a document. It also can give you an overview of a large portion of the document. Although the **Windows Zoom** command changes how much of a document appears on-screen, it does not alter the font, column widths, or related features when the document prints.

Most worksheets exceed the bounds of Excel's window. The worksheet shown in figure 11.1, for example, shows revenue projections for the ABC corporation along with the Window menu and the Zoom command. The projections are displayed on a monthly basis by type of business. Totals for each set of three months summarize income estimates by month, type of business, and overall. Figure 11.1 shows that ABC's income projection for the first quarter is $96,000.

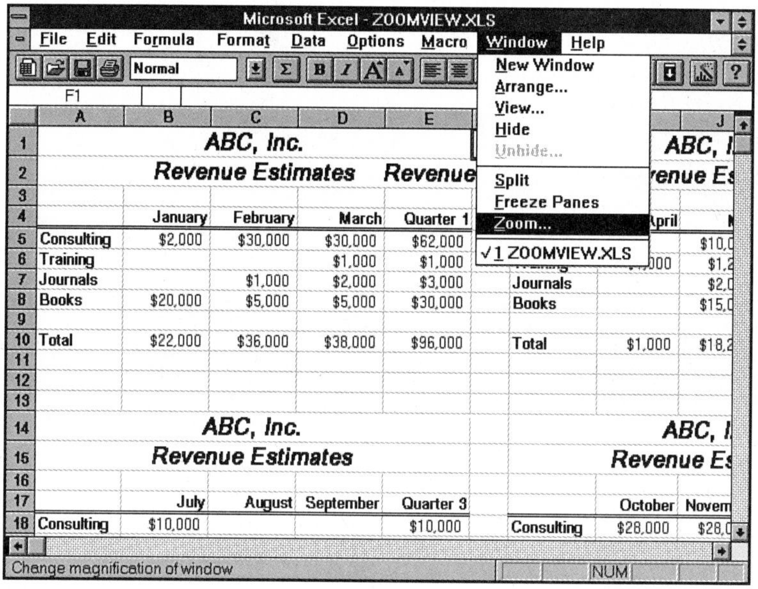

FIG. 11.1

A standard Excel view of a document with four tables. Notice that only one of the tables can be seen completely in this view.

The standard Excel view in figure 11.1 does not span a sufficiently wide portion of the document to show each of the four tables. All of the income table for the first quarter can be seen, but only portions of the remaining three tables are visible.

To change the view, select the Zoom command from the Windows menu. When you choose the Zoom command, Excel displays the Zoom dialog box shown in figure 11.2.

The Zoom dialog box includes five standard zoom settings and two custom settings. The standard view has 100% magnification. The 200% magnification setting provides a closer view of the document that shows about half as many columns and rows as the standard view. The 75% setting presents about 50 percent more rows and columns than the standard view.

To select one of the standard zooms, select the option button and choose OK or press Enter. The new view shows immediately. Figure 11.3 shows a document with 75 percent magnification.

FIG. 11.2

The Zoom dialog box enables you to magnify or reduce your view of the screen.

FIG. 11.3

A 75 percent magnification view of the document shown in figure 11.1.

Although the 75 percent magnification presents all four tables, there may be some minor distortion introduced with this increased viewpoint. Nevertheless, these different perspectives are useful because they show how tables are positioned on a worksheet.

When you need to magnify or reduce a screen by a percentage different than the predefined settings, use the Fit Selection and Custom options. If you have a range you want to expand or contract to fit within Excel's boundaries, select the range and use the Fit Selection option. The range expands or contracts to fit in the boundaries. If you know approximately how much you want the normal view magnified or condensed, enter a percentage in the Custom edit box. To return to the normal view, select the 100 option.

The Zoom tool is available on the Utility toolbar. Chapter 2 describes how to display the Utility toolbar. Chapter 33 describes how to add a tool to any toolbar. Each click on the increase (+) or decrease (-) zoom tool increases or decreases the magnification by one increment in the Zoom dialog box.

Naming and Saving a View

Worksheets are dynamic. You move between different locations and print different areas. By using the **Windows View** command, you can name different views with their display settings and name different print areas and their print settings. To return to the same view or print setup, all you need to do is select the named view that you want.

Saving views or print areas and settings with a name can be helpful in many situations—for example:

- You can see the printed report view that has print ranges predefined and includes the page setup and print titles.

- You can look at the data-entry view with display settings that make the entry form appear like paper with gridlines and rows and columns turned off.

- You can set up data-entry views, formula debugging views, and large-area overviews.

Figures 11.4 and 11.5 show before and after examples of switching between different views and settings onto the same worksheet.

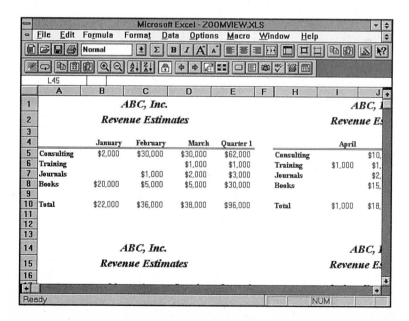

FIG. 11.4

A standard worksheet before the views and settings have been modified.

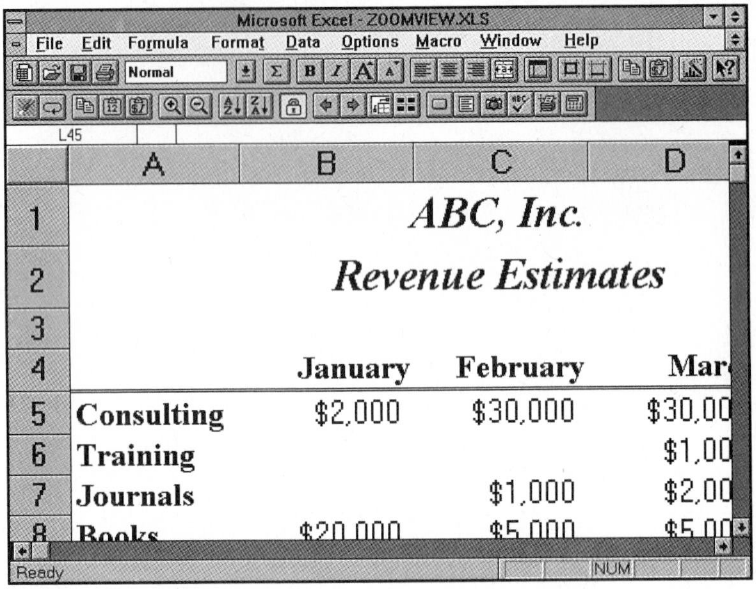

FIG. 11.5

The same worksheet
after the views and
settings have been
changed.

To create a named view, complete the following steps:

1. Create the worksheet or macro sheet.

2. Position the window, add panes by splitting the window, size the row heights and column widths, and set display settings as you want them in the view. If you are naming an area you will use for printed reports, specify the print area, print titles, and page setup settings.

3. Select the cells or ranges you want selected when the view appears.

4. Choose the **Window View** command.

5. Choose the **Add** button.

   The Views dialog box appears, as shown in figure 11.6.

6. Choose the **Add** button. The Add View dialog box appears.

7. Type the view's name in the **Name** box.

8. Select or clear the **Print Settings** and Hidden **Row & Column** Settings check boxes.

9. Choose OK or press Enter.

To change a view you already have named, display the view. Then modify the window, display settings, or print settings as you need. Repeat the process of choosing the **Windows View** command and choosing the **Add** button. Enter the same name you used originally to name the view.

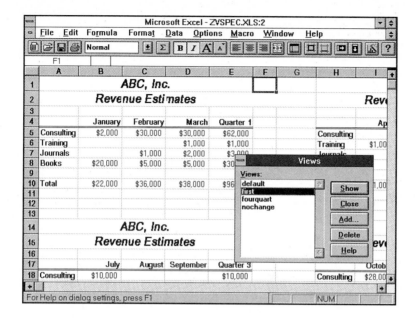

FIG. 11.6

The Views dialog box.

Displaying a Named View

To display a named view, complete the following steps:

1. Choose the **Window View** command.

2. Select the name of the view you want from the **Views** list (refer to fig. 11.6).

3. Choose **Show**.

When your named view is displayed, you can begin work or print by using the **File Print** or **File Print Preview** command.

 NOTE The **View** command is only available when the View add-in has been installed in Excel. The View add-in can be installed during installation or can be added to Excel at any time by using the Add-In Manager. To learn how to add or delete add-ins from Excel by using the Add-In Manager, read Chapter 15.

Deleting a Named View

To delete a view, complete the following steps:

1. Choose the **Window View** command.

2. Select from the **Views** list the name of the view you want to delete.

3. Choose the **D**elete button.

4. Select and delete additional names, or choose the **C**lose button.

FROM HERE...

For Related Information:

▶▶ "Using Other Add-Ins," p. 615.

▶▶ "Printing," p. 643.

Viewing a Window through Multiple Panes

Dividing an Excel window into sections enables you to see two or four different parts of a worksheet. Appropriately, each section of the window is referred to as a *pane*. Multiple panes are particularly useful when you work with databases or large worksheets. The views in each pane are synchronized so that scrolling through one pane scrolls its counterpart in the same direction.

As an illustration, you can display both the criteria range and the extract range of a database at the same time. This technique enables you to enter a criterion and see whether the extract matches what you expected. Figure 11.7 shows the criteria and extract ranges of a sample database displayed in two separate panes.

You can place the data-entry area of a large worksheet in one pane and the results in another. If you divide the worksheet into four panes and use **O**ptions Freeze Panes to freeze the panes containing the headings, you can scroll through the worksheet and still see the worksheet's row and column headings.

Dividing a Window into Multiple Panes

Figure 11.7 shows a database window divided into two panes. Notice how the row numbers jump from 9 to 34. The upper pane shows the database column titles; the lower pane shows the database. With this arrangement, you never lose sight of the column headings as you scroll through a database.

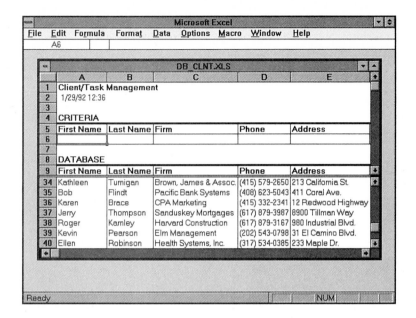

FIG. 11.7

You can view different parts of the same worksheet through panes.

To split a worksheet window at the top-left corner of the active cell, complete the following steps:

1. Activate the window you want to split and position the active cell.

2. Choose the **Window S**plit command.

The window will split above and to the left of the active cell. To split the window horizontally into two sections, move the active cell to column A in the cell below where you want the split, and then choose the command. To split the window vertically into two sections, move the active cell to the first row in the column to the right of where you want the split, and then choose the command.

To remove a split window by using the keyboard, choose the **W**indow Remove **S**plit command. The active cell can be in any location.

Figure 11.8 shows two gray bars positioned to divide the window into four sections. This was done by selecting cell D7 and choosing the **Win**dow **S**plit command. Figure 11.8 shows how the vertical and horizontal scroll bars become split after pressing Enter.

Before you create panes with the mouse, notice that solid black bars appear at the top of the vertical scroll bar and at the left edge of the horizontal scroll bar. To create panes with the mouse, complete the following steps:

1. Drag the solid black bars down the vertical scroll bar or across the horizontal scroll bar. As you drag, a gray pane divider shows where the window will be split.

2. Position the gray pane divider where you want the window split, and then release the mouse button.

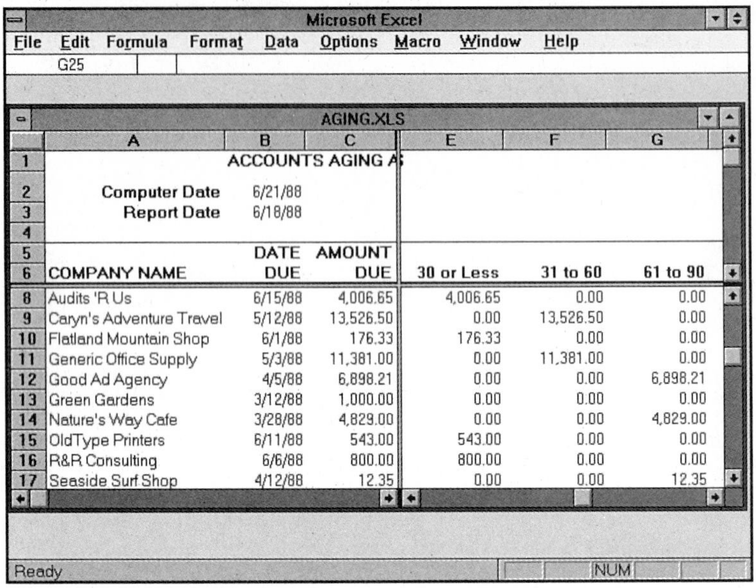

FIG. 11.8

After splitting windows into panes, you can scroll each pane.

To resize panes, drag the solid black bars to a new location. To remove the split, drag the solid black bar past the arrow on the scroll bar, and then release the mouse button.

T I P   If you quickly want to split a window evenly into panes, double-click one of the solid black bars. To quickly remove one of the splits, double-click the solid black bar that is creating the split.

Freezing Headings into Position

You can freeze the panes in position so that you cannot change them accidentally. To freeze panes you already have positioned, choose the **W**indow Freeze Panes command.

When panes are frozen, the gray split bar becomes a thin solid line and you cannot scroll into the frozen area. The top or left pane cannot scroll. You can move the active cell into the frozen area by pressing the arrow keys or clicking a cell. To *thaw* the frozen panes, choose **W**indow Unfreeze Panes.

> **T I P**
>
> If you have not split a worksheet into panes, you can split the window and freeze the panes with a single command. Select a cell positioned below and to the right of where you want the panes to split and freeze, and then choose the **Window Freeze Panes** command. Choose the **Window Unfreeze Panes** command to remove the panes.

You might want to freeze panes in databases that less-experienced operators will be working on. Figure 11.9 shows the worksheet from figure 11.8. The lower-right portion of the worksheet can now be scrolled to the right without losing the row headings on the left. Notice that the divider between panes is invisible. The scroll bar scrolls only the area in the lower-right portion of the window.

	Microsoft Excel							
File	**Edit**	**Formula**	**Format**	**Data**	**Options**	**Macro**	**Window**	**Help**

G25

	AGING.XLS						
	A	**B**	**C**	**E**	**F**	**G**	
1	ACCOUNTS AGING A						
2	Computer Date	6/21/88					
3	Report Date	6/18/88					
4							
5		DATE	AMOUNT				
6	COMPANY NAME	DUE	DUE	30 or Less	31 to 60	61 to 90	
8	Audits 'R Us	6/15/88	4,006.65	4,006.65	0.00	0.00	
9	Caryn's Adventure Travel	5/12/88	13,526.50	0.00	13,526.50	0.00	
10	Flatland Mountain Shop	6/1/88	176.33	176.33	0.00	0.00	
11	Generic Office Supply	5/3/88	11,381.00	0.00	11,381.00	0.00	
12	Good Ad Agency	4/5/88	6,898.21	0.00	0.00	6,898.21	
13	Green Gardens	3/12/88	1,000.00	0.00	0.00	0.00	
14	Nature's Way Cafe	3/28/88	4,829.00	0.00	0.00	4,829.00	
15	OldType Printers	6/11/88	543.00	543.00	0.00	0.00	
16	R&R Consulting	6/6/88	800.00	800.00	0.00	0.00	
17	Seaside Surf Shop	4/12/88	12.35	0.00	0.00	12.35	

Ready   NUM

FIG. 11.9

Freeze panes to prevent scrolling into headings and to prevent panes from moving.

Activating Different Panes

Using the keyboard, you can move the active cell clockwise among panes by pressing F6; press Shift+F6 to move counterclockwise among the panes. The active cell moves to the same cell it occupied the last time it was in the pane. With the mouse, you can shift among panes by clicking in the pane you want to activate. Note that jumping between panes often causes windows to reposition. You cannot move between panes like this if the panes are frozen.

Viewing One Document through Multiple Windows

If you have worked with a large worksheet, you probably have wanted to see different parts of the worksheet at the same time. You can do this in Excel by opening new windows of the same worksheet. Although there is still only one worksheet, you can view it through multiple windows. The method discussed previously uses panes that divide a single window. This method displays additional windows of the same worksheet.

In figure 11.10, you can see that windows opened on the same worksheet have the same name in the title bar, but the title of the first window opened ends with :1, the second ends with :2, and so on. The window titles in the figure are DB_CLNT.XLS:1, DB_CLNT.XLS:2, and DB_CLNT.XLS:3. These windows display the same worksheet. Each window can be located and sized separately.

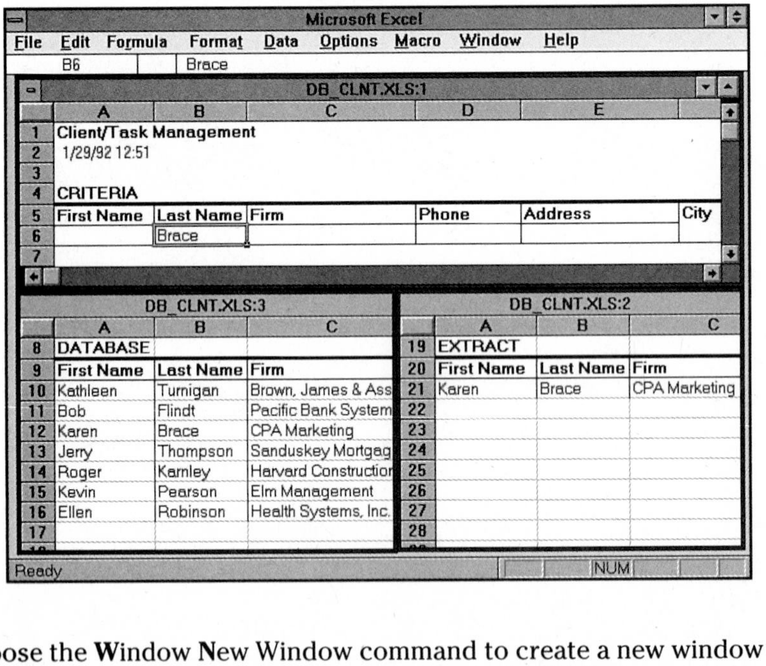

FIG. 11.10

You can open more than one window on a worksheet.

Choose the **Window New** Window command to create a new window in the current worksheet. You can move, size, and split the new window in the same way as the original. Each window can have different formats, column widths, and display arrangements. In fact, each can appear totally different. If, however, you change data or formulas in one window, the change affects all the windows belonging to that worksheet.

Multiple windows increase your power with Excel. The tips that follow show you a few ways you can tap the power of multiple windows.

T I P

Multiple windows can make data entry easier. You can arrange windows so that one window displays the data-entry area. With this arrangement, you can scroll through account codes or prices in one window and make entries in another window.

You also can use multiple windows to create help screens for your programs. Open a window in the instructional area of the worksheet so that users can scroll to the instructions they need.

T I P

Use **Window New** Window to create a second or third window in the active worksheet when you want to debug it. Use **Options Display** Formulas to format the new window so that it displays formulas. The original window still displays the results. This way, you can see the results and formulas at the same time, as shown in figure 11.11. You can see the cell references and the effect of changes more quickly and easily with these two windows.

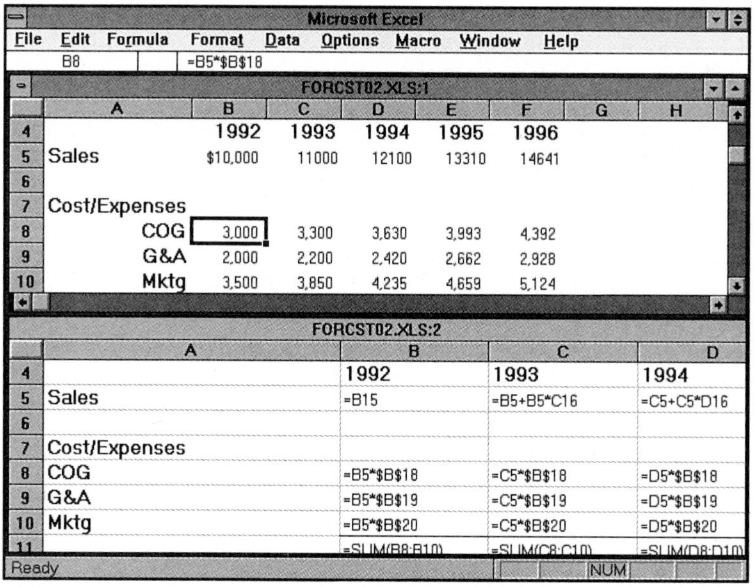

FIG. 11.11

You can see both the results and the formulas by opening a second window on the same worksheet.

T I P Jumping between the criteria range, the database range, and the extract range in a database can slow down your work. Instead, set up a window displaying each range. Arrange the windows in a fashion similar to that shown in figure 11.10. You even can have the windows maximized to full-screen. Whenever you want to use that part of the worksheet shown in another window, press Ctrl+F6 until that window appears on top.

FROM HERE...

For Related Information:

◀◀ "Manipulating Windows," p. 59.

Working with Multiple Documents

Excel enables you to have multiple documents on-screen. Working with multiple documents is a great convenience and time-saver when you want to link worksheets, view worksheets and graphs simultaneously, or just see multiple documents at the same time. A later section in this chapter, "Grouping Documents into Workbooks," describes how you can collect worksheets, charts, and macros into workbooks, which makes it easy to keep a collection together.

Opening Additional Documents

When you need to work with additional worksheets, charts, or macro sheets, open the additional documents with **File O**pen, just as you opened the first document. When you open documents that are linked to other documents, such as a chart that is linked to an unopened worksheet, you are asked whether you want to update the document you are opening by using the data from the unopened document.

Switching to a Window

If you have multiple worksheets or windows on-screen, you can switch to the one you want and work on it. Using the mouse, move the other windows out of the way by dragging their title bars, and then click anywhere in the window you want to work on. That window will appear on top.

With the keyboard, press Ctrl+F6 until the window you want is active; or choose the **W**indow menu, and then choose the window's name from the menu.

Arranging Multiple Windows

You can arrange windows manually by moving and sizing them as explained in Chapter 2. If you have many windows to reorganize, you may want to take advantage of some automated assistance. Choose **W**indow **A**rrange, and from the Arrange Windows dialog box, select how you want the windows arranged. The windows will be resized and rearranged. Figure 11.12 shows three windows before using **W**indow **A**rrange and the Arrange Windows dialog box, and figure 11.13 shows the same three windows afterwards, using the settings shown in figure 11.12.

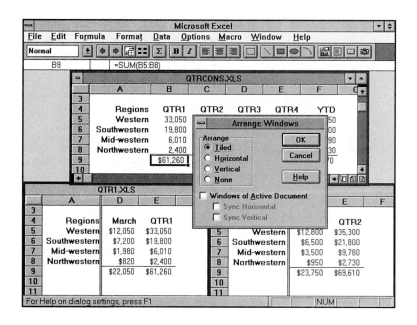

FIG. 11.12

Use the Arrange Windows dialog box to arrange and synchronize windows.

The different Arrange Windows options include the following:

Option	Function
Tiled	Arranges an even number of windows to divide the screen so that the active window becomes the top-left window. Arranges an odd number of windows so that the active window appears vertically along the left edge.
Horizontal	Arranges all the windows in horizontal strips. The active window moves to the top.
Vertical	Arranges all the windows in vertical strips. The active window moves to the far left.
None	This option is selected if you have manually sized and moved multiple windows.
Windows of Active Document	Places all windows of the active document in the foreground; all others in the background.
Sync Horizontal	Causes all windows from the same document to move in a synchronized manner when scrolled horizontally.
Sync Vertical	Causes all windows from the same document to move in a synchronized manner when scrolled vertically.

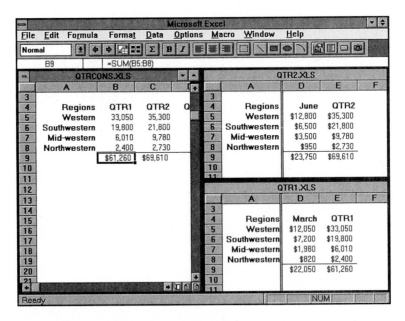

FIG. 11.13

After tiling, windows are easier to use.

Hiding and Unhiding Windows

You do not need to keep all your worksheets, charts, and macro sheets on-screen at one time. You can hide documents from view so that the screen appears more organized and less confusing. Hiding documents also can be valuable when you want to hide a macro sheet from novice operators. A hidden document remains available to other documents with which it is linked.

To hide a window, complete the following steps:

1. Activate the window so that it is on top.

2. Select the **Window Hide** command. The window disappears from the screen, and the **Unhide** command appears as a choice on the **Window** menu.

> To move a worksheet out of the way but to keep it accessible, minimize the worksheet to an icon. To minimize a worksheet, click on the worksheet's minimize icon (a double-headed arrow) at the top-right corner of the worksheet. To restore the worksheet icon into a window, double-click on the icon.
>
> **T I P**

To reveal hidden windows, complete the following steps:

1. Choose the **Window Unhide** command. The Unhide dialog box is displayed (see fig. 11.14).

FIG. 11.14

The Unhide dialog box.

2. From the list box, select the title of the hidden window you want to reveal.

3. Choose OK or press Enter. You are asked for a password if the hidden window is protected.

   The hidden windows reappear in their former position and size.

If all windows are hidden, the **Window** menu disappears and the **Unhide** command appears under the **File** menu.

T I P If you want to hide a worksheet or macro so that it cannot be unhidden, you need to create an add-in document, .XLA. If you want to create a worksheet, chart, or macro sheet that is hidden when opened but can be unhidden, complete the following steps:

1. Make a change in each document that you want to be hidden. This can be as simple as typing a letter in a cell and then deleting it.

2. Hide each document you want to open as hidden.

3. Quit Excel with the **File** E**x**it command.

4. When you are asked whether you want to save one of the files you want hidden, choose OK.

When you exit Excel and then reopen any of these files, they will be hidden because they were saved while hidden. You can unhide them with the **Windows** **U**nhide command.

Locking Windows in Position

After your windows are sized and in the proper positions, you may want to make sure that they stay there. Locking windows in position is a good idea, particularly if the worksheets are used by inexperienced operators or are displayed by macros.

To keep a window from moving or changing size, complete the following steps:

1. Position and size the window as you want it.

2. Choose the **O**ptions **P**rotect Document command.

3. Select the **W**indows check box.

4. Enter a password if you do not want others to remove protection. (A password can be any combination of letters and numbers; letters are case-sensitive. Make sure that you don't forget your password—you cannot unprotect your document if you do.)

5. Choose OK or press Enter. If you entered a password, the Confirm Password dialog box prompts you to retype it.

You can scroll through windows that are locked, but you will not be able to resize or move them (notice that the sizing border disappears from a protected window). You still can, however, enter and edit cells. If cells have been protected with the Format Cell Protection command and if protection for the worksheet is enabled with **O**ptions **P**rotect Document, you cannot edit the cells.

To unlock a worksheet, activate its window and choose the **O**ptions Un**p**rotect Document command. If a password was used to lock the window's position, you are asked to enter the password.

Saving and Closing Multiple Windows

When you save your worksheet to disk, all the windows with their current sizes and shapes are saved. You can set up multiple windows on a worksheet in the arrangement that you use most frequently, and then save the worksheet to disk. When you open the worksheet from disk, all the windows are arranged and sized as you left them.

If you want to save a worksheet with only one window, make sure that you close the extra windows. To close unwanted windows, first activate the window that you want to close. Then double-click in the document Control menu to the left of the document title; you also can select the document Control menu by pressing Alt+hyphen and then choose the **C**lose command; or you can choose the **F**ile **C**lose command.

If you want to close all the open documents, hold down the Shift key as you choose the File menu. A new command, Close All appears in place of the normal Close command. Choosing Close All closes all the open documents. You are prompted to save any changes made to documents that have changed since they were last saved.

T I P

For Related Information:

◄◄ "Manipulating Windows," p. 59.

◄◄ "Protecting Worksheets," p. 309.

FROM HERE...

Grouping Documents into Workbooks

Workbooks are useful whenever you need to group related documents so that they can be retrieved or worked on together. Situations where you might want to group documents include the following:

- When you are consolidating worksheets for an income projection, and you need access to the individual worksheets as well as the consolidated income worksheet.

- When you need to keep two or more linked worksheets together.

- When you want to show instructions for using worksheets in a separate document window.

- When you have a collection of worksheets, charts, and macros you want to copy as a group so that no file is left out.

- When you want to create a system of integrated worksheets, charts, macros, and add-ins that you can package.

- When you want to reference documents by names up to 32 characters long.

A workbook is a collection of two or more documents that are saved—and opened—as a unit. Joining documents as a workbook adds a management window: a Workbook Contents window, which lists each of the documents contained within the workbook. The documents that comprise a workbook may be *bound* into the workbook so that they don't exist separately, or they may be *unbound*, included in the workbook but also existing as individual files.

A workbook saves more than just a collection of documents. It also saves each document's view, size, and order.

Workbooks are ideal for any group of worksheets, charts, and macros that are related and must stay related. Although it is not necessary for workbook documents to be linked or consolidated, saving such documents together in a workbook often is helpful.

Workbook files have the extension XLW. If documents included in a Workbook are unbound, you can open the documents separately. If they are bound, you cannot open them—you can open only the Workbook that contains them. When you open a Workbook, you first see the Workbook Contents window, listing all the documents contained in the workbook. In the background are the Workbook's remaining documents.

Retrieved workbooks show the view displayed at the time the workbook was saved. However, this view can be modified with all the techniques presented in this chapter.

Workbooks can contain both bound and unbound documents.

You should include bound documents in a workbook in the following circumstances:

- When documents work together and you want them packaged as a single unit.

- When documents need to be packaged as a single unit so that documents can be protected and you don't want a document to be forgotten when copied or moved.

- When document management would be easier with file names up to 32 characters long.

You should save documents individually but list them in the workbook Table of Contents in the following circumstances:

- When documents need to be shared with other documents or workbooks.

- When documents need to be used individually or as part of a workbook.

Saving Workbooks

One of the easiest ways to create a workbook is to open and arrange documents as you want them in the workbook. You may want to save documents separately until you are comfortable with workbooks. You then can save the workbook containing these documents with the **File Save Workbook** command. A later section describes how to modify your workbook so that files in the workbook are saved separately or bound into a workbook.

Figure 11.15 shows a pair of linked files. In the top worksheet, HWORDER.XLS, a user can enter a quantity order of two items, Screws and Screw Drivers. This worksheet uses information in the bottom worksheet, HWPRICES.XLS, to determine the appropriate price for each item.

To save this pair of worksheets in a workbook, complete the following steps:

1. Choose the **File Save Workbook** command. Excel displays the Save As dialog box in front of the Workbook screen (see fig. 11.16).

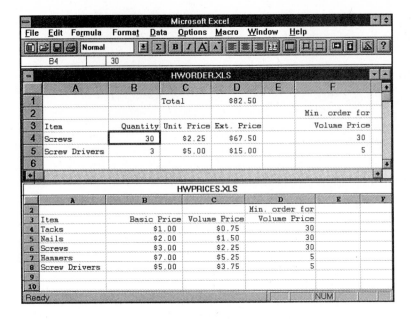

A pair of linked
worksheets.

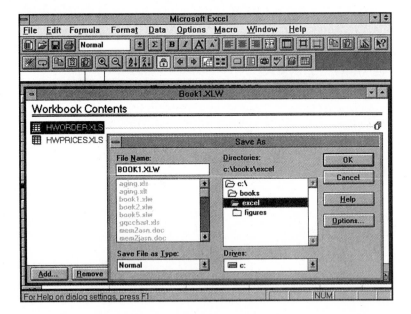

The Save As dialog
box that is ready to
save HWORDER.XLS
and HWPRICES.XLS
as entries in
BOOK1.XLW.

2. Type the name you want for the workbook over the name
   BOOK1.XLW in the File **N**ame text box.

3. Choose OK or press Enter to save the pair of worksheets as a workbook with the name you type and the extension XLW.

The workbook's table of contents shows files that are in memory at the time. You can add and delete files from the workbook. The documents in a workbook can be retrieved separately to form other workbooks or to be used individually.

Figure 11.17 shows the screen after BOOK1.XLW is saved. Notice that the worksheet titles have a new prefix, [BOOK1.XLW], and that the Workbook Contents window has been minimized or moved to the background. This indicates that BOOK1.XLW is in memory and that these files are available as part of that book. Obviously, your workbook will use the title under which you save it.

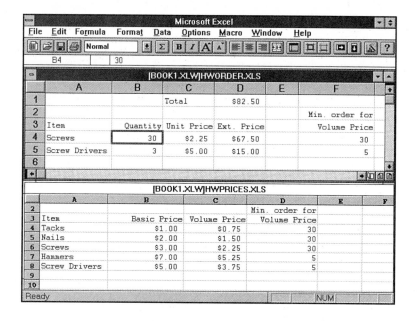

FIG. 11.17

Window titles show the workbook name and the document name.

Retrieving Workbooks

You retrieve a workbook just like a worksheet, except that you specify a workbook name. To open a workbook, complete the following steps:

1. Choose the **File Open** command.

2. Select the name of the workbook you want to retrieve; workbook files end with XLW.

3. Choose OK or press Enter to retrieve the selected workbook.

When the workbook opens, documents appear on-screen as they were when they were saved, with the Workbook Contents window active. Figure 11.18 shows the BOOK1.XLW workbook. If the table of contents window were minimized, you would be able to see the two covered windows for the worksheets in the workbook.

You can cycle through the documents in the workbook by selecting one of the three icons that appear at the bottom-right corner of the active workbook window. The leftmost icon shows an open binder; select it to return to the Workbook Contents window. The middle icon shows a left page; select this icon to activate the previous workbook window. The rightmost icon shows a right page; select it to activate the next workbook window.

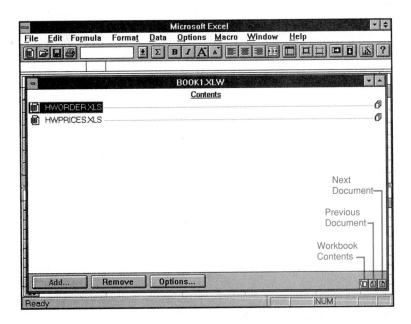

FIG. 11.18

The screen immediately after opening BOOK1.XLW.

Adding Workbook Documents

In most active systems, you will need to add or delete documents from a workbook. In the example used so far, the linked system of files in BOOK1.XLW can benefit from a third file. If an instruction document were added to BOOK1.XLW, users could refer to it as a guide for using the system, and there would be no need to maintain a hard copy of user instructions for the system. The instructions would always be available to anyone with access to the workbook containing the system.

If you are using a mouse, you can drag a document into an existing workbook. Follow these steps:

1. Arrange the Workbook Contents window and the document you want to add to the workbook so that you can see them both on-screen.

2. Activate the Table of Contents window in the workbook.

3. To add a worksheet or macro sheet to the workbook, drag the *Select All* button from the worksheet onto the Table of Contents window and release it.

   The Select All button is the blank square above row 1 heading and left of the column A heading. When clicked, the entire document is selected.

To add a chart to a workbook, select the entire chart by clicking in the chart background or choosing **Chart Select Chart**. Then drag one of the white handles from the chart onto the Table of Contents window and release. Figure 11.19 shows a document being dragged onto a Table of Contents window.

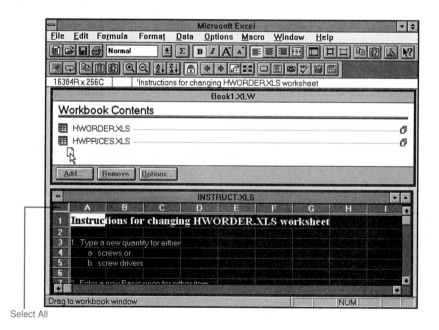

FIG. 11.19

Add documents by dragging the Select All button onto a workbook's Table of Contents window.

You also can use commands to add a document to a workbook. Follow these steps:

1. Choose the **File Open** command and open the workbook.

2. Switch to the workbook table of contents window by clicking it, selecting it from the **W**indow menu, or selecting the Table of Contents icon at the lower-right corner of the workbook.

3. Choose the **A**dd button at the bottom of the table of contents window.

   If you are using a keyboard press, the Tab key until the **A**dd button is selected, and then press Enter.

   The Add To Workbook dialog box, shown in figure 11.20, appears.

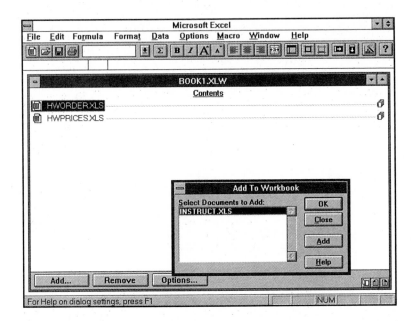

4. Select from the **S**elect Documents to Add list the document you want to add to the workbook.

   If the document you want to add is not open, choose the **O**pen button and open it. If you want to add a new document, choose the New button and select the type of new document you want to add.

5. Repeat step 4 to add more documents. Or choose OK or press Enter.

Figure 11.21 displays the new table of contents after the INSTRUCT.XLS file is added to BOOK1.XLW. The INSTRUCT.XLS document can be displayed from this table of contents by pressing Enter (with the INSTRUCT.XLS file selected) or by double-clicking the INSTRUCT.XLS file name in the table of contents.

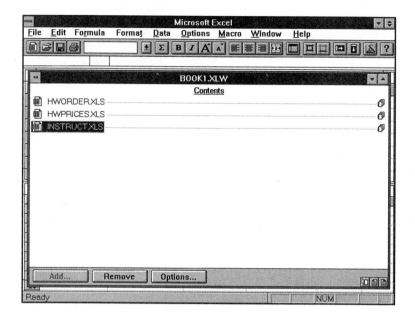

FIG. 11.21

A view of the table of contents window for BOOK1.XLW after INSTRUCT.XLS is added to the workbook.

Double-click the icon to the left of a document name in the table of contents to open that document.

T I P

Removing Workbook Documents

When you want to remove a document from a workbook, go to the workbook table of contents, select the document, and click the Remove button or choose the **E**dit Cl**e**ar command or press Del. You also can remove a document with the mouse by dragging the document's icon out of the table of contents and releasing it outside the workbook. (If you want to add a document back, choose the **A**dd button in the Contents window, select the file from the **S**elect Document to Add list, and choose **A**dd.)

Reorganizing a Workbook's Contents

Use your workbook the same as you would a notebook. Keep documents in the order you use them or in a hierarchical order. When you want to reorganize a workbook, you can drag a document's icon to its new location in the Workbook Contents window, and then release it when the horizontal insertion bar is positioned where you want to move the file. If you are using a keyboard, you can select a document and move it with the Cut and Paste commands on the menu.

Saving Documents in the Workbook or Separately

To see whether a document listed in the workbook table of contents has been saved as part of the workbook, check the bound or unbound icon at the far right in the table of contents. Figure 11.22 shows bound and unbound icons. Bound files are saved within a single workbook file. Unbound files must be saved as separate documents and are only listed in the table of contents.

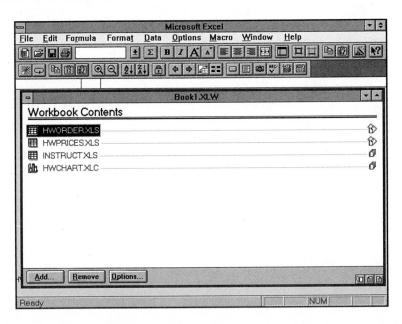

FIG. 11.22

Icons on the right indicate whether a document is bound into the workbook as part of a single file.

To change a file's status between bound or unbound, with the mouse, click the bound or unbound icon to toggle it between bound or unbound. When you save the workbook file, bound documents are saved within the workbook file. You must save unbound documents separately as you would save any document.

To change a file's status with the keyboard, complete the following steps:

1. Select the document in the table of contents.

2. Choose the **O**ptions button by pressing Tab until the button is bold, and then pressing Enter. The Document Options dialog box, in figure 11.23, appears.

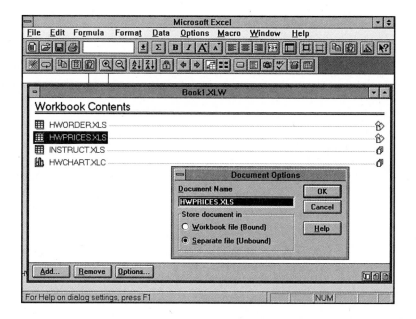

FIG. 11.23

The Document Options dialog box.

3. In the Store Document In group, select the **W**orkbook file (bound) option to save the document as part of a single workbook file. Select the **S**eparate file (unbound) option to save the document's name in the table of contents. The document must be saved separately.

4. Choose OK or press Enter.

You can create long document names by following the previous procedures to display the Document Options dialog box. In the **D**ocument Name box you can type a document name up to 32 characters long.

T I P

Editing and Formatting Groups of Worksheets

If you create or work with multiple worksheets that require the same data, edits, and formats in the same locations, you can save time by using *groups*. Groups tie together worksheets or macro sheets so that you can enter data, edit, format, or change display options in multiple sheets at the same time. Groups are an excellent way to create documents that are the same as each other in structure and format, with variations in content.

Unlike a workbook, which saves files together, a group exists only while files are open. Each file in a group is separate, and when you close the files in a group, the group is gone. Groups are most useful when you need to do identical editing, formatting, or data entry across multiple files.

T I P   The previous section in this chapter explains how to collect documents into workbooks so that they are packaged together. If you frequently edit and format the same group of documents, you may want to put them into a workbook.

Creating a Group

Figure 11.24 illustrates three worksheets built with the same layout, worksheet options, and formatting. Creating worksheets that are duplicates of each other is easy to do with groups. The data is different in each worksheet because each regional office enters its own data, but the structure and format are the same.

To create a group, complete the following steps:

1. Open or create the worksheets and macro sheets that you want in the same group.

2. Activate the worksheet in which you will make changes. Click the worksheet or press Ctrl+F6 until the worksheet is active. This worksheet acts as the master that other sheets will duplicate.

3. Choose the **Options Group Edit** command to display the Group Edit dialog box, shown in figure 11.25. All unhidden sheets appear selected if you have not previously grouped sheets that are now open.

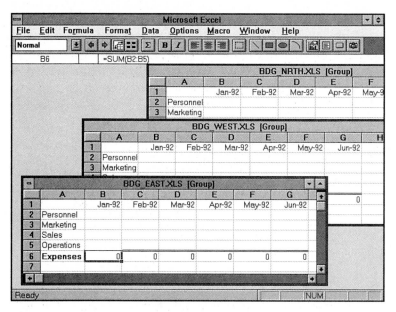

FIG. 11.24

You can group worksheets together to build duplicates of the same sheet.

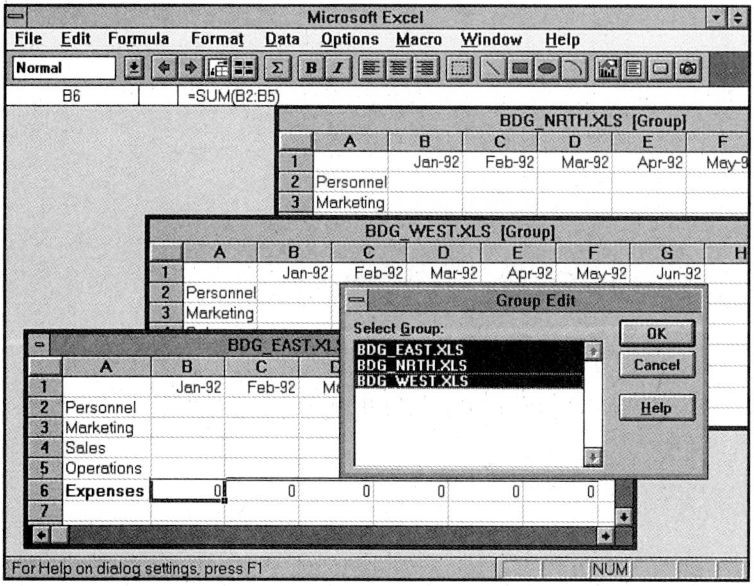

FIG. 11.25

Select the sheets that you want grouped together from the Group Edit dialog box.

4. In the Select **G**roup box, clear the selection from sheets that you do not want in the group by holding down Ctrl as you click worksheet names in the list (click again to reselect files). From the keyboard,

hold down Ctrl as you press the up- or down-arrow key to move to a worksheet name, and then press the Ctrl+space bar to select or clear a worksheet name.

5. Choose OK or press Enter.

Notice in figure 11.24 that [Group] appears in the title bars of selected sheets.

If you want to see only the sheets in the group as you work, choose the **W**indow **A**rrange command and select the Documents of **A**ctive Group check box. When this check box is selected, you can arrange sheets in this group with the other option buttons. Sheets that are part of the current group appear in the **W**indow menu with a check mark.

 While a group is active, the available commands are limited to editing and formatting within the group. You cannot, for example, open a document or a new file.

If you have an existing group and you want to add or remove other sheets, choose the **O**ptions **G**roup Edit command. The selected sheets are those of the most current group. Add or remove other sheets with the following two methods:

■ Hold down the Ctrl key as you click the worksheet name to add or delete from the list box.

■ Hold down the Ctrl key as you move up or down to the worksheet name, and then press the Ctrl+space bar to add or remove a worksheet from the group.

Editing or Modifying Groups

As long as you continue to work in the active worksheet, the group stays intact. As soon as you activate a different document, the group dissolves. The sheets in the last group used are remembered in the Group Edit dialog box. Activate other documents by clicking them, pressing Ctrl+F6, or choosing them from the **W**indow menu.

If you exit a group and want to return to it, choose the **O**ptions **G**roup Edit command. Notice that the sheets in the last group remain selected. All you need to do is choose OK or press Enter.

Entering Formulas and Data in Groups

When you want to enter data or formulas across multiple worksheets, complete the following steps:

1. Create the group.

2. Enter, edit, fill, or copy data or formulas in the active worksheet just as you would normally.

The entries, edits, or changes you make to the active worksheet are duplicated in the same location on other sheets in the group. When you edit a cell's contents in the active worksheet and press Enter (or click the Enter box), you place that entry into all the same cells in the group.

Figure 11.26 shows a SUM() function entered in the active worksheet. Figure 11.27 shows that the SUM() function has been duplicated in other sheets in the group.

If you make a mistake while entering data in a group, choose the Edit Undo command to undo the change in all sheets in the group.

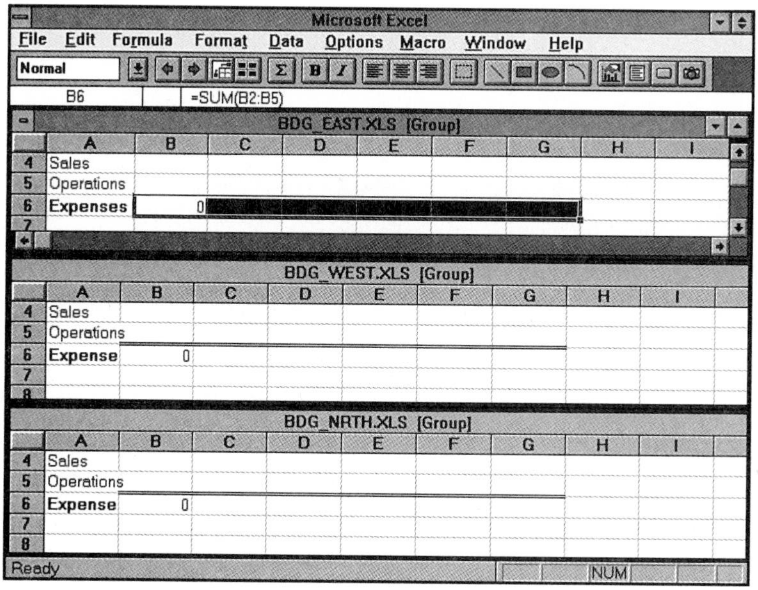

FIG. 11.26

Enter data, a function, or a formula in the active sheet.

The following commands act across the group in the same manner that they act on the active sheet:

Menu	Commands
File	Close, Close All, Page Setup, **Print**
Edit	Clear, **Delete**, **Insert**
Format	Alignment, **Border**, Cell Protection, Column Width, Font, **Number**, **Patterns**, Row Height, Style
Formula	Goto, Paste Function, S**how** Active Cell
Options	Display, Calculate Now, Short Menus, **Workspace**

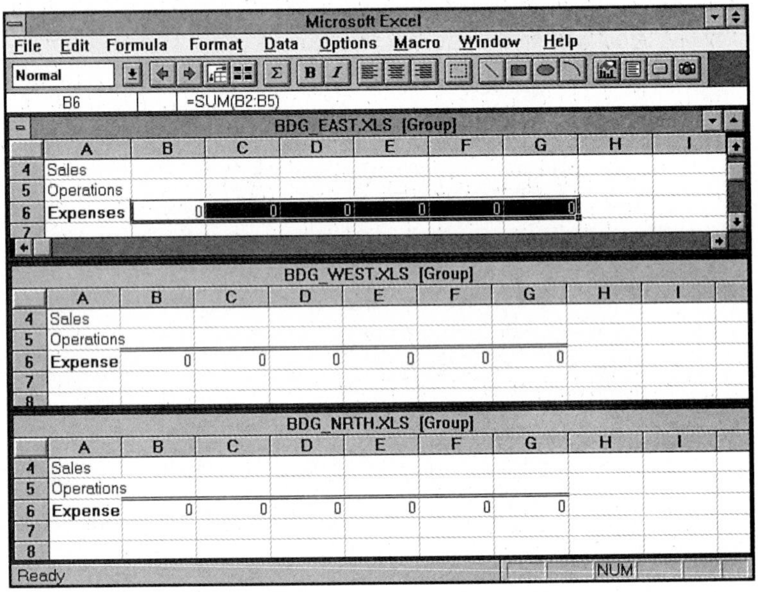

FIG. 11.27

Changes and entries in the active worksheet are duplicated throughout the group.

The following commands act differently on other group sheets than on the active sheet:

Menu	Command	Explanation
Data	Series	Enters a data series in each worksheet of the group. The data series can be different in each worksheet if each worksheet has a different starting value.

Menu	Command	Explanation
Edit	Fill, Down/Up, Left/Right	Fills the initial value or formula in each worksheet into the same range as selected in the active sheet.
		To fill the same value or formula across the same range in all worksheets, create the group first; then enter the initial value in the active sheet; then choose the **F**ill command.
		To fill a unique value or formula across the same range in all worksheets, enter the unique value or formula in each worksheet; then create the group; and choose the **F**ill command.
Macro	Absolute/Relative Record	Changes the cell reference type for all sheets in the group.
	Record	Records on all macro sheets in the group.
	Start Recorder	Works on the single macro sheet in the group in which you selected a cell with the **M**acro Set Recorder command. Do not include this macro sheet in the group or it may be overwritten.

Copying and Filling in Groups

When you have sheets in a group, any copying or filling you do in the active worksheet automatically is repeated in the other sheets in the group. This feature enables you to easily fill a formula into adjacent cells, create a data series, or copy and move new cell contents. In fact even the fill handle and drag and drop techniques are mimicked by other sheets in the group. For information on how to fill copies, create a sequence of data, and move or drag cells to new locations with the mouse, refer to Chapters 6 and 7.

Sometimes, you may have a worksheet containing existing data or formulas and you want to fill that data or formula into other sheets in the group. Use the **E**dit Fill **G**roup command to fill through sheets in the group in the same way that the **E**dit Fill Ri**g**ht and **E**dit Fill Do**w**n commands fill within the same worksheet.

If you have existing data or formulas that you want to copy throughout the same cells or ranges in other sheets, complete the following steps:

1. Create a group.

2. Activate the worksheet that contains the cell contents you want filled into other sheets.

3. Select the cells that you want to fill into other worksheets.

4. Choose the **E**dit Fill **G**roup command to display the Fill Group dialog box.

5. Select the **A**ll option to fill formulas and formats into other sheets. Select Formulas to fill formulas only, or select Formats to fill formats only.

6. Choose OK or press Enter.

Be careful when filling through sheets in a group. You may fill into an area of a worksheet that already contains data or formulas. If you are uncertain about the results of filling, first save the worksheets in the group.

Building Templates

A *template* is a file used as a form to create other worksheets, macro sheets, or charts. Documents created from a template contain the same layout, text, data, formulas, settings, styles, formats, names, and macros as those in the template.

Templates are useful for any documents that you use frequently and that you want to look consistent. Each of the documents created from a template will be a repeated image of others from the template. Templates can be useful for forms, such as data entry and expense accounts, or for ensuring consistency in departmental budget presentations.

Opening a Template

Opening a template creates a new document based on the template. The template remains unchanged. The new document will have a temporary name; if, for example, the template's file name is DATA.XLT, the documents based on the template will be DATA1, DATA2, and so on.

You can make templates readily accessible by saving them in the XLSTART directory, which is under the directory that contains the

EXCEL.EXE program. Templates saved in XLSTART will appear in the list shown in the **File New** command.

You can open a template stored in any directory; however, only those templates in the XLSTART directory appear in the New dialog box from the **File New** command. Templates use the XLT file extension.

Creating a Template

Templates can be based on a blank worksheet containing only settings or on an existing document. To build a template, complete the following steps:

1. Open or create the document that you want the template to use as a pattern.

2. Choose the **File Save As** command.

3. Type the template's name in the File **Name** text box.

4. Select the Template format from the Save File as **Type** list. This step adds an XLT extension to the file name.

5. Change to the directory where you want the template saved.

6. Choose OK twice or press Enter.

 Editing a file extension to become XLT will not save the file as a template. You must select Template from the Save File as **Type** list in the Save As dialog box.

Templates can be saved to or opened from any directory. If you save templates to the XLSTART directory, however, you see them listed in the **File New** dialog box. This listing makes them easy to open. The list of templates in the **File New** dialog box is updated only when you start Excel, so templates added during an Excel session are not shown until you restart Excel.

Templates created from charts do not retain the references to the worksheet data from which the chart was originally created. Chart templates retain only the chart format and use the currently selected worksheet data to create a new chart using the template's format. To create a chart using the format of the template, select the data in the worksheet, choose **File New**, and select the chart template you want.

To delete a template, use the **File Delete** command in Excel or the File Manager in Windows.

Editing a Template

Editing a template is similar to editing the document on which the template was based. There is, however, one extra step. To open the template, choose the **File O**pen command and select the template that you want to edit. Remember that templates use the extension XLT. Do not press Enter. Press Shift+Enter, or hold down the Shift key and click OK. This step opens the template and not a document based on the template.

To save the template after editing, choose the **File S**ave command. Excel remembers that this is a template, so you do not need to change the file format.

Building a System

Large Excel systems are composed of many documents that work to-gether: worksheets, templates, macros, charts, and add-ins. With Excel's features, you can work on-screen simultaneously with many documents that you frequently use together. You even can create workbooks of files that are bundled together or create files that load automatically when you start Excel.

In Excel, building a system of multiple documents consists of a few basic steps. Although every system you build will be different, you may want to follow these guidelines when building a system that you want to open or run automatically:

- Create the worksheets, charts, macro sheets, add-ins, and templates used in the system. The worksheets should contain formatting styles and custom numeric formats that you want to have available. Macros can add shortcut keys, buttons, or menus to the other documents. Templates should be copied to the XLSTART or alternate startup directory for access through the **File N**ew command.

- Select the worksheet settings, such as the following, that you want as defaults when the system opens:

    Hide and protect documents with **W**indow **H**ide and **O**ptions **P**rotect Document

    Worksheet and display settings from **O**ptions **W**orkspace and **D**isplay

    Chart preferences set in **G**allery **P**referred

    Custom color palettes set in **O**ptions Color Palette and **C**hart Color Pale**t**te

■ Define Auto_Open names in worksheets and templates that will start macros when the worksheet or template opens. Define Auto_Close names in worksheets and templates that will start macros when the worksheet or template closes.

■ Arrange all windows and documents on-screen as you want them to appear when the system starts. Create views and reports that users will need.

5. Save all documents separately with their permanent file names if you will need access to individual files.

6. Save groups of worksheets, macros, and charts together in workbooks.

These steps create a system that may involve many documents. You can start the system in several different ways:

■ If you want the system to start when you start Excel, save the file or workbook to the XLSTART directory or your alternate startup directory.

■ If you want to start the system from within Excel, use the File Open command.

■ If you want to start Excel and the system from an icon in the Program Manager, use the Program Manager's File New command to add a program item icon to a group window.

Opening Documents Automatically

If you want a document to open automatically when Excel starts, copy that document into the XLSTART directory, or open the document and save it into the XLSTART directory. This directory is created during installation under the directory containing EXCEL.EXE. Following are the types of files that Excel will open automatically:

Worksheets	Charts
Macro sheets	Workbooks
Add-ins	

Template files, ending with XLT, that are in the XLSTART directory, appear in the list box displayed by the File New command, but they will not open automatically.

If you want a macro to run as soon as a worksheet opens, use the Formula Define Name command to create the name Auto_Open in the worksheet. In the Refers to: text box, enter the name of the macro sheet and the directory where the macro is saved. (For more information on creating Auto-Open macros, see Chapter 28.) The **R**efers to: box might contain this entry:

='C:\FINANCE\FINMACR.XLM'!SETUP

In this example, the macro that will run when that worksheet opens is the SETUP macro on the worksheet FINMACR.XLM, which is located in the C:\FINANCE directory.

Save the macro sheet into the directory you specified, and save the worksheet into the XLSTART directory. When Excel starts, it opens the worksheet in the XLSTART directory. When that worksheet opens, it starts the macro specified by the name Auto_Open.

Chapter Summary

Excel has all the capabilities necessary to create business, scientific, and engineering applications that work within Windows. By using some of the capabilities explained in this chapter along with Excel's macro language, you can create powerful solutions.

When you work with multiple worksheets and charts, linking and consolidation usually are required. Chapter 11 describes in detail how Excel can link cells and ranges between worksheets or consolidate data across multiple worksheets with the same or different layouts.

Excel's macro language is far more extensive than the macro capability found in other spreadsheet programs. You can automate processes in Excel, create custom menus and dialog boxes, control other Windows programs, and control data exchange between Excel and other Windows programs. But it's easy to get started with Excel macros. Chapter 27 demonstrates how the macro recorder and six small modifications quickly help you automate your work.

Linking and Consolidating Worksheets

Excel enables you to work with more than one worksheet at a time. You can copy a chart or worksheet range and embed it as a picture on the worksheet; you can link worksheets so that changes in one worksheet update another worksheet; and you can consolidate worksheets so that data from multiple worksheets accumulates into one worksheet.

You can use linking to divide a large business system into its component worksheets. You can test each worksheet separately, and then link the worksheets together to produce an integrated system. You can create links that always update or that update only on your request.

Excel's capability to link pictures enables you to bring together pictures of cells and charts from different documents and arrange them on one page. This capability gives you the power to work in separate documents but organize the printed results the way you want to present them. The results have the quality of desktop publishing.

Consolidation enables you to bring together data from multiple worksheets into one worksheet. Consolidation is often used to accumulate budgets or forecasts from multiple divisions into a unified corporate budget or forecast. Excel enables you to fix these consolidations so that they don't change or to link them so that the consolidations update when division data changes. Linked consolidations automatically build an outline.

Linking Pictures of Worksheet Cells

You can create two types of picture links within a worksheet. One type links a picture of a worksheet area into another worksheet. The linked picture can be updated. The second type of link links a cell or range in a supporting worksheet to a cell or range in another worksheet. The following section describes how to link a *picture* of a worksheet area to another worksheet. The section "Linking Worksheet Cells and Ranges" describes how to link worksheet cells and ranges.

 NOTE   You also can embed Excel charts in a worksheet. This process is described in Chapter 17, "Chart Quick Start," Chapter 18, "Creating Charts," and Chapter 9, "Drawing and Placing Graphics in Worksheets."

Some Windows programs, such as Excel, enable you to link objects from one document into another document. A linked object from Excel can be a cell, a range, a chart, or a complete Excel document. Embedded documents link an image of the original into another document. You can format and update the linked object whenever you want. The top-right corner of figure 12.1 shows a linked cell picture taken from a separate portion of the same worksheet. This single figure displays (and prints) two charts, a distant part of the worksheet, a text box containing explanation, and arrows and circles.

Desktop Publishing Layouts with Linked Pictures

To create page layouts displaying data from multiple worksheets and charts, you can link a picture of an Excel worksheet area into another worksheet. This linkage is an excellent way to create management information displays that bring together data from disparate sources. Linked cell pictures have the following advantages over cell or range links (described later in this chapter in the section "Linking Worksheet Cells and Ranges"):

- Linked cell pictures can be opened and updated quickly. When a linked cell picture is double-clicked, the entire supporting worksheet is activated and the pictured range is selected. If the worksheet is not open, Excel opens it and selects the range so that you can easily change data or make major corrections to the linked cell picture.

- Linked cell pictures can be formatted with most of the same features as text boxes (described in Chapter 9). This formatting makes the cell pictures attractive and easier to read.

- Linked worksheet objects can be resized and moved, unfettered by cell locations. This flexibility enables you to create attractive page layouts involving multiple linked worksheet ranges and charts.

- Linked cell pictures and charts print together on the page in which they appear.

- Linked cell pictures can be linked to macros; when such a cell picture is selected, it runs a macro.

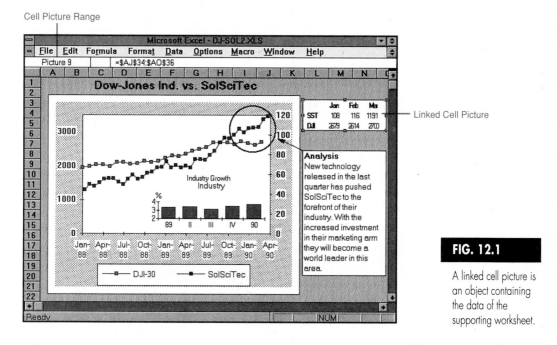

FIG. 12.1

A linked cell picture is an object containing the data of the supporting worksheet.

Linked cell pictures have the following disadvantages:

- Linked cell pictures are not actual cells, so you cannot enter data in them.

- Linked cell pictures cannot be used in calculations. If you need to perform calculations with the information in the cells, use the methods in the following sections that describe linking cells and ranges.

Linking Cell Pictures

Embedding a range from one range on a worksheet into another area of the same or different worksheet involves *taking a picture* of the *server* range that supplies the data and pasting that picture in the *client* worksheet. One worksheet may be both a client and server if the linked picture appears on the same worksheet that supplied the cell picture.

To link a picture of the worksheet by using the toolbar and the mouse, follow these steps:

1. Select the range on the *server* worksheet that you want to take a picture of.

2. Click on the Camera icon in the Utility or Microsoft Excel 3.0 toolbar.

3. Activate the *client* worksheet that will receive the picture. If you are pasting the picture into the source worksheet, scroll the worksheet to where you want the picture.

4. Click on the cell where you want the cell picture to appear.

To link a cell picture by using a keyboard, perform the following steps:

1. Open the worksheet that will supply the picture (server) and the worksheet that will receive the linked cell picture (client).

2. Activate the server worksheet supplying the picture.

3. Select the range of the worksheet to be pictured.

4. Choose the **E**dit **C**opy command.

5. Switch to the client worksheet by clicking on it or by choosing it from the **W**indow menu (or pressing Ctrl+F6). If you are pasting the picture into the source worksheet, then scroll the worksheet to where you want the picture.

6. Select the cell at the top-left corner of the area where you want the cell picture to appear.

7. Hold down the Shift key as you choose the Edit Paste Picture Link command.

A picture with black handles around it will appear on the worksheet. Notice the black handles at the corners and edges of the picture in figure 12.1. Notice that the reference formula linking this formula to the worksheet cells appears in the Formula Bar while the embedded worksheet is selected. In this figure, the cell picture is from the same worksheet that the picture is embedded on. If the picture is from a different worksheet, the Formula Bar shows an external cell reference.

The cell reference formula that links the supporting worksheet to the client worksheet is known as an *external reference formula*. (External reference formulas are described in the section "Linking Worksheet Cells and Ranges" in this chapter.)

 Save the server worksheets before saving the client. By saving server worksheets first, the links in the client worksheet will contain the correct file names for the servers.

To format, resize, position, or protect the embedded cell picture, use the techniques described in the discussion of drawing, formatting, and placing graphics in Chapter 9.

Updating Linked Cell Pictures

When you first open a worksheet containing linked cell pictures, a dialog box will ask whether you want the links updated from source files that are unopened. If you want to update, choose **Yes**. If you want to keep the pictures as they were when last saved, choose No.

To update the cell picture or make changes to the server that supplied the picture, double-click on the linked cell picture. Double-clicking on the linked cell picture opens the server worksheet if it is not already open and activates its window. Excel selects the worksheet range in the picture. Make changes in this server worksheet range, save the changes, and then close the server worksheet if you do not need to make further changes. If the worksheet contains a cell picture from one of its own cells or ranges, you do not need to close the worksheet.

If you have double-clicked on a linked cell picture, the server worksheet and its range appear. To return quickly to the linked cell picture, press the Goto key, F5. Notice that the **R**eference edit box contains the address of the sheet and the location from which you came. Do not make any changes in the Goto box; choose OK or press Enter and you will return immediately to your original location.

Excel has much of the power of executive information systems and management display systems. By using embedded pictures, linked worksheets, and linked outlines, you can create systems that enable short *drill downs* to underlying detail worksheets. Double-clicking on a linked cell or linked cell picture or chart will open and activate the source if it is not already open. Excel also can support large executive information systems by linking Excel to an SQL Server or mainframe database via Q+E on one of the many other access programs available for Windows.

T I P

If you are using a keyboard, you cannot open a source file and update a link to a closed source by double-clicking. You also may need to update multiple pictures simultaneously. Perform the following steps if you need to open and update multiple linked pictures:

1. Activate the worksheet containing linked pictures.

2. Choose the File Links command. The Links dialog box appears (see fig. 12.2).

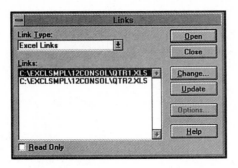

FIG. 12.2

The Links dialog box.

3. Select Excel Links from the Link Type list.

4. Select the source worksheet from the Links list by clicking or by pressing the arrow keys. To select multiple worksheets, press Ctrl while you click on more than one worksheet in the Links list. Using the keyboard, select multiple worksheets by holding Ctrl as you press the up- or down- arrow keys. Press space bar to select or clear a worksheet.

5. Choose Update to refresh the links from disk, or choose Open to open the selected worksheet.

6. Choose Close or press Esc.

Changing Links to Linked Cell Pictures

If you change the server worksheet's name, move it to a different directory, or want to change the source to a different worksheet, you need to edit the embedded picture's cell reference formula. The external reference formulas used by linked cell pictures or objects are the same as those used by linked cells and ranges. You can see this reference formula by selecting a linked cell picture and looking at the Formula Bar.

T I P

You can use the keyboard to select individual objects. Choose the Formula Select Special command, select the Objects option, and then choose OK or press Enter. This procedure selects all objects on the active worksheet. Press Tab to select each object in turn or press Shift+Tab to cycle through the objects in reverse order.

To change or edit all links to the same server worksheet, follow the procedures for File Links in the following section on updating and editing linked worksheets. If you edit a linked cell picture and change it to a server worksheet file that is not open, the linked cell picture appears blank. Use one of the update methods previously described to open the new server worksheet and update the linked pictures. You can close the server worksheet after you update the pictures. The linked cell picture will continue to display data from its new server worksheet.

To change the link to one embedded cell picture without changing other links to the same server worksheet, select the individual linked cell picture. Edit the external reference formula in the Formula Bar to refer to the new server worksheet's path, file, and cell references. Press Enter to reenter the formula. The linked cell picture will be blank if the reference worksheet is not open. Use the update techniques to update the linked picture.

To delete a linked cell picture, select it so that black handles appear on its edges; then press Del or the Backspace key, or choose Edit Clear. Choose Edit Undo immediately to restore a deleted embedded object.

For Related Information:

FROM HERE...

◄◄ "Embedding Pictures of Cells in a Worksheet," p. 331.

◄◄ "Working with Graphic Objects," p. 337.

◄◄ "Grouping Documents into Workbooks," p. 426.

▶▶ "Embedding Data in a Worksheet," p. 1034.

Linking Worksheet Cells and Ranges

Linking data enables you to avoid the problems inherent in large, cumbersome worksheets. You can build small worksheets to accomplish specific tasks and then link all these *modules* together to form a larger *system*.

The following list describes some of the advantages of building systems composed of smaller worksheets that share data by linking:

- Data linked between worksheets passes actual data, numbers, and text that can be used by formulas in the receiving worksheet.

- Linked data can be formatted by using the same formatting techniques you would use on any cell contents.

- Systems require less memory because all worksheets may not need to be open simultaneously. Some worksheets can be linked to worksheets that remain on disk.

- Modules can be built separately by different people as long as the data transfer between modules is planned and coordinated. Such cooperation can mean quicker project completion.

- Systems composed of worksheet modules are flexible and can be updated more easily. One module can be redesigned, tested, and implemented without rebuilding the entire system.

- Smaller worksheets recalculate faster than single, large worksheets.

- You can create data-entry modules that operate on separate computers or in separate locations. At a given time, filled-in modules can be linked into the system. This arrangement has a number of advantages: more people can work on the system at once; people can work in separate locations; the work can be completed faster; and the chance that an inexperienced operator will damage the overall system is reduced.

- Systems are easier to maintain and debug when they are built in modules.

- Worksheet modules can be modified for use in different systems.

T I P   If your system needs to keep its linked worksheets together, consider binding them together into a workbook. Chapter 11 describes workbooks.

Understanding Links

Linking enables one worksheet to share the data in another worksheet. You can link one cell, a range of cells, and a named formula or constant.

The worksheet containing the original data—the source of information—
is the *server worksheet*. The worksheet that receives the linked data is
the *client worksheet*. (You also may see them referred to as the *source*
and the *target* or the *supporting* and the *dependent*.)

Server worksheets can be on-screen or on disk; the client worksheet can
get the information it needs through the link. When the client worksheet
opens, it updates linked data that it reads from the server worksheet, if
the server worksheet is open. If the server worksheet is not open, the
client worksheet asks whether you want to use the data the client
worksheet had when it was saved or whether you want the client
worksheet to read in new data from the server worksheet still on disk.

Figure 12.3 shows worksheets linked by an external reference formula.
QTR1.XLS is the server for the ANNUAL.XLS client worksheet. The external reference formula in ANNUAL.XLS appears in the Formula Bar as
=QTR1.XLS!$E$5, which indicates that cell B5 on the ANNUAL.XLS
worksheet is linked to the contents of cell E5 on the QTR1.XLS
worksheet. When the contents of E5 in the QTR1.XLS worksheet changes,
the value of B5 of the ANNUAL.XLS worksheet also will change.

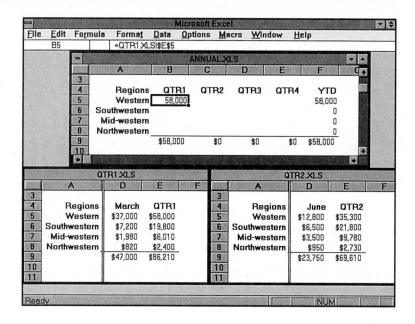

FIG. 12.3

The QTR1.XLS
worksheet serves the
ANNUAL.XLS
worksheet by feeding
data through a link.

External reference formulas use the following form:

    =WorksheetName!CellRef

The following formula is an example external reference formula:

    =QTR1.XLS!$E$5

In this formula, QTR1.XLS is the name of the supporting worksheet that contains the data, and $E5 is the cell that supplies information to the link. An exclamation mark (!) separates the supporting worksheet name from the cell reference.

An external reference also can span a range of cells. The total in B9 on ANNUAL.XLS, for example, can be one formula that totals the range of cells from the QTR1.XLS worksheet. The formula would appear in the following way:

>   =SUM(QTR1.XLS!$E$5:$E$8)

You can link a range of cells to another range of cells of the same size. These links use array formulas and are created with the **Edit Paste Link** command. An external reference formula on ANNUAL.XLS that links B5:B8 to the supporting cells E5:E8 on QTR1.XLS appears as the following array:

>   {=QTR1.XLS!$E$5:$E$8}

The braces, { }, around the formula indicate that it is an array formula. Array formulas act on multiple cells at one time. You must enter and edit array formulas differently than normal single-cell formulas. You cannot type the brace; you must enter them in a special way, described later. (Array formulas are described further in Chapter 13.)

The external reference formula appears differently, depending on whether the server worksheet is open or closed. If the server worksheet is open, the external reference formula appears with only the worksheet name, as in the following example:

>   =QTR1.XLS!$E$5

If the server worksheet is closed, the external reference appears with the full path name, disk, directory, and file name, enclosed in single quotation marks, as shown in the following example:

>   ='C:\EXCEL\FINANCE\QTR1.XLS'!$E$9

Because open server worksheets do not include their path name in the external reference formula, you cannot have two worksheets open with the same name, even if they are from different directories. You can have links to server worksheets with the same names in different directories, but you can have only one of them open at a time.

Linking Cells with Copy and Paste Link Commands

To link a cell or range in a supporting worksheet to a cell or range in the client worksheet, use the **Edit Paste Link** command. In the following steps, the range of E5:E8 on the QTR1.XLS worksheet is linked to cells B5:B8 (the rows do not have to be the same) on the client ANNUAL.XLS worksheet:

1. Open the worksheets that you want to link.

2. Activate the server worksheet.

3. Select the range of cells that provide the data you want linked (see fig. 12.4).

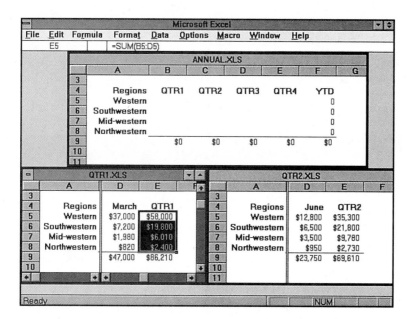

FIG. 12.4

A selected range of cells on the supporting worksheet.

4. Choose the **Edit Copy** command.

5. Activate the client worksheet that will receive the data.

6. Select the top-left cell of the range where you want the link to appear.

   In this example, select cell B5 on the ANNUAL.XLS worksheet. Do not select an entire range to paste into; doing so is unnecessary and increases the chance that you will select the wrong size of range to paste into. You need to select only the single cell at the upper-left corner of the area that you want to paste.

7. Choose the **Edit Paste Link** command.

The link appears, as shown in figure 12.5.

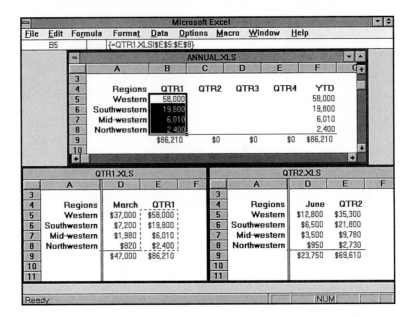

FIG. 12.5

The cells on
ANNUAL.XLS display
data from the
supporting worksheet,
QTR1.XLS.

Notice that in the client worksheet's Formula Bar, braces, { }, enclose cells in the linked range. The braces indicate that the linked range is one array. The entire range is linked, not the individual cells. You cannot change individual cells within the array, but you can edit the entire array, as described in the section "Editing Arrays Made with Paste Link."

If you use **Edit Copy** and **Edit Paste Link** to link a single cell to another single cell, an external reference formula is created that is not an array. You can edit this formula like any other formula.

Linking Cells by Pointing

To create many links that are individual cells or are links within larger formulas, use the pointing method of creating links. You can enter external references in a formula in the same way that you build a formula within one worksheet: by pointing to the cell references you want in the formula, even when the cells are on another worksheet. To point to a cell or range so that it is included in a formula, click on it as you are building the formula or drag across its range.

To link the client cell B5 on ANNUAL.XLS to the server cell, E5 on QTR1.XLS, perform the following steps:

1. Open the client and server worksheets.

2. Activate the client worksheet.

3. Select the cell that you want to contain the link and start your formula. The formula may involve many terms and functions or be as simple as an equals sign (=) and the single linked cell.

In figure 12.6, an equals sign (=) is typed in cell B5 on the ANNUAL.XLS worksheet.

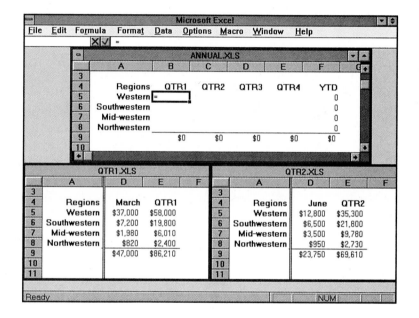

FIG. 12.6

Link cells by typing an = and clicking on the linked cell.

4. Activate the server worksheet, QTR1.XLS.

5. Select the server cell or range supplying data to the link. In the example, click on cell E5 or press the arrow keys to enclose E5 in the dashed marquee.

6. Continue building the formula in the same way you would build any formula, by typing another math operator (math sign) and continuing to select cells or enter terms.

7. After you complete the formula, click on the Enter box in the Formula Bar or press Enter.

As soon as you press Enter or type a math operator, the client worksheet reactivates. Figure 12.7 shows the external reference formula in B5 as =QTR1.XLS!$E$5 just before pressing Enter.

You can use the pointing method to enter external references within complex formulas such as the following:

=2*SIN(READINGS.XLS!$AE$5)/(B12*56)

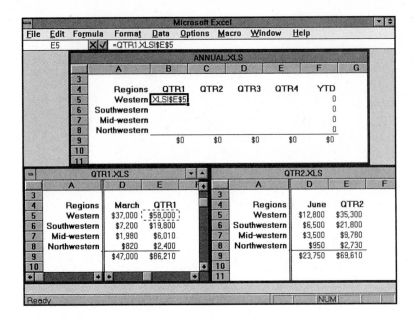

FIG. 12.7

The resulting link in B5
is created by pointing
to a cell on another
worksheet.

You also can point to ranges on other worksheets. Consider the following formula:

=SUM(SUPPORT.XLS!$F$6:$F$8)

This formula was entered by typing =SUM(and then switching to the
server worksheet and dragging across the range F6:F8 with the mouse.
To select the range with the keyboard, hold down the Shift key and press
the arrow keys until the range is selected. Type the closing), and press
Enter.

Linking Cells by Typing

If you need to create links to worksheets on disk without opening the
worksheets, you can type in the external reference formula. This technique is helpful if the server file is too large to load with your existing
worksheet or if you are so familiar with the supporting worksheet that
you can type a reference faster than you can find the cell and click on it.

When you type an external reference to an open worksheet, use a syntax
like that shown in the preceding examples:

=QTR1.XLS!$E$5

or

=SUM(QTR1.XLS!$E$5:$E$8)

or

    =QTR1.XLS!RangeName

When you type an external reference to an unopened worksheet on disk, enclose the full path name, file name, and cell or range in single quotations, as in the following example:

    ='C:\EXCEL\FINANCE\QTR1.XLS'!$E$9

If the server file is in the current directory, Excel enters the path name for you. For example, type the following:

    =QTR1.XLS!$E$9

and press Enter. Excel enters the path.

Typing external reference formulas is easiest when you use the Formula **D**efine Name or the Formula **C**reate Names command to name cells or ranges. Suppose that cell E5 in QTR1.XLS is named Qtr1.Western. If both the ANNUAL.XLS and QTR1.XLS worksheets are open, you can link them by typing the following formula in the ANNUAL.XLS worksheet:

    =QTR1.XLS!Qtr1.Western

This formula contains an external reference. When you type formulas containing an external reference, the answer appears as soon as you enter the formula. (If you use a range name such as Qtr1.Western, that name must exist on the server worksheet. In this example, the Qtr1 in the name Qtr1.Western is not related to the worksheet name QTR1.XLS.)

Editing Arrays Made with Paste Link

When you use Edit Paste **L**ink to link a range of cells, an array is created in the client worksheet that looks similar to {=QTR1.XLS!$E$5:$E$8}. An external reference array formula links a range of cells in one worksheet to a range of cells in another worksheet. Because an array is involved, you must edit the entire range that makes up the array. To edit the entire range, you must select the entire range and edit the formula. A special entry procedure is required, as described later in this chapter. When you have edited the array formula to include a named range, the array formula will look similar to the following example:

    {=QTR1.XLS!Qtr1.Totals}

To add a name to the formula in this case, name the range in the supporting worksheet. In figure 12.5, for example, you could give the name Qtrl.Totals to $E$5:$E$8.

To add the name to the external reference formula in the client worksheet, create the link by using **Edit Paste Link**. With this command, you can paste the formula into a range such as B5:B8 in the ANNUAL.XLS worksheet, as explained in the section "Linking Cells with Copy and Paste Link Commands." Pasting creates the formula {=QTR1.XLS! $E$5:$E$8} in cells B5:B8. Replace $E$5:$E$8 by selecting one of the linked cells involving the range B5:B8. Click in the Formula Bar and notice that the array formula changes to a normal formula. The array brackets disappear. Edit the formula to replace $E$5:$E$8 with Qtr1.Totals.

To reenter the external reference formula as an array in the selected cells, press Shift+Ctrl+Enter. The formula will be {=QTR1.XLS! Qtr1.Totals}. This link will be preserved no matter where you move the range Qtr1.All on the QTR1.XLS worksheet, even if you move the range while the client is not open.

Saving Linked Worksheets

When you save linked worksheets, first save the server worksheet that supplies the data. Next save the client worksheets. This procedure ensures that the client worksheets will store the correct path name and file name of their server worksheets.

If you change the name of a server worksheet, be certain that client worksheets that depend upon it are also open. Save the server worksheet and then resave the client worksheets. This procedure ensures that the client worksheets record the new path name and file name of their server worksheet. If a client worksheet becomes unlinked from its server worksheet, you can relink the worksheets by using the **File Links** command.

Opening Linked Worksheets

The linked data in a client worksheet updates in different ways when the worksheet is opened. If its server worksheets are already open, the client worksheet updates immediately when it opens. If the server worksheets are on disk when the client worksheet opens, the alert box shown in figure 12.8 appears.

If you select **Yes** in the alert box, Excel reads the linked data off the files on disk and updates the client worksheet. If you select **No**, Excel retains the values the client worksheet had when last saved.

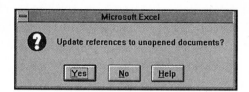

FIG. 12.8

When opening a client worksheet, you can choose to keep the old values or update links to files on disk.

If you already opened a client worksheet and want to open the server worksheets that feed it, perform the following steps:

1. Activate the client sheet containing the links.

2. Choose the **File Links** command to display the Links dialog box, shown in figure 12.9.

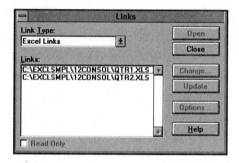

FIG. 12.9

Use the File Links dialog box to change or update links between worksheets.

3. From the Link **Type** pull-down list box, select Excel Links, if it is not already selected.

4. Select the **Links** list, and then select those files you want to open. Unopened files appear with their path name.

   To select multiple adjacent worksheets, click on the first worksheet and then Shift+click on the last worksheet. All worksheets between are selected. To select or clear nonadjacent worksheets, Ctrl+click on the worksheet names.

   Select multiple adjacent worksheets by pressing up- or down-arrow keys to select the first worksheet, and then press Shift+arrow key to select adjacent names. Select nonadjacent worksheets by holding down Ctrl as you press the up- or down-arrow keys to move to different file names. Press the space bar to select or clear each file name.

5. Choose the **O**pen button.

T I P Be certain that the client worksheet is active. If a worksheet without links is active, the File Links command will appear grayed, indicating that the command is not available.

Changing and Updating Links

To maintain a system of linked worksheets properly, you need to know how to reestablish lost links and how to update a large system of links. If server worksheets are renamed or moved to other directories, client worksheets cannot find the data they need. These links are lost and need to be reestablished.

To reestablish links to a worksheet or to link a client worksheet to a different supporting worksheet, perform the following steps:

1. Open the client worksheet.

2. Choose the File Links command to display the Links dialog box.

3. From the Link Type pull-down list box, select Excel Links, if it is not already selected.

4. Select the Links scrolling list and then select the files that you want to open (see fig. 12.10). Unopened files appear with their path name.

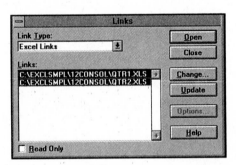

FIG. 12.10

Selected files whose links you want to reestablish or change.

5. Choose the Change button to display the Change Links dialog box, shown in figure 12.11. The current link is displayed at the top of the dialog box.

6. Select a directory and file name to indicate the directory and file of the new supporting worksheet; or type the directory and file name of the file you want to establish as the server.

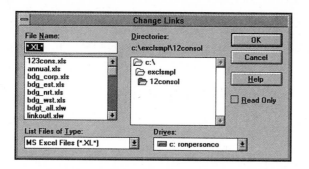

FIG. 12.11

Change links with this dialog box.

7. Choose OK to link to the file name you selected, or choose Cancel to ignore the change.

8. If you selected multiple server files, repeat steps 6 and 7, noting at the top of the dialog box which server worksheet you are changing.

To update an active client worksheet when its server worksheet is on disk, choose the **File Links** command, select the server worksheet from which the client worksheet needs an update, and then choose the **Up**date button. You can select more than one server worksheet by clicking on the first worksheet and then Shift+clicking on the last worksheet.

NOTE You can unknowingly create linked worksheets where changed data does not get passed to all client worksheets. This occurs only when worksheets involved in the links are not open. If worksheet A passes data to B, and B passes data to C, in some cases a change in A will not occur in C. If you change worksheet A, but never open and update B, B will not have the updated data to pass on to C. Consequently, you must know the hierarchy of linked worksheets and update them in order from the lowest server worksheet to the highest client worksheet.

Editing a Link Manually

You can edit one external reference formula linked to a cell or range. Consider the following example:

```
=QTR1.XLS!$E$5
```

Edit the cell as you would edit any formula. Select the cell and then press F2 or click in the Formula Bar to edit.

T I P To find cells that contain external references, choose the Formula Find command and select the Look in Formulas option. Type an exclamation mark (!) in the Find What text box and choose OK. Press F7 to search forward again or Shift+F7 to search backward. This method is helpful for finding cells containing external links that need to be edited selectively.

Links that link a range of cells use array formulas. When you select a cell that is part of an array, the external reference formula will look similar to the following example:

{=QTR1.XLS!$E$5:$E$8}

Editing an external reference *array formula* requires more steps and a special entry keystroke. When you link a range of cells using Edit Paste Link, you create an array formula in the dependent worksheet that looks similar to {=QTR1.XLS!$E$5:$E$8}. This formula spans multiple cells, linking a range in one worksheet to another.

Consider, for example, the following formula:

{=QTR1.XLS!$E$5:$E$8}

To edit this formula, select one cell on the dependent worksheet that involves this array formula. You can select all cells manually or, for a large array, you can select one cell in the array and then choose the Formula Select Special command. Select the Current Array option and choose OK; or you can press the shortcut key, Ctrl+/.

Press F2 or click in the Formula Bar. Notice that the braces, { }, disappear. Edit the formula. You may want to replace the range $E$5:$E$8, for example, with a range name such as Qtr1.All. To reenter the formula as an array, press Shift+Ctrl+Enter; or hold down Shift and Ctrl as you click on the Enter box in the Formula Bar.

To delete an array formula such as the one just described, you must select and then delete all cells involving the array formula.

Freezing Links

To preserve the values from a link but remove the external reference, you can freeze the external reference portion of a formula so that portion becomes a value. To freeze an external reference, select the cell so that the formula appears in the Formula Bar. Click in the Formula Bar or press the Edit Formula key, F2, and select the external reference part of the formula by dragging across it or by pressing Shift+left or right arrow.

Choose **O**ptions Calculate **N**ow or press F9 to change the selected reference into a value. Press Enter to reenter the formula.

You also can freeze formulas by selecting the cell or range that contains
the formulas and choosing the **E**dit **C**opy command. Next, choose **E**dit
Paste **S**pecial with the **V**alues option selected and paste directly on top
of the original cell or range. This procedure replaces entire formulas
with their values.

For Related Information:

◄◄ "Working with Multiple Documents," p. 420.

◄◄ "Grouping Documents into Workbooks," p. 426.

◄◄ "Editing and Formatting Groups of Worksheets," p. 436.

FROM HERE...

Consolidating Worksheets

When you consolidate worksheets, Excel performs calculations on similar
data across multiple worksheets and places the results of calculations in a
consolidation worksheet. You can use this capability to consolidate department budgets into one division budget; you then can consolidate the division budgets into the corporate budget. Consolidations can be more than
just simple totals, however. Excel also can create consolidations that calculate statistical worksheet information such as averages, standard devia-
tions, and counts.

If you use consolidations, be sure to review outlining. A consolidation
can produce an outline automatically. The details within the outline
are the sources of the consolidation.

T I P

The data in the multiple worksheets can have identical physical layouts
or can have different layouts. If the physical layouts of the supporting
worksheets are the same, Excel consolidates data by working with cells
from the same relative location on each supporting worksheet. If the
physical layouts of the server worksheets are different, you can ask Excel to examine the row and column headings in supporting worksheets
to find the data to be consolidated. This method consolidates data by
consolidating those cells having the same row and column headings,
regardless of their physical location.

A common example of a consolidation occurs in corporate budgeting. A corporation accumulates all the division budget forecast worksheets into one budget forecast worksheet for the entire corporation. Each division updates its own worksheets. Each month the corporation can consolidate the individual division budget worksheets into one corporate budget worksheet. Figure 12.12 shows 12 months of budget items from 3 sources, BDG_NRT.XLS, BDG_EST.XLS, and BDG_WST.XLS, which are consolidated with the SUM( ) function into the BDG_CORP.XLS worksheet.

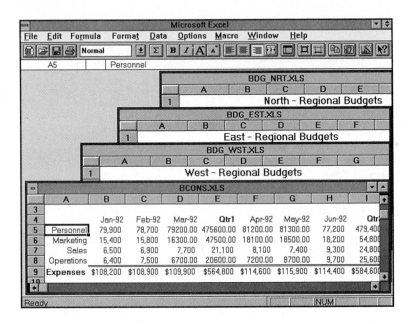

FIG. 12.12

BDG_CORP.XLS contains a SUM ( ) consolidation of three divisional budgets.

T I P

If your office uses a mixture of Excel and 1-2-3, remember that Excel can link and consolidate with 1-2-3 worksheets. Follow the same procedures you use for linking or consolidating with Excel worksheets.

Other examples of business consolidation include sales forecasts and inventory reports. For scientific or engineering uses, consolidation can produce average or standard deviation reports. These reports can include data taken from multiple worksheets produced by various experiments, chromatograph analyzers, well readings, control monitors, and so on.

Understanding Consolidation

When you consolidate, Excel takes data from source areas on different worksheets, calculates the data, and places that data onto a destination area in the consolidation worksheet. The following general steps provide an overview of consolidating multiple source areas into a destination area:

1. Select the destination area where you want the consolidation to appear.

2. Specify the source ranges that hold the data to be consolidated. A consolidation can have as many as 255 source ranges. The sources do not have to be open during consolidation.

3. Select the way that you want to consolidate the cells: by cell position with the source range or by the row or column headings in the source ranges.

4. Select what you want the destination area to contain: fixed values that do not change or links that update when the sources change.

5. Select one of the following types of consolidation:

    AVERAGE

    COUNT

    COUNTA

    MAX

    MIN

    PRODUCT

    STDEV

    STDEVP

    SUM

    VAR

    VARP

Consolidations are handled differently in the destination worksheet, depending on the layout of the destination area that you select, as shown in table 12.1.

Table 12.1. Destinations and Consolidation Results

Destination Selection	Consolidation Result
One cell	Uses as much room on the destination worksheet as needed to consolidate all the categories (items) from the sources.
Row of cells	Fills the consolidation down from the selection. The destination area is only as wide as your selection.
Column of cells	Fills the consolidation to the right of the selection. The destination area is only as tall as your selection.
Range	Consolidates as many categories into the destination as will fit. You are warned if the destination area is not large enough to hold the consolidation.

Consolidating Worksheets by Physical Layout

Consolidate worksheets by their physical layout if the data items, such as budget labels, are in the same position within each source range. The actual location of the source range may be different on each source worksheet. The destination range will have the same layout as the source range. To consolidate by layout, perform the following steps:

1. Select a destination range as described in table 12.1.

   Select only the data range, because text does not consolidate and because you won't want to consolidate dates used as headings.

2. Choose the **Data Consolidate** command to display the Consolidate dialog box, shown in figure 12.13.

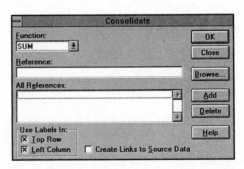

FIG. 12.13

The Consolidate dialog box enables you to consolidate sheets by location or by data headings.

3. Select the **R**eference text box and then select or type a source area. Use an external reference of a form similar to =BDG_EST.XLS! $B$5:$E$8. You can select an area in any open worksheet although the destination worksheet remains the active worksheet. If the source worksheet is on disk, you can type its full path name and source area enclosed in single quotes.

If the source worksheet is open, and you are using a mouse, click on a source worksheet; or choose the **W**indow menu to activate the source worksheet. Select the source area on the worksheet by clicking on it or dragging across it. Move the dialog box, if necessary.

If the source worksheet is open, and you are using the keyboard, press Ctrl+F6; or choose the **W**indow menu to activate the source worksheet. Select the source area by moving to it and then holding the Shift key as you press arrow keys to select, or use the F8 key to extend the selection. Move the dialog box, if necessary.

If the source worksheet is closed, choose the **B**rowse button. The standard File Open dialog box appears. Select the file name you want and choose OK. Excel enters the file name; you must type a range reference or range name.

4. Choose the **A**dd button to add the source entry to the All References list. The Excel screen will now look similar to the screen in figure 12.14, where the BDG_CORP.XLS worksheet is the destination and the source area is one of the BDG.XLS division worksheets.

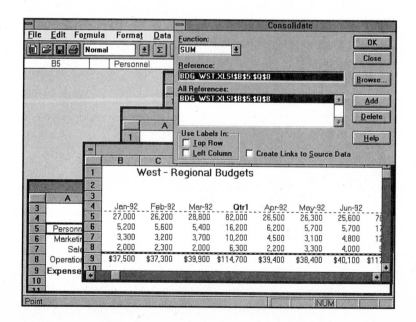

FIG. 12.14

To prepare for consolidation, you select the source range from each source worksheet.

5. Repeat steps 3 and 4 to add all the source areas to the **All Refer-ences** list. If you name all your source worksheets with similar file names, and the source worksheets use the same range names, you only need to edit the **R**eference text box.

6. Select the type of consolidation you want from the **F**unction list.

7. Clear the Use Labels In: **T**op Row and **L**eft Column check boxes.

   The consolidation in this procedure uses cell position within the source range, not labels in the row or column headings.

8. Select the Create Links to **S**ource Data check box if you want the destination range to be linked to the source range.

   Linking the source ranges to the destination ranges makes the con-solidation an outline. Consolidation outlines are described at the end of this chapter.

9. Choose OK or press Enter.

The finished consolidation is shown in figure 12.15.

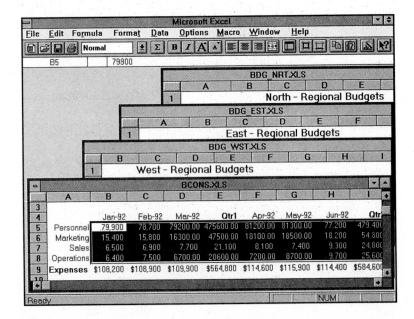

FIG. 12.15

Consolidating by position requires the same physical layout in all source areas.

T I P   Do not include date headings in a consolidation by position. Excel will treat the serial date number in a cell as a number to be consolidated. The serial date number will throw off the consolidation of numeric data.

Be aware of how much space the consolidation will take if you select one cell as the destination area. One cell can use an unlimited destination area, which means that as many rows and columns are used for the consolidation as necessary. The consolidation may cover cells containing information you need.

> To create worksheets with matching text labels and layouts, use the **O**ptions **G**roup Edit command. To build worksheets that are exactly the same, save a master worksheet under different names. To make only a portion of different worksheets the same, however, use the **O**ptions **G**roup Edit command. While this command is on, edits and entries you make in the active worksheet are repeated in other worksheets in the group. See Chapter 11 for more information about the **O**ptions **G**roup Edit command.

T I P

Text and formulas within the source area are not brought into the destination area. Only values are brought in and formatted. If you are consolidating on a blank worksheet, copy text from divisional worksheets for use as headings.

You can specify multiple worksheet source areas by using wild cards in the worksheet names. Instead of specifying all three sheets— BDG_EST.XLS, BDG_WST.XLS, and BDG_NRT.XLS—and their source areas in the All **R**eferences list, enter the name in the **R**eference box with a wild card, such as BDG_*.XLS. The asterisk (*) wild card refers to WST, EST, and NRT.

NOTE If you use wild cards in the Reference box to reference all the source worksheets, make sure that the wild cards do not match the name of the consolidation worksheet. If the wild card is BDG_*.XLS, for example, do not use BDG_CONS.XLS as the consolidation sheet. You will cause an error because Excel will try to consolidate the consolidation sheet into itself.

You can reduce problems caused in moving or rearranging source areas. Use the Fo**r**mula **D**efine Name command to name the source range on each source worksheet with the same range name. Edit the source areas in the **R**eference text box so that it references range names rather than cell references. You can reference a consolidation area on all the sheets with BDG_*.XLS!BUDGET. The asterisk (*) in the file name is a wild card that refers to EST, WST, and NRT. BUDGET is a range name on each sheet that refers to the range containing the source data.

Consolidating Worksheets by Row and Column Headings

You usually don't want to consolidate worksheets by position. Doing so means that each division's worksheet must have exactly the same line items and column headings in the same order. The various divisions, for example, may have separate budget items or different sales territories selling different products. When you use the following method, source worksheets can contain different items and the headings can be ordered differently, yet the consolidation still works.

When source worksheets have data in different locations or when source worksheets contain different categories to be consolidated, use the names in row or column headings to consolidate. With this method, Excel consolidates data according to the row and column headings of a piece of data and not by the data's cell location. This method is the most flexible way to consolidate. The actual location of the data may be different on each source area.

To consolidate by headings, perform the following steps:

1. Select a destination area. If you want headings in a specific order, include the row or column headings that you want to use as consolidation categories. The headings must be spelled the same as in the source worksheets. If you do not enter headings, Excel will create them for you.

2. Choose the **Data Consolidate** command.

3. Select the **Reference** text box and then select or type a source range. Include the row and column headings in the source range. You can select the source range from any open worksheet. If the source worksheet is on disk, you can type its full path name and source range enclosed in single quotes. Use a form such as =BDGT_EST.XLS!$A$4:$R$8.

   If the source worksheet is open, and you are using a mouse, click on a source worksheet; or choose the **Window** menu and select a worksheet. Select the source area on the worksheet by clicking on it or dragging across it. Move the dialog box, if necessary.

   If the source worksheet is open, and you are using the keyboard, press Ctrl+F6; or choose the **Window** menu to activate the source worksheet. Select the source area by moving to it and then holding the Shift key as you press arrow keys to select, or use the F8 key to extend the selection. Move the dialog box, if necessary.

   If the source worksheet is closed, choose the **Browse** button. The standard File Open dialog box appears. You then can select the file name you want and choose OK. Excel enters the file name; you must type a range reference or range name.

4. Choose the **A**dd button to add the source entry to the All References list.

5. Repeat steps 3 and 4 to add all the source areas to the All References list.

6. Select the type of consolidation that you want from the **F**unction list.

7. Select the headings in the source areas by which you want to consolidate. Select one or both of the following: the Use Labels In: **T**op Row and the **L**eft Column check boxes.

8. Select the Create Links to **S**ource Data check box if you want the destination area to be linked to the source areas. This step makes the consolidation an outline. (Consolidation outlines are described at the end of this chapter.)

9. Choose OK or press Enter.

When you use headings to consolidate, you can specify which categories to consolidate and the order in which you want categories placed in the destination area. Enter the headings in the top row or left column of the destination area. Then include those headings in the selection you make before you start consolidation (step 1 in the preceding instructions).

Figure 12.16 shows a destination area with headings down the left column in an order different from the headings in the source areas. Notice that after consolidation, Excel has arranged the consolidated data in the correct rows by headings (see fig. 12.17).

Reduce problems caused by moving or rearranging source areas by editing the source areas in the **R**eference text box to use range names instead of cell references.

Deleting or Editing Links

You can add new source ranges to the All References list by opening the Consolidate dialog box, selecting the **R**eference text box, and then selecting the source range on a worksheet. Choose the **A**dd button to add the new range area to the All References list.

Delete source ranges from future consolidations by selecting the source range in the All References list and then choosing the **D**elete button.

Edit a source area by selecting it from the All References list, editing it in the **R**eference text box, and then choosing the **A**dd button. Delete the original source area from the list, if necessary.

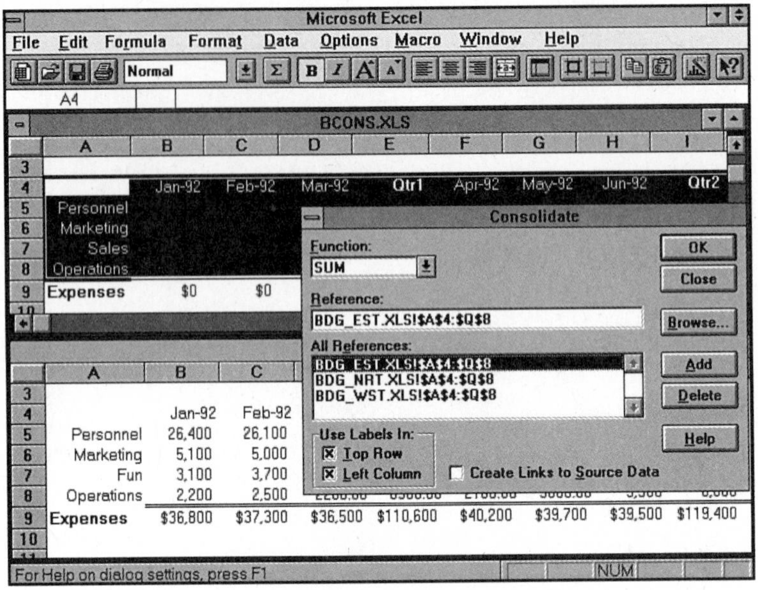

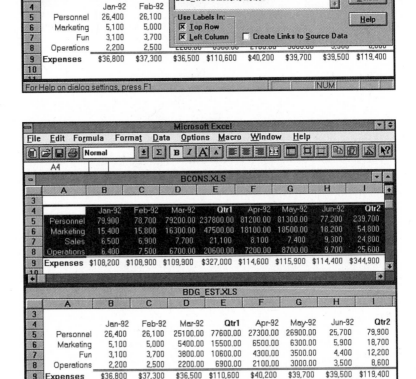

FIG. 12.16

Enter row or column headings first in the destination area to specify the consolidation order.

FIG. 12.17

The consolidation is arranged to match existing headings in the destination area.

Linking Consolidated Worksheets

When you select the Create Links to Source Data check box, Excel consolidates and inserts detailed rows/columns that are linked to the source data in rows and columns between the consolidated results. These inserted rows and columns contain external reference formulas that link cells in the consolidation area to cells in each source area. These new rows and columns become part of a worksheet outline. The highest level of the outline shows the consolidation; the lower levels of the outline contain the links to source worksheets. Chapter 13 describes worksheet outlining in more detail.

Figure 12.18 shows a destination area in BDG_CORP.XLS created with headings and linking selected. Figure 12.19 shows the same destination area with the outline feature turned on. The highest level of the outline is the consolidation. Lower levels contain links that feed into the consolidation.

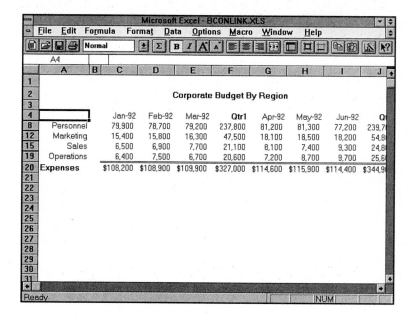

FIG. 12.18

The consolidation area in BDG_CORP.XLS is linked to its sources and uses the headings specified in the dependent worksheet for the consolidation.

Formatting Consolidated Worksheets

You need to understand the relation of linked consolidations and outlines for two important reasons. You can give each level in an outline and the linked consolidation a different formatting style; you can expand or contract linked consolidations to show summary or detail views of the consolidated data.

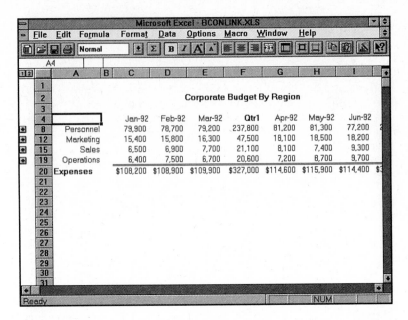

By clicking on the row-level buttons on the left side of the screen (shown with a plus sign (+), as in figure 12.19), the outline for rows opens to reveal the links that supply the consolidated cells. Figure 12.20 shows the hidden rows revealed. The consolidation results are actually SUM( ) functions that total the external references in these hidden rows.

If you double-click on a detail row, its source worksheet will open and activate.

To apply outline styles to an existing linked consolidation, select the destination area, choose the Formula Outline command, and choose the Apply Styles button. Refer to Chapter 13 for information on outlining. Refer to Chapter 8 to learn how to change the definitions of outline styles to produce the outline formatting you want.

Consolidating Worksheets Manually

When you need to transfer only values between worksheets, and you do not want those values automatically updated, use Edit Paste Special. With Paste Special, you combine the values from one worksheet into another. Paste Special enables you to combine data by pasting values or by adding, subtracting, multiplying, or dividing values with existing cell contents. Because a link is not established, values are not updated when the supporting worksheet changes.

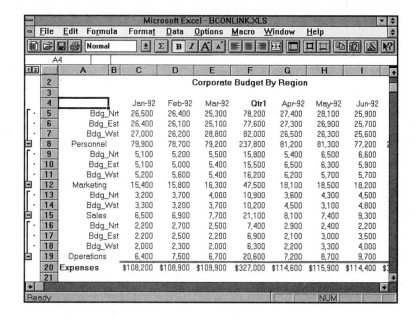

FIG. 12.20

Expanding the outline's
rows reveals the
external reference
formulas that link to the
source areas.

To consolidate data between worksheets, use **Edit Copy** to copy cell
contents from one worksheet. Activate the other worksheet and paste
with the **Edit Paste Special** command. Select the **Values** option to paste
the values from the source worksheet. To perform a math operation with
the data as it is pasted, select a math operation such as **Add** from the
Operation option group.

For Related Information:

FROM HERE...

◄◄ "Working with Multiple Documents," p. 420.

◄◄ "Grouping Documents into Workbooks," p. 426.

◄◄ "Editing and Formatting Groups of Worksheets," p. 436.

▶▶ "Outlining Worksheets," p. 517.

Chapter Summary

Excel's capability to display multiple worksheets, to link pictures, and to
link or consolidate open or disk-based worksheets gives your systems a

great deal of flexibility and power. In Excel, you also can use Q+E to link worksheets to disk-based database files. Q+E is described in Chapter 25, "Linking Excel to Databases with Q+E."

Using Power Worksheet Features

E xcel contains many commands and features that can reduce your workload. This chapter describes the commands and techniques to help you accomplish more work in less time.

You learn how to enter a series of numbers or dates, how to use formulas to manipulate text, and how to write formulas that make decisions based on conditions that you specify. You also learn how to test input values to make sure that these values are in the correct range, use lookup tables to find tax or commission rates, and use arrays to enter formulas and save memory. The section that covers creating worksheet outlines teaches you how to present large sheets of summary and detailed information. This chapter ends with a section on troubleshooting worksheets.

For information on advanced methods of data analysis, Chapter 14 contains information that helps you perform more advanced data analysis, solve for the optimum solution, find solutions from multiple sets of input data, and add more worksheet functions.

T I P

482

Entering a Series of Numbers or Dates

When you build forecasts, budgets, or trend analyses, you often need a series of dates, numbers, or text. You can enter a series quickly with the **Data Series** command or by dragging across existing cells that contain a series. A data series can number the items in a database, enter a series of consecutive dates, create quarterly or dated headings, or create a series of data-entry values for a table of solutions that you generate with the **Data Table** command.

T I P You can use series techniques for trend analysis. To perform a trend analysis on data, you can use series techniques to create the forecasted series. To learn how to perform a linear or growth best-fit analysis by using data series techniques, read the section, "Analyzing Trends," later in this chapter.

Figure 13.1 shows examples of numeric and date series, entered with the **Data Series** command. Note that the dates for the days and months are created with a custom date format. This format is described in a following section.

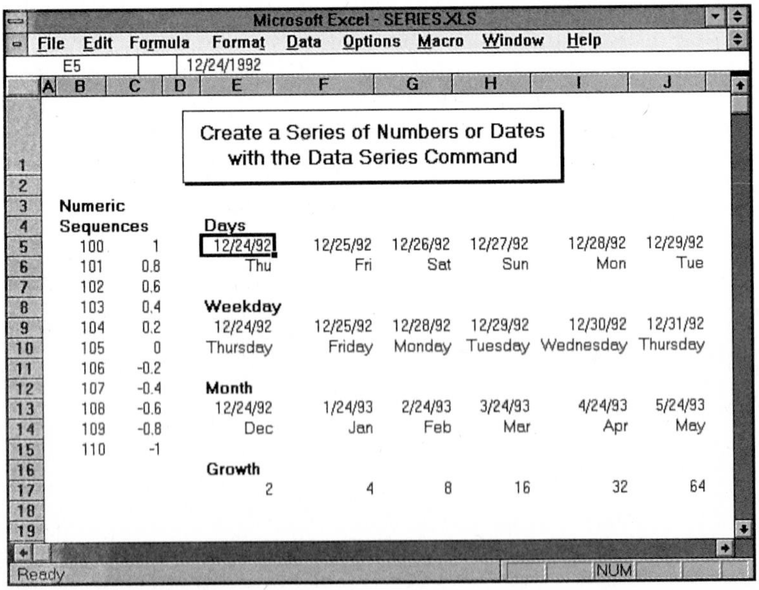

FIG. 13.1

Create numeric or date series with the Data Series command.

You can create a series in two ways. The easiest method for creating a *linear series*, a series that progresses in equal steps, uses the mouse to drag the fill handle. The second method uses a command and gives you the capability to create many kinds of series.

Creating a Linear Series

To create a linear series that increments in equal steps, perform the following steps:

1. Enter the first two pieces of data in the series in adjacent cells, as shown in figure 13.2.

   Excel uses these two data to determine the amount to increment in each step and the starting number for the series.

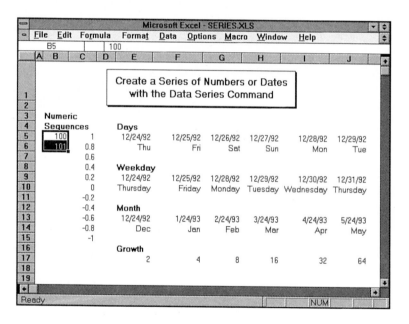

FIG. 13.2

Select the first two numbers in the series.

2. Select these two cells, as shown in figure 13.2.

3. Drag the fill handle down or right to enclose the area you want filled with a series of numbers. Figure 13.3 shows the fill handle dragged down to prepare for creating a series. The fill handle is the small square located at the lower right corner of a selection.

4. Release the mouse button.

The area enclosed with the gray border fills with a series determined by the first two cells you selected.

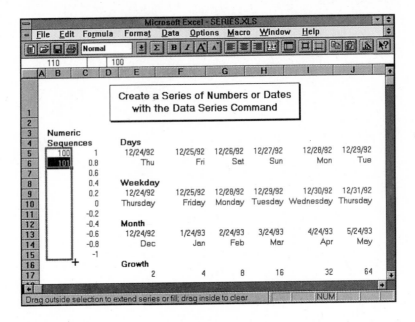

FIG. 13.3

Drag the fill handle across cells you want filled with a series.

You can create a series up or left by dragging the fill handle up a column or left across a row if you need a series that goes up or left from the two starting *seed* cells. Make sure that you end the selection outside the original cells, however, or part of the original selection will be cleared.

T I P   If you select more than two cells that contain data and drag the fill handle, Excel will replace the cells dragged across with values that fit the straight trend line (linear regression). To learn how you can create a trend line with the fill handles, see "Analyzing Trends," later in this chapter.

To create a series of numbers or dates by using the **Data Series** command, complete the following steps:

1. In the first cell, enter the first number or date.

2. Select the range of cells you want filled (see fig. 13.4).

3. To display the Series dialog box, choose **Data Series** (see fig. 13.5).

4. Verify that the **C**olumns or **R**ows option matches the type of range you want filled.

5. Select the **T**rend check box if you want selected values to be replaced by values for a linear or exponential best-fit. This selection limits step 6 to **L**inear or **G**rowth options.

6. Select one of the following Type options:

Linear	Adds the **S**tep Value to the preceding number in the series. If **T**rend is selected, the trend values will be a linear trend.
Growth	Multiplies the **S**tep Value by the preceding number in the series. If **T**rend is selected, the trend values will be an exponential growth trend.
Date	Enables the Date Unit group so that the increment applies to a **D**ay, **W**eekday, **M**onth, or **Y**ear.
Aut**o**fill	Creates automatic series that may include text dates and labels. This is described in the next section, "Creating Series of Text and Headings."

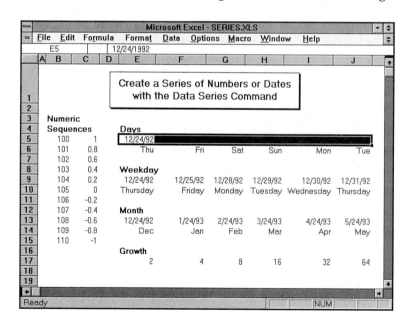

FIG. 13.4

Start a data series with the first number or date.

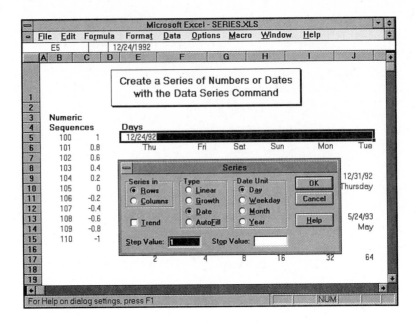

FIG. 13.5

The Data Series
dialog box.

Now, depending on the kind of series you want to create, use one of the following sets of steps.

If, in step 6, you are entering a series of numbers and you choose either **Linear** or **Growth**, continue with the following steps:

1. Enter the **S**tep Value. This number is the constant amount by which the series changes from cell to cell. The **S**tep Value may be positive or negative.

   Figure 13.4 shows how a –2 **S**tep Value decreases the numbers in column C.

2. Enter the St**o**p Value only if you think that you highlighted too many cells when you selected the range to fill.

3. Choose OK or press Enter.

When the series reaches either the end of the selected range or the St**o**p Value, Excel stops. If you use a negative **S**tep Value, the St**o**p Value must be *less* than the starting value. You can type a date or time as the stop value if you type in a format that Excel recognizes.

If, in step 6, you are entering a series of dates and you choose **D**ate, complete the following steps:

1. From the Date Unit area of the Data Series dialog box, select either **D**ay, **W**eekday, **M**onth, or **Y**ear to designate the date increment. (**W**eekday gives you dates without Saturdays and Sundays.)

2. To specify the increment amount, enter the **S**tep Value. If the starting value is 12/1/91, for example, and you choose Month as the Date Unit and 2 as the **S**tep Value, the second date in the series becomes 2/1/92, and the third date becomes 4/1/92.

3. If you think that you highlighted too many cells, enter the St**o**p Value.

   The St**o**p Value indicates the last date in the series. You also can use one of Excel's predefined date formats, such as the format shown in figure 13.6, as the St**o**p Value.

4. Choose OK or press Enter.

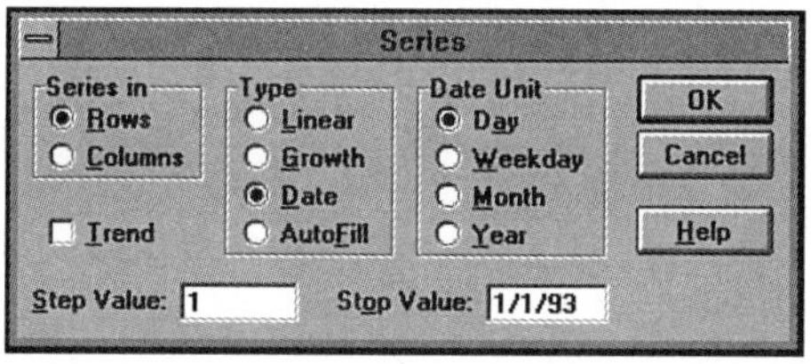

<table>
<tr><td colspan="4">Series</td></tr>
<tr><td>Series in
⦿ Rows
○ Columns

☐ Trend</td><td>Type
○ Linear
○ Growth
⦿ Date
○ AutoFill</td><td>Date Unit
⦿ Day
○ Weekday
○ Month
○ Year</td><td>OK
Cancel
Help</td></tr>
<tr><td colspan="4">Step Value: 1   Stop Value: 1/1/93</td></tr>
</table>

FIG. 13.6

For the Stop Value, use a date or time in one of Excel's predefined formats.

> **T I P**
>
> You can display text dates. To display only the name of the month or the day of the week, as shown in rows 6, 10, and 14 of figure 13.1, use custom date formatting. Custom numeric and date formats are described in detail in Chapter 8.

Creating Series of Text and Headings

Some headings or series that you create may not be dates or numbers. These items, for example, may be a text heading that includes a number, such as Quarter1, QTR3, Task1, Project 52, or Tuesday (see fig. 13.7). Excel also can extend these kinds of series.

The AutoFill feature extends text series that Excel can recognize. The text series that Excel recognizes include the text shown in the following listing:

Type	Example
Day	Tuesday, Wednesday, or Tue, Wed
Month	September, October, or Sep, Oct
Text	Project, Task
Text *number*	Task 1, Task 2 Paragraph 1.2, Paragraph 1.3
Quarterly	Quarter 1, Quarter 2 Qtr 2, Qtr 3 Q1, Q2

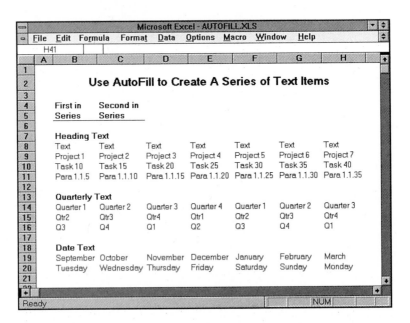

FIG. 13.7

Excel can create series of text and number items for use in headings.

Excel recognizes key words, such as days of the week, month names, and Quarterly abbreviations. Excel knows how these series run and repeat and extends a series to repeat correctly; for example, Qtr1 follows Qtr4 and then the series continues.

If you use two data cells to start a series, like rows 10 and 11 in figure 13.7, Excel determines how the number used with the text is incremented. Cells B11 and C11, for example, dictate that the legal Paragraph numbering in row 11 increments by 0.0.5 with each new number.

To use the fill handles to create a series that increases by one increment in each cell, complete the following steps:

1. Select the first cell that contains data.

2. To outline the cells you want filled, drag across or down, as shown in figure 13.8.

3. Release the mouse button.

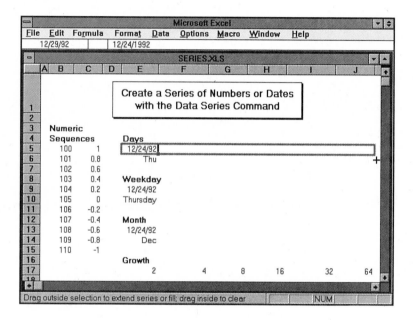

To use a command to create a series that increases by one increment in each cell, complete the following steps:

1. Select the first cell and the cells that you want to fill.

2. Choose the **Data Series** command.

3. Select the AutoFill option.

4. Choose OK or press Enter.

When you need to fill in a series that increments by more than one unit at a time, you need to enter two seeds in adjacent cells. In figure 13.7, for example, B10 and C10 are seeds for incrementing the Task number by 5. Cells B11 and C11 are seeds for incrementing the legal Paragraph number by 0.0.5. When you have AutoFill selected, however, Excel calculates for you what the increment will be. To create a similar series by dragging the fill handle, complete the following steps:

1. Select both seed cells.

2. To select the cells you want filled, drag the fill handle.

3. Release the mouse button.

To use the **D**ata Series command to fill with increments of more than one unit, follow the AutoFill procedure described previously. Make sure that both seeds cells are the first two cells of the selection before you choose the **D**ata Series command and select the AutoFill option. Figure 13.9 illustrates a selection before the command is executed. You also can use the fill handle to create linear trends. This is described in the section, "Analyzing Trends," later in this chapter.

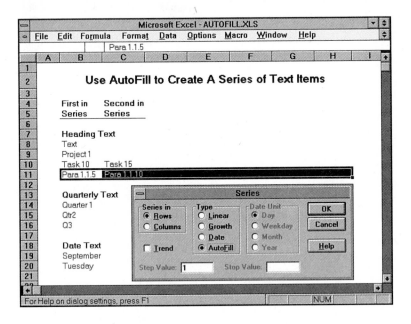

FIG. 13.9

Select both seed cells, then give the command.

Manipulating Text

Excel enables you to manipulate text, numbers, and dates. Text manipulation is handy for combining text and numbers in printed invoices, creating titles from numeric results, and using data from a database to create a mailing list. With Excel, you can use formulas to manipulate text in the same way you use formulas to calculate numeric results.

Use the concatenation operator, the & (ampersand), to join text, numbers, or cell contents to create a text string. Enclose text in quotation marks. You don't need to enclose numbers in quotation marks. Do not enclose cell references in quotation marks. You can reference cells that contain text or numbers. For example, consider the following formula:

="This "&"and That"

This formula displays the following text:

This and That

 NOTE Text used in a formula always must be enclosed in quotes. Excel assumes that text not in quotes is a name. This situation causes a #NAME? error if a name with this spelling is not defined.

You also can join text by referring to the cell address. If A12 contains the text, John, and B12 contains the text, McDougall, you can use the following formula to combine the first and last names:

=A12&" "&B12

The result of the formula is the following full name:

John McDougall

Notice that a space between the two quotation marks in the formula separates the text contained in cells A12 and B12.

Excel also enables you to convert a number to text. You can refer to a number as you refer to a cell filled with text. If A12 contains 99 and B12 contains the text, Stone St., use the following formula to create the full street address:

=A12&" "&B12

The result of the formula is the address:

99 Stone St.

When you refer to a number or date in a text formula, the number or date appears in the General format, not as the number or date appears in the formatted display. Suppose that cell B23 contains the date 12/24/91 and that you enter the following formula:

="Merry Christmas! Today is "&B23

The result of this formula is the following display:

Merry Christmas! Today is 33596

You can change the format of the number with the FIXED(), DOLLAR(), and TEXT() functions. These functions change numbers and dates to text in the format you want. With dates, for example, you can use the TEXT() function to produce the following formula:

="Merry Christmas! Today is "&TEXT(B23,"mmm dd, yy")

The result appears as the following text:

Merry Christmas! Today is Dec 24, 91

You can use any predefined or custom numeric or date format between the quotation marks of the TEXT() function.

The TEXT() function is a handy way to trick large numbers into exceeding the width of a column without producing the #### signs that indicate a narrow column. The TEXT() function also is useful for numeric titles. If you want the number $5,000,000 stored in A36 to fit in a narrow column, for example, use the following formula, which displays the formatted number as text so that the number can exceed the column width:

=TEXT(A36,"$#,##0")

FROM HERE...

For Related Information:

◄◄   "Changing Character Fonts, Sizes, Styles, and Colors," p. 257.

◄◄   "Aligning Text and Numbers," p. 264.

◄◄   "Text Functions," p. 400.

Using Formulas To Make Decisions

Excel's IF() function can make decisions based on whether a test condition is true or false. Use IF(), for example, to test whether the time has come to reorder a part, whether data was entered correctly, or which of two results or formulas to use.

The IF() function uses the following format:

IF(*logical_test*,*value_if_true*,*value_if_false*)

If the *logical_test* (condition) is true, the result is *value_if_true*; but if the *logical_test* is false, the result is *value_if_false*. The result values can display text, calculate a formula, or display the contents of a cell. IF() functions are valuable in macros for testing different conditions and acting according to the results of the test conditions.

Consider the following formula:

=IF(B34>50,B34*2,"Entry too low!")

In this example, the IF() function produces the answer 110 if B34 is 55. If B34 is 12, however, the cell that contains the function displays this text:

```
Entry too low!
```

Making Simple Decisions

IF() functions frequently are used to make comparisons. Figure 13.10 shows an Accounts Aging Analysis worksheet in which Excel checks how long an amount has been owed. Using IF() functions and the age of the account, Excel displays the amount in the correct column.

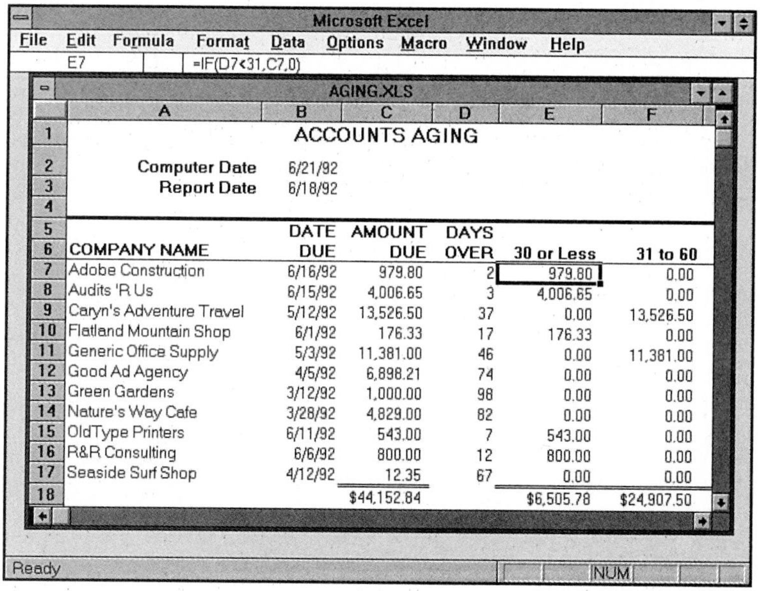

File **Edit** **Formula** **Format** **Data** **Options** **Macro** **Window** **Help**						
E7	=IF(D7<31,C7,0)					

AGING.XLS

	A	B	C	D	E	F
1		ACCOUNTS AGING				
2	Computer Date	6/21/92				
3	Report Date	6/18/92				
4						
5		DATE	AMOUNT	DAYS		
6	COMPANY NAME	DUE	DUE	OVER	30 or Less	31 to 60
7	Adobe Construction	6/16/92	979.80	2	979.80	0.00
8	Audits 'R Us	6/15/92	4,006.65	3	4,006.65	0.00
9	Caryn's Adventure Travel	5/12/92	13,526.50	37	0.00	13,526.50
10	Flatland Mountain Shop	6/1/92	176.33	17	176.33	0.00
11	Generic Office Supply	5/3/92	11,381.00	46	0.00	11,381.00
12	Good Ad Agency	4/5/92	6,898.21	74	0.00	0.00
13	Green Gardens	3/12/92	1,000.00	98	0.00	0.00
14	Nature's Way Cafe	3/28/92	4,829.00	82	0.00	0.00
15	OldType Printers	6/11/92	543.00	7	543.00	0.00
16	R&R Consulting	6/6/92	800.00	12	800.00	0.00
17	Seaside Surf Shop	4/12/92	12.35	67	0.00	0.00
18			$44,152.84		$6,505.78	$24,907.50

Ready | NUM

FIG. 13.10

Use IF( ) functions to test ranges, such as the ages of these accounts.

The first few times you use IF() statements, you may want to write an English sentence that states the *logical_test,* or the question you want to ask. The question also should state both the results if true and if false. For example, each cell from E7 through E16 uses an IF() statement equivalent to the following sentence:

> IF DAYS OVER is less than 31, show the AMOUNT DUE; but if DAYS OVER is not more than 31, show nothing.

The IF() function equivalent of this statement for cell E7 appears in the Formula Bar as the following formula:

=IF(D7<31,C7,0)

In this example, D7 contains the DAYS OVER for row 7, and C7 contains the AMOUNT DUE for the row. To prevent the display of all zeros on the sheet, choose **O**ptions **D**isplay and clear **Z**ero Values.

T I P

To display a blank cell for specific conditions, use a formula similar to the following:

=IF(D7<31,C7,"")

Nothing is entered between the quotation marks, so this function displays a blank cell for the false condition. Remember that Excel can hide zeros for the entire worksheet if you choose the **O**ptions **D**isplay and deselect the **Z**ero Values option.

Making Complex Decisions

In column F of the worksheet shown in figure 13.10, the IF() question needs to be more complex:

IF DAYS OVER is greater than 30 and DAYS OVER is less than 61, show the AMOUNT DUE; but show nothing if these conditions aren't true.

The IF functions in F7 through F17 use the following formula to check for DAYS OVER in the range from 31 to 60:

=IF(AND(D7>30,D7<61),C7,0)

The AND() function produces a TRUE response only when all the elements within the parentheses meet the conditions: D7>30 is true *AND* D7<61 is true. When the AND() function produces TRUE, the IF() formula produces the value found in C7.

When you want to check for a number within a range of values, use an AND() function as shown here; for the AND() function to be TRUE, all the arguments must be true. When you check for a specific number, use an OR() function. With an OR() function, all true arguments produce a TRUE result. AND() and OR() functions are described in greater detail in Chapter 23.

Checking Data Entry

IF() functions also are useful for verifying that data falls within allowable limits. You can put an IF() function in a cell adjacent to the entry cell to warn the operator when data is out of limits. Consider, for example, the following formula:

=IF(AND(B6>250,B6<500),"","Enter values between 250 and 500")

This formula results in the following warning when the value entered in B6 is not between 250 and 500:

```
Enter values between 250 and 500
```

For Related Information:

◄◄ "Entering Formulas," p. 175.

◄◄ "Entering Worksheet Functions," p. 356.

◄◄ "Logical Functions," p. 381.

FROM HERE...

Using Formulas To Look Up Data in Tables

You can build a table in Excel and look up the contents of various cells within the table. Lookup tables provide an efficient way of producing numbers or text that you cannot calculate with a formula. For example, you may not be able to calculate a tax table or commission table. In these cases, looking up values from a table is much easier. Tables also enable you to cross-check typed data against a list of allowable values.

Excel has two techniques for looking up information from tables. The first method uses three types of LOOKUP() functions, similar to the functions found in Lotus 1-2-3. Although easy to use, these functions have the disadvantage of giving you an answer whether or not the function finds an exact match. The list in the table also needs to be in sorted order— another disadvantage. This method is good in some situations, however, such as creating volume discount tables.

The second method is more precise and uses a combination of the IN-DEX() and MATCH() functions to find an exact match in a table, regardless of whether the list in the table is sorted. If Excel cannot find an exact match, the function returns an error so that you know an exact match wasn't found. This method is good for exact matches, such as looking up the quantity on hand for a specific product.

Looking up close or exact matches from tables is valuable for calculating commissions, shipping rates, or checking entered part numbers or descriptions against a known list. Looking up exact matches from tables can save time in locating information or cross-checking data entry.

Using LOOKUP Functions on Tables

Excel has three LOOKUP() functions. The VLOOKUP() function looks down the vertical column on the left side of the table until the appropriate comparison value is found. The HLOOKUP() function looks across the horizontal row at the top of the table until the appropriate comparison value is found. The third form, LOOKUP(), is described in Chapter 10, "Using Functions."

The VLOOKUP() and HLOOKUP() functions use the following forms:

VLOOKUP(*lookup_value,table_array,col_index*)

HLOOKUP(*lookup_value,table_array,row_index_num*)

The VLOOKUP() function tries to match the value in the left column of the table; the HLOOKUP() function tries to match the value in the top row. These values are the *lookup_values*. The *table_array* describes the range that contains the table and lookup values. The *col_index* for the VLOOKUP() function or the *row_index_num* for HLOOKUP() tells the function which column or row, respectively, contains the result. The first column or row in the table always is numbered 1.

The list you use for comparison in the table must be in ascending order. For the lookup function to work correctly, the cells in C11:C15, in figure 13.11, must be sorted in ascending order. The function searches down column one in a VLOOKUP() table or across row one in an HLOOKUP() table until it meets a value larger than the *lookup_value*. If the *lookup_values* are not in ascending order, the function can be misled.

Figure 13.11 shows an example of a VLOOKUP() table that locates sales commissions. The VLOOKUP() and HLOOKUP() commands are helpful for looking up data in commission or tax tables because these tables contain data that may be difficult to calculate exactly. The sales upon which a commission is based, for example, may fall between two numbers in the list. The formula that finds this sales commission is in cell D5. The VLOOKUP() function, as shown in the Formula Bar of the example, is used in the following formula:

=VLOOKUP(D3,C11:F15,D4+1)

The VLOOKUP() formula looks down the left column of the table displayed in the range C11:F15 until a Sales $ amount larger than D3 ($12,425) is found. VLOOKUP() then backs up to the previous row and looks across the table to the column specified by D4+1. The formula D4+1 results in 2, the second column of the table. (Sales $ is column 1. The value 1 is added to D4 so that the lookup starts in the Product Class portion of the table.) The VLOOKUP() function returns the value .045 from the table. The commission is calculated by multiplying .045 by the amount of sale, which is $12,452.

The LOOKUP() functions don't use the headings in row 10. These headings are shown for the user's benefit.

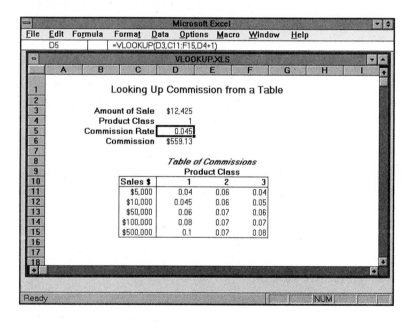

FIG. 13.11

The VLOOKUP() function finds information in a vertical table.

Using MATCH and INDEX Functions

Excel also can look up data from a table and use an exact match to find the information. The list that you use for comparison doesn't have to be in sorted order. The data you are looking up can be text or numbers. If

Excel doesn't find an exact match in the list, an error warns you that the table contained no matches.

Using exact matches against a list is one way to prevent data-entry errors. Imagine a case in which an operator must enter an item number and an item description that belongs to this number. If the description is misspelled or doesn't match the item number, telling the operator to enter the item description can introduce errors. A better plan is to have the operator enter only the item number and have Excel look up the description. This technique not only reduces typing but cross-checks the item number by displaying either an accurate description or an error message if the number is incorrect.

In figure 13.12, Excel enters the item description when the item number is entered. If the item number is nonexistent, the worksheet displays #N/A in the Description cell (C8).

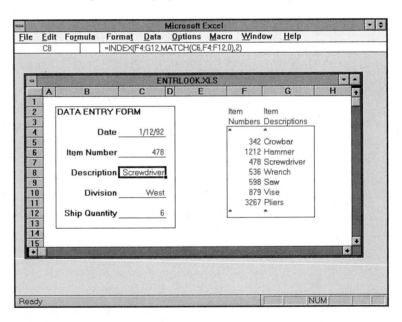

FIG. 13.12

Use an exact match to look up and enter data.

The following formula found in cell C8 looks up and enters the description:

=INDEX(F4:G12,MATCH(C6,F4:F12,0),2)

The two functions used in this formula follow this syntax:

=INDEX(*array,row_num,column_num*)

=MATCH(*lookup_value,lookup_array,match_type*)

In the INDEX() function, *array* is the entire range that contains data. The *row_num* and *column_num* arguments designate the row and column that specify a value in the *array*. For example, for the range F4:G12, a *row_num* of 5 and a *column_num* of 2 causes INDEX() to return Wrench.

In the MATCH() function, the *lookup_value* is the value for which you are searching. In the example, this value is the item number found in C6. The *lookup_array* is an array in a row or column that contains the list of values that you are searching. In the example, this array is the column of item numbers F4:F12. The *match_type* specifies the kind of match required. In the example, 0 specifies an exact match.

In the example, therefore, the MATCH() function looks through the range F4:F12 until an exact match for the contents of cell C6 is found. When an exact match is found, the MATCH() function returns the position of the match—row 4 of the specified range. Notice that the MATCH() function finds the first match in the range. For an exact match, the contents of the range F4:F12 do not have to be in ascending order.

You also can omit the *match_type* or specify *1* or *-1*. If the *match_type* is omitted or is 1, then MATCH() finds the largest value in the *lookup_array* equal to or less than the *lookup_value*. If *match_type* is omitted or is 1, the *lookup-array* must be in ascending order. If the *match_type* is -1, MATCH() finds the smallest value greater than or equal to the *lookup_value*. If the *match_type* is -1, the *lookup_array* must be in descending order.

In the formula shown in figure 13.12, the INDEX() function looks in the range F4:G12. The function returns the contents of the cell located at the intersection of column 2 and row 4, as specified by the MATCH() function. The result is Screwdriver.

The item numbers and descriptions in the table are outlined to identify the table. The asterisks (*) at the top and bottom of the table mark the corners of the ranges. The function continues to work correctly as long as you insert all new data item codes and descriptions between the asterisks.

For Related Information:

◄◄ "Lookup and Reference Functions," p. 383.

FROM HERE...

Calculating Tables of Answers

Because of the *what if* game made possible by electronic worksheets, worksheets are extremely useful in business. Worksheets provide immediate feedback to questions, such as: "What if we reduce costs by .5 percent?", "What if we sell 11 percent more?", and "What if we don't get that loan?"

T I P   If you find data tables useful, examine the Scenario Manager, described in Chapter 14, along with other more advanced methods of analysis. If you need to test a set of data inputs and find the myriad of results, then look to the Scenario Manager.

When you test how small changes in input affect the result of a worksheet, you are conducting a *sensitivity analysis.* You can use Excel's **Data Table** command to conduct sensitivity analyses across a wide range of inputs.

Excel can create a table that shows the inputs you want to test and displays the results so that you don't have to enter all the possible inputs at the keyboard. Using a combination of a data table and the D*functions*, you can do quick but extensive database analysis of finance, marketing, or research information.

You can have more than one data table in a worksheet so that you can analyze different variables or database statistics at one time.

You can use **D**ata **T**able in the following two ways:

- Change one input to see the resulting effect on one or more formulas.

- Change two inputs to see the resulting effect on only one formula.

One Changing Variable and Many Formulas

Among the best (and most frequently used) examples of sensitivity analysis is a data table that calculates the loan payments for different interest rates. The single-input data table described in this section creates a chart of monthly payments for a series of loan interest rates.

Before you create a data table, you need to build a worksheet that solves the problem you want to test. The worksheet in figure 13.13 calculates a house or car mortgage payment. The following formula in cell D8 handles the following task:

=PMT(D5/12,D6*12,D4)

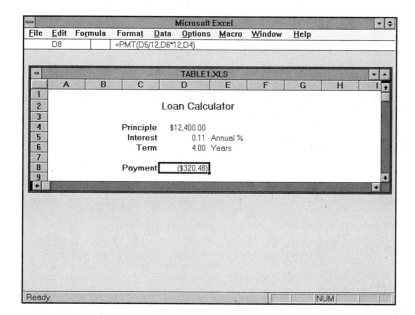

FIG. 13.13

Build a worksheet
with a result you
want to analyze.

To build a data table, complete the following steps:

1. Build the worksheet.

2. Enter the different values that you want tested. You can enter the values in any sequence.

   Cells C11:C17 in figure 13.14 show the interest rates to be used as inputs in the sensitivity analysis.

3. In the top row of the table, above where the results appear, enter the address of each formula for which you want answers. In this cell, you also can enter the formula.

   In figure 13.14, cell D10 contains =D8. Therefore, the results for the payment formula in D8 are calculated for each interest rate in the table. To see the results of other formulas in the table, enter these formulas in other cells across the top of the table. For example, you can enter more formulas in E10, F10, and so on.

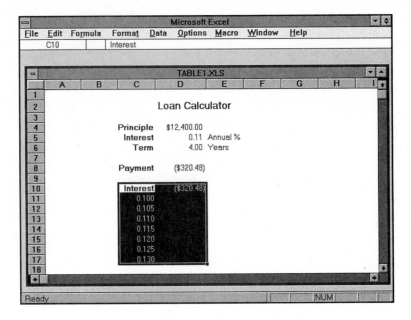

FIG. 13.14

Enter interest rates to
be evaluated.

4. Select the cells that enclose the table. Include the input values in the left column and the row of formulas at the top, as shown in figure 13.14.

5. Choose the **Data Table** command to display the Table dialog box (see fig. 13.15).

6. Enter the **Row** Input Cell or **Column** Input Cell. Click on or point to the cell in which you want to type the variable numbers listed in the table.

   Here, the **Column** Input Cell is $D$5. $D$5 is entered in the **Column** Input Cell text box because the variable inputs go down the columns in the table. The reference $D$5 tells Excel to take each value from column C11:C17 and substitute the values one at a time into cell D5. After each substitution, the result for the value appears in the range D11:D17.

7. Choose OK or press Enter.

The data table fills with the payment amounts that correspond to each interest rate in the table (see fig. 13.16).

If the Table dialog box covers the cells that you want to select as the row or column inputs, move the dialog box. To move the box, drag the title bar; or press Alt and then the space bar and select **Move**.

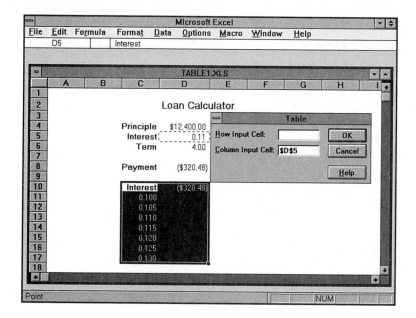

FIG. 13.15

The Table
dialog box.

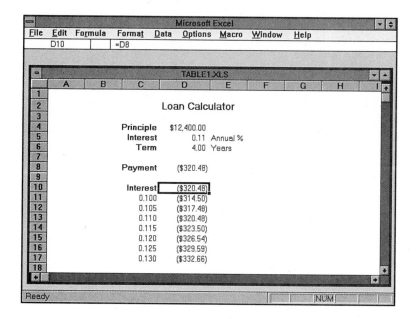

FIG. 13.16

The Data Table fills
with results for each
value in the left
column.

You can create a sequence of input values by using the **Data** Series command or by dragging a fill handle across a series to create a sequence of evenly incremented numbers for use as input values in the data table. Creating a series of numbers is described earlier in this chapter.

Two Changing Variables and One Formula

Figure 13.17 shows how to create a data table that changes two input values, interest and principal (the loan's starting amount). The worksheet calculates the result of a formula for all combinations of those values. The top row of the table area, row 10, contains different principal amounts for cell D3, the **R**ow Input Cell. The left column of the table still contains the sequence of interest rates to use in cell D4. (If you are duplicating this example, notice that cell references in the example have changed by one row from the previous example.)

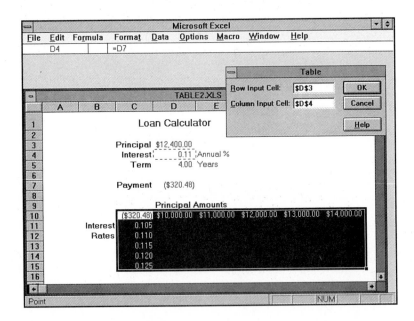

FIG. 13.17

Data tables also can change two input values used by one formula.

Notice that when you use two different input values, you can test the results from only one formula. The formula or a reference to the formula must be in the top-left corner of the table. In figure 13.17, cell C10 contains the reference =D7 to the payment formula to be tested.

The Table dialog box in figure 13.17 shows how the **R**ow Input Cell is entered as $D$3 because the values from the top row of the table are substituted into cell D3. The **C**olumn Input Cell is entered as $D$4 because the values from the left column of the table are substituted into cell D4.

Figure 13.18 shows the result of a two-input data table. Each dollar value is the amount you pay on a loan with this principal amount and annual interest rate. Because each monthly payment represents a cash outflow, the results appear in parentheses to show that the amounts are negative.

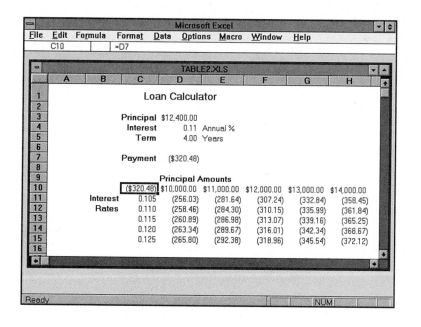

FIG. 13.18

The completed data table with the results of combinations from two input values, interest and principal.

Editing Data Tables

After the data table is complete, you can change values in the worksheet on which the data table depends. Using the new values, the table recalculates. In the example in figure 13.18, typing a new Term in D5 causes new Payment amounts to appear.

You also can change the numbers or text in the rows and columns of input values and see the resulting change in the data table. In the example in figure 13.18, you can type new numbers or use the **Data Series** command to replace the numbers in C11:C15 or in D10:H10. If automatic recalculation is selected, the data table updates by default.

You cannot edit a single formula within the data table. All the formulas in this area are array formulas of the following form:

$$\{=TABLE(row\_input, column\_input)\}$$

To rebuild or just expand the data table, select all the cells that contain the {=TABLE( )} array formula and clear these cells with **E**dit **C**lear or by pressing Del and then Enter. Change the data table, select the table area, and choose again the **Data Table** command.

Calculating Data Tables

Large data tables or many data tables may slow down calculation. If you want the worksheet—but not the data tables—to recalculate, choose the **O**ptions **C**alculation command and select the Automatic except **T**ables option. Recalculate the tables by pressing F9 to calculate all worksheets or press Shift+F9 to calculate the active worksheet. If you are performing a large database analysis, you may not want the worksheet and the related tables to recalculate before saving, which is the normal process. To save without recalculating, choose the **O**ptions **C**alculation command, select the **M**anual option, and clear the Recalculate Before **S**ave check box.

FROM HERE...

For Related Information:

▶▶ "Building Database Reports with the Crosstab Wizard," p. 882.

▶▶ "Using Data Tables," p. 897.

Calculating with Arrays

Arrays are rectangular ranges of formulas or values that Excel treats as a single group. Some array formulas or functions return an array of results that appear in many cells. Other formulas or functions affect an entire array of cells, yet return the result in a single cell.

Arrays are a powerful method of performing a large amount of calculation in a small space. When used to replace repetitive formulas, arrays also can save memory. Some Excel functions, such as the trend analysis functions discussed in this chapter under "Analyzing Trends," require some knowledge of arrays.

Entering Array Formulas

Rather than entering or copying a repetitive formula in each cell of a range, you can save memory by entering an array formula. Excel stores an array of formulas in memory as a single formula even if the array affects many cells. Some Excel functions also must be entered as arrays that span a range of cells because the function produces multiple results and each result appears only in one cell.

Figure 13.19 shows a worksheet for cost estimating with Price in column D and Quantity in column E. Using standard formulas, you find the sum of the products in column D times column E by entering a formula, such as =D5*E5 in F5, and copy it down column F. This method requires a formula for each cell that produced a result.

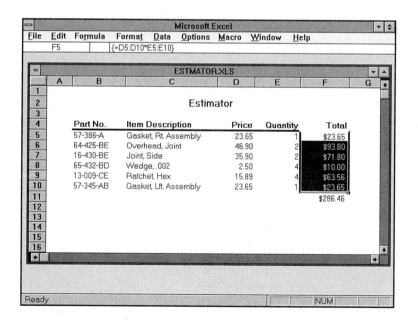

FIG. 13.19

Entering a repetitive formula as an array formula.

Instead, you can enter a single array formula in cell F5 that fills the range from F5 through F10 and uses only the memory and storage required for a single formula. Notice that the entire range F5:F10 reflects a different kind of formula shown in the Formula Bar. This array formula appears enclosed in braces, ({}).

To enter a single array formula, perform the following steps:

1. Select the range to contain the array formula—F5:F10 (see fig. 13.20).

2. Enter the formula that uses ranges by typing the formula or pointing with the mouse. The formula in cell F5 is =D5:D10*E5:E10.

3. To enter the formula or function as an array, press Shift+Ctrl+Enter.

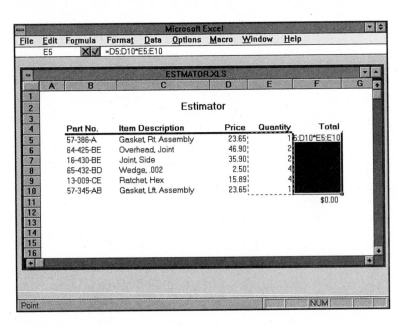

FIG. 13.20

Select the range, and then enter the array formula with Shift+Ctrl+Enter.

Rather than multiplying two cells, the formula shown in the Formula Bar of figure 13.19 multiplies the two arrays D5:D10 and E5:E10 by taking each corresponding element from the two arrays and multiplying them in pairs—for example, D5*E5, then D6*E6, and so on. The corresponding result is placed in each cell of the range F5:F10, which were selected before entry.

Notice that the formula in figure 13.19 is enclosed in braces ({}). Each cell in the array range F5:F10 contains the same formula in braces. The braces signify that the formula is an array formula and that the array range must be treated as a single entity. You cannot insert cells or rows within the array range, delete part of the range, or edit a single cell within the range. To change an array, you must select and change the entire array.

You can enter functions that operate on corresponding values in ranges with array math. *Array functions* use an array of values as an input and produce an array of results as an output. Enter array functions the same way you enter an array formula. Select a range of the correct size to hold the results of the array function and enter the array formula or function specifying the ranges on which the formula or function works. Then press Shift+Ctrl+Enter.

Suppose that you want only the total in cell F11 of figure 13.19 and do not need the total price for each part. You can calculate and sum the products in a single cell with an array formula. To see this result, type the following formula in cell F14:

=SUM(D5:D10*E5:E10)

Enter the formula by pressing Shift+Ctrl+Enter so that Excel treats the formula as an array formula. Excel calculates the sum of the array product. The SUM() formula appears in the Formula Bar, enclosed in braces.

Selecting an Array Range

Usually, the range you select in which to enter an array formula or function should be the same size and shape as the arrays used for input. If the array range you select for the result is too small, you cannot see all the results. If the array range is too large, the unnecessary cells appear with the #N/A message. If an array of a single cell, a single row, or a single column is entered in too large a selection, this element, row, or column is repeated to expand the array to the appropriate size.

In figure 13.19, the array range for each column is 6-by-1 (six rows by one column). The result of multiplying these two arrays is a 6-by-1 array. Therefore, the range from F5 through F10 is selected.

Calculating Array Results

Figure 13.21 shows how a single array formula can perform the work of multiple formulas in a range of extensive database analysis. The formulas in cells C15 and D15 match the entry in cell B15 against the list of Part No. For example, in the formula in cell C15, when the part number in cell

B15 matches a part in the range B5:B10, the corresponding value from E5:E10 is added to a total. The result of the total displays in cell C15.

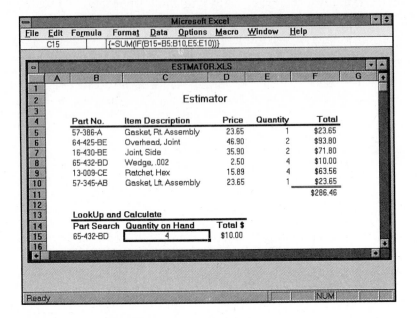

FIG. 13.21

Array formulas can do extensive lookups and calculations in a single cell.

The following line shows the formula in cell C15:

{=SUM(IF(B15=B5:B10,E5:E10))}

This formula was entered as an array formula in C15 by typing the formula and pressing Shift+Ctrl+Enter.

The formula in cell C15 uses the IF() function to compare the contents of cell B15 with each cell in the range B5:B10. When a match is found, the corresponding cell in the range E5:E10 is added to a total kept by SUM(). For this formula to work, you must enter the formula as an array formula.

The following line shows the formula in cell D15:

=SUM(IF(B15=B5:B10,D5:D10*E5:E10))

This formula is entered as an array formula in C15 by typing the formula and pressing Shift+Ctrl+Enter.

The formula in cell D15 works almost exactly as the formula in C15 but adds an extra calculation. When a match is found between the contents of B15 and a cell in the range B5:B10, the calculation of the correspond-ing cells in columns D and E are multiplied. The result of this multiplica-tion is totalled by the SUM() function. This formula must be entered as an array formula.

Editing Array Formulas and Functions

To edit an array formula or function, complete the following steps:

1. Move the pointer within the array range.

2. Click in the Formula Bar, or press F2 (the Edit key).

3. Edit the array formula or function.

4. To reenter the array, press Shift+Ctrl+Enter.

For Related Information:

FROM HERE...

◀◀ "Entering Formulas," p. 175.

◀◀ "Logical Functions," p. 381.

◀◀ "Matrix Functions," p. 394.

▶▶ "Using the Analysis ToolPak," p. 573.

Analyzing Trends

Excel can calculate a best-fit line that passes through a series of data. You can use the result of these calculations to analyze trends and make short-term forecasts. Two ways of calculating the data for these trends are available. You can drag across numbers using the fill handles, or you can use worksheet functions.

If you need to extend existing data by a few periods (cells) but don't need the corresponding best-fit data for the existing cells, you can use the method of dragging on fill handles to extend the data. By using the **D**ata Series command, you have multiple methods of creating a best-fit trend line. If, however, you need both original data and the correspond-ing best-fit data for the same periods—for example, to show original data and a best-fit line through the data—then use the worksheet function method.

Calculating Trends with Fill Handles

Figure 13.22 shows known data for regional housing starts. If you need to project this data into the empty cells to the right by using a linear best-fit, select the cells as shown in figure 13.22. To fill the data in the empty cells, drag the fill handle to the right to enclose the area you want extended, then release the mouse button. Figure 13.23 shows the results of this procedure.

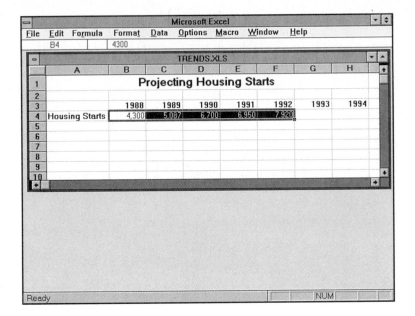

FIG. 13.22

Using linear best-fit, extend a series by dragging the fill handle.

Calculating Trends with the Data Series Command

You may remember back in science class recording a number of data points on a chart and then trying to draw a line through the points so that the line gave the trend of the data with the least errors. That line was a best-fit line. Points on that line are the best-fit data. Using Excel's **Data Series** command, you can create best-fit data that replace or extend the original data. You also can chart the best-fit data to create a best-fit line.

The **Data Series** command creates a linear (straight line) or exponential growth trend line. Using the **Data Series** command, you can create these two types of trend lines in two ways. Figure 13.24 illustrates the different types of trend data produced.

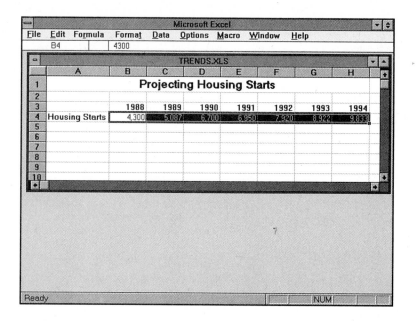

FIG. 13.23

Data filled into the empty cells are projections using a linear best-fit.

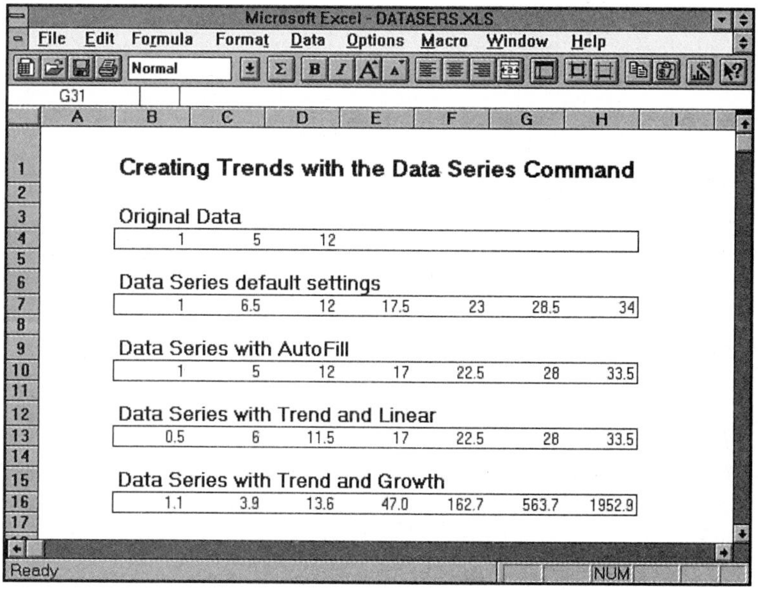

FIG 13.24

Use the Data Series command to quickly produce trend data.

The original data used to produce the trends in the figure are the numbers 1, 5, and 12 shown in B4:D4. The selected range used with each command was in each of the rows from column B to column H. The different types of trend data produced used these combinations of settings:

Settings	Description of Resulting Trend
Data Series default settings	A linear trend is produced starting with the original first data point. Calculated data replaces the original data. If charted, the trend line is forced to go through the first data point.
Data Series AutoFill	A linear trend is produced. The original data remains. Selected cells beyond the original data fill with data points for the linear trend.
Data Series with Trend and Linear	A linear trend is produced and the trend is not forced to pass through the first original data point. Original data is replaced with trend data.
Data Series with Trend and Growth	An exponential growth trend is produced and the trend is not forced to pass through the first original data point. Original data is replaced with trend data.

To create a trend using the **Data Series** command, perform the following steps:

1. Select the original data and as many additional cells as you want the trend data to extend into. In figure 13.24, for example, the cells B4:H4 might be selected.

2. Choose the **Data Series** command.

3. Choose one of the following combinations of options:

Setting	Result
Default (no changes)	Linear trend through first data point. Trend replaces original data.
AutoFill	Linear trend through first data point. Trend fills in blank selected cells.
Trend/Linear	Linear trend. Fills all cells.
Trend/Growth	Exponential growth trend. Fills all cells.

Calculating Trends with Worksheet Functions

Excel's trend functions work by calculating the best-fit equation for the straight line or exponential growth line that passes through the data. The LINEST() and LOGEST() functions calculate the parameters for the straight-line and exponential growth-line equations. The TREND() or

GROWTH() functions calculate the values along the straight line or exponential growth line needed to draw a curve or forecast a short-range value.

Before you can use the trend analysis functions, become familiar with dependent and independent variables. The value of a *dependent variable* changes when the *independent variable* changes. Frequently, the independent variable is time but also can be other items, such as the price of raw materials, the temperature, or a population size. The independent variable's actual data is entered as the *known-x* argument in the function, and the dependent variable's actual data is entered as the function's *known-y* argument.

Imagine that you own a concrete business that depends on new residential construction. You want to plan for future growth or decline so that you can best manage your firm's assets and people.

After research with the help of the local economic advisory boards, you assemble statistics on housing starts in the service area for the previous five years. In figure 13.22, row 4 shows the housing starts by year. After meeting with county planners, you are convinced that this area may continue to grow at the same or a slightly higher rate. You still need to estimate, however, the number of housing starts in 1993 and 1994.

In the figure, the independent variables of time (*known_x*) are entered in B3:F3. The dependent variables of housing starts (*known_y*) are entered in B4:F4. If the trend from the past five years continues, you can project the estimated housing starts for the next two years with the following steps:

1. Select the range of cells that you want the straight-line projection to fill, B6:H6, as shown in figure 13.25.

2. Choose the Formula Paste Function command.

3. From the list box, select TREND.

4. Ensure that the Paste Arguments check box is selected so that prompts for arguments are pasted between the function's parentheses.

5. Enter the arguments for the TREND() function so that the formula appears as shown in figure 13.25. The following line shows the syntax for the TREND() function:

    TREND(*known_y's,known_x's,new_x's*)

    Replace the *known_y*'s argument with B4:F4. (Housing Starts are y's because these numbers are dependent on the Year value.)

    Replace the *known_x*'s argument with B3:F3. (Year is the independent variable.)

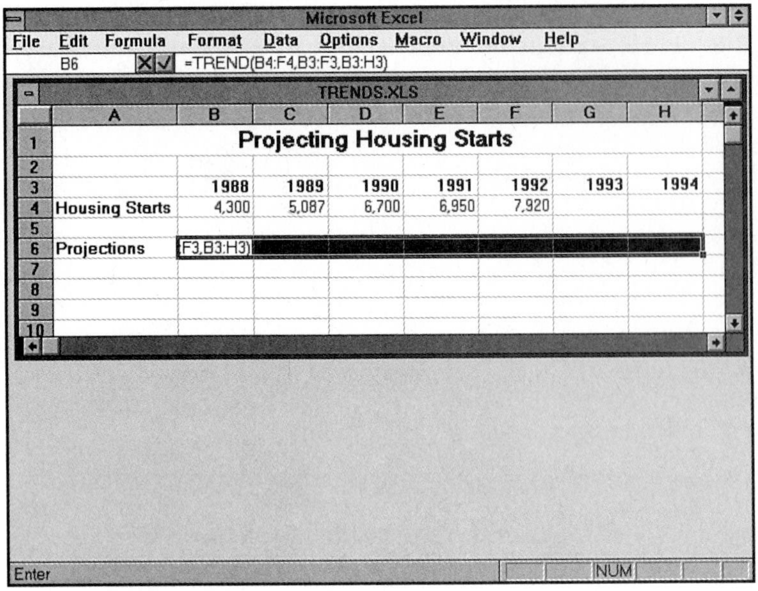

	Microsoft Excel							
File	Edit	Formula	Format	Data	Options	Macro	Window	Help

B6 ☒✓ =TREND(B4:F4,B3:F3,B3:H3)

TRENDS.XLS

	A	B	C	D	E	F	G	H
1			**Projecting Housing Starts**					
2								
3		1988	1989	1990	1991	1992	1993	1994
4	Housing Starts	4,300	5,087	6,700	6,950	7,920		
5								
6	Projections	[F3,B3:H3]						
7								
8								
9								
10								

Enter   NUM

FIG. 13.25

Select the range
before creating the
array formula.

Replace *new_x*'s with B3:H3, which are the years for which you
want to know the values that describe a trend line.

Notice that the selected area in figure 13.25 covers the room for the
resulting calculated *y* values.

6. To enter the TREND() function as an array function in the selected
    range, press Shift+Ctrl+Enter.

If the present trend continues, the result shown in figure 13.26 illustrates
that years 1993 and 1994 may have housing starts of about 8922 and
9833.

Notice that the new *y* values in cells B6:F6 don't exactly match the
known *y* values in B3:F3 because the TREND() function calculated the
housing starts for these years according to its trend equation (a linear
regression). The real number of housing starts in each year undoubtedly
will be different. The greater the differences between the real housing
starts and projected housing starts, the less accurate the projection
becomes.

FROM HERE...

For Related Information:

◄◄ "Entering Worksheet Functions," p. 356.

◄◄ "Statistical Functions," p. 395.

►► "Using the Analysis ToolPak," p. 573.

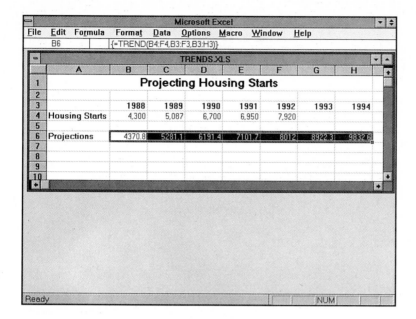

FIG. 13.26

The trend values can help you make short-term projections.

Outlining Worksheets

With Excel you can display summary and detail information efficiently in an outline (see fig. 13.27). When you condense an outline, only the summary information shows. When you expand an outline, the summary and the detailed information show.

Figure 13.27 shows the history of sales as an outline. East, West, North, South, and Corporate rows are summary rows that contain the detail of product sales. Columns E, I, M, and Q contain, respectively, each quarter's monthly detail.

Notice that some rows and columns are hidden and show only summary information. North and South rows are collapsed to show only the regional summary. The East and West regions are expanded to show the product detail these cells contain. Similarly, the quarterly columns can be expanded to show the monthly detail these cells contain. The Annual column can be collapsed to contain the quarterly as well as monthly columns.

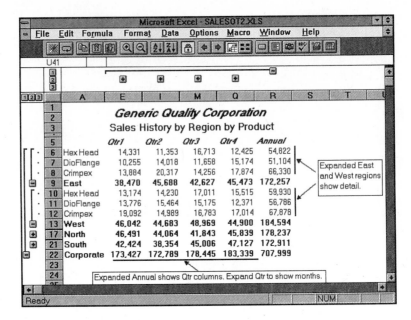

FIG. 13.27

Outlines can display
data at different
summary or detail
levels.

Showing selected levels of information on-screen is a real advantage
when you need to work with or print worksheets that contain different
levels of information. The outline enables you to display or print only the
amount of information you need. For example, budgets often contain
subordinate line items. Operational managers need to see these details
but managers at a different level may need to see the summary level
only.

Engineers and scientists also find outlines useful. Engineers who review
large amounts of instrument recordings may want to see only hourly
summary statistics of readings taken each minute. When hourly statistics look abnormal, the engineer can expand the outline to show the
detail of the recordings taken each minute.

Figure 13.28 shows a history of sales dollars in which time appears horizontally on the worksheet and regions and products appear vertically.
The summary and detail information all are shown. Products are summarized by region in rows 9, 13, 17, and 21. Row 22 is a corporate summary.
Summaries by quarter are in columns E, I, M, and Q. The Annual summary is in column R. Each summary is a SUM() function of the data
above or to the left of the function.

	A	B	C	D	E	F	G	H	I
	Microsoft Excel - SALESOUT.XLS								
	File Edit Formula Format Data Options Macro Window Help								
	A1								
2				*Generic Quality Corporation*					
3				Sales by Region by Product					
5		Jan	Feb	Mar	Qtr1	Apr	May	Jun	Qtr2
6	Hex Head	4,318	5,955	4,059	14,331	4,412	3,233	3,708	11,353
7	DioFlange	3,223	3,276	3,755	10,255	5,521	5,209	3,287	14,018
8	Crimpex	4,562	4,857	4,464	13,884	6,564	6,946	6,807	20,317
9	East	12,103	14,088	12,279	38,470	16,498	15,387	13,803	45,688
10	Hex Head	4,154	3,565	5,455	13,174	3,299	5,403	5,527	14,230
11	DioFlange	4,014	4,415	5,347	13,776	6,783	4,489	4,192	15,464
12	Crimpex	6,104	6,986	6,002	19,092	4,687	3,801	6,500	14,989
13	West	14,272	14,967	16,804	46,042	14,769	13,694	16,220	44,683
14	Hex Head	6,859	6,000	6,932	19,792	6,859	5,431	5,616	17,906
15	DioFlange	5,194	3,379	4,833	13,406	4,020	5,919	3,582	13,522
16	Crimpex	4,730	3,449	5,115	13,293	3,560	4,089	4,987	12,636
17	North	16,783	12,828	16,880	46,491	14,440	15,440	14,185	44,064
18	Hex Head	5,370	5,210	5,228	15,808	5,519	6,582	4,244	16,346
19	DioFlange	3,281	3,732	3,783	10,796	3,856	3,287	4,697	11,840
20	Crimpex	5,009	6,755	4,056	15,819	3,396	3,441	3,331	10,169
21	South	13,660	15,697	13,067	42,424	12,772	13,311	12,272	38,354

Ready   NUM

FIG. 13.28

Usually, worksheets display both detailed and summary data.

Understanding the Outline Display

Figure 13.29 shows a picture of the outlining symbols and tools on the Utility toolbar. Outlining tools also are available on the Microsoft Excel 3.0 toolbar. Outlining tools in the toolbar are used to create, display, change, or select data at a specific outline level. The outlining tools and descriptions are shown in the following list:

Tool	Description
Promote	Raises a row or column to a higher level in the outline.
Demote	Lowers a row or column to a lower level in the outline.
Show Outline	Displays or hides the outline and its buttons.
Select Visible Cells	Selects only the cells at the levels displayed in the outline.

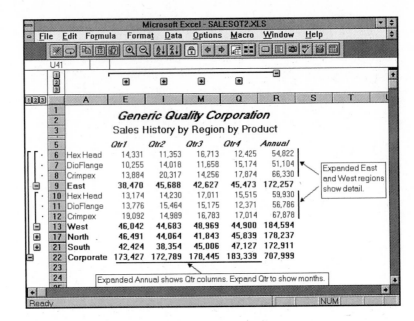

FIG. 13.29

Outlining uses two
tools and special
symbols to expand
and collapse outlines.

While an outline is displayed, you see outlining symbols along the left
edge and top of the worksheet that contains the outline. These outlining
symbols and tools expand and collapse levels. You can selectively expand or collapse a selected row or column and the related levels, or you
can expand or collapse all rows or columns at a specific level. The outlining symbols are shown in the following list:

Symbol	Description
Expand(+)	Specifies a level that contains lower levels of hidden data. Click to expand and display these levels for the selected row or column.
Collapse (–)	Specifies a summary level within which lower levels may be collapsed. Click to collapse and hide these levels for the selected row or column.
Row or column level number buttons	Specifies the number of the row or column level to display throughout the outline.
Level bars	Specifies all rows or columns at a specific level.

Understanding Outline Layout

Using Excel, you can create an outline at the keyboard by specifying a level for each row or column; or you can let Excel create an outline on the worksheet for you. When you use the keyboard to create an outline, you use the Promote or Demote symbol to specify an outline level for a row or column. You must organize the levels in the outline.

If Excel creates the outline, Excel examines the contents of each cell in the range to be outlined. Depending on the data and formulas in rows and columns, Excel then creates an outline with appropriate levels. The outline can use up to seven levels of rows and columns.

Excel examines the range of cells you want to outline, searching for constant data and formulas or functions that show a consistent pattern (see fig. 13.30). Excel checks whether all the SUM() functions in a column total the columns to the left. When consistent relationships are found, Excel makes these rows or columns summary rows or columns. These rows or columns appear at a higher level in the outline than the summarized rows or columns.

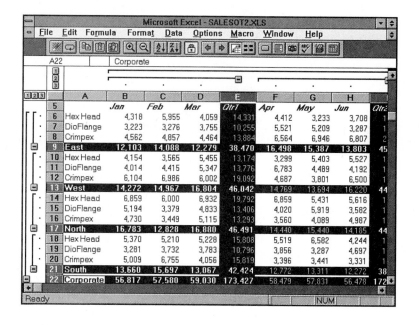

FIG. 13.30

Excel examines the layout of summary formulas to determine an outline's organization.

T I P You can use dates as the top row of an outline. When you create an outline, serial date numbers along the top row of the outline may be mistaken for data and disrupt this outline level. If this problem occurs, you can open the old file, type text dates—such as *May* or ="1/1/92"—in this row, and then re-create the outline. You also can manually adjust the levels of rows and columns to correct the outline. To create a series of text dates, such as May, June, and so on, review the AutoFill function described in the section "Creating Series of Text and Headings," earlier in this chapter.

The selected cells contain summarizing functions or formulas. The outline symbols show these rows and columns as a higher level in the outline. For example, cells in column E use SUM() to total the cells in B, C, and D to the left. Cells in row 9 use SUM() to total the cells in rows 6, 7, and 8 above.

The highest levels in the outline are row 22 and column R, shown in figure 13.29. These levels contain simple addition formulas that total lower level SUM() functions. Row 22 contains the Corporate total by region; for example, =B9+B13+B17+B21. Column R contains the total of all quarters; for example, =Q6+M6+I6+E6.

NOTE All summary directions must be consistent. For automatic outlining to work, all summary columns must have the data on the same side, and all summary rows must have the data either all above or all below. If the outline mixes the direction in which data is summarized, use the manual method to create an outline.

When you create an outline automatically, Excel assumes that summary rows are below detail rows and summary columns are to the right of detail columns. If you use the Formula Outline command to create the outline, you can specify that summary rows are above detail and summary columns are to the left of detail. The summary functions must summarize in the directions specified by the options for the outline to work correctly.

NOTE A worksheet can contain only one outline, but the outline can be disjointed and spread over different parts of a worksheet.

Creating an Outline

You can create an outline by using a menu command or the Show Outline tool from the utility and Excel 3.0 toolbars.

If you are using a mouse and have the toolbar on-screen, you can quickly create an outline if an outline doesn't currently exist. To use this shortcut, complete the following steps:

1. To outline the cells in the range, select a range. To outline the entire worksheet, select a single cell.

2. Click on the Show Outline tool. If no outline exists on the worksheet, the dialog box in figure 13.31 appears.

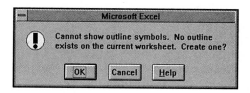

FIG. 13.31

If an outline doesn't exist, this alert box appears and asks whether you want to make an outline.

3. Choose OK or press Enter.

To create an outline by using the menu, complete the following steps:

1. Examine the cells you want to outline. Notice whether the summary column is to the left or right of the column data and whether summary rows are above or below the row data.

2. To outline the cells in the range, select a range. To outline the entire worksheet, select a single cell.

3. Choose the Formula Outline command. The dialog box in figure 13.32 appears.

FIG. 13.32

The Outline dialog box
enables you to specify
the orientation of your
outline.

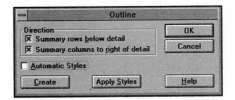

4. If you want to apply predefined styles to different outline levels, select the **A**utomatic Styles check box.

5. Select the check boxes that define the location of detail data with respect to summary rows and columns:

    If formulas or functions in rows are below the data they summarize, select the Summary Rows **b**elow Detail check box. Deselect if formulas or functions are above the data.

    If formulas or functions in columns are to the right of data, select the Summary Columns to the **r**ight of Detail check box. Deselect if formulas or functions are to the left of the data.

6. Choose the **C**reate button.

You can apply any desired predefined outline styles whenever you want. Styles and redefining styles are discussed in Chapter 8's section "Creating Styles."

Clearing an Outline

You can remove part, or all, of an outline from the worksheet. To remove rows, columns, or the entire outline, raise the level of this part of the outline until the section is *above* all outline levels. Promoting rows or columns out of the outline doesn't clear these elements from the worksheet.

To remove all or part of an outline, complete the following steps:

1. Select the rows or columns you want to remove by selecting the entire row or column. Click on the row or column heading, or press Shift+space bar or Ctrl+space bar.

    To remove the entire outline, select the entire worksheet by clicking in the empty square at the intersection of the column headings and row headings, or press Shift+Ctrl+space bar.

2. If you selected rows or columns, raise the level of the selection by clicking on the Promote tool (left arrow) in the toolbar or by pressing Alt+Shift+left arrow.

If you select the entire worksheet or only a few cells, the dialog box in figure 13.32 appears. Select whether you want to raise rows or columns to a higher level and choose OK or press Enter.

3. Continue raising the level of the selection until all the contents of the selection are at the same level.

If you remove an outline or parts of an outline and rows or columns remain hidden, select these rows or columns and choose the Format **R**ow Height or Forma**t** **C**olumn Width commands, then select the **U**nhide button.

Creating Outlines Manually

You can use the mouse or keyboard to create an outline or change the levels in an outline by selecting rows or columns and then promoting or demoting the rows or columns. You can create or change outlines this way by using the mouse or the keyboard.

To change or assign a level to a row or column, complete the following steps:

1. Select the rows or columns that you want to change.

2. Click on the Demote or Promote tool in the toolbar. With the keyboard, press Alt+Shift+left arrow to promote or Alt+Shift+right arrow to demote.

3. Continue to demote or promote rows or columns as necessary to change the outline.

If you need to quickly examine the summary formulas to see the direction of reference, press Ctrl+` (grave accent, located on the ~key). This switches the worksheet display to show formulas. Press Ctrl+` again to display formula results.

T I P

If you are creating an outline with the mouse or keyboard, demote rows or columns in the worksheet to the level necessary for the outline. When you demote a row or column, the outline symbols appear. You can toggle the outline symbols on or off by clicking on the Show Outline Symbols tool in the toolbar or by pressing Ctrl+8.

If you didn't select an entire row or column, a dialog box appears and asks whether you want to change a row or column. Select which you want to change, and then choose OK or press Enter.

Expanding and Collapsing the Outline

The real value of an outline is apparent when you expand and collapse the outline to display or work with different levels of data or summary. Although using the mouse is the easiest method to expand and collapse, you also can use the keyboard.

T I P Text boxes and graphic objects that overlap an outline may become distorted or disappear when you expand or collapse the outline. To prevent this kind of distortion, format the text boxes or graphic objects with the Format Object Placement command. Although situations vary, you usually can format worksheet or outline titles in a text box with the Don't Move or Size with Cells option. Format arrows with the Move and Size with Cells option. Text boxes that explain data in the outline usually use Move but Don't Size with Cells. This procedure keeps titles over the correct areas, adjusts the length of arrows appropriately, and moves explanatory text boxes without distorting the text inside.

To expand or collapse an outline with the mouse or keyboard, complete the following steps:

1. Display the toolbar by choosing the Options Display command, selecting the Toolbar check box, and choosing OK. You can toggle the toolbar on or off by pressing Ctrl+7.

2. Display the outline symbols by clicking on the Show Outline tool in the toolbar, choosing the Options Display command, and selecting Outline Symbols or pressing Ctrl+0.

3. Expand or collapse specific rows and columns or an entire level with one of the following actions:

    Expand a specific row or column by clicking on the related Expand (+) symbol.

    Expand to an entire level by clicking on the appropriate Level number button. To display all levels, click on the highest numbered button.

    Collapse a specific row or column by clicking on the element's Demote (−) symbol.

    Collapse to an entire level by clicking on the appropriate Level Number button. To collapse all levels, click on the lowest numbered button.

If you are using a keyboard, you can expand areas of an outline by select-ing rows or columns, choosing the Format **R**ow Height or Format **C**olumn Width commands, and selecting the **U**nhide check box.

Formatting Outlines

Excel applies predefined formatting styles to each level of the outline. This feature can make report and display formatting easier.

To apply styles when you create the outline, select the **A**utomatic Styles check box from the Outline dialog box.

To apply styles to an existing outline, complete the following steps:

1. Select the parts of the outline to which you want to apply styles.

2. Choose the Fo**r**mula **O**utline command. The Outline dialog box appears.

3. Choose the Apply **S**tyles button.

Chapter 8 describes how to change the definition of a style. By changing the definition of a style, you reformat all cells in the worksheet to which this style applies. This method enables you to efficiently change the appearance of a report.

Copying and Charting from Specific Outline Levels

The worksheet contains all the data at different levels, even levels not currently displayed. If you copy or chart from a selection in the outline, the copied area or chart includes data at levels below those displayed.

To work with data from the displayed level in the worksheet only, you must specify that you want to work with visible selected cells only. To specify that you want to work with visible cells only, complete the fol-lowing steps:

1. Select the cells with which you want to work.

2. Click on the Select Visible Cells tool in the toolbar; or choose the Fo**r**mula **S**elect Special command, select the **V**isible Cells option, and then choose OK or press Enter.

   You see a separation between cells that contain nonvisible data, as shown in figure 13.33.

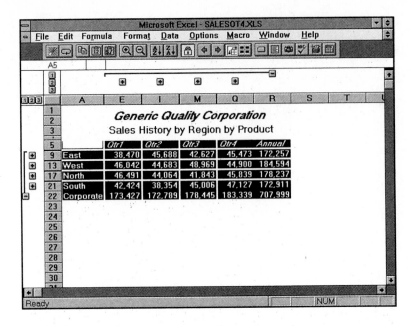

FIG. 13.33

Select only visible cells
to work with displayed
data.

3. Continue working by using commands, such as the commands in
   the following list:

   Chart Edit Series
   Edit Copy
   Edit Fill Down/Up
   Edit Paste
   Edit Paste Link
   File New Chart

   When you paste summary data, the summary formulas are changed to
   constant values.

For Related Information:

FROM HERE...

◄◄ "Creating Styles," p. 297.

◄◄ "Working with Multiple Documents," p. 420.

◄◄ "Grouping Documents into Workbooks," p. 426

◄◄ "Editing and Formatting Groups of Worksheets," p. 436.

◄◄ "Linking Consolidated Worksheets," p. 477.

Troubleshooting Worksheets

Surveys show that 30 percent of all electronic worksheets contain errors. This statistic can be terrifying but believable when you consider that most users are given little or no training, and few are trained in designing or auditing worksheets. Few companies have policies for auditing or documenting worksheets.

Correct worksheets require careful planning and execution. Always be sure that you cross-check and review a new worksheet before using it for a critical decision. Excel has built-in commands, macros, and error values to help you discover trouble spots in your worksheets.

Excel includes two features, the Formula Select Special command and the AUDIT.XLA add-in, to make troubleshooting Excel worksheets easier. This section describes these features and includes other tips and techniques to help you resolve problems and find errors in worksheets.

Problem:

After pressing Enter to enter a formula, Excel beeps and displays an alert box warning that an error exists in the formula.

Solution:

Press the F1 key for Help when you see this kind of alert box. Excel displays a Help window that lists the most common errors that occur in worksheets. If, after reading the Help, you cannot find the error in the formula, delete the equals sign (=) at the front of the formula and press Enter. This step enters the formula as text so that you can return later and work on it. To turn the text back into a formula, just reenter the equals sign at the front of the formula and press Enter.

Problem:

When typing a complicated formula that includes many pairs of parentheses, you miss, and cannot locate, one of the parentheses.

Solution:

Excel highlights matching pairs of parentheses as you move the insertion point across one parenthesis of a pair. To see these highlighted, move the insertion point into the Formula Bar, and then press the right- or left-arrow keys to move the insertion point across a parenthesis. Watch for an opposing parenthesis to highlight. If the highlighted parenthesis doesn't enclose the correct term in the formula, you have found the terms that require another parenthesis.

Problem:

Everything within a function appears correct, but Excel doesn't accept the entry.

Solution:

A frequent mistake when typing functions is to miss or delete a comma between arguments. You can reduce the chance of omitting commas and entering arguments incorrectly by entering functions with Formula Paste Function and selecting the Paste Arguments option. To select an argument to replace, double-click on the argument prompt you pasted and then type or click on the needed cell. This procedure selects only the argument prompt between commas and replaces this argument with data you type or information from the cell on which you click. Another common error is mismatched parentheses in a formula or function. To find the match to a parenthesis, move the insertion point in the Formula Bar next to a parenthesis. Press the arrow key to move across the parenthesis. As the insertion point moves over a parenthesis, the parenthesis and its match change to bold.

Problem:

When auditing a worksheet, you want to see more than one formula or determine the range names that a cell is part of.

Solution:

You can switch the worksheet to display formulas by choosing the Options Display command and selecting the Formulas option. The shortcut key is Ctrl+` (grave accent). Open a second window to the worksheet with the Window New Window command; then format one worksheet to show results and the other to show formulas.

To see the range names, formulas, and formats that involve a cell, select the cell and then choose the Options Workspace command and select the Info Window check box to display an Information window. A new menu appears while the Info Window is active. Select from the Info menu the attributes you want to see about the active cell. When troubleshooting a worksheet, leave the Information window open. When you select a new cell, you can switch to the Info window for this cell by pressing Ctrl+F6 to display the Info window updated for the current cell.

If you selected exactly the same cells used by a range name, the name appears in the Reference area at the top-left corner of the worksheet.

Problem:

Large Excel worksheets are difficult to understand without a map that shows areas and regions.

Solution:

Use Excel's **Window Zoom** command to shrink the worksheet so that you can see more. This shows the actual worksheet results. You also can create a map showing text, values, and formulas. Use the AUDIT.XLA add-in that comes free with Excel to add the Audit command to the Formula menu. The Audit command enables you to create a miniature map that shows all the regions of a worksheet and the varieties of values or formulas these regions contain. AUDIT.XLA, an add-in program that you can install with the Add-in Manager, is described in Chapter 15.

Problem:

The Circular (Circ) indicator appears at the bottom of the worksheet. Although no data has changed, with every recalculation of the worksheet, some of the results grow larger or grow smaller.

Solution:

The worksheet has a circular error—a formula that refers to another cell that contains a formula that refers to the first. This error may happen through a chain involving many cells. The formula feeds on itself with progressing recalculations. Therefore, like a snake devouring its tail, each recalculation reduces the results; or the results can grow larger, depending on how the formula is built. To find all the cells involved in a circular error, add the Audit command to the Formula menu. AUDIT.XLA is an add-in program that you can install with the Add-in Manager, which is described in Chapter 15.

Problem:

In a long formula that contains many parts, one of the smaller terms in the formula is incorrect. You cannot find the part of the formula that produces these incorrect results.

Solution:

To see how a term or function within a formula evaluates, complete the following steps:

1. Select the cell that produces the incorrect result or an error value.

2. In the Formula Bar, select the smallest portion of the formula that may cause this problem. The term you select must be a complete function or portion of a formula that can be calculated by itself. Figure 13.34 shows a portion of an IF() function selected. Notice that the complete AND() function, including both parentheses and all arguments, is selected.

3. To calculate the portion you selected, press the F9 key. Figure 13.35 shows how the selected portion in the formula changes to the related calculated result, FALSE. If the selected portion results in a number, text, error, or array you see these values.

4. Select and calculate other parts of the formula until you find the portion causing the error.

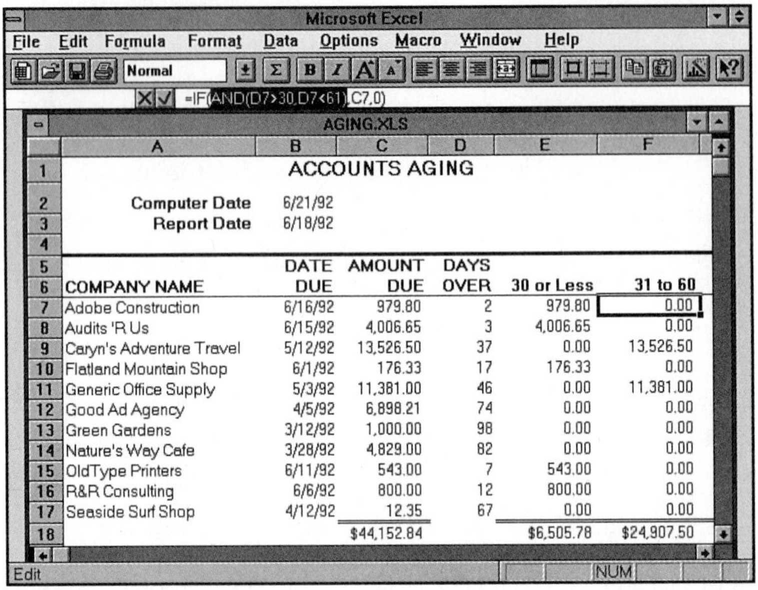

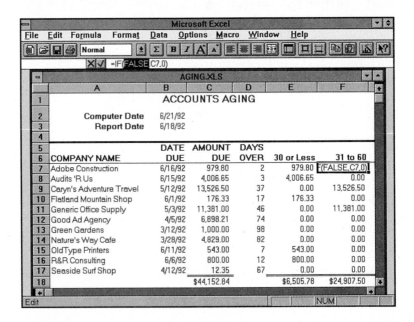

FIG. 13.34

Select the portion of
the formula that you
want to check.

FIG. 13.35

Only the selected
portion is calculated.

5. To return the formula to the original form, press Esc or click on the Cancel box in the Formula Bar. If you enter the formula, the result of the formula replaces the equation.

6. Correct the portion of the formula that returned the incorrect answer.

The preceding method of calculating part of a formula displays the contents of arrays. If, in the Formula Bar, you select a function that returns an array of values and press F9, you see the values within the array, as in the following example:

{2,3,"four";5,6,"seven"}

Commas separate array values into columns. Semicolons separate rows.

Problem:

Error messages appear in cells.

Solution:

When Excel cannot evaluate a formula or function, the program displays an error value in the offending cell. Error values begin with a pound sign (#). Excel has seven kinds of error values with self-explanatory names (see table 13.1). The AUDIT.XLA add-in described in Chapter 15 creates an audit report that shows the location of all error values on the worksheet and also finds all names that cause errors and all formulas that reference a blank cell.

Table 13.1. Excel Error Values

Value	Meaning
#DIV/0!	The formula or macro is attempting to divide by zero.
	Check: Examine cell references for blanks or zeros. You may have accidentally deleted an area of the worksheet needed by this formula. An incorrectly written formula may be attempting to divide by zero.
#N/A	The formula refers to a cell that has a #N/A entry.
	Check: You can type *#N/A* in mandatory data-entry cells. Then, if data isn't entered to replace the #N/A, formulas that depend on this cell display #N/A. This error value warns you that not all the data was entered.

continues

Table 13.1. Continued

Value	Meaning
	An array argument is the wrong size, and #N/A is returned in some cells.
	HLOOKUP(), VLOOKUP(), LOOKUP(), MATCH(), or other functions have incorrect arguments. In some instances these functions return an error value when they cannot find a match.
	You omitted an argument from a function. If Excel cannot correctly evaluate the arguments that you entered, some functions return #N/A. See the function's description in Chapter 10 for more information on the function.
#NAME?	Excel does not recognize a name.
	Check: Use the Formula **D**efine Name command to see whether the name exists. Create a name, if necessary.
	Verify the spelling of the name. Make sure that no spaces exist.
	Verify that functions are spelled correctly. Spaces are okay almost everywhere, except between the function name and the opening parenthesis. Novice users frequently type a space between the last character in the function name and the first parenthesis.
	See whether you used text in a formula without enclosing the text in quotation marks. Excel considers the text as a name rather than as text.
	See whether you forgot to replace one of the Paste **A**rguments prompts pasted into a function.
	Check whether you mistyped an address or range so that this information appears to Excel as a name, such as the cell ABB5 (two Bs) or the range B12C45 (a missing :).
	See whether you referred to an incorrect or nonexistent name in a linked worksheet.
#NULL!	The formula specifies two areas that don't intersect.

Value	Meaning
	Check: See whether the cell or range reference is entered incorrectly.
#NUM!	The formula has a problem with a number.
	Check: See whether the numeric argument is out of the acceptable range of inputs, or whether the function can find an answer given the arguments you entered.
#REF!	The cell reference is incorrect.
	Check: See whether you have deleted cells, rows, or columns referenced by formulas. Other causes may include indexes that exceed a range used in a function or offsets that are outside worksheet boundaries.
	See whether external worksheet references are still valid. Use the **File Links** command to open source worksheets. If you need to change a link to a worksheet with a different name or directory, use the **File Links** command with the **Change** button on, described in Chapter 12, in the section on linking worksheets.
	See whether a macro has returned a #REF! value from an unopened or incorrect function macro.
	See whether a Dynamic Data Exchange (DDE) topic is incorrectly entered or is not available.
#VALUE!	The value is not the kind expected by the argument or the result from an intersect operation when the ranges being evaluated do not intersect.
	Check: Verify that values used as arguments are of the kind listed in Chapter 10, "Using Functions."

Problem:

Searching individual formulas for errors or related formulas takes too long. You want to quickly select cells that contain errors, feed into the formula in the active cell, or depend on the result of the active cell.

Solution:

The Formula **S**elect Special command is a powerful ally in auditing and troubleshooting a worksheet. From the Select Special dialog box (see fig. 13.36), you can select specific parts of a worksheet or cell contents.

Table 13.2 describes the Formula Select Special options you can use when auditing a worksheet. Finding errors, such as #REF! or #N/A, in a worksheet or in a range is easy. Select the Formulas option and deselect all check boxes except the Formulas option, and select Errors.

When debugging a worksheet, find the cells that feed information in the active cell and the cells that depend on the results in the active cell. To see which cells feed into the active cell, select the **Pre**cedents option; select the **D**ependents option to see cells that depend upon the active cell. The Di**r**ect Only option selects cells that immediately feed or depend on the active cell. The All Levels option selects cells that feed into or depend on the active cell at all levels. The **D**irect Only option is like selecting only your parents or your children. The **A**ll Levels option is like selecting the entire family tree, backward or forward.

Typing a number over a formula is a common error in worksheets. To see cells that contain formulas and cells that contain values, select the range you want to troubleshoot and select the **C**onstants or Formulas options from the Select Special dialog box. Usually, you leave all the related check boxes selected. You may be surprised to find a constant value in the middle of what you believed were formulas!

Press Tab or Shift+Tab to move the active cell between the selected cells, while keeping all other cells selected. Read each cell's contents in the Formula Bar until you find the cell that contains an error.

Table 13.2. Formula Select Special Options Used in Auditing

Option	Action
Constants	Specifies that constants of the type you specify are selected. Available types are numbers, text, logicals, and errors.
Formulas	Specifies that formulas with results of the type you specify are selected.
Numbers	Selects constants or formulas that result in numbers.
Text	Selects constants or formulas that result in text.
Logicals	Selects constants or formulas that result in logicals (true/false).
Errors	Selects cells with error values.
Precedents	Selects cells that support the active cell.
Dependents	Selects cells that depend on the active cell.
Row Differences	Selects cells in the same row that have a different reference *pattern*.
Column Differences	Selects cells in the same column that have a different reference *pattern*.

For Related Information:

FROM HERE...

◄◄ "Selecting Cells by Their Type of Content," p. 156.

►► "Adding a Worksheet Auditor and Troubleshooter," p. 613.

►► "Troubleshooting Databases," p. 903.

Chapter Summary

The techniques described in this chapter work best when combined with other commands, functions, and techniques. You can find more techniques, tips, and functions in Chapter 10, "Using Functions," Chapter 26, "Building Extensive Databases," and Chapter 14, "Using Analytical Tools."

Chapter 14 describes more advanced analysis tools, including Goal Seek, the Solver, the Analysis ToolPak, and the Scenario Manager. To find the optimum solution, need advanced statistical, financial or engineering functions, or need to test multiple sets of input data, examine Chapter 14.

Using Analytical Tools

xcel comes with several tools to help you analyze data on worksheets. These tools include the Formula Goal Seek command,
the Solver add-in, the Scenario Manager add-in, and the Analysis ToolPak
add-in. The Goal Seek command helps you find the input value that will
give you the answer you want. Solver is a mathematical tool that can help
you find the best solution to certain types of problems. The Scenario
Manager enables you to keep and compare various input values for a
single worksheet. The Analysis ToolPak is a large collection of commands
and functions for use by financial analysts and engineers, but several of
its tools are useful in many business situations.

The Scenario Manager and the Analysis ToolPak are new with the current
version. The Solver has many new features to help you work faster and
better. This chapter helps you get the most out of these powerful analytical tools.

Deciding Which Tool To Use

Excel provides many tools—each one is best for different situations.
Some of these are add-in programs. For information on how to install and
activate add-in programs, see Chapter 15. Following are the major what-if
tools in Excel:

Tool	When To Use It
What-If add-in	If you have one or two input values and want to cycle between the choices. See Chapter 15 for more information on the What-if add-in.
Data Tables	If you have one input value and multiple result formulas, or two input values and a single result formula and want to create a table of results for each input value. The table is built with dynamic calculating formulas. See Chapter 13 for more information about Data Tables.
Solver	If you have one or more input values, and have constraints on the solution; if you want to obtain an optimal solution; or both. The Scenario Manager remembers named solutions found by the Solver so that you can create Scenario Manager reports of optimal solutions.
Scenario Manager	If you have one set of multiple input values, you can choose named sets of input and see the results in the worksheet. If you have more than one set of input values, you can create a report showing tables of each set of input values and that table's results.

Using the Goal Seek Feature

When you know the answer you want, and you need to work backward to find the input value that gives you that answer, use the Formula Goal Seek command. With this command, you first specify a solution and then the cell that should be changed to reach that solution. Excel finds the value that results in the specific answer you want. To find the answer, the command operates as if it were making repetitive, educated guesses.

The Goal Seek command can save you time when you need to *back into* solutions. You may need to use this command to determine the needed growth rate to reach a sales goal or to determine how many units must be sold to break even.

When you're using the Formula Goal Seek command, the cell being changed must affect the cell you have specified to reach a specific answer. Because you cannot put restraints on the command, you may end up with solutions that do not make sense, or you may have problems where no input value is possible. If you face situations like this, you will want to use Data Tables or the Scenario Manager to test different input values, or you may want to use the Solver to find the optimum solution within constraints that you specify.

Solving for a Single Solution

Figure 14.1 shows the worksheet that you may have created if you followed the instructions in Chapter 3, "Worksheet Quick Start." Suppose that you want to use the Goal Seek feature to vary cell D16 until cell F12 reaches the solution of $3,000.

To solve for a specific answer with Goal Seek, complete the following steps:

1. Select a cell that contains a formula for which you want to produce a specific answer. In the example, this cell is F12.

2. Choose the Formula Goal Seek command. The Goal Seek dialog box appears (see fig 14.1). Notice that the **S**et cell field already contains the cell you selected in step 1.

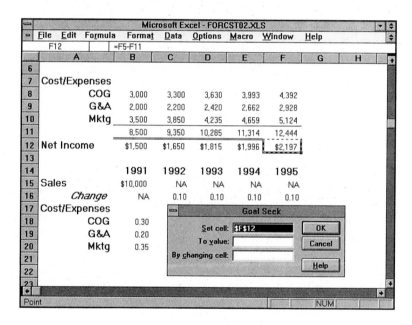

FIG. 14.1

The Goal Seek dialog box.

3. In the To **v**alue: text box, type the solution you want to reach. In the example, the desired solution is $3,000.

4. Select the By **c**hanging cell: text box, and enter the cell reference of the input cell. This cell must directly or indirectly feed into the formula in step 1. In the example, the cell being changed is $D$16.

   Figure 14.2 shows the completed Goal Seek dialog box.

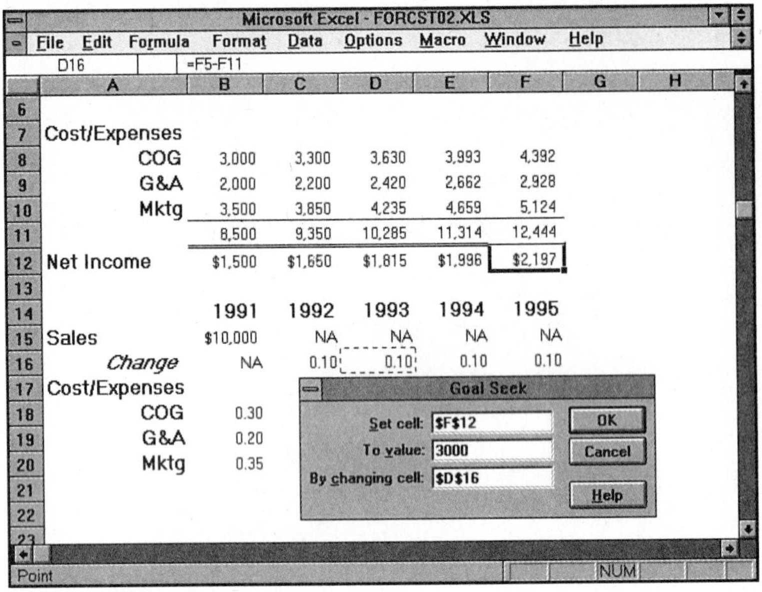

FIG. 14.2

Enter the solution you want and the cell you want to change to get that solution.

5. Choose OK or press Enter.

   Goal Seek begins substituting input values into cell D16. It substitutes high and low values and attempts to converge as close as possible to the solution you want.

6. If you want to pause or cancel the goal-seeking during a long goal-seeking process, choose the **P**ause or Cancel button. Step through the iteration solution process by choosing the **S**tep button. As you step, you can see the current solution value in the dialog box. To continue after pausing, choose the **C**ontinue button.

The input cell selected in step 4 must feed directly or indirectly into the set cell and must not contain a formula. To see which cells are precedents (feed into) the set cell, select the set cell. Choose the For**m**ula **S**elect Special command. Select the **P**recedents **A**ll Levels option; then choose OK or press Enter. All cells feeding into the set cell are selected. Press Tab or Enter to move among these cells while keeping them selected.

After a solution has been found, you can replace the values in the original worksheet with the new values that show on-screen by choosing OK. Keep the original values by choosing Cancel.

Moving a Chart Marker To Seek a Goal

You can use a chart to search for the goal you want to meet. To do so, you must be in a 2-D column, bar, or line chart. When you drag a marker to a new value position, the Goal Seek dialog box and worksheet appear. Excel then asks which cell you want changed to make the chart value come true.

To find a solution graphically from a chart, complete the following steps:

1. Open the worksheet and chart you want to manipulate. Activate the chart.

2. Hold down the Ctrl key as you click the data series marker (column, bar, or line symbol) that you want to change to a new value in the chart. A black handle appears on the marker, as shown in the marker at the right in figure 14.3.

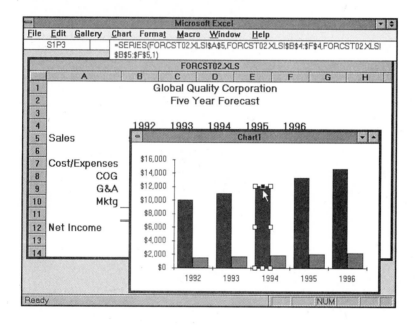

FIG. 14.3

Display the black handle on a chart marker.

3. Drag the black handle so that the end of the marker moves to a new value. In the example, drag the black handle up or down to change the height of the column. When you release the mouse button, the Goal Seek dialog box appears with the worksheet to which the chart marker is linked. Figure 14.4 shows the Goal Seek dialog box and worksheet.

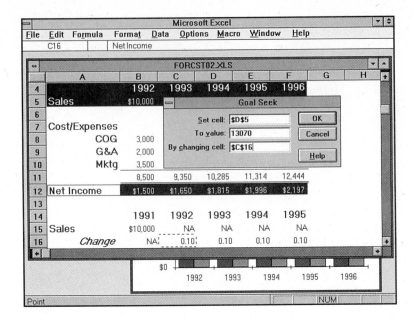

FIG. 14.4

Use Goal Seek to work backward and find a solution that matches your chart.

4. In the Goal Seek dialog box, the To **value:** text box is already filled with the value from the chart marker. Change the To **value:** if you need a different value. The **S**et cell: box contains the cell linked to the marker.

5. Select the By **c**hanging cell: text box, and type or select the cell reference you want to change.

6. Choose OK or press Enter.

Follow the described Goal Seek procedure to find the input value that produces the correct value for the chart marker.

As you drag the marker, notice that the numeric value of the marker appears in the Reference Area to the left of the Formula bar. This reference enables you to see the value of the marker as you reposition it.

If the chart marker is linked to a cell that contains a number and not a formula, the Goal Seek dialog box does not appear. The number in the worksheet changes to reflect the marker value. This feature helps you to easily enter values into a worksheet when you need a set of values that reflects a certain chart configuration.

Using Solver

Many worksheets are too complex for the Formula Goal Seek command to find a solution. A valid solution in these more complex models may require multiple inputs and may have limiting constraints on some of the input values or the output.

Where the Goal Seek feature finds a specific solution, the Solver program finds the best or optimal solution. To do that, Solver can vary multiple input cells while ensuring that other formulas in the worksheet stay within limits you set. The Solver works the way problems in the real world work—more than one variable must be changed to find an answer, yet other areas of the problem must be watched to make sure that they stay within realistic limits.

In many cases, you may need to rework your worksheet to fit the type of model with which Solver works best. To set up such a worksheet, you must have a good understanding of the relationships among variables and formulas. Solver's payback for your efforts, however, can be extremely high. Solver can save you from wasting resources with mis-managed schedules; help you earn higher rates through better cash management; and show you what mix of manufacturing, inventory, and products produces the best profit.

Understanding When To Use Solver

Use Solver to find the best solution to a problem. Solver is normally help-ful for the following types of problems:

- *Product Mix.* Maximizing the return on products given limited re-sources to build those products.

- *Staff Scheduling.* Meeting staffing levels at minimum cost within specified employee satisfaction levels.

- *Optimal Routing.* Minimizing transportation costs between a manu-facturing site and sale sites.

- *Blending.* Blending mixtures of materials to achieve a quality level at minimum cost.

The types of problems with which Solver can work have three import-ant parts. First, problems must have a single objective—for example, to maximize profit or minimize time. Second, problems must have constraints that are typically given as inequalities—for example, the materials used cannot exceed inventory, or the machine hours sched-uled cannot exceed 24 hours less maintenance time. Third, the problems must have input values that directly or indirectly affect both the con-straints and the values being optimized.

These problems usually fall within two mathematical types: linear and nonlinear. Solver can solve both types of problems. *Linear problems* are those in which the relationship between input and output results in a straight line or flat plane when graphed. If you have a linear problem, Solver has an option for finding solutions faster by using linear programming techniques. Linear formulas are usually simple and have the following form:

X=A*Y1+B*Y2+C*Y3...

In this syntax, X is the result; A, B, and C are constants; and Y1, Y2, and Y3 are variables.

Solver also solves for the best solution in worksheets involving nonlinear relationships. The following are examples of *nonlinear problems*:

- Sales approach a certain volume and then level off.

- Product quality increases at a decreasing level as production-line staffing increases.

- Advertising response increases with ad frequency but then diminishes.

- Product costs vary with different sales volumes.

Some of the forms involving nonlinear relationships include the following:

X=Y1/Y2

X=Y1^.5

X=A+Y1*Y2

where X is the result, A is a constant, and Y1 and Y2 are input values.

Creating the Sample Worksheet

The worksheet in figure 14.5 illustrates a simple model built to work with Solver. In this worksheet, a city government has started a service named Dirt Cheap, Inc. The service uses many existing resources to produce a positive income stream for the city. In addition, Dirt Cheap reduces and recycles garbage and landscape trimmings.

T I P Excel reads names to the top and left of the set cell and constraints and uses them to generate printed reports. Cells with long or confusing names may result in Solver-generated reports that are difficult to read.

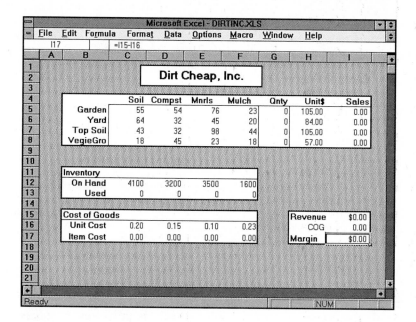

FIG. 14.5

The Dirt Cheap worksheet solves for the best combination of materials to reach the highest margin.

Dirt Cheap has a collection program for organic garbage, park trimmings, Christmas trees, and so on. The service mulches or composts these items and combines them in different blends with soil and mineral additives to produce high-quality mulch, soil, and growing mixtures. Some of the labor is volunteer, and materials costs are low except for collection costs.

The worksheet calculates the best combination of raw materials to produce the highest margin, shown in cell I17. No real problem is this simple, but Solver can work within the constraints of the real world to recalculate the best solution given changing conditions.

Much of the Dirt Cheap worksheet is text and constant numbers. To build the worksheet, type the text shown in figure 14.5 to use as a skeleton. Then enter the following numbers and formulas:

Cells	Item	Enter			
		Column Headings			
C5:F8	Mixture amounts	**C**	**D**	**E**	**F**
	Row Headings:	**5** 55	54	76	23
		6 64	32	45	20
		7 43	32	98	44
		8 18	45	23	18

continues

Cells	Item	Enter
G5:G8	Product amount	0
H5:H8	Product price	Numbers 105, 84, 105, 57
I5	Product $ sold	=G5*H5; then fill down into I6:I8
C12:F12	Inv. on hand	Numbers 4100, 3200, 3500, 1600
C13	Inv. used	=$G5*C5+$G6*C6+$G7*C7+$G8*C8; then fill right into D13:F13
C16	Unit cost	Numbers 0.20, 0.15, 0.10, 0.23
C17	Item cost	=C16*C13; then fill right into D17:F17
I15	Revenue	=SUM(I5:I8)
I16	Cost of goods	=SUM(C17:F17)
I17	Margin	=I15-I16

In the model, the values from C5:F5 are the mixture amounts necessary to create a soil product called *Garden Blend*. The retail price for a unit of Garden Blend is $105.00. Solver finds the best quantity, G5, to make of Garden Blend. After the best quantity is found, the sales amount in I5 is calculated by multiplying G5 times H5. This same technique is used for each soil product.

One constraint is that a limited amount of material exists to make the products. The inventory on hand of materials—Soil, Compost, Minerals, and Mulch—is specified in cells C12:F12. Cells C13:F13 calculate the amount of each material used to find the best combination of products. Of course, the amount of materials used cannot exceed the amount of materials on hand.

The cost of each material used is found by multiplying the unit cost for the materials, C16:F16, by the material used, C13:F13. This cost formula is in C17:F17.

The revenue is calculated in cell I15 by totaling the sales, I5:I8. The cost of goods, COG in cell I16, is the total of item costs, C17:F17. The margin is revenue minus cost.

Before you run the Solver, save this worksheet to disk by using the File Save **As** command.

Installing Solver

Solver involves a special Dynamic Link Library that works with Excel. If you didn't install Solver when you installed Excel, rerun the Excel install procedure and select the option to install Solver. You do not have to reinstall all of Excel or Windows.

When you have the Solver files on disk, you can load Solver in one of two ways. If you do not normally use Solver, you do not need to do anything until you begin to use it. The first time you choose the Formula Solver command, the Solver program starts. Watch the Reference Area to the left of the File menu to see the percentage of loading completed.

Solving for the Best Solution

Suppose that for this model, the city council mandates that the goal is to find the optimum (maximum) dollar return in cell I17. This objective will help expand the recycling and composting done by Dirt Cheap and may reduce taxes.

The input values that are changed to find the best margin are the quantities of each soil product to be created. At this point, the city sells all the product it makes, so it doesn't have to worry about limits on a product. Limiting an item's production or availability of resources is explained in the sections "Changing Constraints" and "Changing a Limited Resource." The input values that Solver will solve for are in G5:G8. For this example, the input values started with are 0. In models that take a long time to calculate, you can reduce calculation time by starting with input values that you believe are near the best solution.

The constraint on the solution is that the inventory used cannot exceed the inventory on hand. In spreadsheet terms, the calculated totals in cells C13:F13 cannot exceed the corresponding values in C12:F12. In addition, the values in G5:G8 must be greater than 0 because you cannot produce a negative amount of soil.

After the Solver Parameters dialog box is filled in with the cell optimized, the cells are changed and the constraints on the solution appear as shown in figure 14.6.

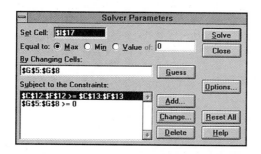

FIG. 14.6

The completed Solver Parameters dialog box finds the optimal combination of soil mixes.

To solve for the best solution, complete the following steps:

1. Select the cell you want to optimize. In the example, this cell is I17.

2. Choose the Formula Solver command. The Solver loads if it didn't when Excel started, and the Solver Parameters dialog box, shown in figure 14.7, appears.

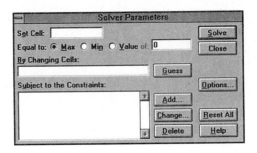

3. In the Set Cell box, enter the cell you want to optimize.

4. Define the type of relation between the Set Cell and a solution value by selecting one of the following Equal To options:

   Max   Find the maximum result for the set cell.

   Min   Find the minimum result for the set cell.

   Value of   Find an exact value for the amount typed in the Value of text box.

   For this example, select the Equal to **Max** option.

5. Select the **B**y Changing Cells text box; then select the adjustable cells that Solver should change while attempting to find the best answer. For this example, the cells are $G$5:$G$8. You can type the entry, select each cell with the keyboard, or drag the mouse across the cells. If the cells you need are not visible, you can move the Solver Parameters dialog box or scroll the worksheet.

6. Select the **Add** button to add constraints to the list of constraints. The Add Constraint dialog box appears, as shown in figure 14.8.

7. Enter the first constraint. In this example, the values in $G$5:$G$8 must be greater than 0. This constraint ensures that Solver looks for solutions that produce only a positive or zero quantity of soil.

Select the Cell **R**eference text box and enter $G$5:$G$8. You can type the cell reference, select it by using the keyboard, or drag across the cells. If the cells you need are not visible, you can move the Add Constraint dialog box or scroll the worksheet.

To move to the comparison signs, press Tab or click the down arrow. Then select the >= comparison sign by clicking it or by pressing the down-arrow key.

Select the **C**onstraint text box and enter 0.

The completed Add Constraint dialog box for this example appears in figure 14.9.

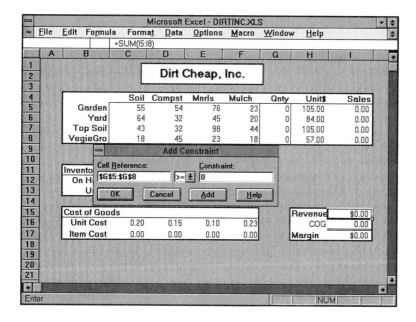

FIG. 14.9

A completed constraint.

8. Choose the **A**dd button so that you can add another constraint. When the Add Constraint dialog box reappears, enter the second constraint. For this example, the constraint is $C$12:$F$12> =$C$13:$F$13, which indicates that the inventory used must always be less than the inventory on hand.

9. Choose the OK button. The completed Solver Parameters dialog box appears (see fig. 14.6).

10. Choose the **S**olve button to run Solver and find the optimal combination of soil products that gives the maximum margin.

11. When Solver finds a solution, another dialog box appears, as shown in figure 14.10. Select Keep Solver Solution to keep the solution shown in the worksheet. Select Restore Original Values to return to the original worksheet values. For this example, select Keep Solver Solution and choose OK or press Enter. In this dialog box, you also choose the reports you want to generate, as explained later in this chapter in "Printing Solver Reports."

Solver tells you that you can achieve the best margin if you make 11 units of Garden, 49 units of Yard, no Top Soil, and 21 units of VegieGro. With this combination, the maximized margin is $4,425.89.

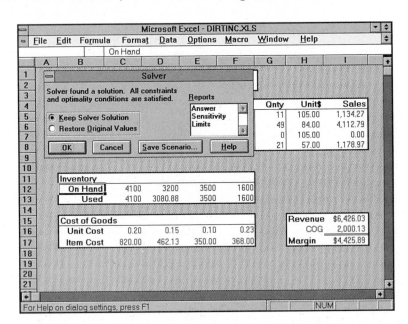

FIG. 14.10

Choose to keep the solution, return to the original answers, or generate reports.

T I P In some linear-programming programs, you are required to set up constraints as comparison formulas that produce a TRUE or FALSE result. With Solver, you do not need to use this setup. If you have worksheets or mainframe data from programs requiring that method, however, you still can use them with Solver. In the Subject to the Constraints box of Solver, set the constraint equal to a TRUE or FALSE. Do not use 1 or 0 to indicate TRUE or FALSE.

NOTE Do not change the values on the worksheet if you want to try the exercises that follow in this chapter.

You can stop the solver process at any time by pressing Esc. A dialog box appears and asks whether you want to let Solver continue or keep the current trial and stop the solver process. This gives you an opportunity to switch to another application, do some work, and then switch back to Excel and continue solving.

T I P

Solver stores the dialog box settings in the worksheet that contains the problem. The settings are stored in named formulas. Because the Solver Parameters dialog box stores previous settings, rerunning Solver with different constraints is easy. You can reset the worksheet by entering zeros into G5:G8 and rerunning Solver. You then see the settings of your most recent solution. This procedure is explained in the section "Saving and Loading Solver Data" later in this chapter.

After you find a solution, you also can save the references used in **By** Changing Cells for use in the **C**hanging Cells box of the Scenario Manager. If you want to use the Scenario Manager to run the solution found by Solver, choose the **S**ave Scenario button shown in figure 14.10. When the Save Scenario dialog box appears, type the name you want. This name stores the values the Solver determined for the **B**y Changing Cells edit box. You can save several scenarios of answers, and then review and compare them using the Scenario Manager. Detailed instructions on using the Scenario Manager is covered in the "Using the Scenario Manager" section, later in this chapter.

If you want to store settings without running Solver, enter the settings as explained in the preceding instructions and choose OK. To remove the Solver dialog box without running Solver and without storing settings made with **O**ptions, **A**dd, **C**hange, or **D**elete, choose Cancel.

Changing a Limited Resource

In real-world situations, the limits on production resources change. You can see the effect of this change on the solution by changing resources in the worksheet and rerunning Solver. The effect of such changes is known as the *dual value* or *shadow price*. A shadow price tells you what a change in inventory or resources does to the bottom line.

Suppose that the people at Dirt Cheap get a phone call telling them that they can have a hundred pounds of minerals for the cost of the gas required to haul them. For $10, Dirt Cheap can get 100 more pounds of minerals. This exchange throws off the average mineral price slightly, but are the minerals worth $10?

To find the return margin for 100 more pounds of minerals, change the mineral inventory in cell E12 from 3,500 to 3,600. Enter 0s in G5:G8. Rerun Solver by using the same settings as in the previous problem. Keep this solution so that your worksheet will match the next situation.

Adding 100 pounds of minerals takes the margin from $4,425.89 at 3,500 pounds of minerals to $4,464.24 with 3,600 pounds of minerals. The minerals cost $10 but contributed $38.35 to the margin. They are a good value.

Changing Constraints

The real world doesn't stay steady for long. Things are always changing. But with Solver, you can resolve to find an optimal solution quickly even when conditions change.

Suppose that a major purchaser of Dirt Cheap's soils calls to say that she must have 10 units of top soil. On checking the printout, Dirt Cheap's manager finds that no top soil was going to be mixed in this run. She decides to add a constraint that 10 units of top soil must be made for this customer, however. What effect does that change have on the margin?

To see the effect of requiring 10 units of top soil, choose the Formula Solver command to open the Solver Parameters dialog box. You need to change the constraints and rerun Solver. To change the constraints, complete the following steps:

1. Select the Subject to the Constraints box and select the following constraint:

   $G$5:$G$8>=0

2. Choose the Change button.

3. Change the constraint to the following line:

   $G$5:$G$6>=0

   Then choose OK.

4. Choose the Add button and enter the following constraint:

   $G$7>=10

   This statement indicates that at least 10 units of top soil must be made. Choose OK.

5. Choose the **Add** button, enter the following constraint,

   $G$8>=0

   and choose OK.

6. Choose Solve to solve for the best margin.

The new solution, with a new limit of 10 units of top soil and the additional 100 pounds of minerals, yields a result of $4,039.10. This amount is $325.14 less than the margin after adding the 100 pounds of minerals. Satisfying this long-term customer will cost money in the short run but may have gained loyalty and word-of-mouth advertising.

You can delete constraints by selecting them and choosing the Delete button. Choose Reset to reset all settings, cell references, and constraints.

Setting Integer Constraints

According to cell $G$5, Solver currently is recommending that you make 1 unit of garden soil. If you select cell G5 and look in the Formula Bar, however, you can see that Solver actually calculated an optimal value of 0.879608026131595. The value displayed was rounded to an integer because of the formatting of the cells. To force Solver to allow only integer values for the units, choose the Formula Solver command to open the Solver Parameters dialog box, add an integer constraint, and rerun Solver. To add the integer constraint, complete the following steps:

1. Choose the **Add** button.

2. Select cells $G$5:$G$8 as the cell reference.

3. Select int from the drop-down list of comparison signs. The Constraint box changes to Integer.

4. Choose the OK button. The constraint $G$5:$G$8 = Integer now appears in the Constraints list.

5. Choose the **S**olve button. Solver calculates a solution in which all the unit values are integers. Integer constraints make the calculation much slower.

The new solution results in a margin of $4,023.11. The value is less than before, but it is more precise because all the quantities are true integers.

Changing Operational Settings

You can change the technique used by Solver to find answers and change how long Solver works or how precise an answer it attempts to find. Choosing the **O**ptions button in the Solver Parameters dialog box displays the Solver Options dialog box, shown in figure 14.11. Use these options to control how Solver works. The default settings are appropriate for most problems. Table 14.1 shows the options and their capabilities.

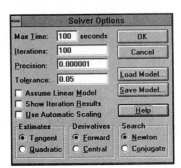

FIG. 14.11

The Solver Options dialog box enables you to control how Solver works.

Table 14.1. Solver Option Settings

Option	Control
Max Time	Specifies the time in seconds Solver spends finding a solution.
Iterations	Specifies the number of times Solver recalculates with attempted solutions.
Precision	Specifies how far apart two trial solutions must be before a best solution is declared.
Tolerance	Specifies how close the answer must be by percentage to the best possible solution when working with integer problems. Setting a higher tolerance can speed up calculation considerably when working with complex integer problems. Use only with integer models.

Option	Control
Assume Linear **M**odel	Sets Solver to use a linear programming solution method that speeds solutions that are linear. You are warned if the worksheet is not linear.
Show Iteration **R**esults	Shows trial solutions when they make significant jumps toward a best solution.
Use Auto Scaling	Enables the Solver to set some of the changing cells to radically larger or smaller values than others.
Estimates	Additional solution methods are **T**angent and **Q**uadratic. Use Quadratic if the worksheet involves complex formulas that are highly nonlinear.
Derivatives	Specifies the method of partial derivatives, using **F**orward or **C**entral differencing. Central difference can take longer but may result in a closer solution.
Search	Specifies a quasi-**N**ewton or **C**onjugate gradient method of searching.

Printing Solver Reports

Solver generates reports that summarize the results of its solutions. These reports are helpful when you're comparing different constraint conditions or calculating shadow prices that show the effects of changes on final results.

Solver generates three reports: the Answer report, the Sensitivity report, and the Limit report. To generate a report after you have solved a model, select one or more of the reports from the **R**eports list when the solution box is displayed (see fig. 14.10). To select more than one report from the list, select the first report, hold down the Control key, and click one or both of the other reports. These reports are generated in their own windows. The Solver worksheet is left as the active window after reports are generated. Press Ctrl+F6 or choose the report sheets from the Window menu.

The Answer report, shown in figure 14.12, shows the original and final values for the set cell and the adjustable cells. The report also shows the constraints. The constraint analysis tells you whether a constraint was Binding because it equaled the constraint limit, Not Binding because it met the constraint but wasn't bound by it, or Not Satisfied because the constraint could not be met. The Slack values in the report show the differences between the constraints and the final values. In this chapter's example, the *Slack* is the amount of inventory remaining.

Microsoft Excel - Answer Report 1			

File Edit Formula Format Data Options Macro Window Help

A1 — Microsoft Excel 4.0 Answer Report

Microsoft Excel 4.0 Answer Report
Worksheet: DIRT02.XLS
Report Created: 5/14/92 11:05

Target Cell (Max)

Cell	Name	Original Value	Final Value
$I$17	Margin Sales	$0.00	$4,481.62

Adjustable Cells

Cell	Name	Original Value	Final Value
$G$5	Garden Qnty	0	13
$G$6	Yard Qnty	0	48
$G$7	Top Soil Qnty	0	-1
$G$8	VegieGro Qnty	0	23

Constraints

Cell	Name	Cell Value	Formula	Status	Slack
$C$12	Onhand Soil	4100	$C$12>=$C$13	Binding	0
$D$12	Onhand Compst	3200	$D$12>=$D$13	Binding	-4.10459E-05
$E$12	Onhand Marle	3500	$E$12>=$E$13	Binding	0

Ready — NUM

FIG. 14.12

The Answer report shows original and final results.

The Sensitivity report has two sections. The first shows each adjustable cell, the cell name, the value, and the amount the target cell would increase (or decrease) for each unit increase in that adjustable cell. The second section shows each constraint cell, its name, value, and the amount the target cell would increase (or decrease) for each unit increase in that constraint. This report can show you how much difference it would make to change either the adjustable or constraint cell values. When Solver is working with a Linear Model, the Sensitivity report also shows how much the cell value could increase or decrease before the target cell would change (see fig. 14.13).

The Limit report shows the set cell value, adjustable cell values, upper and lower limits, and the target result. The upper and lower limits specify how much the adjustable cell can change and still satisfy all constraints. The target result is the set cell value when the adjustable cell value is at its upper or lower limit. This report can show you how much variance is available in adjustable cells. Figure 14.14 shows the Limit report.

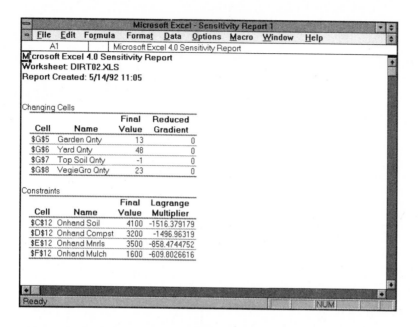

FIG. 14.13

The Sensitivity report shows the solutions' sensitivity to changes in input or constraints.

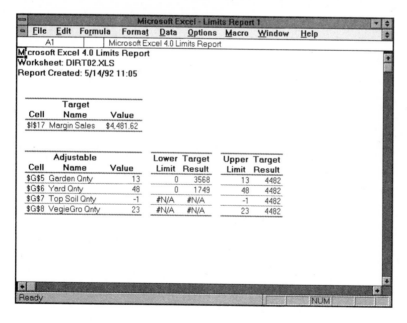

FIG. 14.14

The Limit report shows how much adjustable cells can change within constraints.

Saving and Loading Solver Data

Solver stores in the worksheet the last settings used to solve a problem or settings that were in the dialog box when you chose OK. As mentioned previously, the last settings used are stored in named formulas. The next time you open that worksheet and run Solver, the Solver Parameters dialog box is set as you last used it.

In some cases, you may want to store predefined settings for the Solver Parameters dialog box. You may, for example, have specific sets of constraints that you must consider. You can store each of these sets of constraints in cells on the worksheet and quickly load the settings you need.

You can save and load different Solver models (settings) by using the Options button in the Solver Parameters dialog box. To save Solver settings, complete the following steps:

1. Set up the Solver Parameters dialog box with the settings you want to save. Choose OK.

2. On the worksheet, select a range of cells equal to the number of constraints plus two cells for the set cell and adjustable cells.

   If your constraints include a range of cells, be sure to include a cell on the worksheet for each cell in the constraint's range. The range can be any shape. Making it too large doesn't hurt. Excel advises you if the range is not large enough.

3. Choose the Formula Solver command. When the dialog box opens, choose the **O**ptions button.

4. Choose the **S**ave Model button. Choose Cancel when the Solver Parameters dialog box reappears.

The range fills with the settings from the Solver Parameters dialog box. Figure 14.15 shows an example of saved settings.

To load settings when you want to rerun a Solver model you have saved on the worksheet, complete the following steps:

1. Select the range of cells that contains the model.

2. Choose the Formula Solver command.

3. Choose the **O**ptions button.

4. Choose the **L**oad Model button.

5. When the Solver reappears with the settings loaded, you can run the Solver or choose OK and run it later.

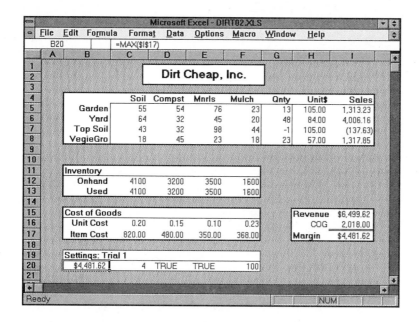

FIG. 14.15

Save Solver settings on the worksheet for later use.

T I P

When you use the preceding steps to save the model, you save all the information needed for Solver to work: the adjustable cell references, the optimization type, the constraints, and any options. This information enables you to switch between completely different ways of looking at the problem. When you use **S**ave Scenario at the completion of a Solver calculation, you are saving only the values for the adjustable cells. You then can use the Scenario Manager, explained later in this chapter, to switch quickly among different results from different Solver problems, or even to build a report of the alternate solutions.

Understanding the Free Solver Samples

Excel comes with several free example worksheets that use Solver to find an optimal or best solution. Although simplified, these examples cover many of the classes of problems for which Solver is designed. For these types of problems, Solver saves time over trial-and-error methods.

These example files are located in the EXAMPLES\SOLVER directory. This directory is located under the directory in which Excel is installed. Use the File Open command to open the example file, and then choose the Formula Solver command. You can examine the settings in the Solver Parameters dialog box. You may want to write down the settings and limitations and then return to the worksheet to see how they relate to the problem.

To run Solver on an example, open a worksheet, choose the Formula Solver command, and choose the **S**olve button. If you choose to keep the solutions that are found, save the worksheet with a different name to preserve the original example.

The example worksheets and their purposes follow.

File name	Purpose
SOLVER1	Finds the maximum profit by changing the production mix of electronic products where the products share common parts and the sales margin diminishes with increased volume due to sales costs.
SOLVER2	Minimizes the shipping costs from a set of production plants to warehouses while meeting warehouse needs without exceeding plant production.
SOLVER3	Finds an employee schedule that meets all shift requirements while minimizing unnecessary staffing.
SOLVER4	Finds the best combination of certificates of deposit and deposit times so that the interest earned is maximized while ensuring that cash-on-hand is available for forecasted needs.
SOLVER5	Finds the combination of stocks in a portfolio that gives the best rate of return for a specific level of risk.
SOLVER6	Finds the value of a resistor that will discharge a circuit to a specific amount within a specific time frame.

FROM HERE...

For Related Information:

◄◄ "Calculating Tables of Answers," p. 500

▶▶ "Using Other Add-Ins," p. 615

Using the Scenario Manager

Worksheets are ideally suited for *what-if* analysis. You enter values into key cells and watch what happens to the results. This procedure enables you to easily enter new alternatives, but reconstructing the preceding values is often tedious. In many situations, you need to look at several alternatives.

The Scenario Manager is an add-in tool that comes with Microsoft Excel. It appears on the Formula menu, but the file is not loaded into memory until you choose the Formula Solver command the first time during a work session.

Scenario Manager stores values for input data cells in names that you assign. These values are stored in the worksheet as hidden names. You can keep several versions—or *scenarios*—of input values and switch easily among them. When you want to view the results from a different scenario of input values, you just choose a different named scenario.

 NOTE The Scenario Manager is an add-in. To use the Scenario Manager, you must have installed the add-ins during Excel installation. You can add or remove the Scenario Manager as an add-in, while leaving its file on disk, by using the Add-in Manager. The Add-in Manager and other add-ins are described in Chapter 15.

For Related Information:

▶▶ "Adding the Scenario Manager," p. 616

FROM HERE...

Preparing Your Model

A model with named scenarios should have a clear set of one or more key input values and a clear set of one or more result values that will change based on the inputs. Figure 14.16 shows the Five Year Forecast model built in the quick start from Chapter 3, adapted for use with Named Scenarios.

By changing the model to use expected annual growth rates for each line item to project future values, you have a clear set of input values that directly affect the results.

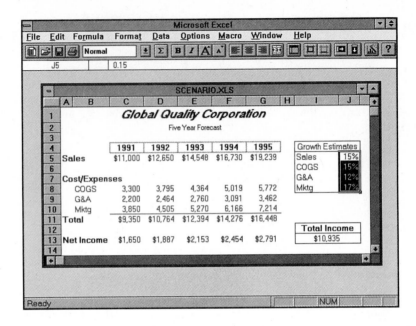

FIG. 14.16

The Five Year Forecast uses growth estimates to calculate income levels.

To convert the model to use growth rates for the forecast, complete the following steps:

1. Group the growth estimates in cells J5:J8, and put appropriate labels in I5:I8. Enter the numeric values as shown in figure 14.16. These values will be the input values saved by the Scenario Manager.

   The Scenario Manager does not require the input cells to be in a block, but grouping them can help you highlight the key input values for the model.

2. Enter the following numbers that will be used as annual growth rates for Sales, COGS, G&A, and Mktg. These constants are the starting values for the first year.

Item	Cell	Enter number
Sales	C5	$11,000
COGS	C8	3,300
G&A	C9	2,200
Mktg	C10	3,850

3. Enter the following formulas to calculate the growth of each item for the first year. Each formula has the appropriate absolute reference ($) so that it can be copied to the right across each row.

Item	Cell	Enter number
Sales	D5	=C5*(1+$J$5)
COGS	D8	=C8*(1+$J$6)
G&A	D9	=C9*(1+$J$7)
Mktg	D10	=D10*(1+$J$8)

4. Enter the formula =SUM(C8:C10) into cell C11 and enter the label *Total* into A11. Select cells C11:G11 and choose the **Edit Fill Right** command.

5. Enter the formula =C5–C11 into cell C13 and enter the label *Net Income* into A13. Select cells C13:G13 and choose the **Edit Fill Right** command.

6. Enter the formula =SUM(C13:G13) into cell I13 and enter the label *Total Income* into I12. You can watch this cell to see the overall effect of changes to the input variables.

7. Select cell I13 and choose the **Formula Define** Name command. Type *Total_Income* in the Name box if it does not already show; then choose OK or press Enter.

Now, when you type new numbers for the growth estimates in range J5:J8, the Income figures will adjust themselves automatically and you can see the new Total Income. You have a clear set of input values as well as a clear result value.

Using Named Cells

Before running the Scenario Manager, you should give names to the input and result cells. The Scenario Manager does not require that cells have names, but if they do have names, the dialog boxes and reports in the Scenario Manager will display the names rather than difficult-to-understand cell addresses. To name the input and result cells, complete the following steps:

1. Select cells I5:J8.

2. Choose the Formula **C**reate Names command, and select the **L**eft Column check box if it is not already selected.

3. Choose OK or press Enter.

4. Select cells I12:I13.

5. Choose the Formula Create Names command, and select the **Left Column** check box if it is not already selected.

6. Choose OK or press Enter.

This process used the text labels in the left column to create names for the cells in the right column. To check the names you have created, press the Goto key, F5, select one of the names you created, and choose OK. The active cell should move to that name.

Save the modified worksheet to disk with a different name by using the File Save **As** command.

NOTE   The Scenario Manager will use a name instead of a cell reference if there is a name that applies specifically to that cell. If a name applies to more than the single cell, the Scenario Manager ignores the name.

Adding Named Scenarios

Suppose that you need to create three scenarios for this model: a best-guess estimate, a best-case estimate, and a worst-case estimate. These estimates will enable you to get a sense of the range of options for the future.

To add the best-guess scenarios to your worksheet, complete the following steps:

1. Select cells J5:J8, the input values, and enter the following best guess numbers into the cells: *15%* for Sales, *15%* for COGS, *12%* for G&A, and *17%* for Marketing. Keep these cells selected.

   The Scenario Manager uses the currently selected cells, with their current values, as the default Changing Cells.

2. Choose the Formula Scenario **Manager** command.

   The first time you choose this command, Excel takes a few seconds to load the add-in file into memory. Then the Scenario Manager dialog box, shown in figure 14.17, appears.

3. If you didn't preselect the input cells, select them now and choose **Add** or press Enter. The Add Scenario dialog box appears, as shown in figure 14.18. Your Scenario dialog box will reflect the cell contents and names in your worksheet.

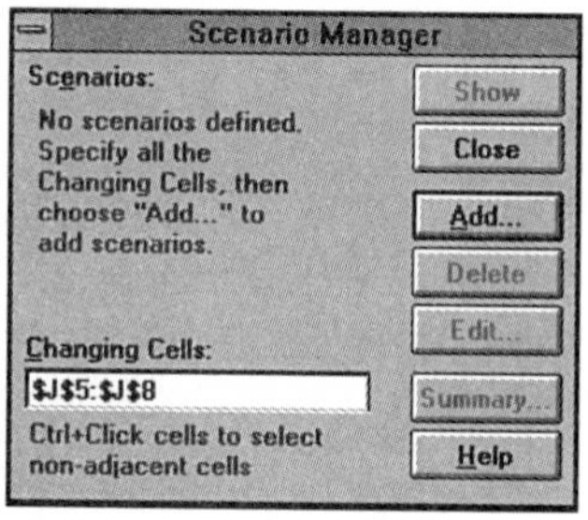

Scenario Manager

Scenarios:

No scenarios defined. Specify all the Changing Cells, then choose "Add..." to add scenarios.

Changing Cells:
$J$5:$J$8

Ctrl+Click cells to select non-adjacent cells

Show | Close | Add... | Delete | Edit... | Summary... | Help

FIG. 14.17

The Scenario Manager dialog box before any scenarios have been created.

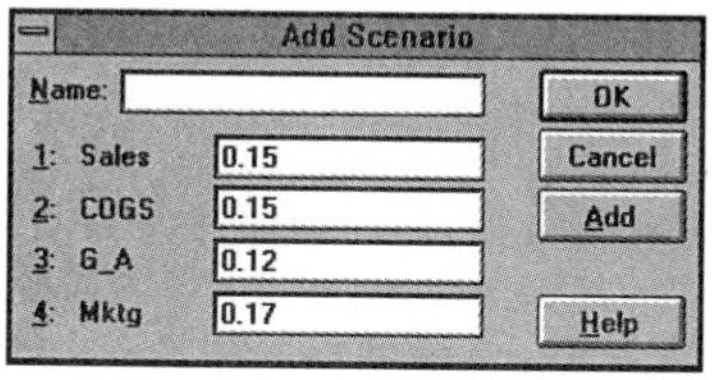

Add Scenario

Name:		OK
1: Sales	0.15	Cancel
2: COGS	0.15	Add
3: G_A	0.12	
4: Mktg	0.17	Help

FIG. 14.18

The Add Scenario dialog box.

4. Enter *Best Guess* in the Name box and choose OK or press Enter.

5. Choose Close or press Esc to close the Scenario Manager Dialog box.

You now have a single scenario stored in the worksheet. If you save the worksheet now, the Changing cells for the scenarios, as well as the scenario name and values, will be stored with the worksheet. A single scenario doesn't enable you to do very much, however. Follow these steps to add the Best Case Scenario.

1. Select cells J5:J8 and change the values to those of the Best Case scenario: *20%* for Sales, *18%* for COGS, *18%* for G&A, and *19%* for Mktg.

2. Choose the Formula Scenario **M**anager command. The Scenario Manager dialog box appears, but you have existing scenarios on the sheet so it is different now, as you can see by comparing figure 14.19 with figure 14.17.

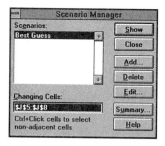

Scenario Manager

Scenarios:
Best Guess

Changing Cells:
$J$5:$J$8

Ctrl+Click cells to select non-adjacent cells

Show | Close | Add... | Delete | Edit... | Summary... | Help

FIG. 14.19

The Scenario Manager dialog box with one scenario listed.

3. Choose **Add.** When there were no scenarios, **Add** was the default button, so you could just press Enter. On a sheet with existing scenarios, **S**how is the default button, so you must choose the **Add** button.

4. Type *Best Case* for the Scenario **N**ame. The numbers entered on the sheet appear in the edit boxes as default values (see fig. 14.18). Do not select OK.

5. Select **Add** to add the best-case scenario. Excel leaves you in the Add Scenario dialog box, ready to add another scenario.

For both scenarios so far, you entered the values on the worksheet, so they already appeared in the dialog box. You also can add multiple scenarios at one time by using the **Add** button in the Add Scenario dialog box and typing the values in number boxes. To enter the worst-case scenario directly in the dialog box, complete the following steps:

1. Type *Worst Case* as the scenario **N**ame.

2. Enter these worst-case values into the input value boxes: *12%* for Sales, *14%* for COGS, *18%* for G_A, and *20%* for Mktg. Notice that the label G&A on the sheet became G_A when Excel made it into a name, and it is the Excel name that appears in the dialog box.

T I P Although the Add Scenario dialog box displays the percent values you entered on the sheet using decimal notation, you are not required to enter them that way. You can enter numbers into the dialog box using any valid Excel number format.

3. Choose OK or press Enter to accept the worst-case scenario. The Scenario Manager Dialog box reappears—this time, with all three Scenarios listed, as shown in figure 14.20

FIG. 14.20

The Scenario Manager dialog box with all three scenarios.

4. Choose Close or press Esc to close the Scenario Manager Dialog box.

You now have all three scenarios on the worksheet ready to review, but you must first save the updated worksheet to disk by using the File **S**ave command. Because the named scenarios are stored in hidden names in the worksheet when you save the worksheet, you save the scenarios you have just created.

Switching between Scenarios

Now that you have some named scenarios on the worksheet, you can quickly switch the model from one scenario to another. Follow these steps to switch scenarios:

1. Choose the Fo**r**mula Scenario **M**anager command.

2. Drag the dialog box so that the most interesting parts of the screen remain visible.

   You can even drag the dialog box over the Excel menu bars to reveal most of the screen, as shown in figure 14.21. When you leave the Scenario Manager and then reactivate it, Excel remembers where you left the dialog box.

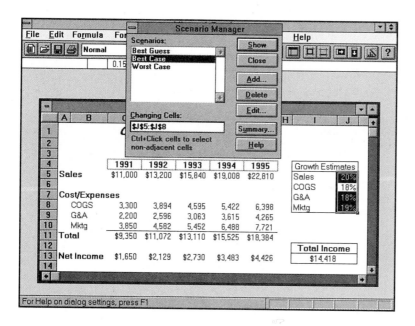

FIG. 14.21

Position the Scenario Manager dialog box to a place where it isn't in the way.

3. Select a different scenario from the **S**cenarios list box and choose **S**how or press Enter. The values for the scenario you chose appear in the changing cells, and the worksheet is recalculated.

> **NOTE** If you are using the keyboard to select the scenario, make sure that the Scenario list box is active before you press the up- or down-arrow keys. Otherwise, you may be changing the cell references of the changing cells.

4. When you have finished browsing the scenarios, display the one you want to keep, and then choose Close or press Esc.

Creating a Summary Table

Switching among different scenarios is useful, but many times you also will need to see a single summary table with the results for all the scenarios. The Scenario Manager provides this capability. To create a summary of the inputs and results of all the scenarios, complete the following steps:

1. Choose Formula Scenario Manager.

2. Choose the Summary button. The Scenario Summary dialog box appears, as shown in figure 14.22.

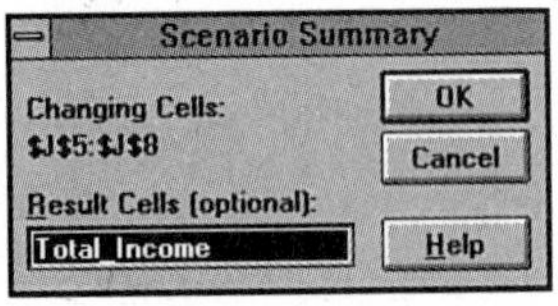

FIG. 14.22

The Scenario Summary dialog box makes an intelligent guess of the result cells in your model.

> **Scenario Summary**
>
> Changing Cells:
> $J$5:$J$8
>
> Result Cells (optional):
> Total_Income
>
> OK
> Cancel
> Help

3. If needed, change the Result Cells by pointing on the sheet. The result cell is the cell that contains the answer to be printed. Use a reference or a name.

4. Choose OK or press Enter. After a few seconds, Excel displays a new sheet with a summary table of the scenario inputs and results, as shown in figure 14.23.

Because the summary is a separate Excel worksheet, you can print or close it, save it with its own name, or save it as part of a workbook with the main worksheet. The summary is not linked to the worksheet, however, so if you change any values or formulas on the worksheet, you need to create a new summary table.

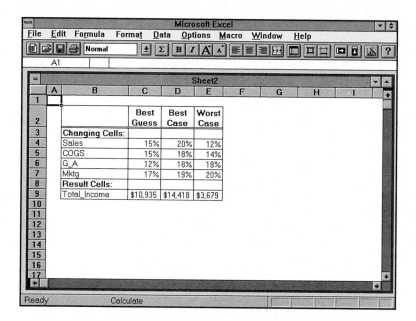

	Best Guess	Best Case	Worst Case
Changing Cells:			
Sales	15%	20%	12%
COGS	15%	18%	14%
G_A	12%	18%	18%
Mktg	17%	19%	20%
Result Cells:			
Total_Income	$10,935	$14,418	$3,679

FIG. 14.23

The summary creates a new worksheet to display each scenario with its input and result cells.

> You can select more than one result cell for the summary report, but you should be sure to give each of the result cells a name in Excel before you create the report. Otherwise, the report will display cell addresses rather than readable names.
>
> **T I P**

Changing the Scenario Values

After you have named scenarios in your worksheet, you can go back and change the values for a given scenario. To edit the values for a scenario, complete the following steps:

1. Choose the Formula Scenario Manager command to display the Scenario Manager dialog box.

2. Choose the scenario you want to change from the Scenarios list box.

3. Choose the Edit button. You see the Add Scenario dialog box in which you can make your changes.

4. After making the changes, choose OK or press Enter to accept the changes.

5. Choose Close or press Esc to close the dialog box.

If you want to replace all the values in a scenario and prefer to enter numbers on the worksheet rather than in the dialog box, you can change them on the worksheet, and then simply create a new scenario with the same name as the one you want to replace.

Changing the Scenario Cells

You can have only one set of scenarios on a worksheet at a time, and they must all reference the same changing cells. To create a different scenario, you change the changing cells in the Scenario Manager dialog box. If any of the new cells overlap existing changing cells, the Scenario Manager displays the warning message shown in figure 14.24. In this case, the old scenarios are not destroyed, but some of the values may be lost. On the other hand, if none of the cells overlap, the Scenario Manager warns you that it will delete all existing scenarios.

FIG. 14.24

If some of the new changing cells were in the old scenarios, Excel will keep all the values it can.

To create scenarios with new changing cells, complete the following steps:

1. Choose the Formula Scenario **M**anager command.

2. Select the **C**hanging Cells reference box.

3. Enter the reference of the new changing cells or point at the new changing cells with the mouse.

4. Choose **A**dd or press Enter. The Scenario Manager asks whether you want to change the existing cells.

FROM HERE...

For Related Information:

◄◄ "Naming Cells," p. 210

◄◄ "Naming and Saving a View," p. 411

◄◄ "Calculating Tables of Answers," p. 500

▶▶ "Using Other Add-Ins," p. 615

▶▶ "Creating Reports," p. 644

Using the Analysis ToolPak

The Analysis ToolPak is an extensive and powerful collection of new tools added to Microsoft Excel 4. These new features are added with the help of add-in macro sheets, but they are implemented using very fast and efficient dynamic link libraries.

Most of the commands and functions in the ToolPak are designed for specific, technical purposes. If you don't know what they mean, you probably don't need them. However, if you are not a very technical user, don't just skip over this chapter. Some of these tools are useful for a wide variety of problems. This section will help you sift through the ToolPak to find the parts you can put to use. Technical users also learn how to apply these tools; they all work in a consistent way.

First, you need to have some idea of what the ToolPak is and how it works. The Analysis ToolPak contains two parts:

- New commands that are available through a new Analysis Tools command on the **O**ptions menu. The ToolPak includes 17 new Statistical commands and 2 new Engineering commands. Table 14.3 at the end of this chapter includes a summary list of all the new commands.

- New functions that can be used from a worksheet just like any other function. The ToolPak includes 51 new Math and Engineering functions and 41 new Financial functions. Table 14.4 at the end of this chapter includes a list of all these new functions.

Excel also includes many new statistical functions that are built into the program itself and are therefore not technically part of the Analysis ToolPak. You may have some related functions for a much smaller Add-in Functions tool that came with Excel 3.0. Table 14.2 will help you to see how the new features relate to existing features.

NOTE Not all of the functions shown in table 14.2 are immediately accessible. If you have installed the Analysis ToolPak, but some of the engineering functions are not available, open ANALYSF.XLA. The file ANALYSF.XLA is located in the LIBRARY\ANALYSIS directory under Excel's directory.

Table 14.2. Comparison of New and Existing Analytical Features		
Features Built into EXCEL.EXE	**Features in Analysis ToolPak**	**Features in Add-in Functions**
Statistics	14 Existing Functions 67 New Functions	17 New Commands (ANALYSIS.XLA)
Math and Engineering	16 Existing Functions	51 New Functions (ENG.DLL and ANALYSF.XLA), 2 New Commands (ANALYSIS.XLA), and 5 Existing Functions (ADDINFNS.XLA)
Financial Analysis	14 Existing Functions	41 New Functions (FIN.DLL and ANALYSF.XLA)

Using Analysis Tools Commands

Most of the Analysis Tools commands perform sophisticated statistical analyses on input data. These are tools for the statistician, researcher, scientist, or engineer. Hidden among these tools, however, are several tools that can be readily applied in a wide variety of situations. This section covers three common tasks that you can accomplish by using the Analysis Tools:

- Creating realistic sample data.
- Evaluating performance.
- Smoothing time-series data.

Creating Realistic Sample Data

Random numbers have many uses. One common use is to create realistic sample data while a model is under development. Suppose that you want to create a model to analyze Dirt Cheap's orders. One of the charts is a histogram of number of orders per day. Eventually, you will have actual data to put into the model, but you want to create a prototype chart to show your managers what the model results will look like. A histogram is a table that reflects how data is distributed. The histogram is made of "bins" where each bin contains the number of items that satisfy the requirement for that bin. Each bin usually holds items in a specific numeric range or in a range of dates. Bins also can be used for text items.

You know that your company sales force makes approximately 200 calls per day and about 10 percent of the people called purchase your product, so the company has an average of 20 orders per day. You could simply create a data series with the average for each day, but then the histogram becomes simply a single spike. You know that is not at all close to what will really happen. Most of the time Dirt Cheap gets between 10 and 30 orders per day. You can use the Analysis ToolPak to create a series of random numbers between 10 and 30.

To create a uniform random series, complete the following steps:

1. Find a location on the worksheet where you want to enter the set of random numbers. You can enter these numbers in a range. Note the top-left corner and the number of rows and columns you will need.

2. Select the **O**ptions Analysis Tools command. The Analysis Tools dialog box, shown in figure 14.25, appears.

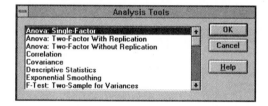

FIG. 14.25

The Analysis Tools dialog box.

3. Select Random Number Generation from the list. Choose OK or press Enter.

   The Random Number Generation dialog box, shown in figure 14.26, appears.

4. Select Uniform in the **D**istribution list box. This is the default.

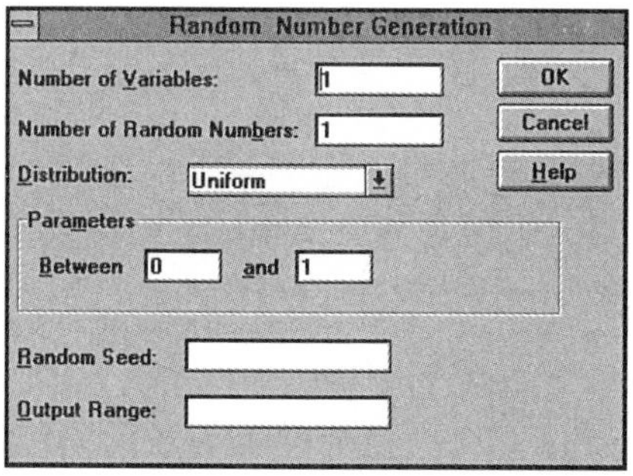

FIG. 14.26

The Random Number Generation dialog box.

5. Type *1* in the Number of **Variables** box. This is the number of columns into which you want to put random numbers.

6. Type *180* in the Number of Random Num**b**ers box. This is the number of rows for entry, because you want to create six months worth of daily orders.

7. Type *10* and *30* for the upper- and lower-limit values in the **B**etween and the **a**nd boxes.

8. Type a number into the Random **S**eed box if you want to create the same series of random numbers each time. The seed can be used again to duplicate this series. Otherwise, leave the box blank.

9. Enter the top-left cell of the range where the random numbers should go into the **O**utput Range box. (You specified the number of rows and columns in steps 4 and 5.)

10. Choose OK or press Enter. If data is already in the output range, Excel asks whether you're sure you want it replaced.

The generator fills down the column the random numbers it generated. From these numbers, you can create a histogram that graphically shows the distribution of numbers in the columns. The next section, "Creating Histograms and Frequency Distributions," describes how to create frequency tables and the chart shown in figure 14.27.

After combining the data in buckets, which you learn how to do in the next section, the histogram looks something like figure 14.27. This figure is a more realistic distribution of numbers. In real life, distributions tend to be clumped around the average more than this.

The Random Number Generator can create other kinds of random numbers that may be closer to your needs. One potentially useful choice is the Normal distribution. The Normal distribution creates what is commonly known as a bell curve. For the Normal distribution, you specify the desired average, along with a standard deviation. Most of the data will fall within one standard deviation on either side of the average. The Normal distribution works very well for things like test scores or performance rankings.

FIG. 14.27

A Histogram with uniformly distributed random numbers.

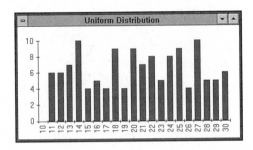

For Dirt Cheap's orders, however, there is an even better choice. In this sample situation, 200 customers each day choose to order or not to order, and an average of 10 percent say yes. This situation is very similar to that of tossing a coin—but a *loaded* coin. The Binomial distribution exactly models this situation. For the Binomial distribution, you specify how many coin tosses for each sample, and what average percent of them should be heads. To create 180 random numbers using the Binomial distribution, complete the following steps:

1. Select the **O**ptions Analysis Tools command.

2. Select **R**andom Number Generation from the list and choose OK or press Enter.

3. Select Binomial from the **D**istribution drop-down list box. Select the distribution type before entering any other parameters, or you may lose the values for the other parameters. The Random Number Generation dialog box changes to the parameters for the Binomial distribution, as shown in figure 14.28.

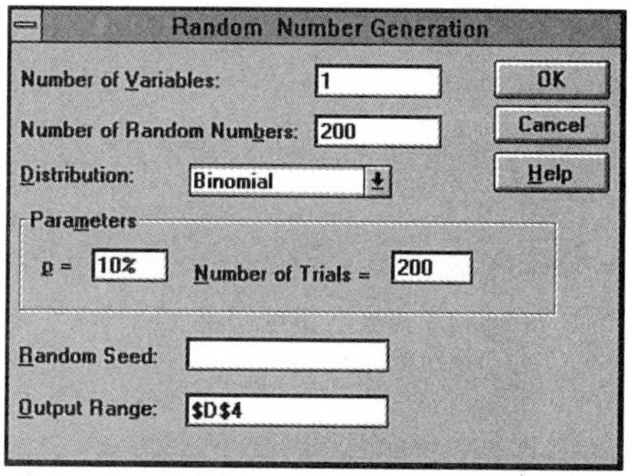

FIG. 14.28

The Parameters for the Random Number Generation dialog box change when the Distribution type changes.

4. Enter *1* in the Number of **V**ariables box.

5. Enter *180* in the Number of Random Num**b**ers box.

6. Enter *10%* for the **p** parameter and *200* in the **N**umber of Trials box.

7. Enter the top left cell of the range where the random numbers should go in the **O**utput Range box.

8. Choose OK or press Enter. Excel generates the random numbers and enters them in the sheet.

When you create a histogram of these numbers, the numeric distribution is very realistic, as you can see in figure 14.29. This chart gives management a good sense of what the final chart will look like. (Creating a histogram chart and frequency distribution table is described in the next section.)

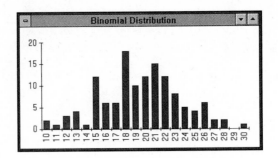

FIG. 14.29

A histogram of
numbers created with
a Binomial distribution.

Creating Histograms and Frequency Distributions

Just about any performance measure compares one item against others.
It is necessary to see how many people or widgets or orders per day fit
into performance bands. One of the tools in Excel's Analysis ToolPak—
the Histogram—provides this capability. A *histogram* is a table where
values in a data set are counted into bins. A histogram is sometimes
called a *frequency distribution*. Histograms are used to get a picture of the
spread of data, whether it is of number of orders per day, or of the number of students who fell into each grade category. Figure 14.30 shows a
worksheet with random orders per day.

	A	B	C	D	E	F	G	H	I
1									
2									
3		Date	Orders		Rate				
4		5/1/92	19		10				
5		5/4/92	15		12				
6		5/5/92	26		14				
7		5/6/92	28		16				
8		5/7/92	18		18				
9		5/8/92	22		20				
10		5/11/92	23		22				
11		5/12/92	20		24				
12		5/13/92	18		26				
13		5/14/92	15		28				
14		5/15/92	15		30				
15		5/18/92	18						
16		5/19/92	24						
17		5/20/92	20						
18		5/21/92	18						

FIG. 14.30

Random orders per
day ready to be
grouped with a
histogram. The Bins
are the numbers under
the Rate heading.

> The Histogram in Excel does essentially the same thing as the Data Distribution command in 1-2-3.
>
> **TIP**

To categorize those orders into bins, complete the following steps:

1. Create a set of numbers to use as bins. These numbers do not have to be a regular series, but they do need to be sorted in ascending order. In figure 14.30, the numbers defining the bins are in E4 through E14.
2. Select the input data for the histogram. This is the data in column C in the figure. The Analysis Tools use the current selection as the default input range.
3. Select the **O**ptions Ana**l**ysis Tools command.
4. Select **H**istogram from the list, and choose OK or press Enter. The Histogram dialog box in figure 14.31 appears.

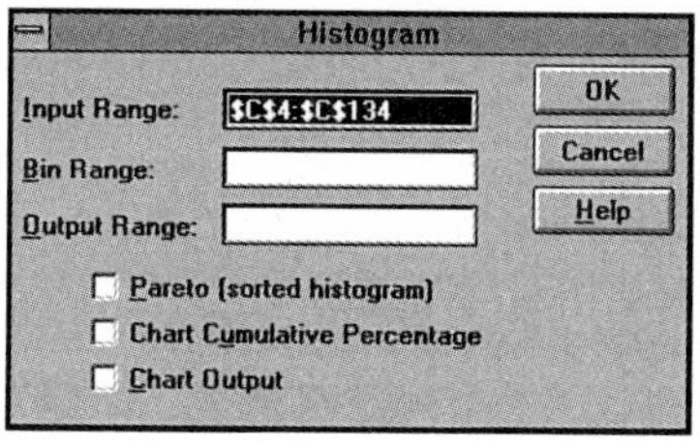

FIG. 14.31

The Histogram dialog box.

5. Select the **B**in Range edit box, and then drag across the range E4:E14.
6. Select the **O**utput Range edit box and click the top-left cell of where you want the output to go. The resulting report fills down and right, so be certain that you select in an area where there is room. The Histogram command will put titles in the first row and also copy the bin values to the first column.
7. Leave the other check boxes blank, and choose OK or press Enter.

   The report is generated with headings. Figure 14.32 shows the histogram report.

The checkboxes in the Histogram dialog box add additional powerful capabilities to the Histogram. The **P**areto check box creates an extra copy of the report, and then that copy is sorted, with the bucket that contains the most items first. The Chart Cumulative Percentage check box does not create a chart, but it does put an additional column into the output report that shows the cumulative percent of total for each bucket and, if a chart is requested, the percentages are used for the chart. If the Create Chart check box is checked, Excel actually creates a new chart based on the report results.

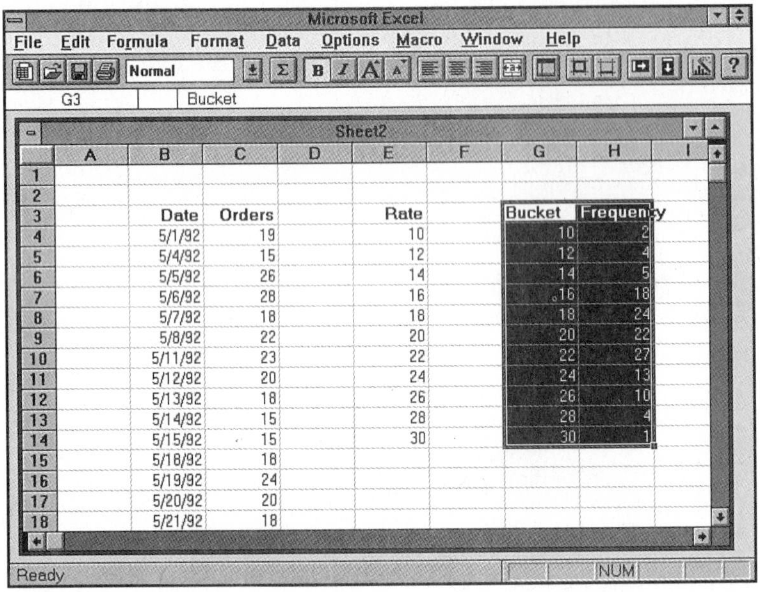

FIG. 14.32

The resulting simple histogram report.

T I P If an open chart or an unopened chart is in the current directory named HISTOGRM.XLC, Excel modifies that chart to reflect the histogram.

NOTE The Analysis ToolPak Add-in must be loaded for add-in functions, such as FREQUENCY(), RANK(), and PERCENTRANK(), to work.

The Histogram command is convenient because it walks you through all the steps of creating the histogram. The values in the Frequency column of the report, however, are frozen values, not linked formulas. With a little extra work, you can use one of Excel's new built-in statistical functions to create a hot-linked histogram that will actually change when the input data changes. To create a histogram table with linked formulas, complete the following steps:

1. The formula is much easier to create if the input and bin ranges are named. Select from cell C3 to the bottom of the data.

2. Choose Formula Create Names.

3. Choose OK or press Enter.

4. Select the range E3:E14 and create names again. This step assigns the name at the top of each column to the cells below.

5. Select cells F4:F14. This range is where the function for the histogram will go.

6. Select the Formula Paste Function command.

7. Choose the Statistical Function Category.

8. Choose FREQUENCY from the Paste Function list, as shown in figure 14.33.

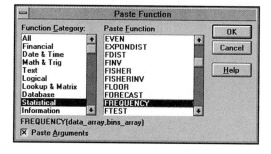

FIG. 14.33

Select the Frequency function from the Statistical category.

9. Choose OK or press Enter. The FREQUENCY() function appears in the Formula Bar with the data_array parameter highlighted and ready to edit.

10. Replace the data_array parameter with the name *Orders*, the name of the input range. Double-click the bins_array parameter to select it, and then replace it with the name *Rate*, the name of the bins range.

11. Press Shift+Ctrl+Enter to enter the function as an array. See Chapter 13 for more information about array formulas.

The FREQUENCY() function fills the cells. These values are linked to the data, however, so if the underlying data values change, the histogram automatically updates.

> **T I P** Another useful command for evaluating performance is the Ranking and Percent command. This command works much like the Histogram command but produces a report that shows both the ordinal ranking and also the percentile ranking—the percent of items in the sample scoring the same or worse than the current sample. You can use the command version in the Analysis ToolPak or, if you prefer hot-linked formulas, use RANK() and PERCENTRANK() statistical functions.

Smoothing Time-Series Data

As you start to track and chart Dirt Cheap's orders over time, you will see that orders fluctuate a great deal. Sometimes it is difficult to tell whether orders are improving over time or dropping off. You need a way to smooth out the random variations in orders to see the underlying trends more clearly. The Analysis ToolPak provides two new commands to help smooth time-series data: Moving Average and Exponential Smoothing.

The Moving Average command puts the average of the last few periods into each period. You can specify how many periods to include in the average. Exponential Smoothing averages the smoothed value for the previous period with the actual data for the previous data point. This feature automatically includes all previous periods in the average. You can specify how much to weight the current period.

Figure 14.34 shows a worksheet with the last 20 days of Dirt Cheap orders. As you can see in the chart, it is difficult to see any trends in the data. You should try Moving Average and Exponential Smoothing.

To smooth the line with a moving average, complete the following steps:

1. Select the order data to be smoothed.

2. Select the **Options Analysis Tools** command, and then select Moving Average. The Moving Average dialog box appears (see fig. 14.35).

3. Edit and select boxes as necessary. Figure 14.35 shows a completed box. The following table explains the available options:

Input Range	Contains the data being smoothed. Should be filled with the current selection.
Output Range	Contains the cell where you want the smoothed data entered. The results will be one column wide and as long as the input range.

Interval	Enables you to control the number of periods back included in the average. The default is 3. Increasing the interval smooths the curve more but increases the inertia of the line, so the line does not reflect changes in trends as quickly. Leave the default, for the example.
Standard Errors check box	Creates an additional column of error statistics. Leave this box empty for the example.
Chart Output check box	Creates a chart. The example already has a chart, so this is not necessary. Leave this box empty for the example.

4. Choose OK or press Enter.

The smoothed data fills the worksheet starting in cell D4. The first two periods will have #N/A because there were not yet three periods of data available to average. The number of #N/A reflects the number you used for the interval.

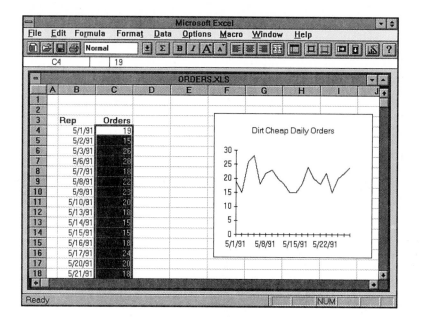

FIG. 14.34

The last 20 days of Dirt Cheap orders need to be smoothed.

FIG. 14.35

The Moving Average dialog box.

Now you need to add the exponential smoothing. To smooth out the data using exponential smoothing, complete the following steps:

1. Verify that the data to be smoothed is selected.

2. Select the **O**ptions Analysis Tools command.

3. Select Exponential Smoothing from the list and choose OK or press Enter. The Exponential Smoothing dialog box, shown in figure 14.36, appears.

4. Select the **O**utput Range and click cell E4. The **D**amping factor gives the amount of weighting to be applied to the prior average. A higher damping factor produces a smoother line.

5. Choose OK or press Enter.

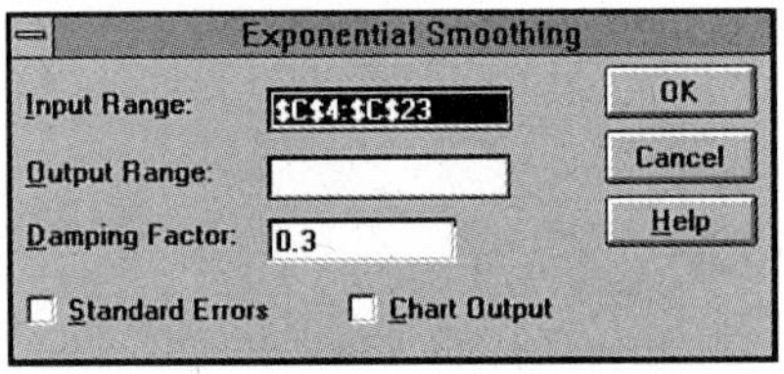

FIG. 14.36

The Exponential Smoothing dialog box.

For the example, the exponentially smoothed data is entered starting in cell E4.

If you use these two lines of data in the chart, you get something close to what is shown in figure 14.37. With the smoothed data on the chart, you can see that Dirt Cheap orders were dropping off in the first half of the month, but have been picking up again in the second half.

T I P   The Moving Average and Exponential Smoothing Analysis tools commands are the only commands that actually put formulas in the cells. If you change the input values, the smoothed data is updated.

Overview of ToolPak Commands and Functions

The Analysis ToolPak contains many new commands and functions. The following tables give an overview of these commands and functions, the new built-in statistical functions, and the existing add-in functions from Excel 3.0.

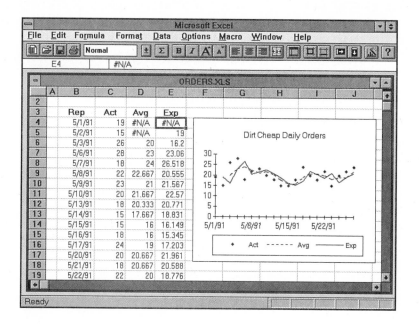

FIG. 14.37

The worksheet with both types of smoothing and a chart comparing the different types of data.

NOTE The Analysis ToolPak consists of functions available through the Formula Paste Function command and commands available through the Options Analysis Tools. Installing the Analysis ToolPak provides access to most of these functions and commands. If functions you need do not appear in the Paste Function list when the Analysis ToolPak is loaded, then open the file named ANALYSF.XLA located in the LIBRARY\ANALYSIS directory under Excel.

Table 14.3. Analysis ToolPak Commands

Command	Description	Macro*
ANOVA: Single Factor	Simple Analysis of Variance	ANOVA1
ANOVA: Two-Factor with Replication	Analysis of Variance including more than one sample for each data group	ANOVA2
ANOVA: Two-Factor Without Replication	Analysis of Variance not including more than one sample for each data group	ANOVA3
Correlation	Measurement-independent correlation between data sets	MCORREL

continues

Table 14.3. Continued

Command	Description	Macro*
Covariance	Measurement-dependent correlation between two sets	MCOVAR
Descriptive Statistics	Report of univariate statistics for sample	DESCR
Exponential Smoothing	Smooths data, weighting most recent data more	EXPON
F-Test: Two-Sample for Variances	Two-Sample F:Test to compare population variances	FTEST
Histogram	Counts occurrences in each of several data bins	HISTOGRAM
Moving Average	Smooths data series by averaging the last few periods	MOVEAVG
Random Number Generation	Creates any of several types of random numbers	RANDOM
Uniform	Uniform random numbers between upper and lower bounds	
Normal	Normally distributed numbers based on mean and standard deviation	
Bernoulli	Ones and zeros with a specified probability of success	
Binomial	Sum of several Bernoulli trials	
Poisson	A Poisson distribution of random numbers given desired Lambda	
Patterned	A sequence of numbers at a specific interval (cf. Data Series)	
Discrete	Probabilities based on predefined percents of total	
Rank and Percentile	Creates report of ranking and percentile distribution	RANKPERC
Regression	Creates table of statistics that result from least-squares regression	REGRESS
t-Test: Paired Two-Sample for Means	Paired two-sample student's t-Test	PTTESTM

Command	Description	Macro*
t-Test: Two-Sample Assuming Equal Variances	Paired two-sample t-Test assuming equal means	PTTESTV
t-Test: Two-Sample Assuming Unequal Variances	Homoscedastic -test	TTESTM
z-Test: Two-Sample for Means	Two-sample z-test for means with known variances	ZTESTM
Engineering Commands		
Fourier Analysis	DFT or FFT method, including reverse transforms	FOURIER
Sampling	Samples a population randomly or periodically	SAMPLE

* The Macro column gives the name of the command name if you want to run it from a macro.

Table 14.4. New Analysis ToolPak Engineering Functions*

Function	Description
BESSELI	Returns the modified Bessel function In(x).
BESSELJ	Returns the Bessel function Jn(x).
BESSELK	Returns the modified Bessel function Kn(x).
BESSELY	Returns the Bessel function Yn(x).
BIN2DEC	Converts a number from binary notation to decimal.
BIN2HEX	Converts a number from binary notation to hexa-decimal.
BIN2OCT	Converts a number from binary notation to octal.
COMPLEX	Converts two real numbers to a single complex number.
CONVERT	Converts a number from one measurement system to another.
DEC2BIN	Converts a number from decimal notation to binary.
DEC2HEX	Converts a number from decimal notation to hexa-decimal.
DEC2OCT	Converts a number from decimal notation to octal.

continues

Table 14.4. Continued

Function	Description
DELTA	Returns 1 if two numbers are equal; 0 if not.
ERF	Returns the error function between limits.
ERFC	Returns the complementary ERF function.
FACTDOUBLE	Returns the double factorial.
GCD	Returns the greatest common divisor of two numbers.
GESTEP	Returns 1 if a number is greater than a specified step.
HEX2BIN	Converts a number from hexadecimal notation to binary.
HEX2DEC	Converts a number from hexadecimal notation to decimal.
HEX2OCT	Converts a number from hexadecimal notation to octal.
IMABS	Returns the absolute value of a complex number.
IMAGINARY	Returns the imaginary component of a complex number.
IMCONJUGATE	Returns the complex conjugate of a complex number.
IMCOS	Returns the cosine of a complex number.
IMDIV	Divides one complex number by another.
IMEXP	Returns the exponential of a complex number.
IMLN	Returns the natural logarithm of a complex number.
IMLOG10	Returns the base-10 logarithm of a complex number.
IMLOG2	Returns the base-2 logarithm of a complex number.
IMPOWER	Returns a complex number raised to an integer power.
IMPRODUCT	Returns the product of two complex numbers.
IMREAL	Returns the real component of a complex number.
IMSIN	Returns the sine of a complex number.
IMSQRT	Returns the square root of a complex number.
IMSUB	Returns the difference of two complex numbers.
IMSUM	Returns the sum of two complex numbers.
ISEVEN	Returns 1 if a number is even; 0 if it is odd.

Function	Description
ISODD	Returns 1 if a number is odd; 0 if it is even.
LCM	Returns the least common multiple of 1-12 integers.
MROUND	Rounds a number to a multiple of a specified number.
MULTINOMIAL	Divides the factorial of several numbers added by the product of the factorial of each number.
OCT2BIN	Converts a number from octal notation to binary.
OCT2DEC	Converts a number from octal notation to decimal.
OCT2HEX	Converts a number from octal notation to hexadecimal.
QUOTIENT	Returns the integer part of the answer to a division. Equivalent to TRUNC(x/y).
SERIESSUM	Returns the sum of a power series.
SQRTPI	Returns the square root of a specified number times PI. Equivalent to SQRT(PI()*x).
WEIGHTAVG	Returns the weighted average of 1-14 arrays.

*To access these functions, the file ANALYSISF.XLA must be open.

Table 14.5. Analysis ToolPak Financial Functions*

Function	Description
ACCRINT	Returns the accrued interest for a security.
ACCRINTM	Returns the accrued interest for a security that pays at maturity.
COUPDAYBS	Returns the number of days for a coupon before settlement.
COUPDAYS	Returns the number of days for a coupon in its last period.
COUPDAYSNC	Returns the difference between COUPDAYS and COUPDAYSBS.
COUPNCD	Returns the next coupon date after the settlement date.
COUPNUM	Returns the number of coupons between the settlement date and the maturity date.
COUPPCD	Returns the previous coupon date before the settlement date.
CUMIPMT	Returns the cumulative interest on a loan between two periods.

continues

Table 14.5. Continued

Function	Description
CUMPRINC	Returns the cumulative principal on a loan between two periods.
DISC	Returns the discount rate for a security.
DOLLARDE	Converts fractional dollars to decimal dollars.
DOLLARFR	Converts decimal dollars to fractional dollars.
DURATION	Returns the annual duration of a security.
EFFECT	Returns the effective interest rate of a loan.
INTRATE	Returns the interest rate for a fully invested security.
MDURATION	Returns the modified duration of a security.
NETWORKDAYS	Returns the net count of working days between two dates.
NEWMONTH	Returns a date a specified number of months from a base date. (Appears in documentation as MONTHCHANGE.)
NEWMONTHE	Returns the last day of the month ending a specified number of months relative to a base date. (Appears in documentation as EOMONTH.)
NOMINAL	Returns the nominal interest rate of a loan.
ODDFPRICE	Returns the price per $100 of a security with an odd first period.
ODDFYIELD	Returns the yield of a security with an odd first period.
ODDLPRICE	Returns the price per $100 of a security with an odd last period.
ODDLYIELD	Returns the yield of a security with an odd last period.
PRICE	Returns the price per $100 of a security.
PRICEDISC	Returns the price per $100 of a discounted security.
PRICEMAT	Returns the price per $100 of a security that pays at maturity.
RECEIVED	Returns the amount received at maturity.
TBILLPRICE	Returns the price per $100 of a treasury bill.
TBILLYIELD	Returns the yield for a treasury bill.
TBILLEQ	Returns the bond-equivalent yield for a treasury bill.
WORKDAY	Returns a date a specified number of work days from a base date.

Function	Description
XIRR	Returns the IRR for irregular cash flows.
XNPV	Returns the NPV for irregular cash flows.
YEARFRAC	Returns the fraction of a year between two dates.
YIELD	Returns the yield of a security.
YIELDDISC	Returns the yield of a discounted security.
YIELDMAT	Returns the yield of a security that pays at maturity.

*To access these functions, the file ANALYSISF.XLA must be open.

Table 14.6. Built-in Statistical Functions*

Function	Description
AVEDEV	Returns the average absolute deviation from the mean.
BETADIST	Returns the cumulative beta probability density function.
BETAINV	Returns the inverse of the cumulative beta probability density function.
BINOMDIST	Returns the individual term binomial distribution probability.
CEILING	Returns a number rounded up to the next highest multiple of a specified value.
CHIDIST	Returns the chi-squared distribution.
CHIINV	Returns the inverse of the chi-squared distribution.
CHITEST	Returns the test for independence.
COMBIN	Returns the number of ways that a specified number of objects can be chosen from another specified number of objects.
CONFIDENCE	Returns the confidence interval for a population mean.
CORREL	Returns the correlation coefficient of two arrays.
COVAR	Returns the covariance for data point pairs.
CRITBINOM	Returns the smallest integer where the cumulative binomial distribution is less than a specified value.
DEVSQ	Returns the sum of squares of deviations.
EVEN	Returns a number rounded up to the next even integer.

continues

Table 14.6. Continued

Function	Description
EXPONDIST	Returns the exponential distribution function.
FDIST	Returns the F probability distribution.
FINV	Returns the inverse of the F probability distribution.
FISHER	Returns the Fisher transformation.
FISHERINV	Returns the inverse of the Fisher transformation.
FLOOR	Returns a number rounded down to the next lower multiple of a specified value.
FORECAST	Returns the predicted value for x based on a linear regression.
FREQUENCY	Returns a histogram distribution for a given set of values and bins.
FTEST	Returns the results of an F-test.
GAMMADIST	Returns the gamma distribution function.
GAMMAINV	Returns the inverse of the gamma cumulative distribution.
GAMMALN	Returns the natural logarithm of the gamma function.
GEOMEAN	Returns the geometric mean of an array.
HARMEAN	Returns the harmonic mean of an array.
HYPGEOMDIST	Returns the hypergeometric distribution.
INTERCEPT	Returns the intercept of a linear regression line.
KURT	Returns the kurtosis of a data set.
LARGE	Returns the value a specified position from the largest value in a data set.
LOGINV	Returns the inverse of the lognormal cumulative distribution function.
LOGNORMDIST	Returns the lognormal cumulative distribution function.
MEDIAN	Returns the median of a set of numbers.
MODE	Returns the mode of a set of numbers.
NEGBINOMDIST	Returns the negative binomial distribution.
NORMDIST	Returns the normal cumulative distribution.
NORMINV	Returns the inverse of the normal cumulative distribution.

Function	Description
NORMSDIST	Returns the standard normal cumulative distribution.
NORMSINV	Returns the inverse of the standard normal cumulative distribution.
ODD	Returns a number rounded up to the next larger odd number.
PEARSON	Returns the Pearson product moment correlation coefficient.
PERCENTILE	Returns the value from an array at the specified percentile.
PERCENTRANK	Returns the percentage rank of a value in a data set.
PERMUT	Returns the number of permutations of a number chosen from another number.
POISSON	Returns the Poisson probability distribution.
PROB	Returns the probability that values in a range are between a lower and upper limit.
QUARTILE	Returns the specified quartile value from a data set.
RANK	Returns the rank of a number in a data set.
RSQ	Returns the square of the Pearson product moment correlation coefficient.
SKEW	Returns the skewness of a distribution.
SLOPE	Returns the slope of a linear regression line.
SMALL	Returns the value a specified position from the smallest value in a data set.
STANDARDIZE	Returns a normalized value from a distribution.
STEYX	Returns the standard error of the regression of y on x.
SUMSQUARES	Returns the sum of the squares of a set of numbers.
SUMX2MY2	Returns the sum of the difference of squares of corresponding values in two arrays.
SUMX2PY2	Returns the sum of the sum of squares of corresponding values in two arrays.
SUMXMY2	Returns the sum of squares' differences of corresponding values in two arrays.
TDIST	Returns the student's distribution.
TINV	Returns the inverse of the student's distribution.
TRIMMEAN	Returns the average of a set, excluding a specified percentage of data points from the tails.

continues

Table 14.6. Continued

Function	Description
TTEST	Returns the probability associated with a student's *t*-test.
WEIBULL	Returns the Weibull distribution.
ZTEST	Returns the *p* value of a two-tailed *z*-test.

*These functions are built into Excel and are always available.

Table 14.7. Additional Related Functions*

Function	Description
DEGREES	Converts a number from radians to degrees.
RADIANS	Converts a number from degrees to radians.
RANDBETWEEN	Returns a random number between specified limits.
BASE	Converts a number from base 10 to a desired base.
FASTMATCH	Uses binary search to find a match on a large array.

*To access these functions, the file ADDINS.XLA must be open.

FROM HERE...

For Related Information:

◄◄ "Entering Worksheet Functions," p. 356

◄◄ "Excel Function Dictionary," p. 361

▶▶ "Using Other Add-Ins," p. 615

▶▶ "Building Database Reports with the Crosstab Wizard," p. 882

▶▶ "Using Data Tables," p. 897

Chapter Summary

The tools described in this chapter extend far beyond the capabilities of most electronic spreadsheets. They give you the ability to solve problems that a few years ago required minicomputers.

The Scenario Manager is a tool everyone can use. Now when you present your conclusions, you can use a report from the Scenario Manager to show how you came to your conclusions and what backup alternative solutions are available. Combined with the Report Manager and saved Views, the Scenario Manager is a productive tool that every worksheet user should use.

Worksheets involving Solver can be more difficult to set up but can produce solutions to problems that previously required mainframe computational power. Many of these problems formerly could be solved only by companies with large computers. With Excel and Solver and higher-speed 386 and 486 computers, some of those problems can now be solved on a desktop by large and small companies.

The Analysis ToolPak is a specialized tool that brings Excel to professionals that required hard-coded programs to solve specific financial, statistical, or scientific problems. With the Analysis ToolPak, disciplines with specialized needs have the advanced functions they need to use a worksheet.

If you find the tools described in this chapter useful and important, then you will want to learn about macros. Excel has two types of macros; *function* macros and *command* macros. Function macros enable you to add your own math, logical, or text functions to Excel's Paste Functions list. Function macros work as though they were built into Excel. Command macros enable you to build automated procedures that range from your own custom shortcut keys to complete custom applications. Macros are explained in Chapters 27 through 30.

Using Excel's Add-In Macros

Even with its ease of use, Excel has a more comprehensive set of features than other worksheets offer. But no matter how extensive Excel's features, special industries or special situations are bound to require more. With Excel, anyone who can record or write macros can add features, functions, and commands to Excel so that it works the way it's needed.

Excel comes with add-in programs that add new features and serve as examples of how you can add new features. These programs are built with command macros, function macros, and dynamic link libraries.

This chapter describes the add-in macros (programs) that come with Excel and add helpful and sometimes extensive capabilities. If you want to learn how to create your own add-in macros, see Chapters 27 to 30.

T I P

When you initially installed Excel, you had the opportunity to install a set of add-in macros that add more features to Excel. If you chose a Complete installation, the macros were installed immediately. If you chose a Custom installation, you may have installed these add-ins by installing the Macro Library Files, the Microsoft Solver, and Q+E. If you chose a Minimum installation, none of these add-ins were installed. If you did not install them, you can rerun the Excel setup program and install the add-in macros. These add-in macros use an XLA, DLL, or XLL extension and are saved into the LIBRARY directory under Excel. Some add-ins have their own subdirectory under LIBRARY.

Add-in files are located in the LIBRARY directory below Excel unless indicated otherwise. The following listing describes the available add-ins.

Feature Name	Command	File To Load with Add-In Manager	Description
Add-In Manager	**O**ptions Add-ins	ADDINMGR.XLA	Adds or removes other add-ins from the menus.
Alternate Startup	N/A	ALTSTART.XLA	Specifies a second startup directory after the XLSTART directory.
Analysis ToolPak	**O**ptions Analysis Tools	ANALYSIS.XLA; other associated files are loaded automatically	Adds statistical, financial, and engineering functions and features.
Auto Save	**O**ptions Au**t**o Save	AUTOSAVE.XLA	Adds a monitor that prompts you to save your work at different time and work intervals.
Checkup	Runs when file opened	\LIBRARY\CHECKUP\ CHECKUP.XLM	Finds and displays technical information.
Crosstab	**D**ata Cross**t**ab	\LIBRARY\CROSSTAB\ CROSSDEF.XLA	Creates cross-tabulation reports from databases.
Custom Color Palettes	**O**ptions Custom Palettes	\LIBRARY\COLOR\ PALETTES.XLA	Changes color palettes to predefined sets of colors.
Document Summary	**F**ile Su**m**mary Info	SUMMARY.XLA	Adds a summary sheet to a work-sheet or macro sheet that stores vital information about authorship, revision date, and so on.

Feature Name	Command	File To Load with Add-In Manager	Description
File Functions	Macro function	FILEFNS.XLA	Adds four macro commands that enable you to manipulate directories or test whether a file exists.
Flat File Exporter	Data Smart Parse; Data Export	FLATFILE.XLA	Adds another method of parsing (separating) text files into worksheet cells. Adds command to export text flat file.
Glossary	Edit Glossary	GLOSSARY.XLA	Adds a glossary feature that stores or inserts frequently used text, numbers, or formulas.
Macro Debugger	Macro Debug	DEBUG.XLA	Adds macro-troubleshooting features.
Name Changer	Formula Change Name	CHANGER.XLA	Adds a command to quickly change or redefine names in a worksheet.
Q+E	Data commands	†\QE\QE.XLA; †\QE\QESTART.XLA	Adds commands to the Data menu to link Excel to databases outside the worksheet.
Report Manager	File Print Report	REPORTS.XLA	Prints reports from multiple worksheets, views, and scenarios.
Scenario Manager	Formula Scenario Manager	SCENARIO.XLA	Uses multiple input data sets to create multiple sets of solutions.

continues

Feature Name	Command	File To Load with Add-In Manager	Description
Slide Show	Open SLIDES template from File New	SLIDES.XLA; SLIDES.XLT	Adds a slideshow display system that displays charts, sheets, and graphics with flashy transitions and sound.
Solver	Formula Solver	SOLVER.XLA	Finds optimal solutions by using linear and non-linear optimization techniques.
Switch To		SWITCHTO.XLA	Adds tools to toolbar so that you can switch to other Windows applications.
View Manager	Window View	VIEWS.XLA	Stores commonly used locations, display settings, and print settings.
What If	Formula Goal Seek	WHATIF.XLA	Adds the capability of testing multiple input values and seeing the results for different combinations of these inputs.
Worksheet Auditor	Formula Worksheet Auditor	AUDIT.XLA	Adds worksheet troubleshooting features and reports.
Worksheet Comparison	Formula Compare	COMPARE.XLA	Adds a command to compare two worksheets or macro sheets for differences.

†Files not located under LIBRARY directory.

For additional information on add-in macros, choose the **Help Con-**
tents command or press F1, and then select the Macro Library help
topic located under the Reference section. This topic lists all the macros and information about them.

T I P

For Related Information:

▶▶ "Building Command Macros," p. 915.

▶▶ "Building Function Macros," p. 926.

▶▶ "Creating Add-In Macros," p. 945.

FROM HERE...

Using Add-In Programs

Excel's free add-in programs are stored in files ending with the XLA extension. Additional files needed by the add-ins use the extensions XLL
and DLL. You can find them in the LIBRARY subdirectory under the directory containing Excel. These XLA files are special macros that add
features to Excel as though the features were built in. In this section, you
learn how to start these add-in macros and how to use the Add-In Manager to manage them. To learn how you can make your own recorded or
written macros into add-ins, read about macros in Chapters 27 through 30.

Starting Add-Ins

You start an add-in macro when you open the XLA file containing the
add-in macro. When that file opens, special commands, shortcuts, functions, or features available through the add-in become accessible. Although XLA files can be opened with the **File Open** command, they are
more manageable when added to menus with the Add-in Manager. When
you install an add-in with the Add-In Manager, the new command appears on the menu, but the add-in file is not opened until the command
is chosen. This process makes add-ins available without using system
resources unnecessarily. The add-in macros that come with Excel—except for Q+E macros—are stored in the LIBRARY directory under the
Excel directory. Some add-in macros have their own subdirectories
under LIBRARY.

Using the Add-In Manager

The Add-In Manager helps you by opening a collection of add-ins you specify. The Add-In Manager is installed when you install add-ins during installation (see fig. 15.1). (If you did not install the add-ins and macro library, you can rerun the setup program to install them.)

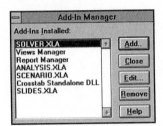

FIG. 15.1

The Add-In Manager
dialog box.

Add add-in macros to the Add-In Manager by choosing the **A**dd button. A Files dialog box—the same one as the File Open dialog box—appears. Select from this dialog box the XLA file you want to open; then choose OK. When you open the XLA file, the corresponding add-in's name is added to the list in the Add-In Manager dialog box. Repeat the procedure to add more add-ins or worksheets. Choose the **C**lose button when you are finished. Menu commands will now be available to run the add-ins you installed.

If you move an add-in macro file to a different directory, you can edit its path and file name by selecting the add-in's name from the list in the Add-In Manager dialog box. Then choose the **E**dit button, select the **P**ath text box, and correct the path. Remove add-in macros from the Add-In Manager list by selecting them and then choosing the **R**emove button.

Adding an Auto Save Feature

The AUTOSAVE.XLA add-in saves Excel files for you at the frequency you specify. This macro helps you remember to save. When AUTOSAVE.XLA loads, it adds the A**u**to Save command to the **O**ptions menu. Choose the **O**ptions A**u**to Save command to display the AutoSave dialog box, shown in figure 15.2.

FIG. 15.2

The AutoSave
dialog box.

For the Save Frequency setting, you can choose one of the following
options:

Option	Frequency
High	Save approximately every 3 minutes.
Medium	Save approximately every 9 minutes.
Low	Save approximately every 30 minutes.
Never	Do not save.

The other options on the AutoSave dialog box are **P**rompt Before Saving
and **S**ave All Files. Select **P**rompt Before Saving if you want the program
to prompt you before saving. This method is helpful if you prefer to save
with a different file name and version number each time. Select **S**ave All
Files to save all open Excel documents. Deselect to save only the active
document.

Changing Custom Color Palettes

If you are tired of using the default color palettes and don't want to create your own or you need to ensure that everyone uses exactly the same
palette, or you want to specify the automatic colors of chart markers
and the 3-D surface charts, then use Custom Color Palettes. Figure 15.3
shows the Custom Color Palettes dialog box available from **O**ptions or
Chart **Cu**stom Palettes command. The PALETTES.XLA file is located in
the LIBRARY\COLORS directory under Excel.

From the list, you can select a predefined color palette and apply it to
the active worksheet or chart.

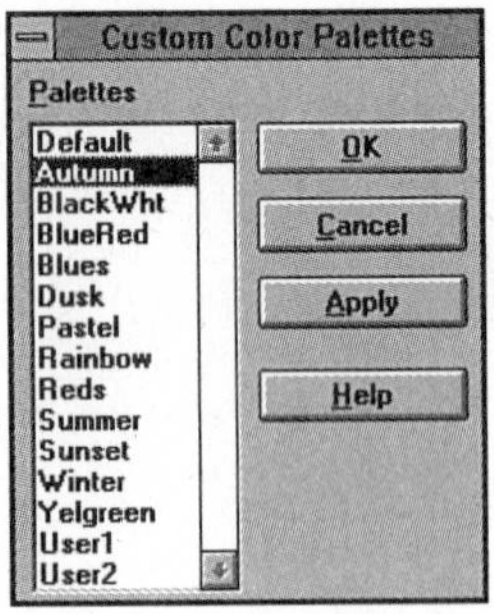

FIG. 15.3

The Custom Color
Palettes dialog box.

T I P   To add your own custom color palette, open a blank worksheet and
use the **Options** or **Chart Color Palette** command to specify a new
palette. Save this worksheet to the LIBRARY\COLORS directory and
use the name you want to appear in the **Palettes** list.

Adding Directory Commands

The FILEFNS.XLA add-in gives you four macro functions with which you
can create, delete, and find information about directories. These four
macro functions are described in the following paragraphs. These functions work only when used within macro sheets.

CREATE.DIRECTORY(*path_text*)

This macro function creates a directory. For example, the following function

CREATE.DIRECTORY("BUDGET")

creates the directory named BUDGET as a subdirectory of the current
directory. The following function

CREATE.DIRECTORY("D:\FINANCE\BUDGET")

creates the directory BUDGET as a subdirectory under FINANCE on the
D drive. FINANCE must exist.

DELETE.DIRECTORY(*path_text*)

This macro function deletes an empty directory. It returns FALSE if the directory cannot be deleted. This macro uses the same argument syntax as CREATE.DIRECTORY().

FILE.EXISTS(*path_text*)

This macro function returns TRUE if the specified file or directory exists, or FALSE otherwise. The function uses the same argument syntax as CREATE.DIRECTORY(). Be sure to include the file name in the argument when you're testing for the presence of a file.

DIRECTORIES(*path_text*)

This macro function returns a horizontal array of all subdirectories in the current directory or of all subdirectories in the path you specify. Use the INDEX() function to retrieve a specific name within the returned array. Use the COLUMNS() function to test the returned array for its total number of directories.

The following is an example of how this function can be used in a macro:

    SET.NAME("Dir3",INDEX(DIRECTORIES("C:\FINANCE"),0,3))

stores the name of the third subdirectory under C:\FINANCE in the name Dir3.

Adding a Document Summary

The SUMMARY.XLA add-in enables you to store summary information easily with the worksheet. This feature is valuable for auditing worksheets or when more than one person updates a worksheet. The summary stores information, such as the worksheet title, its size, the date saved and revision number, topics, comments, and the author's name.

To add the Summary Info command to the File menu, add the SUMMARY.XLA file using the Add-in Manager. Select the Summary Info command to display the Summary Info dialog box, shown in figure 15.4. You can edit all information in the Summary Info dialog box except the creation date. Information from the dialog box is stored in hidden names within the worksheet. Use the NAMES() macro function within a macro to retrieve an array of hidden names.

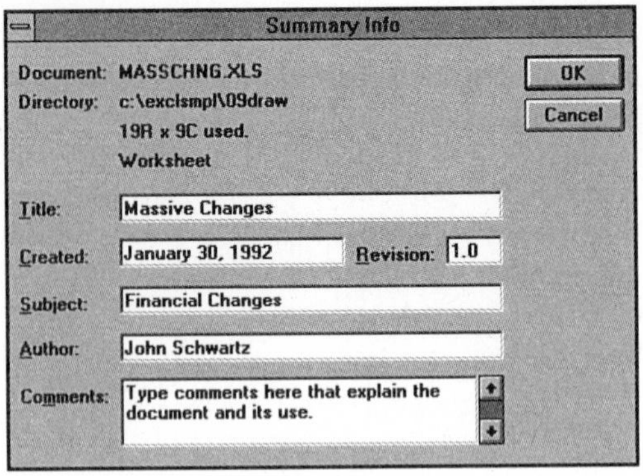

FIG. 15.4

The Summary Info
dialog box.

Adding Functions

The ADDINFNS.XLA add-in adds to Excel six worksheet functions that you can use in your worksheets or macro sheets. Adding the file with the Add-in Manager makes these functions available as though they were built-in. You can type them without specifying the sheet name, or you can select them from the Formula Paste Functions list.

The added functions are described in the following paragraphs.

BASE(*number,target_base,precision*)

Returns a number as text in the target_base system when given a base-10 number. The target base must be between 2 and 36; the default is 16. The precision argument refers to the number of decimal places.

DEGREES(*angle_in_radians*)

Returns degrees when given radians.

FASTMATCH(*lookup_value,lookup_array,type_of_match*)

Returns the relative position of the lookup_value within the lookup-array. Different types of matches are made depending upon the type_of_match. Use FASTMATCH() rather than the MATCH() function when you're searching large arrays. See the discussion of the MATCH() function in Chapter 10 for more information.

RADIANS(*angle_in_degrees*)

Returns radians when given degrees.

RANDBETWEEN(*bottom,top*)

Returns a random integer between the top and bottom numbers. This function is included for compatibility with earlier versions of Excel. You may want to review the other ways of creating random numbers by using the Analysis ToolPak. The Analysis ToolPak is described in Chapter 14.

SUMSQUARE(*reference*)

Returns the sum of the squares of all numbers within the reference or array. This function is included for compatibility with earlier versions. Text and logical values in the reference are ignored. Before using this function, see the built-in sum or squares functions listed in Chapter 10.

Adding a Glossary Feature

The glossary add-in is a boon to any operator who frequently enters the same labels, titles, or formulas. The glossary stores frequently used cell references and ranges and inserts them at your request. It replaces many keystrokes with a few. This add-in is similar to the glossary feature available in Word for Windows or Word.

To add the **G**lossary command to the **E**dit menu, use the Add-in Manager to add the GLOSSARY.XLA file.

To add text or formulas to the glossary, complete the following steps:

1. Select the cell or range containing the information you want added to the glossary.

2. Choose the **E**dit **G**lossary command. The Glossary dialog box, shown in figure 15.5, appears.

3. In the **N**ame text box, type a short name or abbreviation you want to assign to the contents of the selected cells.

4. Choose the **D**efine button.

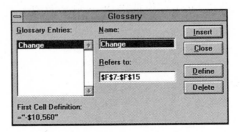

To insert something from the glossary into a worksheet, complete the following steps:

1. Select the cell or cells in which you want to insert the information.

2. Choose the **E**dit **G**lossary command.

3. Select from the **G**lossary Entries list the name you assigned to the glossary contents you need.

4. Choose the **I**nsert button.

Delete glossary entries by selecting the glossary name in the dialog box and choosing the **D**elete button. Choose Cancel to exit the dialog box.

Adding the Macro Debugger

The macro debugger can help you troubleshoot your macros. You add the macro debugger by using the Add-In Manager to open the DEBUG.XLA file. The debugger gives you additional commands and a new work space in which to run and debug (troubleshoot) your macros. You also can set *tracepoints* and *breakpoints* in macro cells. When a macro runs and reaches a tracepoint, the macro stops and enters Step mode. When a breakpoint is reached, the values and names of cells you previously requested are displayed. From there you can continue, enter Single Step mode, or halt.

To insert a tracepoint that puts the macro into Step mode, select the cell that you want to use as a tracepoint, and then choose the **D**ebug **S**et **T**race Point command.

To insert a breakpoint that shows a message or displays variables, select the cell where you want the breakpoint, and then choose **D**ebug **S**et **B**reakpoint. Type a message that should appear when the breakpoint is reached, and choose OK.

To display variables at a breakpoint, choose the **D**ebug **B**reakpoint **O**utput command. Type the range or variable name or cell reference you want to display, and choose OK. The value of the reference or name appears when the breakpoint is reached during the macro's operation. To remove a variable from the breakpoint, select the variable from the Variables to **O**utput list and choose the **D**elete button.

Remove tracepoints or breakpoints by selecting the cell containing them and choosing the **D**ebug **E**rase Debug Point command.

When you want to run the macro, press Ctrl+F6 repeatedly until the worksheet on which you want to run the macro appears; then choose **D**ebug **R**un Macro. Select the macro from the list, and choose OK. The macro runs as it would normally, but when tracepoints or breakpoints are reached, you enter Step mode or see the variables you requested. If your macro switches menu bars away from the Debug menu bar, press Ctrl+R to return to the Debug menu bar.

Other commands on the Debug menu bar are self-explanatory and can help you select or display information useful to debugging macros. For more information on debugging macros, read Chapter 28 in the macro section of this book.

Adding a Name Changer

The name changer is available when you add the CHANGER.XLA macro. With this feature, you quickly can change the definition of names or replace one name with another. The macro also makes the related change to all uses of the name in formulas throughout the worksheet.

The name changer will not affect names used in external reference formulas. Use the **E**dit **R**eplace command to search and replace those names.

T I P

To change names by using the Changer, perform the following steps:

1. Choose Change Name to display the Rename a Name dialog box, shown in figure 15.6, so that you can change names on your worksheet.

2. Select the name you want to change from the From box.

FIG. 15.6

Use the Rename a Name dialog box to change cell and range names.

3. Type the new name in the To box.

4. Choose the Rename button.

You can repeat this procedure until you choose the Close button. You also can delete names from within the Rename a Name dialog box by selecting them and choosing the Delete button.

Adding Text File Commands

Opening the FLATFILE.XLA add-in gives you additional methods for working with text files. This add-in macro enables you to save files in *column-delimited* format, in which each field of data aligns in a specific character position. With this add-in, you also can *parse*, or separate, files in which values are separated by nonstandard field delimiters.

T I P   If your E-mail system cannot send an XLS file, you can send the values in the file by using the FLATFILE.XLA command to export the worksheet as a text file.

Text files are used to transfer information between Excel and personal computer or mainframe applications. For many situations involving text files, you can save or open text files by using the File Save As command and the CSV format for comma-separated values or the text format for tab-separated values. In some exchanges, however, data files are column-delimited: each field aligns in specific columns of characters.

Before you save a worksheet as a flat (column-delimited) file, seeing how characters on the sheet align is often helpful. Because Excel normally uses proportionally spaced characters, columns of characters may not appear to align. To correct this problem, format all involved cells with a nonproportional text, such as Courier or Line Printer.

To save a worksheet so that it contains only characters and spaces, complete the following steps:

1. Add the FLATFILE.XLA file using the Add-in Manager. This adds the **Export** command to the **Data** menu.

2. Select the cells you want to export to a file.

3. Choose the **Data Export** command.

4. Type the file name in the dialog box.

5. Select the **Retain Cell Formats** check box if you want characters to have the alignment and numeric format shown on-screen. One extra space character is inserted between columns if you choose this option. Do not select the **Retain Cell Formats** check box if you want general alignment and number formatting.

6. Choose the **Export** button.

Before using the **Data Smart Parse** command, you should try using the **File Open** command. Select the Text button to display the Text File Options dialog box. From within this dialog box, you can select the column delimiters and character set used in the file you want to open.

To parse or separate a text file into separate cells, use the **Data Parse** command (a normal Excel command) or the **Data Smart Parse** command (an add-in command). **Data Parse** is described in Chapter 32, "Using Excel with DOS Applications," and is used to separate files in which each field of data is stored in a specific column within a long string of text. The **Data Smart Parse** command is added by the FLATFILE.XLA add-in and enables you to parse (separate) lines of text in which data is separated by a unique character. Each piece of information between those unique characters is put into its own individual cell.

To parse a text file that uses a specific character to separate data, complete the following steps:

1. Open the text file. Text data opens into a single column. The data being parsed must be in one column for the add-in to work.

2. In that column, select the range of cells that you want parsed.

3. Choose the **Data Smart Parse** command to display the Data Smart Parse dialog box, shown in figure 15.7.

4. Select **Blank** Space ( ) if each cell's data is separated from the next cell by a blank space. Select **Slash** (/) if each cell of data is separated from the next cell by a slash. Select the **Other** check box and

enter your own single character if it is neither a blank space nor a slash.

If you want to include spaces as they are in the file, clear the **Re**-move extra blank spaces check box; otherwise, multiple blanks are replaced by single blank characters.

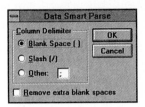

FIG. 15.7

Select the parsing character from the Data Smart Parse dialog box.

When you need to export a range of data from a worksheet, use the Export command that is added to the **D**ata menu. This command enables you to select a range and export it to a file name as a flat file.

Finding Technical Information about Your System

If you're calling for technical assistance from Microsoft and you aren't familiar with your computer's configuration, you may want to run the Checkup add-in. It gives you technical information about your system. To see this technical information, open the file CHECKUP.XLM, located in the \LIBRARY\CHECKUP directory under Excel. Figure 15.8 shows the information displayed by CHECKUP.XLM.

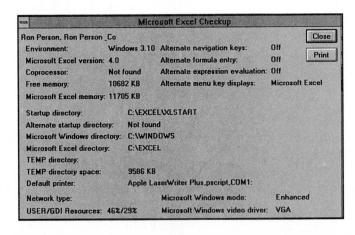

FIG. 15.8

CHECKUP.XLM displays technical information and settings about Excel.

Adding a Worksheet Auditor and Troubleshooter

The Worksheet auditor is a tool that goes beyond the troubleshooting prowess of the Formula Select Special options. When you add the AUDIT.XLA macro with the Add-In Manager, the Formula Worksheet Auditor command is added. This command adds four troubleshooting tools: reports of errors, maps of the worksheet layout, interactive tracing of cell dependencies, and a worksheet information report. Choose the Formula Worksheet Auditor command to display the Worksheet Auditor dialog box, shown in figure 15.9.

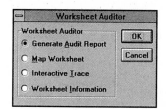

FIG. 15.9

The Worksheet Auditor dialog box.

If you want to see a report of general errors and potential problems on a separate worksheet, select the Generate Audit Report option, click OK or press Enter, and then select check boxes for the following types of reports:

Report	Description
Errors	Prints cells containing error values.
References To Blanks	Prints cell references with formulas that refer to blanks.
References To Text	Prints cell references with formulas that refer to text.
Circular References	Prints cell references and formulas involved in a circular reference. This option can be a life-saver, but it may take a while to run on large worksheets.
Names	Prints names that are unused or that contain errors.

To see a map that shows your worksheet's layout in miniature, reduce Windows' memory use by closing other applications and unnecessary worksheets, activate the worksheet you want to map, and select the **Map** Worksheet option from the Worksheet Auditor dialog box. The map is built on its own worksheet, which you can print.

You can trace dependent or precedent cells from a formula with the Formula **S**elect Special command or the Ctrl+[and Ctrl+] shortcut keys.

An alternative is to use the Interactive **T**race option of the worksheet auditor. Select the cell you want to trace, choose the Formula **W**orksheet Auditor command, and select the Interactive Trace option. The display splits into two windows. The right is the worksheet; the left is the trace information window. To select dependent or precedent cells to the active cell, choose the Find **D**ependents or Find **P**recedents button. To change the active cell, choose the **R**eset Active Cell button and change the active cell. To retrace through traces you have made, choose the Retrace Move **B**ack or Retrace Move **F**orward button. When you are finished tracing cells, choose the **E**xit Trace button.

To see audit information regarding your worksheet and an analysis of its contents by type, select the Worksheet **I**nformation option from the Worksheet Auditor dialog box. Another worksheet is opened to contain this information.

Adding a What-If Generator

The what-if macro quickly tests sets of input values on your worksheet by trying all possible combinations. The what-if macro prompts you for a set of values. Then, with your worksheet displayed, these values are plugged into the appropriate cells each time you press Ctrl+T or Shift+Ctrl+T.

To add the **W**hat If command to the Formula menu, add the WHATIF.XLA file using the Add-in Manager. To set up a data sheet that contains the variables you want tested, choose the Formula **W**hat If command and select the New button. A new sheet appears. When you are prompted, type the name or the cell reference of the input cell you want to receive the values being tested. (You cannot select the cell.) Choose OK. The macro then prompts you for each value you want to test in that input cell. Choose **D**one when you are through entering values.

You are prompted again for the next input cell to be changed. After entering the cell reference, enter the values you want tested in that cell. Choose **D**one after you have entered the last input value for that cell. Continue in this manner until you have entered all input cells and their values. Choose **D**one when the macro prompts you for another input cell reference. All the cell references and input values you have entered have been saved on a worksheet.

To test the input values on your worksheet, activate the worksheet and press Ctrl+Shift+T to cycle through all combinations of input values. To see changes affected by a single input cell, select that cell and press Ctrl+T.

Adding a Worksheet Comparison Command

If you think that minor changes have been made to a worksheet, the COMPARE.XLA add-in can find them. To use it, open the two worksheets you want to compare. Make one of them active.

Open the COMPARE.XLA add-in and choose the new command that becomes available, Formula Compare. From the Compare to sheet list, select the inactive worksheet you want to compare with the active worksheet. A report of all differences is printed on a new worksheet.

Using Other Add-Ins

The following sections offer brief descriptions of additional add-ins you can acquire to make Excel more productive for you. Each section describes the function of the add-in program and directs you to the corresponding section in this book that discusses the add-in.

Adding a Startup Director

To learn about the ALTSTART.XLA add-in and how to add a second startup directory for Excel, see the appropriate section in Chapter 11.

Using the Analysis ToolPak

The Analysis ToolPak is a must for financial, statistical, and some engineering and scientific analysis. It contains functions and models that a few years earlier required minicomputers for solutions. For coverage of the added calculating capabilities available with the Analysis ToolPak, see Chapter 14.

Creating Crosstab Reports

It is nearly impossible to extract trends and patterns from raw database results. However, by using the Crosstab add-in, you can generate reports that make it easy to see information grouped by categories, include total and statistical analysis on groups, and see the relationships between information in different database categories. For detailed information on the Crosstab add-in, see Chapter 26.

Switching to Other Applications

Add the SWITCHTO.XLA add-in to give yourself additional tools for use in toolbars. These tools enable you to switch to other Windows applications when you click the tool. Chapters 2 and 33 describe how to display and customize your toolbars.

Adding the Scenario Manager

The Scenario Manager is a powerful tool that enables you to test multiple sets of input data and see the corresponding results. Electronic worksheets increased proficiency and timeliness in doing calculations. Now, with the Scenario Manager, you get another increase in your ability to test multiple scenarios. Chapter 14 gives a detailed explanation of the Scenario Manager.

T I P   A study on multipaths, who are geniuses in many fields, found that one of their main differences from the rest of us was that they find many solutions to a problem, and then choose the best from the many solutions they come up with. Many people stop when they come up with the first solution. With the Scenario Manager, you have the chance to look like a genius by testing many different possible solutions and choosing the one that's best.

Adding Optimization with the Solver

The Solver add-in gives Excel the power of linear and non-linear optimization. You can let Solver not only find an answer to a problem, but it will also find the best answer given a set of cells it can change, a set of constraints that must be met, and one cell that must be optimized for the greatest, least, or equal to solution. The Solver is described in Chapter 14.

Adding a Slide Show

The SLIDES.XLA macro gives you access to the slide show program, which creates a slide show from Excel charts, worksheets, and graphics or text from other applications. Slide Show includes sound capability and flashy slide transitions. The *slides* that Excel displays can be viewed only from a computer screen or screen projector. They cannot be printed to 35mm or overhead transparency by using this add-in. Use the Add-in Manager to add SLIDES.XLA. It is located in the LIBRARY\SLIDES directory. The Slide Show is described in Chapter 20.

Adding the View Manager

The View Manager enables you to name and save frequently used worksheet locations and their display settings. It also stores print areas and print settings by name. The View Manager is a real time-saver for frequently printed reports or for data-entry screens. You must use the View Manager if you want to use the Report Manager. Add the VIEWS.XLA add-in to use the View Manager. The View Manager is described in Chapter 11.

Adding Commands for External Databases

Excel worksheets can extract information from databases on the hard disk, on an SQL Server, and even in a mainframe by using a companion program that comes free, Q+E. Chapter 25 is devoted to describing how to use Excel and Q+E together.

Adding the File Print Report Command

The Report Manager is a major feature of Excel for anyone who must print charts and reports involving multiple worksheets, multiple views, or different sets of input data. If you need to do a job like this more than once, use the Report Manager. Add the Report Manager by using the Add-in Manager to add REPORTS.XLA. The Report Manager is described in Chapter 16.

Chapter Summary

Add-ins are useful programs that extend and adapt Excel's capabilities. In addition to the free add-ins provided with Excel and described in this chapter, other add-ins are written to adapt Excel to specific industry problems or to fit specific needs within a business. Other Windows applications that work in synergy with Excel come with add-ins so that the two programs can work together as though they were one. Examples of such programs are Solver from Frontline System, Inc., and Q+E from Pioneer Software. Other programs that work well with Excel are listed in the Appendix.

To learn how to create add-in programs for your own use or for use in your company or industry, begin by learning how to record and modify simple macros. Chapters 27 through 30 describe how to record, modify, and program macros. After you have created a command or function macro, you can save it as an add-in.

Printing Worksheets

E xcel enables you to use the full capabilities of your printer. Excel reports printed from laser printers can look as though they have been typeset. You will find that you can achieve better quality with your printer than you ever have before.

Figures 16.1 through 16.4 give you some idea of what you can produce. Excel can produce the equivalent of preprinted invoices or annual report-quality financial statements.

Excel saves you from the trial-and-error process of printing to see the result. You can preview the printed page on-screen before you send it to the printer. You also can adjust margins and column widths in the preview.

When you have many different reports or *views* to print from a worksheet, you can use the **W**indows **V**iews command to assign a name and print settings to each different view. Views are described in Chapter 11.

If your work involves multiple documents that need to be printed in sequence, even including sequential page numbers, you should use the Report Manager. The Report Manager enables you to list the different views and scenarios that you want printed. These views and scenarios are then printed as a single document. (Scenarios are stored collections of input values that enable you to print multiple test results. The Scenario Manager is described in Chapter 14.) The Report Manager is described near the end of this chapter.

The Windows Print Manager also increases your work efficiency. The Print Manager queues material to be printed, enabling the computer to print while you continue working on other projects.

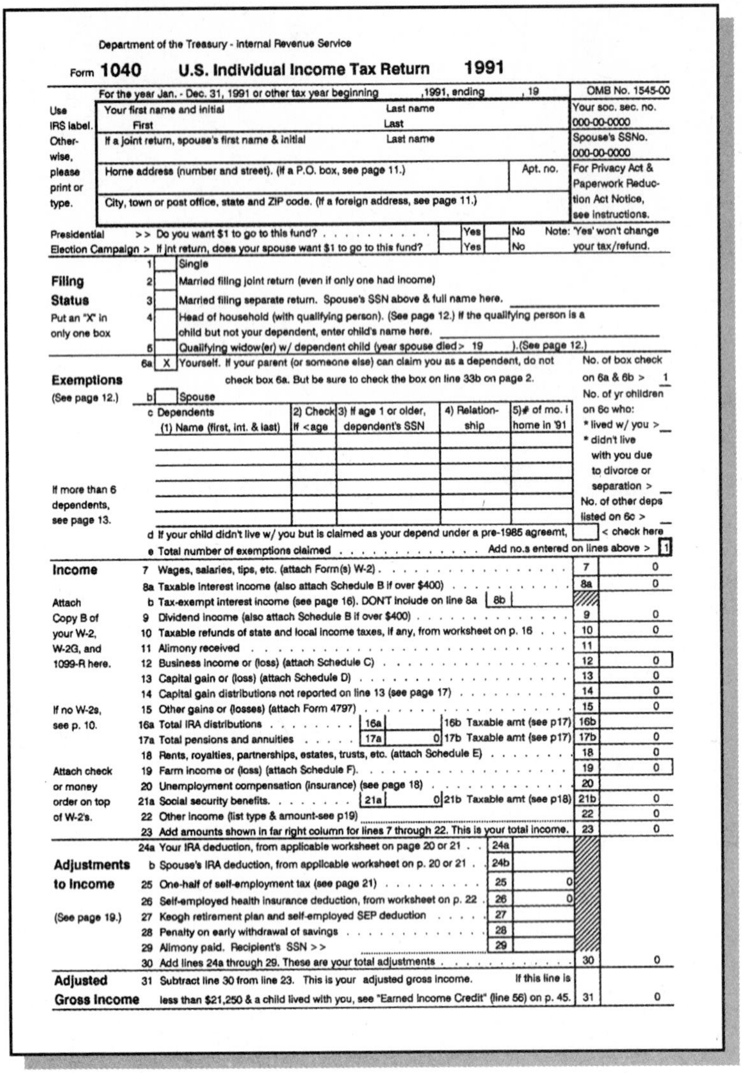

Department of the Treasury - Internal Revenue Service

Form **1040** **U.S. Individual Income Tax Return** **1991**

For the year Jan. - Dec. 31, 1991 or other tax year beginning ,1991, ending , 19 | OMB No. 1545-00

Use IRS label. Other- wise, please print or type.

Your first name and initial: First | Last name: Last | Your soc. sec. no. 000-00-0000

If a joint return, spouse's first name & initial | Last name | Spouse's SSNo. 000-00-0000

Home address (number and street). (If a P.O. box, see page 11.) | Apt. no. | For Privacy Act & Paperwork Reduction Act Notice, see instructions.

City, town or post office, state and ZIP code. (If a foreign address, see page 11.)

Presidential Election Campaign
>> Do you want $1 to go to this fund? . . . . Yes No
> If jnt return, does your spouse want $1 to go to this fund? Yes No
Note: 'Yes' won't change your tax/refund.

Filing Status
Put an "X" in only one box
1 Single
2 Married filing joint return (even if only one had income)
3 Married filing separate return. Spouse's SSN above & full name here.
4 Head of household (with qualifying person). (See page 12.) If the qualifying person is a child but not your dependent, enter child's name here.
5 Qualifying widow(er) w/ dependent child (year spouse died> 19).(See page 12.)

Exemptions
(See page 12.)
6a X Yourself. If your parent (or someone else) can claim you as a dependent, do not check box 6a. But be sure to check the box on line 33b on page 2. | No. of box check on 6a & 6b > 1
b Spouse | No. of yr children on 6c who:
c Dependents

(1) Name (first, int. & last)	2) Check if <age	3) If age 1 or older, dependent's SSN	4) Relationship	5)# of mo. i home in '91

* lived w/ you >
* didn't live with you due to divorce or separation >
No. of other deps listed on 6c >

If more than 6 dependents, see page 13.
d If your child didn't live w/ you but is claimed as your depend under a pre-1985 agreemt, < check here
e Total number of exemptions claimed . . . . Add no.s entered on lines above > 1

Income

	7 Wages, salaries, tips, etc. (attach Form(s) W-2)	7	0
	8a Taxable interest income (also attach Schedule B if over $400)	8a	0
Attach	b Tax-exempt interest income (see page 16). DON'T include on line 8a [8b]		
Copy B of	9 Dividend income (also attach Schedule B if over $400)	9	0
your W-2,	10 Taxable refunds of state and local income taxes, if any, from worksheet on p. 16	10	0
W-2G, and	11 Alimony received	11	
1099-R here.	12 Business income or (loss) (attach Schedule C)	12	0
	13 Capital gain or (loss) (attach Schedule D)	13	0
	14 Capital gain distributions not reported on line 13 (see page 17)	14	0
If no W-2s,	15 Other gains or (losses) (attach Form 4797)	15	0
see p. 10.	16a Total IRA distributions [16a] 16b Taxable amt (see p17)	16b	
	17a Total pensions and annuities [17a 0] 17b Taxable amt (see p17)	17b	0
	18 Rents, royalties, partnerships, estates, trusts, etc. (attach Schedule E)	18	0
Attach check	19 Farm income or (loss) (attach Schedule F)	19	0
or money	20 Unemployment compensation (insurance) (see page 18)	20	
order on top	21a Social security benefits [21a 0] 21b Taxable amt (see p18)	21b	0
of W-2's.	22 Other income (list type & amount-see p19)	22	0
	23 Add amounts shown in far right column for lines 7 through 22. This is your total income.	23	0

Adjustments to Income
(See page 19.)

24a Your IRA deduction, from applicable worksheet on page 20 or 21	24a	
b Spouse's IRA deduction, from applicable worksheet on p. 20 or 21	24b	
25 One-half of self-employment tax (see page 21)	25	0
26 Self-employed health insurance deduction, from worksheet on p. 22	26	0
27 Keogh retirement plan and self-employed SEP deduction	27	
28 Penalty on early withdrawal of savings	28	
29 Alimony paid. Recipient's SSN >>	29	

30 Add lines 24a through 29. These are your total adjustments . . . 30 | 0

Adjusted Gross Income
31 Subtract line 30 from line 23. This is your adjusted gross income. If this line is less than $21,250 & a child lived with you, see "Earned Income Credit" (line 56) on p. 45. 31 | 0

FIG. 16.1

A 1040 U.S. Individual Tax Return form (courtesy of Heizer Software).

Reviewing the Printing Process

Usually, printing consists of the following steps. These steps, along with the available options, are described in detail later in this chapter.

1. Choose the **File** Page Se**t**up command.

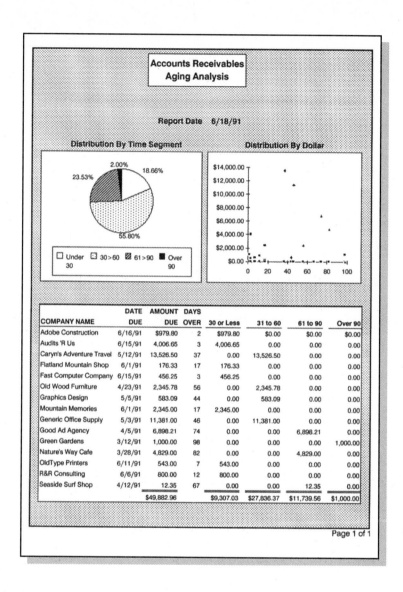

**Accounts Receivables
Aging Analysis**

Report Date 6/18/91

Distribution By Time Segment

2.00%
23.53%
18.66%
55.80%

☐ Under 30 ☐ 30>60 ☒ 61>90 ■ Over 90

Distribution By Dollar

COMPANY NAME	DATE DUE	AMOUNT DUE	DAYS OVER	30 or Less	31 to 60	61 to 90	Over 90
Adobe Construction	6/16/91	$979.80	2	$979.80	$0.00	$0.00	$0.00
Audits 'R Us	6/15/91	4,006.65	3	4,006.65	0.00	0.00	0.00
Caryn's Adventure Travel	5/12/91	13,526.50	37	0.00	13,526.50	0.00	0.00
Flatland Mountain Shop	6/1/91	176.33	17	176.33	0.00	0.00	0.00
Fast Computer Company	6/15/91	456.25	3	456.25	0.00	0.00	0.00
Old Wood Furniture	4/23/91	2,345.78	56	0.00	2,345.78	0.00	0.00
Graphics Design	5/5/91	583.09	44	0.00	583.09	0.00	0.00
Mountain Memories	6/1/91	2,345.00	17	2,345.00	0.00	0.00	0.00
Generic Office Supply	5/3/91	11,381.00	46	0.00	11,381.00	0.00	0.00
Good Ad Agency	4/5/91	6,898.21	74	0.00	0.00	6,898.21	0.00
Green Gardens	3/12/91	1,000.00	98	0.00	0.00	0.00	1,000.00
Nature's Way Cafe	3/28/91	4,829.00	82	0.00	0.00	4,829.00	0.00
OldType Printers	6/11/91	543.00	7	543.00	0.00	0.00	0.00
R&R Consulting	6/6/91	800.00	12	800.00	0.00	0.00	0.00
Seaside Surf Shop	4/12/91	12.35	67	0.00	0.00	12.35	0.00
		$49,882.96		$9,307.03	$27,836.37	$11,739.56	$1,000.00

Page 1 of 1

FIG 16.2

An aging analysis.

2. Choose the Printer Setup button and select your printer. You only need to do this once unless you change printers.

3. Choose the File Page Setup command and set borders, page orientation, resolution, and headers and footers.

4. Select the area to be printed.

5. Click the Set Print Area tool in the Utility toolbar, or choose Options, Set Print Area.

4
VERSION

Global Quality Corporation

Balance Sheet
September 30, 1991

Assets

Current Assets	Current Year	Previous Year	% Change
Current Assets			
Cash	15,007	8,265	181.57%
Accounts Receivable	203,850	448,320	45.47%
Inventory	243,000	241,543	100.60%
Prepaid Expenses	11,400	4,378	260.39%
Investments	95,000	3	0.00%
Total Current Assets	568,257	702,509	80.89%
Fixed Assets			
Buildings	395,577	304,769	129.80%
Leasehold Improvements	3,765	4,356	86.43%
Furniture	27,546	21,587	127.60%
Machinery and Equipment	176,897	87,437	202.31%
	603,785	418,149	144.39%
Less Accumulated Depreciation	156,723	106,734	146.84%
	447,062	311,415	143.56%
Land	89,055	89,055	100.00%
Total Fixed Assets	516,117	380,470	135.65%
	$1,084,374	$1,082,979	100.13%

Liabilities and Shareholder's Equity

Current Liabilities			
Notes Payable	250,000	337,000	74.18%
Trade Accounts Payable	101,900	173,500	58.73%
Accrued Liabilities	35,543	34,200	103.93%
Corporate Income Taxes Payable	21,587	12,423	173.77%
Total Current Liabilities	409,030	557,123	73.42%
Long-Term Debt	213,549	445,638	47.92%
Due to Shareholders	5,690	8,120	70.07%
Deferred Income Tax	4,870	90,230	5.40%
Shareholder's Equity			
Capital Stock	124,000	118,000	105.08%
Opening Retained Earnings	548,789	406,744	134.43%
Dividends Declared	(8,690)	(3,545)	245.13%
Profit/(Loss) for the Period	13,245	4,657	284.41%
Total Shareholder's Equity	675,344	525,856	128.43%
	$1,084,374	$1,082,979	100.13%

FIG. 16.3

A balance sheet.

6. Select the rows or columns that you want to print as headings on each page.

7. Choose the **O**ptions Set Print **T**itles command.

8. Set manual page breaks, if necessary, with **O**ptions Set Page **B**reak.

9. Choose the **File P**rint command or click the Print tool, or choose the **File** Print Preview command if you want to see how the printed document will appear. While in the preview, choose the Print button when you want to print.

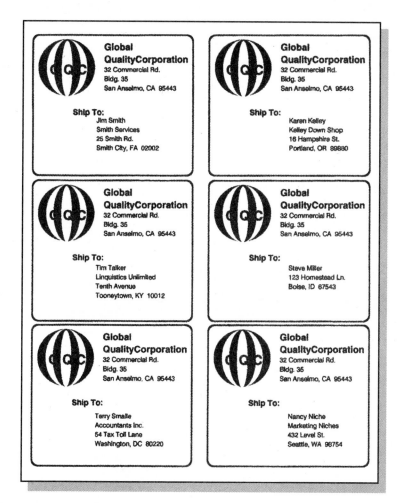

FIG. 16.4

Mailing labels.

Installing Your Printer

When you install Windows, you are asked to select the printers you will use. If you want to install or remove printers after Windows is installed, open the Main window in the Program Manager and start the Control Panel application. Start the Printers application and press F1 for Help about the Printers application. Windows will need to read your original Windows disks to install the printer driver files.

Selecting the Printer

You may have installed more than one printer when you installed Windows, or you may have added additional printers using the Printers application in the Control Panel. To change between printers, follow these steps:

1. Choose the File Page Setup command; then choose the Printer Setup button.

2. Select the printer and the printer port that you want to use from the Printer list.

3. Select the Setup button if you have not used this printer before.

   A dialog box similar to the one shown in figure 16.5 appears. Default settings for your printer are set in this box. After they are set, you should rarely have to use this box again.

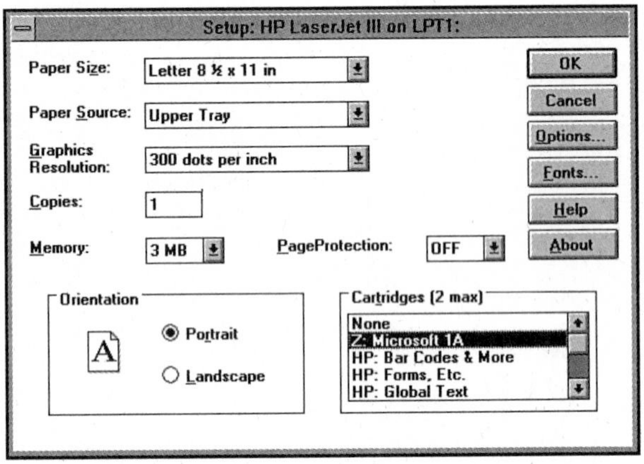

FIG. 16.5

Printer setup dialog boxes vary with each printer.

4. Select Paper Source, Paper Size, Orientation (Portrait or Landscape), and number of Copies. These settings are used as the default settings. Also select options appropriate to any additional memory or font cartridges available in your printer. The Printer Setup dialog box will be different for various printers. Some of the options available are shown in table 16.1.

   Choose the Options button to make additional selections specific to your printer. Choose OK to close the Options dialog box, if necessary.

5. Choose OK or press Enter.

6. Choose OK or press Enter a second time to return to the Page Setup dialog box. Choose OK if you do not want to change page settings.

The printer settings you choose in the Setup dialog box are the default printer settings. These settings remain in effect for all documents, even in other applications, until you change them.

Table 16.1. Printer Setup Options

Option	Description
Copies	Specifies the number of copies to be printed.
Memory	Specifies the exact model of printer and its memory capacity (to ensure that Windows uses all the features of this model).
Paper Size	Lists the sizes and types of paper available.
Paper Source	Lists which of the bins your printer may have for different types of paper.
Orientation	Specifies the placement of print on the page: Portrait prints characters on the page as they appear in a normal letter; Landscape prints sideways on the paper and is useful for making transparencies and charts.
Graphics Resolution	Specifies print quality; printing at high resolution slows the printer speed but produces better graphic images.
Cartridges	Specifies the types of font cartridges available.

If you have questions about the settings available for your printer, choose the **Help** button.

Defining the Page Setup

The **F**ile Page Setup command controls all the settings you normally need to print with. A few of the items controlled from its dialog box include the position of print on the page, paper orientation (vertical or sideways), headers and footers, gridlines, color or black and white, and row and column headings.

To change the page setup for the printed page, complete the following steps:

1. Choose the **F**ile Page Setup command.

2. Change the page options as needed in the Page Setup dialog box (see fig. 16.6). These options are described in more detail in the following sections.

3. Choose the OK button or press Enter.

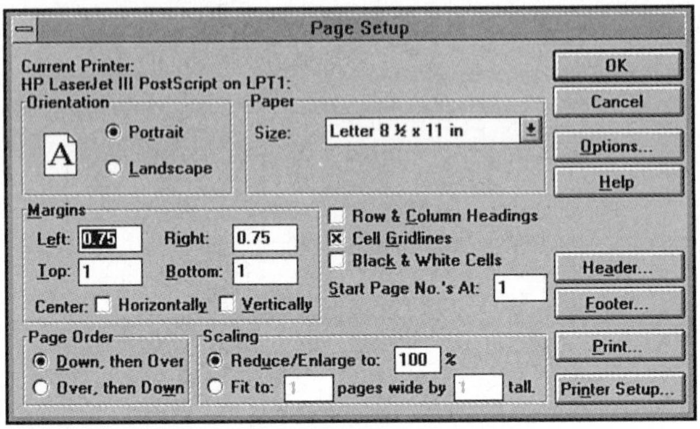

FIG. 16.6

The Page Setup dialog box.

Setting the Paper Margins

Excel's character width changes with each different font size. Consequently, you need to measure your margins in inches rather than by a count of characters. The default settings for margins are shown in table 16.2.

Table 16.2. Default Margin Settings

Margin	Default in Inches
Left	0.75
Right	0.75
Top	1
Bottom	1

Measure the margins from the edge of the paper inward. When you set the top and bottom margins, keep in mind that headers and footers automatically print 1/2 inch from the top or bottom of the paper.

Many laser printers are unable to print to the edge of the paper. Because of this limitation, you may not be able to set margins of less than 1/4 inch.

If you want your document to be centered between margins, select the Center Horizontally or the Center Vertically check box.

Turning Gridlines and Headings On and Off

For most printed reports, you will not want to print gridlines or the row and column headings. If you turn off gridlines in the worksheet using the Options Display command, they also turn off for your printed copies. To change gridlines or row and column headings when printing, clear or select the Row & Column Headings or the Gridlines option.

You probably will want to print row and column headings when you print worksheet documentation showing formulas or when you print notes. If you use Options Display with the Formulas check box selected, you can display the formulas on-screen so that they can be printed.

Creating Headers and Footers

You can create headers and footers that place a title, date, or page number at the top or bottom of each printed page of your worksheet. You also can format them with different fonts, styles, and sizes. Use headers and footers to enter a copyright notice, to document the author, to show the printout date, or to note the source worksheet.

Excel automatically uses the document name as the header and shows the word Page and the page number as the footer. You can delete these or change them.

Headers and footers use a 3/4-inch side margin and a 1/2-inch margin at the top and bottom. The header and footer cannot be moved in this area. If you specify page setup margins that cross these boundaries, the document may print over a header or footer.

To create a header or footer, choose the File Page Setup command. In the Page Setup dialog box, choose the Header or Footer buttons to display the header or footer dialog box. These dialog boxes contain three sections for left-, center-, or right-aligned data. You enter text or codes, such as the date code, into the three sections. The sections are labeled Left Section, Center Section, and Right Section. Figure 16.7 shows the Header dialog box as it first appears.

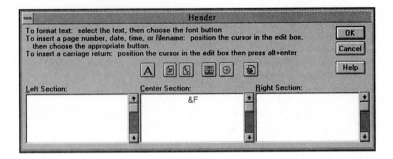

FIG. 16.7

The Header
dialog box.

To enter information into a section with the mouse, click a section and type. Click a code icon to enter a code at the insertion point. To format text, select the text and click the font icon to display the font dialog box; select your font formatting options and choose OK.

To enter information from the keyboard, press the Alt+letter key that moves the insertion point into the section. Type the text and codes listed in table 16.3. Or select code icons by pressing Tab until the icon is selected, then pressing Enter. Use the **H**elp button if you forget the codes. You can create multiple-line headers or footers by pressing Alt+Enter to break a line.

As the following examples illustrate, you can combine the codes shown in table 16.3 with your own text to create the header and footer you need:

Code:

Left	&L&D Page &P of &N
Center	&C&"Tms Rmn"&14&BABC Investment Corp.
Right	&RMortgage Banking Div.

Result:

12/24/92 Page 1 of 3 **ABC Investment Corp.** Mortgage Banking Div.

When you print or preview the document, the result appears as shown in figure 16.8.

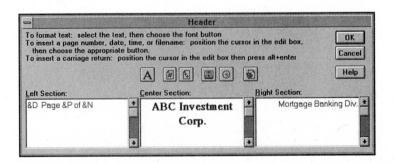

FIG. 16.8

The header or footer
as entered.

Table 16.3. Header and Footer Codes

Icon	Code	Effect
Font and Style Codes		
A	&"*fontname*"	Prints text that follows (or selected text, if you choose the icon) in the font specified. Use the same spelling as in the Format **F**ont dialog box and enclose it in quotes.
A	&*nn*	Prints text that follows (or selected text, if you choose the icon) in the font size specified by *nn*. Use a two-digit point size: 08, 12, or 14.
A	&B	Prints text that follows (or selected text, if you choose the icon) in bold.
A	&I	Prints text that follows (or selected text, if you choose the icon) in italic.
A	&U	Prints text (or selected text, if you choose the icon) that follows <u>underlined</u>.
A	&S	Prints text that follows (or selected text, if you choose the icon) with strikethroughs.
Inserted Data Codes		
Calendar	&D	Inserts the computer's date.
Clock	&T	Inserts the computer's time.
Excel sheet	&F	Inserts the name of the document.
Page Codes		
#	&P	Inserts the page number.
&P+# or &P-#		Inserts the page number plus or minus an amount you specify (#). Use the page code with the plus sign (+) to start printing at a page number greater than the actual page number. Use the page code with the minus sign (-) to start printing at a page number smaller than the actual page number.
+/+	&N	Inserts the total number of pages. For example, the header *Page &P of &N* produces the result *Page 6 of 15*.
Other		
&&		Prints an ampersand.

Headers are printed 1/2 inch from the top of the page, and footers 1/2 inch from the bottom. If text overlaps the header or footer, use **File Page Setup** to change the top or bottom margin.

 If you enter a font name, size, and style, make sure that the name is in quotation marks and that it is spelled the same as it appears in the Font dialog box. Use font styles and sizes that are available in your printer.

Specifying the Page Layout Order

When Excel prints a range larger than will fit on one sheet of paper, it prints down the range, and then goes to the columns to the right of the first page and prints down those. In some cases—wide landscape reports, for example—you may want to print so that Excel prints across the wide range first and then goes to the next lower area and goes across it.

To select how you want Excel to print pages, choose the **File Page Setup** command, and select from the Page Order group either **D**own, then Over or Over, then Down.

Reducing and Enlarging Prints

 If your printer supports scalable type, you can print a document that is proportionally reduced or enlarged. By making a proportional reduction, you can fit a document to a page without losing or redoing the formatting. To scale your document, choose the **File Page Setup** command and select the Reduce/Enlarge to: text box. Enter a number smaller than 100 to reduce the page to that percentage of the original. Enter a number larger than 100 to enlarge the page. If your printer is not capable of scaling the print job to fit the page, the Reduce/ Enlarge and **F**it to Pages boxes are gray.

Printing Color or Black and White

 Your worksheets and charts may use color on-screen, but you want to make sure that they look good on your black-and-white printer. To substitute grays for colors, white background for patterns, and black text for colored text automatically, select the Blac**k** & White Cells check box.

For Related Information:

◄◄ "Using TrueType Fonts," p. 261.

FROM HERE...

Setting the Print Range

By default, Excel prints the entire worksheet unless you specify otherwise. When you need to print only a portion of the worksheet, you must
define that area with **O**ptions Set Print **A**rea. The print area can include
more than one range.

If you have many print ranges on one worksheet, you may want to create
named views of those print ranges and settings. You then can print a
range with its settings by returning to that view. If you have many views
that you want to print, even from multiple documents, make sure that
you read about the Report Manager, described at the end of this
chapter.

When you work with databases or large worksheets, you may be
tempted to put field names or column headings in the header so that
you can see the labels on each page of the printout. *Don't* Labels in
the header are difficult to align with columns and cannot be positioned close to the body of the report. Instead, use **O**ptions Set Print
Titles to set print titles. Print titles are discussed later in this chapter.

T I P

Setting a Print Area

The **O**ptions Set Print **A**rea command controls how much of the document is printed; the command also controls which cell notes are printed.
To define a single print area, select the range of cells that you want
printed and choose the **O**ptions Set Print **A**rea command. Cell notes that
are in the selected range will print if you select the **N**otes or the **B**oth
option from the **F**ile **P**rint command.

After you set the print area, Excel marks the edges of the print area with
dashed lines. Figure 16.9 shows the worksheet created in the Worksheet
Quick Start. Excel marked the calculated area, which is selected in the

figure, as the area to be printed when the **O**ptions Set Print **A**rea command is chosen. In figure 16.10, you can see the dashed lines that mark
the edges of the print area after **O**ptions Set Print **A**rea is chosen.
Dashed lines also indicate manual and automatic page breaks.

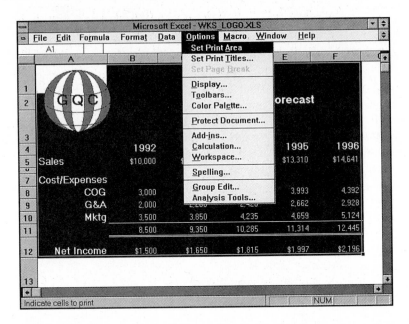

FIG. 16.9

Select the area that
you want to print
before choosing the
Options Set Print **A**rea
command.

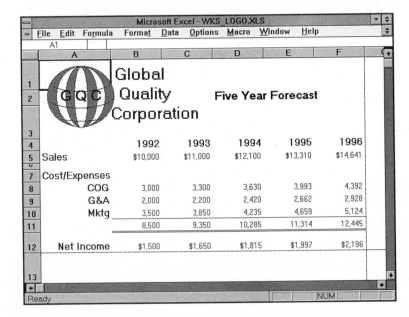

FIG. 16.10

Page breaks mark the
page breaks and the
edges of a print area.

The **O**ptions Set Print **A**rea command creates a named range called *Print_Area*. You can display this range name and its cell references with the **Fo**rmula **D**efine Name command.

Removing a Print Area

If you want to return to printing the entire worksheet, remove the print area. Select the entire worksheet by pressing Shift+Ctrl+space bar or clicking the Select All button above the row 1 heading and to the left of the A column heading. Choose the **O**ptions Remove Print **A**rea command.

Adjusting the Printed Page

After you select a print area, you may need to make adjustments to fit the information on the page. You might, for example, want to change the page breaks to keep related data together. You also might want to change the margins or font size so that you can fit the information on the page.

When you set a print area with **O**ptions Set Print **A**rea, Excel displays dashed lines to mark the page boundaries and automatic page breaks. Automatic page breaks are determined by how much of the print area you have selected will fit within the printable area of the page.

Setting Manual Page Breaks

Sometimes you need to insert a manual page break to override an automatic page break. When you insert manual page breaks, the automatic page breaks reposition automatically.

When you choose the **O**ptions Set Page **B**reak command, the manual page breaks appear above and to the left of the active cell. Figure 16.11 shows page breaks above and to the left of the active cell. Manual page breaks appear on-screen with a longer and bolder dashed line than the automatic page breaks. Page breaks are easier to see on-screen when you remove gridlines with the **O**ptions **D**isplay command.

To insert manual page breaks, move the active cell beneath and to the right of the place you want the break, and then choose **O**ptions Set Page **B**reak. If you want to set page breaks for only the sides, make sure that the active cell is in row 1 before you choose **O**ptions Set Page **B**reak. If you want to set the breaks for only the tops and bottoms of pages, move the active cell to the correct row in column A, and then choose the **O**ptions Set Page **B**reak command.

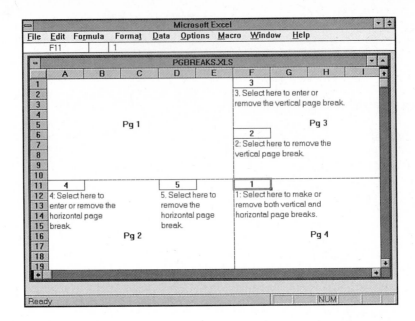

FIG. 16.11

Manual page breaks appear above and to the left of the active cell.

A manual page break stays at the location that you set until you remove it. Remove manual page breaks by first moving the active cell directly below or immediately to the right of the manual page break. Then choose **O**ptions Remove Page **B**reak. This command appears on the menu only when the active cell is positioned correctly. Remove all page breaks by selecting the entire document and choosing the **O**ptions Remove Page **B**reak command.

NOTE   Be sure that you try to remove only manual page breaks. You can drive yourself crazy trying to remove an automatic page break that you mistake for a manual one.

Fitting More Data on a Page

You can fit more information on a page by decreasing the margins, decreasing the column widths or row heights, or choosing a smaller font size. You also can use the fit-to-page feature described in a following section.

If you used styles to format your document, you can change fonts throughout the entire worksheet by redefining the style names used in your worksheet. Normal is the style used in cells that have not been formatted. Use a small font size to fit more data on a page. Save your document before you begin changing fonts so that you can easily return to the original document.

Smaller margins produce more room on the paper. Some laser printers can print only within 1/4 inch of the paper's edge.

You also can narrow columns and reduce row height to fit more data on a page. To make sure that all adjustments are the same, select multiple columns before you narrow a column. All the columns will reduce simultaneously.

You also can use the Reduce/Enlarge To option or the Fit to Page option found in the Page Setup dialog box to fit more of a document on the page. The Fit to Page capability is described in the next section. Reduce/Enlarge To was described earlier under Page Setup.

Setting Multiple Print Areas

Excel can print multiple ranges with a single print command. Although these ranges print sequentially, each range prints on its own sheet.

Select the multiple ranges that you want to print by using Ctrl+drag or F8 and Shift+F8. Select ranges in the order that you want them to print, and then choose the **O**ptions Set Print **A**rea command. This technique works well for creating a single printed report from different areas of a worksheet.

If you frequently print the same parts of a document, save time by learning about the **W**indow View command. View enables you to assign names to print settings and frequently printed ranges. If you need to print multiple views, or need to print the same output with different sets of input data, then learn about the Report Manager at the end of this chapter. The View command is described in Chapter 11.

T I P

For Related Information:

◀◀ "Choosing Commands," p. 35

◀◀ "Moving around the Worksheet," p. 145.

◀◀ "Selecting Cells," p. 147.

FROM HERE...

Printing Titles

Repeating printed titles on each page can make large worksheet or database printouts easier to read. When your worksheet is wider than one page, for example, you can repeat row titles along the left margin of each page. You can repeat column titles at the top of each page of a database that spans multiple pages. The **O**ptions Set Print **T**itles command specifies that selected rows or columns will print at the top or left side of each printed page.

To specify titles, complete the following steps:

1. Select the entire row(s) or columns(s) or both of titles that you want on each page. The rows or columns must be adjacent, as shown in figure 16.12.

2. Choose the **O**ptions Set Print **T**itles command. The Set Print Titles dialog box appears (see fig. 16.12).

3. Choose OK or press Enter.

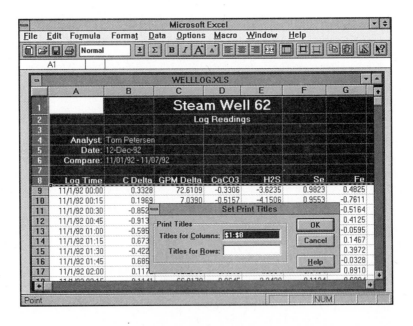

FIG. 16.12

The Options Set Print Titles command repeats rows or columns on each page.

To display the currently selected titles, press the Goto key (F5) and select Print_Titles. To delete Print_Titles, choose the **O**ptions Set Print **T**itles command and clear the edit boxes or select the entire worksheet and choose the **O**ptions Remove Print **T**itles command.

You don't have to limit yourself to one row or column of titles. As long as the title rows or columns are adjacent, you can include as many as you want.

Excel prints titles set with **O**ptions Set Print **T**itles only when the selection being printed includes the same rows or columns as the Print_Titles range. Suppose, for example, that you type titles in rows A3:G4 and create Print Titles of rows 3 and 4. If you print data from B36 to H54, you have the titles that are in cells B3:G4. If you print the area from H54 to K72, you will have as titles whatever is in H3:K4. Because you did not type titles in this range, you may have blanks or unwanted cell values.

T I P

For Related Information:

◀◀ "Entering Data," p. 169.

◀◀ "Editing Text and Formulas," p. 195.

◀◀ "Changing Character Fonts, Sizes, Styles, and Colors," p. 257.

◀◀ "Formatting Rows and Columns," p. 289.

◀◀ "Controlling the Worksheet Display," p. 306.

FROM HERE...

Previewing the Document

Instead of printing to check the appearance of your worksheet, you can view a display of the printout with miniature pages such as the page shown in figure 16.13. When you want to examine a preview page up close, you can zoom into the area you want to see.

To preview pages, select the **F**ile Print Preview command. The preview screen shows you how the page will look when printed.

To zoom into a portion of the page, choose the **Z**oom button or click the mouse pointer—a magnifying glass—over the portion that you want to magnify. Use the cursor keys or scroll bars to move around in the zoomed-in view. Figures 16.14 and 16.15 show the zoom-in and zoom-out views of the document. To zoom out, choose **Z**oom a second time, or click a second time.

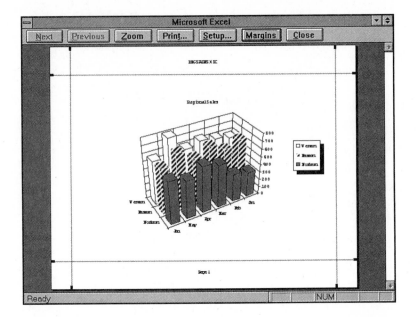

FIG. 16.13

Previewing enables you to see how the document is positioned on the printed page.

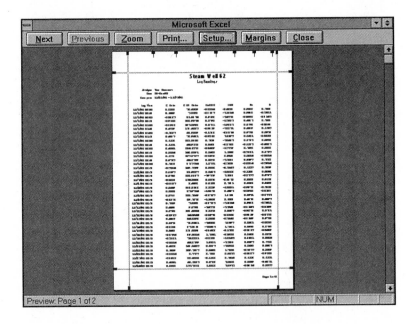

FIG. 16.14

Get the big picture of the page fit when you adjust margins and columns.

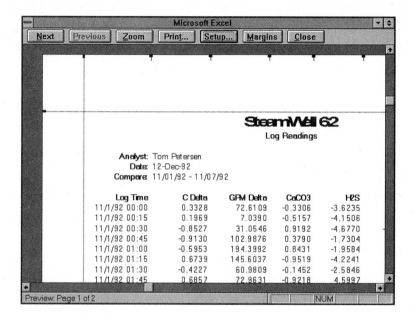

FIG. 16.15

Zoom in for a precise
positioning of margins
and column widths.

To change pages in the preview mode, use the **Next** or **Previous** buttons. These buttons appear gray if there is no next or previous page.

After you preview the worksheet, you can print it from the preview screen by choosing the Print button. If you want to change or see the Page Setup settings, choose the **Setup** button. To return to the document, choose the **Close** button.

For Related Information:

◄◄ "Using the Mouse," p. 27.

◄◄ "Choosing Commands," p. 35.

FROM HERE...

Adjusting Margins and Column Widths While Previewing

You can adjust margins and column widths while in the preview screen. Before adjusting margins with this method, save your document so that you can easily return to the original settings if necessary.

To adjust margins or column widths, complete the following steps:

1. Choose the **F**ile Print Preview command.

2. Choose the **M**argins button. Column and margin markers will appear on the preview page in full page view or when zoomed in.

3. Choose the **Z**oom button or click the magnifying glass pointer to zoom in or out of the preview for more accurate viewing.

4. Drag the margin handles (black squares) or the dotted line to a better position.

5. Drag column handles (black T's) or the column gridline to adjust column widths.

6. Choose **C**lose to return to the document with these new settings, or choose Print to print the document with these settings.

Figures 16.14 and 16.15 show column and margin adjustment from either a magnified or full view.

For Related Information:

◄◄ "Choosing Commands," p. 35.

Compressing Reports To Fit the Paper Size

You may have faced the problem of adjusting row heights, column widths, or margins so that your document would not have a few columns lapping over to an adjacent page or three lines hanging over at the bottom. With Excel's print-to-fit feature, you can compress a report so that it fits snugly in the space you demand.

Compressing Reports to One Page

The most basic way of using the print-to-fit feature is to compress the report enough so that a few lines from a second page move to the first page. This can turn a two-page report into a single-page report.

Figure 16.16 shows two different views of a worksheet that can generate long, multiple page reports.

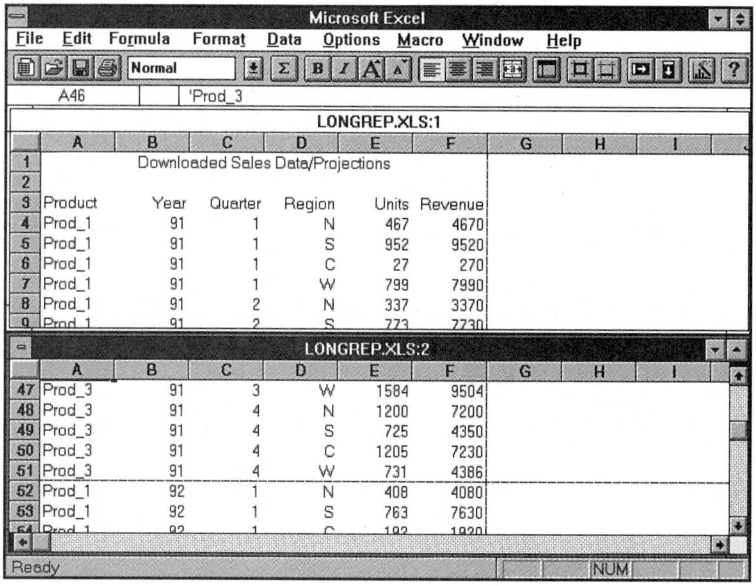

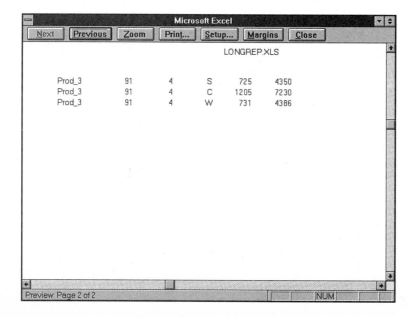

FIG. 16.16

Two views of LONGREP.XLS containing three years of data.

If you print the 1991 data at 100% of its size (Excel's default), three lines will extend to the next page (see fig. 16.17).

FIG. 16.17

A Print Preview screen showing that the report has a few lines on the second page.

The Page Setup dialog box in figure 16.18 shows how you can compress the three lines on the second page of the report to the first page. In the Scaling box, select the **Fit** to: option button. The two text boxes after the **Fit** to: button indicate the print area is to be shrunk to 1 page wide by 1 page tall.

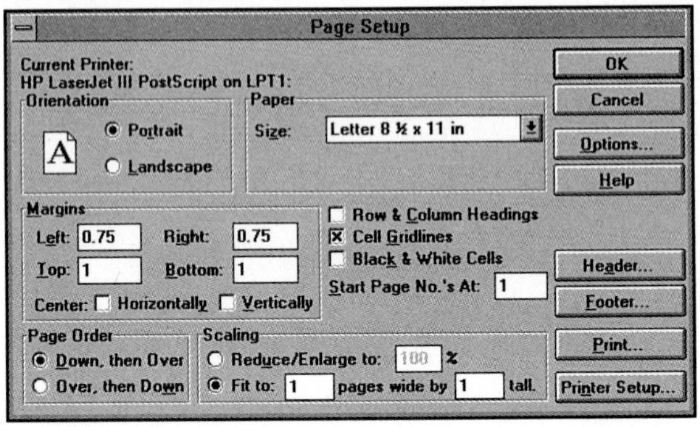
Page Setup
Current Printer:
HP LaserJet III PostScript on LPT1:
Orientation
Portrait
Landscape
Paper
Size:
Letter 8 ½ x 11 in
OK
Cancel
Options...
Help
Margins
Left: 0.75
Right: 0.75
Top: 1
Bottom: 1
Center: Horizontally Vertically
Row & Column Headings
Cell Gridlines
Black & White Cells
Start Page No.'s At: 1
Header...
Footer...
Page Order
Down, then Over
Over, then Down
Scaling
Reduce/Enlarge to: 100 %
Fit to: 1 pages wide by 1 tall.
Print...
Printer Setup...

FIG. 16.18

The printed area will be reduced to fit in an area one page tall by one page wide.

The Print Preview screen in figure 16.19 shows that the whole report, all of the sales data for 1991, fits on a single page.

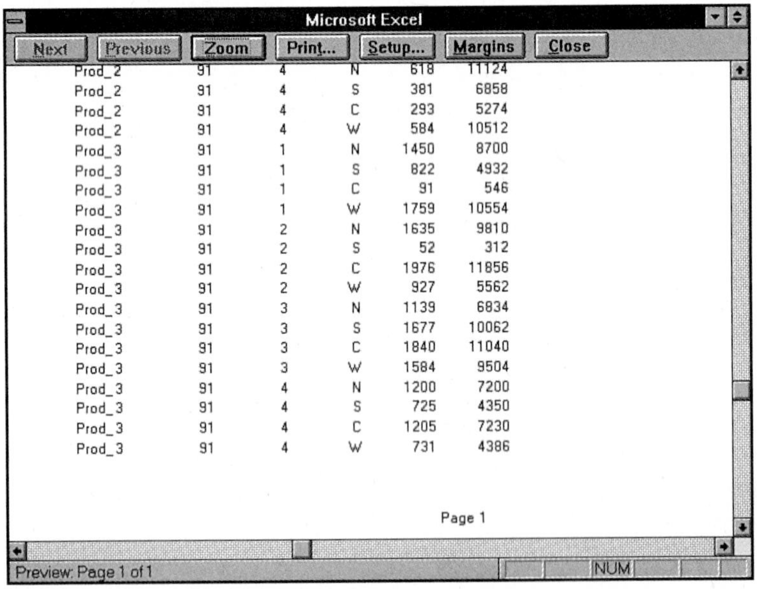
Microsoft Excel
Next
Previous
Zoom
Print...
Setup...
Margins
Close
Prod_2 91 4 N 618 11124
Prod_2 91 4 S 381 6858
Prod_2 91 4 C 293 5274
Prod_2 91 4 W 584 10512
Prod_3 91 1 N 1450 8700
Prod_3 91 1 S 822 4932
Prod_3 91 1 C 91 546
Prod_3 91 1 W 1759 10554
Prod_3 91 2 N 1635 9810
Prod_3 91 2 S 52 312
Prod_3 91 2 C 1976 11856
Prod_3 91 2 W 927 5562
Prod_3 91 3 N 1139 6834
Prod_3 91 3 S 1677 10062
Prod_3 91 3 C 1840 11040
Prod_3 91 3 W 1584 9504
Prod_3 91 4 N 1200 7200
Prod_3 91 4 S 725 4350
Prod_3 91 4 C 1205 7230
Prod_3 91 4 W 731 4386
Page 1
Preview: Page 1 of 1
NUM

FIG. 16.19

The report now fits on one page.

Compressing Longer Reports

Long reports also can be compressed so that they fit exactly on the final page. This prevents the last few lines from dropping over to the last page.

To compress a tall report that is one page wide and 8 1/4 pages long so that it fits on eight pages, enter the following settings in the Fit to: boxes:

Fit to: 1 pages wide by 8 tall

To print a report that is three pages long but one column too wide so that it fits on three pages, enter the following in the Fit to: boxes:

Fit to: 1 pages wide by 3 tall

Printing

With Excel, you can select the range of pages and the number of copies that you want to print. In addition, you can preview the printout on-screen before printing to paper.

After you are ready to print, choose the File **Print** command to display the print options in the Print dialog box, as shown in figure 16.20.

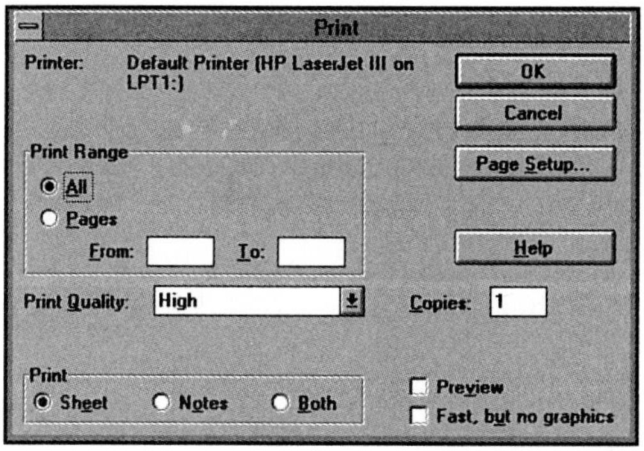

FIG. 16.20

The Print dialog box.

In the **Copies** text box, enter the number of copies you want to print. Specify the range of pages that you want to print; select the **All** option to print the entire print area, or you can enter page numbers in the **From** and **To** text boxes.

When you need a quick print, select the Print **Quality** list and select lower resolution printing, such as Low or Medium, if your printer supports it. The result is faster, but the quality may be lower. If you want to see a preview before printing, choose the Preview check box.

Specify what you want to print by selecting the Sheet, Notes, or Both options. Sheet prints only the document; Notes prints only the notes; and Both prints the document followed by the notes. If you have set a print area, only the document and notes in that area are printed. To print the cell reference along with each note, make sure that the Row & Column Headings check box is selected from the Page Setup dialog box.

To print, just choose the OK button. Make sure that your printer is turned on and is on-line.

For Related Information:

FROM HERE...

◄◄ "Choosing Commands," p. 35.

◄◄ "Selecting Cells," p. 147.

Creating Reports

The Report Manager automates the printing of worksheets that may have unique print ranges and different sets of input data. The finished product from the Report Manager is a report that appears to have been compiled from one all-encompassing worksheet.

You can compile, print, and edit sequences of reports with the File Print Report command. The individual reports, which are compiled into report sequences, must be created from views of a worksheet and input scenarios. Views include named print areas and their associated print settings. Views are described in Chapter 11. The Scenario Manager controls multiple sets of data used as inputs for your worksheet. The Scenario Manager is described in Chapter 14.

NOTE   The Report Manager is an add-in installed during Excel installation. If you do not see the Print Report command under the File menu, then refer to Chapter 15 to learn how to add the Report Manager.

The Report Manager enables you to put together a collection of views that will print in sequence as one large report. You also can print sequential page numbers. If you also have specified sets of data to be controlled by the Scenario Manager, the reports can print the results from each set of data.

Creating a Sequence of Reports

Before you can create a report, you must have already created the views you want to print. You do not need to create scenarios to use the Report Manager. Follow these steps to create a sequence of reports:

1. Choose the **F**ile Print **R**eport command.

   The Print Report dialog box is displayed (see fig. 16.21).

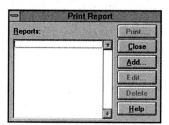

FIG. 16.21

The Print Report
dialog box.

2. Choose the **A**dd button. You see the Add Report dialog box (see fig. 16.22).

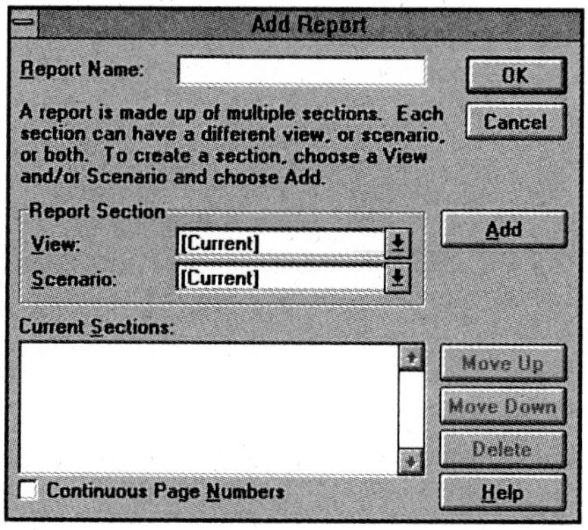

FIG. 16.22

The Add Report
dialog box.

3. Type the name of the report you are creating in the **R**eport Name box.

4. Select the name of the view from the **V**iew pull-down list.

5. Select the name of the scenario from the **S**cenario pull-down list. You do not need a scenario for a report.

   Enter views and scenarios in the order in which you want them to print in the report. You can reorder items after you have built your list.

6. Choose the Add button to add the view and scenario to the bottom of the Current Sections list.

7. If you want the report to print with continuous page numbers, select the Continuous Page Numbers check box.

8. Return to step 4 if you want to add more views and scenarios.

9. Choose OK or press Enter.

Figure 16.23 shows a complete Current Selection list. Views appear as the first item followed by the associated scenario.

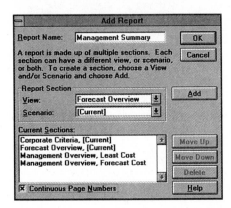

FIG. 16.23

A complete Current Selection list showing views and scenarios and their order in the report.

Reorganizing Report Sequences

After a sequence of views and scenarios is created, you may need to edit and reorganize it. For example, a client may prefer to see reports printed in a different order, or you may need to add or delete reports.

To edit a report sequence, choose the File Print Report command. When the Print Report dialog box appears, choose the Edit button. When the Add Report dialog box appears, select from the Current Sections list the view and scenario you want to change. To delete a scenario, choose the Delete button. To move the selected item up or down in the list, choose the Move Up or Move Down button. Choose OK or press Enter when you are finished.

Printing a Report Sequence

You can create several different report sequences. When you are ready to print one of them, complete the following steps:

1. Choose the File Print Report command.
2. Select the name of the report you want to print.
3. Choose the Print button.
4. Enter the number of copies and choose OK or press Enter.

For Related Information:

◄◄ "Linking or Consolidating Worksheets," p. 107.

◄◄ "Checking Spelling," p. 205.

◄◄ "Changing Worksheet Layout," p. 222.

◄◄ "Changing Character Fonts, Sizes, Styles, and Colors," p. 257.

◄◄ "Aligning Text and Numbers," p. 264.

◄◄ "Formatting Numbers," p. 272.

FROM HERE...

Chapter Summary

Excel has always been known for excellent quality of its printing. With the power for views, scenarios, and the Report Manager, you now can automate the printing of reports you must do frequently. Don't forget to use Excel's print preview so that you can see what's going to print without wasting a trip to the printer and a ream of paper. Other areas that relate to printing include the topic of views, described in Chapter 11, and scenarios, described in Chapter 14.

Excel Charts

PART

III

OUTLINE

Chart Quick Start

T his Quick Start teaches you how to create and customize the chart shown in figure 17.1 by using a mouse and Excel's ChartWizard. The ChartWizard guides you through the process of making a chart. To work through the instructions in the Quick Start, you need to start with a worksheet that contains data.

This Quick Start uses the forecast worksheet created in Chapter 3, "Worksheet Quick Start." If you did not complete or save that worksheet, enter the numbers and text as you see them in figure 17.2. You do not need to enter the formulas; entering the numbers and text in rows 4, 5, and 12 will give you enough data to create a chart.

NOTE   To create a chart by using the keyboard, see "Creating a Chart Automatically" in Chapter 18.

Remember that you can get help by choosing the **Help I**ndex command and selecting Chart. Whenever a dialog box is displayed, you can get help by pressing the F1 key.

Using the ChartWizard

Excel automatically creates a chart from the worksheet data you select. After you have created a basic chart, you can change the type of chart or enhance the chart.

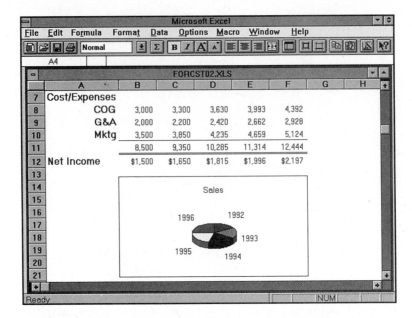

Microsoft Excel
File Edit Formula Format Data Options Macro Window Help
Normal

FIG. 17.1

You create this chart in this Quick Start.

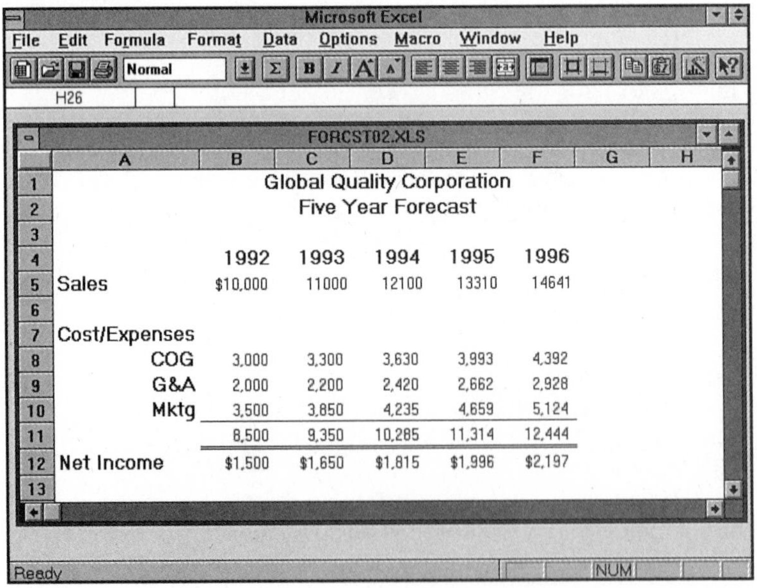

FIG. 17.2

This forecast worksheet is used to create the chart.

Excel uses two types of charts. You can create a chart as a separate document in its own window, or you can create a chart that is embedded in a worksheet along with worksheet or database information. Embedded charts display and print with the worksheet. The following steps show you how to create a chart as an embedded document.

> Excel automatically creates a chart from the data selected in the worksheet. Excel positions the category (X) axis labels according to these rules:
>
> ■ If the selection is wider than tall, the category axis labels are in the row along the top.
>
> ■ If the selection is taller than wide, the category axis labels are in the column along the left edge of the selection.
>
> The next chapter describes how to create a chart manually and choose which data is used on the category axis. When you include data labels, such as the word *Sales* in cell A5, in the selection, you enable Excel to create titles and legends from text in the worksheet automatically.

T I P

Embedded charts exist on a worksheet, display on the worksheet, and print with the worksheet. Using a mouse, you can simultaneously create and embed a chart in a worksheet. If you use a keyboard, you embed charts in the worksheet by creating them as separate documents and then pasting the charts into the worksheet. Chapter 18 describes how to embed charts by keyboard.

In this example, you create an embedded chart by using the Chart-Wizard. The ChartWizard is a collection of dialog boxes that help you complete a task by asking you a series of related questions. In this case, the ChartWizard asks you what data you want to graph, what type of chart you want to create, and so on.

Before you embed a chart in the worksheet, make room for where it will appear below the worksheet results. To insert rows in the worksheet, perform the following steps:

1. Select the row headings from rows 14 to 24 by clicking the number 14 at the far left of row 14 and dragging down to row 24.

2. Choose the **Edit Insert** command.

After you make room for the chart, embed it by following these steps:

1. Select the cells to be charted. In this case, start in cell A4 and select cells A4:F5. Include the text label in cell A5.

2. Click the ChartWizard tool in the toolbar.

Notice that the mouse pointer changes to a cross hair and the prompt in the Status Bar tells you `Click and drag in document to create a chart`. The ChartWizard tool is shown in figure 17.3.

ChartWizard

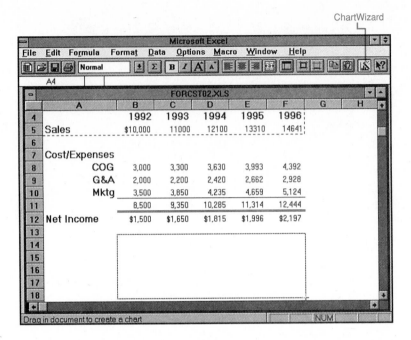

FIG. 17.3

After clicking the
ChartWizard tool, you
are prompted to drag
across where you want
the embedded chart.

3. Click the down arrow in the scroll bar until cell A14 is visible.

4. To draw a shadow box where the embedded chart will appear, drag
   from the center of cell A14 to the center of cell F24. As you touch a
   screen boundary with the cross hair, the window scrolls to give
   you more room. The embedded chart does not have to match cell
   boundaries.

5. Release the mouse button, and the first ChartWizard dialog box
   appears (see fig. 17.4).

6. If the range of data to be charted is not correct, drag across the
   new range or edit the range reference in the dialog box.

7. Click the Next button or press the Enter key to continue to the next
   ChartWizard dialog box.

T I P   Clicking the Fast Forward button (>>) bypasses the intermediate steps
and produces a column chart. You can back up and make alternative
choices anytime by clicking on the <Back button.

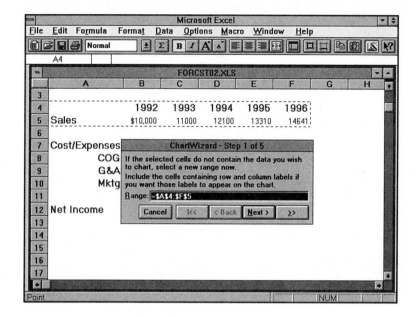

FIG. 17.4

The first ChartWizard
dialog box.

Choosing a Chart Type

Figure 17.5 shows the second ChartWizard dialog box, which indicates
the chart types you can choose.

Perform the following steps to select the type of chart you want to create
from the dialog box:

1. Choose 3-D Pie, and click Next.

   Figure 17.6 shows the third ChartWizard dialog box, which displays
   the different types of 3-D pie charts. Pie charts plot only the first
   series of data points. Therefore, if you had selected multiple rows of
   data, the pie chart would plot only the first row.

2. Choose the labeled pie chart (5), and choose Next.

Specifying the Data Orientation

Figure 17.7 shows a sample of how the completed chart will appear. The
sample that you see in the step 4 dialog box uses the data you selected.

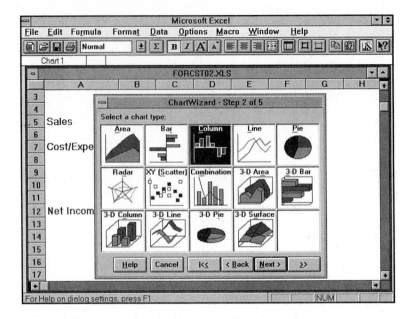

FIG. 17.5

The second ChartWizard dialog box showing available chart types.

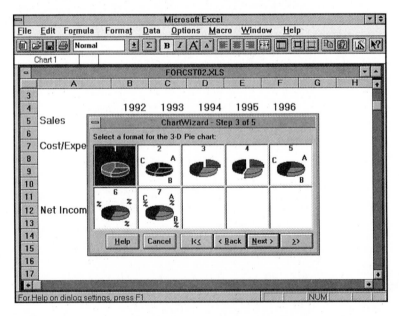

FIG. 17.6

The third ChartWizard dialog box showing different types of 3-D pie charts.

At this point, you can change how Excel plots the data in the range. If, for example, Excel interpreted the layout of your data and labels incorrectly you can change the chart orientation with these options. If data is plotted on the incorrect axis or if data is plotted as labels, you can select options and see the change in the sample.

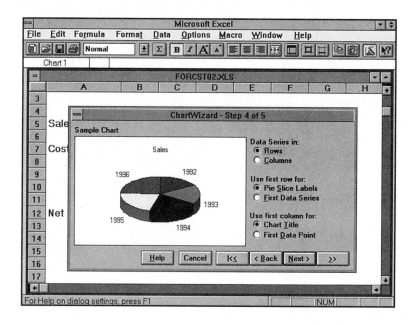

FIG. 17.7

The fourth dialog box shows a sample of your actual chart.

For this example, you do not need to make changes to the settings in the Step 4 of 5 dialog box. Choose the Next button.

Adding a Legend

Figure 17.8 shows the fifth ChartWizard dialog box, which enables you to specify whether you want a legend to appear and provides text edit boxes for entering chart titles and axis labels (on appropriate charts).

The chart type you have chosen already has the pie wedges labeled, so no legend is necessary. Be certain that **No** is selected for legend. Excel already has picked up the *Sales* title from the worksheet, so you do not need to enter a new title. Choose the OK button. Excel embeds a chart on the worksheet (see fig. 17.9).

Formatting a Chart

While the chart is embedded in a worksheet, it is a graphical object. You can format the frame enclosing the embedded chart; you can round its edge, put in a shadow border, protect the chart, or move and resize it. But, if you want to edit, enhance, or format the contents of an embedded chart, you must open it in a window.

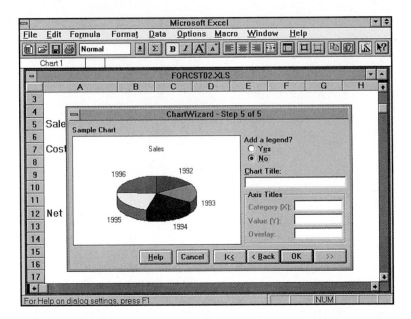

FIG. 17.8

The fifth dialog box enables you to add titles and legends.

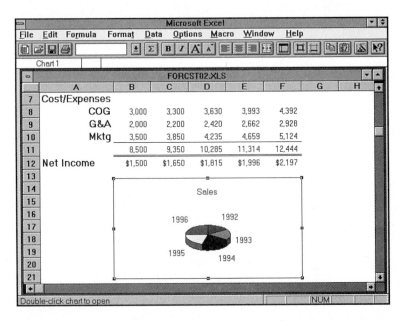

FIG. 17.9

An embedded chart.

To open the embedded chart in a window, double-click the embedded chart (see fig. 17.10). The chart will open into a document window. To return this chart to its embedded location, close the chart's window. Keep the window open while completing the following steps.

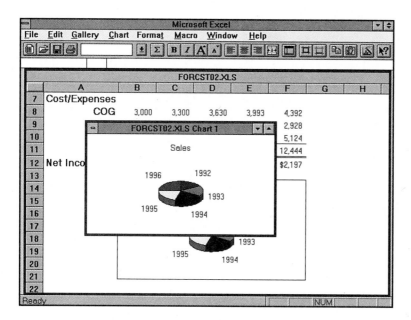

FIG. 17.10

Double-clicking on an embedded chart places it in a window.

Keep the chart's window the same size as the embedded chart in the worksheet. If you change the chart's format while it is enlarged, the new format may not look good when the chart is reduced to fit back into its embedded location. (If all your windows are maximized, click on the double-headed arrow in the menu bar at the far right side.)

Notice that while the chart is in a window, the menus change to chart menus. Chapters 18-20 describe using these menus to format charts in a window.

Moving Pie Chart Wedges

By using a mouse, you can click and drag wedges in and out of the pie chart, as shown in figure 17.11.

Notice that when black handles appear around selected graphical objects, you can move the objects with the mouse. As you withdraw a wedge, the size of the pie decreases. For a presentation, pull the wedge out only a short distance.

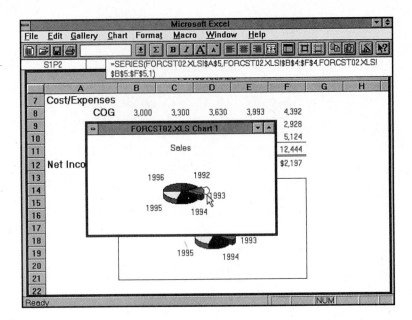

The black handles (squares) that appear around some objects when selected indicate that you can drag the object to a new location. White handles around a selected object indicate that the object is in a fixed position. You can drag legends to new locations on a chart. You also can drag bars, columns, and line markers in 2-D charts to new positions.

Closing an Embedded Chart Window

While an embedded chart is in a window, you can change its format. To return the chart to its original embedded object, close the window. Choose the **File Close** command, or double-click on the chart's Control menu icon.

Saving a Chart

If you created an embedded chart, saving the worksheet saves the chart in it. If you want to save the embedded chart as a separate document, double-click the embedded chart so that it appears in its own window (refer to fig. 17.11). Save the chart with the **File Save As** command.

Printing a Chart

To print a chart that is embedded in a worksheet, simply print the worksheet. To print a chart that is a separate document, perform the following steps:

1. Activate the chart window by pressing Ctrl+F6 or by choosing the chart from the **Windows** menu.

2. Choose the **File Print** Preview command.

3. Choose OK or press Enter.

4. Change margins by clicking the **Margins** button and dragging a margin handle to a new location.

5. To print, choose the **Print** button. To close the preview without printing, choose the **Close** button.

Chapter Summary

If you leave your chart open in its own window, you can experiment with it while you skim through the chapters on charting. You might want to explore how you can replace columns and bars with pictures. You can, for example, create a picture chart using pictures, such as stacked cars, for the columns. You also can rotate and zoom 3-D charts. If you are interested in drawing on a worksheet or including graphical images from other programs or scanners, read Chapter 9, "Drawing and Placing Graphics in Worksheets."

Creating Charts

By using Excel, you can create charts that are appropriate for any boardroom presentation. When you analyze a worksheet or database and need to visually present your results, you can use any of Excel's predesigned formats or completely customize the chart by adding text, arrows, titles, and legends as well as change shading, overlay, patterns, and borders. When you print the chart on a laser printer or plotter, the quality rivals that of charts created by graphic art firms.

This chapter explains the details of creating a chart. The next chapter explains the custom formatting features available for Excel charts and how to create picture charts. After finishing these two chapters, you will be able to meet the majority of business charting needs. The final charting chapter explains how to analyze worksheet data by moving chart markers, how to use advanced techniques for manipulating charts, and how to troubleshoot problems in charts.

Figures 18.1 and 18.2 are examples of charts you can create by using Excel. Figure 18.1 is a chart in its own document. Figure 18.2 illustrates how you can embed charts on a worksheet. Embedded charts display and print with the worksheet.

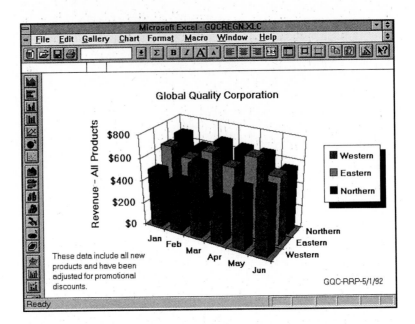

FIG. 18.1

A sample Excel chart.

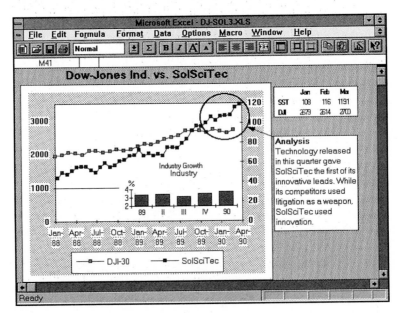

FIG. 18.2

Embed or paste charts
on worksheets for
better understanding.

You can improve 1-2-3 graphs by using Excel. Retrieve the 1-2-3 worksheet and its current and named graphs by choosing Excel's File Open command, changing the file name wild cards from *.XL* to *.WK* so that you can see 1-2-3 file names, and opening the 1-2-3 worksheet that contains the graphs. When Excel automatically translates and opens the 1-2-3 files, the program also converts the active 1-2-3 graph and any named graphs into Excel charts. Then you can use Excel's charting power to change, enhance, or print the chart as you want it.

Excel does not translate 1-2-3 PrintGraph files that use the file extension PIC. Only graphs in the worksheet are translated. When you save the translated 1-2-3 worksheet, save it as an Excel document with File Save As. Select the Save File as Type pull-down list and select Normal, the type designation for Excel 4 files. (Changing the file extension to an XLS extension will not work. You must use the pull-down list.) Charts created from 1-2-3 worksheets opened in Excel cannot be saved back to 1-2-3.

T I P

Reviewing the Charting Process

Excel creates charts for you from data you select. To draw the chart, the application uses certain rules that are based on how the data is configured. The data orientation determines which cells will be used for the *category axis,* the labels along the bottom or x-axis, and which cells will be used for the *legend* labels. In most cases, the rules fit standard data layout, so Excel charts come out correctly without your intervention.

Defining Chart Terms

Excel charts contain many different objects that you can select and modify individually. Figure 18.3 shows some of these objects, and each object is described in table 18.1.

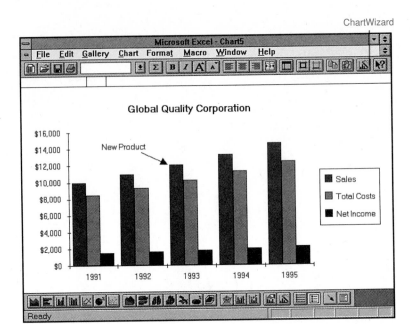

ChartWizard

FIG. 18.3

The parts of a chart.

Table 18.1. The Parts of an Excel Chart

Object	Description
Arrow	A movable and sizable object that you can format as an arrow or a line. Charts can have multiple arrows.
Axis	The category axis and value axis form the boundaries of a chart and contain the scale against which data plots. The category axis is the horizontal or x-axis along the bottom of most charts and frequently refers to time series. The value axis is the vertical or y-axis against which data points are measured. A z-axis is used for the third dimension on 3-D charts. (Axes for bar charts are reversed. Pie charts have no axes.)
Data point	A single piece of data, such as sales for one year.
Data series	A collection of data points, such as sales for the years from 1991 to 1996. In a line chart, all points in a data series are connected by the same line.

Object	Description
Legend	A guide that explains the symbols, patterns, or colors used to differentiate data series. The name of each data series is used as a legend title. Legends may be moved anywhere on a chart.
Marker	An object representing a data point in a chart. Bars, pie wedges, and symbols are examples of markers. All the markers belonging to the same data series appear as the same shape, symbol, and color. In 2-D line, bar, column, and XY scatter charts, Excel can use pictures drawn in Windows graphics programs as markers.
Plot area	The rectangular area bounded by the two axes. This area also exists around a pie chart. A pie chart does not exceed the plot area when wedges are extracted.
Series formula	An external reference formula that tells Excel where to look on a specific worksheet to find the data for a chart. A chart may be linked to multiple worksheets.
Text	Attached text, such as titles or axis titles, cannot be moved. Unattached text can be moved to any location on the chart and also may be used as text or blank boxes.
Tick mark	A division mark along the category (X) axis.
Toolbar	A special toolbar is available with charting tools.

Understanding How To Create a Chart

Excel has three different methods by which you can create a chart. With any of these methods, you must first select the data to be charted.

If you have a mouse, Excel will guide you through the process of embedding a chart within a worksheet. To embed a chart you must first select the data, then choose the ChartWizard tool found in the Standard toolbar. The ChartWizard presents a series of screens with alternatives. Using the ChartWizard is the easiest method of creating a chart which you can then enhance with commands. The section "Creating Charts with the ChartWizard" describes this process.

You also can create a chart by selecting data and opening a chart document by using the File New command. Excel automatically creates a chart as a separate document that is linked to the worksheet. Chart documents can be fully customized the same as embedded charts. This chart document can be saved and printed separately. If you want to embed a chart document into a worksheet, you can copy it and paste it into a worksheet. The section "Creating a Chart Automatically" describes this process.

You also can create a chart manually by opening a blank chart and pasting data into it. This technique is useful when creating complex XY scatter charts or when creating charts with data from different worksheets. The section "Creating a Chart Manually" describes this process.

The chart you create can be in its own chart window, as a separate document, or embedded within a worksheet. Charts that are a separate document maintain link to data in a worksheet. They print separately from the worksheet. Embedded charts also maintain links to their source date, but they can be printed as part of the worksheet.

Creating Charts with the ChartWizard

The easiest method of creating charts is using the mouse and the ChartWizard. The ChartWizard guides you through the creation process and shows you a sample of the chart you are creating, so that you can see the effect of your choices before the chart is complete. This method is especially helpful when you are using data that is not arranged in a layout that Excel automatically recognizes.

The ChartWizard tool looks like a magic wand inside a chart. The ChartWizard tool is located on the right side of the Standard toolbar when it is docked under the menu (refer to fig. 18.3). You must use a mouse to operate the ChartWizard.

The ChartWizard embeds a chart in your worksheet. This process places the chart in the worksheet next to tables, calculations, and text. Figure 18.2 shows an embedded chart. Before you can embed a chart, you should insert rows, columns, or cells in the worksheet to make room for the chart.

Selecting the Data

To create a chart with the ChartWizard, complete the following steps:

1. Select the data you want to chart.

2. Click on the ChartWizard tool.

3. Drag across the cells you want to contain the chart; then release the mouse button.

You can drag to the edges or middle of cells; you are not restricted to keeping the chart aligned with cell boundaries.

The first of a series of ChartWizard dialog boxes will appear. Follow the directions in these boxes. The next sections describe each of the ChartWizard dialog boxes you will see.

> If you want to align the chart with cell edges, hold down the Alt key as you drag across where the chart will be embedded. If you want the chart to be square, hold down the Shift key as you drag.
>
> **T I P**

The following are some of the rules for selecting cells for the ChartWizard:

- Select non contiguous data, if necessary, by holding down the Ctrl key as you drag across each additional series of data.

- If one series of data includes a cell with a label, then all must include a cell in the same position, even if the cell is blank.

For a greater clarification of how Excel builds a chart from different data layouts, see the sections "Understanding Excel's Standard Data Layout" and "Understanding Excel's Non-Standard Data Layout" in this chapter.

Understanding ChartWizard Dialog Boxes

The ChartWizard dialog boxes display control buttons similar to VCR controls. Figure 18.4 shows one of the ChartWizard dialog boxes with the buttons labeled.

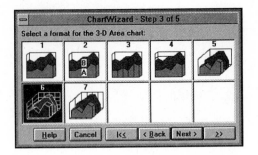

FIG. 18.4

ChartWizard dialog
boxes use buttons
similar to those on a
VCR.

The ChartWizard buttons control the following actions:

Button	Action
Next>	Go to the next step in the ChartWizard.
<Back	Go to the previous step in the ChartWizard.
>>	Fast forward; complete the chart by using the selections made so far.
|<<	Fast reverse; return to the first step of the ChartWizard.
Cancel	Return to the worksheet without creating a chart.
Help	Display a Help window describing what to do at this point.

T I P   Choosing the >> button in the first step of the ChartWizard creates the
chart by using the preferred chart format. If you have not set a preferred chart format, Excel creates a chart in the default format, 2-D
column.

Verifying the Chart Data Range

The ChartWizard displays a series of dialog boxes that guide you
through making the chart. The first dialog box, shown in figure 18.5, enables you to correct your data selection if it is incorrect. You can edit
the data range in the **R**ange edit box. Edit as you would in the Formula
Bar. Click in the reference range, or press F2, the edit key. You can reenter ranges or cells by dragging across the worksheet behind the dialog
box. Ranges of noncontiguous data are separated in the **R**ange box by a
comma.

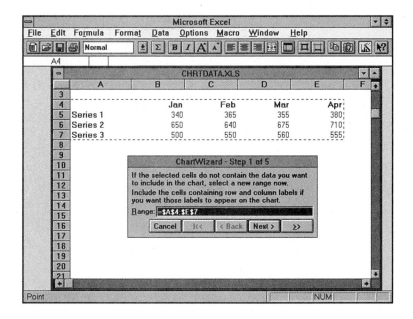

FIG. 18.5

The first dialog box enables you to change the range.

Add a data series to a chart by extending the reference in the **R**ange edit box in the Step 1 dialog box. Click the insertion point at the end of the existing range, type a comma, then drag across the cells you want included. (A comma separates a series of data.) If the original data ranges included a cell with a label, the added range should include a cell.

T I P

Defining the Chart Type

When you verify the range and choose the Next button, the second dialog box, shown in figure 18.6, appears. This dialog box enables you to choose one of the many types of Excel charts. In figure 18.6, the 3-D Column type has been selected. These chart types are described later in this chapter. Click on the chart type you want, or press the arrow keys to select a format; then press Enter. The default chart type will be the preferred chart format.

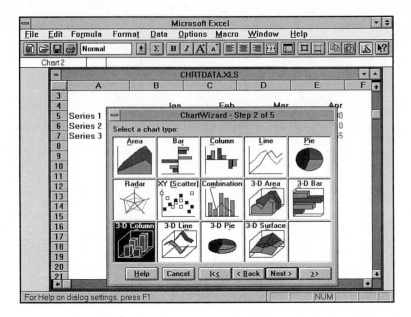

FIG. 18.6

You can choose from many basic chart types in the second dialog box.

Choose the Next button to confirm the chart type. The third Chart-Wizard dialog box enables you to choose the predefined format used for the chart type you selected. In figure 18.7, format 6 is selected. You can choose from 14 chart types, and each has many predefined formats. Examples of these predefined formats can be found in the section "Choosing a Predefined Chart Format." Predefined formats may include gridlines, marker overlaps, and labeling.

Changing How Excel Interprets Data Layout

After you define the chart type and its predefined format, the fourth dialog box appears. This dialog box displays a sample chart using the actual data and labels you have selected (see fig. 18.8).

In this dialog box, you have the opportunity to make corrections if Excel has not correctly drawn the chart. Excel may not draw a chart correctly if the data is not in a layout that Excel understands. The sections "Understanding Excel's Standard Data Layout" and "Understanding Excel's Non-Standard Data Layout" describe how Excel expects data to be laid out on a worksheet.

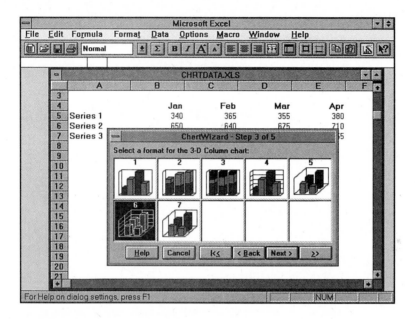

FIG. 18.7

Choose a predefined format for your basic chart type from dialog box 3.

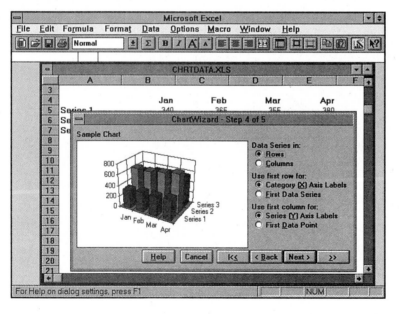

FIG. 18.8

Change a chart's orientation if Excel did not understand the data layout.

If the sample chart does not correctly portray your data and labels, select the clear option of a pair to reverse how Excel interprets the data selection. The following table explains how the options affect the chart. Choose Next to go to the next dialog box.

Changing the options haphazardly can create a confusing chart. In dialog box 4, the titles for the groups of option will change depending upon your selection of Data Series in: options. Begin at the top option group and work down. Consider the following troubleshooting guidelines if your chart does not appear correct:

- If Category (X) Axis Labels appear in the legend, and vice versa, then select the other option in Data Series in:.

- If the sample chart displays numbers as Category (X) Axis Labels and it should display labels, then select the Category (**X**) Axis Labels option.

- If you did not include a series of Category (X) Axis Labels and the sample chart is missing a series of data, then select the **F**irst Data Series option.

- If you included a label in each data series you selected but no labels appear on the Series (Y) Axis or in the legend, then select the Series (**Y**) Axis Labels option.

- If you did not include a label in each data series you selected and your sample chart is missing one data point, then select the First **D**ata Point option.

Add Legends and Titles

The final ChartWizard dialog box enables you to add or remove a legend, which is a box that labels colors or patterns used (see fig. 18.9). Legends also contain text edit boxes so that you can add titles that are fixed in locations on the chart. If your preferred chart format uses a legend, then a legend will be preselected. Depending on the type of chart you are making, some titles may not be available to you.

Add a title as you would edit in a dialog box. Click in the edit box, and type or press Alt+letter and type.

When you type a title in an edit box, do not press Enter. Type the title, then tab to the next title, and the title will appear in the sample chart. You can edit in these text edit boxes as you would normally. When you're satisfied with the titles, choose OK or press Enter.

After you choose OK or press Enter in the final ChartWizard dialog box, Excel will embed the chart you created into the area you selected on the worksheet (see fig. 18.10).

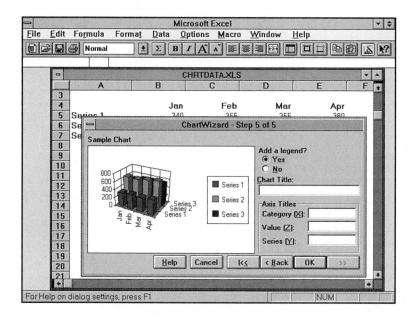

FIG. 18.9

Add legends and fixed titles in the final ChartWizard dialog box.

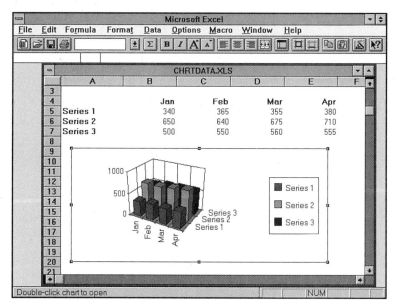

FIG. 18.10

The ChartWizard embeds its chart in the worksheet.

The embedded chart is now part of the worksheet. It will save and open with the worksheet. To enhance the chart or make formatting changes, you must open the chart into its own window.

Opening an Embedded Chart for Formatting

A chart embedded in the worksheet prints and saves with the worksheet. You must open an embedded chart into its own window if you want to edit or format it.

To open the embedded chart into a document window so that it can be edited or saved as a separate document, double-click on it. The chart appears in a window the same size as when embedded. You can use any of the editing or enhancing techniques described in the remaining chart chapters while the chart is in a window. While the embedded chart is in a window, you also can save a duplicate of it as a separate chart file. Use the **File Save** or **Save As** command if you wish to save it separately.

When you are finished enhancing or editing, return the embedded chart to its document by closing the chart's window. Use the **File Close** command, press Ctrl+F4, or double-click on the window's Control menu icon to close the window.

T I P Do not change the size of the chart window for embedded charts. To edit or enhance an embedded chart, you must open the embedded chart into a window by double-clicking on the chart. The chart opens into a window that is the same size as the embedded chart. If you change the size of the window, add arrows or floating text, or change font sizes, you may find that items move out of position or text is the wrong size when you put the chart back into the document.

FROM HERE...

For Related Information:

◄◄ "Using the ChartWizard," p. 651.

►► "Adding and Formatting Text," p. 717.

►► "Adding and Formatting Legends," p. 724.

Creating a Chart Automatically

Although using the ChartWizard is the easiest method for creating charts, you also can easily create charts by using the keyboard with menu commands or shortcut keys. If the data is in a layout that Excel can interpret, you need only to select the data and press F11 to create a chart. (Press Alt+F1 if you don't have an F11 key.)

Excel uses three rules to decide how a chart will be created from the selected cells. If the cells you have selected do not meet these rules, you must create your chart by using the procedures in the section "Creating a Chart Manually."

Understanding How Excel Builds a Chart

Excel can automatically build a chart for you from selected data and labels if the selected area follows three rules. Excel uses these rules to understand what should be on the horizontal Category (X) axis, what should be on the vertical Value (Y) axis, and where cell labels used for legend titles are located.

Before you learn the rules, you must understand the terms *series* and *point*. These terms describe how the data will be used by a chart. Understanding how Excel builds a chart from the data on a worksheet will prevent you from building charts with reversed axes or labels.

A *series* is a collection of associated data, such as the dollar amounts sold of the Global Quality bicycle, the forecast in units for specific products, or the readings from each of three specific medical instruments. When charted, the data from a series appears as a single line or as bars or columns of the same color.

A *point* is a single piece of data within any of the series. Examples of points in most charts are time sequences, such as years, quarters, or months. A point appears in a chart as a single dot on a line or one column out of a series.

Labels for the Category (X) axis and legends can be entered in cells in the worksheet and Excel will use them as labels in the chart. When charted correctly, the label for each point—month for example—appears along the horizontal Category (X) axis. The series labels appear as titles in the legend (see fig. 18.11).

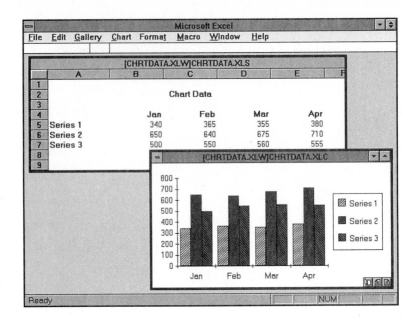

FIG. 18.11

A selection wider than it is tall plots its graph with category labels from the top row.

Excel uses the following three rules to interpret how series and points are laid out on the worksheet:

- When Excel examines the data you have selected, the program assumes that the Category (X) axis runs along the longest side of the selection. If the selection is square or wider than it is tall, as in figure 18.11, then Excel assumes that the category labels run across the top row of the selection. If the selection is taller than it is wide, as in figure 18.12, then Excel assumes that the category labels run down the left column of the selection.

- Excel assumes that labels in cells along the short side of the selection should be used as titles in the legend for each data series. If only one data series exists, Excel uses that label to title the chart. If more than one data series is selected, Excel uses the labels in cells to title the legend.

- If the contents of the cells that Excel wants to use as category labels are numbers (not text or dates), then Excel displays the dialog box shown in figure 18.13. This dialog box enables you to tell Excel whether a side of the data range contains the first data series, Category (X) axis labels, or the X values for an XY scattergram chart.

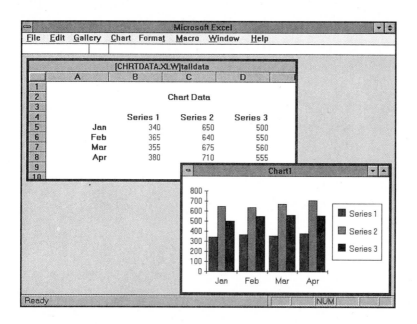

FIG. 18.12

A selection taller than it is wide plots with category labels from the left column.

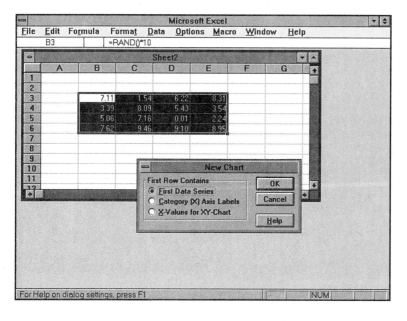

FIG. 18.13

This dialog box asks you to specify the contents of the long side of the selection.

If the dialog box shown in figure 18.13 displays, select one of the following options to describe the data along the longest side of your selection. (Your dialog box may request a description for the first row or column.)

■ Choose **F**irst Data Series if the data along the longest side of the selection is a series of data that should be plotted as a line, bar, or column. Because no category labels exist, Excel uses numbers (1, 2, 3,...) for category labels.

■ Choose **C**ategory (X) Axis Labels if the data along the longest side of the selection should be used as labels for the Category (X) axis.

■ Choose **X**-Values for XY-Chart if the data along the longest side of the selection should be used as X data for a scattergram or an XY chart. The chart then is created as an XY or a scattergram type.

Creating a Chart Automatically

To build a chart that has the correct orientation of category data along the longest side, complete the following steps:

1. Select the data and labels, as shown in figure 18.14.

   Notice that the selected range includes more data points—the months—than data series; the range has three series and four data points in each series. A data series in this example is a collection of related data—all the sales for one product, for example.

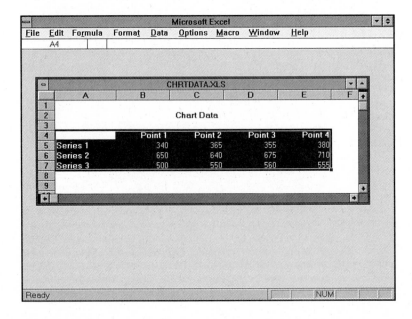

FIG. 18.14

A worksheet with three data series.

2. Press F11. (Press Alt+F1 if you don't have an F11 key.)

Or Choose the **File New** command, select Chart, and then choose OK or press Enter.

Excel plots the data in the preferred chart type; the default is the 2-D column chart. Figure 18.15 shows a column chart created with the preceding steps.

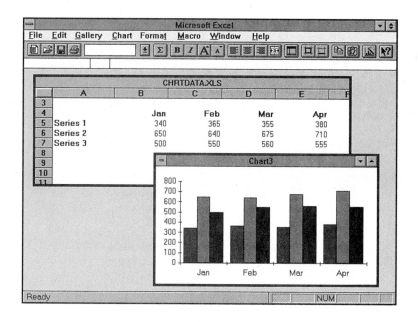

FIG. 18.15

An example of a column chart.

In the chart in figure 18.15, notice that the points (months from the top row of the worksheet data) are used as category labels below the Category (X) axis. What would happen if a series of data was listed down a column as in figure 18.16? If you select the data shown in figure 18.16 and press F11, the chart in figure 18.17 appears. Notice that the chart still is drawn correctly. In this case, Excel assumes that the data series again goes in the long direction. Because the long direction is in columns, Category (X) axis labels are taken from the left column.

In the preceding two examples, Excel drew a correct chart. Excel, however, can create an incorrectly oriented chart if the data is laid out so that it doesn't match the rules Excel uses. When this happens, you need to create your chart manually, as described in the following section.

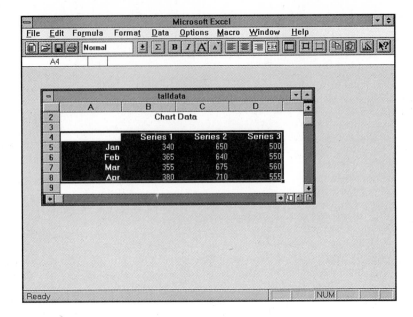

FIG. 18.16

A worksheet with the
data series down a
column.

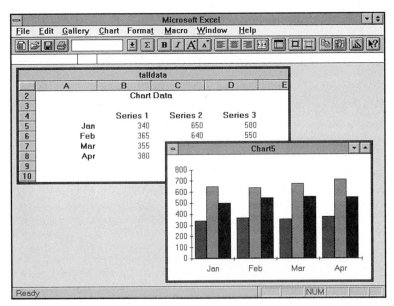

FIG. 18.17

The chart created from
the vertical data series.

T I P

Numbers along the category axis indicate that you forgot to select category labels. If you did not include a row or column of labels for the Category (X) axis, the chart will show a sequence of numbers beginning with 1 along that axis.

If you want to create a chart from data that is not in adjacent rows or columns, such as the selection shown in figure 18.18, select the rows or columns by using the Ctrl drag method with the mouse or by pressing Shift+F8 on the keyboard. Select the Category (X) axis cells first; then select Value (Y) data cells in the same order in which you want the value series to appear on the chart.

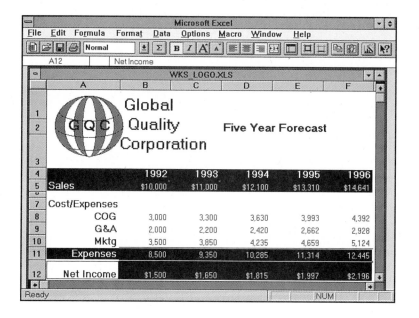

FIG. 18.18

Select nonadjacent cells to chart nonadjacent data.

Creating a Chart Manually

When your data is laid out in a nonstandard way so that Excel cannot automatically create a chart, you must change the layout of your data or create the chart manually. This section describes how to create charts manually by copying data from the worksheet and pasting the data into a blank chart.

Understanding Non-Standard Data Layout

When the data you select for a chart does not meet Excel's three rules for charting, Excel still may create a chart, but it may not be correct. A typical problem indicating that you need to create a chart manually is that your chart's horizontal Category (X) labels appear in the legend and labels used for the series appear in the Category (X) axis (see fig. 18.19).

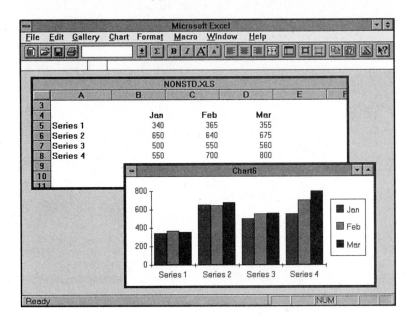

FIG. 18.19

A chart where series and points are reversed.

Another problem occurs if Excel cannot find cell contents along the long side of the selection to use as Category (X) labels. When this errpr happens, the Category (X) axis displays a series of integers—1, 2, 3, and so on. Figure 18.20 shows how such a chart looks.

The following rules describe when to create a chart manually:

- When the Category (X) axis labels, such as months, are along the short side of the selection, create the chart manually.

- When the labels along the long side of the selection should be used in the legend, create the chart manually.

- When a number appears in the top-left corner of the selection, Excel may misinterpret whether the first row or column is data or labels; you may need to create the chart manually.

- When you try to create a chart and don't get what you want, create your chart manually by using the procedures for a nonstandard data layout.

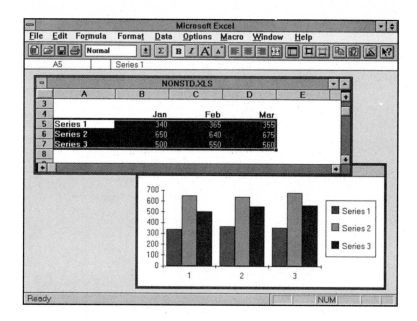

FIG. 18.20

A chart that did not have labels for use along the category axis.

Creating a Chart Manually

To create a chart manually, you copy the selected data from the worksheet and then paste the data into a blank chart document. When you paste into the blank chart, a dialog box asks for the correct orientation of data series and where labels are located.

Suppose, for example, that you have a column chart with more series than it has data points. In other words, the Category (X) axis is along the short side of the selection. Also, suppose that the selection includes series labels that may be needed later for legend titles. If created automatically, the chart appears as shown in figure 18.21. The series labels appear along the Category (X) axis and the point labels appear in the legend, which is the reverse of the configuration you want.

Use the ChartWizard with nonstandard data layout when possible. When you create charts from the ChartWizard, you have the opportunity to specify whether series are in columns or rows and whether a row contains Category (X) labels or contains legend titles. When you try these different alternatives in the ChartWizard, you can see the effect in the sample chart and that chart uses your actual data.

T I P

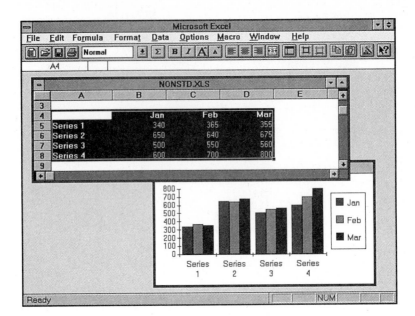

FIG. 18.21

An automatically created chart with series and points reversed.

To create a chart manually, complete the following steps:

1. Select the data as shown in figure 18.22.

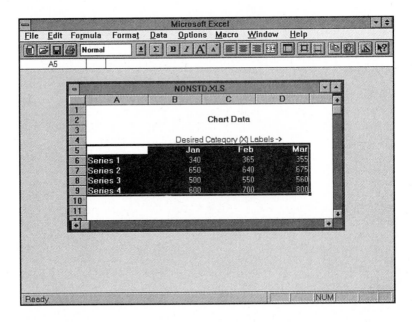

FIG. 18.22

A layout of data from which Excel does not create the correct chart automatically.

Notice that the data selected violates rules for automatic charting. The actual Category (X) axis side of the data is narrower than the number of series.

2. Later in the procedure, you must make selections from a dialog box to orient your chart correctly. Consider the following pieces of information about your data:

   ■ Which way are Y values (a plotted line) oriented: across rows or down columns? These are the series.

   ■ If Category (X) labels exist, are they across the top row or down the left column?

   ■ If series (legend) labels exist, are they across the top row or down the left column?

3. Choose the Edit Copy command.

4. Press F11. Or choose File New, Chart, and OK.

5. Choose the Edit Paste Special command to display the dialog box shown in figure 18.23.

   The Paste Special dialog box appears with options selected that would create a chart automatically. If the chart Excel created automatically had its series and data labels reversed, select the opposite option from the one that appears selected in Values (Y) in Rows/Columns.

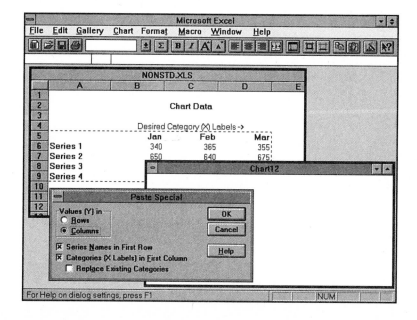

FIG. 18.23

The Paste Special dialog box enables you to change chart orientation and determine which labels are used.

6. Select Values (Y) in **R**ows if each series of Y data goes across a row, or select Values (Y) in **C**olumns if each series of Y data goes down a column.

7. If your selection includes series names (used in legend titles) for each set of Y values, select Series **N**ames in First Column (Row).

NOTE The text in the Paste Special dialog box changes between Column and Row, depending on your selection in step 6. For the book's example, you select Series **N**ames in First Column. If you are not aware that the text changes, the dialog box options can be confusing.

8. If your selection encloses Category (X) labels, select the Categories (X Labels) in **F**irst Row (Column) option.

NOTE The option text here changes between Row and Column, depending on your selection in step 6. For the book's example, you select Categories (X Labels) in **F**irst Row.

9. Choose OK or press Enter.

10. Choose the **G**allery menu, and select the chart type you want.

Figure 18.24 shows a completed column chart and data.

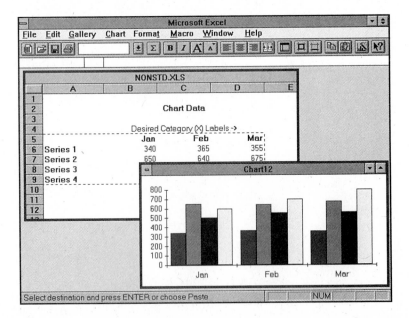

FIG. 18.24

The manually created chart.

For Related Information:

◀◀ "Combining Data and Charts on the Same Page," p. 328.

◀◀ "Embedding Linked Pictures of Charts in a Worksheet," p. 329.

FROM HERE...

Embedding a Chart Document

You can create a chart on a worksheet in two ways. You can embed the chart on the worksheet, as described in the ChartWizard section at the beginning of the chapter (see fig. 18.25). Or you can create a chart in its own document window, as the previous sections describe, and then copy and paste the chart onto a worksheet.

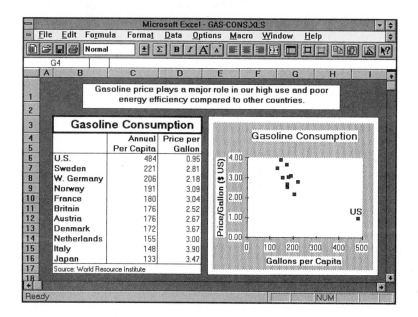

FIG. 18.25

A chart embedded on a worksheet.

To create an embedded chart when the Chart toolbar is displayed, perform the following steps:

1. Select the data to be charted.

2. Click on the chart tool that shows the format you want.

3. Drag across the worksheet where you want the chart embedded.

Perform the following steps to embed a chart in a window into a worksheet:

1. With the chart window active, select the chart by choosing the **C**hart Select **C**hart command.

2. Choose the **E**dit **C**opy command.

3. Activate the worksheet, and select the cell at which you want to place the top-left corner of the chart.

4. Choose the **E**dit **P**aste command to embed the chart into the worksheet.

For Related Information:

◄◄ "Combining Data and Charts on the Same Page," p. 328.

◄◄ "Embedding Linked Pictures of Charts in a Worksheet," p. 329.

Choosing a Predefined Chart Format

Excel offers you eight different 2-D chart types and six different 3-D chart types. Within each of these general types, you can select predefined formats. The easiest way to create charts is to select the predefined chart closest to the type you want. Then you can customize the predefined chart until it fits your needs. You should select a predefined chart format before you begin customizing your chart.

 NOTE   Choosing a new chart type from the gallery or the toolbar may remove some custom formatting from your chart. Instead of choosing from the gallery to change a basic chart type, use the Format **M**ain Chart or Forma**t O**verlay commands. They enable you to change types but preserve formats.

 To choose a chart type from the Chart toolbar, perform the following steps:

1. Activate the chart you want to change.

2. Click on the chart tool for the type of chart you want.

You can see the name of the chart type in the Status Bar if you click and hold on the tool. If this is not the type of chart you want, drag off the tool before releasing the mouse button.

To apply a predefined chart, perform the following steps:

1. Activate the chart you want to change by clicking the chart window, pressing Ctrl+F6, or choosing the chart's name from the **W**indow menu.

2. Select the **G**allery command.

3. From the menu, choose one of these charts:

> **A**rea
>
> **B**ar
>
> **C**olumn
>
> **L**ine
>
> **P**ie
>
> R**a**dar
>
> **S**catter
>
> **C**ombination
>
> 3-D Area
>
> **3**-D Bar
>
> 3-D **C**olumn
>
> 3-D **L**ine
>
> 3-D **P**ie
>
> 3-D S**u**rface

After you make your choice, you see a dialog box showing the different predefined formats available for that chart. Figure 18.26 shows the gallery of formats available for area charts.

4. Select the chart format you want by clicking the square or typing the number.

Or, if the chart you want is not visible, choose the **N**ext or **P**revious button to go to the next or previous type in the gallery until you reach the chart type you want. Then select a predefined format.

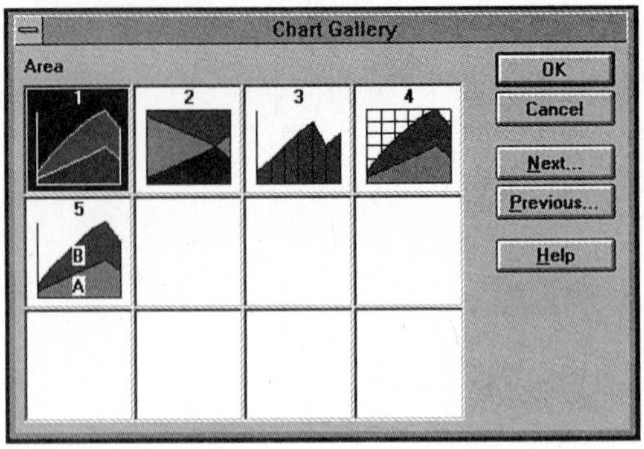

FIG. 18.26

The gallery of predefined area chart formats.

5. Choose OK or press Enter.

T I P
To select the predefined chart type you want in the gallery, double-click the box containing the chart. This technique selects the type and chooses OK.

Reviewing Types of 2-D Charts

Excel's six 2-D chart types plus combination charts give you many options. This section examines how each type of chart generally is used. This information will help you select the correct type of chart to match your data.

Area Charts

The gallery of area charts is shown in figure 18.26. An *area chart* compares the continuous change in volume of series of data. This type of chart adds the data from all the individual series to create the top line that encloses the area, giving the viewer an impression of how different series contribute to the total volume. Use the area chart in sales and production to show how volume changes over time and to emphasize the amount or volume of change. The subjects of area charts may be similar to line charts, such as units shipped per day or the volume of orders over time.

Bar Charts

The gallery of bar charts is shown in figure 18.27. A *bar chart* is used for comparing distinct (noncontinuous), unrelated items over time. This chart type gives little impression of time but uses horizontal bars to show positive or negative variation from a center point. You can use a bar chart to give a *single point in time* snapshot of budget variance for different items. Bars to the left of center have negative variance, and those to the right have positive variance.

In 2-D bar charts, you can drag a point to a new position, and the worksheet solves backward to meet that result.

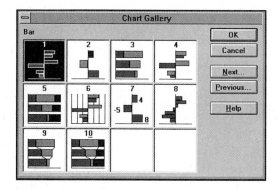

FIG. 18.27

The gallery of bar charts.

Column Charts

The gallery of column charts is shown in figure 18.28. *Column charts* often compare separate (noncontinuous) items as they vary over time. This chart type uses vertical columns to give the impression of distinct measurements made at different intervals. Column charts frequently are used for comparing different items by placing them side-by-side. In the chart Quick Start in Chapter 17, for example, the total sales and total costs are charted in columns by the month.

In a 2-D column chart, you can drag a point to a new position, and the worksheet solves backward to meet that result.

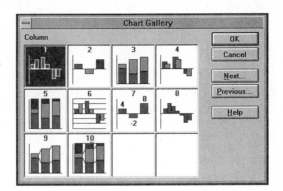

FIG. 18.28

The gallery of column charts.

Line Charts

The gallery of line charts is shown in figure 18.29. A *line chart* compares trends over even time or measurement intervals plotted on the Category (X) axis. (If your Category [X] data points are at uneven intervals, use an XY scatter chart.) Use the line chart in production, sales, or stock market charts to show the trend of revenue or sales over time. In the hi-lo and hi-lo-close charts, numbers 7 and 8 in the gallery, point lines extend from the highest to the lowest value in each category. In the stock market, hi-lo-close charts show the high, low, and closing stock prices on each day.

In a 2-D line chart, you can drag a point to a new position, and the worksheet solves backward to meet that result.

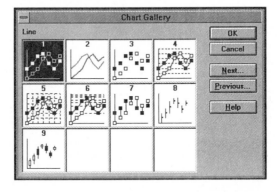

FIG. 18.29

The gallery of line charts.

Pie Charts

The gallery of pie charts is shown in figure 18.30. A *pie chart* compares the size of each of the pieces in a whole unit. Use this type of chart when the parts total 100 percent for a single series of data. Only the first data series in a worksheet selection is plotted. Pie charts work well to show the percentage of mix in products shipped, mix in income sources, or mix in target populations. Wedges in pie charts can be pulled from the pie.

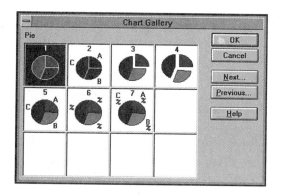

Radar Charts

The gallery of radar charts is shown in figure 18.31. Use radar charts to show the relationship between each of the data series and between a specific series and the whole of the other series.

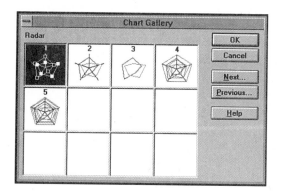

Each category (series label) in the chart has its own axis (spoke). Data points plot along the spoke. Lines that connect the data points define the area covered by the items. For example, radar charts can be used to show how much time is spent on each task in a project. Each task would be a series.

Each spoke on the radar chart represents time spent on a specific task. If all tasks receive the same time, the chart will create a near circle. The larger the total area covered by the plot, the more total time spent on the project.

XY Scatter Charts

The gallery of XY (scatter) charts is shown in figure 18.32. A *scattergram* or *XY chart* compares trends over uneven time or measurement intervals plotted on the Category (X) axis. (If your Category [X] data is at even intervals, use a line chart.) Scatter charts also display patterns from discrete X and Y data measurements. Use scatter charts when you must plot data in which the independent variable is recorded at uneven intervals or the Category (X) data points are not specified in even increments. For example, survey data, when plotted with response on the Value (Y) axis and age on the Category (X) axis, can reveal opinion clusters by age. Much scientific and engineering data is charted with scatter charts.

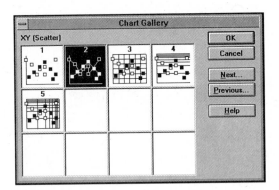

FIG. 18.32

The gallery of XY scatter charts.

Combination Charts

The gallery of combination charts is shown in figure 18.33. A *combination chart* lays one chart over another. This type of chart is helpful when you're comparing data of different types or data requiring different axis scales. After a combination chart is created, you can change the type of chart to be used for the main or overlaid chart by using the Format **Main** Chart or Format **Overlay** command.

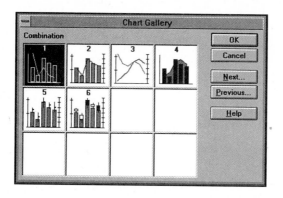

FIG. 18.33

The gallery of
combination charts.

Reviewing Types of 3-D Charts

Excel's 3-D charts are attractive and work well for presentations or marketing materials. When you are using charts for analytical work, you may find more exact data comparison easier on 2-D charts.

3-D Area Charts

3-D area charts are similar to 2-D area charts. The gallery of 3-D area charts is shown in figure 18.34. Use 3-D area charts for the same types of data as those used in 2-D area charts.

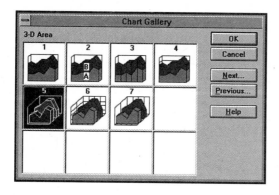

FIG. 18.34

The gallery of 3-D
area charts.

3-D Bar Charts

3-D bar charts are used to show comparison of times over time or against each other. The gallery of 3-D bar charts is shown in figure 18.35.

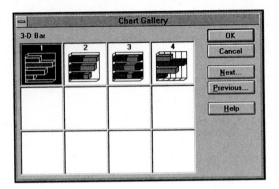

FIG. 18.35

The gallery of 3-D bar charts.

3-D Column Charts

You can create 3-D column charts with the columns adjacent to each other or layered into the third dimension. The gallery of 3-D column charts is shown in figure 18.36. Use 3-D column charts for the same types of data as those used in 2-D column charts.

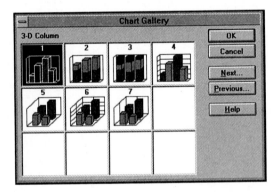

FIG. 18.36

The gallery of 3-D column charts.

3-D Line Charts

3-D line charts also are known as *ribbon charts*. The gallery of 3-D line charts is shown in figure 18.37. Use 3-D line charts for the same types of data as those used in 2-D line charts.

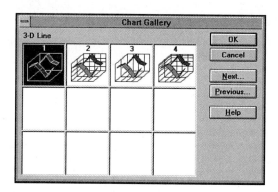

FIG. 18.37

The gallery of 3-D line charts.

3-D Pie Charts

The gallery of 3-D pie charts is shown in figure 18.38. These types of charts work well for marketing materials or presentations in which an overall impression is required. You can pull the wedges from the pie when you need to discuss the contents of that wedge. Excel can show labels or calculate percentages for wedges. Only the first data series from a selection is charted as a pie.

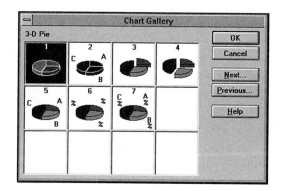

FIG. 18.38

The gallery of 3-D pie charts.

3-D Surface Charts

Surface charts are like topographic maps. They show the high and low points along a surface. Surface charts are an excellent way of visually locating high and low points resulting from two changing variables.

The gallery provides wire frame as well as surface displays (see fig. 18.39). The surface chart, choice 1, shows a surface stretched between points. The color of the surface helps distinguish its value. A color contour chart, choice 3, acts like a topographical map by showing elevations according to color. If you want to see the surface map from a different point of view, click on one of the chart axis corners. When black handles appear at the corners (it may take a moment), drag the handles to rotate the chart. This procedure is described in more detail in later chapters.

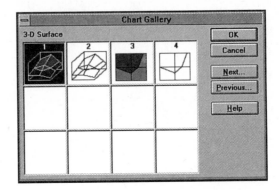

FIG. 18.39

The gallery of 3-D surface charts.

Surface chart types 1 and 2 display a three-dimensional view of the surface. Types 3 and 4 appear more like topographical maps that show changes in elevation with contour lines and colors. Types 2 and 4 display data in a wire frame. The wire frame enables you to more easily compare data points that may be hidden.

T I P   The colors used in 3-D surface maps are defined by the current palette. The number of colors used depends upon the scaling of the vertical axis.

Choosing Line or XY (Scatter) Charts

Line and XY (scatter) charts can be similar in appearance, but they treat data differently when charted. You need to be aware of the differences if you want accurate charts.

You should use a line chart when the Category (X) data points are evenly spaced or when the category data points are text and spacing does not matter. Category (X) data should be in ascending or descending order. Line charts are most commonly used with business or financial charts in which data is distributed evenly over time or in such categories as Sales, Costs, and so on. Such Category (X) data as time should be sequential with no data missing.

You should use an XY (scatter) chart when data is intermittent or un-evenly spaced. When Excel creates a scatter chart, the program reads the lowest and highest values in the Category (X) data and uses these values as the end points for the Category (X) axis. The tick marks in between are placed at even intervals between end points. The data then plots along that Category (X) axis according to the X data value—not at evenly spaced intervals as it would in a line chart.

Figure 18.40 shows data plotted in a line chart that should have been plotted in an XY (scatter) chart. The correctly plotted data in an XY (scatter) chart appears in figure 18.41. Notice the difference in the spacing of missed days in the two charts.

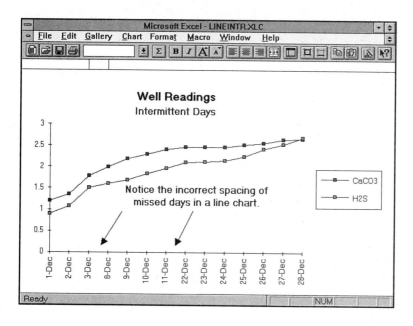

FIG. 18.40

Intermittent data plotted in a line chart, which gives an incorrect impression.

Changing the Chart Type

Using the **G**allery command to change the chart type in an existing chart removes some of the custom formatting you may have added and re-turns the chart to its default colors and patterns. If you need to change the chart type on an existing chart, choose the Forma**t M**ain Chart com-mand to display the Main Chart dialog box shown in figure 18.42. Select the type of chart you want from the Main Chart **Type** list. Then select the specific format for that type from the miniature charts shown in the Data View.

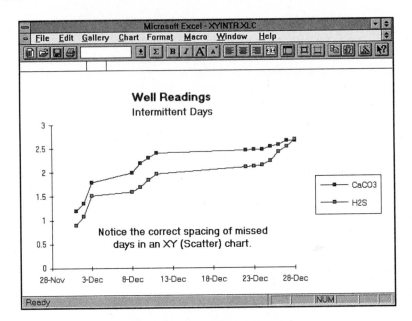

FIG. 18.41

The same data plotted in an XY (scatter) chart, which shows the correct relationships.

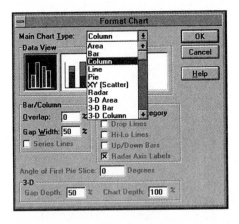

FIG. 18.42

The Format Chart dialog box changes the chart type of existing charts and preserves custom formatting.

Combination charts use two different chart types in one chart. To change the type of chart used in the main or the overlay chart, do not select another type of combination from the **Gallery** menu. Doing so removes your custom format. Instead, use the Format **Main** Chart or Format **Overlay** command to change the type of chart used in the main chart or in the overlay chart. (See Chapter 19 for more detailed information on using the Format Main and Format Overlay Chart commands.)

Choosing a Preferred Chart Format

If you deal with the same chart type and format regularly, you may want to designate a specific type and format for Excel to use as the default for new charts you create. Usually, Excel's preferred chart type is the first predefined 2-D column chart. To change Excel's default chart type and format, activate a chart that has the type and custom formatting you want as the default. Choose the Gallery Set Preferred command. Future charts created during this work session will use your preferred format when they first display. If during this work session you want the active chart to revert to the preferred format, choose the Gallery Preferred command or click on the Preferred Chart tool in the chart toolbar. When you exit Excel, the preferred format is not saved.

If you want to use the preferred format at other times, save the chart as a template that you can open instead of choosing Chart from the File New command. You also can save the chart as part of a workbook. (Workbooks are described in Chapter 11.)

For Related Information:

◄◄ "Working with Multiple Documents," p. 420.

◄◄ "Grouping Documents into Workbooks," p. 426.

►► "Creating a Chart Template," p. 741.

►► "Changing and Modifying Chart Types," p. 743.

FROM HERE...

Adding or Deleting Data

You can add data to your existing charts, regardless of whether they were created automatically or manually. You can choose from two ways to add or delete data from a chart. You can edit the data series, as described in Chapter 20, or you can use the following methods.

To add data to charts, simply copy the data from the worksheet and paste the data onto the chart. If the data that created the chart included cells containing labels, the new data you copy also must include cells for labels, even if those cells are blank.

If you are adding data with a standard layout so that the Category (X) axis is along the longest side of the selection, then choose **E**dit **C**opy to copy the selection, activate the chart, and choose **E**dit **P**aste. The data appears in the chart as a new series.

If the data you want to add uses a nonstandard layout and its Category (X) axis is along the short side of the selection, then choose **E**dit **C**opy to copy the selection, activate the chart, and choose **E**dit Paste **S**pecial. Select from the Paste Special dialog box the options that describe the layout of the data. Usually, you must select the opposite option button from the one selected in the Values (Y) in group option when the box first displays. If the box appears with **R**ows selected, for example, then select **C**olumns. After you change the options button, then select the appropriate check boxes that describe where labels are located. Choose OK to paste the data as a new series onto the chart.

FROM HERE...

For Related Information:

▶▶ "Clearing Chart Formats or Contents," p. 743.

▶▶ "Changing the Data Range with the ChartWizard," p. 756.

▶▶ "Deleting a Data Series," p. 760.

▶▶ "Editing a Data Series," p. 761.

Saving Charts

Embedded charts are saved when you save the worksheet in which they are embedded. Charts in a document window are saved as individual files that contain links to worksheet files.

Save a chart by activating it and then choosing **F**ile Save **A**s. If you attempt to close a chart that has not been saved or that has been changed, Excel asks you to confirm whether you want to save the chart.

Save your worksheet first, then save the chart. Saving in this order stores the correct worksheet name within the saved chart.

For Related Information:

◀◀ "Saving a Chart," p. 660.

FROM HERE...

Changing Chart and Worksheet Links

Charts in document windows are linked to a worksheet file. This link can be lost if you save the worksheet with a new name, change the name of the worksheet file, move the worksheet file to a different directory, or delete the worksheet file.

If one of your charts loses its link to its worksheet, or you need to link a chart to a different worksheet, perform the following steps:

1. Open the chart.

2. If you want to establish a link with a different worksheet, open that worksheet.

3. Activate the chart.

4. Choose the **File Links** command to display the dialog box shown in figure 18.43.

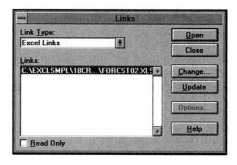

FIG. 18.43

Use the File Links command to open or change source worksheets.

5. Select the worksheet link you want to change in the **Links** list box.

6. Choose the **Change** button.

7. Select from the File **Names** list box the name of the worksheet with which you want to establish or reestablish a link. You may need to change directories or disks to find the file. Use the same directory and drive-changing techniques you use in the File Open or File Save As dialog box.

8. Choose OK or press Enter.

9. Save the worksheet.

10. Save the chart.

Opening Charts

A chart can be in its own document window or embedded in a worksheet. Either chart can be reformatted.

To open a chart embedded in a worksheet, double-click the embedded chart. It opens into a chart window. When you are finished formatting the embedded chart, close its document window by choosing **File Close** or by pressing Ctrl+F4. The chart returns to its embedded area.

To open a chart that is its own document, choose the **File Open** command, select the appropriate file name ending with XLC, and choose OK. When you open a chart in its own document window without opening its source worksheet, a dialog box asks whether you want to update the chart (see fig. 18.44). If you choose **Yes**, the chart uses the current values stored in the worksheet file. Choose **No**, however, and the chart uses the values with which it was saved.

To open the worksheets linked to charts that are already open, choose the **File Links** command. Select the worksheet file name in the **Links** box, and choose the **Open** button.

Printing Charts

Printing charts is similar to printing worksheets. You can print directly from the screen, or you can preview the chart before printing. Previewing a chart gives you a much more accurate view of how the chart will appear when printed. Charts embedded on worksheets print with the worksheets.

> When charts are embedded on a worksheet, you can print them by using the same techniques you use to print worksheets. You can store views and scenarios that involve the embedded charts, then use the File Print Report command to print those views with different scenarios.
>
> **T I P**

Before you print a chart that is in its own document window, decide how large you want the chart to be on the page. Set the size of the chart on the page by using the File Page Setup command to change margins or the File Print Preview command with the Margins button to change margins. The Page Setup dialog box appears when you choose the File Page Setup command. Figure 18.45 shows the dialog box for an HP Series III printer.

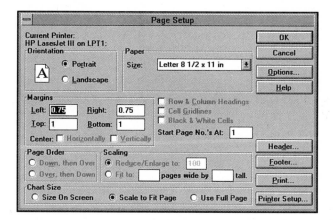

FIG. 18.45

Use the Page Setup dialog box to set a chart's size and other print options.

If you choose fonts that your printer cannot print, the printed chart will not look as it does on-screen. To ensure that your charts use fonts available in your printer, select fonts from the Format Font command dialog box that show a printer icon or the TT icon that indicates TrueType.

Charts react to print area margins in three ways. If you want the chart to print in the approximate size shown on-screen, select the Chart Size group at the bottom of the Page Setup dialog box. If you want the chart to expand proportionally until margins are touched, select Scale to Fit Page. The results of a Scale to Fit Page setting are shown in figure 18.46. If you want the chart to expand in both height and width until margins in all directions are reached, select Use Full Page. The same chart in figure 18.46 is shown with the Use Full Page option in figure 18.47.

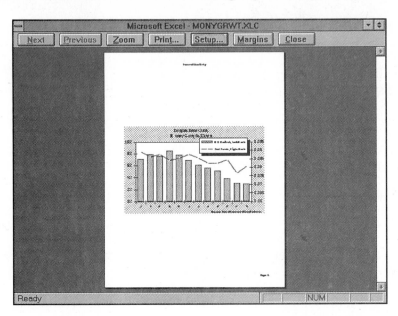

FIG. 18.46

Scale to Fit Page expands a chart proportionally until a page margin is reached.

To preview your chart before printing or to use the mouse to visually adjust chart size or margins, perform the following steps:

1. Choose the File Print Preview command.

2. Examine detail and positioning on the chart by zooming in or out on the page. To zoom in, move the pointer, which is a magnifying glass, over an area of interest and click. Click the zoomed page to return to expanded view. With the keyboard, choose the Zoom button to zoom and unzoom by keyboard.

3. Return to the Page Setup dialog box by selecting the Setup button. If you want the chart to expand in height and width, select the Use Full Page option from the Page Setup dialog box.

4. Adjust margins and the size of the chart by clicking the Margins button. Drag the black handles shown in figure 18.47 to change margins and to change the chart size.

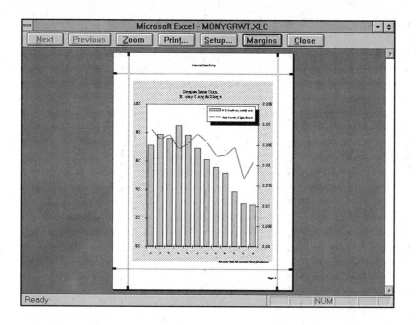

FIG. 18.47

Use Full Page expands a chart on all sides until page margins are reached.

5. Choose **P**rint to display the Print dialog box, or choose **C**lose to return to the chart document.

To print your chart, choose the **F**ile **P**rint command and complete the dialog box. Follow the same procedures as you would for printing a worksheet as described in Chapter 16, "Printing Worksheets."

For Related Information:

FROM HERE...

◄◄ "Combining Data and Charts on the Same Page," p. 328.

◄◄ "Previewing the Document," p. 637.

◄◄ "Creating Reports," p. 644.

◄◄ "Printing a Chart," p. 661.

Chapter Summary

Charts are valuable for communicating information quickly. They enable people to see relationships and detect trends faster than from a table of numbers. If you want to be guided through the building of a chart by ChartWizard and by command, go to the preceding chapter, Chapter 17, "Chart Quick Start," and work through the short exercise.

In the next chapter, you learn how to add your own custom formatting to charts. If you can select a chart item, then you can change its appearance.

Formatting Charts

I n the preceding chapter, you learned that you can produce most charts quickly and easily with Excel. In this chapter, you learn how to apply custom formats to Excel's predefined chart formats.

After you have selected a predefined chart format, you can add lines, arrows, titles, legends, and floating text. You also can create picture charts, in which pictures take the place of columns, bars, or lines.

After you select a predefined chart format, you can change the colors, patterns, and borders of chart items; the type and color of the fonts; the position and size of some chart items; and you can add lines, arrows, titles, legends, and floating text. By selecting an axis and then a format command, you can change the scale and the appearance of tick marks and labels. You also can rotate 3-D charts and create picture charts.

Understanding How To Format Chart Items

After you select one of the predefined chart types, you can customize your chart. You can make it more attractive and easier to understand, while emphasizing the point you want to make.

Customize charts by using the same concept you use with worksheets: select, then do. Perform the following steps to customize a chart:

1. Select the chart item you want to customize by clicking on it or by pressing an arrow key.

2. Choose the Format command to customize the item, or choose the Chart command to add or delete an item such as a legend, an arrow, or attached text.

3. Select the changes you want to make from the dialog box that appears.

4. Choose OK or press Enter.

These steps are explained in detail in the sections that follow.

T I P   Use chart tools to make quick changes. You can change the chart type and add or delete such chart items as legends, arrows, and gridlines by clicking on the appropriate tool in the Chart toolbar. If the Chart toolbar is not visible, activate a worksheet, choose the Options Toolbar command, and select the Chart toolbar. Many of the chart tools change the chart type and may cause a custom-formatted chart to lose some of its formatting. To change chart types without losing formatting, use the Format Main Chart or Format Overlay.

T I P   Use shortcut menus in charts. Click on an item in a chart with the right mouse button to display the shortcut menu for that item.

Using the Chart Toolbar

To add the Chart toolbar, click with the right mouse button on any displayed toolbar, then choose Chart from the shortcut menu. If a toolbar is not displayed, choose the Options Toolbars command, select Chart from the Toolbars dialog box, and choose OK or press Enter.

The tools available on the Chart toolbar are shown in figure 19.1.

You can change a chart type by clicking on the tool for a different type. For example, you can switch from a column chart to a 3-D pie chart by clicking on the 3D Pie tool.

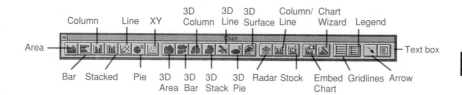

FIG. 19.1

The Chart toolbar.

NOTE Changing chart types by clicking on a tool may clear some custom formatting, just as changing chart types by using the Gallery menu does. If you already have formatted a chart and wish to change types, use the Format **M**ain or Format **O**verlay commands.

Using Shortcut Menus

In charts and worksheets, you can display shortcut menus by clicking on an item with the right mouse button. A shortcut menu appears with the most frequently used commands for that item. Figure 19.2 shows a shortcut menu for the Value axis on a 3-D Surface chart.

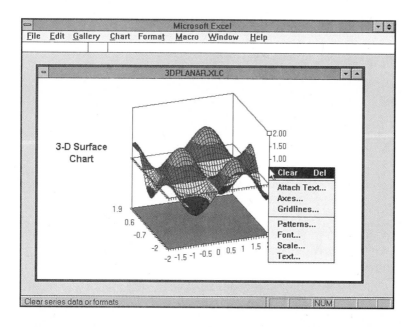

FIG. 19.2

A shortcut menu.

When the shortcut menu appears, you can click with the left or right mouse button to select a command. The easiest way to select a command is to click with the right mouse button, drag down to the command you want, and then release.

Selecting Chart Items

Charts are composed of items such as markers, legends, axes, and text. When you customize charts, you add items to the chart or you format existing items with a new appearance. Before you can format a chart item, you must select it.

To select an item on the chart with the mouse, click on that item. To select a single data point in a series, Ctrl-click on that point.

To select an item on the chart with the keyboard, first select the class of the item by pressing the up or down arrow key. The following items are classes of chart items:

Chart background

Axes

Legend

Arrows

Hi-lo lines

Markers

Drop lines

Plot area

Gridlines

Text

Next, select the specific item from within its class by pressing the left or right arrow key. When you reach the first or last item in a class, the selection skips to items in the adjacent class.

You can select the two largest chart items—the plot area and the chart background—with the Select Chart or Select Plot Area commands from the Chart menu. You also can click inside the rectangle formed by the axes to select the plot area or outside this rectangle to select the chart.

Selected items have white or black squares, called *handles*, at their corners. You cannot move or size items enclosed in white squares (see fig. 19.3). You can move or size items enclosed in black squares with the mouse or the keyboard (see fig. 19.4).

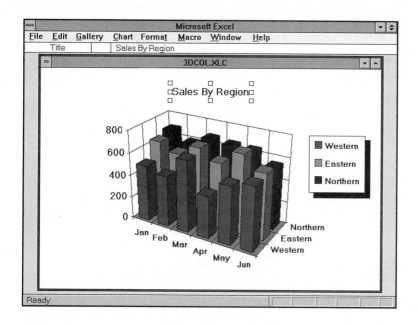

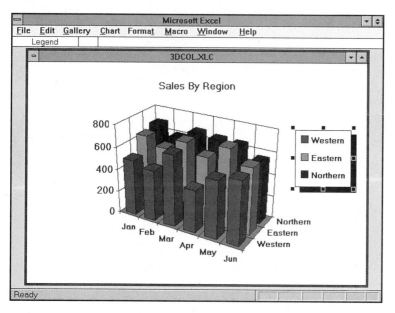

Moving and Sizing Chart Items

You can move or resize items that display black handles when selected, such as the legend, arrows, and boxes of text.

To move an item anywhere on-screen, perform the following steps:

1. Select the item.

2. Move the item.

   If you are using a mouse, drag the item to its new location; then release the mouse button. To move an arrow or text, drag from the center. Do not drag on a black box or you may change the size of the item. A rectangle shows the location of the item as it is moved.

   From the keyboard, choose the Format Move command. Press the arrow keys to move the item. Press Enter when the item reaches the correct location. (Before pressing Enter, you can return the item to its original location by pressing Esc.)

To resize an item, perform the following steps:

1. Select the item.

2. Size the item.

   If you are using a mouse, drag one of the black boxes to expand or contract the item. Drag a handle on the edge of a text box to keep the item's other dimension the same. Drag a handle on the corner of a text box to change two dimensions at once. Words of the text wrap to fit the new box size.

   If you are using the keyboard, choose Format Size and press the arrow keys to reposition the upper-left corner of the box, making it larger or smaller. You may need to move the box after resizing it.

T I P If the arrow keys provide movements or size changes that are too large, hold down the Ctrl key as you press the arrow keys. Each press of the arrow key makes a significantly smaller change.

Excel automatically resizes pie wedges when you move them. The farther you move them from the center, the smaller the wedges and pie become.

Resizing unattached text does not change the size of the text; it changes only the size of the background box surrounding the text.

For Related Information:

◄◄ "Choosing Commands," p. 35.

◄◄ "Choosing Commands from Shortcut Menus," p. 37.

◄◄ "Using the Toolbars," p. 47.

Adding and Formatting Chart Items

You can add many types of items to Excel charts to make them easier to understand or to pinpoint specific information. This section describes how to add text and text boxes, arrows and lines, legends, and gridlines.

Adding and Formatting Text

Excel charts contain three types of text. First, the chart background includes labels along the category (X) and value (Y) or (Z) axes. Excel gets this text from the worksheet data. Excel's second form of text is attached to a specific item such as a title, an axis, or a data point. The third form of text is not attached to other items and can be positioned anywhere. Unattached text is useful for text labels, text comments alongside a chart, or hiding portions of the screen.

> To make a line break to create a two-line title or to break unattached text into separate lines, press Alt+Enter. You can remove the line break by moving to the right of it and pressing the backspace key.
>
> **T I P**

Attaching Text

The chart shown in figure 19.5 has text attached to the title position and to each of the three axes. To attach text, perform the following steps:

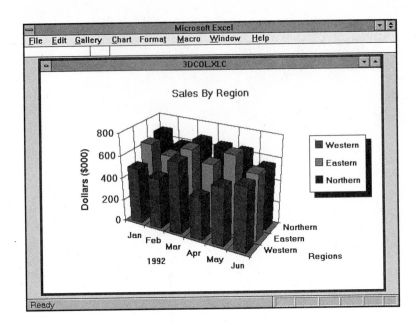

FIG. 19.5

Attached text used for
the chart title and axis
titles.

1. To attach text to a data point, select that data point. To attach a text title, begin with step 2.

2. Choose the **Chart Attach Text** command.

3. Select from the following list the location for the attached text.

Item	Location
Chart Title	Centers the temporary text `Title` above the chart.
Value Axis	Centers the temporary text Y beside the value (Y) axis in 2-D charts or beside the value (Z) axis in 3-D charts.
Category Axis	Centers the temporary text X under category (X) axis.
Series (Y) Axis	Centers the temporary text Y under the series (Y) axis on 3-D charts.
Series or Data Point	Attaches the value number to the specified data point. On area charts, attaches text to the center of a series.
Overlay Value (Y) Axis	Centers a temporary Y beside the overlay's value (Y) axis.
Overlay Category (X) Axis	Centers a temporary X under the overlay's category (X) axis.

4. If you chose Series or **D**ata Point, enter the number of the series in **S**eries Number and the number of the data point in **P**oint Number. On area charts, you need only specify the series. If you selected the data point in step 1, these numbers already are entered for you.

In a column chart, the first series is the column closest to the vertical (Y) axis. In a bar chart, the first series is the bar closest to the horizontal (X) axis.

A data point is one marker within a series. In a column chart, data points are numbered starting with the one closest to the vertical axis. In a bar chart, data point number one is closest to the horizontal axis.

5. Choose OK or press Enter.

Temporary text is attached to the point you specified and remains selected. The surrounding white squares indicate that the text is selected but not movable. You can edit this text or type over it.

6. Edit the temporary text as you would a formula: click in the Formula Bar or press F2, and then edit.

7. Choose OK or press Enter.

You can customize the attached text further by changing its font, size, color, and background, using the procedures described in this chapter.

Deleting Attached Text

To delete attached text, perform the following steps:

1. Select the text in the chart. The text will appear in the Formula Bar.

2. Press the Delete or Backspace key to delete the text from the Formula Bar.

Add or delete chart axes titles by choosing the **C**hart A**x**es command. From the dialog box that appears, select or deselect axes titles that you want or do not want in the chart. Excel reads these chart titles from the chart data on the worksheet.

Adding Unattached Text

In Excel, creating text that can be placed anywhere on a chart is easy and extremely useful. Figure 19.6 illustrates how you can use floating text in a comment box to label an arrow.

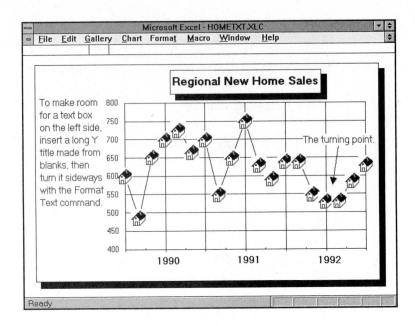

FIG. 19.6

Floating text in a chart.

To add unattached text to a chart, perform the following steps:

1. Select a nontext item.

2. Type the unattached text. Text appears in the Formula Bar, where you can edit it with normal editing procedures.

3. Press Enter or click on the check box when the text is complete.

Small black squares surround the text on the chart, indicating that you can move and size the text background.

To move unattached text with the mouse, select the text and then drag the center of the text block to its new location. Size text blocks by selecting the text and dragging one of the black squares to expand or contract the block. Drag a corner to change two dimensions at once. Words within the text box wrap to fit the new block size.

To move or size unattached text with the keyboard, perform the following steps:

1. Select the text by pressing the up- or down-arrow key until any unattached text on-screen is selected.

2. Press the right or left arrow key to select the specific unattached text.

3. Choose the Format Move or Format Size command.

4. Move the text or change its size with the arrow keys.

5. Press Enter to fix the text's position or size, or, to abandon the process, press Esc.

As you change the size of the text block, the words wrap to fit the new space.

You can edit or delete unattached text at any time. Select the text and then press Del or choose the Edit Clear command.

Formatting Text

After you have selected a block of unattached text, you can use Format commands to change its appearance. To reach format commands quickly, display a shortcut menu by clicking on the text with the right mouse button, and then click on the command you want. Figure 19.7 shows the shortcuts menu displayed for an attached title.

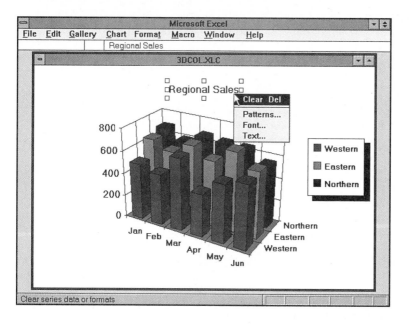

FIG. 19.7

A shortcut menus displayed by clicking on an item with the right mouse button.

A number of tools are available for formatting text. You can use text-formatting tools for alignment, to add bold and italic formatting, and to increase or decrease the font size. To use a tool to format text, select the text and then click on the tool.

As an alternative to the shortcut menus, you can select the text, and then choose Format **P**atterns; or double-click on the text. You can change the appearance of the text box from the Patterns dialog box (see fig. 19.8).

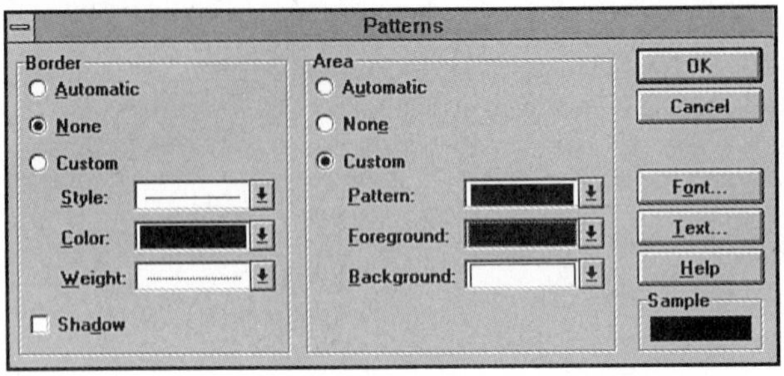

FIG. 19.8

Use the Patterns dialog box to change the appearance of the box surrounding the text.

From within text-formatting dialog boxes, such as the one shown in figure 19.8, you can *tunnel* through to other formatting commands by choosing a tunnel button such as **F**ont or **T**ext.

T   I   P   If you choose fonts that are not available in your printer, the printed chart will not look like it does on-screen. Use fonts that appear in the Font list with a TT icon (TrueType) or with a printer icon (printer resident fonts).

When you select Font from the shortcut menu, the Font dialog box appears, from which you can change the text font, style, and color (see fig. 19.9). You also can change the immediate background behind the text, which is useful for text that overlaps lines or patterns. Select Auto**m**atic to use the default background pattern, T**r**ansparent to let the area show through, and Op**a**que to remove any pattern behind characters but keep the foreground color.

T   I   P   The procedure for hiding selected parts of a chart is similar to the procedure for creating unattached text. Create an *empty*, unattached text box by making an unattached text box that contains only one space character. (If the space appears as a blank character in the pattern, select the text and choose Format Font. Next, select Background Transparent to make the character's background invisible.) While the text block is selected, choose Format **P**atterns and select a Foreground and **B**ackground color that matches the area being covered. Move the box in front of what you want to hide.

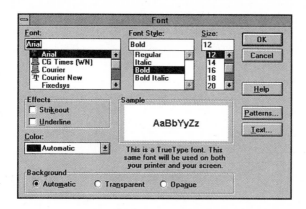

FIG. 19.9

The Font dialog box.

The Format **T**ext command or shortcut Text command or Text button displays the Text dialog box, from which you can change the text alignment and its horizontal or vertical orientation (see fig. 19.10). The capability to change the text's orientation enables you to rotate axis titles or text boxes containing explanations.

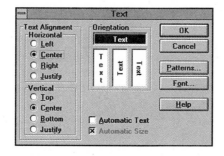

FIG. 19.10

The Text dialog box.

Checking Spelling in Charts

To check the spelling of attached and unattached text in your charts, use the **Chart S**pelling command. The spelling checker works the same as it does in a worksheet. For a description on how to operate the spelling checker, see Chapter 7.

The spelling checker checks attached and unattached text. If any text in a chart is linked to a worksheet, as described in Chapter 20, check that text in the worksheet.

Adding and Formatting Legends

Legends explain the markers or symbols used in a chart. Excel creates legends from the labels on the shorter side of the worksheet data series. Figure 19.11 shows an example of a legend. The legend in the figure was customized with border, pattern, and font selections.

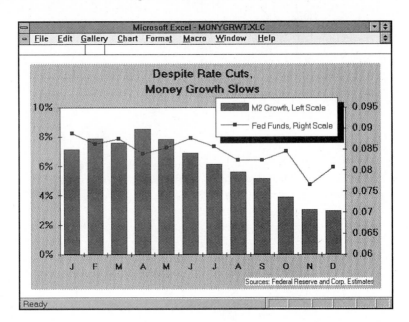

If you used the ChartWizard to create the chart, you can add a legend by selecting the Yes option button in response to the Add a legend question in step 5. (For additional information on the ChartWizard, see Chapter 17). At any later time, you can add a legend by choosing the Chart Add Legend command or by clicking on the Legend tool in the Chart toolbar. The legend appears on the right side of the chart (refer to fig. 19.11). When a chart has a legend, the Add Legend menu item changes to Delete Legend. Use that command to delete a legend, or select the legend and press the Del key.

In the same way that you changed the display characteristics of attached and unattached text, you can change the appearance of a legend. First, select the legend you want to customize (white squares appear at its corners). Choose Format Font command or click with the right mouse button on the legend to access the shortcut menu from which you can choose the Font command. You can change the text font, style, size, color, and background. Use Format Patterns to change the border and the foreground and background colors of the area pattern. If you want the legend to blend into the chart so that you do not see the legend's border and background, choose the Invisible option for Border and for Area under Format Patterns.

You can move the legend to any location on the chart by selecting it and then dragging it with the mouse. If you move the legend against a chart edge, a black line will appear across the edge to indicate that the chart will move to accommodate the legend. If you move the legend to a central part of the chart, the legend will stay where you leave it. Figure 19.11 shows a legend over a central area of the chart.

From the keyboard, position the legend by selecting it and then choosing Format Legend. Choose a location from the Legend dialog box, shown in figure 19.12.

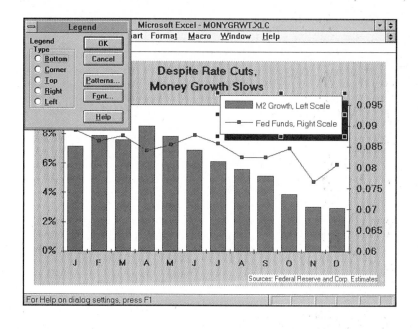

FIG. 19.12

The Legend dialog box.

Adding and Formatting Arrows

Use arrows and unattached text to point to places on a chart that you want to identify or explain. Headless arrows serve as straight lines in charts.

To add an arrow when the Chart toolbar is visible, click on the Arrow tool. Drag in the chart from the foot of where you want the arrows to its tip, then release. Drag the head and tail of the arrow to position the arrow. Clicking on the Arrow tool a second time creates another arrow on top of the last arrow.

To add an arrow or a straight line to an active chart, perform the following steps:

1. Choose the **C**hart Add **A**rrow command.

   An arrow appears, pointing from the upper-left corner to midscreen.

2. Move the arrow until its tail is in the correct position.

   If you are using the mouse, drag the center of the arrow until the arrow is positioned and then release the mouse button.

   From the keyboard, choose Forma**t** Move and then press the arrow keys to position the arrow. Press Enter.

3. Size the arrow so that it points to the correct spot.

   If you are using a mouse, drag the black square at the arrow's head to move the head to the correct spot, and then release the mouse button.

   From the keyboard, choose Forma**t** Size and then press the arrow keys to position the arrow's head. Press Enter.

   Move or size arrows in small increments by holding down the Ctrl key as you press an arrow key.

You cannot add another arrow while an arrow is selected, because the Chart Add Arrow command is replaced by **C**hart Delete **A**rrow. If you need additional arrows, first select a different item on the chart. The Add Arrow command then appears.

To remove an arrow, select the arrow you want to remove and then choose the **C**hart Delete **A**rrow command, or press the Del key.

Move an existing arrow by dragging its middle with the mouse. You can drag on the black square at either end of the arrow to change the arrow's size and position.

Change an arrow's appearance by double-clicking on the arrow to display the Pattern dialog box, by clicking with the right mouse button to display the shortcut Pattern command, or by selecting the arrow and choose Format **P**atterns. Use the dialog box shown in figure 19.13 to modify the arrow. Notice that the Arrow Head drop-down list boxes enable you to use many different arrowhead shapes and to change an arrow into a line.

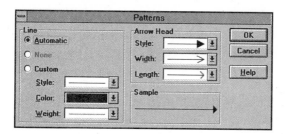

FIG. 19.13

The Patterns dialog box.

Change an arrow to a line by selecting the arrow and then displaying the Patterns dialog box. The dialog box shown in figure 19.13 has many alternatives for the color, weight, and style of the arrow's shaft and head. To make a straight line, select the straight line from the Arrow Head Style drop-down list.

T   I   P

Scaling and Customizing an Axis

You can scale and customize axes. To change the scale, tick marks, fonts, or colors, perform the following steps:

1. Select the axis by clicking on one of the axis lines or by pressing the arrow keys until the axis is selected. White handles appear at either end of the axis.

2. Click with the right mouse button on the axis to display the short-cut menu or choose the Format Patterns, Font, or Scale command. A dialog box displays the formatting alternatives.

3. Select the formatting options you want.

4. Choose OK or press Enter.

Another shortcut with the mouse is to double-click on the axis with the left button to display the Patterns dialog box. When the dialog box for axis patterns appears, select any desired pattern options; then select the Font, Text, or Scale tunnel buttons to make other changes without re-turning to the Format menu.

Use the dialog box for axis patterns to customize the axis line and the positions of tick marks and labels. Figure 19.14 shows the Patterns dialog box for a value (Y) axis.

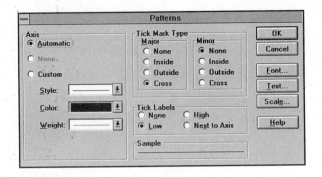

FIG. 19.14

Use the Axis Patterns dialog box to customize lines, tick marks, and thick labels.

You can use the dialog box for axis fonts to choose among type styles, sizes, and colors (see fig. 19.15). Be sure to choose printer fonts or TrueType fonts to ensure that your chart fonts match the fonts available in your printer.

FIG. 19.15

The Font dialog box.

The dialog box to change the scale of an axis is different for the category and the value axes. Display the Scale dialog box by clicking with the right mouse button on a scale and then choosing Scale from the shortcut menu, or by selecting a scale and then choosing the Format Scale command. The Category (X) Axis Scale dialog box, shown in figure 19.16, enables you to choose where the vertical axis will cross, how frequently to show category labels, how frequently to display tick marks, whether to replot categories in reverse (right to left) order, and whether to reverse the crossing point for the scales.

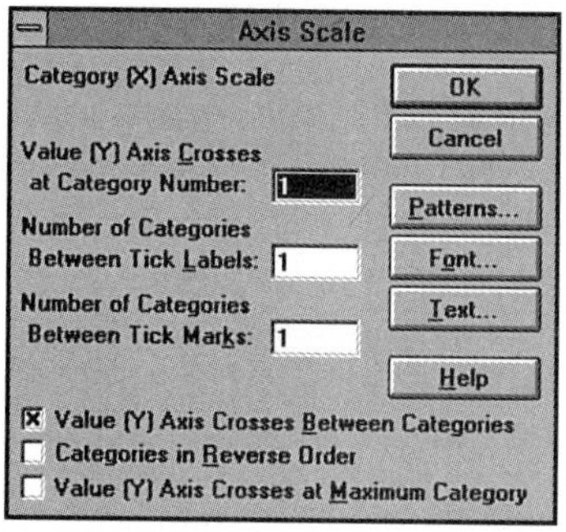

FIG. 19.16

The Category (X) Axis Scale dialog box.

> When you need to change multiple axes settings, change one setting at a time, see the result, and then change another. Otherwise, the results can become confusing.

T I P

In a Scatter (XY) chart, the Category (X) Axis Scale dialog box (see fig. 19.17) enables you to specify the range of the scale and the frequency of major and minor units. Select the Auto check boxes to return the chart to its automatic scaling factors. Change the Minimum and Maximum numbers to change the end points of the category axis. Select the Logarithmic check box to use a log scale on the category axis. To make the value (Y) axis cross at a different point on the category axis, enter the number where you want the value axis to cross in the Crosses At text box.

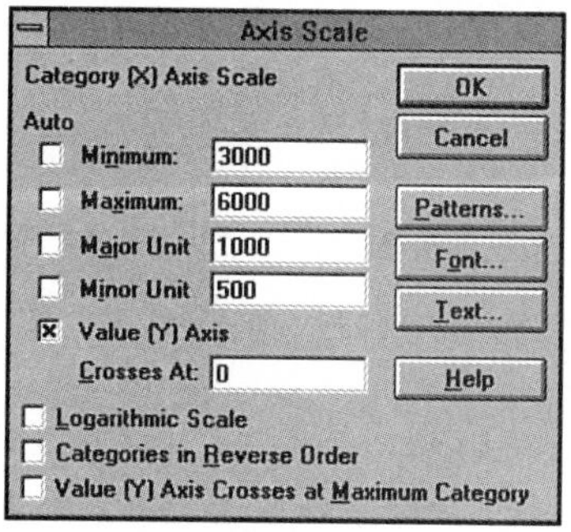

FIG. 19.17

The Category (X) Axis Scale dialog box for a Scatter (XY) chart.

In figure 19.17, notice that dates on the category (X) axis appear as numbers in the Minimum and Maximum text boxes. These numbers are the numbers of days from the beginning of the century to the specified starting and ending dates. Because months have an unequal number of days, no Major Unit value is available to produce the same date on the axis for each month. One way to create evenly spaced month/day labels on the category (X) axis is to use a Major Unit value of 29.5. After the axis is scaled, you can correct any month that has a day different from the others by using a floating text label to cover month/day combinations that aren't exact.

The Value (Y) Axis Scale dialog box enables you to choose the units and range of the scale and the point where the category (X) axis crosses (see fig. 19.18). Set the top and bottom limits on the scale by changing the Maximum and Minimum text boxes. Choose the Auto check boxes to return to the default scaling. You also can convert the scale to logarithmic display.

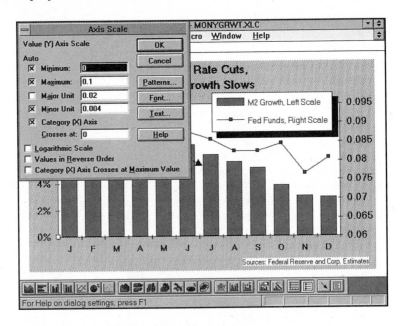

FIG. 19.18

The Value (Y) Axis
Scale dialog box.

T I P   Do not crowd tick marks and axis labels. Some charts, such as charts of stock prices or instrument readings, contain so many data points that the labels and tick marks crowd one another. To reduce this clutter, select the category (X) axis and choose Format Scale. Enter larger numbers into the text boxes for Number of Categories Between Tick Labels and for Number of Categories Between Tick Marks. The larger the numbers you enter, the more distance between labels and between tick marks.

Adding and Formatting Gridlines

Gridlines help viewers compare markers and read values. You can add gridlines that originate from the category (X) axis or from the value (Y) axis. You also can choose whether gridlines originate only from major divisions on the axis or whether they also originate from points between major divisions.

To add or delete horizontal gridlines from the major value (Y) axis, click on the Gridline tool in the Chart toolbar. The Gridline tool looks like a miniature chart with horizontal lines.

If you are using a keyboard, choose the **Chart Gridlines** command. Select the type of gridlines you want from the Gridlines dialog box, shown in figure 19.19, then choose OK.

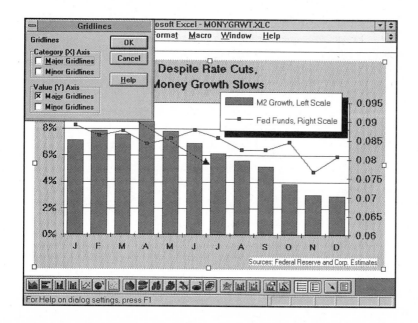

FIG. 19.19

Add gridlines to either axis.

Format the type of line used by gridlines by selecting a vertical or horizontal gridline and choosing the Format Pattern command. Select from the different line styles and weights.

Too many gridlines obscure the chart, making it messy and confusing. In general, do not use gridlines if the chart is for overhead projection. Instead, use gridlines in printed materials where readers need to read charts more precisely.

Displaying Data Values with Columns or Bars

To display the exact value of a marker, perform the following steps:

1. Select the series to which you want to attach text by clicking on the line, column, or bar or by pressing arrow keys until the series is selected.

2. If you want data attached to a specific marker you can see, Ctrl+click on the marker.

3. Choose the Chart Attach Text command. The Attach text box shown in figure 19.20 is displayed.

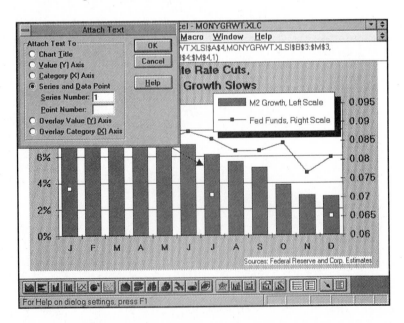

FIG. 19.20

You can attach text or data to any chart marker.

4. Select the Series and **D**ata Point option.

5. If you selected the correct series, the series number appears in the **S**eries Number edit box. Change the number, if necessary.

6. Type the number of the data point in the **P**oint Number box. This number indicates which point in the series will have an attached number. If you Ctrl+clicked on a marker, the number already is in the **P**oint Number box.

7. Choose OK or press Enter.

In a column chart, for example, this procedure places the numeric value for the column above the column. The value changes and floats as the column changes or moves. Figure 19.21 shows a data point value above markers.

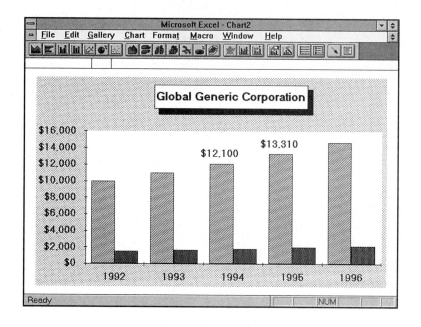

FIG. 19.21

Data point values
above markers.

The data point values that attach to markers use the format of the corresponding cell in the worksheet. To change a number's format in the chart, format its worksheet cell.

T I P

Changing Item Colors, Patterns, and Borders

If you can select an item on a chart, you can change its fill color and pattern, border weight and color, and font type and color. You can customize the appearance of anything that shows handles.

T I P To use colors that are different from the 16 default colors, you can use the Chart Color Palette command to select your own set of 16 colors from a wide range of colors. This command and the Options Color Palette for worksheets are described in Chapter 33, "Customizing Excel."

To change the appearance of items, perform the following steps:

1. Double-click on the item to display the Patterns dialog box, click with the right mouse button on the item and choose Patterns, or select the item, then choose the Format Pattern command. A dialog box similar to the one shown in figure 19.22 will appear.

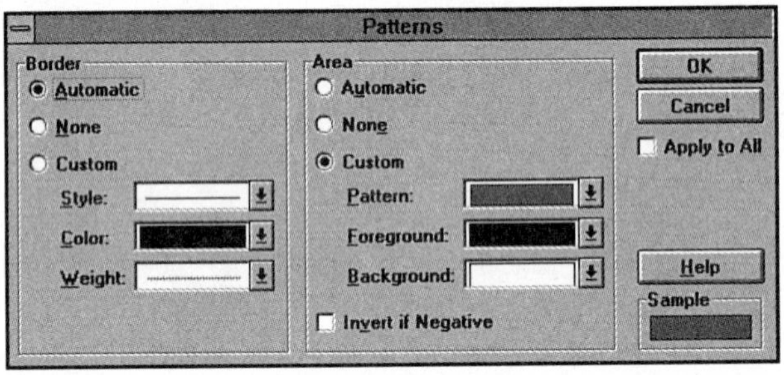

FIG. 19.22

Patterns dialog boxes are similar for all items.

2. Make selections from the dialog box. The lists in pattern boxes are drop-down list boxes, so the list appears only when you select the list box. Click on the down arrow or press Alt+down arrow. Figure 19.23 shows a pattern box with the Area Pattern list dropped down.

3. If tunnel buttons such as Font, Text, or Legend appear in the dialog box, choose the button for the format you want to change next; or choose OK or press Enter.

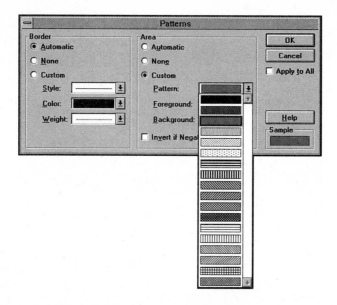

FIG. 19.23

A drop-down list in a pattern box.

> Format a single marker by holding down Ctrl, then double-click on the marker to bring up pattern dialog box for that marker.   **T I P**

Pattern dialog boxes are similar for all items. The left group in the dialog box displays formatting alternatives for the border or line in the item. The right group in the box displays formatting alternatives for the fill pattern in the item. A sample of the completed format appears in the lower-right corner.

The following are the options in a Pattern dialog box:

Option	Description
Border	
Automatic	Uses default settings.
None	Uses no border.
Custom	
Style	Changes type of line.
Color	Changes color of line. Choose from 16 alternatives.
Weight	Changes the thickness of line.

continues

Option	Description
Area	
Automatic	Uses default settings.
No**ne**	Uses no fill (background shows through).
Custom	
Pattern	Uses a pattern or shade created from a fore-ground and background pattern.
Foreground	Changes the top color in the pattern. Choose from 16 alternatives.
Background	Changes the bottom color in the pattern. Choose from 16 alternatives.
Tunnel buttons	Buttons such as Text, Font, or Scale enable you to go to another format command from the pattern box without returning to the Chart menu.
Sample	The Sample box shows you how your selections will appear.

Pattern boxes for items such as arrows include different types of lines and arrowhead shapes.

The largest areas in a chart are the chart background and the plot area. The chart background includes the entire chart; the plot area includes only the area within the axes. You can change the colors, patterns, and boundaries of both areas. Click on the background area or choose **C**hart Select **C**hart or **C**hart Select Plot **A**rea before choosing the format command. Figure 19.24 shows a chart with patterns for the chart background and plot area, and with the text for the axes in boldface.

For Related Information:

◀◀ "Changing Character Fonts, Styles, and Colors," p. 257.

◀◀ "Using TrueType Fonts," p. 261.

Rotating 3-D Charts

3-D charts may display data in such a way that some series are difficult to see. In figure 19.25, for example, the first series blocks the second series from view. To avoid this problem, you can rotate and adjust

3-D charts by using the Format **3**-D View command. After rotation, the same 3-D chart appears as shown in figure 19.24. The following sections explain how to rotate a 3-D chart.

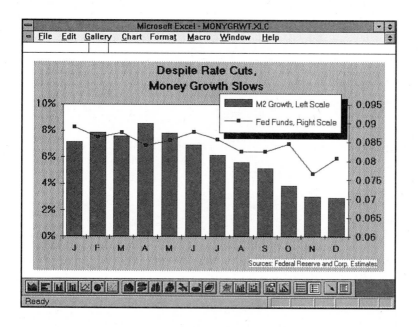

FIG. 19.24

A chart and plot area formatted for a standout appearance.

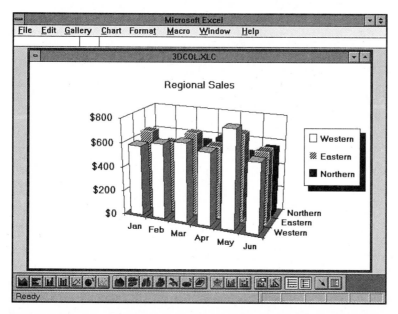

FIG. 19.25

A 3-D chart with data series blocked from view.

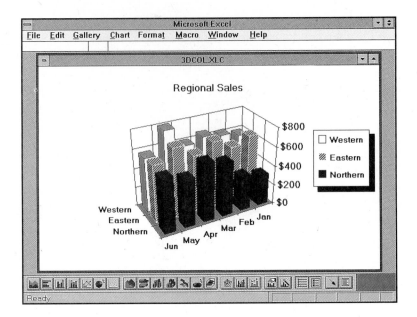

FIG. 19.26

Rotating and adjusting
the perspective of a
3-D chart displays the
series from a better
angle.

Rotating a 3-D Chart by Dragging

With a mouse, you can rotate a 3-D chart in any direction by dragging
one end of an axis. To rotate a 3-D chart by dragging, perform the following steps:

1. Click at the tip of one of the axis.

   Black handles appear at the end of all eight tips (see fig. 19.27).

2. Drag one of the handles on the side close to you. Drag in the direction you want the chart to rotate. Imagine that the chart is within a
   sphere, and you are dragging the mouse along the surface of that
   sphere. As you drag, a wire-frame outline of the chart depicts the
   chart's orientation, as shown in figure 19.28.

3. Release the mouse button when the outline appears in the correct
   orientation. Excel will redraw the chart, as shown in figure 19.29.

T   I   P   Drag different handles as the chart rotates. Use one of the handles
closest to you when you begin dragging the chart. After the chart
passes approximately 90 degrees of rotation, you may have difficulty
visualizing how the chart is rotating. Release the handle you were
dragging and begin dragging one of the handles that is now in front.

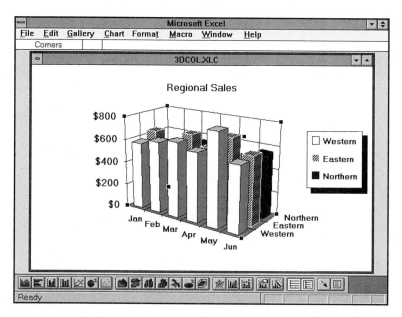

FIG. 19.27

Rotate 3-D charts by dragging a black handle at the tip of an axis.

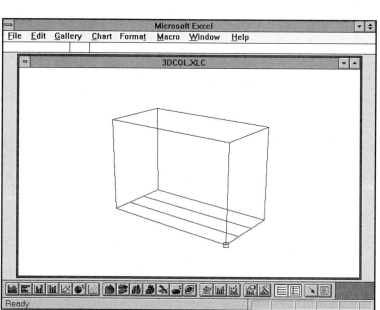

FIG. 19.28

3-D charts rotate as though inside a sphere.

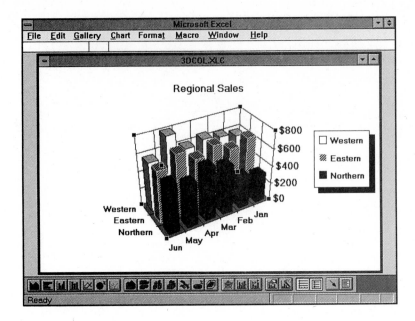

FIG. 19.29

A rotated chart displays a totally different view.

Rotating a 3-D Chart by Command

When you choose the Forma**t** **3**-D View command, the dialog box shown in figure 19.30 appears. Selections in this dialog box change the angle and perspective from which the 3-D chart is drawn.

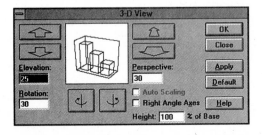

FIG. 19.30

Rotate the wire-framed chart to rotate your 3-D chart.

You can use a mouse or a keyboard to rotate or adjust the viewpoint shown in the 3-D View dialog box. Using the mouse is faster and easier.

If you are using the mouse to rotate or adjust the viewpoint, click on the appropriate directional button to rotate or adjust the viewpoint.

To rotate or adjust the viewpoint with the keyboard, select a text box and then type in a number within the range. The following table lists the available options:

Option	Effect on Chart
Elevation	Changes the height from which you see the chart. Use an angle from –90 to +90 degrees for all charts except pie charts. Use an angle from 10 to 80 degrees for pie charts.
Rotation	Rotates the chart around the vertical (Z) axis. The range is from 0 to 360 degrees.
Perspective	Controls the vanishing point or the sense of depth in the chart. Use a number between 0 and 100 to specify the ratio of the front of the chart to its back.
Height _ % of Base	Controls the height of the vertical (Z) axis as a percentage of the chart width (X) axis. Enter a number between 5 and 500.
Right Angle Axes	Freezes axis angles at 90 degrees. Perspective is turned off.

When the wire-frame chart has the orientation you want, choose OK. By choosing the **A**pply button, you can keep the dialog box on-screen and apply the current settings to the chart so that you can see how they look. Choose the **D**efault button to return all dialog box settings to default values.

Creating a Chart Template

When your work requires that you create similar charts many times, consider creating a template. A template contains all the formatting and attached text used by your repetitive charts. The template can be used with any data that fits the type of chart created by the template.

To create a chart template, perform the following steps:

1. Create a chart that is the same as the chart you frequently need.

2. Choose the **F**ile Save **A**s command.

3. If you want the template to appear in the **F**ile **N**ew dialog box, change to the EXCEL\XLSTART directory so that the file is saved there. You can save a template into any directory, but they appear only in **F**ile **N**ew if they have been saved in XLSTART.

4. Enter a name for the template in the File **N**ame box.

5. Select Template from the Save File as **T**ype list. The extension changes to XLT.

6. Choose OK or press Enter.

When you want to create a chart using this template as a guide, do the following:

1. Select the appropriate type of data in the active worksheet. The data selection does not need to be the same number of categories or data points.

2. Choose the **File New** command.

3. Select the name of your template from the **New** list.

 NOTE   Templates appear in **File New** only if they are saved to the XLSTART directory. If the template is in a different directory, open it by using **File Open**.

Your chart will open using the data you selected but will have the formatting of the chart you used to create the template. The chart you open will have a numbered name such as *template1* to show the template on which it was based. Format and save your chart as you would any other.

To remove a template from the New list, use the **File Delete** command to delete the template, any file ending with .XLT, from the XLSTART directory.

FROM HERE...

For Related Information:

▶▶ "Grouping Documents into Workbooks," p. 426.

▶▶ "Building Templates," p. 442.

Transferring Chart Formats

After you create a chart, you can apply formatting from another chart. To transfer a chart format, use the **Paste Special** command to copy the formatting from one chart and paste it onto another chart. Perform the following steps to transfer a chart format:

1. Activate the chart that has the format you want to copy.

2. Choose the **Chart Select Chart** command.

3. Choose the **Edit Copy** command.

4. Activate the chart you want to format.

5. Choose **E**dit Paste **S**pecial.

6. Select Forma**t**s from the Paste dialog box.

7. Choose OK or press Enter.

Clearing Chart Formats or Contents

You do not have to create a new chart from the worksheet when you want to change all the data or formats. You can clear the unwanted data or formats from the chart by using the following steps:

1. Choose the **C**hart Select **C**hart command.

2. Choose the **E**dit **C**lear command or press Delete.

3. Select one of the following options:

Button	Action
All	Clears the chart.
Formats	Clears the formats but retains the data series.
Formulas	Clears the data series but retains the formats.

4. Choose OK or press Enter.

You can copy and paste new data on top of a chart whose contents you have deleted. The new data will use the format of the preceding chart.

Changing and Modifying Chart Types

If you use the **G**allery menu to change the chart type, Excel erases some of your custom formatting. To change the type of an existing chart and retain custom colors and other formatting, choose the Forma**t M**ain Chart command or click with the right mouse button on the outside chart background and choose Main Chart from the shortcut menu. Select the new chart type from the Format Chart dialog box (see fig. 19.31). If you have created a customized column chart, for example, and you want to switch to a bar chart, select Bar from the Main Chart Type pull-down list. Your custom formatting is preserved, if it is appropriate for the new type of chart.

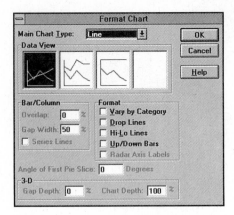

FIG. 19.31

The Format Main
Chart dialog box.

You have many options in the Format Main Chart dialog box. When you
select the type of chart, different combinations of options become available. Unavailable options are dimmed. Table 19.1 shows some of these
options.

Table 19.1. Main Chart Options

Option	Effect
Bar/Column **O**verlap	Overlaps bars or columns by a percentage of their width when you enter a positive number. Creates a gap between bars or columns when you enter a negative number. Limits are −100 to 100.
Bar/Column Gap **W**idth	Creates a gap between groups of bars or columns when you enter a positive number (the percentage of bar or column width). Limits are 0 to 500.
Series Lines	Connects tops of data markers with lines for stacked bar/column charts.
Format **V**ary by Category	When the chart includes only one data series, displays each data point in a different color.
Drop Lines	In line or area charts, drops a line from each marker to the category (X) axis.
Hi-Lo Lines	Extends lines from the highest to the lowest value in each category. Use this option with 2-D line charts.
Up/Down Bars	Shows open and close values for tracking stock prices. Used with line charts (Gallery Line, 9).

Option	Effect
Radar Axis Labels	Determines whether labels are used on the Category axis (spokes) of a radar chart.
Angle of First Pi**e** Slice	Specifies the angle in degrees clockwise from vertical to the start of the first pie wedge.
3-D **G**raph Depth	Specifies the distance, measured as a percentage of column width, between series in a 3-D chart.
Chart Depth	Specifies the depth, measured as a percentage of chart width, of a 3-D chart. Uses 30 to make a chart 30% as deep as it is wide.

For Related Information:

◀◀ "Creating Charts with the ChartWizard," p. 668.

◀◀ "Choosing a Predefined Chart Format," p. 690.

FROM HERE...

Creating Picture Charts

Excel charts can use pictures as markers in place of columns, bars, or lines. You can use this feature to make picture charts that grab the eye and then communicate the information. Figure 19.32 shows how you can use pictures in column charts. Figure 19.33 shows a drawing created in Windows Paintbrush used as a replacement for line markers.

To replace columns, bars, or lines, you can use pictures from any Windows graphics or drawing program that can copy graphics to the Clipboard in the Windows Metafile format. Examples of such programs are Windows Paintbrush (the free program that comes with Windows), CorelDRAW!, and Micrografx Designer. You also can use Excel's worksheet drawing tools to create pictures to copy and paste into charts. Chapter 9, "Drawing and Placing Graphics in Worksheets," describes how to draw on the worksheet.

You can store frequently used pictures in a worksheet that you use as a picture scrapbook. Chapter 9 explains how to paste pictures into worksheets. Copy pictures from the worksheet by selecting them and choosing **E**dit **C**opy.

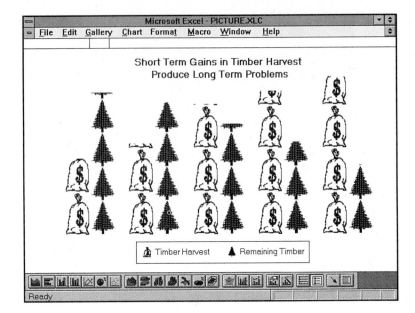

FIG. 19.32

Pictures can replace columns or bars.

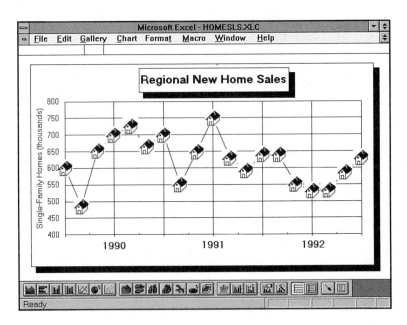

FIG. 19.33

Custom pictures can replace the markers on lines.

To create a picture chart, perform the following steps:

1. Activate your column, bar, or line chart in Excel.

2. Switch to the Windows graphics program in which you want to draw. Press Ctrl+Esc to see the Task List, or press Alt+Tab to cycle between programs.

3. Draw or open the picture you want to use in your chart. (Some graphics programs come with extensive libraries of graphics, called *clip art*.)

4. Select the picture by using the graphic selection tool for that program, and then choose the **Edit Copy** command. Figure 19.34 shows a picture about to be copied from Windows Paintbrush.

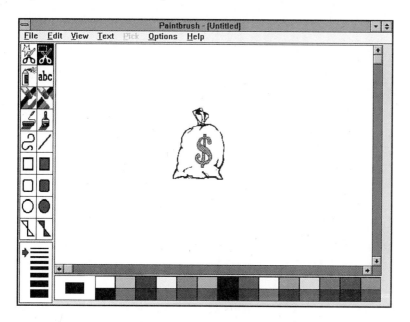

FIG. 19.34

Draw the picture in a Windows program, such as Paintbrush.

5. Switch back to Excel. Press Ctrl+Esc to see the Task List or press Alt+Tab to cycle between programs.

6. Select the column, bar, or line series (as shown in figure 19.35) that you want to contain the picture. Click on the series, or press arrow keys to select the series.

7. Choose the **Edit Paste** command. The picture replaces the series markers, as shown in figure 19.36. The picture may stretch to fit. You can adjust the picture later.

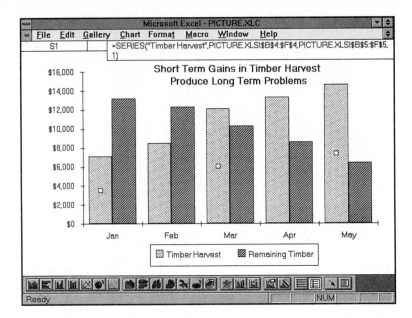

FIG. 19.35

Select the series that
you want to represent
with the picture.

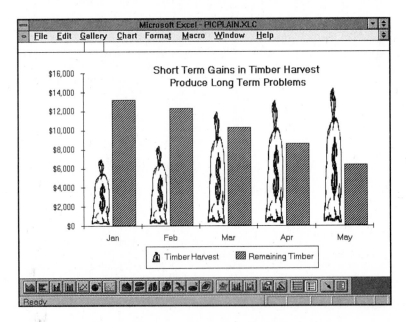

FIG. 19.36

The pasted picture
replaces the series
markers.

To stretch, stack, or stack and scale the pictures in column or bar
charts, select the series containing the picture and choose the Format
Patterns command. From the dialog box shown in figure 19.37, select
one of the picture-formatting options. A stacked picture appears in
figure 19.38.

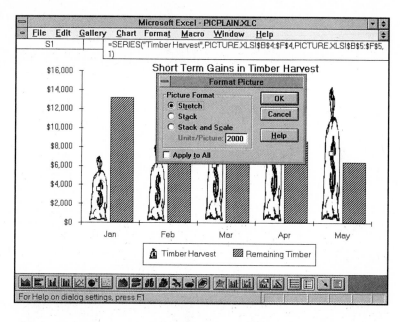

FIG. 19.37

The Format Picture
dialog box.

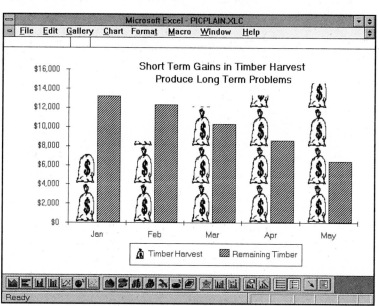

FIG. 19.38

A stacked picture
for a different
representation.

The following table explains the options in the Format Picture Patterns
dialog box:

Option	Effect
Stretch	Stretches the picture to match the value for each data point.
Stack	Stacks the picture in its original proportions to match the value for each data point.
Stack and Scale	Scales the picture's height to equal the value in the Units/Picture text box, and then stacks the picture to match the value for each data point.

To remove a picture from a series, complete the following steps:

1. Select the series

2. Press the Del key to display the Clear dialog box.

3. Select the Formats option.

4. Choose OK, or press Enter.

FROM HERE...

For Related Information:

◄◄ "Creating Graphic Objects," p. 317.

◄◄ "Combining Data and Charts on the Same Page," p. 328.

▶▶ "Understanding the Clipboard," p. 1018.

▶▶ "Copying Data between Applications," p. 1019.

Chapter Summary

You can create impressive, high-quality graphics by using a laser printer or color plotter and the chart formatting techniques described in this chapter. When you reach the point where you need to create overlaid charts, link multiple worksheets to one chart, or do more complex charting, be sure to read Chapter 20, "Building Complex Charts."

If you have a question or run into trouble as you work with charts, remember that you can get help by choosing topics from the Help menu or by pressing F1 when a dialog box is displayed.

Building Complex Charts

![black bar separator]

When you have a situation that requires special charts or you need to go beyond the fundamentals in modifying and formatting charts, the techniques in this chapter will help you. Here, you learn how to solve worksheet problems by moving lines, bars, or columns on a chart; link one chart to multiple worksheets; edit the series formulas to control the order of chart markers and the text used in legends; and overlap two charts. This chapter also describes how to prevent a chart from being scrambled when the worksheet is rearranged and includes tips for troubleshooting common problems with charts.

Chapter 20 also discusses Excel's exceptional slide show capability. With the Slide Show add-in, you can display sequences of worksheets, charts, text, and graphics from other applications. Slides can switch manually or with timed sequences. You select the visual and audio transition used between slides.

Using Charts To Analyze Worksheets

In addition to enlivening presentations, charts make excellent analytical tools. Excel charts are linked to one or more worksheets, so playing *what-if* games on the worksheets updates the charts that are linked to them. Updating can help to reveal profit-loss crossover points, forecast inventory quantities, or quantify trends for different scenarios.

Excel also has the powerful capability to find a worksheet value to match changes in the chart. If you drag a bar, column, or line to a new location in the chart, Excel seeks a new worksheet input that produces the result shown in the chart. This feature provides a quick and easy way to make a visual estimate of a situation and have Excel determine the numbers that correspond.

Analyzing Charts for *What-If* Analysis

By using Excel, you can make changes to your worksheet and watch the chart immediately reflect those changes. This capability is valuable for performing *what-if* types of analysis. Because you can see the effects of your worksheet changes, you can determine emerging trends, crossover points between profit and loss, and mistakes made during data entry.

As figure 20.1 illustrates, you can position worksheet and chart windows so that all windows are visible. As you change a variable in the worksheet, the Sales versus Costs and the Itemized Cost charts reflect the changes immediately. To arrange the windows, use **W**indow commands or drag the sides and title bars. (Read Chapter 15, "Using Excel's Add-In Macros," to learn to add more window-arranging commands to the **W**indow menu.)

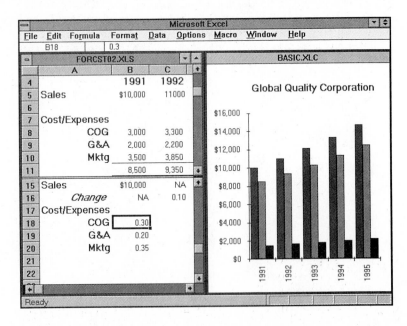

FIG. 20.1

Arrange the windows so that you can watch the changes in the chart as you perform *what-if* analysis in the worksheet.

Moving Markers To Change Worksheet Values

Excel enables you to move column, bar, or line markers on a chart and cause the corresponding data in the worksheet to change. If the data is not a value but a formula, then Excel executes the Formula Goal Seek command to find the input value that makes the worksheet correspond to the chart.

To change values on the worksheet from the chart, perform the following steps:

1. Open the worksheet and chart. Activate the chart. The chart must be a two-dimensional column, bar, line, or XY scatter chart.

2. Hold down the Ctrl key and click on the column, bar, or line marker you want to change. A black handle appears on the marker as shown in figure 20.2.

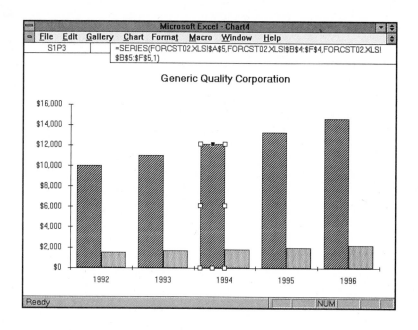

FIG. 20.2

The black handle indicates that this column can be dragged to a new height.

3. Drag the black handle to the location you want. Watch the Reference Area to the left of the formula bar to see the changing numeric value for the marker. A sliding marker shows the position on the value (Y) axis

4. Release the mouse when the marker is at the location you want.

If the column, line, or bar references a number on the worksheet, that number changes. If the column, line, or bar references the result of a formula, Excel activates the Formula Goal Seek command. This command activates the worksheet for the marker and displays the Goal Seek dialog box, as shown in figure 20.3.

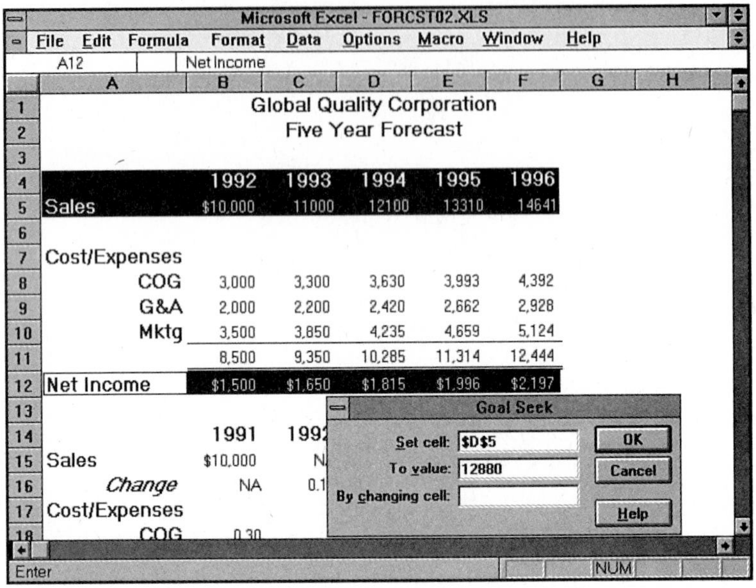

FIG. 20.3

The Goal Seek dialog box asks which worksheet cell should be changed to achieve the result in the chart.

To operate Goal Seek, perform the following steps:

1. In the By changing cell text box, select the cell (or type the cell reference of the cell) that you want to change to produce the result in the chart. The cell you select must not contain a formula.

2. Choose OK or press Enter.

   Goal Seek iterates through input values to find the value that produces the result in the chart. Then, the Goal Seek dialog box displays the solution.

3. Choose OK or press Enter to enter the new input value, or choose Cancel to return to the original worksheet.

When Goal Seek is complete, Excel reactivates the chart. (The Goal Seek command is described in detail in Chapter 14, "Using Analytical Tools.")

For Related Information:

◄◄ "Using the Goal Seek Feature," p. 540.

FROM HERE...

Working with the Series Formula

When you create a chart or add a data series to a chart, Excel links the chart to a data series on a worksheet. Excel creates this link with a series formula. You should understand how to use a series formula if you use the ChartWizard or the Edit **S**eries command to change the data used by a chart.

A series formula tells the chart where the worksheet is located on the disk or network, which worksheet to use, and which cells of that worksheet contain the data to be charted. Each data series has a series formula. As figure 20.4 shows, you can display the series formula in the Formula Bar by selecting one of the markers in the data series. The formula in figure 20.4 belongs to the first data series, which is shown with white squares along the line.

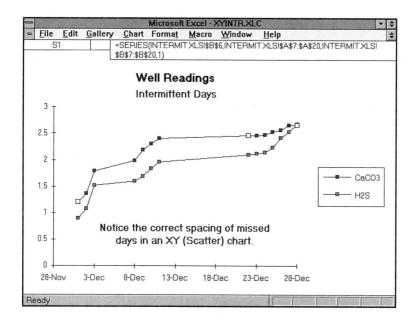

FIG. 20.4

Each set of markers in a chart has a series formula referring to data on a worksheet.

> **T I P** Although you can edit or delete the series formula by hand, using the Chart Edit Series command is easier. This command is described under appropriate topics throughout this chapter. You also may want to change the data used by a chart through the ChartWizard.

When you examine the worksheet and the related chart, you can see how the series formula works. All series formulas are constructed on the following pattern:

=SERIES(*"series_name",worksheet_name!category_reference, worksheet_name!values_reference,marker_order_number*)

The *series_name* is text in quotation marks or an external reference to the cell that contains the text label for the data series. An external reference to a text label in a cell is not enclosed in quotation marks. The *series_name* is used in the legend.

The *worksheet_name!category_reference* is an absolute external reference to the worksheet cells that contain the labels for the category (X) axis. The *worksheet_name!values_reference* specifies which worksheet cells contain the (Y) values for the data series.

The *marker_order_number* dictates the order of the data series. In the example in figure 20.4, the *marker_order_number* is 1. The first series appears first in the legend and appears as the first series of columns in column charts. A *marker_order_number* of 2 would make the markers for this data series the second series of markers on the chart.

Changing the Data Range with the ChartWizard

One of the easiest ways to change the data range that a chart uses is by using the ChartWizard. You need to know how to do this if you need to add or remove another series in the chart or if the series add or delete data points.

To change the data range used by a chart, perform the following steps:

1. If the Standard or Chart toolbar is not displayed, activate a worksheet and choose the **O**ptions **T**oolbar command; then select the Standard or Chart toolbar and choose OK.

2. Open the chart and the worksheet containing the data. Activate the chart.

3. Click on the ChartWizard tool.

The worksheet containing the data will activate with the current chart data selected. A ChartWizard dialog box appears over the worksheet, as shown in figure 20.5.

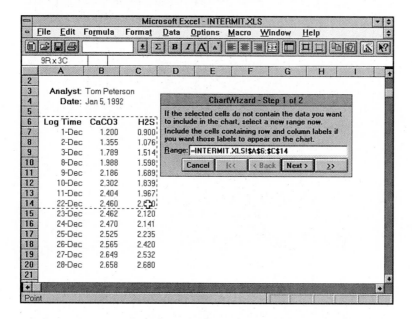

FIG. 20.5

Drag across the new data range you want for the chart.

4. Edit the range or reselect the data range so the ChartWizard's **R**ange edit box displays the new range you want for the chart.

5. Choose the Next button.

   A second dialog box displays and gives you the opportunity to change the chart orientation and labels for the new data layout.

6. Make selections as described in Chapter 18.

7. Choose OK.

Excel redraws your chart by using the new data you selected but keeping the previous data type and formatting.

Pasting a Data Series into a Chart

You can add data series to a chart or change existing data series by using the **E**dit **P**aste, **E**dit Paste **S**pecial, or **C**hart Edit **S**eries commands. Each has advantages in certain situations. With the Edit Series dialog box, you also can link data series from multiple worksheets to a single chart.

You can add a data series to an existing chart by copying data from the source worksheet and pasting it into the chart. The selected data must meet the restrictions described in preceding chapters for height and width orientation. For example, you can create a chart made from the Quick Start worksheet by selecting A4:F5 and pressing F11. This chart is shown in figure 20.6.

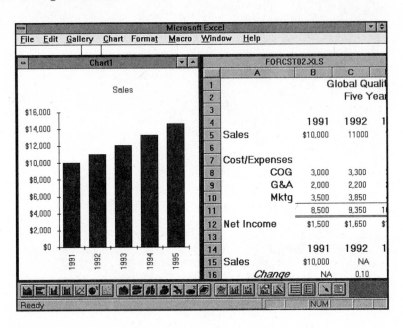

FIG. 20.6

A simple chart created from one data series.

To add the nonadjacent data series A12:F12 to the existing chart, complete the following steps:

1. Select the data in cells A12:F12, as indicated by the cells enclosed in dashed lines in figure 20.7.

2. Choose the **Edit Copy** command.

3. Activate the chart and select the **Edit Paste** command.

This procedure pastes the data into the chart, as shown in figure 20.7.

If the category (X) axis of the data you are pasting into the chart is not the longer axis, then choose the **Edit Paste Special** command. Select the opposite of the current Row or Column selection, and choose OK.

If you are adding additional data to a Scatter (XY) chart, then select both the new X and Y data. The X and Y data must be in adjacent rows or columns, and the X data must be in the top row or the left column. Paste the X and Y data into the chart with the **Edit Paste Special** command. Be sure to select the Category (X) Values in **F**irst Row (Column) check box.

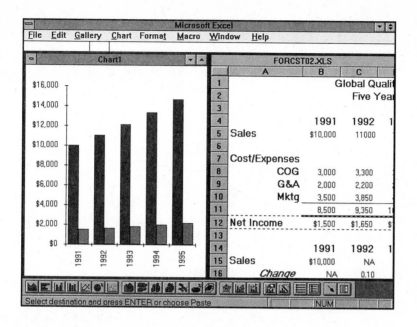

FIG. 20.7

Additional data series can be pasted into the chart.

> A legend on the chart can indicate how Excel is interpreting the data. **T I P**

Adding Data from Multiple Worksheets

After you know how to paste a data series into a chart, you can just as easily create a chart with data from multiple worksheets. You can, for example, create a chart that reflects data from four different quarters, although each quarter is on a different worksheet.

You combine data from multiple worksheets by copying the data from each worksheet and pasting it into the chart. Perform the following steps:

1. Create a chart from the worksheet data you want as the first series in the chart.

2. Activate a different worksheet.

3. Select a data series. Include labels if the original data selection included labels. (If you are adding to a Scatter (XY) chart, the number of data points does not need to be the same, but you must include both X and Y data as described earlier.)

4. Choose the **Edit C**opy command.

5. Activate the chart.

6. Choose the **Edit P**aste command. If you are adding to a Scatter (XY) chart, use the **Edit Paste S**pecial command as described previously.

Deleting a Data Series

When you need to delete a line, area, or series of columns or bars, use the **Chart Edit S**eries command.

Use the ChartWizard to redefine the data being charted. Using the ChartWizard is often the easiest method of changing the data range, but deleting a single series from many is easier if you use the procedure described here.

To delete a series, perform the following steps:

1. Select the series you want to delete.

2. Choose the **Chart Edit S**eries command. The Edit Series dialog box appears, as shown in figure 20.8.

3. Be certain that the series you want to delete is selected in the **S**eries list, and then choose the **D**elete button.

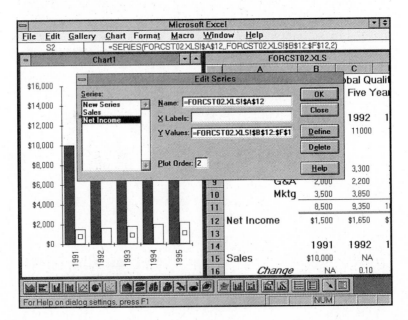

FIG. 20.8

Use the Edit Series
dialog box to change
or delete chart series.

4. Make any additional deletions, additions, or edits, and then choose OK. Choosing Close does not undo the deletion of a series.

A quick way to delete a series is to select the series markers in the chart. Then select and delete the series formula that appears in the Formula Bar. Finally, press Enter.

T I P

Editing a Data Series

When you extend a series of data on a worksheet, you probably will want to extend the related chart as well. You can use the ChartWizard as described earlier to make these changes. Another method is using the **Chart Edit Series** command to extend the range of the data series by editing the series formula. For example, to add a new year for Sales to the existing chart from the FORCAST.XLS worksheet, complete the following steps:

1. Open the worksheet and the chart. Activate the chart.

2. Select the markers (data series) you want to edit. In this example, select the Sales series.

3. Choose the **Chart Edit Series** command to display the Edit Series dialog box shown in figure 20.9.

4. Select the Name, **X** Labels, or **Y** Values text boxes.

   The **Name** text box references the cell from which the legend name is taken. You can type in a legend name.

   The **X** Labels text box contains the external reference formula for data used to create the category (X) axis. Excel uses the **X** Labels for the first data series to determine category (X) axis labels. The **Y** Values text box contains the external reference formula for the value represented by chart markers.

5. Manually edit the external reference formula in each text box, or select the new data range by dragging across it with the mouse.

   Manually edit the reference if it needs only minor changes. For significant changes, such as referencing a distant worksheet range or using a data series from a different worksheet, activate the worksheet and scroll to the data area. The Edit Series dialog box remains on top, but can be moved if necessary. Select the text in the **Name**, **X** Label, or **Y** Label text box you want to change. Select the cells you want to reference by the **Name**, **X** Label, or **Y** Value text box.

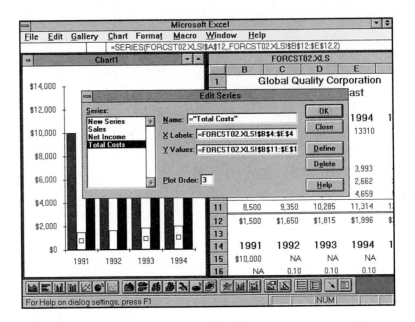

FIG. 20.9

The Edit Series dialog box before the external references are extended to include more cells.

Notice that in figure 20.9 the X labels and Y values external references do not extend to column F and do not include the added numbers for 1995. Figure 20.10 shows the updated Edit Series dialog box with the X and Y data ranges extended to include an additional year's data.

6. Repeat steps 4 and 5 to edit all text boxes to include the correct locations of other data. Choose the **D**efine button to accept your changes and keep the dialog box open.

7. Choose OK after you have made all changes.

Rearranging the Markers

The series formula also controls the order of bars or columns in a chart. In their series formulas, the data series have marker order numbers from 1 to the total number of data series in the chart. To reorder the bars or columns, follow the same procedure as you would to edit a data series.

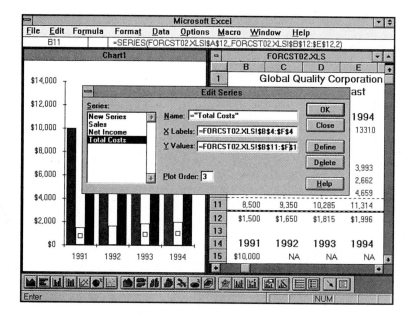

FIG. 20.10

The updated Edit
Series dialog box
shows extended
external reference
formulas that include
the additional data
locations.

Begin by choosing the **C**hart Edit **S**eries command. Be certain that the
data series you want to move is selected in the **S**eries list. Select the **P**lot
Order text box, and type the number you want the selected series to
have. Choose OK. The **C**hart Edit **S**eries command renumbers the other
markers accordingly and redraws the chart with the columns and bars in
their new order.

NOTE   Excel uses the X Labels reference for Series 1 to create Category (X) Labels. If you change the order of the series, the
new Series 1 may not include a reference to the Category (X)
labels, and your chart appears without Category (X) labels.
To repair this problem, enter in the **X** Labels box a reference
for Category (X) labels for the new Series 1.

For Related Information:

◀◀ "Creating Charts with the ChartWizard," p. 668.

◀◀ "Adding or Deleting Data," p. 703.

◀◀ "Clearing Chart Formats or Contents," p. 743.

FROM HERE...

Linking Chart Text to Worksheet Cells

The capability to link worksheet text or numbers to attached or unattached (free-floating) chart text is helpful. This technique can be used to update chart or axis titles when titles on the worksheet change or to link comments in a worksheet cell to a chart. Figure 20.11 shows a text box that displays the contents of a worksheet cell.

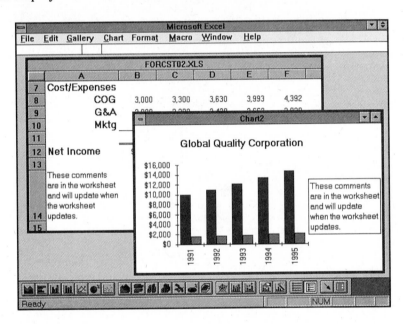

FIG. 20.11

You can link the contents of a worksheet cell to a text box in the chart.

When you edit the worksheet comments, the change appears in the chart text. You also can link a worksheet cell's contents to the data series numbers that are attached to the top of columns or bars. Then the worksheet cell's contents also appear at the top of the column or end of the bar.

To link a worksheet cell's contents to attached or unattached text in a chart, perform the following steps:

1. Open the worksheet and the chart. Activate the chart.

2. Create attached text, such as titles or data series numbers, if you want the cell contents to appear at these points.

3. If you are creating unattached text linked to a worksheet cell, be certain that no text object is selected, and enter an equals (=) sign.

If you want a cell's contents to appear at an attached text location, select the attached text and replace it with an equals (=) sign.

4. Activate the worksheet by clicking on it (if you can see it), or choose the worksheet from the **W**indow menu.

5. Select the cell containing the text you want to link. You also can select cells containing numbers. If the worksheet cell is named, you can enter the name by using the Formula **P**aste Name command.

6. Press Enter.

Figure 20.11 shows a worksheet containing information linked to a chart. The unattached text in the chart is selected so that the external reference formula that links the text box in the chart to the worksheet appears in the Formula Bar.

Creating Combination Charts

Combination charts present two or more series of data on the same chart; they may use two chart types. Combination charts work well to compare trends in two types of data or to look for possible interactions between two sets of data. The two charts are called the *main* chart and the *overlay* chart.

Figure 20.12 shows a combination column chart and line chart created by pasting in a data series, then choosing the **C**hart Add **O**verlay command. Marketing expenses were added to the chart created in Chapter 17, "Chart Quick Start," so that the chart now has three data series. In the figure, the third series of data appears as the line.

Figure 20.13 shows a combination chart where both charts are line charts. This combination enables you to use two value (Y) axes with different scales.

You can create a combination chart in two ways. The method you choose depends on whether you are creating a new chart or customizing an existing one.

If you are creating a new chart or are working with a chart that has not been customized, you can create a combination chart by choosing the **G**allery Combination command. You can select from five combination formats.

If your chart has custom features that you do not want to lose, or if you want a combination not included in the gallery combinations, choose **C**hart Add **O**verlay to create your combination chart. One or more of the charts series will be converted to the default overlay format. You can alter the type of overlay by choosing Format **O**verlay, as described in the section "Changing the Overlay Chart Format" later in this chapter. The Format Overlay command is available only when the chart has an overlay.

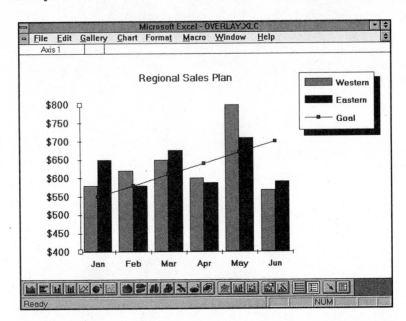

FIG. 20.12

Combination charts combine two types of charts.

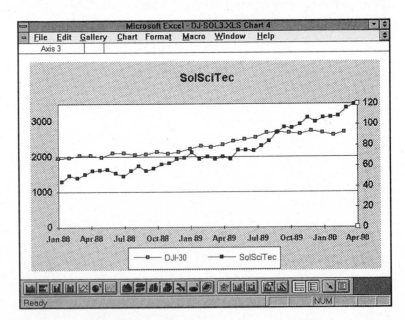

FIG. 20.13

Use combination charts to plot data series that have different value (Y) axes.

In combination charts, the chart in the background is the main chart, and the one in the foreground is the overlay. Choosing **C**hart Add **O**verlay divides the data series evenly, putting the first half of the data series on the main chart and the second half of the data series on the overlay chart. If an odd number of data series exists, then the main chart includes the extra series. A following section "Changing the Overlay Chart Format" describes how to change the number of series in the overlay chart. For example, if five lines are being charted, then three will be on the main chart and two will be on the overlay. When an overlay chart already exists on the current chart, the menu command becomes **C**hart Delete **O**verlay.

Changing the Main Chart Format

You may want to change the type of the main chart during analysis. For example, you might change the main chart from a **L**ine to a **C**olumn and then to an **A**rea to see whether different graphic representations reveal something unique. While switching among these chart types with the Format **M**ain Chart command, you can customize the chart with such features as hi-lo lines or overlapping columns.

To change the main chart, perform the following steps:

1. Choose the Forma**t M**ain Chart command. Figure 20.14 shows the Main Chart dialog box that appears.

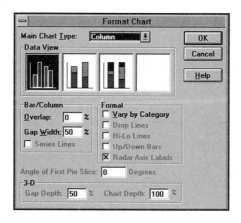

FIG. 20.14

Use the Main Chart dialog box to change chart types without losing customization.

2. Select from table 20.1 the options you want to use for the main (background) chart.

Only the options that make sense for the chart type you selected in the **Type** list are available. Unavailable options are dimmed.

3. Choose OK or press Enter.

Table 20.1. Main Chart Formats

Option	Description
Main Chart Type	Changes the chart type to one of the types shown in the **G**allery menu, but custom formats are retained. Types available are: Area, Bar, Column, Line, Pie, and XY (Scatter). Choosing one of these types removes any overlay.
Data View	Changes the type of marker or axis presentation within a specific chart type.
Bar/Column Overlap	Specifies how much bars or columns overlap. Enter a positive number as the percentage of overlap. 50 is full overlap. A negative number separates individual bars or columns.
Bar/Column Gap Width	Specifies the space between groups of bars or columns. Measured as a percentage of one bar or column width.
Series Lines	Draws a line between types of markers in stacked bar and stacked column charts.
Format Vary	Specifies a different color or pattern by category for each marker in all pie charts or any chart with one data series.
Format Drop Lines	Drops a vertical line from a marker to the category (X) axis. Used on line or area charts.
Format Hi-Lo Lines	Draws a line between the highest and lowest lines at a specific category. Used on 2-D line charts.
Up/Down Bars	Used in stock market charts to draw a rectangle between opening and closing prices. Creates an open-high-low chart. Use only on line charts. If series are in rows, then Hi data should be in the first row; Open data in the second row; and Close data in the third row.
Radar Axis Labels	Creates labels for the category axis (spokes) on radar charts.
Angle of First	Specifies the starting angle in Pie Slice degrees for the first wedge in a pie chart. Vertical is zero degrees.

Option	Description
3-D **G**ap Depth	Specifies the spacing in depth between markers as a percentage of a marker. 50 changes the space of the depth between markers to 50 percent of a marker width. Because the chart depth has not changed, this action makes markers thinner. Number must be between 0 and 500.
3-D **C**hart Depth	Specifies how deep a 3-D chart is relative to its width. Enter a number as a percentage of the chart width. 50 makes the depth 50 percent of the width. Number must be between 20 and 2000.

Changing the Overlay Chart Format

As you work with your charts, you may find that a different overlay chart type helps you to more accurately compare data between the main chart and the overlay chart. To change the type of overlay chart, choose the Format **O**verlay command and select the options appropriate to the type of overlay chart you select.

The Format Overlay dialog box is shown in figure 20.15. The options in the Format Overlay box are the same as those described for the Format Main Chart dialog box with the exception of the Series Distribution group.

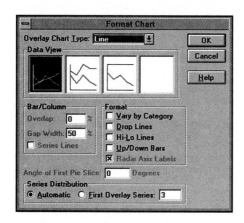

FIG. 20.15

Use the Format Overlay dialog box to change the type of overlay or the data series used in the overlay.

The Series Distribution options define where data series are split between the main chart and the overlay chart in a combination chart. If you select the **A**utomatic option, the data series are split evenly between the main and the overlay chart. The first half of the series are assigned to the main chart. If the number of data series is uneven, the main chart receives one extra data series. If there are five data series, for example, the first three data series are used in the main chart and the last two are used in the overlay.

If you want the split between main and overlay charts to begin with a specific data series, select the **F**irst Overlay Series and type the number of the first overlay data series in the text box.

T   I   P   The Series Distribution option specifies where the split between the main and overlay chart occurs. To change the order in which data series appear, choose the **C**hart **E**dit **S**eries command, select the series you want to reposition from the **S**eries list, and then enter the new position in the **P**lot Order text box.

Whenever a chart with an overlay is active, the **C**hart menu displays the Delete **O**verlay command. Choosing Delete **O**verlay removes the overlay chart and displays all data series on the main chart.

FROM HERE...

For Related Information:

Creating Slide Show Presentations

The Slides add-in enables you to create slide shows. With the Slide Show, you can display timed or manually controlled sequences of worksheets, charts, graphics and text. Slide Show is perfect for making presentations through LCD overhead projectors or video projector systems. The slide shows you create can use special visual and audio effects when moving between slides.

The Slides add-in gives you control over the following features:

- A slide's display time

- Manually controlled slide changes

- Special visual transition effects

- Audio transition effects (available with sound boards)

- Which slide begins a presentation

If you wish to use the special sound effects available when changing between slides, you must be using Windows 3.1 or running Windows 3.0 with the Multimedia Extensions Version 1.0 or later. You also need sound boards or multimedia boards and speakers compatible with Windows multimedia.

 Slide shows created with the add-in can appear only on a screen. You can not direct slides to a printer, plotter, or other output device.

Installing the Slide Add-In

You can determine that the Slide add-in is available if you choose the File New command and Slide is an available template. If Slide is not shown in the list of templates, then you need to install the Slide add-in.

Before you can create or run a slide show, you must install the Slide add-in. If you installed the macro library during Excel installation, the appropriate files will be on your system. If you did not install the add-ins, you can rerun Excel's setup software and elect to install only the macro add-ins.

To install the Slide add-in, perform the following steps:

1. Choose the **O**ptions Add-**i**ns command.

2. Choose the **A**dd button from the Add-In Manager dialog box. The File Open dialog box will appear.

3. Change to the \LIBRARY\SLIDES directory under the directory containing Excel.

4. Select the file SLIDES.XLA, and choose OK.

5. When the Add-In Manager dialog box reappears, notice that Slides is shown in the Add-Ins **I**nstalled list. Choose **C**lose, or press Enter.

The preceding procedure installs the macro sheet necessary for Slides to run. Unlike other add-ins, Slide does not add commands to your menus. Instead, the slide commands are accessed from buttons on a slide worksheet.

Two methods are available for opening a slide template. You can use the File Open command to open the SLIDES.XLT template located in the LIBRARY\SLIDES directory located under Excel. Or you can make the Slide template appear in the File New list of templates.

To make the slide template appear in the list of templates, use the File Manager to copy the file SLIDES.XLT from the LIBRARY\SLIDES directory into the EXCEL\XLSTART directory. You should keep your original SLIDES.XLT for safekeeping. Place a copy of SLIDES.XLT into the XLSTART directory by holding down the Ctrl key before you begin to drag the SLIDES.XLT from LIBRARY\SLIDES into XLSTART.

Creating a New Slide Show

You build slide shows by copying worksheets, charts, text, or graphics from Excel or other programs and then pasting them into the slide template. Any images included in a slide show must exist in the slide show template and in their original worksheet.

To create a slide show, open a new slide template by completing the following steps:

1. Choose the File New command.

2. Select Slides from the New dialog box.

3. Choose OK or press Enter.

The slide template shown in figure 20.16 enables you to create, edit, and run slide shows. You will use the buttons at the top of a slide worksheet to manage the slide show. Table 20.2 describes the buttons.

Table 20.2. Slide Show Buttons

Button	Result
Paste Slide	Pastes the contents of the Clipboard into the slide worksheet. Data is captured for a slide by copying it into the Clipboard and then pasting it into the slide worksheet.
Set Defaults	Changes the default settings for transition times and transition effects.

Button	Result
Edit Slide	Changes the transition from the current slide to the next slide.
Cut Row	Cuts a slide's information so that it can be moved to a different location in the slide show sequence.
Cop**y** Row	Copies a slide's information so that it can be moved to a different location in the slide show sequence.
Paste Row	Pastes a row of slide information into the active row.
De**l**ete Row	Removes a slide from the slide show.
Start Show	Starts the slide show and prompt for whether the show should be automatic or manually controlled.
Help	Displays information about the Slide Show program.

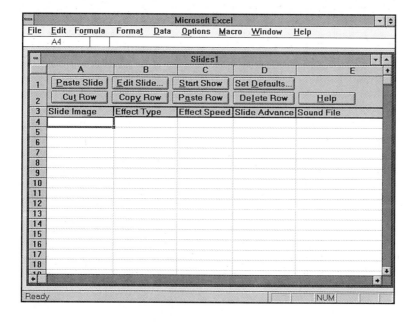

FIG. 20.16

Use the buttons on a
slide worksheet to
manage a slide show.

After a slide worksheet is open, you can add data to the slide worksheet.
Figure 20.17 shows a slide worksheet containing data for a slide show.
Each row in the slide worksheet contains information about a slide. From
left to right, the cells contain a copy of the slide, the type of visual transition effect, the speed of transition, how long the slide is visible, and the
audio transition effect.

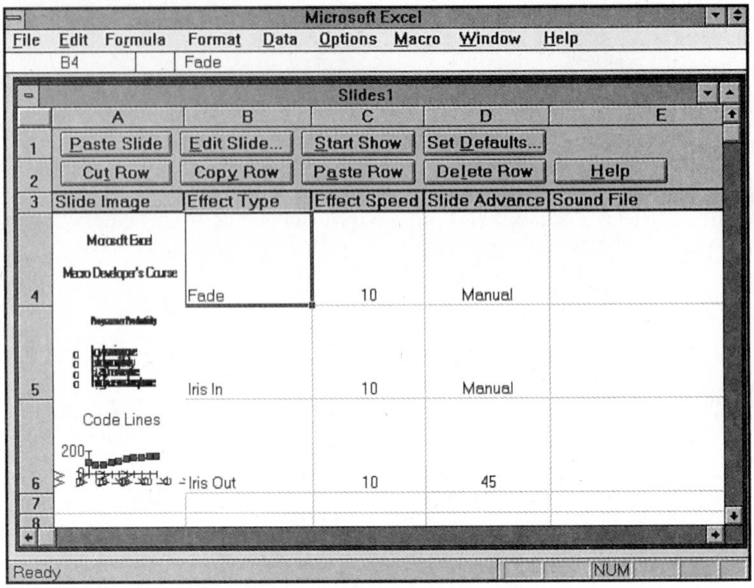

FIG. 20.17

Manage your slide
show in a slide
worksheet.

You should plan your slide show. Although you can edit the order in which slides appear, initially pasting them into the slide sheet in approximately the correct order is much faster. To copy Excel cells, Excel charts, or graphics from a Windows application into a slide, complete the following steps:

1. Select worksheet cells. Select all cells over which the characters you want to include extend. Format the worksheet and use the **Op**tions **D**isplay command to set gridlines and colors as you want them to appear in the slide.

   Or

   Select the chart you want as a slide.

   Or

   Select the object or graphic from another Windows application.

2. Choose the **E**dit **C**opy command.

3. Activate Excel if you are in another application; then activate the slide worksheet window.

4. Choose the **P**aste Slide button to copy the contents of the Windows clipboard into the first free row in column A on the slide worksheet.

   The Edit Slide dialog box appears, as shown in figure 20.18.

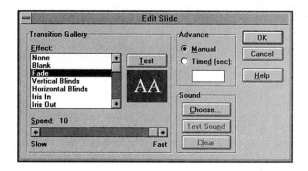

FIG. 20.18

Select the transition
times and effects from
the Edit Slide
dialog box.

5. Select the options to control this slide, which are described in the following table.

6. Choose OK, or press Enter.

7. If you want to create another slide, return to step 1.

   Your slide and its options will paste into the first available row in the slide worksheet.

> If text or graphics from another application will not display in the slide show, paste it first into an Excel worksheet; then save the worksheet. Now create a slide by using the text or graphic located on the Excel worksheet.
>
> **T I P**

8. Change the defaults for transitions between all pairs of slides.

9. Edit transitions between individual pairs of slides.

10. Move, copy, or delete individual slides.

11. Start the slide show.

12. Save the slide show.

The Edit Slide dialog box controls three characteristics of the transition from the previous slide to the current one. Select the following options you want for the transition from the current slide.

Transition Gallery

Effect	The visual transition effect, such as fading from one to another, sliding one on and the other off, creating a venetian blind effect, or opening an iris or shutter.
Test	See a sample of how the effect works.
Speed	The speed of the transition in seconds.

Advance

Manual	Begin transition to the next slide when you press the space bar or click a mouse button.
Time**d**	Begin transition to the next slide in the seconds you enter in the edit box.

Sound

Choose	Select a sound to play during the transition. (Only available with multimedia hardware and drivers installed.)
Test Sound	Play the select sound.
Clear	Remove the sound for this transition.

Editing Transitions

The Edit Slide dialog box displays with default settings. If you frequently use different settings than those that appear, change the default settings. To change a slide show's defaults for transitions, choose the Set **D**efaults button on the slide template. The Sets **D**efaults dialog box appears. From this dialog box, you make selections as you would in the **E**dit Slide dialog box. When you next choose the **P**aste Slide button, the **E**dit Slide dialog box appears with the new default settings.

To edit a slide's transition effects after it is pasted into a slide presentation, follow these steps:

1. Select a cell in the row with the slide you want to edit. The first cell containing a copy of the slide is protected. Select a cell to the right of the first cell.

2. Choose the **E**dit Slide button on the slide template. The Edit Slide dialog box appears.

3. Select the options you want from the dialog box.

4. Choose OK or press Enter.

Reordering a Slide Show

The steps for moving or copying one or more slides in a slide show are similar. In either case, you cut or copy a slide row from one location and paste it into another location. To move one or more slides, perform the following steps:

1. Select a cell in the row with the slide you want to move. Select more than one row to move more than one slide. The first cell containing a copy of the slide is protected. Select a cell to the right.

2. Choose the Cut Row or Copy Row button on the slide template.

3. Select the slide above which you want to insert the slide(s).

4. Choose the Paste Row button on the slide template.

To delete one or more slides, select them from the slide show template. Then, choose the Delete Row button from the template.

Starting a Slide Show

To run the slide show perform the following steps:

1. Activate the slide worksheet containing your slide show.

2. Choose the Start Show button. The Start Show dialog box displays, as shown in figure 20.19.

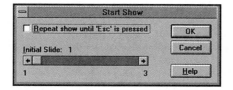

FIG. 20.19

Use the Start Show dialog box to control the start of your slide show.

3. Select the Repeat Show until 'Esc' is pressed check box if you want the show to run continuously. Otherwise the show runs through one time then stops.

4. Select the Initial Slide bar, and move the slide to the number of the slide at which you want the show to start. Drag the box with the mouse, or use the arrow keys to select a starting slide.

5. Choose OK or press Enter.

Stopping, Pausing, or Restarting a Slide Show

To interrupt a slide show, press the Esc key. This action displays the Slide Show Options dialog box. This box enables you to choose to stop the show, continue running the slide show, or go to a specific slide.

When you press Esc, the Slide Show Options dialog box displays, as shown in figure 20.20. The slide show pauses while this box displays.

FIG. 20.20

You can stop, interrupt, or repeat slides from the Slide Show Options dialog box.

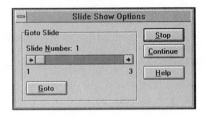

From the Slide Show options dialog box, you can stop the slide show by choosing the **S**top button. To continue the show, choose the **C**ontinue button.

If you want to return to a specific slide or restart the entire slide show, select the Slide **N**umber bar and move the box to the slide at which you want to begin. Drag the box or press arrow keys to move it. Choose the **G**oto button to display the slide you have chosen and continue the show.

Modifying Slides in the Slide Show

Slides actually are embedded or linked data. To modify a slide that is linked to worksheet data, open the worksheet containing the data and make your changes. Save the worksheet to preserve the changes. When you change the server worksheet, the slide changes.

Charts that are pasted are pasted as embedded charts. To update them you must unprotect the slide sheet by using the **O**ptions Un**p**rotect Document command. (Excel does not use a password to protect the template.) Double-click on the chart to put it into a chart window; then change its format.

After the slide sheet is unprotected, you can use any of the updating methods described in Chapters 9 and 12 to update linked data. For example, if you have multiple files you need to open and update, then choose the **F**ile **L**inks command, select the files you want to open and choose **O**pen. When you are finished updating source sheets and charts, remember to save the source documents. After source documents are saved, use the **O**ptions **P**rotect Document command to reprotect the slide sheet. If you want to ensure that no changes are made to the slide show, use a password. Save the slide show sheet.

Maintaining the Links to Original Slide Data

The slide show actually displays data that is linked to original worksheet or chart files. If the worksheets or charts that create the slide show are moved or renamed, the slide show cannot find the documents it needs. By using the same procedure for changing links in worksheets and charts, you can change links in the slide sheet. You also can redirect a slide, for example, by changing a slide from a chart of January data to a chart of February data.

Use the following steps to change where the Slide Show looks for the original data that supplies each slide:

1. Open the slide show sheet.

2. Choose the **O**ptions Un**p**rotect Document command.

3. Choose the **F**ile **L**inks command.

4. Select the source worksheet or chart you need to change.

5. Choose the **C**hange button. The Change Links dialog box displays and looks like a File Open dialog box.

6. Select the drive, directory, and file to which you want the slide linked.

7. Choose OK or press Enter.

   The Links dialog box reappears.

8. Select the file to which the link has just been changed, and choose the **O**pen button.

This procedure opens the new source document and updates the contents of the slide sheet. Save the slide sheet to preserve the new link.

If your slide show needs to be transferred to other computers you may want to *bind* all the documents needed for the slide show into a workbook. This process ensures that some of the original documents will not get lost. Workbooks are described in Chapter 11.

T I P

Saving a Slide Show

After you have designed a slide to match your specifications, or if you must move on to other activities, you can save the slide show. To save a show, perform the same steps that you use to save a normal worksheet:

1. Activate the slide show sheet.

2. Choose the **File Save As** command.

3. Type a name for the template.

4. Choose OK, or press Enter.

Modifying an Existing Slide Show

Modifying an existing slide show is just like editing a new one—except that you open a previously composed slide show sheet instead of opening the template from **File New**. Perform the following steps to open an existing slide show:

1. Choose the **File Open** command.

2. Select the slide show worksheet you want to open.

3. Choose OK, or press Enter.

If the slide show has graphics linked to other documents, you will be prompted to update the links. Respond with **Yes** if you want slides to use the most current data from the files on disk.

FROM HERE...

For Related Information:

◄◄ "Linking Pictures of Worksheet Cells," p. 448.

◄◄ "Linking Worksheet Cells and Ranges," p. 453.

Troubleshooting Charts

You can create enlightening charts from your worksheets. However, even Excel's charts can produce unusual results if you do something outside normal chart operations. The troubleshooting tips that follow reveal some of the ways charts can produce a different result than you expected. These tips also suggest ways you can solve common problems.

Problem:

Excel does not update or redraw the chart after you change data on the worksheet or after you edit one of the chart-related series formulas.

Solution:

Excel may be set for manual recalculation. To update the chart by using new worksheet data or a new series formula, choose **C**hart **C**alculate **N**ow, or reset to automatic with **O**ption **C**alculation **A**utomatic.

Problem:

You opened a chart without updating it to see the chart using old data. Now you want to update the chart without opening the worksheet.

Solution:

Choose the **F**ile **L**inks command, select from the **L**inks list the worksheet from which you want an update, and then choose the **U**pdate button.

Problem:

The numbers along the value (Y) axis have too many decimal places and have a format that just doesn't look right with the rest of the chart. What command formats the numbers along the value axis?

Solution:

Excel does not have a command to directly format numbers along the value axis. Formats along the value axis reflect the formats in the worksheet. To change the format of numbers on the value axis, use **F**ormat **N**umber to format the numbers in the cells of the first data series in the worksheet.

If you need to scale down the numbers on the axis, divide them by 100, 1,000, or another appropriate number in the worksheet. Use the numbers resulting from this division to create the chart. You also can use a custom numeric format in the worksheet, such as:

    ###,

Because no #s or 0s are to the right of the command, Excel formats the numeric display to display without those digits. The entire number is still used in calculation.

Problem:

When plotting a large amount of data in a line chart, the category X labels and tick marks are too close together. How can their appearance be improved?

Solution:

To display fewer labels or tick marks along the category axis but still keep all the data, use the **F**ormat **S**cale command in the following steps:

1. Select the category axis, then choose **F**ormat **S**cale.

2. Select the text boxes for either or both options: Number of Categories Between Tick Labels and Number of Categories Between Tick Marks.

3. Enter a number larger than the one displayed in the box.

4. Choose OK or press Enter.

If the labels or tick marks are still too close together, repeat the process and use a larger number. As an alternative, you can use the Format **Text** command to rotate the labels along an axis.

Problem:

Some combinations of colors and patterns on charts are aesthetically offensive (ugly). How are colors and patterns returned to their original selections?

Solution:

You can return to the default colors and patterns by selecting the chart items you want to change, choosing the Format **P**atterns command, and then selecting the Automatic option. You also can select the object and press the Del key; then select the Formats option, and choose OK.

Problem:

Selecting the embedded chart in a worksheet does not make the chart menu appear.

Solution:

To change or format embedded charts, double-click on the embedded chart so that it opens into a window. While the chart is in a window you can format it. To put the chart back into the worksheet, close the window the chart is in.

Problem:

The printed copies of the chart do not look the same as the chart looks in the window. Why does this difference exist, and what can be done about it?

Solution:

Always use printer fonts or TrueType fonts in your charts. Printer fonts have a small printer icon next to them in the Font list and TrueType fonts have a small TT icon. If you create a chart with fonts your printer does not have available, the printer makes a substitution, which can cause problems with spacing, style and size.

If you need to format embedded charts, do not maximize their windows when you format them. After you double-click on the embedded chart, the window it appears in will be the same size as the embedded chart. Format the chart within this window. This process ensures that you are seeing a more accurate representation of how the chart will print.

Problem:

Changing the chart type removes custom formats.

Solution:

Clicking on a chart type tool or choosing a chart type from the **G**allery menu may destroy custom formats you have applied. When you want to change the chart type of a custom formatted chart, choose the Forma**t M**ain Chart command. To change the type of the overlay chart in a combination chart, choose the Format **O**verlay command. These dialog boxes enable you to change chart types while preserving custom features that are appropriate to the new chart type.

Problem:

After moving a chart or its supporting worksheet to a different directory, the chart loses its link to the worksheet because it cannot locate the worksheet. How can the chart be relinked to its worksheet?

Solution:

Use the **F**ile **O**pen command to find the worksheet and open it. Activate the chart so that it is on top. Choose **F**ile Links and select the name of the worksheet that was originally linked to the chart. Choose the **C**hange button, and select the replacement worksheet's drive, directory, and file name from the list boxes. Choose OK or press Enter. The old directory and file name of the supporting worksheet is replaced in the chart's series formula by the directory and file name you chose from the list boxes. Save your updated chart.

For Related Information:

◄◄ "Troubleshooting Worksheets," p. 529.

FROM HERE...

Chapter Summary

Keep in mind that Excel charts have a wide variety of uses. You can create charts quickly and use them for data analysis, yet they can have the quality of professionally created graphics.

To use your charts inside other Windows programs and some standard DOS applications, refer to Chapter 31, "Using Excel with Windows Applications," and Chapter 32, "Using Excel with DOS Applications." In those chapters, you learn how to put Excel charts into other applications.

Excel Databases

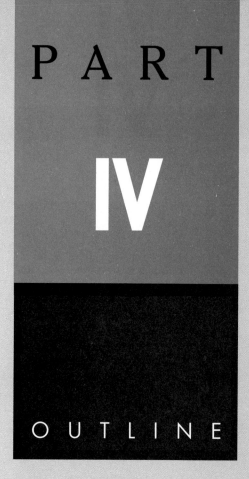

PART

IV

OUTLINE

Designing Databases

This chapter helps you understand important database terms and concepts. The chapter describes a database, explains the parts of a database, advises how to choose the contents for a database, and shows you how to lay out a database on the worksheet. The following Chapters 22-26 explain the details of building and operating databases.

Defining a Database

The first example of a database that most people encounter is the familiar rolling card file (see fig. 21.1). You quickly can flip through a card file to find information, such as a client's address, phone number, or favorite restaurant. Card files are easy to use as long as the cards are kept in alphabetical order according to a single key word, such as the client's name. Card files can present problems, however, when you want to do anything other than find a client by name. If, for example, you wanted to find all the financial analysts in San Francisco, using a card file could take considerable time.

Excel's database handles basic functions, such as finding the kind of information you would write on a card, quickly and easily. Excel also handles complex database jobs, such as analyzing and extracting information in the database.

```
Turnigan, Kathleen      (415) 579-2650

Financial Analyst

Brown, James & Assoc.
213 California St.
San Francisco, CA 94003

Background:          Interned w/Peterman, M.B.A., Stanford

Expertise:           Bond portfolio analysis

Computer experience: Excel expert
```

The file card for Kathleen Turnigan contains information related to Kathleen Turnigan. In a computer database, that information is a record. All the information from one file card goes into one database *record*, or a row of related information. In that row, individual items are stored in *fields* (cells).

Each individual piece of data in the record (row) must be entered in a separate cell. Kathleen's first name, for example, goes in one cell (the First Name field), her last name in another cell (the Last Name field), the firm name in a third (the Firm field), and so on. To keep the information organized, each field is assigned to a specific column. For example, first names belong only in column A, last names belong in column B, and so on. Each column is given a unique *field name*. Figure 21.2 shows how part of Kathleen's card would be entered in the first record of an Excel database in row 10.

An Excel database will have many records. When looking for related information, you must tell Excel what field (column) to search. To do this, you must give Excel the exact field name or the field's column number. To find the records in a database for everyone in San Francisco, for example, you might tell Excel to search a field named City. Field names must be text or text formulas. Figure 21.2 shows how the field names and data are arranged within an Excel worksheet.

Figure 21.2 shows that the information from the card in figure 21.1 now appears in a single record (row) of the database; each cell in the row contains a different field of data. From the field names at the top of each database column, you easily can tell the data each field contains.

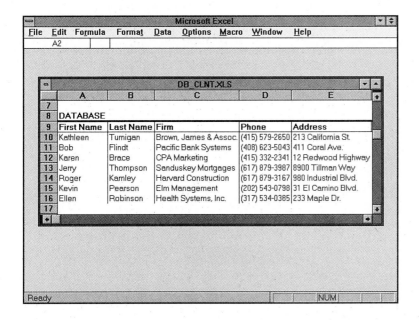

FIG. 21.2

An Excel database
with field names as
column headings.

Defining the Parts of a Database

A fully functional database contains the following three parts:

Range	Description
Database	Where information is kept. An Excel database is kept in a worksheet; related information is entered in rows. Each column of information has a unique field name. With the use of Q+E, you can link Excel to databases on your hard disk, SQL server, or mainframe.
Criteria	Where you indicate what you want to find or analyze in the database. Contains field names and an area in which you type a specification describing the information you want.
Extract	Where Excel copies desired information from the database. Contains field names of the data you want and an area in which the copy will be pasted.

Before you can use Excel's database, you must indicate the database being used. In most cases, the database is a range on a worksheet. The range must contain both the data and the field names in the database. You tell Excel the location of the database range by selecting the field names and data records, as shown in figure 21.3. Next, choose **Data Set Database**. This command gives the database and its field names the range name *Database*. Remember that field names must occupy only a single row. If you use Q+E to link Excel to a database on your disk or the network, you must tell Q+E which file and table contain the data you want to use.

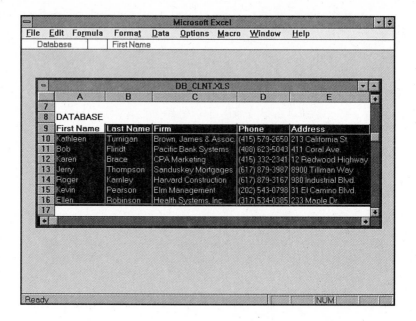

FIG. 21.3

The selected database range.

After you name the database range, you can begin to add, delete, edit, and find information. Choosing the **Data Form** command automatically creates a database form with buttons. The form enables you to view one record at a time. Figure 21.4 shows the form created for the database in figure 21.3. Notice that the form shows all the fields that were not immediately visible and those on the screen.

If you want to conduct complex searches or extract information from the database, you also need to specify a criteria range. Figure 21.5 shows a criteria range selected before choosing the **Data Set Criteria** command. The criteria range must contain the field names on top and at least one blank row underneath. The criteria range does not need to include all the fields in the database. The field names must be exactly the same as those in the database. In the blank row, you enter the criteria that specifies what you are searching for. Figure 21.5 shows the criteria range selected. You do not have to place borders around the criteria range.

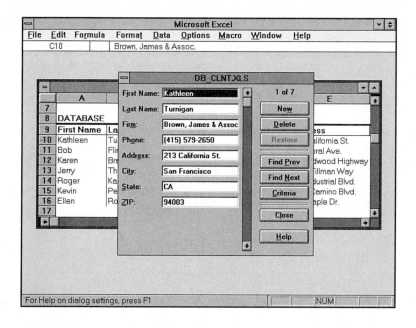

FIG. 21.4

Excel automatically
creates a database
form for you.

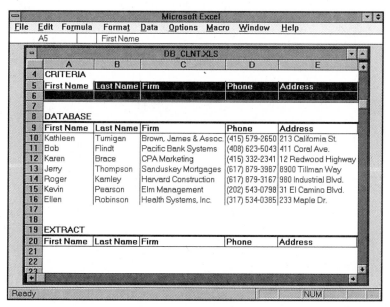

FIG. 21.5

The criteria range is
where you indicate for
what you are looking.

The last database area you need to know is the extract range. The extract range is where Excel copies records that meet the criteria. You could, for example, request an extract of all addresses in a specific ZIP code. Excel would copy the addresses into the extract range. Another excellent use of this feature is to create smaller databases or reports from the original database.

Figure 21.6 shows a single row of headings selected in preparation for choosing **D**ata Extract. Because only a single row of field names has been selected, all cells below the selected extract headings will be cleared before the extracted data is copied under the field names in the extract range.

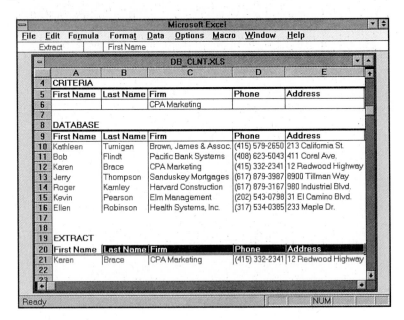

FIG. 21.6

Use the extract range to make duplicate copies of information meeting your criteria.

For Related Information:

FROM HERE...

▶▶ "Matching Simple Criteria," p. 828.

▶▶ "Extracting Data," p. 845.

▶▶ "Using External Database Commands," p. 866.

Choosing the Contents for a Database

You can save yourself time and trouble by planning your database before building it. As a simple checklist for what data to include in a database and how to name it, consider these points:

■ List the groups of data you want in each record, such as Company Info and Personal Info.

■ Break these groups of data into the smallest elements that you will ever consider using. Personal Info, for example, might be divided into separate fields such as First_Name, Last_Name, and Title. This technique makes searching the database easier and enables you to reorder data in new structures. Use only text or text formulas in field names. Do not use numeric or date values.

■ Cross out fields you probably will never use. For example, don't use fields that can be calculated in a report. Why waste memory storing information that can be calculated?

Choose fields that are small and contain the most usable part of the data. For example, instead of using Name as a single field containing an entire name, use three fields: Title, First_Name, and Last_Name. This technique gives you the option of reordering the data in many different combinations. Suppose, for example, that your data looks like the following:

Title	*First_Name*	*Last_Name*
Ms.	Kathleen	Turnigan

From this data, you later can create any of the following combinations:

Ms. Turnigan

Kathleen

Ms. Kathleen Turnigan

Kathleen Turnigan

You also should keep ZIP codes as a separate field. Never include the ZIP code in the city and state fields. Demographic and market data may be tied to the ZIP code. In addition, you can reduce postage rates by sorting mailings by ZIP code.

Be on the lean side when including data fields. Many business information systems lie unused because some well-meaning person wanted the database to contain too much information. The result is a database that is expensive, time-consuming, and tedious to maintain. When a database isn't maintained, it isn't used. Include only data you can use and keep up-to-date.

Organizing Your Database

Before building your database, consider how it fits with the rest of the worksheet and how to coordinate it with other worksheets and databases for your business. Remember that Excel databases and worksheets in different files can be linked together. The following are some additional points to consider:

- Draw diagrams of other databases and worksheets in your business, and notice where the data is stored twice. Can the data be stored in separate files and recombined as needed with the aid of Excel or Q+E? If you frequently need to join files or if the databases involve more than a few thousand records (rows), you should use a relational database instead of a worksheet like Excel.

- Be certain that nothing lies below an unlimited extract range. Extracting to an unlimited extract range clears all cells below the extract field names.

- Position the database so that room is available for it to expand downward. If you use Data Form to add records (rows) to your database, records are added without pushing down the information below the database. If not enough room is available to insert data for the new records, the database form will not let you add a new record.

- If you want to insert rows to add records to the middle of a database, insert cells within all columns of the database. Inserting a row through a database also inserts a row through anything on the sides of the database.

Chapter Summary

To get started with your database, read Chapter 22, "Entering and Sorting Data," and Chapter 23, "Finding and Editing Data." If you need to perform complex queries or extract information from the database to create a report, refer to Chapter 24, "Extracting and Maintaining Data." If you have large databases or want to link Excel to databases created by other PC programs or from a mainframe, then read Chapter 25, "Linking Excel to Databases with Q+E." Chapter 26, "Building Extensive Databases," shows you how to link databases that are on separate documents and how to analyze database contents, create cross-tabulation reports, cross-check data entry, and troubleshoot database operations.

Entering and Sorting Data

This and the following chapters describe how to build and use a database that resides on an Excel worksheet. A database is like an automated card-file system that enables you to find information quickly, and then edit, sort, extract and print, or analyze it. The three parts of an Excel database—database, criteria, and extract range—are explained more fully in Chapter 21.

Although Excel is primarily a worksheet, it does have database capability that can help you analyze stock market trends, track client names and addresses, save expense account data, and monitor sales figures. The combination of database functions, powerful worksheet analysis capabilities, and charting capabilities makes Excel an excellent tool for business analysis and management systems.

Excel provides two methods for working with a database. The first method uses Excel's automatically generated data form for quick and simple data entry, editing, deleting, and searching. The second method gives you the ability to query the database with complex questions and find or extract the information you need. The database is specified in one range of the worksheet, and another range is used for criteria or questions. A third range is specified to hold extracted information.

Excel's database can hold a single row of data or an entire worksheet full of information. You can put your Excel database on one worksheet and your criteria (questions) on another and have analysis and reports done on yet another worksheet. If the database is too large to fit in a worksheet or the design requires a disk-based database, you can use the Q+E add-in that comes with Excel to link Excel to database files on your hard disk, on the network server, or in some mainframe files. Q+E is explained in Chapter 25, "Linking Excel to Databases with Q+E."

In this chapter, you learn how to build a database and how to enter information into your database. If you want to keep just a few records of information, you will find the discussion on the automatic database form interesting. If you want to enter information in a list (more like the worksheet format), you will prefer the other methods.

After creating your database, you may want to keep it sorted for better presentation in reports. Excel's Sort command enables you to sort your data in ascending or descending order using as many fields to sort on as you want.

Entering the Field Names

The database must have unique field names in a single row across the top of the database. These field names identify each column of data. The database must have at least one row of data directly below the field names.

Figure 22.1 shows a sample database and the criteria range where questions are asked. The formatting shown in the figure is not a requirement; it serves to enhance the database's appearance and to reduce errors. Figure 22.2 shows the only mandatory parts of a database: the single row of field headings in row 10 and the data in rows 11-19.

When you enter field names across the top of the database, you must keep the following points in mind:

- Field names must be text or text formulas, such as ="9540".

- Field names cannot be numbers, dates, nontext formulas, logical values, error values, or blanks.

- Field names can include up to 255 characters, but short names are easier to see in a cell.

- Only the names in the row directly above the data are used as field names. You can add explanatory names, such as those in cells A9 and B9 of figure 22.1, but only the field names in the row directly above the data are used by Excel.

- Names must be different from each other.

After you create field names, you need to add a row or two of data before building the rest of the database. Add one or two rows of data with normal worksheet entry techniques. After you create the database, you can use more convenient methods of entering data that are described later.

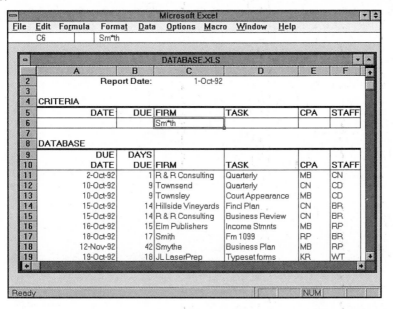

FIG. 22.1

This sample database is formatted with borders so that it is easier to read.

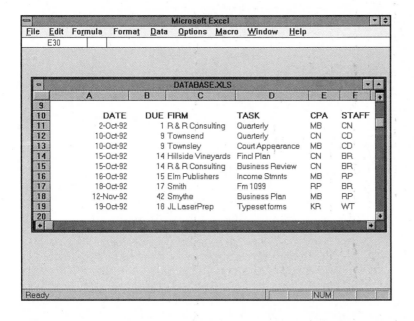

FIG. 22.2

The essential parts of a database: the field names and data.

Setting the Database Range

After creating field names and adding at least one row of data, you need to set the database range so that Excel will know where the database is located on the worksheet. The database range contains the field names in the single row above data and the data itself. Figure 22.3 shows a selected database range. Notice that only the row of field names directly above the data has been selected.

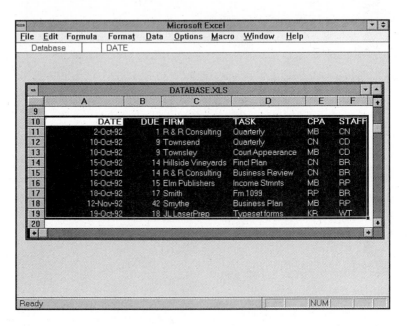

FIG. 22.3

The database range includes data and a single row of field names above the data.

To define the location of the database, complete the following steps:

1. Select the field names and data underneath the field names.

2. Choose the **D**ata Set Data**b**ase command.

This procedure creates a named range called *Database*. You can view the currently selected database range at any time by choosing the Fo**r**mula **G**oto command (F5) and selecting Database from the list box.

You can define only one database at a time with the **D**ata Set Data**b**ase command. To use a different database, you need to name the new database range by selecting it and choosing **D**ata Set Data**b**ase. The following steps explain a fast way to perform this action. (This method will not work when data is added with the **D**ata F**o**rm command, because the names of the ranges will not automatically expand.)

T I P

If your database has only a single row of field names and no filled cells are touching the field names or data, as shown in figure 22.3, then you quickly can select the entire database by clicking a filled cell in the field names or database and pressing Ctrl+* (Shift+Ctrl+8). This process is the same as the Formula Select Special command with the Current Region check box selected.

Quickly change between different databases by giving each database a range name with the Formula Define Name command. Names such as DB.AR, DB.Client, or DB.Sales will make the databases easier to find and remember. After each database range is named, you can switch quickly between databases by completing the following steps:

1. Choose the Formula Goto command (F5).

2. Select the name of the database you want to use, such as DB.AR, and press Enter, or double-click the name in the list.

3. Choose the Data Set Database command.

T I P

To speed up this process even more, record a command macro that performs steps 1 to 3. After the macro is recorded, insert a question mark into the macro. The question mark pauses the Goto dialog box so that you can choose any range name to be set as the database name. To make the Goto box pause, insert a question mark as follows:

=FORMULA.GOTO?("DB.AR")

This formula pauses the Goto dialog box with the name DB.AR selected as the default. The macro enables you to pop up a dialog box with a Ctrl+key combination and select the new database from the Goto list. Sample macros in Chapter 30 illustrate macros that quickly change database and print ranges.

For Related Information:

FROM HERE...

◄◄ "Naming Cells," p. 210.

►► "Building Command Macros," p. 915.

Entering Data

Now that you have entered the field headings and initial data and have selected the database range, you can use many different methods for entering data. Some methods include the following:

- You can use Excel's automatic database form to enter data. This is a quick and easy method of entering data.

- You can enter data into blank rows or cells inserted in the database.

- Use a macro to automate either of these methods or to create a custom dialog box that accepts, verifies, and enters data. The macro portion of this book demonstrates custom dialog boxes that enter data into a database.

Using the Database Form

The easiest method of entering data is with Excel's automatically generated database form. After you have set the database range with **D**ata Set Data**b**ase, you can use the form to enter data by following these steps:

1. Choose the **D**ata F**o**rm command.

   A database form similar to the one shown in figure 22.4 appears over the worksheet.

2. Select the Ne**w** button.

3. After typing data in a field's text box, press Tab or Shift+Tab to travel forward or backward between fields. You also can click a text box if you use a mouse. Be careful not to press Enter until you are ready to move to the next record.

4. To enter additional records, repeat steps 2 and 3.

5. Choose the Close button to close the form and return to the worksheet.

   The data form will display calculated field results, but you cannot edit the contents. To hide fields in the form, hide the calculated field's column in the worksheet.

Selecting the **N**ew button or pressing Enter places the new record you have typed in the form into the database. Therefore, use Tab and Shift+Tab only until you are ready to save. After selecting Close, you may want to save the worksheet to record the additions on disk.

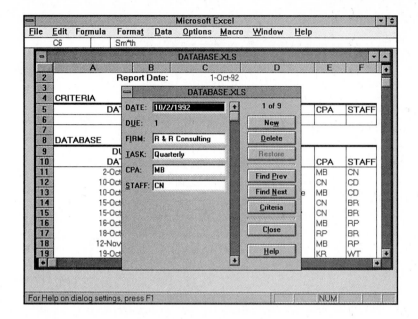

FIG. 22.4

The automatic database form with the first record displayed.

The records added with the Data Form are placed below the last row of the database. The database range is extended automatically to include the added records. Information below the database is not pushed down.

The data form will not let you add new records if there are not enough blank cells below the current database range. When you create your database, choose a location in the worksheet with enough room for your database to expand.

You can change the data in the new record until you have selected **New** or **Close** to add the record to the database. After you have added the new data, use any of the data find and edit techniques described in Chapter 23, "Finding and Editing Data," to make changes.

  The Data Form automatically expands the range name Database as new data is added to the bottom. Ranges that overlap the database are not automatically expanded.

Entering Data Directly

A second method for entering data is typing the data directly into rows in the worksheet. Before you use this data-entry method, you must make room in the database range for new records.

To preserve the named range, Database, insert new rows or cells be-tween existing database records (rows). If you insert new rows or cells below the last record of the database, those rows or cells will not be included in the database range. If you insert new rows or cells directly under the field headings, the format of the heading will be copied into the new row, not the format of other data cells.

If you add new records below the existing database instead of between records, you must re-create the database range. To re-create the data-base range, reselect the field names next to the data and the data, includ-ing the new data, and choose the **D**ata Set Data**b**ase command.

T I P
To move quickly through your databases from top to bottom or side to side, use a Ctrl+arrow key combination. You move the active cell across filled cells until the edge of the database is reached. To select cells as you move, also hold down the Shift key (Shift+Ctrl+arrow key).

Inserting entire rows through the database moves everything in the worksheet below that row. To move down only the cells directly below the database, only select a range that matches the database's columns before inserting rows. Insert cells in the database when you don't want to disturb areas to the right or left of the database.

In figure 22.5, the cells of the middle two records have been selected so that they can be moved down to allow for the addition of two more records. Cells outside the database are not selected. Notice the markers in column G; these indicate the cell locations outside the selected cells.

Choose the **E**dit **I**nsert command to display the dialog box, shown in figure 22.5, for inserting cells. In this box, you specify whether the cells should be moved down or right. For a database, you should shift cells down. Choosing OK moves everything below the selected cells, as shown in figure 22.6. The markers in column G have not moved.

To enter data in the blank cells that you have inserted in the database, complete the following steps:

1. Select the cells that will receive data. If you just inserted them, they are still selected.

2. Type data into the active cell.

3. Press one of the keys shown in table 22.1 to enter the data and move the active cell.

4. After the data is entered, press an arrow key to deselect the range.

5. Format the columns of data if necessary.

6. Create and copy formulas down the appropriate columns.

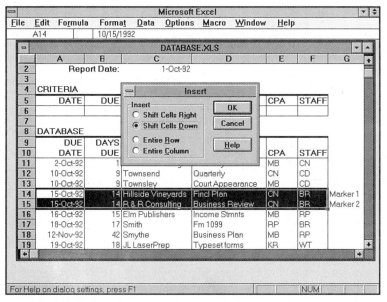

FIG. 22.5

Inserting cells into a database, rather than rows, preserves the position of information alongside the database.

FIG. 22.6

Blank cells have been inserted into the database range without moving adjacent cells.

While you are working within a selected data-entry range, the active cell remains in the data-entry area. The active cell automatically wraps from one edge of the selected range to the next edge.

Table 22.1. Data-Entry Keys

Key	Action
Tab	Enters data and moves right
Shift+Tab	Enters data and moves left
Enter	Enters data and moves down
Shift+Enter	Enters data and moves up

Excel has five shortcut key combinations that can speed your data-entry work. The key combinations are shown in table 22.2.

Table 22.2. Shortcut Keys for Data Entry

Key combination	Action
Ctrl+; (semicolon)	Enters the computer's current date
Ctrl+: (colon)	Enters the computer's current time
Ctrl+' (apostrophe)	Copies the formula from the cell above without adjusting cell references
Ctrl+" (double quotation marks)	Copies the value from the cell above
Ctrl+arrow	Moves over filled cells to the last filled cell, or moves over blank cells to the first filled cell

Speeding Up Data Entry

Excel recalculates only the formulas that depend on the changed cells. While Excel is calculating, you can continue to enter data; Excel will stop its calculations momentarily to accept your entry or command. In large databases containing many formulas, constant recalculation can slow data entry.

To speed up data entry, turn off automatic recalculation by choosing **O**ptions **C**alculation, selecting the **M**anual option, and pressing Enter. If automatic calculation is off and you plan to read the database while it remains on disk through worksheet links or Q+E, be certain that you press the F9 key or select the Recalculate Before Save check box.

Recalculating before the save, when Manual option is on, ensures that the database is accurate even while saved on disk.

While Excel is in manual calculation mode, the program will not update the formulas as you enter data. When you make a change that affects a formula in the worksheet, a `Calculate` indicator appears in the Status Bar at the bottom of the Excel screen. When you see the `Calculate` indicator, do not trust formula results displayed on-screen.

To recalculate all open worksheets while staying in manual calculation mode, choose **O**ptions Calculate **N**ow, press F9, or click the Calculate Now tool. If you want to recalculate only the active document, choose Shift+**O**ptions Calculate Docume**n**t, or press Shift+F9.

After making your database entries, you can return to automatic calculation by choosing the **O**ptions **C**alculation command and selecting the **A**utomatic option.

For Related Information:

◀◀ "Entering Formulas," p. 175.

◀◀ "Editing Text and Formulas," p. 195.

▶▶ "Drawing Dialog Boxes," p. 991.

FROM HERE...

Sorting Data

Sorting organizes your data in ascending or descending alphabetic and numeric order. Excel can sort the rows of a database or the columns of a worksheet.

Excel sorts thousands of rows or columns in the time it would take you to manually sort just a few. It sorts on three fields at a time in case duplicates exist in one of the sorted fields. With a simple trick, you can sort on an unlimited number of rows or columns.

When you select **D**ata **S**ort, Excel displays the Sort dialog box, shown in figure 22.7. The items that you can select in the box include sort keys and sort order.

The keys indicate which fields Excel sorts on. In a telephone book, for example, the first key is Last Name and the second key is First Name. If there are several people with the name Smith, their first names are used to put all the Smiths in sorted order. In the database shown in figure 22.8, the first sort key is column A (Due Date), the second key is column E (CPA), and the third key is column F (Staff). Notice that the key is a cell reference that can be anywhere in the column you want to sort.

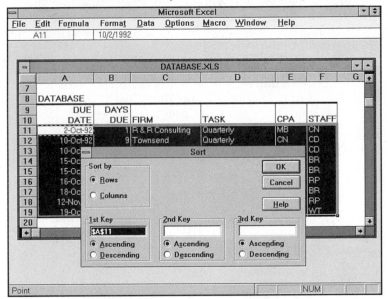

FIG. 22.7

The Sort dialog box enables you to reorganize database rows or worksheet columns.

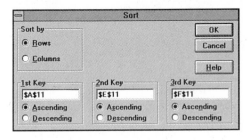

FIG. 22.8

Excel sorts on three columns or rows at a time.

The Ascending and Descending options beneath each key tell Excel to sort in A to Z and Z to A order, respectively. Excel sorts in ascending order from top to bottom for rows, or left to right for columns. The Descending option reverses this order. Blanks always sort to the bottom in ascending or descending sort. In addition, the program uses the following order of priority:

Numbers from largest negative to largest positive

Text

FALSE results

TRUE results

Error values

Blanks

Excel ignores the difference between upper- and lowercase letters, and Excel does not recognize international accent marks. This feature makes finding entries easier.

If you have set international character settings through the Windows Control Panel, Excel will sort in the order used by the country specified.

Be careful when you sort databases that contain formulas. When the rows in the database change order, formulas in the rows adjust to their new locations, which may produce references that provide incorrect results. To avoid this problem, remember that a database row should refer to other cells in the same row. If the formula needs to reference a cell outside the database range, that reference should be an absolute reference so that it doesn't change during sorting.

If you want numbers to sort as text, enter them as text. In the following list of numbers, for example, the first three are sorted as numbers. The others are sorted as text. Notice how the numbers entered as text mix with the alphanumeric combinations.

1	number
2	number
3	number
1	left-aligned text preceded by '
1a	left-aligned text preceded by '
2	left-aligned text preceded by '
2a	left-aligned text preceded by '
3	left-aligned text preceded by '
3a	left-aligned text preceded by '

You also can enter numbers as text formulas, for example,

="321"

NOTE Arithmetic operators, such as + or –, will coerce a text-number into its numeric equivalent. Numbers preceded by ' will calculate. Excel functions, such as SUM(), do not coerce a text-number. They treat these text-numbers as 0. To coerce a single text-number into a number that can be used by a function, use the VALUE() function.

Sorting by Command

Sorting is easy to use and is helpful for any type of list, not just data-bases. In fact, you can create quick and useful reports by just sorting database-like information so that the information you need ends up in adjacent rows. The result may not look as pretty as a full-fledged data-base, but it gets the job done quickly.

To sort a database or worksheet, complete the following steps:

1. Choose the File Save As command. Save the worksheet with a dif-ferent file name in case you scramble the data during sorting.

2. Select the data you want to sort.

   Do not select field names at the top of databases. If you include the field names, they will be sorted into the data.

   Select the full width of the database records if you are sorting by Rows, or the full height of the columns if you are sorting by Col-umns. Failing to include the full width (rows) or height (columns) can scramble your database or worksheet, leaving part sorted and part unsorted.

3. Choose the Data Sort command.

4. Enter the 1st Key.

   If you are sorting a database by rows (the usual method of sorting), select any cell in the column you want to sort on. If you are sorting by columns (reordering columns), select any cell in the row you want to sort on.

5. Select Ascending or Descending sort order on the 1st Key.

6. Move to the 2nd or 3rd Key, and repeat the procedures in steps 4 and 5.

   The second key is only used if there is duplicate data in the first key. The third key is only used if there is duplicate data in the first and second key.

7. Select Rows to keep individual rows intact when sorting databases or Columns to keep individual columns intact. (Sorting by columns is covered in more detail later in this chapter.)

8. Choose OK or press Enter.

Because you selected only part of the record, the problem of scrambling the database occurs most frequently when the database extends past the right of the screen, and you select only the cells visible on-screen. If you sort by columns, the same problem can occur if you do not select the full column height. If you immediately recognize that the sort has created a problem, choose the **Edit Undo Sort** command. If you cannot undo a problem, hope that you did not skip step 1. If you see a problem, retrieve the original copy.

 NOTE If you select less than the entire width of your database, the sort function may scramble the database. A database must have its full width selected before sorting but not necessarily its full height. If, for example, you select the First_Name and Last_Name fields in the sort area but do not include the Phone and Address fields, the First_Name and Last_Name cells will be sorted into a different order than the Phone and Address cells.

Sorting with the Toolbar

The Utility toolbar contains two tools that sort in ascending or descending order. These tools show A over Z for ascending sort and Z over A for descending sort. To sort with these tools perform the following steps:

1. Select the range you want sorted.

2. Move the active cell to the column you want as the first sort key: the column to be sorted on.

3. Click the Ascending or Descending sort tool.

The sort tools sort on only one key.

Returning a Sort to Its Original Order

When you want to sort a database and later return it to the original order, you need to add a record index to your database. This method does not help databases that have been torn asunder by incorrect sorting. A record index assigns a number to each record according to the record's position, date and time of entry, or some other unique numeric record indicator. Figure 22.9 shows an index in column A for a database. You can insert a column or cells to make room for an index.

To index the database records so that you can return them to a previous order, complete the following steps:

1. Insert a column. (If you are sorting a database, insert through the database so the new column is within the named database range.)

2. Type a number, such as *1*, in the top cell of the column.

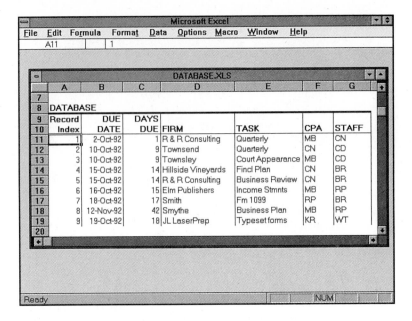

FIG. 22.9

A record index
enables you to return
the database to its
previous order.

3. Select the cell with the number, along with all cells in that column, through the height of the database.

4. Choose the **Data** **Series** command and fill the column with numbers in increasing order. These numbers are the index numbers.

T I P Use the fill handles to fill in a series of numbers quickly. Insert a blank column through the database. Type *1* in the top cell and *2* in the next cell down in the blank column. Select both cells. Drag the fill handle down the length of the database.

When you sort, always make sure that you include the column containing the index numbers. When you want to return to the original order, use the column of index numbers in ascending order as the first key.

Sorting by Date and Time

Excel sorts date fields by the serial number created by dates and times entered in cells. Sorting works correctly on only dates and times entered with a date and time format that Excel recognizes, or created with date or time functions. Check Chapters 7 and 8 for information on entering and formatting dates and times. If you enter dates and times that Excel does not recognize, Excel stores them as text and they are sorted in text order, not date-time order.

In many cases, you can change text dates into serial date numbers by inserting a column and entering a formula into the column that converts the adjacent date entry. Chapter 10 describes several functions that may be helpful in this process. (TRIM) removes unwanted blanks; (DATE) converts month, day, and year to a serial number; and (LEFT), (RIGHT), (MIDDLE), and (LEN) can take apart text so that pieces from within text can be used to calculate the date or time.

Sorting Account Codes, Service Codes, or Part Numbers

Sorting account codes, service codes, and part numbers may seem confusing at first, because these codes may contain a prefix, body, and suffix. For example, your business may use codes such as the following:

AE-576-12

02-88022-09

0001-6589

PRE-56983-LBL

Sorting part and service codes may be difficult because a segment of one code may overlap the character position of a different segment of another code. The result is incorrect sorting. For example, different sections of a code may have different numbers of characters for different items, such as AE-576-12 and AE-2576-12. In this case, AE-576-12 sorts before AE-2576-12, and that's not what you want.

You can solve this problem by verifying that each code segment has exactly the same number of characters. You can, for example, enter the examples in the preceding paragraph as AE-0576-12 and AE-2576-12. Because you have added a zero to the middle section of the first code, both codes have the same number of characters.

Another problem that may exist is numbers that drop their leading zeroes. For entries that require a specific number of zero placeholders, you can use the custom numeric formats that Chapter 8, "Formatting Worksheets," describes.

Following are three methods of entering the number 0056:

What Is Typed	Numeric Format	Display
56	0000	0056
="0056"	Any format	0056
'0056	Any format	0056

The first method is a number formatted to display with leading zeros. This method can be used in math, and it is sorted before text, as are normal numbers. The second and third methods change the numbers to text. The text sorts with alphabetic characters.

Sorting on More than Three Fields

With Excel's **Data Sort** command, you can sort on as many fields as you want. You are not limited to just three. You can re-sort on additional fields as many times as necessary, without losing the ordered result from previous sorts. The guideline for sorting on more than three keys is to sort the lowest levels first, working your way up to the highest level.

If, for example, you want to sort column A as the **1**st Key, column B as the **2**nd Key, column C as the **3**rd Key, and so on for six keys, you would need a sort like the following:

Key	1	2	3	4	5	6
Column	A	B	C	D	E	F

Although Excel has only three sort keys, you still can sort by the six columns needed. Your first sort uses the lowest level columns, such as the following:

Key	1	2	3
Column	D	E	F

A second sort sorts the higher level columns with the following keys:

Key	1	2	3
Column	A	B	C

Sorting Calculated Results

You are not confined to sorting on the contents of a given cell. You can include in your database formulas that calculate new data from existing data.

In figure 22.10, column F contains the following function:

=RIGHT(E8,5)

This function extracts the last five characters of cell E8, the ZIP code. After you have the ZIP codes in column F, you can sort on column F. If you want to convert these calculated ZIP codes into text permanently, copy them and paste them over the originals by using the Edit Paste Special command with the Values option selected.

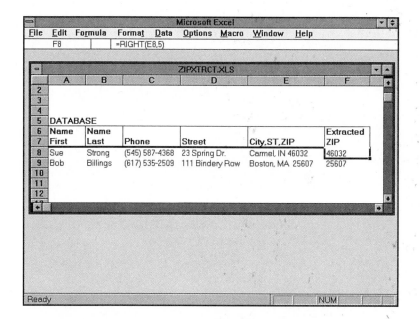

FIG. 22.10

The RIGHT() function pulls ZIP code information out of an address field.

Rearranging Database Columns

Excel can sort columns as well as rows. This capability enables you to rearrange the columns in your database without extensive cutting and pasting.

Figure 22.11 shows the sample database about to be sorted into a new column order. Row 9 contains numbers indicating the desired column order. Notice that the Days Due column must remain directly to the right of Due Date in order for the formula in Days Due to calculate correctly. The Sort dialog box shows that the sort will be by columns and that row 9, the row containing the new column order, will be sorted on.

Figure 22.12 shows the database after the columns have been sorted in the order specified in row 9. If the Days Due column had not stayed directly to the right of the Due Date column, the formulas would display the error #VALUE!. This error would display because the formulas in Days Due would refer to cells containing text and not dates.

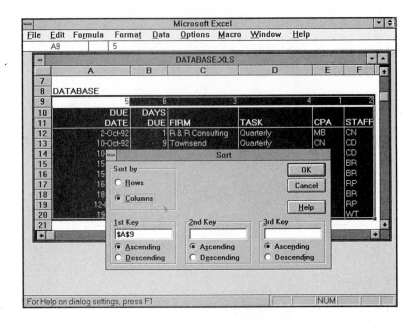

FIG. 22.11

Columns in the database are rearranged according to assigned numbers.

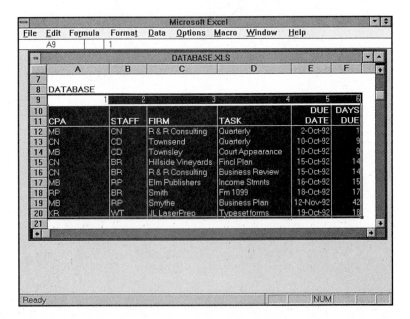

FIG. 22.12

The database after being sorted to rearrange columns.

NOTE You probably will have to adjust column widths after you reorder columns in a database. If columns are too narrow to display a number or date in the required format, the cell displays #####.

Be careful when you perform a column sort on a worksheet, such as the one in figure 22.12. Formulas refer to the same relative addresses (for example, two cells left) or refer to an absolute address. When you shift worksheet columns around, the appropriate cell may no longer be where it is expected.

For Related Information:

◄◄ "Entering Data," p. 169.

◄◄ "Formatting Dates and Times," p. 285.

FROM HERE...

Chapter Summary

When you have your database set up and data entered, you probably will want to find records that meet criteria you set. Chapter 23, "Finding and Editing Data," shows you how to search the database for records. You should read Chapter 23 and understand what a criterion is before you go on to Chapter 24, "Extracting and Maintaining Data." Chapter 24 describes how to extract information from the database to create a second database or a report.

Finding and Editing Data

Databases are used most frequently to find specific information. Excel provides four ways of finding and editing information. The worksheet editing commands Formula Find and Formula Replace can find and replace individual words or phrases in a worksheet or database. These commands are described in Chapter 7, "Entering and Editing Worksheet Data." Excel's Data Form command, which displays the automatically generated database form, enables you to find data quickly and easily by using simple search specifications. If you need to specify a more complex search, you must establish a criteria range and use the Data Find command.

By using the information in this chapter, you will be able to find and edit any type of data in your database. The concepts in this chapter act as a base for learning how to extract information from a database. Extracting data is described in Chapter 24, "Extracting and Maintaining Data." You also can use the methods you learn here to work with external databases on a hard disk or mainframe; these methods are described in Chapter 25, "Linking Excel to Databases with Q+E."

Finding Data

The process of finding data in your database consists of the following four general steps:

1. Decide what you want to find.

2. Define a pattern that specifies the types of information you want to find. What you find must match this criteria.

3. Enter that pattern in the database form or criteria range.

4. Choose the Find **Next** button on the database form, or choose the **Data** **Find** command when you are working in the worksheet.

You enter criteria in a special range called the *criteria range*. The simplest of criteria are exact matches. For example, if you want to find someone named John, you type *John* below the Last Name field in the criteria range. Criteria can specify text, dates, numbers, numeric ranges, or logical values (TRUE or FALSE). Criteria can be simple comparisons or complex formulas that involve calculations; criteria can include multiple comparisons or ranges of dates or numbers.

You can use two database commands to find information. The easiest method uses the **Data** **Form** command. The data form accepts only simple comparisons as criteria. The second method of finding information uses a criteria range. After you enter simple or complex criteria in the criteria range, you can use the **Data** **Find** command to search the database for matching records. This chapter describes both the **Data** **Form** and **Data** **Find** methods of finding records.

Using the Database Form

Excel's database form is excellent for finding records that satisfy simple comparisons. You enter criteria in a blank form and request the next or previous record that matches your criteria. The database form then displays the next or previous record that matches your criteria.

To use the database form to search for records, complete the following steps:

1. If you have not done so, prepare the database by selecting the database range and choosing the **Data** **Set Database** command.

2. Choose the **Data** **Form** command to display the database form.

3. Select the **Criteria** button.

Selecting **C**riteria changes the buttons on the database form and clears the text box next to each field. Figure 23.1 shows the form ready to accept criteria.

4. Select the text box next to the field you want to search. Click in the box or press Tab for the next box, Shift+Tab for the previous box, or press the Alt+key combination for a particular field.

5. Type the criteria, but do not press the Enter key.

6. Press Tab to move to the next box if you want to type additional criteria.

7. Choose Find **N**ext or Find **P**rev to move from the current record to the record that meets the entered criteria.

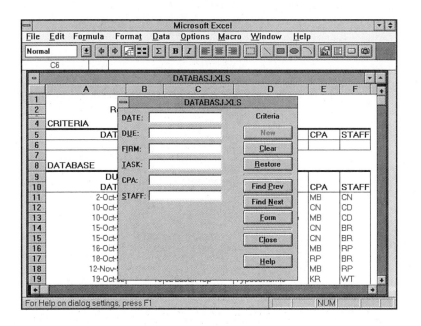

The database form ready to accept criteria.

Figure 23.2 shows a database form with criteria entered that will match records where the CPA has the initials MB. In figure 23.3, the criteria in the DUE field indicates that items with less than 15 days will be found. You also can search for dates by entering criteria, such as >10-Oct-92 in the Date criteria box. You also can find records that must satisfy criteria in more than one field. For example, the criteria in figure 23.4 specify a search for records with a CPA who has initials CN, the date DUE less than 15 days, and the FIRM name starting with H.

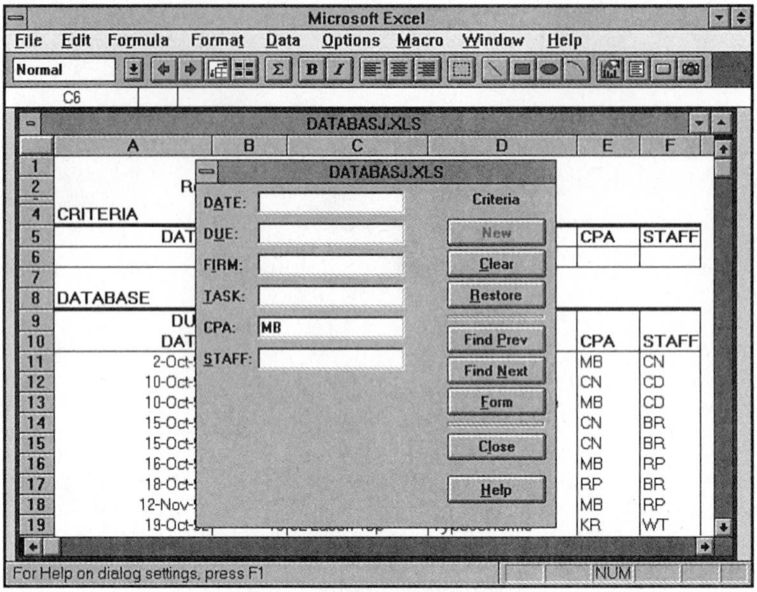

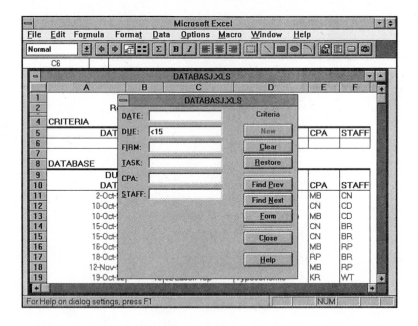

FIG. 23.2

A database form
specifying MB for
CPA's initials as the
criteria.

FIG. 23.3

A database form
specifying a date DUE
of less than 15 days
as the criteria.

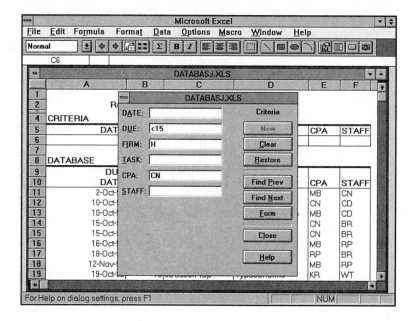

FIG. 23.4

A form specifying that the date DUE must be less than 15, the FIRM name must start with H, and the CPA's initials must be CN.

You can use the form to find only simple or multiple comparisons. You cannot use the form to find calculated comparisons or complex AND and OR comparisons.

All comparisons in the criteria must be true for a record to be found. For example, in figure 23.4, the only records that will be found are those where *all three* criteria are true. Later in this chapter, table 23.2 shows the different types of comparison operators that you can use in the database form and criteria range.

Because the database form is so easy to use, you will be able to search for data after only a few minutes of practice. If you want to search for matches that involve calculated comparisons or complex uses of AND and OR in the criteria, use the **Data Find** command. The **Data Find** command requires you to type criteria into a criteria range. Criteria in the criteria range do not affect searches done with the data form or criteria entered into the data form.

Using the Data Find Command

Although using the **Data Find** command involves more work than using the database form, the command enables you to search for data that must match calculated criteria or matches involving complicated AND and OR criteria. In addition, the command prepares you to use more powerful database features, such as extracting a copy of specific data from a database for use in reports. The command also uses the same concepts required for using Excel's database analysis functions and data tables.

Setting the Criteria Range

If you plan to use the **D**ata **F**ind command, you need to create and define a criteria range after you have set the database with the **D**ata **S**et Data-**b**ase command. The top row of the criteria range contains field names that must be spelled exactly the same as the field names above the data-base. The criteria range also includes at least one blank row below the field names. You enter in this row criteria that the records you are searching for must match. Excel matches the criteria under a field name in the criteria range against the data under the same field name in the database.

Do not use more than one blank row unless you will be entering multiple criteria in all the rows, as explained in the section "Matching Multiple Criteria."

Figure 23.5 shows a selected criteria range. In this example, Forma**t** **B**order was used to outline selected cells.

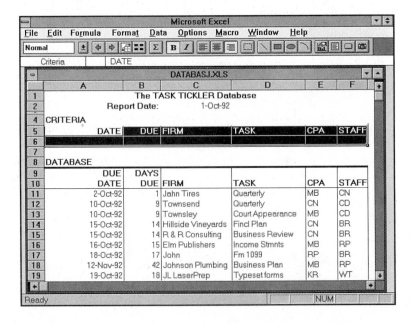

FIG. 23.5

Borders around a criteria range help identify where to enter questions.

You define the criteria range in much the same way as you set the database range. Perform the following steps to define a criteria range:

1. Copy the field names from the top of the database range to the top row of the criteria range. Copying the field names reduces the chance of mistakes from retyping.

2. Select all the field names and one blank row below the field names.

3. Choose the **D**ata Set **C**riteria command.

4. Choose the Forma**t B**order command while the range is selected and format a border around the criteria range to make it easy to identify.

If the field names in the criteria range do not match those in the database, the **D**ata **F**ind command will not work. To be certain that your criteria field names match the database field names exactly, copy them from the database with the **E**dit **C**opy and **E**dit **P**aste commands or with shortcut keys or tools. You do not need to include every field name in the criteria range. You can include the names in any order you like, as long as they exactly match the field names used in the database. (The field names in the criteria range must be either text or formulas that produce text.)

When you choose **D**ata Set **C**riteria, the selected range is named Criteria. Use Fo**r**mula **D**efine Name to see the cell address reference or delete the range name Criteria. Use the F5, Formula Goto key, to go to and select the range named Criteria.

 NOTE Do not include unused blank rows in the criteria range. Blank rows in the criteria range tell Excel to match against all records in the database. You can see the size of the criteria range by pressing the F5 key and selecting the criteria range from the Goto list. If unneeded blank rows are in the criteria range, redefine the criteria range without the blank rows.

Although you can have only one named criteria range at a time, you can quickly switch between criteria ranges. Chapter 22, "Entering and Sorting Data," contains a tip on changing databases quickly. You can use this same tip to quickly change criteria ranges.

Searching for Records

After you set the database and criteria ranges, you are ready to search for records in the database. Complete the following steps to enter the criteria and invoke the search:

1. Enter your criteria in the criteria range.

   The criteria range can contain simple criteria, such as Townsend below the FIRM field name in figure 23.6.

   The criteria range also can contain entries that match ranges of numbers, calculate criteria, and contain TRUE/FALSE comparisons. Later sections in this chapter describe simple, complex, and calculated criteria.

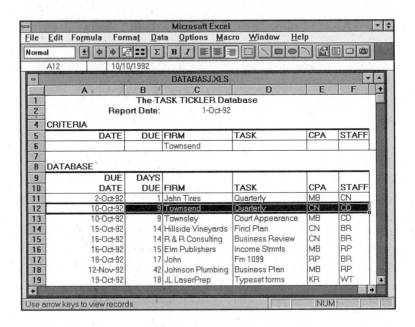

FIG. 23.6

The database appears in the window with the found record selected.

2. Select a cell outside the database to begin the search at the first database record. To begin the search at a specific record in the database, select a cell in that record.

3. Choose the **Data Find** command. To search backward from the active cell through the database, hold down Shift while choosing **Data Find**.

   When Excel encounters a record that matches the criteria you have specified, the window scrolls to display the database record; the Status Bar displays the word Find; and the number of the found record appears in the Reference Area, left of the Formula Bar. The found record appears selected, as shown in figure 23.6. If no records meet the criteria, Excel beeps and displays an alert box.

4. Press the up- or down-arrow keys, or click on the scroll arrows, to move to the next or previous matching record. If there are no more matching records, Excel beeps and you are unable to move the cursor.

5. Choose the **D**ata Exit **F**ind command, press Esc, or click on a cell outside the database range to exit Find mode.

Use the **W**indow **S**plit command to see the criteria range and database simultaneously. Enter your criteria in one pane, then select a cell above your database in the other pane. When you search for data by using the **D**ata **F**ind command, the window scrolls so that the found record is near the top. (These commands are described further in Chapter 11.)

T I P

While in Find mode, you can scroll through the records that meet the criteria. Use the commands listed in table 23.1 to scroll the database.

Table 23.1. Scrolling a Database

Result	Action
Mouse	
Move to next matching record	Click on down scroll arrow
Move to previous matching record	Click on up scroll arrow
Jump to match at least one window away	Click in scroll bar
Keyboard	
Move to next matching record	Press down-arrow key
Move to previous matching record	Press up-arrow key
Move active cell right	Press Tab
Move active cell left	Press Shift+Tab
Scroll right	Press right-arrow key
Scroll left	Press left-arrow key
Move to next matching record at least one window away	Press PgDn
Move to previous matching record at least one window away	Press PgUp

While in Find mode, you cannot scroll outside the database either vertically or horizontally.

When you are ready to exit from **Data Find**, choose **Data Exit Find**, press Esc, or select a cell by clicking outside the database.

Matching Simple Criteria

Comparative criteria involve finding exact matches or simple ranges of greater- or less-than comparisons. Comparative criteria do not involve mathematical calculations or logical operators AND or OR. You can use comparative criteria in the database form and in the criteria range. If you need to use complex or calculated criteria, you must use a criteria range. (See the section "Matching Calculated and Compound Criteria" later in this chapter.)

The simplest and easiest criteria specify text for which you are searching. Figures 23.7 and 23.8 show how text criteria for the name John is entered in the database form (fig. 23.7) and in the criteria range (fig. 23.8) You can see that the criteria is typed exactly as you expect it to be entered in the database. Text criteria is not case-sensitive, so you can match against upper- or lowercase text.

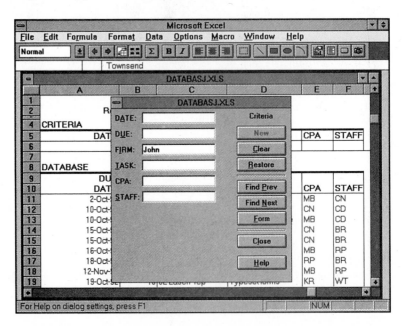

FIG. 23.7

Text criteria in the database form.

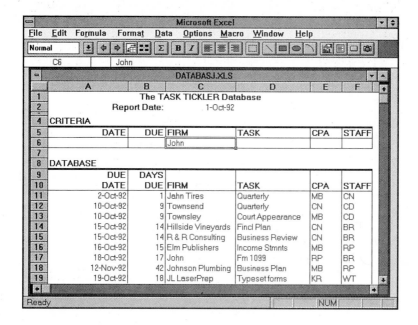

FIG. 23.8

Text criteria in the
criteria range.

If you selected the **D**ata **F**ind command, or in the form the Find **N**ext button, by using John, as shown in figures 23.7 and 23.8, you would find records containing the following:

> John
> Johnson Plumbing

Notice that Excel may match more words than just *John*. Depending on the options currently selected, Excel can match the text you enter and accept any spaces or text after the last character in the criteria. This feature helps you to find records even if a blank space was accidentally typed after the last character.

If you always want to find exact matches to a text entry and not match extra trailing characters, enter your text criteria as a text formula. Use ="John" or '=John, for example.

The most frequent database problem is caused by incorrectly clearing the criteria range. If you do not clear criteria from the criteria range, Excel will try to find records that match the old and new criteria.

To clear the criteria row correctly, select the cells containing the old criteria. Next, choose the **E**dit **C**lear command; or press Del, then Enter.

NOTE When the Alternate Expression Evaluation check box is selected under the Options Calculation command, Excel criteria follow the database search rules used by 1-2-3. If your database does not seem to be using the rules listed here, check whether the Alternate Expression Evaluation check box is cleared.

Do not clear cells by pressing the space bar and then pressing Enter. This procedure enters a blank character in the criteria row. Excel then will attempt to find records that contain a blank character in that field.

Finding Near Matches

If you are not sure of the spelling of a word in the database, or you need to find records containing similar but not identical text, you will need a couple of extra cards up your sleeve. In Excel, these are called *wild cards*, and they are part of the searching game.

You can use the two text criteria wild cards: the asterisk (*) and the question mark (?). The two wild cards represent the following characters:

?   Any single character in the same position

*   Any group of characters in the same position

The question mark (?) is useful if you are uncertain how the word you want to match is spelled. For example, if a name in the FIRM field could be John or Jahn, then you would enter your criteria as the following:

J?hn*

The ? matches any single letter between the *J* and *h*. The * at the end accepts the Tires that follows Jahn in cell C11 in figure 23.8. Because Excel does not distinguish between upper- and lowercase when matching, the program also matches the lowercase to capitals.

The asterisk (*) matches groups of characters. You can use it at any location in the text criteria: beginning, middle, or end. To locate data in a field with a name like Gallon_Cans, you might use the criteria * *paint*. This criteria would find the following matches:

blue paint
red paint
yellow paint

If you need to find the actual symbols * or ? in a database, then type a tilde (~) before the * or ?. The tilde indicates that you are not using the * or ? as a wild card.

Matching Numeric Criteria

To find an exact match for a number, enter the number in the criteria row directly below the appropriate field name. For example, you might enter a number below the Due field in a criteria range or in a database form.

> You can use comparisons to find ranges of text as well as numbers. For example, to find all text entries that start with T or letters after T, you can use the criteria >T.
>
> **T I P**

If you want to find numbers greater than or less than a number, enter comparison criteria, such as the criteria in figures 23.3 and 23.4. In this case, the expression <15 tells Excel to search the DUE field (column) for database values that are less than 15. Table 23.2 shows other comparison operators that you can use in the criteria range or database form.

Table 23.2. Comparison Operators

Operator	Meaning	Criteria	Finds
=	Equals	=200	Fields equal to 200
=	Equals	=	Fields equal to blank
>	Greater than	>200	Fields greater than 200
>=	Greater than or equal to	>=200	Fields greater than or equal to 200
<	Less than	<200	Fields less than 200
<=	Less than or equal to	<=200	Fields less than or equal to 200
< >	Not equal to	<>200	Fields not equal to 200
< >	Not equal to	<>	Fields that are not blank

> To find fields that are blank, use = with nothing following as a criteria. To find fields that are filled, use <> with nothing following.
>
> **T I P**

Matching Date Criteria

When you search for dates by using comparison criteria, use the comparative operators from table 23.2. Type dates the same way you would type them into a worksheet cell. For example, to search the database shown in figure 23.8 for dates greater than October 14, 1992, you could enter the following criteria under DATE:

>10/14/93

or

>14 Oct 93

You can use a date that is in any of Excel's predefined date formats in the criteria.

Matching Multiple Criteria

You can define multiple criteria in the database form by specifying criteria for each field in the form. When you define multiple criteria, all the criteria must be true in a record for Excel to find that record. For example, figure 23.9 finds records that have a date DUE greater than 14 AND have a CPA's initials of CN.

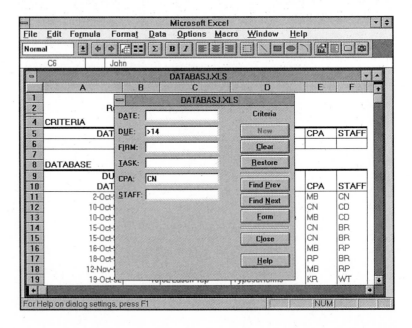

FIG. 23.9

Multiple criteria in the database form must all be true to find a record.

When using **D**ata **F**ind, you can enter multiple criteria on the same row in the criteria range. When you enter multiple criteria on the same criteria row, then *all* the criteria must be met in order for a record to qualify as a match. Figure 23.10 shows the criteria range where DAYS DUE must be greater than 14 AND CPA must be MB. Because both of these criteria are in the same row of the criteria range, a database record must meet both criteria for Excel to find the record. The records in rows 16 and 18 will be found.

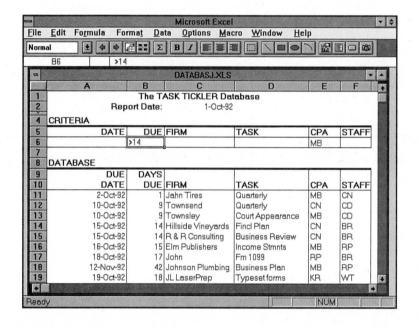

FIG. 23.10

Criteria in the same row of the criteria range must all be true for Excel to find a record.

To find records where one OR the other criteria is met, use the criteria range with more than one row and **D**ata **F**ind. Insert an additional row in the criteria range for each acceptable criterion. Figure 23.11 shows a criteria range with two rows for criteria. Be certain that the extra row is in the criteria range by reselecting the criteria range and choosing the **D**ata **S**et **C**riteria command. The criteria entries shown below CPA tell Excel to find records where the CPA is MB OR the CPA is CN.

Whenever you insert rows through the criteria range, be certain that you check that the name Criteria identifies the expanded area. Do this by pressing the F5 key and choosing the Criteria name from the list. The Criteria range and your extra rows should be selected. If the correct range is not selected, then redefine the range with the **D**ata **S**et **C**riteria range command.

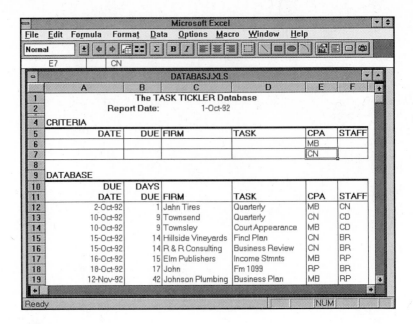

NOTE Be careful when you use two or more rows in the criteria
range. A blank row tells Excel to find all records in the database. Therefore, if you leave a row blank in the criteria range,
Excel finds, extracts, or deletes all data in the database. If you
are unsure of the size of your criteria range, you can see the
range by pressing F5 (Goto), selecting the name Criteria, and
pressing Enter.

Figure 23.12 shows how you can combine simple criteria to ask complex
questions of your database. The criteria range uses two rows so that you
can find records matching one value or the other. All the criteria within
either row must be true for Excel to find a record. When the Alternate
Expression Evaluation check box for the **O**ptions **C**alculation command
is off, the English equivalent of the criteria range in the figure is the following expression.

Find all records where:

    The DAYS DUE are less than 15 AND the CPA is CN.

    OR

    The DUE DATE is 18-Oct-92 AND the FIRM name is John.

Excel finds the records that meet these criteria in rows 13, 15, 16, and 18.

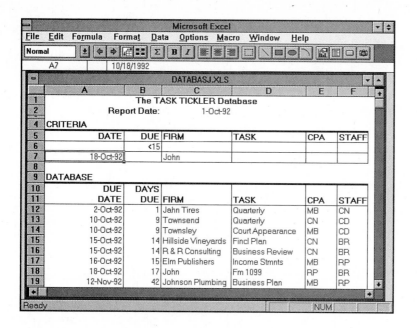

FIG. 23.12

Multiple criteria specifying AND in the same rows and specifying OR between rows.

For Related Information:

◄◄ "Entering Formulas," p. 175.

FROM HERE...

Matching Calculated and Compound Criteria

Using simple comparative criteria is helpful and quick, but in some cases you need to specify more exact data. You may want to find dates between two ranges or even use formulas to calculate what you are searching for. In these cases, you will need to use calculated criteria.

Matching Calculated Criteria

You can select records according to any calculation that results in a TRUE or FALSE logical value as a criteria. Calculated criteria are needed, for example, when you want to find records where inventory quantities are less than a calculated reorder quantity, where a range of dates is needed but some dates within the range are excluded, or where a mailing list has the ZIP code included with the City and State field.

Figure 23.13 shows an example of calculated criteria that find Parts that were sold for less than 90 percent of Retail price. Notice that the calculated criteria, =E9<0.9*D9, must be entered in the criteria range below a *name that does not exist* in the database. In this example, the name Calc was inserted in the middle of the criteria range; Calc is not used as a field name in the database. *You can use any text name above the calculated criteria, if it has not been used in the database field names.*

NOTE You must enter calculated criteria in the criteria range below names that are not used as field names in the database. Use a field name that is different from any field name in the database.

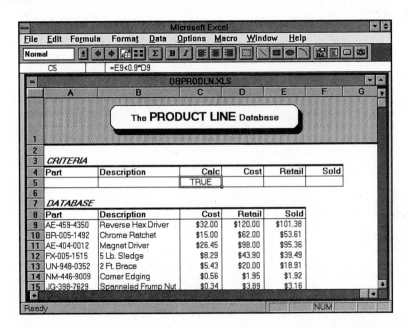

FIG. 23.13

Calculated criteria must use a new field name in the criteria range.

In your calculated criteria formula, use cell references that refer to cells in the top data row of the database. Use relative reference addresses (without $ signs) for references within the database, as shown in figure 23.14. Use absolute cell references to refer to any cell outside the database that is involved in the calculated criteria.

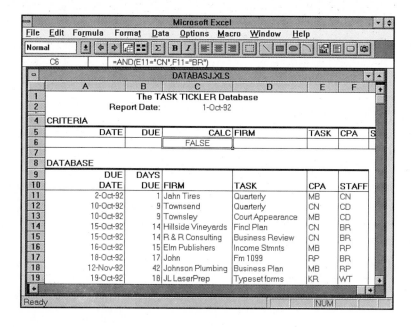

FIG. 23.14

Using relative
reference addresses
for references within
the database.

Calculated criteria can involve multiple fields and equations, but the
result must produce a TRUE or FALSE condition. The Excel database
commands select those records that produce a TRUE result. Some
simple calculated criteria, where the first data row is row 36, are illus-
trated in table 23.3. Remember that calculated criteria must compare
the value found in the first row of data in the database.

Table 23.3. Simple Calculated Criteria

Criteria	Explanation
=B36=G36	Compares the values of fields in the same record. Selects the record when the value in column B equals the value in column G.
=B36<G36/2	Compares the value in B36 to one half the value in G36. Both cells are in the same record. Selects the record when the value in column B is less than half of the value in column G.
=B36−G36>10	Compares two values in the same database record. Selects the record when a value in column B minus a value in column G is greater than 10.

T I P   If you use the correct syntax when you enter a calculated criteria formula, Excel displays TRUE or FALSE in the cell after you enter the formula. TRUE or FALSE applies to the specific cells you used in the formula. Check to see whether TRUE or FALSE corresponds correctly to the evaluation of the cells you used in the criteria formula.

More complex but extremely useful calculated criteria include comparisons between values in a record with other records or with values outside the database. These types of criteria are useful when you want to compare records or use criteria calculated elsewhere in the worksheet. The following shows some examples of these types of criteria; assume that the first data row (record) is row 36.

Criteria	Explanation
=B36–G37>10	Compares values in adjacent database records. Selects the record when the value in column B of one record is more than 10 greater than the value in column G of the next record. Usually you will want to sort the database before doing this type of comparison so that columns B and G are in an order that makes sense for the comparison.
=B36=$C$24	Compares a value in a record to a value outside the database. Selects the record when the value in column B equals the value in $C$24, where C24 is a cell outside the database. This is how you can refer to a criteria that is calculated or entered elsewhere in the worksheet.

As you can see from the examples, calculated criteria can involve cell references that are outside the database. However, you must use an absolute reference to refer to any location outside the database range.

Matching Compound Criteria with AND and OR

You can use Excel's AND(), OR(), and NOT() functions to create complex compound criteria. This method is useful for specifying complex criteria that cannot be handled by inserting additional rows in the criteria range.

You can use any of the following functions in your compound criteria. These are the AND(), OR(), and NOT() functions that are used as worksheet and macro functions. The conditions that are being matched are used as arguments within the functions. For an AND(), OR(), or NOT() function to be TRUE so that a record matches, the arguments within them must match the following conditions:

AND All conditions (arguments) must be TRUE.

OR One condition (argument) out of all the conditions must be TRUE.

NOT The condition used with NOT is reversed. TRUE changes to FALSE; FALSE changes to TRUE.

Just as you can enter calculated criteria that results in a TRUE or FALSE value, you can enter AND(), OR(), and NOT() functions that evaluate to TRUE or FALSE. For example, consider the database in figure 23.14. For each of the following queries stated in English syntax, the associated compound criteria formula is presented, and the resulting records that Excel finds are listed:

English statement: The CPA is CN AND the STAFF is BR.
Compound criteria: =AND(E11="CN",F11="BR")
Result: Finds the records in rows 14 and 15.

English statement: The FIRM is Townsley OR the FIRM is John.
Compound criteria: =OR(C11="Townsley",C11="John")
Result: Finds the records in rows 13 and 17.

English statement: The FIRM is NOT Townsley AND the DAYS DUE is 9.
Compound criteria: =AND(NOT(C11="Townsley"),B11=9)
Result: Finds the record in row 12.

NOTE AND() and OR() are easy to confuse. If you are searching a single field for two different text entries (for example, Smith and Jones), use the OR() function. An OR() function specifies that one name OR the other can be found (TRUE). An AND() function specifies that Smith AND Jones must be in the field at the same time—something that will not happen.

Editing Data

Keeping a database current involves two basic functions: continuous updating of individual records and periodic deleting to get rid of old records. The balance of this chapter describes how to edit records. The following chapter describes how to manage a database by deleting large numbers of records that meet a specific criteria.

The following descriptions cover two methods of editing the database: editing in the database form and editing directly in the worksheet. In cases where you will be editing one or two records that are easy to find, the database form may be preferable. However, when you need to perform a complex search to find the records or when you can make one change and copy it down a column, then you will want to edit directly in the worksheet.

Editing with the Database Form

The easiest way to edit individual records is with the database form. If you can find the record by using the simple comparative criteria available in the database form, then use the form to do your editing.

Begin by defining the database range with **D**ata Set Database. After you have defined the range, perform the following steps to find the records you want, and then edit them:

1. Choose the **D**ata **F**orm command.

2. Select the **C**riteria button.

3. To define the records you want to edit, type the criteria. Press Tab or Shift+Tab to move between fields in the criteria form. Do not press Enter.

4. Select the Find **N**ext button to find the next record matching the criteria.

5. Edit the field contents by using normal mouse or keyboard techniques. Press the appropriate Alt+key combination to select a text box, or press the Tab key to move between boxes. Figure 23.15 shows the **T**ask text box selected after pressing Alt+T. Don't press Enter until you're ready to accept changes.

6. Press Enter or scroll up or down to save the change and move to the next record. Choose the **R**estore button to restore the changes made during editing. Choosing **R**estore after you leave the record will not restore the data.

7. Select C**l**ose to save the changes and return to the worksheet.

If you need to delete a record you have found with the form, choose the **D**elete button on the form. The alert message, shown in figure 23.16, will warn that you are about to delete the current record. Choose OK or press Enter to complete the deletion. Keep in mind that deleted records cannot be recovered.

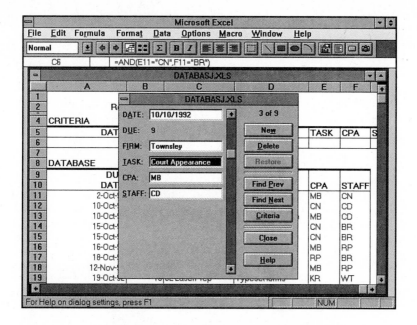

FIG. 23.15

The Task text box
ready for editing.

FIG. 23.16

The alert box warns
that you are about to
delete a record.

Editing Data Directly in the Worksheet

Some of the records you want to edit may require finding calculated or
compound criteria. At other times, you may want to edit or format adjacent rows simultaneously. In these cases, you can enter the criteria in
the criteria range, use **D**ata **F**ind to find the records, and make your
changes directly in the worksheet.

To find the appropriate records with the help of the **D**ata **F**ind command
and edit data directly in the worksheet, complete the following steps:

1. Enter the criteria in the criteria range for the records you want to
   edit.

2. Choose the **D**ata **F**ind command.

3. Move to the record you want to edit.

4. Select the cell you want to edit by clicking on the cell or pressing Tab or Shift+Tab to move to the cell. If you select a cell outside of the database, the Find mode is turned off.

5. Edit the cell contents by clicking in the Formula Bar or by pressing F2 (the Edit key) and making changes. Going into Edit mode throws Excel out of Find mode. You are now back to editing in a normal worksheet.

6. Press Enter to complete the change.

Usually, you will need to make changes to multiple records that all meet the same search criteria. However, as soon as you begin to edit a found record, Excel takes you out of the Find mode and puts you back into the normal worksheet. To find the next record, you again must choose **Data Find**. Excel will begin its searching for matches from the record containing the active cell.

You can conveniently edit a record, then without moving from the record, choose **Data Find** to find the next record to be changed. You may want to create a simple command macro that replaces the three keystrokes needed to choose **Data Find** with a single Ctrl+key combination.

If you want to delete a record directly from the worksheet, complete the following steps:

1. Use the **Data Find** command to find the record, then press Esc to return to normal worksheet mode.

2. Select the row or cells you want to delete. If you select cells, be sure to select the full width of the record.

3. Choose the **Edit Delete** command.

4. If you are deleting cells, the Delete dialog box asks whether you want to shift the remaining cells up or left. Select the Shift Cells **Up** option from the dialog box.

5. Choose OK or press Enter.

> **CAUTION:** Be careful if you delete the entire spreadsheet row passing through a database. You may delete information on either side of the database.

If you need to delete or edit a number of similar records, you may want to sort the database first. Sorting will put similar records together and enable you to find and delete multiple records at once. Sorting is described in Chapter 22, "Entering and Sorting Data." You also can use the **Data Delete** command to delete records that meet the criteria you specify. The **Data Delete** command is described in Chapter 24.

For Related Information:

◄◄ "Editing Text and Formulas," p. 195.

◄◄ "Increasing Data-Entry Efficiency," p. 198.

◄◄ "Filling or Copying Cell Contents," p. 234.

FROM HERE...

Chapter Summary

Two important database topics have not yet been discussed in this text: extracting information for reports and maintaining a database. These topics are covered in Chapter 24, "Extracting and Maintaining Data."

If you analyze information kept in databases, such as accounting data, marketing information, or scientific readings from instruments, you also should read Chapter 26, "Building Extensive Databases," to discover how to use database functions and data tables. These features can save you hours of work doing analysis.

Extracting and Maintaining Data

This chapter shows you how to extract copies of information from a database to create reports or other databases. It also describes some of the procedures you need to follow to maintain your database. In this chapter, you learn to use the **Data Extract** command with what you already learned about criteria in Chapter 23. You can copy extracted data to another worksheet or extract directly onto a worksheet separate from the database. You also learn how to delete groups of records that you no longer need.

Extracting Data

The **Data Extract** command makes a copy of data that meets the criteria in a criteria range. The copy, which is placed in a section of the worksheet separate from the original database, is useful for creating special reports, for making subsets of the original database, and for preparing data for transfer to other programs. A special option of the **Extract** command extracts only those records that are unique. The original database remains intact after you extract a copy of the data that matches the criteria.

To make the **Data Extract** command work, you need to specify the database and criteria ranges. You also must specify where to put the copied information and how to arrange the columns of data.

A set of field names, which are exact duplicates of the database field names, at the top of the extract range tells Excel which data you want extracted and how you want it arranged. Figure 24.1 shows a small database with the three parts that are important to extracting: the criteria range in A5:F6, the database range in A10:F19, and the field names for the extract range in A22:F22. In figure 24.2, the data meeting the criteria is extracted from the database and copied below the field names in the extract range. Notice that, in figure 24.2, the two extracted records each indicate 14 days due, which matches the criteria set in row 6 (refer to fig. 24.1).

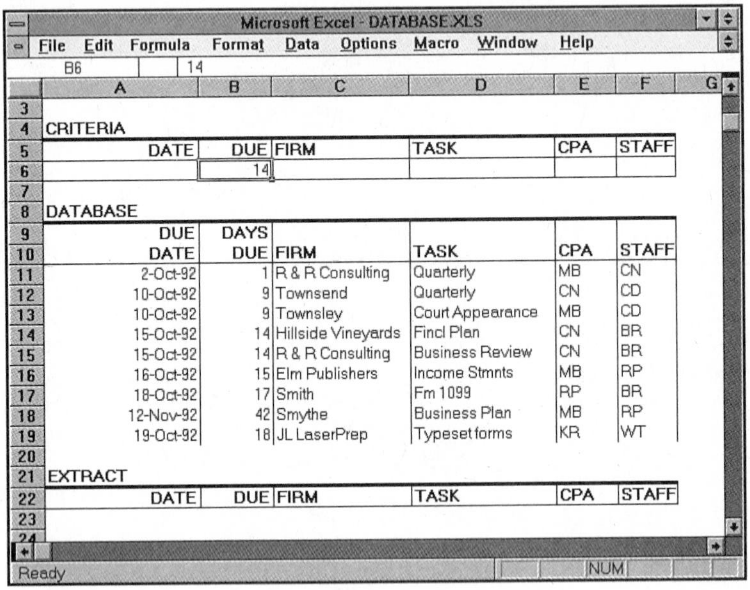

FIG. 24.1

The database, criteria, and extract ranges.

The extract range is separate and distinct from the criteria and database ranges. In figures 24.1 and 24.2, notice that three ranges are used. The row of field names selected for **Data Extract** must be separate from the rows of field names that head the database and criteria ranges.

The field names at the top of the extract range must be identical to the field names used at the top of the database range. The best way to prepare your extract range is to copy the field names that you want from the top of the database.

As figures 24.3 and 24.4 illustrate, however, you don't have to include in the extract range all the field names from the database range, nor must the field names be in the same order as they appear in the database. You can create reports with only the information you need and in the column order you want. Use selected field names and reorder the names as you want them to appear in the extracted data.

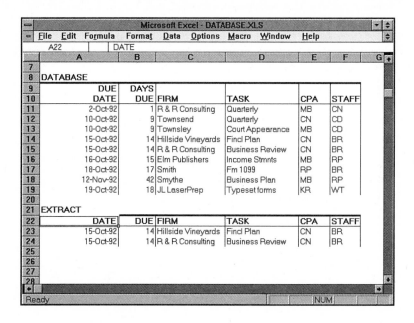

FIG. 24.2

Extracted data is copied from the database and placed below the extract field names.

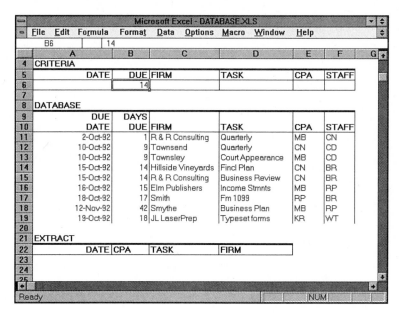

FIG. 24.3

Extract field names in a different order from those in the database.

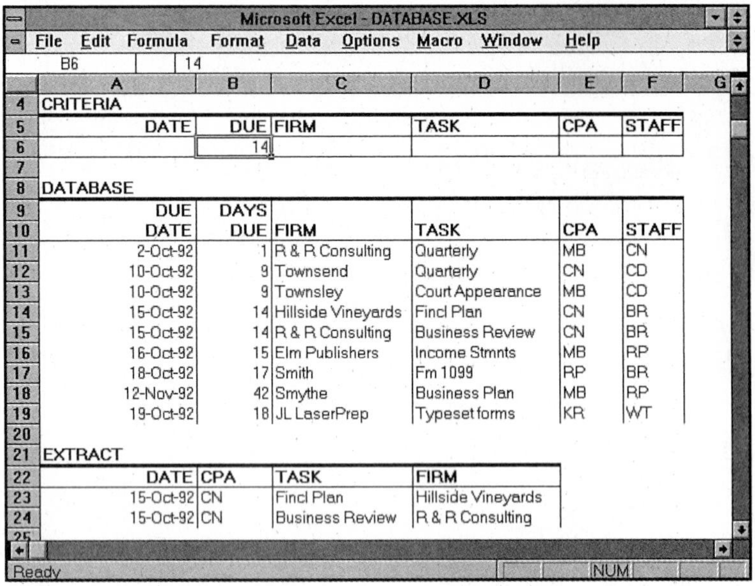

FIG. 24.4

Reordering field names enables you to structure reports.

You can define the extract range in two ways. You can name the range in which data will be extracted *Extract*, or you can use the currently selected area of the worksheet. Naming an area is convenient if you usually extract the same report and headings. By using the currently selected cells as the extract region, you can easily change where the extract will go.

T I P

The two methods of extracting data are exclusive of each other. If you used the **D**ata Set **E**xtract command previously, the name Extract already is defined in your worksheet. You cannot extract to the currently selected cells if the name Extract exists on the worksheet. Use the **F**ormula **D**efine Name command to delete the name Extract.

You can specify two sizes of extract ranges, limited and unlimited. A *limited extract range* includes the field names at the top of the range and a limited number of cells below the names. The extracted information fills only the cells available in the extract range. Excel leaves out extracted data that will not fit and gives you a warning message.

In an *unlimited extract range*, you select only the field names or name only the field names with **D**ata Set **E**xtract. You can fill the resulting extract range with data, beginning with the field names and extending to the bottom of the worksheet. If you don't know how much data will be extracted, use an unlimited extract range.

> **CAUTION:** The worksheet below unlimited extracts is erased. Old data or parts of the worksheet below the field names of an unlimited extract range are cleared. Do not put anything between the field names of an unlimited extract range and the bottom of the worksheet. Excel will not warn you that all cells below the extract headings will be cleared. When you choose the **D**ata Extract command, Excel clears this area automatically to avoid mingling the old data with the new.

> **T I P**
>
> You may need to recalculate before you extract data. If Excel is set to recalculate formulas manually, and the worksheet needs to be recalculated, the word Calculate appears at the bottom of the screen. To ensure that all cells contain current values before the extraction, press F9 (Recalculate) before executing the Extract command.

Use the following basic procedure to extract from the database the information you want. Note that each step is described in greater detail in the sections that follow.

1. Create field names for an extract range by copying the single row of field names from the top of the database range. Arrange the field names in the order you want the columns of data to appear.

2. Enter the criteria in the criteria range.

3. Use one of the following methods to set the extract range:

   If you want an extract range that you can change quickly, select the field names and as many cells down as the number of records you want to extract. For an unlimited extract, select only the field names. Previous use of the **D**ata Set Extract command overrides this method unless you use the **F**ormula **D**efine Name command to delete the name Extract.

   To name an extract range that you can reuse, select only the field names for an unlimited extract range; or select the field names and a limited number of cells below, and then choose the **D**ata Set Extract command.

Figure 24.5 shows field names selected to create an unlimited range. Figure 24.6 shows a limited range selected.

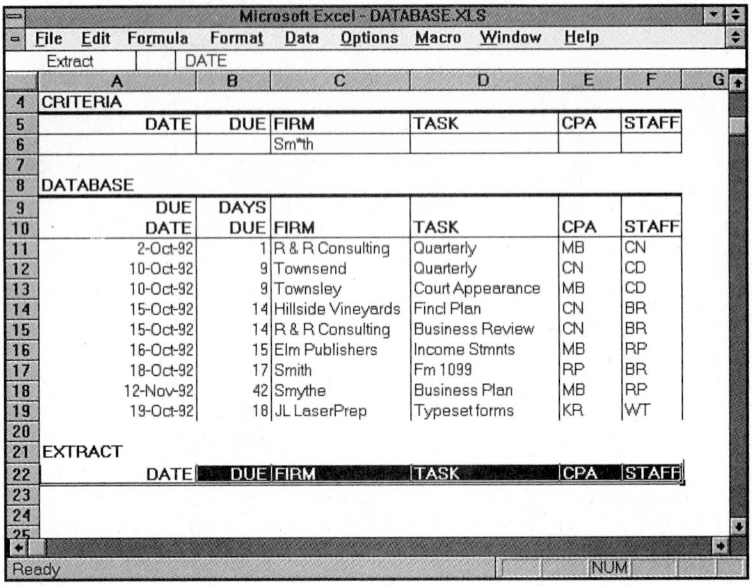

FIG. 24.5

Field names selected to create an unlimited extract range.

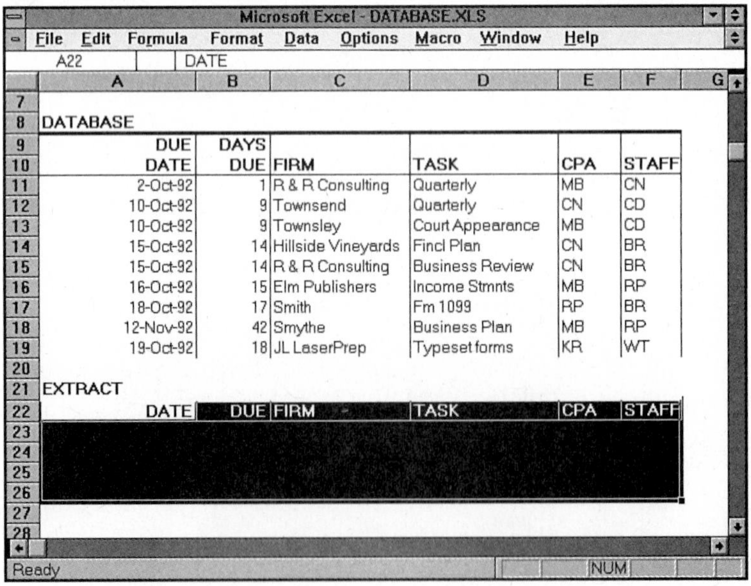

FIG. 24.6

Field names and a limited number of cells below selected to create a limited extract range.

4. Choose the **D**ata **E**xtract command.

5. Select the **U**nique Records Only check box if you do not want duplicate records to appear.

6. Choose OK or press Enter.

Selecting the Extract Range

This section explains in detail the procedures for extracting data in the two sizes of extract range. The benefit of an unlimited extract range is that it enables you to extract an unlimited number of records. This type of extract works well when you don't know how many records will be extracted.

The second, or limited, type of extract range predetermines the area that will hold extracted records. This type of extract works best in a crowded worksheet with limited space.

Extracting a Limited Amount of Data

To extract a limited amount of data, you must select the extract range before you choose the **D**ata **E**xtract command. Select the extract cell that contains the field names and then select as many cells below as you need to hold the extracted data. Figure 24.6 shows an extract range with the field names selected and a few cells for extracted data.

Excel clears the extract range before copying the extracted data into the range. In this way, the program prevents old and new extract data from mixing.

If Excel attempts to extract more data than will fit into the range you select, the extract continues; however, an alert box like the one shown in figure 24.7 appears. The alert box tells you that the extract range is full. This message indicates that you can extract still more data.

When you see the alert box and choose OK, you have four options. You can accept the limited amount of data that was extracted. If you need a larger but still limited number of records, reselect a larger extract range and repeat the extract. You may want to keep the same size extract range and limit the criteria so that fewer records are extracted. Finally, you may want to see all the extracted records by creating an unlimited extract range.

FIG. 24.7

An alert box warns
you when the extract
range cannot hold all
the extracted data.

Extracting Unlimited Rows of Data

You probably will use an unlimited extract range when you are not sure how much data will be extracted. In this case, select only the field names of the extract range, as shown in figure 24.5. Excel extracts all the appropriate data and copies it below the extract field names.

Be careful when designing a worksheet with an unlimited extract range. During the extraction process, Excel clears the cells in all columns below the extract field names to prevent mixing old and new data. *Never put anything below an unlimited extract range.*

Figures 24.8 and 24.9 illustrate the process of extracting data to an unlimited range. In figure 24.8, markers are displayed beneath and to the side of the extract range. Figure 24.9 shows the result of the **Data Extract** command; the marker underneath the extract range is cleared to make room for the extracted data. Notice that the markers on the side are still intact.

FIG. 24.8

An unlimited extract
range before
extraction; markers
appear below and to
the right of the range.

	Microsoft Excel - DATABASE.XLS						
File	Edit	Formula	Format	Data	Options	Macro	Window	Help

C27   Marker 3

	A	B	C	D	E	F	G
8	DATABASE						
9	DUE	DAYS					
10	DATE	DUE	FIRM	TASK	CPA	STAFF	
11	2-Oct-92	1	R & R Consulting	Quarterly	MB	CN	
12	10-Oct-92	9	Townsend	Quarterly	CN	CD	
13	10-Oct-92	9	Townsley	Court Appearance	MB	CD	
14	15-Oct-92	14	Hillside Vineyards	Fincl Plan	CN	BR	
15	15-Oct-92	14	R & R Consulting	Business Review	CN	BR	
16	16-Oct-92	15	Elm Publishers	Income Stmnts	MB	RP	
17	18-Oct-92	17	Smith	Fm 1099	RP	BR	
18	12-Nov-92	42	Smythe	Business Plan	MB	RP	
19	19-Oct-92	18	JL LaserPrep	Typeset forms	KR	WT	
20							
21	EXTRACT						
22	DATE	DUE	FIRM	TASK	CPA	STAFF	
23							Marker 1
24							Marker 2
25							
26							
27			Marker 3				
28							
29							

Ready   NUM

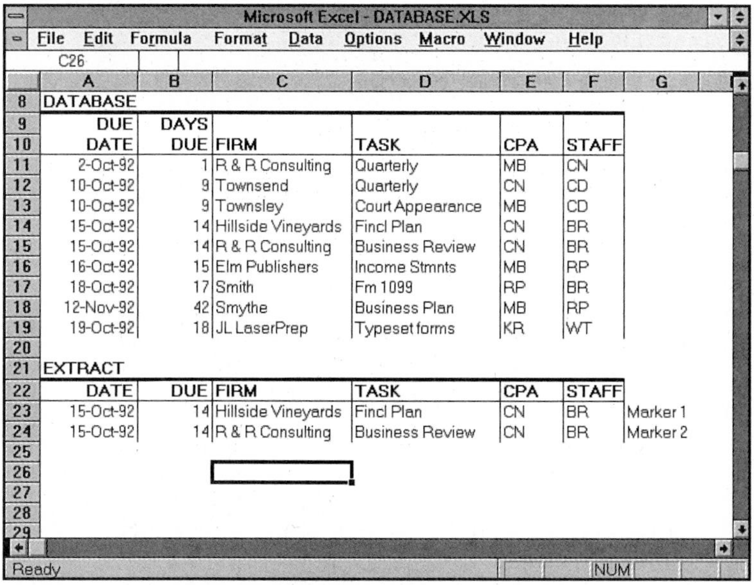

	A	B	C	D	E	F	G
8	DATABASE						
9	DUE	DAYS					
10	DATE	DUE	FIRM	TASK	CPA	STAFF	
11	2-Oct-92	1	R & R Consulting	Quarterly	MB	CN	
12	10-Oct-92	9	Townsend	Quarterly	CN	CD	
13	10-Oct-92	9	Townsley	Court Appearance	MB	CD	
14	15-Oct-92	14	Hillside Vineyards	Fincl Plan	CN	BR	
15	15-Oct-92	14	R & R Consulting	Business Review	CN	BR	
16	16-Oct-92	15	Elm Publishers	Income Stmnts	MB	RP	
17	18-Oct-92	17	Smith	Fm 1099	RP	BR	
18	12-Nov-92	42	Smythe	Business Plan	MB	RP	
19	19-Oct-92	18	JL LaserPrep	Typeset forms	KR	WT	
20							
21	EXTRACT						
22	DATE	DUE	FIRM	TASK	CPA	STAFF	
23	15-Oct-92	14	Hillside Vineyards	Fincl Plan	CN	BR	Marker 1
24	15-Oct-92	14	R & R Consulting	Business Review	CN	BR	Marker 2
25							
26							
27							
28							
29							

Fig. 24.9

After extraction, Marker 3 below the extract range has been deleted.

Extracting Unique Records

After you choose **Data Extract**, Excel displays the Extract dialog box, shown in figure 24.10. If you do not want to copy any duplicate data, select the **Unique Records Only option.

In figure 24.11, for example, the records in rows 14 and 15 are the same except for one field. If you extract with *all* field headings and the Unique Records Only option, both records appear in the extract range.

FIG. 24.10

The Extract dialog box enables you to eliminate duplicate records from the extract.

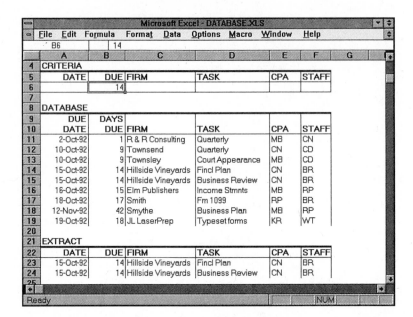

FIG. 24.11

Unique Records Only affects only those records with every field the same.

	A	B	C	D	E	F	G
4	CRITERIA						
5	DATE	DUE	FIRM	TASK	CPA	STAFF	
6		14					
7							
8	DATABASE						
9	DUE	DAYS					
10	DATE	DUE	FIRM	TASK	CPA	STAFF	
11	2-Oct-92	1	R & R Consulting	Quarterly	MB	CN	
12	10-Oct-92	9	Townsend	Quarterly	CN	CD	
13	10-Oct-92	9	Townsley	Court Appearance	MB	CD	
14	15-Oct-92	14	Hillside Vineyards	Fincl Plan	CN	BR	
15	15-Oct-92	14	Hillside Vineyards	Business Review	CN	BR	
16	16-Oct-92	15	Elm Publishers	Income Stmnts	MB	RP	
17	18-Oct-92	17	Smith	Fm 1099	RP	BR	
18	12-Nov-92	42	Smythe	Business Plan	MB	RP	
19	19-Oct-92	18	JL LaserPrep	Typeset forms	KR	WT	
20							
21	EXTRACT						
22	DATE	DUE	FIRM	TASK	CPA	STAFF	
23	15-Oct-92	14	Hillside Vineyards	Fincl Plan	CN	BR	
24	15-Oct-92	14	Hillside Vineyards	Business Review	CN	BR	
25							

T I P   Use a unique extract to cross-check databases for typographical errors. Suppose that you entered a list of part names into a database, with 16 different part names into a total of 320 records. To cross-check for misspelled part names, you can extract unique records by using only the field containing the part names. Each of the 16 correctly spelled part names appears once in the extract range. Any misspelled part name appears in the extract range as an additional item. Use **Data Form, Data Find,** or **Formula Find** to locate the misspelled part name within the database. You can use **Formula Replace** to search for and replace the mistake or use **Options Spelling** to correct mistakes.

Before you print hundreds of mailing labels from an Excel database, use a unique extract to make sure that you don't print duplicate labels.

If, however, the TASK field is removed from the extract range, only one record is extracted. Without the data in the TASK field, the two records are duplicates. Figure 24.12 shows the result of an extraction where the TASK field name is not part of the extract range.

	A	B	C	D	E	F	G
				Microsoft Excel - DATABASE.XLS			
	File	**Edit**	**Formula**	**Format**	**Data**	**Options**	**Macro**	**Window**	**Help**
	B6		14				
4	CRITERIA						
5	DATE	DUE	FIRM		TASK	CPA	STAFF
6		14					
7							
8	DATABASE						
9	DUE	DAYS					
10	DATE	DUE	FIRM		TASK	CPA	STAFF
11	2-Oct-92	1	R & R Consulting		Quarterly	MB	CN
12	10-Oct-92	9	Townsend		Quarterly	CN	CD
13	10-Oct-92	9	Townsley		Court Appearance	MB	CD
14	15-Oct-92	14	Hillside Vineyards		Fincl Plan	CN	BR
15	15-Oct-92	14	Hillside Vineyards		Business Review	CN	BR
16	16-Oct-92	15	Elm Publishers		Income Stmnts	MB	RP
17	18-Oct-92	17	Smith		Fm 1099	RP	BR
18	12-Nov-92	42	Smythe		Business Plan	MB	RP
19	19-Oct-92	18	JL LaserPrep		Typeset forms	KR	WT
20							
21	EXTRACT						
22	DATE	DUE	FIRM		CPA	STAFF	
23	15-Oct-92	14	Hillside Vineyards		CN	BR	
24							
25							

Ready NUM

FIG. 24.12

A unique extract does not show duplicate data.

Extracting from Another Worksheet

You can extract data to one worksheet from a database on another worksheet. In the following example, all items with a Quantity field greater than 10 will be extracted from the database on the FLIMINV.XLS worksheet and placed in the extract range on the FLIMXTRC.XLS worksheet.

Figure 24.13 shows the two worksheets. The FLIMINV.XLS worksheet contains a database in the range A5:C14 that was named Database with the **D**ata Set Data**b**ase command.

The FLIMXTRC.XLS worksheet contains a criteria range and an extract range. The criteria range of A5:C6 was set with the **D**ata Set Criteria command. The field names that act as headings for the extract in FLIMXTRC.XLS are in cells A9:C9. The extract range is set on this worksheet with the **D**ata Set E**x**tract range.

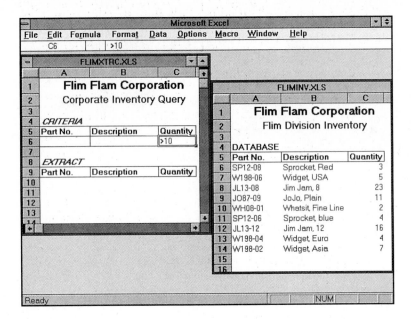

FIG. 24.13

Criteria and extract
ranges on a worksheet
separate from the
database.

By choosing the **Data Extract** command, you ask Excel to extract data
from the range named Database. In this case, however, the desired Database range is on another worksheet. You must tell Excel where to look
for the Database range.

Activate the FLIMINV.XLS worksheet and use the **Data Set Data**base command to name the database. This action creates the range name Database for the area A5:C14. Save the FLIMINV.XLS worksheet.

Next, you need to tell the FLIMXTRC.XLS worksheet where the external
database is located. Activate FLIMXTRC.XLS and choose the Formula
Define Name command. In the Define Name dialog box, type a definition of the name Database that tells Excel that the name Database
in FLIMXTRC.XLS actually refers to a database on the worksheet
FLIMINV.XLS. Type the name *Database* in the **N**ame text box. In the **Re**-
fers to text box, type the external reference for the FLIMINV.XLS database in the following way:

=FLIMINV.XLS!Database

The Define Name dialog box should now look like figure 24.14. This process has defined the Database range on FLIMXTRC.XLS as an external
reference to the Database range on the FLIMINV.XLS worksheet.

Now use normal extract procedures on the FLIMXTRC.XLS worksheet
to extract data. Figure 24.13, for example, shows the FLIMXTRC.XLS
worksheet set up for an extract where the criteria in cell C6 is >10, so

extracted records must have a quantity greater than 10. Figure 24.15 shows the resulting extract from the FLIMINV.XLS database to the FLIMXTRC.XLS extract range.

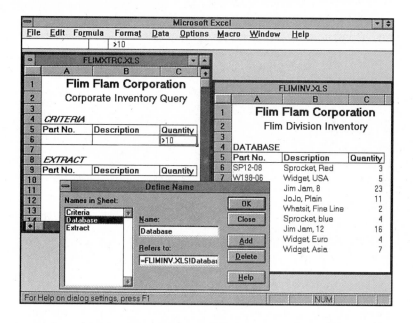

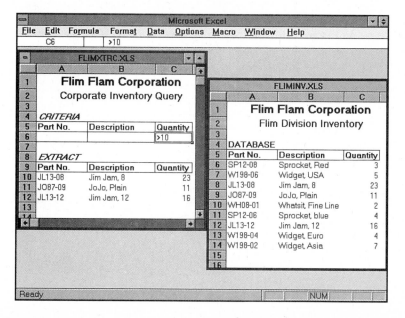

Extracting Database Reports

As figure 24.12 illustrates, you can display extracted columns of data in any order you want. Change the column order of extracted data by changing the order of the field names in the extract range. Keep in mind that you can extract the data you want by using only the field names that you need. Make sure that the field names you use are identical to the field names used in the database.

T I P   Use the **Window View** command to save print or viewed report settings. Chapter 11 describes how to use the **Window View** command to name and save the screen arrangements and to print the ranges and settings you use most frequently. If you have many reports to print or different views for entering and reviewing data, refer to Chapter 11 to learn to use **Window View**.

If you think that you may need to reformat or create summary and detail views of your database, consider using styles and outlines. If your reports show summary and detail lines, use the Formula Outline command to create an outline from the report, or use a mouse and the Promote or Demote tools in the toolbar to promote or demote rows or columns. Outlines enable you to expand a report to show detail or to contract it to show it in summary. Use the Formula Outline command with the Apply styles option to apply styles to an outline. Changing the definition of the styles used in the outline changes the appearance of all rows or columns with that style. Experiment with this process on a simple outline before using it on a large database.

You can save memory by formatting entire rows or entire columns in a database or report. Select the entire row or the entire column and then choose the formatting commands you need.

T I P   Reports for different people may contain data reflecting different levels of security or confidentiality. A report you send to sales managers may contain the commissions earned by all salespersons, whereas the report you send to product managers should not contain that confidential information. You can use one report for both public and confidential reports by hiding selected columns or rows. After you extract data, use the Format Column Width or Format Row Height commands with the Hide button to hide columns or rows.

For Related Information:

◀◀ "Outlining Worksheets," p. 517.

FROM HERE...

Maintaining Data

Databases have a tendency to grow. Eventually, memory and speed limitations dictate that you clean up. As part of this process, you need to make backup copies of the old information before removing it from the working database.

Backing Up Your Data

An unpleasant surprise awaits you if you continually save your worksheet to the same file name. When you choose **File Save**, the current Excel file replaces the original file on disk. This practice is fine as long as you never make a mistake. What if you accidentally delete the wrong records, make a number of incorrect edits, or add some incorrect data? If you save a bad file over the good, you are left with only the bad file.

A conservative policy is to save a printed copy and a disk file of the old data before deleting it from your working database. Suppose that you want to delete all April records. Use the **Data Extract** command to create a printed report of the April records. Cut out the April extract report and paste it into a new document. Save this new document as a file containing only the records that will be deleted.

If you prefer more security, save the database you are editing every 15 to 30 minutes by using the **File Save As** command. Each time you save with **File Save As**, edit the file name to make it different from the previous name. For example, you may want to use a sequence of file names such as the following:

ACCTS_01.XLS

ACCTS_02.XLS

ACCTS_03.XLS

The last two characters before the extension indicate the file's version number. This numbering technique enables you to return to an older file to recover previous data. When files are old enough that you know you will not need them again, use File Delete to erase them from the disk; or switch to the File Manager and erase multiple files all at once.

Keep more than one copy of your important database files and do not keep the backup copy in the same building as the original. Take the backup files to a different building or to a bank vault. If your building burns or a thief takes the computers and disks, you still have your data.

Deleting a Group of Records

Your database is of little use unless someone maintains it. You must edit, add, and delete single records yourself, but Excel can help you delete groups of records. You delete a group of records in much the same way as you extract a group of specific records. Use the **Data Delete** command to delete from the database all records that meet the criteria you specify. Because you cannot undo deleted records, however, adhere to the safety procedures outlined in the following steps:

1. Choose the File Save **As** command and save your worksheet with a file name different from the normal name. This file will be your back up file in case you save incorrectly edited data over your original file.

2. Enter the criteria for the records you want to delete.

3. Choose the **Data Find** command and scroll up and down to be certain that the criteria selects only what you want deleted.

4. Choose the **Data Delete** command to delete records matching the criteria. Excel displays the alert box shown in figure 24.16.

FIG. 24.16

An alert box warns you that records will be deleted permanently.

5. Select the OK button or press Enter if you are sure that you want to delete the records.

6. Choose the File Save **As** command and save the resulting worksheet with the file name of the original worksheet.

The original file name now contains the worksheet with the up-to-date database. The file name saved in step 1 contains a backup copy of the database as it was before deleting.

NOTE The **Edit Undo** command will not restore deleted records.

The **Data Delete** command shifts records upward to fill gaps left by deleted records. The command also automatically redefines the database range. The rest of the worksheet remains unchanged. Figure 24.17 shows the sample database with a new report date of 16-Oct-92. The criteria range is set to select records where the DAYS DUE has past (where the Days Due field is negative). In figure 24.18, records matching this criterion have been deleted, and the database has closed up to fill the gaps.

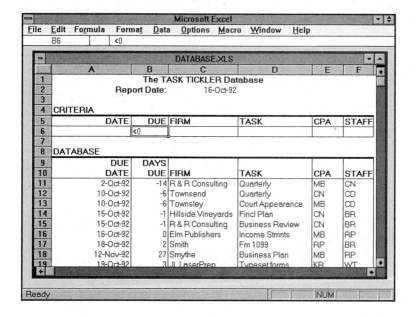

FIG. 24.17

The database before records are deleted with the criterion to delete past records.

If you have only a few records to delete or records that may be difficult to describe with criteria, you may want to delete them manually. Use **Data Form** to find the records and then select the **Delete** button on the form to delete the current record.

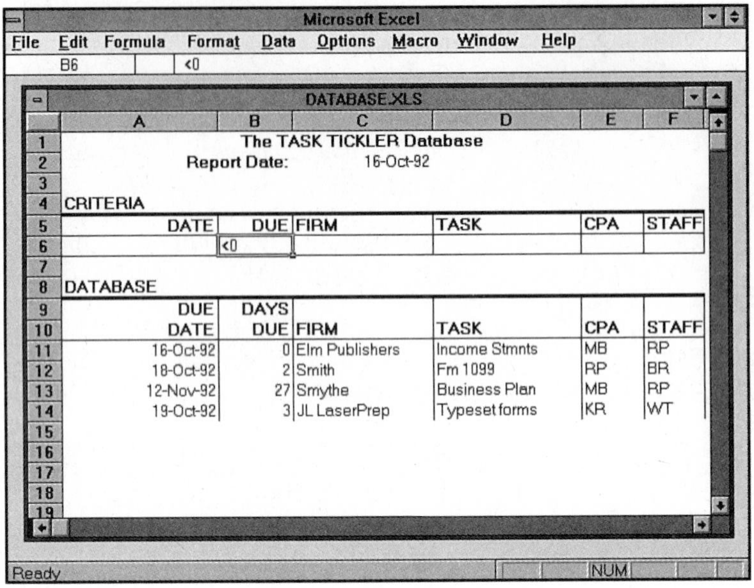

FIG. 24.18

The database after records specified in the criteria range are deleted.

Chapter Summary

If you work with large databases and need to extract information from them, or if you need to join material from two databases, read Chapter 25, "Linking Excel to Databases with Q+E."

Chapter 26, "Building Extensive Databases," shows you a number of ways to combine worksheet commands and techniques in the database. Even if you do not plan to use these techniques now, skim through that chapter for ideas that may help you in your future work.

Linking Excel to Databases with Q+E

One of the features that makes Excel powerful is its capability to work with databases that reside on disk, on an SQL Server, or on a mainframe. These databases can be personal computer databases, such as dBASE III Plus or dBASE IV; SQL Server databases on a network; a mainframe database, such as ORACLE; or a text file downloaded from a mainframe. Excel can link worksheets to these databases, copy information from them onto a worksheet, or extract information from a database and put the result on a worksheet.

Excel uses a program called Q+E to work with databases on disk. Q+E is a separate Windows application designed to query and edit databases stored in a personal computer or some mainframes. Q+E and Excel exchange information through Dynamic Data Exchange (DDE). Dynamic Data Exchange enables Windows applications to pass data and information.

Pioneer Software, the maker of Q+E, continually updates and develops additional database drivers and Q+E enhancements. For more information, contact Pioneer Software; the address is listed in the Appendix of this book.

T I P

This chapter describes only how to use those Q+E features that are available from the Excel **D**ata menu. Q+E is a database query and edit program in its own right and would require many chapters or a book of its own to cover fully. A Q+E manual comes with your copy of Microsoft Excel.

NOTE   You cannot edit or append database files from within Excel by using the add-in macros that come with Excel and Q+E. To edit these files, switch to Q+E and make your changes by using the Q+E program.

Using Q+E

Q+E is a program that enables you to work with different types of database files from within Windows. Because Q+E uses Dynamic Data Exchange, you can closely couple it with some Windows applications, such as Excel and Word for Windows, and give database access capabilities to these programs. Figure 25.1 shows an Excel worksheet containing information brought into it by Q+E from a dBASE file on disk.

	Q+E			
File	**Edit** **Sort** **Select** **Search** **Layout** **Window**			**Help**

Query1 (ADDRESS.DBF)

	FIRM	STREET	CITY	STATE	ZIP
1	Adobe Construction	83 San Carlos	San Jose	CA	94956
2	Audits 'R Us	5 Apian Way	Nevada City	CA	94506
3	Caryn's Adventure Trav	34 Mountain Dr.	Newark	NJ	20254
4	Flatland Mountain Shop	8 Snowside St.	Aspen	CO	80800
5	Generic Office Supply	32 Dona Dr.	Healds	OH	43026
6	Good Ad Agency	9 S.E. St.	Columbus	OH	43000
7	Green Gardens	16 Terrace Trl.	Ashland	OR	87324
8	Nature's Way Cafe	89 Seaside	Redmond	WA	87654
9	OldType Printers	32 Inkblot Ct.	Miami	FL	65098
10	R&R Consulting	90 Gracey Ln.	Louisville	KY	32431
11	Seaside Surf Shop	8 Mouse Rd.	Minot	ND	12039

Dr. Watson   File Manager   Microsoft Excel Microsoft Word - XL25QE12.DOC

FIG. 25.1

Q+E is a separate program that links database files to many Windows applications.

Q+E works with a variety of database systems. Q+E comes with *drivers* that enable the system to manipulate databases in dBASE II, III, and IV;

Excel files, text files; and Microsoft SQL Server, ORACLE, and OS/2 Extended Edition. With Excel and Q+E, you also can access and manipulate Excel database worksheets on disk, as well as access different types of personal computer text files. Because you have Q+E, you can query and edit these files, although you do not have the database program.

This chapter describes how to use Q+E from within Excel by using Excel's **D**ata menu. The end of the chapter shows a simple example of how Q+E can be controlled by Excel macros so that data retrieval is automatic and transparent to the operator.

Even if you are unfamiliar with database concepts, after reading this chapter you will be able to use Excel's **D**ata menu to access dBASE, Excel, or text files on disk. The add-in macros, QE.XLA and QESTART.XLA, add new Excel database commands and modify existing Excel commands so that Excel can extract information from files on disk. You will use the knowledge you acquired in previous Excel database chapters.

Q+E is a powerful program. It enables operators to open database files and tables, to query tables based on complex search criteria specified through dialog boxes, or to create and save queries based on SQL SELECT statements. Q+E also can join tables, which enables you to create a single new database by linking information from two databases containing a common field.

> You can learn more about Q+E's power by choosing Help. Help information is available on-line while Q+E is active. To get Help, access the **H**elp menu or press F1.
>
> **T I P**

After Q+E opens data in a file, you can read and sort the data brought in, edit the file and save it, perform such calculations as subtotals, and specify report formats. When files are read into Q+E, you can copy and paste or link them to Excel. When linked data in a file changes, Excel's worksheet updates.

Installing Q+E

To operate Q+E with Excel, you must install Q+E. You can install Q+E when you install Excel. If Q+E is not available to you, you can reinstall Excel and choose to install Q+E without installing the existing portions of Excel. (For more information on Excel's add-in programs, see Chapter 15.)

If you are not sure whether Q+E is installed, use the **F**ile **O**pen command to look for QE.EXE and QE.HLP in the EXCEL\QE directory. The subdirectory QE under the Excel directory should contain practice files and add-in macros.

To install Q+E if it is not installed, rerun the Excel installation program but request to install only Q+E. The Setup program will give you a Q+E button that enables you to select which databases you want to access. Most personal computer-based users will want access to Excel, dBASE, and text files. Consult your PC coordinator or Information Systems division to determine whether you should install drivers for Microsoft SQL Server, ORACLE, and OS/2 Extended Edition.

Using External Database Commands

The use of Q+E as an integral part of Excel demonstrates how well some Windows applications work together. Q+E comes with two add-in macros that provide commands and features in Excel. The following section demonstrates how to open and use the add-in macro that adds external database extract commands to the **D**ata menu.

Adding External Database Commands

You can use three methods to set up Excel so that it adds the external database commands. These methods are presented by how frequently you need to use Q+E.

If you rarely use an external database, you can add the external database commands and load the Q+E program by choosing the **F**ile **O**pen command in Excel, changing to the EXCEL\QE directory, and opening the add-in macro, QE.XLA. This procedure adds and modifies commands under the **D**ata menu. Q+E does not start until you use one of the external database commands

If you always want the external database commands available on the menu, use the File Manager to copy the file QESTART.XLA from the EXCEL\QE directory into the XLSTART directory. Because QESTART.XLA is small, Excel starts more quickly. Then at startup, Excel opens the QESTART.XLA add-in macro, which adds and modifies commands under the **D**ata menu. The first time you use one of the external database commands, the QE.XLA add-in opens. This method makes Q+E readily accessible. (Chapter 15 explains how to use the Add-in Manager as another method of installing QESTART.XLA.)

If you always want external database commands available, copy the QE.XLA file from the EXCEL\QE directory into the XLSTART directory. When Excel starts, the program adds the external commands. Because this method loads the larger QE.XLA add-in during Excel's startup, Excel starts more slowly; however, the external database commands react more quickly the first time they are used. Do not leave the QESTART.XLA macro in the XLSTART directory with QE.XLA. If during installation you chose the Drivers button and the option to load Q+E on startup, the QE.XLA file was copied into the XLSTART directory for you. (Chapter 15 explains how to use the Add-in Manager as another method of installing QE.XLA.)

NOTE When using the File Manager, you can easily drag the QE.XLA or QESTART.XLA files from the EXCEL\QE directory into the EXCEL\XLSTART directory. However, dragging them causes the files to move to the new directory. If you later delete these files from XLSTART, you will not have copies. Instead, use Ctrl+drag to copy the QE.XLA or QESTART.XLA files from the EXCEL\QE directory into EXCEL\XLSTART. Ctrl+drag creates a copy and leaves you with original files in EXCEL\QE.

When you open QESTART.XLA or QE.XLA, the **Data Extract**, **Data Delete** and **Data Set Database** commands are modified to work with external databases. The **Data Find** commands do not work while an external database is set. The following three additional commands are added to the **Data** menu:

Command	Description
Paste Fieldnames	Reads field names from an external database so that you can choose the names you want pasted onto the worksheet at the top of criteria and extract ranges.
SQL **Query**	Presents a dialog box in which you can write an SQL query that extracts information from an external database.
Activate Q+E	Activates Q+E if it is running, placing Excel in the background. If Q+E is not running, this command starts it.

Understanding How External Commands Work

Most external database commands work similarly to the commands you learned in previous database chapters. A major difference is that you will specify a database that is in a file and not on a worksheet. You will not be able to see the field names at the top of each column, because the files are on disk.

NOTE   Some commands are disabled for external databases. The **Data Form** and **Data Find** commands are disabled when you set the database as external. You cannot display, scroll through, find, or edit information in the file by using the QE.XLA or QESTART.XLA macros. These macros can extract or delete information from a file. Full editing and search capabilities for disk files are available if you work directly within Q+E.

By using the new **Data** menu commands, you can paste external database field names onto the worksheet. You will paste these file names as headings into a criteria and extract range; these ranges work the same as the criteria and extract ranges you used with a worksheet database.

After you set the database range and create criteria and extract ranges with appropriate headings, you can extract or delete information from the file on disk.

Setting the Database

You can have a database on the worksheet and multiple databases specified on disk. The **Data Set Database** command tracks which database is active; the command also enables you to switch between databases. The following figures use the sample dBASE files, .DBF, that come with Excel and Q+E and are located in the EXCEL\QE directory.

To set the first external database of a working session, complete the following steps:

1. Choose the **Data Set Database** command. Figure 25.2 shows the database selection dialog box.

FIG. 25.2

Indicate the current selection or an external database.

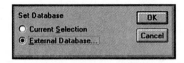

2. If you want to use the selected range on the worksheet as the database, select the Current **S**election option. Choose OK or press Enter. (The Current **S**election option is the same as the normal Set

Database command.) Work with your worksheet database by using the procedures described in previous chapters.

or

If you want to use an external database, select the **External Database** option, and then choose OK or press Enter. Figure 25.3 shows the dialog box that appears.

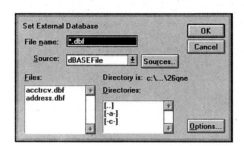

FIG. 25.3

Set the source and location of the external database.

3. Select the type of file to which you are connecting from the **Source** pull-down list. Some common file types are Excel, dBASE, and Text. If your database is not on your computer's disk, select the Sources button. From the Source Connections dialog box, you can log on to the database system containing the information you need. (The drivers for these sources must be installed during Q+E installation for the database system to appear in the Sources list.)

4. Choose OK.

5. Select the location of the file from the **Directories** list box. (The name of this box may vary for different sources. Sample dBASE and text files are located in the EXCEL\QE directory.)

6. Select the file from the **Files** list.

7. Choose OK or press Enter. This step returns you to the Set Database dialog box.

8. Choose the **Change** or **Add** button to change an existing external database or to add more databases. Choose OK when you are finished.

After you set an external database, the Set Database dialog box expands to include the names of external databases that have been set. Figure 25.4 shows the dialog box with multiple external databases set. Choose the **Change** or **Add** buttons to change existing database connections or to add more.

When you are finished with the connection to a remote external database, such as SQL Server or ORACLE, you can free system resources by choosing the **Change** button, and then choosing the Source button and logging off.

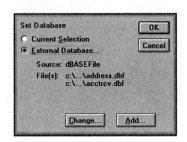

The Set Database dialog box displays all the external databases that are set.

Pasting Field Names

Although the database is in an external file, you still need field names on the worksheet for use in the criteria and extract ranges. The **Data Paste Fieldnames** command added to the **Data** menu by QE.XLA or QESTART.XLA enables you to pull the field names out of a file and paste them into the worksheet. If Q+E is querying only one database, then field names appear as only a field name, such as FIRM or STREET.

T I P   Field names from multiple files or tables include the file or table name. If you set multiple external databases, you will have field names from multiple databases. To distinguish between names from different databases, each field name is preceded by the file name. A period separates the field name and file name to give a syntax of *databasefile.FIELDNAME*.

To paste field names onto the worksheet from a file, complete the following steps:

1. Select the left-most cell of the location at which you want to paste the field names.

2. Choose the **Data Paste Fieldnames** command. The dialog box shown in figure 25.5 appears.

3. If you want to paste all field names in a row to the right of the active cell, choose the Paste All button. You can reorder or delete names by using Excel's cut and paste methods. Do not follow the remainder of these steps.

    or

If you want to paste a few names in a special order, choose the Order Fields button. The dialog box shown in figure 25.6 appears.

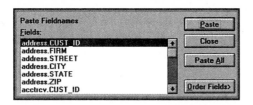

FIG. 25.5

Select the field names you want to use from the Paste Fieldnames dialog box.

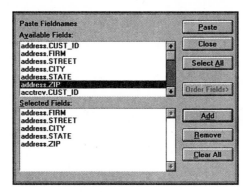

FIG. 25.6

Select the field names and the order in which you want them pasted in this dialog box.

4. Select a field name from the Available Fields list, and then choose the Add button.

5. Select additional field names in the order you want and add them to the list. Delete a name by selecting it from the Selected Fields list and choosing the Remove button.

6. Choose the Paste button to paste the names.

Setting the Criteria Range

When the field names are pasted onto the worksheet, select the names and one blank row below. Next, use the Data Set Criteria command to set the range as the criteria range for the external database. Follow the same procedures as those described in Chapter 23 for setting a criteria range. If you forget to set a criteria range, Excel will extract all the data.

NOTE   You cannot paste field names until you set an external database, because Excel has no way of knowing the field names in an external database.

If you are using a single current external database and you are not using calculated criteria, field names are used in the same way as in a worksheet database. When multiple databases are active, computed criteria or extracts must be set differently.

When you have more than one current external database, specify criteria field names with the following syntax:

databasefile.FIELDNAME

Pasted field names are pasted with the preceding syntax.

Suppose, for example, that multiple databases are active and one database has the name ADDRESS.DBF and the field name STREET. The valid field name in the criteria range would be address.STREET.

Entering Criteria

An extract from an external database through Q+E does not evaluate criteria in the same way as an extract from a worksheet. In Q+E, criteria are case-sensitive; uppercase letters match against uppercase letters, and lowercase letters match against lowercase letters.

If you need computed criteria, do not create the computed criteria as you would for a worksheet database. For example, with a worksheet database, you would use a criteria where the field name above the calculated criteria is a field name that does not exist. In addition, the calculated criteria in a worksheet database is posed as a logical test. For example, the following criteria tests whether the on-hand inventory in column B is less than the reorder quantity in column C plus 5:

Test
=B9<C9+5

Here, the name Test does not exist as a field name in the *worksheet database*. Row nine is the top row of data in the worksheet database and is the first row on which the calculated criteria is tested. (This criteria warns that the on-hand inventory is within five units of needing a reorder.)

To build a calculated criteria for an external database, you must use a syntax that is more English-like and is similar to an SQL query. Use the actual field name that you are testing as the field name for the criteria. The test condition is then a comparative, as in the following example:

ONHAND
<REORDER+5

In this example, ONHAND and REORDER are field names that exist in the external database. The external database is set to a single database, as shown by field names that are not prefixed by the database name.

Extracting Data

Set an extract range for an external database extract in the same way you set an extract for a database on the worksheet. Copy field names for the extract headings from the criteria range, or paste them in the worksheet with the **D**ata Paste Fieldnames command.

To extract from the external database, complete the following steps:

1. Set the external database by using the **D**ata Set Data**b**ase command.

2. Paste names onto the worksheet with the **D**ata Paste Fieldnames command. Arrange and copy those names into criteria and extract range headings.

3. Set the criteria range with **D**ata Set **C**riteria.

4. Enter a criterion.

5. Set the extract range with the **D**ata Set E**x**tract command.

6. Clear the cells in the extract range or below the extract headings.

7. Choose the **D**ata Extract command.

   The dialog box shown in figure 25.7 appears and shows how many records satisfy the criteria.

8. Select the **L**inked or **U**nlinked option to indicate whether you want the data linked to the file via Q+E or whether you want data pasted into cells.

9. Select the **S**ave As button if you want data saved to a text file.

10. Choose OK or press Enter. If you requested that the data be saved to a file, Excel displays the Save As dialog box so that you can enter a file name.

Data that fits your criteria is extracted and copied into the extract range, as shown in figure 25.8.

Clear the previously extracted data. Extracts from external databases do not clear the previous data as do extracts from a worksheet database. If you do not clear previously extracted records, the new records can overlap with the old records and run together.

T I P

FIG. 25.7

In this dialog box, you see how many records satisfy the criteria.

```
11 Records Received          Paste

Paste Options                Save As...
  ○ Linked  ● Unlinked       Cancel
```

FIG. 25.8

Extracted data appear on the worksheet.

	Microsoft Excel					
File Edit Formula Format Data Options Macro Window Help						

A9   address.FIRM

QEADDRSS.XLS

	A	B	C	D	E	F
1						
2	Criteria Range					
3	address.FIRM	address.STREET	address.CITY	address.STATE	address.ZIP	
4				CA		
5				KY		
6						
7						
8	Extract Range					
9	address.FIRM	address.STREET	address.CITY	address.STATE	address.ZIP	
10	Adobe Construction	83 San Carlos	San Jose	CA	94956	
11	Audits 'R Us	5 Apian Way	Nevada City	CA	94506	
12	R&R Consulting	90 Gracey Ln.	Louisville	KY	32431	
13						
14						
15						
16						
17						
18						

Ready   NUM

Joining Database Extracts

An extremely handy feature of Q+E is its capability to join databases. This feature can save you from the necessity of creating huge database files and from repeating data.

For example, with a normal Excel database that contains the names of business clients and their business addresses, you must keep each person's name and business address in a record (row). This database contains many duplicate entries because many people may work at the same address. This type of database also requires extra data-entry time and increases the possibility of errors as duplicate information is typed. Maintenance and changes to this database can be unwieldy.

A more efficient way of building databases is to have one database contain client names with their company and another database contain companies and addresses. This means that only one address is entered for each company. When you need to create mailing labels, you can join the two databases so that each company address is duplicated where needed. The result is an extract that seems to come from a single large database.

By using the sample files, EMP.DBF and DEPT.DBF, available in Q+E, figure 25.9 shows an extract created by joining both files. The field containing data common to both files is emp.DEPT and dept.DEPT_ID. Although the field names are different, they both contain department ID codes. By joining the two files, you can create a list of last names, salaries, and a text name of the department. This information did not exist solely in either file but needed to be created by joining information between the two files.

The join that created this extract was performed by setting the database to both external files with **D**ata Set Data**b**ase. The Add button was chosen to add the second database. Then all the field names from both databases were pasted in with the **D**ata Paste **F**ieldnames command. Unused fieldnames were deleted.

The **D**ata Set **C**riteria and **D**ata Set E**x**tract commands were used to set the criteria and extract ranges. The actual join was created by using the field name containing common data as a criteria. In the example, the field names containing data common to both databases are emp.DEPT and dept.DEPT_ID. By entering dept.DEPT_ID under the field name emp.DEPT, you are specifying that the only records to be extracted will be those having the same data in these two fields. The other limit in this criteria is that emp.SALARY must be greater than 25,000.

The resulting extract found all employees in EMP.DBF whose salary was greater than 25,000. Q+E used the department ID for each record found to find the corresponding department name and department manager ID.

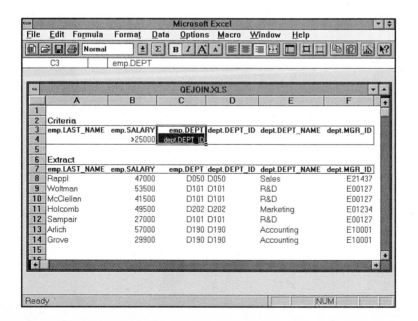

FIG. 25.9

Database files can be joined when they are extracted by Q+E.

Controlling Q+E Links with Macros

Q+E contains its own command language that can be operated under the control of Excel macros. Figure 25.10 shows an example of a macro that opens a Dynamic Data Exchange Channel with Q+E, starts it if necessary, then requests that Q+E retrieve information from a dBASE file. The retrieved information is then transferred into an Excel worksheet. The Q+E command language and sample Excel macros can be found in the Q+E manual that comes with Excel.

You can create and run this sample macro yourself if you are familiar with how to manually create command macros. Cell B1 must be given a command macro name; the name shown is QNE. Cell B3 has been defined with the name *chan*. The text in cell A3 is only a label showing the name of B3. *chan* stands for channel, the Dynamic Data Exchange communication channel opened between Excel and Q+E.

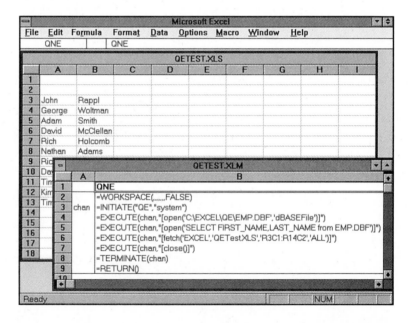

FIG. 25.10

An Excel macro like this can control Q+E by using the Q+E command language.

When you create this macro, be certain that cell B4 uses the correct directory for the sample Q+E file EMP.DBF. The directory shown is the default directory, in which Excel's installation program stores the sample Q+E files. Before you run the macro, you must create a worksheet named QETEST.XLS. QETEST.XLS must be open to receive the data but does need not to be active to receive a data transfer.

The macro works by first using the WORKSPACE() function to be certain that the **I**gnore Remote Requests check box is turned off in the **O**ptions **W**orkspace dialog box. This enables the Dynamic Data Exchange (DDE) communication to occur. The INITIATE command then opens a DDE channel with Q+E. If Q+E is not open, you will be asked whether you want to open it. When a DDE channel is opened, the channel identification number is stored in cell B3. All future communication between this macro and Q+E occurs through this channel number.

> Use Q+E to create SQL statements for you. If you know how to program macros but aren't familiar with SQL statements, you still can make Excel control Q+E. Use Q+E's capability to generate SQL statements from your dialog box choices. Write down the Q+E statement, and retype it into the Excel macro.
>
> **T I P**

Excel's EXEC() function sends Q+E commands to Q+E. The first open() command opens the file named EMP.DBF and tells Q+E to work with a dBASE file. The second open() command sends an SQL statement to select all of the FIRST_NAME and LAST_NAME fields from the EMP.DBF file.

The fetch() command tells Q+E to *fetch* the selected data and transfer the *whole* selection into the R3C1:R14C2 range in the QETEST.XLS worksheet of Excel. You could use a range name in place of the R3C1:R14C2 range reference. Finally the close() function closes the retrieval from Q+E. TERMINATE(chan) closes the DDE channel that the communication has been using.

The macro names and code use the following syntax:

```
        QNE
        =WORKSPACE(,,,,,,,FALSE)
chan =INITIATE("QE","system")
        =EXECUTE(chan,"[open('C:\EXCEL\QE\EMP.DBF','dBASEFile')]")
        =EXECUTE(chan,"[open('SELECT FIRST_NAME,LAST_NAME from
EMP.DBF')]")

=EXECUTE(chan,"[fetch('EXCEL','QETest.XLS','R3C1:R14C2','ALL')]")
        =EXECUTE(chan,"[close()]")
        =TERMINATE(chan)
        =RETURN()
```

FROM HERE...

For Related Information:

◄◄ "Using the Data Find Command," p. 823.

◄◄ "Matching Calculated and Compound Criteria," p. 835.

◄◄ "Extracting Data," p. 845.

▶▶ "Building Command Macros," p. 915.

▶▶ "Manually Creating Macro Names and Shortcut Keys," p. 936.

Chapter Summary

Q+E enables you to use Excel to extract, analyze, report, and chart information that is stored in files from other programs. This capability is especially useful for accounting, finance, marketing, or production systems. Businesses can download data to a text file or dBASE format, or Q+E can directly access the information from many systems. After Q+E can access the data, you can use Excel's capabilities to analyze current data and find up-to-date answers to help manage the business.

Q+E is a program in itself. It has a much wider capability than the Excel-related commands described in this chapter. Q+E includes its own command language and Dynamic Data Exchange so that you can create links between databases and Q+E and Windows applications, such as Excel and Word for Windows. To learn more about Q+E commands, refer to the Q+E reference manual that comes with Excel; or activate Q+E from within Excel by using the **D**ata Acti**v**ate command, and choose Q+E's **H**elp **I**ndex command. The \QE directory under the Excel directory contains practice and demonstration database and index files.

Building Extensive Databases

You can use Excel's database as just an electronic filing system. However, the database has many more uses because it is an integral part of the worksheet. You can use database results within worksheet calculations and analyze database contents with worksheet functions.

The techniques and tips presented in this chapter help you to combine the database with other worksheet functions. The ideas in this chapter also will save you time. The following list contains some of the techniques you will learn:

- How to reduce errors in worksheets and databases by cross-checking data as it is entered

- How to use database functions, such as DSUM( ) and DCOUNT( ), to analyze your database and extract summary information that matches the criteria you set

- How to combine the database functions with the **Data Table** command to produce multiple summaries from the database

 How to analyze and create reports from your database by using the Crosstab Wizard.

Cross-Checking Data Entries

Whether you are entering data in a database form or making entries directly into the cells of a worksheet, you can prevent accidental errors by using formulas that automatically cross-check data as you enter it. Figure 26.1 shows an example of a data-entry form that uses formulas to cross-check entered data. The Formula Bar shows the formula used to check the data in cell D4.

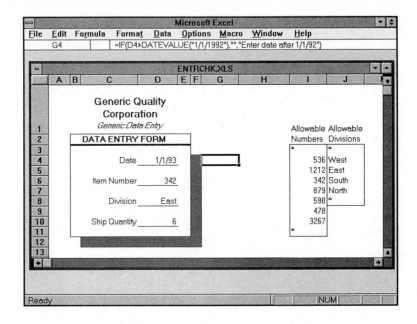

FIG. 26.1

A data-entry form with tables of allowed inputs.

Figure 26.2 shows the same form with incorrect data entered. Notice the warnings that appear to the side of the data-entry cells. The formulas used in those cells are given in the following table:

Cell	Cross-Check	Formula
G4	Date after 1/1/92	=IF(D4>DATEVALUE("1/1/1992"),"","Enter date after 1/1/92")
G6	Item number in list	=IF(ISNA(MATCH(D6,I3:I11,0)),"Invalid Number","")
G8	Division name in list	=IF(ISNA(MATCH(D8, J3:J8,0)),"West, East, South, North","")
G10	Range of quantities	=IF(AND(D10>4,D10<21)," ","5 to 20 units")

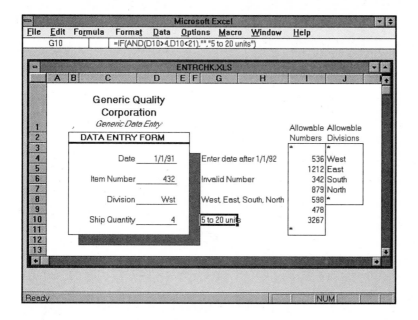

FIG. 26.2

A data-entry form with warnings for incorrect entries.

In each of these formulas, an IF( ) function combined with a conditional test decides whether the entry in column D is correct. The formula in cell G4 checks whether the date serial number from D4 is greater than the date in the IF( ) function. If the serial number is greater, the blank text " " is displayed. If the value in D4 is not greater, the prompting text is displayed.

In cell G6, the MATCH( ) function looks through the values in I3:I11 to find an exact match with the contents of D6. The 0 argument tells MATCH( ) to look for an exact match. When an exact match is not found, the error value #N/A! is returned. The ISNA( ) function detects #N/A! values when a match is not found; it displays the text warning Invalid Number. When a match is found, "" (nothing) is displayed on-screen. Note that when you use MATCH( ), the items in the list do not have to be sorted if you use a 0 *match-type* argument as they do with the LOOKUP( ) functions. MATCH( ) also returns an error if an exact match is not found; whereas a LOOKUP( ) function may return a near but incorrect result.

Cell G8 uses the same MATCH( ) method to check the division name against acceptable spellings. If you use large lists of possible entries that must be entered accurately, you may want to write custom dialog boxes that contain scrolling lists. Custom dialog boxes are described in Chapter 30.

The value of Ship Quantity must be 5 to 20 units. Therefore, the formula in G10 uses an AND( ) statement to check that the number in D10 is greater than 4 *and* less than 21. When both checks are true, nothing is displayed. If the number is out of the range, the message 5 to 20 Units is displayed.

For Related Information:

◄◄ "Logical Functions," p. 381.

◄◄ "Using Formulas To Make Decisions," p. 492.

Building Database Reports with the Crosstab Wizard

The Crosstab Wizard will save you hours of copying, formatting, and calculating. Not only does the Crosstab Wizard save you hours of work, it makes possible reports and database analysis that would be difficult or impossible to automate.

Most Excel databases appear something like figure 26.3. These databases contain rows of information arranged in columns that hold a specific type of information. The database in figure 26.3, for example, contains information about the sales of different light machinery. The database has been sorted by the items in each column from left to right, so all the A division products are together by product line, product, region, and so on. All the information is there for an analysis, but it is difficult to form any type of a comprehensive view. What would make analysis easier is a crosstab table.

Crosstab tables display the finished result of a database analysis. With them, you can analyze values in a database according to related fields. For example, figure 26.4 shows a simple crosstab created by the Crosstab Wizard. It shows product sales by product for each month. Notice that Excel also has created an outline so that each product's summary can be expanded to show the detailed information contained in the summary.

Crosstab tables also can create impressive tables that include statistical analysis on multiple database values, multiple headings, and subtotals (breakfields). The crosstab in figure 26.5 shows a few of the optional crosstab features such as subtotals, multiple value analysis, and multicolumn or multirow headings. Crosstabs are not automatically formatted. The crosstabs in these figures were formatted manually.

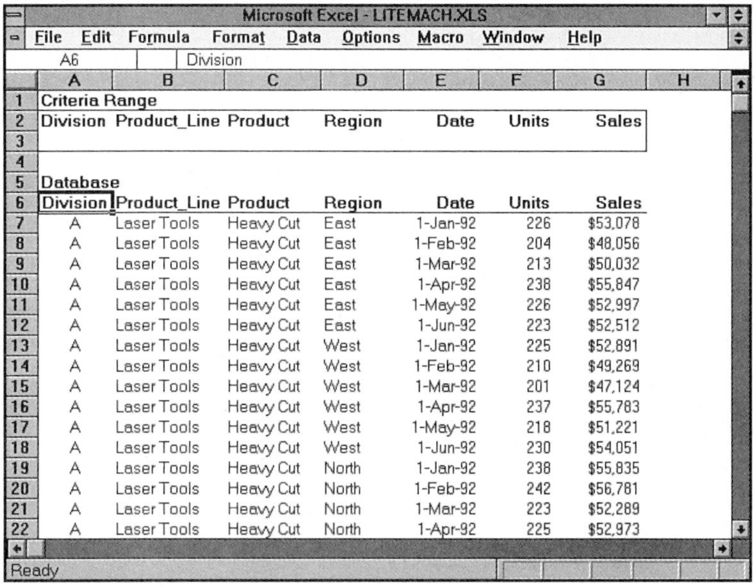

FIG. 26.3

Databases are difficult to analyze if left in the database format.

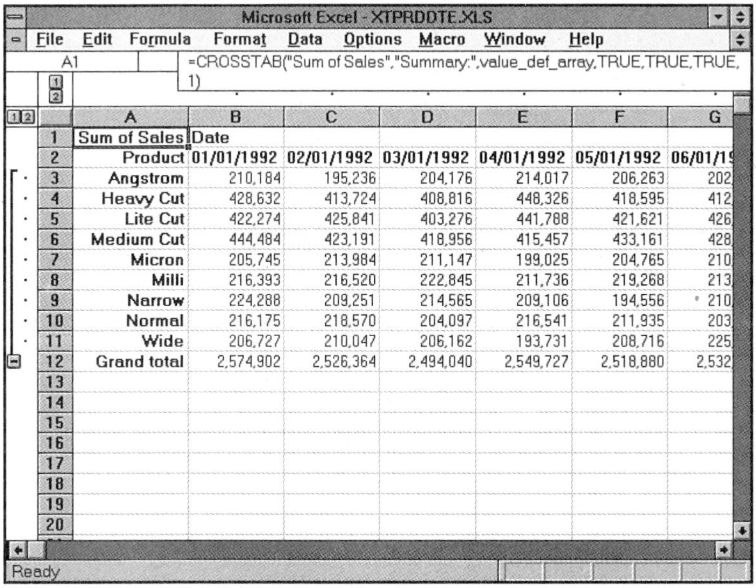

	Microsoft Excel - LITEMACH.XLS								
File	**Edit**	**Formula**	**Format**	**Data**	**Options**	**Macro**	**Window**	**Help**	
A6		Division							
	A	B	C	D	E	F	G	H	
1	Criteria Range								
2	Division	Product_Line	Product	Region	Date	Units	Sales		
3									
4									
5	Database								
6	Division	Product_Line	Product	Region	Date	Units	Sales		
7	A	Laser Tools	Heavy Cut	East	1-Jan-92	226	$53,078		
8	A	Laser Tools	Heavy Cut	East	1-Feb-92	204	$48,056		
9	A	Laser Tools	Heavy Cut	East	1-Mar-92	213	$50,032		
10	A	Laser Tools	Heavy Cut	East	1-Apr-92	238	$55,847		
11	A	Laser Tools	Heavy Cut	East	1-May-92	226	$52,997		
12	A	Laser Tools	Heavy Cut	East	1-Jun-92	223	$52,512		
13	A	Laser Tools	Heavy Cut	West	1-Jan-92	225	$52,891		
14	A	Laser Tools	Heavy Cut	West	1-Feb-92	210	$49,269		
15	A	Laser Tools	Heavy Cut	West	1-Mar-92	201	$47,124		
16	A	Laser Tools	Heavy Cut	West	1-Apr-92	237	$55,783		
17	A	Laser Tools	Heavy Cut	West	1-May-92	218	$51,221		
18	A	Laser Tools	Heavy Cut	West	1-Jun-92	230	$54,051		
19	A	Laser Tools	Heavy Cut	North	1-Jan-92	238	$55,835		
20	A	Laser Tools	Heavy Cut	North	1-Feb-92	242	$56,781		
21	A	Laser Tools	Heavy Cut	North	1-Mar-92	223	$52,289		
22	A	Laser Tools	Heavy Cut	North	1-Apr-92	225	$52,973		

Ready

FIG. 26.4

The Crosstab Wizard can help you build simple reports.

	Microsoft Excel - XTPRDDTE.XLS							
File	**Edit**	**Formula**	**Format**	**Data**	**Options**	**Macro**	**Window**	**Help**
A1		=CROSSTAB("Sum of Sales","Summary:",value_def_array,TRUE,TRUE,TRUE,1)						
	A	B	C	D	E	F	G
1	Sum of Sales	Date					
2	Product	01/01/1992	02/01/1992	03/01/1992	04/01/1992	05/01/1992	06/01/19
3	Angstrom	210,184	195,236	204,176	214,017	206,263	202
4	Heavy Cut	428,632	413,724	408,816	448,326	418,595	412
5	Lite Cut	422,274	425,841	403,276	441,788	421,621	426
6	Medium Cut	444,484	423,191	418,956	415,457	433,161	428
7	Micron	205,745	213,984	211,147	199,025	204,765	210
8	Milli	216,393	216,520	222,845	211,736	219,268	213
9	Narrow	224,288	209,251	214,565	209,106	194,556	210
10	Normal	216,175	218,570	204,097	216,541	211,935	203
11	Wide	206,727	210,047	206,162	193,731	208,716	225
12	Grand total	2,574,902	2,526,364	2,494,040	2,549,727	2,518,880	2,532
13							
14							
15							
16							
17							
18							
19							
20							

Ready

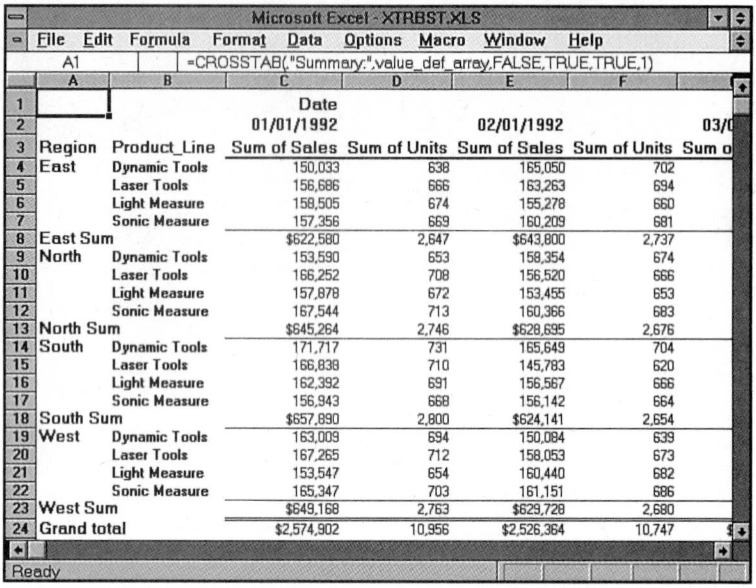

	Microsoft Excel - XTRBST.XLS					
<u>F</u>ile <u>E</u>dit For<u>m</u>ula For<u>m</u>at <u>D</u>ata <u>O</u>ptions <u>M</u>acro <u>W</u>indow <u>H</u>elp						

A1 | =CROSSTAB("Summary:",value_def_array,FALSE,TRUE,TRUE,1)

	A	B	C	D	E	F
1			Date			
2			01/01/1992		02/01/1992	03/0
3	Region	Product_Line	Sum of Sales	Sum of Units	Sum of Sales	Sum of Units	Sum o
4	East	Dynamic Tools	150,033	638	165,050	702
5		Laser Tools	156,686	666	163,263	694
6		Light Measure	158,505	674	155,278	660
7		Sonic Measure	157,356	669	160,209	681
8	East Sum		$622,580	2,647	$643,800	2,737
9	North	Dynamic Tools	153,590	653	158,354	674
10		Laser Tools	166,252	708	156,520	666
11		Light Measure	157,878	672	153,455	653
12		Sonic Measure	167,544	713	160,366	683
13	North Sum		$645,264	2,746	$628,695	2,676
14	South	Dynamic Tools	171,717	731	165,649	704
15		Laser Tools	166,838	710	145,783	620
16		Light Measure	162,392	691	156,567	666
17		Sonic Measure	156,943	668	156,142	664
18	South Sum		$657,890	2,800	$624,141	2,654
19	West	Dynamic Tools	163,009	694	150,084	639
20		Laser Tools	167,265	712	158,053	673
21		Light Measure	153,547	654	160,440	682
22		Sonic Measure	165,347	703	161,151	686
23	West Sum		$649,168	2,763	$629,728	2,680
24	Grand total		$2,574,902	10,956	$2,526,364	10,747

Ready

FIG. 26.5

The Crosstab Wizard will build complex reports with multi-field analysis and subtotals.

The Crosstab Wizard enables you to build reports that include the following elements:

■ Analysis on the values in multiple fields

■ Two levels of headings for multiple fields

■ Automatic outlining

■ Ranges that name the rows and columns in a crosstab

■ Multiple forms of statistical analysis on values

■ Subtotal (breakfields on analysis) on any field

When you build a crosstab using the Crosstab Wizard, you are not building a report in the blind. As you make selections, the Crosstab Wizard shows you a sample crosstab and the consequences of your choices.

Crosstab tables can be built from a database on an Excel worksheet or from a database on a hard disk or server. Crosstabs can be updated when the database changes by running the Crosstab Wizard and recalculating.

If you decide that you don't like the crosstab after it is complete, you can restart the Crosstab Wizard and run forward or backward through its dialog boxes, making changes until you get the crosstab report you want. The Crosstab Wizard gives you the opportunity to put the crosstab on the same worksheet as the database or to place the crosstab on a new worksheet. Only one crosstab is possible for each worksheet, but crosstabs on their own worksheets maintain a link to the original database. By embedding pictures of the crosstabs, you can place multiple crosstabs side-by-side for printing or viewing.

Crosstabs are similar to the database analysis data tables described later in this chapter. The advantages of crosstabs are that you can create complex tables that include subtotals, multi-level headings, and multiple value analysis. Crosstabs are easier to connect to databases on a hard disk or server so that they can reflect data in a network database or mainframe. For most database analysis and reporting situations, you probably want to use the Crosstab Wizard.

Data tables are more dynamic than crosstabs. You can type in new headings in a data table and see the table immediately update. You can have many data tables on one worksheet; whereas you can have only one crosstab per worksheet. (You can paste cell pictures of different crosstabs onto one worksheet for printing or viewing.)

Creating a Crosstab Table

The process of building a simple crosstab table is straightforward: define the database range, start the Crosstab Wizard, and follow the instructions given.

Starting the Crosstab Wizard

The Crosstab Wizard is an add-in application that comes free with Excel. If the **D**ata Crosstab command is not available on your menu, refer to Chapter 15 to learn about installing add-ins. Chapter 15 describes how to rerun the Excel setup application and add features without reinstalling all of Excel.

To build a crosstab table, perform the following steps:

1. Activate a worksheet and select the database on the worksheet. The database must meet the database requirements specified in Chapters 22 and 23. If you are using an external database on disk or on an SQL Server, continue to step 2.

2. If the database is on the worksheet, choose the **D**ata Set Database command. This command assigns the name Database to the range you selected.

   or

If the database is external, choose the **D**ata Set Data**b**ase command and set an external database. Chapter 25 describes how to use the Q+E application that comes with Excel to access external databases from within Excel.

3. Choose the **D**ata Crosstab command.

The Crosstab Wizard begins and guides you through the process of creating a crosstab table.

Running the Crosstab Wizard

The Crosstab Wizard displays dialog boxes that are nearly full screen. Figure 26.6 shows the first Crosstab Wizard dialog box that appears. Notice that these boxes have four parts. The top left shows instructions and a sample of what the crosstab you are building will look like. The top right presents you with options. The lower right displays a VCR-like control panel that enables you to move forward or backward through the Crosstab Wizard. The lower left contains an Explain button that displays help information for you.

The VCR-like buttons in the Crosstab Wizard perform the following actions:

Button	Result
Next>	Move to the next dialog box.
<Back	Move to the preceding dialog box.
>>|	Use current options and move to the last dialog box.
|<<	Return to the first dialog box.
Cancel	Cancel the Crosstab Wizard and return to the worksheet.
Explain	Display an explanation of the options for the current screen. Select Explain a second time to return to the normal screen.

After you choose the **D**ata Crosstab command, the dialog box in figure 26.6 appears. From this point until the crosstab appears in the worksheet, you are working in the Crosstab Wizard.

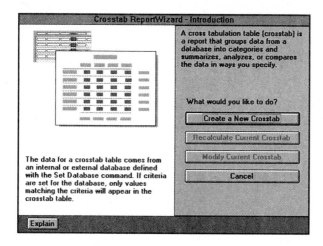

FIG. 26.6

The first Crosstab
Wizard screen.

The following steps guide you through the process of creating a basic
crosstab. Instructions in the following sections describe where to go if
you need to make more advanced selections that produce a more complex crosstab. To complete the Crosstab Wizard dialog boxes, complete
the following steps:

1. Choose the Create A New Crosstab button. The Row Categories
   dialog box displays.

2. Select a Row Category heading from the Fields in Database list and
   choose the Add button to select a field to be used as a row heading
   down the left side of the crosstab. Notice that the heading you
   selected now appears on the left side of the dialog box under Row
   Categories.

   You can repeat step 2 to select more than one Row Category heading. Multiple headings are nested hierarchically as the Product
   names are nested under the region in figure 26.7. Figure 26.7
   shows a Row Category heading selected for the database shown
   in figure 26.3.

3. Choose the Next>> button.

   The Column Categories dialog box appears.

4. Select a Column Category heading from the Fields in Database list,
   and choose the Add button to select a field to be used as a column
   heading across the top of the crosstab.

   Notice that the heading you selected now appears on the left side
   of the dialog box under Column Categories. You can repeat step 4
   to select more than one Column Category heading. Figure 26.8
   shows a field selected as a Column Category heading.

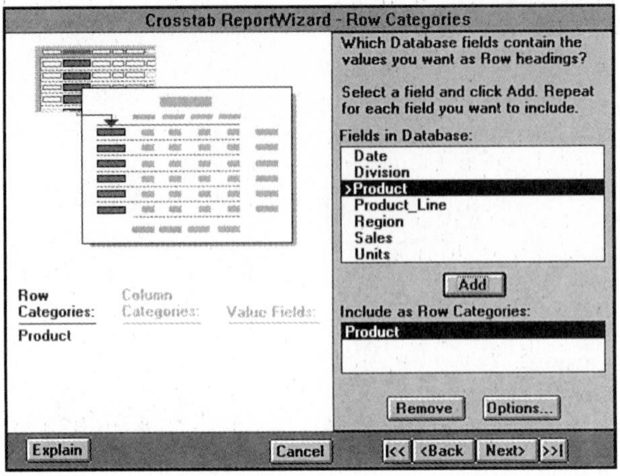

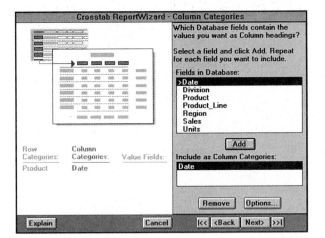

FIG. 26.7

First, you select row headings.

FIG. 26.8

Second, you select column headings.

5. Choose the Next>> button.

   The Value Fields dialog box appears.

6. Select a Value Field from the Fields in Database list, and choose the Add button to select the field to be analyzed. For example, the Sales field could be totalled or averaged. (The default analysis sums numeric values and counts text values.)

   Notice that the field you selected now appears on the left side of the dialog box under `Value Fields`. You can repeat step 6 to select additional value fields. If you select multiple value fields, you should read a following section titled, "Displaying Multiple Values." Figure 26.9 shows a field selected as a value field.

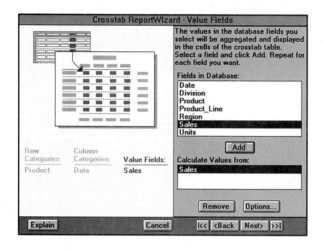

FIG. 26.9

Third, you select which field will be analyzed.

7. Choose the Next>> button. The final Crosstab Wizard dialog box appears, as shown in figure 26.10. If you choose multiple value fields, a Multiple Value Field dialog box appears asking you to select how data should be arranged. This dialog box is described in a following section.

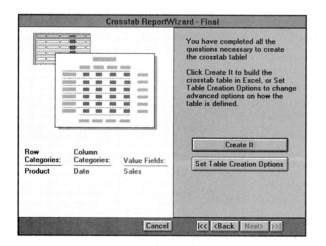

FIG. 26.10

The final Crosstab Wizard dialog box.

8. Choose the Create It button to create a crosstab.

Figure 26.11 shows the crosstab created by using the selections described and the default settings on the database shown in figure 26.3. By using the default settings in the Crosstab Wizard, the crosstab is placed on a new worksheet in outline form. Notice that formatting has not been applied yet, so columns need adjustment, and numbers need formatting.

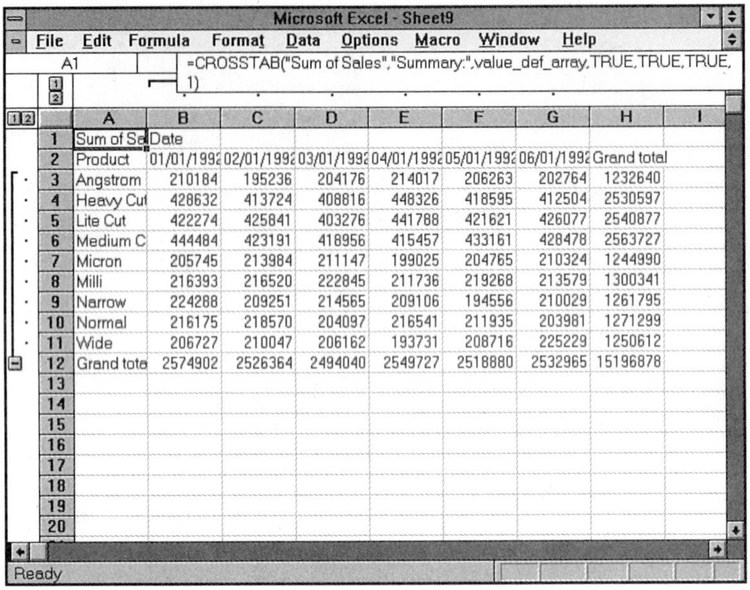

FIG. 26.11

A simple crosstab results from choosing the default buttons.

Choosing a single field at each step and selecting the Next>> button produces a simple crosstab that is very useful. If you want to compile more information into a single crosstab, however, you can select multiple fields at each step and select the Option button to add special analysis or formatting.

Options for Row Category Headings

The Crosstab Wizard gives you a number of ways of controlling values specified by the row headings. Modify Row Category headings when you want to limit the range the category covers (for example, from 1000 to 2000); when you want to group dates into weeks, months, quarters, or years; or when you want to specify how a row subtotal (breakfield) is analyzed.

When the second Crosstab Wizard dialog box displays to accept Row Categories, pick your row categories and complete the following steps:

1. Select the field you want to modify from the Include as Row Categories list at the lower right.

2. Choose the Options button to display the Row Categories Options dialog box (see fig. 26.12).

3. Change settings in the Row Categories Options dialog box by using the following options:

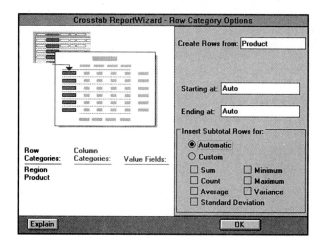

FIG. 26.12

Modify row headings
with the Row
Categories Options
dialog box.

Option	Effect
Create Rows from	Shows the field you selected in step 1.
Starting at	Auto for text. Used to limit numeric or date ranges. Enter dates by using an Excel-recognized format; 7/1/92.
Ending at	Auto for text. Used to limit numeric or date ranges. Enter dates by using an Excel-recognized format; 9/30/92.
In Groups of	Appears for date headings. Values under a date field can be accumulated by (each), Day, Week, Month, 30 Day, and Year. (each) indicates that the data is listed in the database.
Insert Subtotal	Select Automatic to total numbers and count Rows for text. Use Custom to specify one or more statistical analysis in a row below the data.

4. Choose OK to return to the Row Category dialog box. In the Row Category Dialog box, you can select and modify another Row Category or choose Next>>.

Options for Column Headings

Like the Row Category, Column Categories also can be modified. Modify Column Category headings when you want to limit the range the category covers (for example, from 1000 to 2000); when you want to group dates into weeks, months, quarters, or years; or when you want to specify how a column subtotal is analyzed.

When the third Crosstab Wizard dialog box displays to accept Column Categories, pick your column categories and complete the following steps:

1. Select the field you want to modify from the Include as Column Categories list at the lower right.

2. Choose the Options button to display the Column Categories Options dialog box.

3. Change settings in the Column Categories Options dialog box in the same ways listed in the preceding section for Row Categories Options. You can group date headings so that values accumulate into date groups, such as weeks or months (see fig. 26.13).

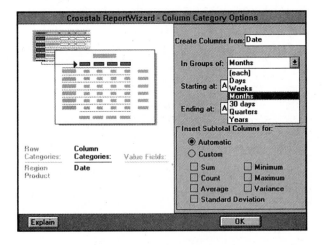

FIG. 26.13

Grouped date headings.

4. Choose OK to return to the Column Category dialog box. In the Column Category dialog box, you can select and modify another Column Category or choose Next>>.

Changing the Value Analysis

The default analysis on the data in the Value field is a total of numeric value fields and a count in text value fields. However, you can change how Excel evaluates the value fields when you get to the Value Field Options dialog box (see fig. 26.14).

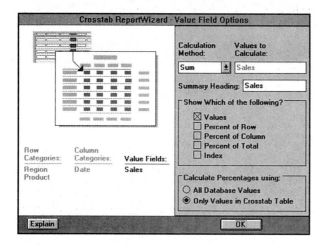

FIG. 26.14

Modify how a value
field is analyzed in this
dialog box.

When the fourth Crosstab Wizard dialog box displays to accept Value
Fields, pick your value fields to be analyzed and then complete the
following steps:

1. Select the field you want to modify from the Calculate Values From
   list at the lower right.

2. Choose the Options button to display the Value Field Options
   dialog box.

3. Change settings in the Value Field Options dialog box. The different
   settings available include the following options:

Option	Effect
Calculation option	Lists the different statistical evaluations available.
Value to Calculate	Displays the value you selected in step 1.
Summary Heading	Shows the editable text used as a worksheet label.
Show Which of the Following	Presents alternatives for showing the value, (the default), percentage or ordinal rank of the values.
Calculate Percentage	Determines whether a percent is calculated from only the data in the table or from all data in the database.

4. Choose OK to return to the Value Field dialog box. In the Value
   Field dialog box, you can select and modify another Value Field or
   choose Next>>.

Displaying Multiple Values

If you selected multiple value fields from the Value Fields dialog box, when you choose Next>>, you are presented with a Multiple Value Field Layout dialog box. This dialog box gives you the opportunity to specify how multiple value headings are arranged under row or column field headings (see fig. 26.15).

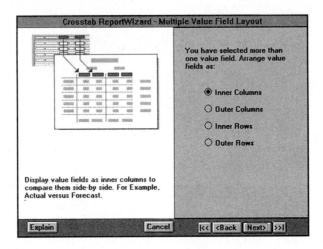

FIG. 26.15

If you use multiple value fields, you are asked how to arrange them.

You have two options for arranging multiple value fields under row or column category headings: Inner-Column or Outer-Column. These options are best explained by example. If the Column Category heading is months and you are totaling two Value fields, Unit and Sales, you are asked to select a layout.

Inner-Column produces column headings grouped together *inside* the *Column* Category. Column headings appear as the following:

Jan		**Feb**		**Mar**	
Unit	Sales	Unit	Sales	Unit	Sales

Outer-Column produces values grouped together *without* the Column Category headings. Column headings appear as the following:

Unit			**Sales**		
Jan	Feb	Mar	Jan	Feb	Mar

Row headings react in the same way to Inner and Outer Row groupings.

Specifying Report Options

At the final Crosstab Wizard dialog box, you have the opportunity to create the crosstab by choosing the Create It button. At that point, you also can choose the Set Table Creation Options button to change how the crosstab is created. Figure 26.16 illustrates the Create Options dialog box.

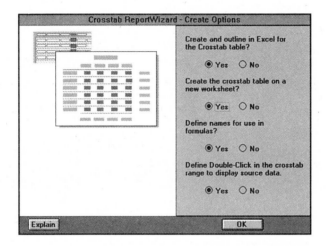

FIG. 26.16

At the end, you choose the way in which the crosstab is generated.

You can choose to create the crosstab as an outline. Figure 26.4 shows an outline used in a crosstab. Outlines enable you to expand the summary data to show the details from which the summary was compiled.

If you need the crosstab located next to the database, you can create the crosstab on the worksheet containing the database. To use this option, you must locate the active cell so that the crosstab can fill down and right across the worksheet without writing over other cells.

Another option names rows and columns using the row and column headings. These names can be useful in formulas. The entire crosstab range always is assigned the name Crosstab_range.

If you are building an Executive Information System, you may want to create the crosstab so that double-clicking on a cell displays the worksheet range from which the data was compiled.

Recalculating a Crosstab

If data in the database has changed, you may want to recalculate the crosstab to ensure that it is accurate. To recalculate a crosstab, activate the worksheet containing the crosstab and then choose the **Data**

Crosstab command. From the first dialog box in the Crosstab Wizard, choose the Recalculate Current Crosstab button.

Modifying and Formatting a Crosstab

You can use the Crosstab Wizard to modify crosstabs that it previously created. All you need to do is activate the worksheet containing the crosstab and select the **D**ata Crosstab command. From the first Crosstab Wizard dialog box, select the Modify Current Crosstab button. From that point, you can use the Next>> or <<Back buttons to traverse the Crosstab Wizard and modify the chart.

Using Criteria To Limit a Crosstab Analysis

You can limit which data Excel analyzes when building a new crosstab. To limit the data that Excel analyzes, build and name a criteria range as you would for any Excel or external database. Enter criteria to limit a data search, and then run the Crosstab Wizard. The criteria limits the values the Crosstab Wizard evaluates just as it limits a search or extract. Chapter 23 describes how to create and use criteria.

Changing Row or Column Headings

The crosstab actually is created by using the CROSSTAB() function. You can edit the title of row or column headings of existing crosstab tables by selecting a heading created by a CROSSTAB() function. The CROSSTAB() formula appears in the Formula Bar. Replace the first argument in the formula with the text you want to appear as a label. When you type this argument remember to enclose the new heading in quotes.

Formatting with AutoFormats

Familiarity with the Format AutoFormats command can save you time in formatting crosstabs. AutoFormats can apply predefined sets of formatting to tables like that built by the Crosstab Wizard. For more information concerning AutoFormats, refer to Chapter 8.

For Related Information:

◀◀ "Formatting with AutoFormats," p. 254.

◀◀ "Linking Pictures of Worksheet Cells," p. 448.

◀◀ "Outlining Worksheets," p. 517.

◀◀ "Finding Data," p. 820.

FROM HERE...

Using Data Tables

If you ever have analyzed a database by hand, you know it can be a great deal of work. For example, if you have a small job-cost database, you may need to manually total amounts by job code. This can take hours. The techniques in this section reduce those hours to less than a minute. Excel can search your database for you and calculate totals, count items, and even perform statistical analysis on data in your database. For example, you can use Excel to count the number of client contacts by sales representative, total the amount for specific account codes by month, or see how repairs are distributed by type.

> Evaluate Excel's Crosstab Wizard before using the data tables. You may find that the Crosstab Wizard gives you more flexibility and generates a more complex report with less effort than the data table method.
>
> **T I P**

Using Basic Database Functions

Database functions can perform such operations as counting, averaging, or totaling the values in a field for only those records that meet your criteria. Three frequently used database functions are DSUM(), DCOUNT(), and DCOUNTA(), which are similar to SUM(), COUNT(), and COUNTA(). DSUM() totals items in a field; DCOUNT() counts only numeric values in a field; and DCOUNTA() counts all nonblank cells in a field.

Excel has many other database-analysis functions: DMIN(), DMAX(), DAVERAGE(), DSTD(), DSTDP(), DVAR(), DVARP(), DGET(), and DPRODUCT(). These functions are described in Chapter 10, "Using Functions." Use the same procedure described in the following section for all of these functions.

When you use database functions, you need to specify three arguments: the range where the database is located, the column on which the function will act in the database range, and the range where the criteria is located. The format for database functions is as follows:

   Dfunction(database, field,criteria)

The *database* and *criteria ranges* can be the same or totally different from the ranges that you use with **D**ata **F**ind, **F**orm, or **E**xtract. Many Excel users set up D*functions* to use the same database range as that set with **D**ata **S**et Data**b**ase while using a totally different criteria range.

The *field* argument in the function can be the column number in the database—the first column in the database is 1—or the field name at the top of the database. If you use a field name, such as CODE, be certain that you enclose it in quotation marks ("). If it is not in quotation marks, Excel expects it to be a name that refers to a cell with the field name.

T   I   P   If you are accustomed to using 1-2-3 database functions, *be careful.* When counting the columns in a database for the field argument, 1-2-3 starts with zero for the first column or field. Excel starts with one for the first column or field. You may want to review Chapter 5 for information about how Excel differs from 1-2-3 and how to make Excel act like 1-2-3.

In figure 26.17, the DSUM() formula in cell F18 totals the Amount column for all records having an Exp Code of 12. Notice the following formula in F18:

   =DSUM(B5:F15,"Amount",B18:B19)

The range B5:F15 is the database, which includes the field names. The range B18:B19 is the criteria to be used by this function only. The column being summed is "Amount". This argument also could be specified as 5, or the fifth column. If you used the Formula Define Name command to name the range B5:F15 as ChkDatabase and the range B18:B19 as ChkCriterial, you could enter the formula as the following:

   =DSUM(ChkDatabase,"*Amount*",ChkCriteria)

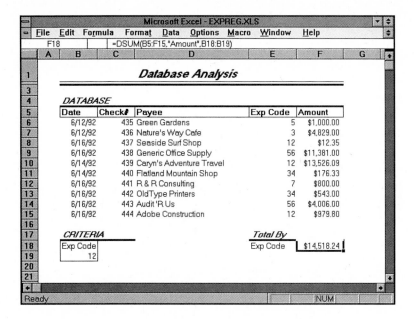

FIG. 26.17

A DSUM() formula in cell F18 totals the Amount column for all records having an Exp Code of 12.

In figure 26.18, the criteria range has been reset to B18:C19, and the field name Date has been added to the criteria range. Now, only those records with an Exp Code of 12 and a Date of 6/16/92 are totaled.

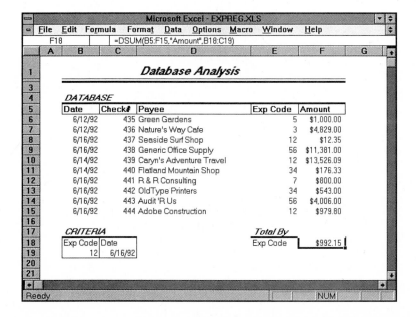

FIG. 26.18

The criteria range is now extended to total the Amount column for records that have an Exp Code of 12 and a date of 6/16/92.

Combining Database Functions with Data Tables

Although database functions are quite useful, they can require a great deal of time if you have many different criteria to type into the criteria range. In the check register shown in figure 26.18, if you want a total for each exp code, for example, you must type six different Exp Codes into the criteria range and then write down a total. Imagine that you were analyzing 50 or 150 codes. Wouldn't it be easier and faster to let Excel build a table for you that shows all the codes and all the database analysis results? In fact, by combining the database functions with the **Data Table** command, you can have Excel build such a table for you.

The **Data Table** command along with the DSUM() function in cell F18 takes the expense codes in E19:E24 and produces the total amounts for each expense code, as shown in F19:F24. **Data Table** takes each code from column E and inserts it into the criteria in cell B19. The DSUM() result from that criteria is then placed under the DSUM() formula in the cell next to the appropriate expense code.

In figure 26.19, the DSUM() function combined with the Data Table command produces a table of expense codes and their totals. The table is in E18:F24, and the DSUM() formula is in cell F18. The left column lists each expense code, and the right column lists the resulting total amount for the corresponding expense code.

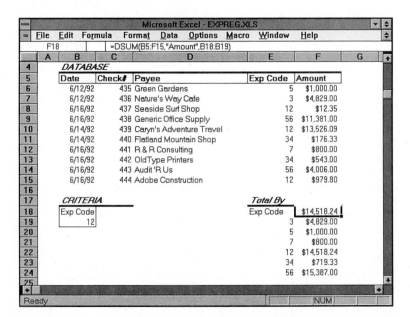

The DSUM formula in cell F18 is the following:

=DSUM(B5:F15,"Amount",B18:B19)

This is the same formula used in 26.17. The criteria range, B18:B19, again holds the criteria for the Exp Code field. The **D**ata **T**able command takes each value from the left side of the data table and places the values one at a time into the criteria cell B19. The command then records the DSUM() total for that criteria and puts it in the adjacent cell on the right side of the data table. Chapter 13, "Using Power Worksheet Features," describes how to select the range and use the **D**ata **T**able command to fill in the table.

If figure 26.19 contained 537 different expense codes, the process of entering them in column E down the left side of the data table would be quite time-consuming. Instead, **D**ata E**x**tract is used to create a list of all the expense codes used in the database. To create this list of codes, **D**ata **S**et Data**b**ase and **D**ata **S**et **C**riteria are used to specify the database and criteria ranges. An unlimited criteria is set so that all Exp Codes are extracted. Because all expense codes should be extracted, no criteria is entered.

The field name Exp Code is copied to cell E18. Then the Exp Code in cell E18 is selected, as shown in figure 26.20, and set as the extract by using the **D**ata **S**et E**x**tract command. Then the **E**xtract command with the **U**nique Records Only option is used to extract unique expense codes from the database. Expense codes are extracted on the field name Exp Code.

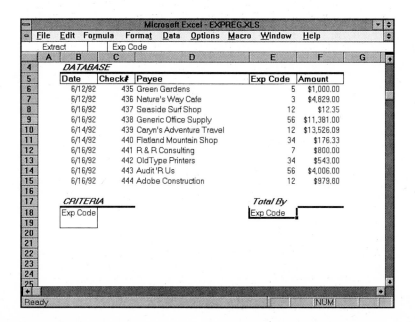

FIG. 26.20

The Exp Code field heading copied and selected in preparation for extracting expense codes.

Figure 26.21 shows the result of using the heading Exp Code as an extract range. Because the **Unique Records Only** option was selected, only one of each of the expense codes was extracted. You can use the **Data Sort** command to rearrange the expense codes.

			Microsoft Excel - EXPREG.XLS			
File	**Edit**	**Formula**	**Format** **Data** **Options** **Macro** **Window**	**Help**		
Extract		Exp Code				
A	B	C	D	E	F	G
4	*DATABASE*					
5	Date	Check#	Payee	Exp Code	Amount	
6	6/12/92	435	Green Gardens	5	$1,000.00	
7	6/12/92	436	Nature's Way Cafe	3	$4,829.00	
8	6/16/92	437	Seaside Surf Shop	12	$12.35	
9	6/16/92	438	Generic Office Supply	56	$11,381.00	
10	6/14/92	439	Caryn's Adventure Travel	12	$13,526.09	
11	6/14/92	440	Flatland Mountain Shop	34	$176.33	
12	6/16/92	441	R & R Consulting	7	$800.00	
13	6/16/92	442	OldType Printers	34	$543.00	
14	6/16/92	443	Audit 'R Us	56	$4,006.00	
15	6/16/92	444	Adobe Construction	12	$979.80	
16						
17	*CRITERIA*			*Total By*		
18	Exp Code			Exp Code		
19				5		
20				3		
21				12		
22				56		
23				34		
24				7		
25						
Ready					NUM	

FIG. 26.21

Extracted expense codes need only to be sorted for use in a data table.

Chapter 13 explains how to select and create a table by using the **Data Table** command.

NOTE   The **Data Extract** command erases all cells below the extract heading. You may want to move the extract heading to a safe area of the worksheet before you extract numbers. Then you can cut and paste the data to the appropriate place on your worksheet after the extraction.

T I P   Large data tables or multiple data tables may require a long time to recalculate. If you want to recalculate the worksheet but not the tables, choose the **Option Calculation** command and choose the Automatic Except Tables option. (Make sure you return this to the Automatic option when you recalculate the table.)

For Related Information:

◀◀ "Database Functions," p. 362.

◀◀ "Calculating Tables of Answers," p. 500.

◀◀ "Finding Data," p. 820.

◀◀ "Matching Simple Criteria," p. 828.

◀◀ "Matching Calculated and Compound Criteria," p. 835.

Troubleshooting Databases

The following section describes some of the more common problems people have when working with an Excel database.

Problem:

Entries in the criteria range that once worked no longer work.

Solution:

Check to see whether you may have changed the Alternate Expression Evaluation check box found within the **Options Calculation** command. When this check box is selected, database queries use the database rules used by 1-2-3. (See Chapter 5.)

Problem:

The database commands do not work at all.

Solution:

Use the following checklist of steps to find the problem:

1. Choose the **Formula Goto** command or press F5, select the Database range name or the Criteria range, and choose OK. Be certain that each range includes a single row of field names at the top of the selected range. The Criteria range should contain at least one row in addition to field names. The Database range should include one row of field names and all data.

2. Select the rows under the field names in the criteria range, and use **Edit Clear** to remove any hidden space characters in the criteria range.

3. Be certain that field names in the criteria and extract ranges are spelled exactly the same as they are in the database range. Use only text names or formulas that produce text names for headings.

Field names cannot be numeric. If you must use a numeric field name at the top of a database column, change it into text with a formula, such as the following:

   ="9540"

4. Be certain that a third set of field names is used for the extract range. The extract range with field names at the top of the range must be set with the **Data Set Extract** command, or it must be selected when you choose the **Data Extract** command.

Problem:

Calculated criteria does not produce a find or an extract result.

Solution:

Calculated criteria must be entered in the criteria range beneath a heading that is *not* a field name. To use a calculated criteria, create a new field heading that is *different* from any field name in the database. Replace an existing field heading in the criteria range with this new heading, or extend the criteria range to make room for the additional heading.

Problem:

Formulas in the database that refer to values outside the database return incorrect results.

Solution

Be certain that database formulas that refer to cells or names outside the database use absolute references.

Problem:

The **Data Find, Extract,** and **Delete** commands act on the entire database and ignore the criteria.

Solution:

Choose Formula **G**oto, select Criteria, and choose the OK button. This action selects the criteria range so that you can see it on-screen. Be certain that blank rows do *not* appear in the criteria range.

Problem:

The **Data Find, Extract,** and **Delete** commands do not act on records that obviously satisfy the criteria.

Solution:

Complete the following steps:

1. Be certain that the field names at the top of the criteria rows are exactly the same as the field names that head each database column. Use **Edit Copy** and **Edit Paste** to duplicate field names.

2. Use **Formula Goto** to select and verify that the database and criteria ranges are correct.

3. Use **Edit Clear** to erase all blank cells in the criteria range. Cells may appear blank, even when they contain blank characters entered with the space bar. Excel tries to find fields that match these blank characters.

4. Check the **Options Calculate** command and see whether the Alternate Expression Evaluation check box is selected. If yes, criteria are evaluated by using 1-2-3 rules.

Problem:

A complex criteria using AND and OR does not work as expected.

Solution:

AND statements must satisfy the first condition *and* the second condition simultaneously. OR statements can satisfy *one* of the conditions *or* both conditions. Consider the following example:

=AND(A15>500,A15<750)

This formula finds records where the data in column A is between 500 and 750. Those are the only values where both conditions are true. Remember that if you are searching for values between two points, such as in a numeric or date range, use AND. If you are searching for multiple text occurrences, such as two names, use OR.

Problem:

The database does not work correctly with dates.

Solution:

Be certain that dates have been entered with a method that produces a serial date number. Without a serial date number, database functions treat your date entry as text or as a number. For more information, read the sections on entering dates in Chapter 7, "Entering and Editing Worksheet Data."

Problem:

Part of the worksheet disappears whenever **Data Extract** is used.

Solution:

When you select only the field names in the extract range and then use the **D**ata **E**xtract command, Excel assumes that you are extracting an unlimited amount of data. Excel then clears the area below the field names in the selected extract range so that extracted data is not mixed with previously extracted data. To review how to extract limited amounts of data, see Chapter 24.

Problem:

Data at the bottom of the database is not found or extracted.

Solution

Use For**m**ula **G**oto to be certain that the bottom rows are included in the database range. To display each corner of the selected database range, press Ctrl+. (period). If the database range does not include all records, reselect the database and choose the **D**ata **S**et Data**b**ase command. Use **D**ata **F**orm to add data and preserve the database, or insert new rows through the middle of the database range.

Problem:

Data on the left side of the records does not align with the appropriate data on the right side.

Solution:

The database may have been torn in half and scrambled by a sort operation that did not include all columns. No way exists to repair the problem. Use a previously saved version.

Chapter Summary

After reviewing this and previous chapters, you should be very familiar with Excel's worksheet and database capabilities. To increase your productivity even more, read Chapter 27 to learn how to automate procedures you perform frequently. By using the macro recorder and six simple modifiers, you can create impressive macros that will automate many of your tasks.

Excel Macros

P A R T

V

O U T L I N E

Creating Macros

M acros are sequences of commands and functions that run Excel operations for you. You can create macros to replace simple repetitive keystrokes, such as setting a numeric format and selecting a font. On the other hand, you can create macros that turn Excel into a specialized program designed to perform specific, complex tasks, such as medical accounting or inventory analysis.

Macros are composed of functions similar to worksheet functions. Each function is the equivalent of a command, action, or worksheet function. The names of most macro functions make their functions easy to figure out. FORMAT.FONT, for example, does the same thing as the Format Font command. Macros also can use worksheet functions to make calculations.

Many menu commands, such as Edit Copy or Formula Paste Function, work the same in a macro sheet as they do in a worksheet. You can apply everything you already learned about editing worksheets to macros.

Macro functions run down a column in the macro sheet, one function to a cell. Each macro function performs some command or action according to the arguments found in the parentheses, much the same as a worksheet function. These arguments define the selected options, such as the font and style selected by the FORMAT.FONT function.

Understanding the Types of Macros

There are two kinds of macros: *command macros* and *function macros*. Command macros store action sequences containing commands from the menu, as well as keystrokes and mouse actions. These macros also can contain additional Excel commands not available from the menu. You activate command macros by pressing a Ctrl+key combination that you define or by choosing the macro name from a list box. You also can run command macros from custom menus that you create.

Command macros can range from the simple, such as range formatting, to the complex, such as industry-specific applications with custom menus, help windows, and dialog boxes. Excel macros can even operate and control other Windows programs. Following are some uses for command macros:

- Formatting a selected range with bold and currency format.
- Printing frequently used reports in a specific order.
- Accepting and cross-checking data entry.
- Automating the preparation and upload of data to a mainframe.
- Automating the download, analysis, charting, and printing of data from a mainframe.
- Creating custom menus, help files, and alert and dialog boxes.
- Linking and controlling other Windows applications.
- Calling C language programs that perform specialized operations.
- Building custom applications.

The second kind of macros—*function macros*—contain custom worksheet functions, which can be used in worksheets in the same way built-in Excel functions (such as SUM( )and MIRR( )) are used. Function macros do not use menu commands and cannot produce an action. They are used only for calculations. Function macros cannot be recorded; you must type or paste them into the macro sheet.

Running Command Macros

If you inherited files from another user, installed Excel's EXAMPLE or LIBRARY directories, or purchased an Excel *template*, you already may have macros. To run an existing macro, you first must open the macro sheet in which the macro resides.

Opening Macro Sheets

You can use two kinds of macro sheets. Normal macro sheet files end with the extension XLM. These macro sheets can be visible when loaded, and the names of the macros on the sheet appear in the **M**acro **R**un dialog box. Another kind of macro sheet, which uses the extension XLA, is used for add-in macros. These macros are designed to be invisible to the operator. When these macro sheets are opened, their macros appear to be an integral part of Excel. Excel comes with several XLA macros that are described in Chapter 15, "Using Excel's Add-In Macros." Chapter 28, "Modifying and Programming Macros," describes how to save recorded or written macros to work as add-in macros. Both XLM and XLA sheets can contain command and function macros.

Follow these steps to open a macro sheet so that you can use the macros the sheet contains:

1. Choose the **File O**pen command.

2. Look in the list box for files with the extension XLM, or change the name in the file name box to *.XLM, or choose MS Excel Macros (*.XLM, *.XLA) from the List Files of **T**ype pull-down list. This file-name pattern lists only macro files.

3. Press Enter to display the macro file names.

4. Select the macro sheet you want.

5. Choose OK or press Enter.

You probably will want to load some macros with the worksheets they control. One way to load multiple documents is to save them as a group with the **F**ile Save **W**orkbook command. Workbooks are described in Chapter 11. A second way to open a macro by default when you open a worksheet is to create an Auto_Open macro. This process is described in Chapter 28.

Understanding the Global Macro Sheet

The Global macro sheet is the only macro sheet that always opens when you start Excel. You normally cannot see the Global macro sheet because it is hidden.

The Global macro sheet is useful for storing function and command macros that you use frequently and always want loaded. Because the Global macro sheet, GLOBAL.XLM, is saved by Excel into the XLSTART directory, the file loads automatically when Excel starts. Therefore, the functions and macros on the Global macro sheet are available to you as soon as you start Excel.

T I P   Avoid routinely adding recorded macros to the Global macro sheet. Limit the Global macros to those you use frequently. Having too many global macros fills the **M**acro **R**un list with so many names that finding macros may be difficult. Too many macros may also cause conflicts with shortcut keys, if global macros use a lot of shortcut keys.

When you record a command macro, you can choose whether you want to record the macro on a new worksheet or on the Global macro sheet. If you want to write command or function macros, you can put them on the Global macro sheet, but you must first unhide the sheet. To unhide the Global macro sheet, choose the **W**indow **U**nhide command, select the GLOBAL.XLM macro from the list, and choose OK or press Enter. After you write or modify macros on the Global macro sheet, be certain that you hide the sheet again before exiting Excel. When GLOBAL.XLM is active, choose the **W**indow **H**ide command to hide the file.

You delete unwanted global macros by unhiding GLOBAL.XLM. Erase the code and documentation for the macro, and use the **F**ormula **D**efine Name command to find and delete the names and shortcut keys for the macro you no longer need. Be certain that you hide the GLOBAL.XLM sheet when you are finished.

If you have recorded a global macro or entered or modified macros on the Global macro sheet, Excel will prompt you to save the Global macro sheet when you exit Excel. If you want to keep the changes to Global macro, save the sheet when prompted.

If the Global macro is not hidden when you exit Excel, it will be visible the next time you start the application. Remedy this problem by hiding the GLOBAL.XLM macro sheet before you exit the next time.

> **CAUTION:** If you delete the XLSTART directory located under the Excel directory, Excel will have no place to create or load the Global macro sheet.

Running Command Macros

When the macro sheet is open, you can run one of the existing command macros in five different ways. You can execute a macro by pressing the related shortcut key combination—that is, holding down the Ctrl key and pressing the macro's associated character. You also can activate a macro by choosing the **M**acro **R**un command, selecting the macro name from the list box (see fig. 27.1), and pressing Enter. You can choose a custom menu command that runs a macro. Custom menus and commands are described in Chapter 29. If you have graphic objects or macro buttons on a worksheet or macro sheet, you can assign the macro to one of them. Or if you created toolbars, you can assign a macro to a tool, as described in Chapter 33.

Be aware that some macros are designed to work with a specific range selected or are designed to work under specific conditions. If, for example, you run a worksheet macro when a chart is active, the macro probably will fail, and the Step box used for troubleshooting will appear.

If you have more than one macro sheet open, you can tell the macros apart because the name of each macro sheet precedes the macro name in the list box of the **M**acro **R**un command. Figure 27.1 shows the Run list box.

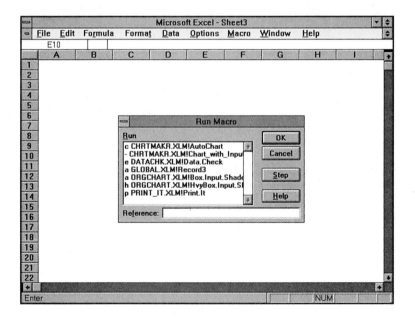

FIG. 27.1

Run macros by name from the Run list box.

You can assign the shortcut key—a Ctrl+key combination—to the macro after you build the macro. If you forget the shortcut key combination for a macro, choose **M**acro **R**un and look at the letter or number on the left side of the list box. The shortcut key also appears at the bottom of the **Fo**rmula **D**efine Name dialog box when you select a command macro.

To watch a macro operate one function at a time, choose the **Macro Run** command, select the macro name, and then choose the **S**tep button. When the macro runs, a Single Step dialog box appears. The dialog box enables you to run the macro one step at a time. This Single Step dialog box is described in the next section and in Chapter 28.

NOTE When two macros have the same shortcut key, the macro appearing first in the list box of the **Macro Run** Command is the one that will be activated. You cannot give the same name to two macros on the same sheet; naming the second macro reassigns the name away from the first macro. Macros on different sheets, however, can have the same name.

Excel discriminates between shortcut keys with upper- and lowercase letters. Therefore, you have 52 shortcut key combinations for running macros. If macro shortcut keys are difficult to remember, start the macro from the **Macro Run** box.

Stopping Macros

You can stop most macros by pressing Esc. Pressing Esc stops the macro and displays a Single Step dialog box used for troubleshooting, like the one shown in figure 27.2. The box shows the cell on which the macro stopped and gives you a chance to **H**alt, **S**tep Into the next macro function, Step **O**ver the next function, **E**valuate the intermediate results of a macro function, **G**oto a macro location, **P**ause macro operation while you make manual changes, or **C**ontinue without stepping. If a macro displays a dialog box, you must respond to the dialog box. The dialog box takes precedence over the Single Step box. Troubleshooting macros with the Single Step dialog box and STEP( ) function is more fully explained in Chapter 28.

```
┌──────────────────────────────────────┐
│  ⊟            Single Step             │
├──────────────────────────────────────┤
│  Cell:  DATACHK.XLM!B5                │
│  Formula:                            │
│  =IF(AND(Num>2,Num<7),GOTO(Good))    │
│                                      │
│                                      │
│  ┌─────────┐┌────────┐┌──────┐┌──────┐│
│  │Step Into││Evaluate││ Halt ││ Goto ││
│  └─────────┘└────────┘└──────┘└──────┘│
│  ┌─────────┐┌────────┐┌────────┐┌─────┐│
│  │Step Over││ Pause  ││Continue││Help ││
│  └─────────┘└────────┘└────────┘└─────┘│
└──────────────────────────────────────┘
```

FIG. 27.2

The Single Step box appears when you stop a macro with Esc.

Some macros also may add a macro function that prevents the Esc key from stopping the macro. If this condition is present with a macro you are using, you must use the method designed by the programmer who wrote the macro.

For Related Information:

◀◀ "Managing Files," p. 158.

◀◀ "Working with Multiple Documents," p. 420.

FROM HERE...

Building Command Macros

You can build macros in three ways: recording macros, recording them and then modifying them, or programming them without the recorder.

In the first method, you record the entire macro and then the macro replays exactly as recorded, selecting the same menu items and dialog box options. This process works well for simple jobs, such as preparing cells with frequently used formats, fonts, and borders.

The second method of creating macros is most effective for the majority of Excel users. You build the main structure of the macro with the re-corder, and then edit this structure to add features and generalize. You can, for example, use the macro recorder to insert and format new rows in a database. You then can add INPUT( ), FORMULA( ), and IF( ) macro functions that request the data for entry and cross-check before entering the data in a database. Another valuable modification is inserting a ques-tion mark (?) after a macro function, such as FORMAT.FONT?( ), to make that macro function's dialog box pause for changes. These techniques are covered in Chapter 28.

The third method of building macros takes advantage of Excel's exten-sive programming language. With Excel's programming language, you can manipulate files, automate extensive data analysis and charting, add custom menus and dialog boxes, link and control other Microsoft Win-dows applications, and build custom application programs. In these more complex applications, a skeleton of routines is usually created with the recorder, and then these skeletons are extensively modified by hand coding. Entry-level and more in-depth programming are discussed in Chapters 28 and 29.

Understanding How Command Macros Work

Figure 27.3 shows a simple macro that has been recorded. The macro name is in the topmost cell of column A. The explanation should be typed by you in column B. The name is created and placed here by the macro recorder or named and placed here from the keyboard.

> **NOTE** The macro must be named either by the recorder or with the Formula **D**efine Name command. The top cell of the macro is named in the same way that you name a worksheet cell or range. Recording a macro with **M**acro Re**c**ord creates the name for you. If you manually create a command or function macro, you must use the Formula **D**efine Name command to name the top cell. Use the **F**unction or **C**ommand option buttons at the bottom of the Define Name dialog box to specify the kind of macro.

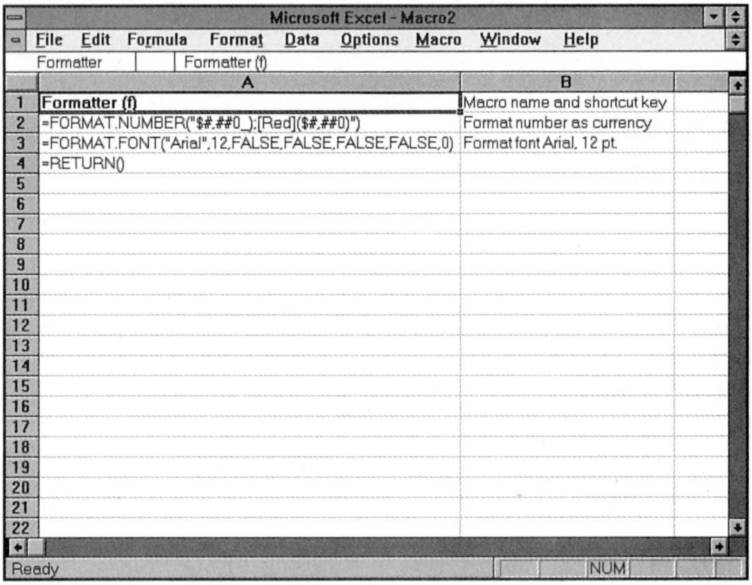

	Microsoft Excel - Macro2	
	File **Edit** **Formula** **Format** **Data** **Options** **Macro** **Window** **Help**	
	Formatter	Formatter (f)	

	A	B
1	Formatter (f)	Macro name and shortcut key
2	=FORMAT.NUMBER("$#,##0_);[Red]($#,##0)")	Format number as currency
3	=FORMAT.FONT("Arial",12,FALSE,FALSE,FALSE,FALSE,0)	Format font Arial, 12 pt.
4	=RETURN()	
5		
6		
7		
8		
9		
10		
11		
12		
13		
14		
15		
16		
17		
18		
19		
20		
21		
22		

Ready   NUM

FIG. 27.3

A simple recorded macro in column A and the typed explanation in column B.

When you run a macro, Excel looks for the appropriate macro sheet and the name on that sheet. The macro starts in the named cell and proceeds down the column, reading and calculating each cell's contents. Text or blank cells are ignored. Contents beginning with an equal sign are evaluated as macro functions. A macro stops when a macro function, such as RETURN( ) or HALT( ) is reached.

T I P The result of a macro function in a cell appears behind the macro function. This process is the opposite of a macro function in a worksheet, where the result appears over the top of the formula.

The macro sheet is, in one respect, the reverse of a normal worksheet. On a worksheet, you see the results of hidden formulas. On a macro sheet, you see the formulas and macro functions, but the results are hidden. The results of macro functions can be either a TRUE/FALSE logic result, a calculated result, or an entered result. A TRUE result indicates that a macro function operated correctly. A FALSE result can indicate that a Cancel button was chosen from a dialog box. Some functions, such as an INPUT box function, return to the cell whatever the operator typed into the Input dialog box. A function that contains syntax errors or cannot operate correctly returns an error value. Because macro functions return different values to cells, you can use these returned values to control how the program operates, check data, or move data from an Input box to the active cell on the worksheet.

Using the Macro Toolbars

The Macro toolbars help you record, stop, troubleshoot, and resume the playing of macros. The Stop Macro and Pause Macro toolbars appear automatically when needed if another toolbar is already displayed. Figure 27.4 shows the macro toolbars. The individual macro tools are explained in the following sections in the context in which the tool is used.

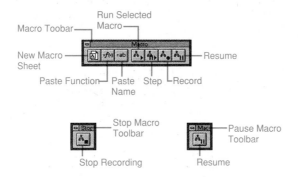

FIG. 27.4

The macro toolbars make running and troubleshooting macro easier.

Recording a Command Macro

Even the newest Excel user can learn to record command macros. Command macros save time and work, yet are easy to create and use.

When you build a command macro, Excel records all your menu choices, mouse actions, and keyboard entries as functions on a macro sheet. A macro sheet looks like a worksheet with some of the commands in the menu bar disabled when the macro sheet is active; the **O**ptions **D**isplay command is preset to display functions, not their results. Columns in macro sheets are wider than in worksheets so that you can see the macro functions more easily.

Macro functions that represent commands and actions will seem familiar. For example, the macro equivalent of the Format Font command is FORMAT.FONT. The equivalent of selecting a range of cells is SELECT. Figure 27.3 shows one such simple macro that was recorded. The explanations in the adjacent cells in column B describe what each of the macro functions in column A does. The RETURN( ) function ends the macro. The macro recorder enters only the functions in column A; the explanations in column B were added manually afterward.

You can use two commands to record a macro: **M**acro **R**ecord and **M**acro **S**tart Recorder. The **M**acro **R**ecord command records and names a new macro. Use the **M**acro **S**tart Recorder when you want to add macro functions to an existing macro. The following sections discuss each command.

T I P   If the Macro toolbar is displayed on-screen, you also can start, stop, and single step through the macro with the tools on the toolbar.

Recording a Command Macro on a New Macro Sheet

Before recording a macro, practice two or three times the keystrokes you want to record so that you understand the commands and options necessary for accomplishing what you need done. Don't, however, worry about making small errors or opening the wrong dialog box while recording. You can delete unwanted macro functions from a macro sheet the same way that you delete formulas in a worksheet. If you open a dialog box that you don't want while the recorder is on, just choose Cancel or press Esc, and the command choice isn't recorded.

To open a macro sheet and record a new macro, complete the following steps:

1. Activate the worksheet or chart on which you want to use the macro.

2. If you want to use this macro on any selected worksheet range or on a selected object in any chart, select cells or chart objects before you begin the macro recording. If you start the recorder and then select cells or objects, the macro records the specific cells or objects that you select.

3. Choose the **M**acro Re**c**ord command, or click the Record Macro tool.

   If a new macro sheet isn't open, the command automatically opens a new macro sheet and asks you to name the macro and shortcut key and specify whether the macro should be recorded on a new macro sheet or added to the Global macro sheet. The macro starts recording in the first cell of the first column. Excel puts the macro name and shortcut key for the macro in the first cell, and then places all the recorded macro functions in cells going down the column.

   The Record Macro dialog box appears after you choose the **M**acro Re**c**ord command (see fig. 27.5).

FIG. 27.5

The Record Macro dialog box asks for the macro name and shortcut key.

4. Type the **N**ame of the macro in the Record Macro dialog box.

   The name you type becomes the name of this macro. The name must conform to Excel's rules for names. Start with a letter; do not use spaces or symbols. Instead of spaces, you can use the hyphen (-) and the underscore (_).

5. Select the **K**ey text box, and delete the character that is there if you do not want Excel's recommendation; then type a single character for use in the Ctrl+key combination. Delete the character before typing a new character. This step is optional; you do not have to assign a key combination to a command macro.

6. Select the **G**lobal Macro Sheet or the **M**acro Sheet option to specify whether the macro will be recorded on the Global sheet or a new sheet.

7. Choose OK or press Enter.

   The macro name and the Ctrl+key combination give you two ways of activating the macro. Later you can start the macro by choosing the macro name from the **M**acro **R**un command's list box or by pressing the Ctrl+key combination. Ctrl+c, for example, might format preselected cells with a custom currency format.

The key character can be an upper- or a lowercase letter. Because Excel can distinguish between upper- and lowercase letters, you can have up to 52 different Ctrl+key combinations.

NOTE The shortcut keys assigned to your macros override Excel's built-in shortcut keys. The quick reference card inside the back cover of this book lists Excel's built-in shortcut keys.

Notice that the word Recording appears in the Status Bar at the bottom of the screen. From this point on, Excel records menu choices and mouse or keyboard actions.

Excel records macros in either relative or absolute reference mode. A macro recorded in relative reference mode refers to the cells on which the macro acts relative to the position of the last active cell in the worksheet. Macros that use absolute reference mode move the active cell in the worksheet to exactly the same cell that you selected during the recording.

8. Choose **Macro Relative Record** if you want cell movements or selections to be recorded relative to the currently active cell. Choose **Macro Absolute Record** if you want cell movements or selections to be recorded in the same location on playback as during the recording. Because this command toggles between the two command names, if the command **Absolute Record** is available for selection, you are currently in the Relative Record mode. You can switch between absolute and relative recording at any time.

9. Make the menu choices and perform the keyboard or mouse actions that you want recorded. With each menu command chosen or action taken, the recorder adds another macro function to the column. Figure 27.6 shows macro functions extending down a column. The macro has not stopped recording yet.

Excel ignores menu selections that you make from dialog boxes when you select the Cancel button or press Esc.

If you make a mistake while you are recording the macro, continue recording, if possible. You can use the **Edit** commands to remove or correct the incorrect macro functions after you stop the recorder. Use the **Edit** commands to make the corrections after you stop the recorder. Do not try to remove a macro function with the UNDO() macro command while you are recording. With the recorder on, choosing **Edit Undo** enters the UNDO() function into the macro.

10. Choose **Macro Stop Recorder**, or click on the Record tool when you are finished recording. Check the Status Bar at the bottom of the screen to verify that the word Recording is no longer displayed.

Choosing the stop command inserts a RETURN( ) macro function at the end of the macro. RETURN( ) marks the end of the macro. It also means that the macro is now usable.

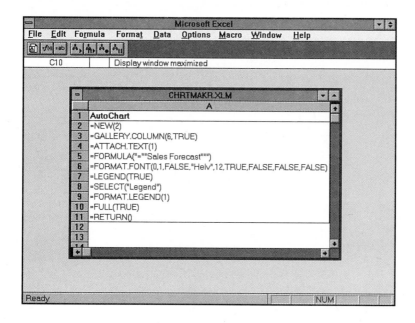

11. Activate the macro sheet by selecting it from the bottom of the **W**indow menu; then choose the **F**ile Save **A**s command to name and save the macro sheet. Macro sheets are saved with the XLM file extension.

NOTE Be careful about choosing what appear to be similar commands. The **M**acro Re**c**ord command prompts you for a new name, defines the macro name, and starts recording a new macro in the next available column. The **M**acro **S**tart Recorder command starts entering recorded macro functions at the point on the macro sheet where the last macro stopped. If you previously recorded macros and accidentally choose **M**acro **S**tart Recorder to add what you think will be a new macro, the new recording is added to the end of the previous macro.

Use the techniques in the next section to add a macro to an existing macro sheet. Don't forget to add documentation in the columns adjacent to the macro. Documentation should describe how the macro works and what each function or section of the macro does. Documentation makes a macro's operation and functions easier to remember.

To see the macro you created, activate the macro sheet with the **W**indow # command, where # is the number of the macro sheet.

Recording a New Macro on an Existing Macro Sheet

Another method of recording macros places the recorded macro on an existing macro sheet in a position that you specify. This method is used most frequently to record macros on a sheet and modify them.

To record a new macro on an existing macro sheet, complete the following steps:

1. Choose the **File O**pen command and open the macro sheet to which you want to add a macro. Macro sheets use the file extension XLM.

    Alternately, if the macro sheet is open, you can choose the **W**indow # command to activate the macro sheet you want to open.

2. Select the cell where you want the macro name to appear. This will be the top, title cell of the macro. Normally, this cell appears at the top of an adjacent blank column, or you can insert a few blank cells below the RETURN of an existing macro. Recorded macro functions will go in cells down the column below this name.

3. Choose the **M**acro Se**t** Recorder command to assign the name *Recorder* to the range from the selected cell to the bottom of the worksheet. Macro Record records into the top cell of Recorder if the range is blank; otherwise, Macro Record resets Recorder to the first blank column and starts at the top of that column.

4. Activate the worksheet and choose the **M**acro Re**c**ord command.

5. Type the macro name and shortcut key in the Record Macro dialog box. Choose OK or press Enter.

6. Choose the **M**acro Rela**t**ive Record command or the **M**acro **A**bsolute Record command.

7. Make the menu choices and perform the keyboard or mouse actions that you want recorded.

8. Choose the **M**acro **S**top Recorder command, or click the Record tool when you are finished recording.

9. Before testing the macro, save the macro sheet as described previously.

Recording Changes to an Existing Macro

After you create a macro, you may find that you want to add more recorded commands or change the dialog box settings in a macro. You do not need to be a programmer to make these changes. You can record changes almost as easily as recording on an existing macro sheet.

To record additions or changes on a macro sheet, you insert cells in the existing macro to make room for the new functions you will record. Then you set the Recorder name at the top of the blank cells. This is where Excel will put its macro recording. Macro functions will fill down the blank cells you inserted.

Complete these steps to record changes or additions to an existing macro:

1. Select the cells where you want to insert new or different macro functions.

   Create a safe margin by selecting more cells than the commands you plan to record. Figure 27.7 shows a macro with cells selected prior to inserting space. If you use additional columns to contain documentation, make sure that you select cells across all columns that the macro and documentation uses.

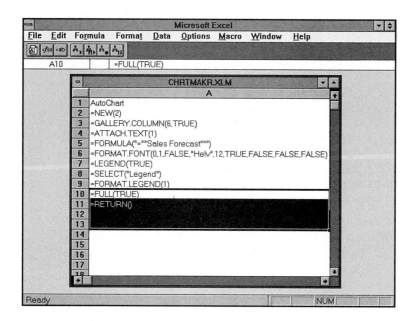

FIG. 27.7

Select cells where you want to insert additional recorded functions.

2. Choose the **Edit Insert** command, select the Shift Cells **Down** option, and then choose OK. The shortcut key is Ctrl+plus sign (+). The macro opens to give room to record inside.

3. Select the top cell in the opened space and choose the **Macro Set** Recorder command. This assigns the name Recorder to this cell and below. If the first cell is blank, recorded functions starts here. Figure 27.8 shows the macro after cells have been inserted and the new Recorder location is set.

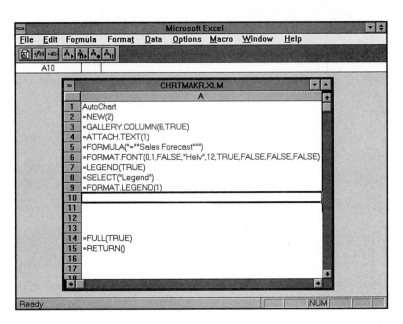

FIG. 27.8

The macro sheet after cells have been inserted and the new Recorder location is set.

4. Activate the worksheet or chart where the macro is used. Put the worksheet or chart in the configuration and settings required for this point in the macro—for example, selecting specific cells or displaying a window to duplicate the conditions the macro expects to be present.

5. Choose the **Macro Start Recorder** command to start recording without creating a new macro.

6. Record the commands that you want to add. Select dialog box options as you want them to be recorded.

   If you did not insert enough cells in the macro you are recording in, the macro recorder stops when there are no blank cells left. The

Recorder does not write over existing cells. An alert box tells you when recording stops.

7. Choose the **M**acro **S**top Recorder command.

8. Activate the macro sheet. If the recorder inserted an unnecessary RETURN( ) macro function, delete it. Delete blank cells by selecting them, and then choose the **E**dit **D**elete command and select the Shift Cells **U**p command. The delete shortcut key is Ctrl+ – (minus). Make sure that you also delete cells in documentation columns so that documentation cells and function cells remain together.

Figure 27.9 shows the AutoChart macro after a legend is added and is formatted for the bottom position (1 represents the first option button in the Format Legend dialog box). Removing the blank cells and the un-wanted RETURN( ) in cell A9 will complete this modification. The next time the AutoChart macro runs, it will add a legend and move the legend to the bottom.

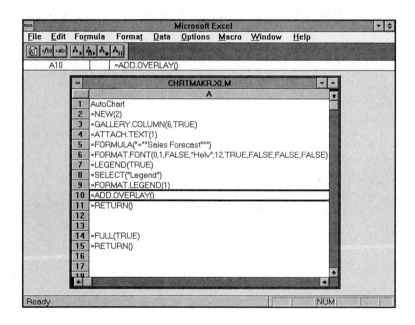

FIG. 27.9

Recording in an existing macro is an easy way to add to a macro.

Chapter 28 describes many easy ways to modify recorded macros. With simple changes, you can make dialog boxes pause for operator selection, have input boxes request data, and have IF( ) functions check for incorrect data.

Building Function Macros

Excel has a wide selection of built-in math, financial, logical, and text functions. With the addition of the Analysis ToolPak, Excel's calculating power by far exceeds any other worksheet. But you may want functions specific to your business or specialty. Imagine the time and errors you can save if the formulas you frequently use are built-in functions.

Excel gives you the power to make that happen. You can create custom function macros that work just like Excel's built-in functions, such as SUM( ) or LOOKUP( ).

The difference between function macros and built-in functions is that you define how the function macros work. After you define a function macro on a macro sheet, you can use it the same as you would any built-in function. You can put function macros on the same sheet as command macros.

Figure 27.10 shows a macro function that calculates calories when given the fat, carbohydrates, and protein in grams that a food contains.

The function is entered in a worksheet with a format like the following:

=FUNCTION.XLM!Calories(*Fat,Carbohydrates,Protein*)

The argument prompts, *Fat*, *Carbohydrates*, and *Protein*, are pasted along with the function when you choose the Formula Paste Function command with the Paste Arguments check box selected. When you use the function in a worksheet, you replace these prompts with cell references or numbers. A completed macro function in a worksheet cell might look like the following:

=FUNCTION.XLM!Calories(*A12,B36,R42*)

Building custom functions increases the accuracy of formulas, reduces repetitive typing, hides complex formulas from novices, presents a cleaner and clearer worksheet, and ensures that the formulas used are those approved by management or an audit team.

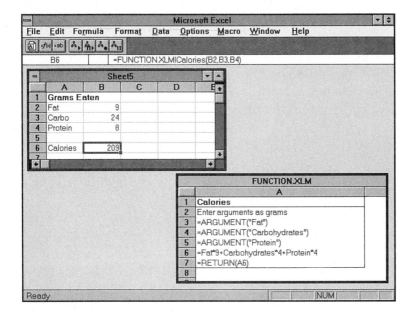

FIG. 27.10

Function macros create
functions that are used
in worksheets.

Understanding How Function Macros Work

Function macros do calculations. They do not produce actions as
command macros do.

A function macro also has a name at the top. Below that name are the
arguments. Arguments specify what information from the worksheet will
be used in the macro's calculations. On the worksheet, the arguments
are the items in the parentheses of a function.

Arguments in a function macro accept information in the order the arguments appear in parentheses in the worksheet. Each argument received
is assigned to a name, such as Sales. These names are then used in calculations. In addition to the simple math shown in these examples, you can
use all the worksheet functions to do calculations in a function macro.

The result of a function macro's calculations is returned to the macro
function in the worksheet. This can produce a result in a cell or a result
used in a larger worksheet formula.

The macro sheet that contains the function macros must be open for a
function macro to return an answer. If the function macro sheet is not
open, the worksheet cell that depends on the macro function produces a
#REF! error. If you want a specific set of function macro sheets to open
when Excel starts, copy those sheets into the XLSTART directory.

Function macros on open sheets appear at the bottom of the Formula Paste Function list box preceded by the name of the macro sheet. This feature enables you to paste in the functions without having to memorize them. Saving a function macro sheet as an XLA add-in macro adds the custom function macros to the Paste Function list just as though the macros were built into Excel.

Creating a Function Macro

Creating a function macro is similar to manually typing a command macro. Function macros cannot be recorded, because they cannot contain action or menu commands. You enter macro and worksheet functions in function macros by typing them or by pasting them into cells from the Formula Paste Function list box. Excel also includes pasted arguments for your functions.

Function macros must be built in a specific order. The macro in figure 27.10 is an example of that order. After you open a new or existing macro sheet, the order of entries as you work down a column on the macro sheet is as follows:

1. Enter a name for the function macro in the top cell where you want the function macro.

2. Enter a RESULT function to specify the kind of result returned to the worksheet.

   This function is optional and is not shown in the figure. If the function calculates a result of a different kind, the function returns an error. (1 specifies numeric result; 2 specifies text. Others are listed in the macro directory.)

3. Enter ARGUMENT( ) functions down the column in the same order that arguments appear between parentheses in the function macro.

4. Enter the formulas that the function macro uses to calculate its result. Use the names of the arguments as the variables in formulas.

5. Enter the RETURN( ) function and specify which cell in the macro contains the final calculated answer. For example,

   =RETURN(B36)

   returns to the worksheet the calculation the macro made in its cell B36.

6. Select the cell containing the macro name at the top of the macro.

7. Choose the Formula Define Name command and select the Function option.

8. Choose OK or press Enter.

Enter an ARGUMENT( ) function for each variable used in the calculation. Rather than typing in functions, you can paste them in using the
Formula Paste Function command. A function can have up to 14 arguments. The order in which the arguments are entered in the macro
dictates the order in which you must enter variable values between
parentheses in the worksheet.

There are two forms for the ARGUMENT( ) function. The first form is the
following:

> **=ARGUMENT(*name_text*,*data_type_num*)**

In this form, *name_text* is a text name in quotation marks that describes
that argument—for example, ARGUMENT("Sales").

The second form of the ARGUMENT function is the following:

> **=ARGUMENT**(*name_text,data_type_num,**ref**)*

This form names the cell address *ref* with the name of *name_text*. The
value associated with *name_text* is entered in the *ref* cell on the macro
sheet.

For both of the forms, *data_type_num* is a number that specifies the kind
of data, such as text or numeric. If no number is specified, the argument
assumes text, a number, or a logical value as the type. If a worksheet
passes an incorrect argument type, the macro returns a #VALUE! error to
the worksheet.

The RETURN function must reference the cell containing the final result
of the calculations. This reference is how the answer gets back to the
cell in the worksheet where you entered the custom function.
RETURN(C4), for example, returns to the worksheet the calculations the
macro made in cell C4.

There are actual calculated results in a macro sheet. Just as a worksheet
shows results and hides formulas, a macro sheet shows its functions and
hides the results. After you run a macro, you can see the results (including errors) produced in each cell of the macro. You can switch a macro
sheet or worksheet so that you can see their results or the formulas and
functions. To switch the display, choose the **Options D**isplay command
and select or clear the Formula option. The shortcut key to switch between displaying functions and results is Ctrl+`. The ` (gravè) is on the
same key as the ~ (tilde) key.

Using Function Macros

Function macros work only when their macro sheet is open. Use **F**ile
Open to open any macro sheet containing the function macros you want.

Remember that macro sheet names end with XLM. If you want a set of function macros always to be available, copy the XLM files into the XLSTART directory or copy these files into the GLOBAL.XLM macro. To learn how to change function macros into add-in macros, read Chapter 28.

After the macro sheet is open, you can paste the name of a function macro in a worksheet cell or macro sheet cell with Formula Paste Function, just as you paste built-in worksheet functions. Function macros appear in the User Defined Category in the Paste Function dialog box, as shown in figure 27.11. Function macros must be preceded by the name of the macro sheet on which the macros reside. For this reason, pasting— not typing—a function macro is much easier and safer.

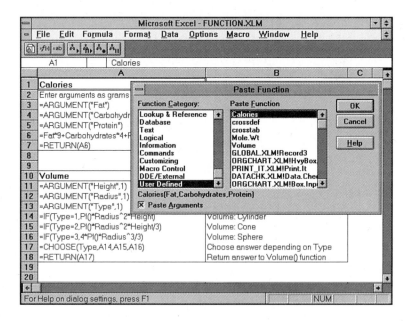

FIG. 27.11

Function macros are easiesr to use if pasted from the Paste Functions dialog box.

FROM HERE...

For Related Information:

◄◄ "Using the Toolbars," p. 47.

◄◄ "Entering Formulas," p. 175.

◄◄ "Editing Text and Formulas," p. 195.

◄◄ "Entering Worksheet Functions," p. 356.

Chapter Summary

Recorded command macros are easy to create and can save you a great deal of extra work on repetitive jobs. With a few simple modifications, you find that these recorded macros can do even more. Chapter 28 describes simple changes that enable macros to pause dialog boxes for changes, display data-entry boxes, and check results with IF functions.

Function macros are very powerful for companies that do a considerable amount of scientific, engineering, or financial work involving specialized formulas. Everyone in a company can use the same macro sheet containing the same functions. This practice increases the probability that worksheets use approved formulas and constants and reduces the chance for typing errors in formulas.

The following three chapters explain how to create custom applications in Excel. Although Excel has a full programming language, you do not need to become a programmer to become more productive. As you will see in the next chapter, you easily can record macros, and then make them much more powerful with simple modifications. Although you may want to eventually do some programming, you will find you can greatly increase productivity by recording and modifying macros.

Modifying and Programming Macros

Recorded macros can add a great deal of productivity to Excel. Modifying recorded macros can increase your productivity even further. The first part of this chapter describes how to make a few simple modifications to macros. These easy modifications enable macros to display messages, ask for data, check the data, and display dialog boxes that usually are displayed by menu commands.

Later in the chapter, you learn to enhance the capabilities of Excel by programming with macro functions. You use these functions in the same way you program with a language such as BASIC or dBASE. Excel has as many as or more commands in its language than a language like BASIC or dBASE. This chapter describes how to use control functions and subroutines within Excel. Chapter 29 describes how to create custom menus and dialog boxes. This chapter describes how to assign your macros to tools on toolbars. The result can be a totally customized application that looks little like the original Excel but contains all the analytical, database, and charting capabilities of Excel.

Two macro features described in this chapter make macros easier to use. The first feature turns your recorded, modified, or programmed macros into add-in macros. The macro sheet for an add-in macro is invisible to operators; the macro sheet adds commands and functions just as though they were built into Excel. (Chapter 15 describes the add-in macros that come with Excel.) With the second feature, you can assign a macro to a button, worksheet graphic object, or tool. The macro will run when you click on this assigned button, graphic object, or tool.

Designing Macros

Creating and modifying your own macros is much easier when you understand some basic guidelines for automating a task. If you are making a simple recorded macro that uses a few of the modifications described later, you may not need the following steps. The more complex the task you are automating, the more you need a structure for creating your macro.

The process of automating a task by using a recorded macro as a foundation usually requires the following steps:

1. Think through the process.   What major processes need to be done and in what order? What commands are used? Is any preparation necessary for these processes?

2. Do it manually.   Manually go through the process you want to automate. Write down notes about which steps to take in order. Write down areas of concern such as "Calculate at this point the size of the range the macro will work on?"

3. Write psuedocode.   Convert your written notes into one line comments. Some Excel users write these single line comments into the column to the right of where the macro functions are entered. This helps them understand what is being done and which parts need to be modified.

4. Record the foundation.   Use the macro recorder to record the basic process you want to automate. (Before you record, save the worksheet the macro modifies so you can use it to test the macro later.) Use your notes from steps 2 and 3 to be certain that you do the process in the correct order. Run your recorded macro to make sure that it does what you want it to do.

5. Modify the recorded macro.   Use the seven modifications described later in this chapter to modify your macro so that dialog

boxes stay open for selections, to pause the macro, to request data entry, to test if a condition is met, or to branch to a new part of the macro.

6. Test your modified macro. — As you modify your macro, test it after only a few modifications. By testing frequently, you can tell more easily which modification has caused a problem.

7. Add data-entry checking. — Add macro functions to check if Cancel buttons were selected or to check if entered data is correct.

8. Test your macro. — Harden your macro against improper user entries or responses. Operate your macro using bad data, choosing Cancel buttons, and making inappropriate selections.

9. Include error checking. — Include error trapping and handling on functions that can halt the macro if they work incorrectly. For example, if an OPEN function cannot find the file name you recorded the macro will halt.

10. Improve speed. — Use some of the techniques described in this chapter to improve performance. For example, the FORMULA and OFFSET commands can be used to transfer data between worksheets significantly faster than the ACTIVATE, COPY, and PASTE commands that are recorded.

Running Macros

Macros can be run a number of ways in addition to choosing a name from the Run Macro dialog box or pressing a shortcut key. You also can assign a macro to a macro button or graphic object so that the macro runs when the button or object is clicked. Another useful feature is assigning a macro to a tool on a toolbar. Click the tool and your macro runs.

Manually Creating Macro Names and Shortcut Keys

You may want to name a manually entered macro, rename an existing macro, or change a Ctrl+key combination. The macro must have its first cell named, or the macro does not work. You can use the Formula **D**efine Name command to assign the macro name to the cell containing the text name of the macro.

If you create a macro by using the **M**acro Re**c**ord command, the macro is named with the name you enter in the Record dialog box. If you manually enter the entire macro, you have to name the first cell yourself. You can create a shortcut key at the same time that you name the macro with the Formula **D**efine Name command.

To create a macro name and shortcut key for a macro you created manually instead of with the **M**acro Re**c**ord command, follow these steps:

1. Activate the macro sheet containing the macro that is unnamed. The first cell in the macro should contain the name you want to use for this macro.

2. Select the cell containing the name of the macro at the top of the column of macro functions.

3. Choose the Formula **D**efine Name command. The Define Name dialog box appears, as shown in figure 28.1. Notice that this dialog box has more options than the Define Name dialog box in a worksheet.

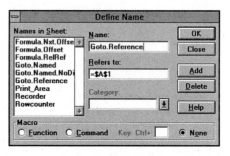

FIG. 28.1

The Define Name dialog box on a macro sheet.

4. Select the **N**ame box and type a legal Excel name (use no blank spaces and do not start with a number). If you selected the cell containing the macro title, the **N**ame box displays the text in the cell (see fig. 28.2).

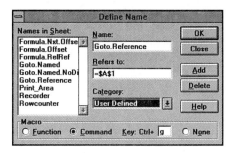

FIG. 28.2

Edit a macro name or shortcut key with the Define Name box.

5. Select the **C**ommand option; then if you want a shortcut key, select the **K**ey: Ctrl+edit box and enter a single letter. Excel differentiates between upper- and lowercase shortcut keys.

6. If you want the capability to paste macro names into your macro sheet, choose the Category pull-down list and select the category in which you want to store this command macro.

7. Choose OK or press Enter.

Subroutines are macros that can be run by other macros. If you have macros that can be used as subroutines, you may want to perform step 6. Step 6 enables you to assign your macro name to a category in the Paste Functions list. This procedure will make the macro you just named easier to enter as a subroutine within another macro because you can paste in the macro name.

To paste a command macro's name into a cell in a macro sheet, choose the Formula Paste Function command, and select the category from the Function Category list; then select the macro name from the Paste Function list, and choose OK. This procedure pastes the name of your command macro into a cell. If your command macro is used as a subroutine and includes ARGUMENT() functions, the prompts for the arguments also are pasted if the Paste Arguments check box in the Paste Function dialog box is selected.

To change a macro name or add a shortcut key, follow these steps:

1. Activate the macro sheet containing the macro you want to change.

2. Choose the Formula **D**efine Name command to display the Define Name dialog box.

3. Select from the Names in **S**heet list box the macro name for which you want to change the name or the shortcut key.

4. If you want to change a name, select the **Name** box and edit the name.

5. If you want to change a shortcut key, select the **Command Key** box and edit the Ctrl+key character.

6. Choose the **A**dd button.

7. Select the old name from the Names in **S**heet list.

8. Choose the **D**elete button.

9. Choose OK, or press Enter.

Assigning Macros to Macro Buttons or Graphic Objects

If you want an easy way to run a macro on a specific worksheet, assign the macro to a macro button or graphic object. Clicking on the button or object will run the macro. Buttons are useful for macros that will be run by people with little Excel experience using systems that will run from a graphical menu.

Using Objects and Buttons

Figure 28.3 shows buttons for data entry, calculation, and printing along the top of the worksheet. Clicking on one of these buttons displays input boxes for data entry, recalculates the worksheet, prints specified reports, or sets the data-entry values back to defaults.

Figure 28.4 shows a graphical front end to a business information system that extracts information from a local or mainframe database. An operator can click on a portion of the world map in which the company does business. The operator then can click on one of the buttons to retrieve specific information on business in that area. You can make the map selections possible by using a map as a background and overlaying it with invisible graphic circles or rectangles drawn with tools from the toolbar. After a macro is assigned to these circles or rectangles, you can make the circles or rectangles invisible by changing their border and fill patterns to a None option.

To run a macro from a button or graphic object, move the mouse pointer over the button or graphic object. If the button or object has a macro assigned to it, the pointer changes to the selection hand you have seen in the Help window. When the hand is over the button or object, click once.

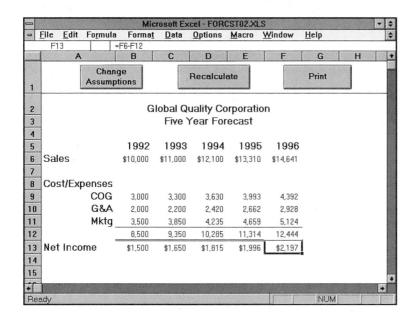

FIG. 28.3

Use macro buttons on frequently changed or printed worksheets.

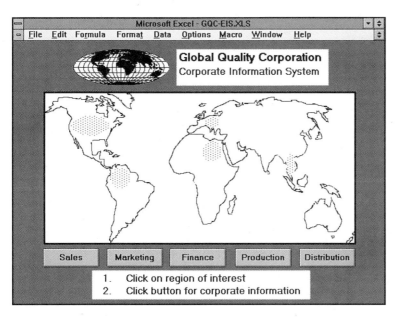

FIG. 28.4

Create visual menus by assigning macros to graphics or buttons.

Creating a Macro Button

To create a button and assign a macro to it, perform the following steps:

1. Open the macro sheet containing the macro you want to assign to a button. Activate the worksheet.

2. Select the Button tool from the Utility or Microsoft Excel 3.0 toolbar. This tool appears as a shadowed box to the left of the Camera icon.

3. Move the pointer cross hair to where you want one corner of the button.

4. If you want a square button, hold down Shift. If you want the button aligned with the shape of gridlines, hold down Alt.

5. Drag across the worksheet to mark the size of the macro button. When you release the mouse button, the macro button appears on the worksheet where you have drawn it and the Assign to Object dialog box shown in figure 28.5 appears.

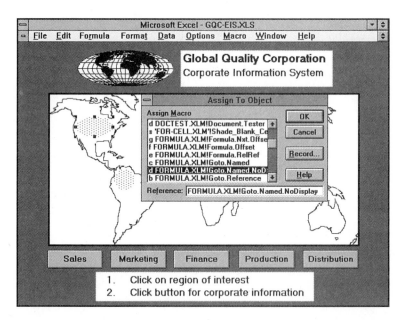

FIG. 28.5

The Assign To Object dialog box.

6. From the Assign Macro list, select the macro you want, and then choose OK or press Enter.

7. Type the text you want to appear as a label on the button in the still-selected macro button.

Before you can run the macro assigned to the button, you must click off the button so that it is not selected.

Assigning a Macro to a Graphic Object

To assign a macro to a graphic object, follow these steps:

1. Open the macro sheet containing the macro you want to run. Activate the worksheet.

2. Select the graphic object on the worksheet that you want to trigger the macro.

3. Choose the **M**acro Assign to **O**bject command. The Assign To Macro dialog box appears.

4. From the Assign **M**acro list, select the macro you want to run, and then choose OK or press Enter.

To change the macro assigned to a button or graphic object, follow these steps:

1. Open the macro sheet containing the macro you want to reassign. Activate the worksheet containing the button.

2. Hold down the Ctrl key, and click on the button or graphic object.

3. Choose the **M**acro Assign to **O**bject command.

4. From the Assign to Object dialog box, select the name of the macro you want to assign.

5. Choose OK or press Enter.

To format a macro button or graphic object that has an assigned macro, hold down the Ctrl key and select the macro button or graphic object. Select all or a portion of the text inside the macro button and use the Forma**t** Font command or the toolbar icons to format the text. To align the text, use the Forma**t** **T**ext command to align or turn the text in the macro button in the same way that you format text boxes. If you want the macro button to adjust its size for a best fit around the text, select the A**u**tomatic Size check box.

If you need to change the macro assigned to a button or object, perform the following steps:

1. Choose the **F**ile **L**inks command.

2. Select from the **L**inks list the link containing the old macro sheet file name.

3. Choose the **C**hange button.

4. Select the name of the new sheet you want to use.

5. Choose OK or press Enter in the Change Links dialog box.

6. Choose the Close button from the Links dialog box.

T I P   Buttons or graphic objects that are on the worksheet scroll out of view when you scroll in the worksheet. Therefore, the objects are inaccessible when you want to click on them to run their macro. If you face this problem, you may need to assign the macro to a tool on a toolbar or make a pane so that a portion of the window will not split. Use the **W**indow **S**plit command to split the window so that it has a top pane and/or a left pane. Put your macro buttons or objects in these panes, and then choose the **W**indow **F**reeze Panes command. This procedure will keep buttons and objects in the top pane visible when you scroll up or down. Buttons and objects in the left pane remain visible when you scroll left or right.

 ## Assigning Macros to a Tool

You can create your own toolbars, customize tools with faces you draw, and then assign macros to the tools. Toolbars make macros readily accessible. Chapter 33 describes how to create your own toolbars, add tools to the toolbar, and create your own tools with tool faces you draw in PaintBrush.

When you drag a custom tool onto a toolbar, you immediately are given the opportunity to assign a macro or record a macro. To create a custom toolbar, perform the following steps:

1. Choose the **O**ptions **T**oolbars command.

2. Type the name of the new toolbar in the Toolbar **N**ame edit box.

3. Choose OK to create a blank toolbar.

To drag a custom tool to the new or existing toolbar and assign a macro to the tool, perform the following steps:

1. Display the custom or predefined toolbar.

2. If the Customize dialog box is not displayed, click with the right mouse button on the toolbar to display the shortcut menu and choose the Customize command. The Customize dialog box shown in figure 28.6 appears.

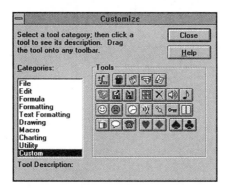

FIG. 28.6

The Customize dialog box with Custom tools displayed.

3. Select Custom from the **C**ategories list.

4. Drag one of the custom tools onto the toolbar.

   The Assign To Tool dialog box immediately appears (see fig. 28.7).

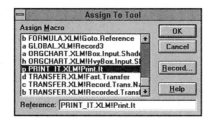

FIG. 28.7

The Assign To Tool dialog box.

5. Assign a macro to the tool by selecting the macro name from the Assign **M**acro list, then choose OK or press Enter. If you want to immediately record a macro to be assigned to this tool, choose **R**ecord tool.

Running Macros Automatically

You will always want some macros available. For example, you may want a specific macro sheet to open whenever you open a specific worksheet. Or you may want a macro to immediately add commands and menus to the menu bar as soon as you open the macro.

You can make macros run automatically from a worksheet or macro sheet. The automatic macros can run when a file opens or closes or when its window activates or deactivates.

To create an Auto_Open, Auto_Close, Auto_Activate, or Auto_Deactivate macro, perform the following steps:

1. Activate the worksheet or macro sheet that will cause the macro to run.

2. Choose the Formula **D**efine Name command.

3. Select the **N**ame text box and type the name *Auto_Open*, *Auto_Close*, *Auto_Activate*, or *Auto_Deactivate*.

4. Select the **R**efers to text box, and enter the name of the macro sheet and macro you want to run automatically.

5. Choose OK, and then resave the worksheet.

Auto macros that include the external reference to the macro open the macro sheet if it is not already opened. If the worksheet and macro sheet are in the same directory, for example, enter the macro in the **R**efers to box in the following way:

=DBAID.XLM!DataEntry

If the macro is in a different directory from the worksheet, enter the macro in the Refers to box in the following way:

='C:\EXCEL\CLIENTS\DBAID.XLM'!DataEntry

You can open a worksheet or macro sheet without the automatic macro running by holding down the Shift key as you choose OK or pressing Enter from the Open dialog box.

Opening or Running Macros When Excel Starts

You can make macros available when Excel starts in one of two ways. You can create or copy them in the Global macro sheet, or you can copy the macro into the XLSTART directory. The XLSTART directory is located under the directory in which you installed Excel. Use the File Manager to copy an XLM or XLA (add-in) file into XLSTART. The next time you start Excel, the macro or add-in will open automatically. If you want a macro on the sheet to run when the sheet opens, use the method in the preceding section to assign the name Auto_Open to the name of the macro you want to run.

Another method of making macros always available is to create or add them to the Global macro sheet. The GLOBAL macro sheet is located in the XLSTART directory under Excel. When you record a macro, as described in Chapter 27, you can make the recording in the Global macro sheet. If you have already created a macro and want it to be on the Global macro sheet, then copy the macro and its names and description from its current sheet and paste it onto the Global macro sheet. Recreate the macros command or function name by using the Formula **D**efine Name command. Recreate any names used in the macro, and be certain that no macro names conflict with existing names. Use the CHANGER.XLA add-in described in Chapter 15 and the Formula **R**eplace commands to update macro functions to update names that have changed.

Creating Add-In Macros

Add-in command or function macros act as though they were built into Excel. Add-in macros are an excellent way to add custom features to your work environment so that Excel appears to have been designed especially for your work. Command macro names on an add-in sheet do not appear in the Macro Run list, and function macros on an add-in sheet appear in the Paste Functions list box in alphabetical order, without being preceded by their worksheet name. Add-in macro sheets are hidden, and you cannot unhide them by using the **W**indow **U**nhide command.

You can change any Excel macro sheet into an add-in macro by saving its macro sheet with the add-in file format. To save a macro sheet as an add-in, complete the following steps:

1. Activate the macro sheet.
2. Choose the **F**ile Save **A**s command.
3. Type a new name if desired.
4. Select Add-In from the Save File as **T**ype list.
5. Choose OK, or press Enter.

Add-in macro files end with the file extension XLA. (You cannot just change the file extension to XLA to create a macro; you must select Add-In from the Save File as Type list.) If you want the add-in macro to run when Excel starts, copy the appropriate XLA file into the XLSTART subdirectory.

Whenever an add-in macro sheet is open, function macros display within the Paste Functions list box the same as Excel's predefined macros. You can use command macros on an add-in macro sheet as subroutines within other macro sheets without specifying the sheet name. For example, instead of using the following subroutine:

    =REPORTS.XLM!Print_It()

you can run the same subroutine on any other macro sheet with the
following:

=Print_It( )

If you want to open an add-in macro sheet as a normal macro that you
can edit, hold down the Shift key as you choose OK or press Enter from
the Open dialog box.

Editing Macros

You can use the same formula and sheet-editing procedures for a macro
sheet that you use in the worksheet. Select the cell to edit; then press F2
or click in the Formula Bar to edit the macro function argument. To copy
or clear parts of a macro and to insert or delete cells, use the same Edit
commands that you use in worksheets.

You can enter additional macro functions into an existing macro by inserting cells or rows into the macro sheet. Use the Edit Insert command
to insert cells or rows; then use the Formula Paste Function command to
paste the macro functions you need in the new cells.

Be careful when inserting rows: if your macros are in adjacent columns,
inserting rows through one macro may insert a blank row through other
macros. This blank row affects the appearance of the macro but does
not stop the macro from running; however, a blank row through a menu
description area spoils the appearance of the menu, and a blank row
through a dialog box description causes an error.

 If the recorder is on while you edit a macro, all your Edit commands and actions appear as macro functions in the macro
being edited. Be certain that the macro recorder is off; otherwise, the result can be quite a mess.

Use upper- and lowercase letters when you define names, and type your
macro functions and names in lowercase characters. Then, when you
press Enter, the functions that Excel recognizes as correctly spelled are
converted to uppercase, and your names are shifted to upper- and lowercase. You can spot mistakes in an entry when you see that a function
remains in lowercase.

Use the Formula Paste Function and Formula Paste Name commands to
paste functions and names into the Formula Bar whenever you are modifying or writing macros. Always keep the Paste Argument check box
selected when pasting functions.

Pasting functions helps prevent typographical errors and accidental
deletion of commas, and helps you enter arguments in the correct order.

You can copy sections from an existing macro and paste them into a macro you are writing. If you copy and paste an entire macro be certain that you examine the names in the pasted macro. Names may need to be recreated or changed so that they do not conflict with existing names on the macro sheet.

Understanding Functions and Returned Values

The macro sheet displays functions; but these functions return results, just as the formulas return results in a worksheet error value. A result can be a number, text, or logical value (TRUE/FALSE). The value that a macro function returns is useful when you're performing calculations, making decisions, and controlling macro operation.

You can see the results returned by macro functions by activating the macro window, selecting the **O**ptions **D**isplay command, and clearing the **F**ormulas box. Figure 28.8 shows the DATACHK macro in two windows. The left window shows macro functions; the right window displays the values returned by each function. For example, if OK is chosen in the input dialog box, cell B3 contains the value the operator typed. If the Cancel button is chosen, cell B3 contains a FALSE result.

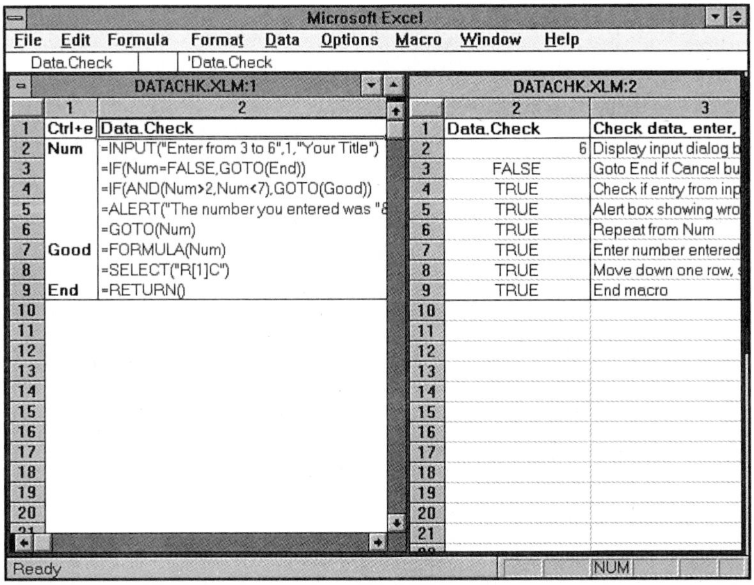

FIG. 28.8

Displaying the values returned by functions.

If you want to toggle a sheet quickly between displaying functions and their results, press Ctrl+`. The ` accent is on the same key with the tilde (~). Press Ctrl+` again to toggle the screen back to its previous view. This method also toggles worksheet displays between results and formulas.

You also can see the results that functions return while the macro operates. The troubleshooting section of this chapter describes how to step through a macro one function at a time by using STEP (). While you are in this Single Step mode, choosing the Evaluate button shows you the result of each function within a cell. If the cell contains multiple functions or nested functions, you see each term evaluated separately.

Understanding Cell and Range References

Macros can reference cells and ranges in more than one way. Macros can use the A1 style, which you are accustomed to using on a worksheet, or the R1C1 style. The best way of dealing with cell and range references in a macro is by using named ranges. The reference type also depends on whether the macro refers to an absolute reference or a relative reference and again on whether it refers to the active sheet, the macro sheet, or a specific named sheet.

References can be relative to the active cell, when a macro runs, or absolute so that they always run in the same cells. When you record a macro, you can switch between relative and absolute by choosing the **M**acro **R**elative Record or the **M**acro **A**bsolute Record command. The following sections explain the reference forms you can use in macros.

Understanding the Types of References

Excel uses different ways of referencing cells and ranges. Some of these methods are very easy to understand and use, and others can be difficult to understand and troubleshoot. The easiest and most preferred method of referencing a specific cell or range on a worksheet or macro sheet is to assign a name to it and then use the name in all references. When you need to move the active cell or current selection a relative distance, the most useful method is to use the OFFSET() function to calculate the new reference.

Referencing Ranges on the Active or Specific Sheets

When you record the selection of a cell with the macro recorder, the cell's location is referenced in R1C1 text style. Because this is a text style, the reference must be enclosed in quotation marks. For example, the following function selects cell B2 on whichever sheet is active:

=SELECT("R2C2")

References can refer to the macro sheet, any active worksheet or macro sheet, or to a specific worksheet or macro sheet. To refer to the active worksheet precede a reference with ! (exclamation mark). To refer to a specific worksheet or macro sheet, precede a reference with the sheet's file name, path name (if in a different directory), and an exclamation mark. Consider the following:

Reference	Refers to
!$A$12	An absolute reference to cell A12 on the active sheet
BUDGET.XLS!$A$12	An absolute reference to cell A12 on the worksheet named BUDGET

> You do not need to type references to another worksheet's cell, ranges, or names. While you are entering a function in the Formula Bar, activate the worksheet you want to refer to and select the cell or range you want to reference. While the worksheet is active, you can choose the Formula **P**aste Name command and paste in a name that resides on the worksheet. The external file name and the cell reference or name will appear in the macro function you are entering.
>
> **T I P**

Possible reference styles within macros include the following:

A! Style	R1C1 Style	Description
$A$1	R1C1	Absolute reference to a cell on the same macro sheet
A1	R[1]C[1]	Relative reference to a cell on the same macro sheet
!A1	!R1C1	Absolute reference to a cell on the active sheet

continues

A! Style	R1C1 Style	Description
!$A$1	!R[1]C[1]	**Never use this style.** Relative reference to a cell on the active sheet, but the relative reference is with respect to the cell containing the macro function using this reference
filename.ext!$A$1	*filename.ext*!R1C1	Absolute reference in a named sheet
filename.ext!A1	*filename.ext*!R[1]C[1]	Relative reference in a named sheet

Using Names for Cell and Range References

The preferred method of referencing cells or ranges on macro sheets or worksheets is by using names. Use the Formula **D**efine Names or Formula **C**reate Names command to create the names. Reference styles are the following:

Reference	Meaning
range_name	Named location on the same macro sheet
!*range_name*	Named location on the active macro sheet or worksheet
filename.ext!*range_name*	Named location on a specific sheet

Using names in worksheets and macros adds a little time to their creation, but it saves much work later. The use of names in macros can be even more important than their use in worksheets.

Macros that refer to named cells or ranges on a worksheet continue to work even when that worksheet has been rearranged. And macros that reference other cells on the macro sheet are much easier to read and maintain.

If your worksheet contains cells or ranges that are named, you can select a cell or range on the active worksheet during your recording by pressing the F5 (Goto) key to select the named area and then continuing with the commands to affect that area. If you have a report that changes in size each month, for example, name the report area Month_Report. A macro to select and print this area each month would look like the following:

```
Print.Report
=FORMULA.GOTO("Month_Report")
=SET.PRINT.AREA( )
=PRINT(1,,,1,FALSE,FALSE,1,FALSE,1)
=RETURN( )
```

Names make macros significantly easier to understand and maintain. Figure 28.9 shows the DATACHK.XLM macro. The labels in column A refer to the adjacent cells in column B. (The cells in column B are named; column A shows only text labels to make the names more apparent.) Using names in this way makes it easy for the macro to reference cell contents and helps you figure out what the macro is doing.

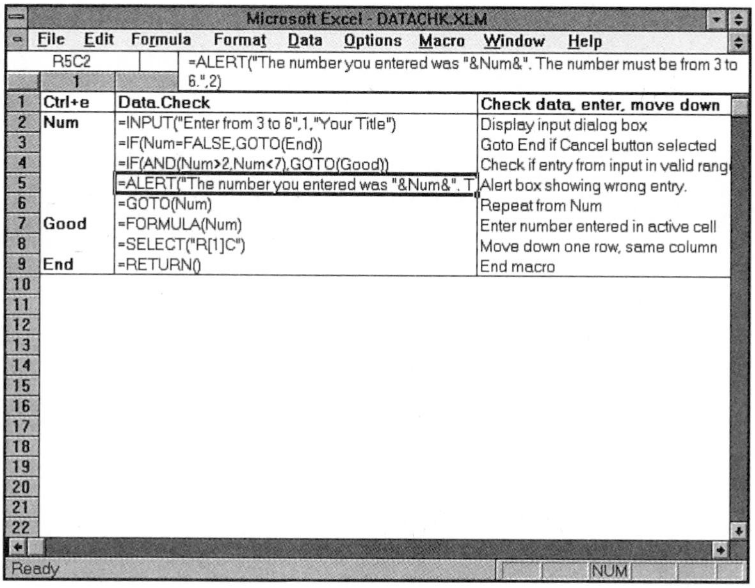

FIG. 28.9

Named cells make macro cell-referencing easier to understand.

To use the labels in column A to name the adjacent cells in column B, perform the following steps:

1. Enter labels down the left column. Select a range that includes both the labels and the cells to be named, as shown in figure 28.10.

2. Choose Formula Create Names; then select the Left Column check box to use the names in the left column. Verify that other check boxes are off.

3. Choose OK or press Enter. You now can use the names in place of cell references.

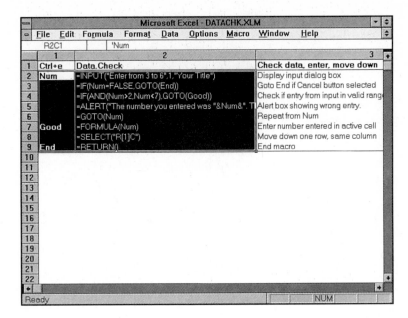

FIG. 28.10

Select the labels in
column A and the cells
you want named in
column B.

Using OFFSET To Calculate Cell and Range References

Although R1C1 references are easy to understand, they can be difficult and slow to manipulate. Using the OFFSET() function to calculate new references is faster and easier to use.

OFFSET() returns a cell or range reference that is offset by a specified distance from a known location. If you were entering data and using OFFSET() to calculate where the data should go, the process would rest in one cell in the worksheet and throw values at a cell three rows down and two columns over.

OFFSET() can be combined with the SELECT() function to move the active cell to a new selection or to select a new range to be formatted. OFFSET() also can be used as the second argument in the FORMULA() function to calculate the reference where data should be entered. The form for OFFSET() is the following:

OFFSET(*reference,rows,cols,height,width*)

The height and width do not need to be specified. *reference* is the base point from which the new reference is offset. The base point does not have to be a single cell, it can be a range. The arguments *rows* and *cols* specify the number of rows and columns that the offset is distanced from the base point. OFFSET() returns a range reference the same size as the base point unless you specify otherwise. If you want an offset to specify a range different from the base point, specify the *height* and *width* for the reference returned.

> Use functions that return a reference, such as ACTIVE.CELL, OFFSET, or SELECTION, within another function. Entering ACTIVE.CELL, OFFSET, or SELECTION in a macro cell by itself does not store the reference it returns. These entries store the contents of the reference they return. If you want to store a reference for later use, for example, and save the current active cell so that it can be returned to later, read the following section, "Storing References for Later Use."

T I P

OFFSET's value comes from being able to use it to calculate new references. Imagine that you need to enter the number 500 in a cell that is one row below the cell named Data and six columns to the right, because this is the sixth month. To perform this entry, you would use the following:

=FORMULA(500,OFFSET(!Data,1,Data.Month))

where !Data is the base point named Data on the active worksheet. 1 indicates one row below the base point, and Data.Month is a name storing the number 6. You could calculate the number six and store it in Data.Month by using many methods. This macro will now enter data into the appropriate cell determined by the month stored in Data.Month.

If you want to select a cell, then you need to enclose OFFSET() within a SELECT() function. To select the cells two rows below the active cell and one cell to the right, and then format that cell as bold, for example, use the following:

=SELECT(OFFSET(ACTIVE.CELL(),2,-1))

=FORMAT.FONT(,,TRUE)

The base point here is ACTIVE.CELL(). The SELECT() function moves the active cell down two rows and left one column. The FORMAT.FONT() then leaves other font formatting as it is and changes only the bold.

Storing References for Later Use

You occasionally will need to store a cell location so you can later use it or return to it. One of the easiest ways of storing is using the SET.NAME() function to store the cell reference in a name. You can later use the name as a reference. For example, in the following macro named Test, SET.NAME() stores the reference for the active cell in the name Here. When PAUSE() is reached, the macro pauses so you can move to any other location. When you click on the Resume tool or choose the **M**acro **R**esume command, Excel resumes the macro. The FORMULA() function then enters 500 into the cell that used to be the active cell. FORMULA() uses the reference stored in Here as its data entry reference. Use the following as your store macro:

```
Test
=SET.NAME("Here",ACTIVE.CELL())
=PAUSE(FALSE)
=FORMULA(500,Here)
=RETURN()
```

Converting References to Content and Vice Versa

Excel macros automatically convert most function results between value and cell reference. For example, the OFFSET() function normally returns a cell reference. But when necessary, OFFSET() will return the contents of a cell. This happens with other functions that return a cell reference, such as ACTIVE.CELL() and SELECTION.() ACTIVE.CELL() returns the reference of the currently active cell and SELECTION() returns the reference of the current range. For example, the following function:

```
=SELECT(OFFSET(ACTIVE.CELL(),1,1))
```

moves the active cell one row down and one column right of its current location. But the following function:

```
=ALERT("The contents are: "&OFFSET(ACTIVE.CELL(),1,1),2)
```

displays an alert box with the message "The contents are: 5" if the cell one down and right of the active cell contains the number five. In this case the ALERT() function needed the value in a cell, so OFFSET() was *coerced* into being a value instead of a reference.

Making Simple Modifications to Recorded Macros

You don't need to be a programmer to make useful macros. You can record the basic process you want automated, then use some or all of these seven simple modifications that add power and flexibility to the recording. The seven simple modifiers are the following:

Macro Function	Description
?	Displays the function and pauses its dialog box so you can select options. The macro continues when you choose the OK or Cancel button. Insert the ? after the function name and before the first parenthesis.
	For example, =ALIGNMENT?(3,FALSE,3,0) displays the Format Alignment dialog box and waits for you to make selections. The arguments in the function specify the default settings when the dialog box displays. Only use a ? with macro functions that display a dialog box, such as Format Font or File Save As.
PAUSE()	Pauses the operation of a macro. When the macro reaches this function it pauses and returns control to you. You can make changes to your worksheet or chart or even run another macro. To restart the macro that is paused, choose the Resume tool or choose the **Macro Resume** command. Arguments in the PAUSE() function determine whether the Macro Paused toolbar displays with the Resume tool.
ALERT()	Displays an alert box with your custom message giving users a warning, a message or letting them choose between an OK or a Cancel button. You can use the result of their choice of OK or Cancel to make your macro do two different things, such as, "Choose OK to print again, or choose Cancel to stop."
MESSAGE()	Displays a message in the Status Bar at the bottom of the screen. Use the message to let operators know what to do next, which part of the macro is running, or approximately how much time remains until the program is finished operating.
INPUT()	Displays a data entry dialog box that displays your message and can include a default entry value. You can specify that the box will accept a specific data type: text, numbers, integers, logical values, references, or formulas. The box contains OK and Cancel buttons that can be used by IF() functions to test whether the Cancel button was chosen.

Macro Function	Description
IF()	Controls decision making within the macro operation. Values entered in an INPUT box, for example, can produce different results depending upon *if* they are greater or less than a certain amount. IF() is also used to test *if* a Cancel button was chosen, then GOTO() a different part of the macro.
GOTO()	Branches the flow of the macro operation. Macros execute their functions down the column. When a GOTO() is reached, the macro operation branches to the location specified by the GOTO(). When combined with an IF() function GOTO() enables the macro to skip over functions that you do not want run or to return to an earlier location so the functions repeat.

Programming Constructs and Techniques

Excel contains hundreds of macro functions, but most programming results come from approximately 20 macro functions. The following functions and techniques can be used in addition to what you record.

Selecting Cells and Ranges

You must select a cell or range if you want to change the format. To select a cell or range, you first must activate the worksheet on which you are selecting, or the SELECT() will return an error and stop the macro.

A worksheet must be active for SELECT() to work. To activate a worksheet before selecting cells use the ACTIVATE() function. For example, to select the range named Data on the worksheet named BUDGET.XLS, use the following functions:

    =ACTIVATE("BUDGET.XLS")

    =SELECT(BUDGET.XLS!Data)

Selecting Cells or Moving the Active Cell

Move the active cell or select new ranges by using the SELECT() function. Combine the SELECT() function with OFFSET() to calculate a new active cell relative to the current active cell or to a named cell. Examples of this can be found in the earlier sections dealing with OFFSET() in this chapter and in Chapter 30.

Selecting Ranges

Most commands that affect a cell or range require the cell or range to be selected. To be selected, the cell or range must be in the active worksheet, so be certain that you use the ACTIVATE() command before SELECT().

To select a named cell or range, use functions like the following:

Function	Result
=SELECT(!Data)	Selects the named range on the active worksheet. An error returns if there is no range named Data.
=SELECT(BUDGET.XLS!Data)	Selects the named range on BUDGET.XLS. An error returns if BUDGET.XLS is not active.
=SELECT(BUDGET.XLS!Header:BUDGET.XLS!Bottom)	Selects the range between the named cells or ranges Header and Bottom on the worksheet BUDGET.XLS.

If you can select one cell within a block of cells, you can select the entire block by using the Formula Select Special command with the Current Region option. For example, you can record a Formula Goto to a named cell, such as Data, then use the Formula Select Special to select a rectangular block of all filled cells touching the active cell. A recorded macro using this method looks like the following:

Select.Region
=ACTIVATE("BUDGET.XLS")
=SELECT(BUDGET.XLS!Data)
=SELECT.SPECIAL(5)
=RETURN()

This method works well to select ranges that may have had additional data added to them—data that was added adjacent to, but outside the original named range.

Another type of selection is useful if you need to select a specific row or column from within a range. After you have the entire range selected, you can calculate how many rows it has by using ROWS() and how many columns it has by using COLUMNS(). This procedure enables you to calculate and select any column or row within the larger region. Consider the following example:

```
Select.Column
=ACTIVATE("BUDGET.XLS")
=SELECT(BUDGET.XLS!Data)
=SELECT.SPECIAL(5)
=SET.NAME("Row.Num",ROWS(SELECTION()))
=SET.NAME("Col.Num",COLUMNS(SELECTION()))
=SELECT(OFFSET(ACTIVE.CELL(),0,3):OFFSET(ACTIVE.CELL(),Row.Num,3))
=RETURN()
```

This example selects the fourth column in a range of data, even if that data area and the fourth column have blank cells scattered throughout. The first three cells of the macro activate the worksheet, select the cell named Data within the area to be selected, and then select the current region. When the region is selected the new active cell moves to the top left of the selected region. (The active cell will later be used as a base point for an offset to the column.) This procedure works like the previous example.

The ROWS() and COLUMN() functions calculate the number of rows and columns in the selection and the SET.NAME functions store those numbers in Row.Num and Col.Num so they can be used later. (COLUMNS is there for illustration; it is not actually used to select the third column of data.)

The fourth column is selected by the last SELECT() function. The top-left corner of the selection is specified by OFFSET() as being in the same row (0) and three columns right from the active cell. The active cell is now at the top left corner of the selection. This procedure selects the top of the fourth column.

The bottom of the fourth column is specified by the second OFFSET() in the last SELECT(). The OFFSET() specifies that the bottom of the selection will be three columns offset to the right and Row.Num down from the active cell. Row.Num was the calculated height of the entire selection.

The same principle can be used with the Col.Num name to calculate and select any row within a range.

Displaying Messages

Use the ALERT() and MESSAGE() functions to generate custom messages and warnings.

Displaying an ALERT box

ALERT() displays a dialog box containing a message. The user must choose the OK button to close the dialog box and continue. The syntax for an ALERT() function is the following:

> =ALERT(*message_text,type_num,help_ref*)

In this syntax, the *message_text* is the text that shows up in the alert box. Be certain that you put the text in quotes. The *type_num* is a number specifies which of three types of alert boxes to display. The type numbers are the following:

type_num	alert box
1	Question mark icon. Displays OK and Cancel button. Includes a Help button if the help file is defined.
2	Information icon. Displays information and an OK button.
3	Exclamation icon. Cautionary information and an OK button.

You can use ALERT boxes to create decision branches in your program, such as "Choose OK to print again or choose Cancel to stop." To create decision branches, use a *type_num* of 1. Choosing the OK button returns TRUE to the cell containing ALERT; choosing Cancel returns FALSE. The TRUE or FALSE can change how your program operates with the use of an IF() function and subroutines or GOTO() functions. Consider the following function:

> =IF(B12,GOTO(B36))

If B12 contains the ALERT box, then choosing OK branches the macro to cell B36. Instead of the GOTO(), you can also use subroutines as one of the IF() function arguments. Figure 28.11 shows an alert box created with the *type_num* of 1.

Displaying Messages in the Status Bar

A more subtle way of sending messages to the user is by putting a message on the Status Bar at the bottom of the screen. In fact, this method is so subtle that many users never see the messages, so you may want to start a macro with an ALERT box telling them to watch the Status Bar for messages.

The syntax for a message is the following:

=MESSAGE(*logical,text*)

To display a message, use the following format:

=MESSAGE(TRUE,"This macro is 50% complete")

To return the Status Bar to normal, use the following format:

=MESSAGE(FALSE)

To clear the Status Bar, use the following format:

=MESSAGE(TRUE)

Pausing Command Dialog Boxes

When you run a recorded macro, you usually do not get a chance to make any changes to the dialog box selections. The macro runs as recorded without letting you select different options. One easy and useful change you can make to your recorded macros causes dialog boxes to wait for your selections. The options you selected during the recording become the default settings when the dialog box opens.

Identify the dialog boxes that you want displayed by inserting a question mark (?) after the function name and before its opening parenthesis. Figure 28.12 shows formatting functions with question marks inserted. When the macro reaches these functions, the macro stops, displays the appropriate dialog box, and waits for your selections or dialog box input. Note that the selections in the dialog box you recorded become the default selections in the dialog box when it pauses. With the box displayed, you can make changes to the selections and choose OK or press Enter to continue with the macro.

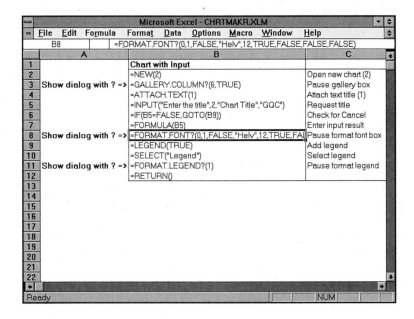

	Microsoft Excel - CHRTMAKR.XLM		

File   Edit   Formula   Format   Data   Options   Macro   Window   Help

B8	=FORMAT.FONT?(0,1,FALSE,"Helv",12,TRUE,FALSE,FALSE,FALSE)	

	A	B	C
1		Chart with Input	
2		=NEW(2)	Open new chart (2)
3	Show dialog with ? =>	=GALLERY.COLUMN?(6,TRUE)	Pause gallery box
4		=ATTACH.TEXT(1)	Attach text title (1)
5		=INPUT("Enter the title",2,"Chart Title","GQC")	Request title
6		=IF(B5=FALSE,GOTO(B9))	Check for Cancel
7		=FORMULA(B5)	Enter input result
8	Show dialog with ? =>	=FORMAT.FONT?(0,1,FALSE,"Helv",12,TRUE,FAl	Pause format font box
9		=LEGEND(TRUE)	Add legend
10		=SELECT("Legend")	Select legend
11	Show dialog with ? =>	=FORMAT.LEGEND?(1)	Pause format legend
12		=RETURN()	
13			
14			
15			
16			
17			
18			
19			
20			
21			
22			

Ready   NUM

FIG. 28.12

A question mark inserted after a macro function name pauses a dialog box for operator selections.

T   I   P

In general, any command you record that displays a dialog box can have its macro function modified with a question mark. For example, the FORMAT.FONT() or PAGE.SETUP() functions accept a question mark.

Macro functions that display dialog boxes accept default values for arguments. For example, FORMAT.NUMBER can use two formats—one with and one without a question mark. In these formats, the bold italic arguments are mandatory and the italic arguments are optional:

FORMAT.NUMBER(*format_text*)

FORMAT.NUMBER?(*format_text*)

Here, *format_text* is the same type of expression you see in the Format Numbers list box; however, the expression is enclosed in quotation marks. If you do not enter the optional *format_text* argument in the version with a question mark, the dialog box displays standard defaults.

Pausing Macro Operation

Excel offers a way of pausing a macro so that you can take control of Excel and perform manual operations. When you are finished entering data, formatting, or other manual operations, you can resume the macro at the point at which it paused.

The syntax for PAUSE() is the following:

=PAUSE(*no_tool*)

When *no_tool* is TRUE, the Macro toolbar does not display. When *no_tool* is FALSE, the Macro toolbar displays with the Resume tool.

To restart the macro after it has paused, click on the Resume macro tool or choose the **M**acro **R**esume command.

Prompting for Data Entry

Use the INPUT() function to prompt the user to enter data. Numerous examples of the INPUT()function are in the macro chapters including Chapter 30. The syntax for the INPUT() function is the following:

=INPUT(*message_text,type_num,title_text,default,x_pos,y_pos,help_ref*)

The *message_text* is text in quotes that displays in the dialog box. The *message_text* is mandatory. Use it as a prompt to remind yourself what to enter. *type_num* is a number that specifies the type of data you must enter. If you type the incorrect type of data, an alert box warns you and you are returned to the INPUT box. The data types are the following:

type_num	accepted data
0	Formula
1	Number
2	Text
4	Logical
8	Reference
16	Error
64	Array

If you need an input box to accept more than one type, add the type numbers together.

title is the title that appears in the title bar at the top of the INPUT box. *default* is what will appear in the INPUT edit box when it first displays. Make sure it is the same type as what you have specified for the INPUT box. If the default is text, put it in quotes. *x_pos* and *y_pos* specify the x and y positions of the top left corner of the box. The INPUT box is centered if they are left out. *help_ref* is the topic in a custom on-line Help file that you must create. If it is specified, then a Help button appears in the INPUT box.

Entering Data in Worksheets and Charts

If you imagine the FORMULA() function as what you put in the Formula Bar, then you will understand that whatever is the argument of the FORMULA() function is entered in the active cell, a specified cell, or the active chart text item.

The syntax for FORMULA() is the following:

=FORMULA(*formula_text,reference*)

The *formula_text* can be a numeric or text value, a formula, or a reference. Text values must be in quotes. Formulas must use quoted R1C1 format. References can use the reference types shown in the earlier sections.

Entering Data in the Active Cell or Item

If you do not enter a *reference* in FORMULA(), the data is placed in the active cell. The following formula:

=FORMULA(INPUT("Type, then press Enter",2))

puts whatever you type in the active cell. Because cancelling an INPUT box results in a FALSE, if you choose Cancel you will see the word FALSE in the active cell. If the INPUT() function was in cell B12 on the macro sheet, then you also could have used the following function:

=FORMULA(A12)

to enter the contents of A12 on the macro sheet into the active cell on the active worksheet or macro sheet.

Don't use FORMULA() to enter data into the macro sheet. Instead use the SET.VALUE() function. SET.VALUE() puts the value you specify into the cell you reference on the macro sheet.

T I P

Entering in a Reference or Range

Use FORMULA() to enter data into a specific cell on the active worksheet or a specific named worksheet. Because you do not need to select the cell you are entering data into, you can enter or transfer information 10 to 20 times faster than you can when selecting a cell and then using FORMULA(). The following function:

=FORMULA(A12,BUDGET.XLS!Data)

takes the value in A12 on the same macro sheet and enters it into the cell named Data on the BUDGET.XLS worksheet. BUDGET.XLS does not have to be active, but it must be open.

To enter data into a specific cell on any active worksheet, use one of the following examples:

=FORMULA(A12,!$B$36)

=FORMULA(A12,!Data)

Entering in a Calculated Reference

By using the OFFSET() function, you can calculate where you want data to be entered. By using this method you can enter data into a specific cell or fill the cells going across a row in a database. Because you are specifying a *reference* the active cell on the worksheet does not move as FORMULA() enters the data. As an example of using OFFSET(), the following functions move entries across a row of cells:

Enter.Number
=FOR("Row.Num",1,5,1)
=INPUT("Type an entry",2)
=FORMULA(B12,OFFSET(ACTIVE.CELL(),Row.Num,0))
=NEXT()
=RETURN()

In this example, the INPUT() function is in cell B12. It results in an entry that is used as the *formula_text* argument of FORMULA(). The *reference* argument for formula is calculated as an offset from the active cell. Look for further description of this FOR-NEXT loop in the looping section that follows.

For additional information on using OFFSET(), see the previous section, "Using OFFSET To Calculate Cell and Range References."

Transferring Data between Locations

You can transfer information between two worksheets much faster by using FORMULA() than you can using ACTIVATE(), COPY() and PASTE(). The speed improvements can be on the order of 10 to 20 times. Another advantage is that data transferred with FORMULA() does not require active worksheets. They do need to be open, however.

To transfer data between cells on different worksheets just use the reference on the source worksheet as the *formula_text* argument. Use the location on the other worksheet as the *reference* argument. For example, the following function:

    =FORMULA(BUDGET.XLS!Data,ANNUAL.XLS!May)

transfers the data in the cell named Data on the BUDGET.XLS worksheet into the cell named May on the ANNUAL.XLS worksheet.

Combining a calculated reference with the concept of transferring data using FORMULA() produces powerful and useful results. It is how dialog box entries left in a macro sheet are transferred from the macro sheet into a database or worksheet. Examples of data transfer are in Chapter 31.

Getting Worksheet Information

Many macros need to know what a cell contains, what documents are open, and so on. Excel contains many functions that can give you the condition of all parts of the Excel environment, from testing whether a cell is blank, to determining whether Excel is running on a PC or Macintosh.

Checking Cell Contents and Conditions

Some of the functions you can use to test cell, range, chart item, document, and object conditions are IS*functions* and GET.*functions*. The IS*functions*, such as ISBLANK() and ISERROR(), are used to test a reference. For example, the following function:

    =ISBLANK(!Data)

returns TRUE if the named cell Data on the active worksheet is blank. You can test whether a macro function has returned an error with a function like the following:

    =ISERROR(B36)

This function returns a TRUE if the macro function in cell B36 returned an error.

The GET.*functions* can return many different values that define the contents or status of a cell, range, item, object, or document. For example, the syntax of GET.CELL() is the following:

GET.CELL(*type_num,reference*)

The *type_num* specifies what type of information will be examined about the cell specified by *reference*. If no *reference* exists, then the cell is the active cell. There are 52 different *type_num* for just this one GET.*function*. The following function:

=GET.CELL(20)

returns a TRUE if the active cell is bold and returns a FALSE if the active cell is not bold.

Checking Document and Window Names

Test for DOCUMENT and WINDOW names by using the DOCUMENTS() and WINDOWS() functions. These functions do not return a single name; they return an array of names. To test whether a specific document is open, you can match that document's name against the names returned in the DOCUMENTS() function. Use an OR() function to return a TRUE when a specific document is open. Consider the following function:

=OR("BUDGET.XLS"=DOCUMENTS())

This function returns a TRUE if BUDGET.XLS is open. It returns a FALSE if it is not open. An IF() function or block IF() then can use this TRUE or FALSE to activate the document if it is open or to open it if it is closed. See Chapter 30 for an example.

Making Decisions in the Macro

IF() functions make the decisions in your programs. There are two types of IF() functions. One type of IF() makes TRUE and FALSE decisions and can have two consequences. The other is a block IF(), and it can make multiple decisions with multiple consequences.

Making TRUE/FALSE Decisions with IF

Use the simple IF() function to test for TRUE/FALSE conditions such as, "Is the result from this INPUT box FALSE?" If it is false, then Cancel was chosen in the INPUT box.

IF() uses the following syntax:

=IF(*logical_test,result_if_true,result_if_false*)

When the *logical_test* or comparison you enter results in TRUE, then whatever is in the *result_if_true* portion executes. If the test results in FALSE, then whatever is in the *result_if_false* portion executes. You do not need a result in both the *result_if_true* and *result_if_false* arguments. You do need to include commas as necessary for Excel to tell the position of the arguments.

Examples of IF() functions appear throughout the book. They can be used in macros in the same way they are used in the worksheet. In a macro, they also can be used to branch operations with a GOTO() or to run subroutines. Examples can be found in Chapter 30.

Making Multiple Decisions with Block IF

The block IF() function is a powerful feature of Excel that enables you to make multiple decisions that don't fit into TRUE or FALSE categories. A block IF() function can test for many conditions until it finds a condition that is TRUE. When IF finds a TRUE condition, then it runs the functions within that portion of the block.

A block IF() consists of multiple functions, each in different cells. The syntax for a block IF() is the following:

=IF(*logical_test_A*)
   do this if test A is TRUE
=ELSE.IF(*logical_test_B*)
   do this if test B is TRUE
=ELSE.IF(*logical_test_C*)
   do this if test C is TRUE
=ELSE.IF(*logical_test_D*)
   do this if test D is TRUE
=ELSE()
   do this if all other tests were FALSE
=END.IF()

The *logical_test* is used by IF() and ELSE(). IFs can be any type of test that results in a TRUE or FALSE. An example of a block IF() is given in Chapter 30.

Controlling the Flow of Macro Operation

You can control which functions operate next in a macro with the use of GOTO() and subroutines. GOTOs are useful for skipping over functions directly below them. The use of too many GOTOs can make following all the changes of direction very difficult. If you have macro operations that you use over and over, you may want to use them as subroutines that can be shared by other macros.

Using GOTO To Branch to New Operations

Macro functions execute in the order they are listed down the column. You can change this flow of execution, however, in a number of ways. A GOTO() command or a subroutine call can reroute the macro to a different section of the macro. The IF() function is an excellent method of controlling when branching takes place.

GOTO(*ref*) permanently branches macro operation to the cell location specified by *ref*. The macros shown earlier in figures 28.10 and 28.12 show examples of the GOTO() function. If the Cancel button from an input box is chosen, the cell for that input box returns FALSE. An IF() function then can test for that FALSE condition and make the macro operation go to another cell to continue operating.

GOTO() is used in a number of sample macros in Chapter 30. If you need to skip more than once, use a block IF() function instead. If you have repetitive parts of a macro do not use GOTO() to go back to them; instead, make the repetitive portion into a subroutine. Better and more readable programming style uses block IF() functions or subroutines. They are both discussed in this chapter.

T I P You use FORMULA.GOTO() in a macro to go to and select a cell or range on the worksheet. FORMULA.GOTO() is equivalent to the Formula **G**oto command or F5 key on the worksheet. The GOTO() function directs a macro to look at macro functions in a different location. Normally, a macro reads and operates on each function in the cells down the column. GOTO() can redirect macro operation so that the macro begins reading and operating on functions in a different location.

Using Subroutines for Frequent Operations

Use subroutines to prevent snarls of GOTO() commands. *Subroutines* are macros used for accomplishing specific and frequently repeated tasks. When a main macro needs the function that a subroutine performs, the main macro transfers macro operation to that subroutine. When the subroutine is finished, control returns to the original macro and continues from where it left off. Not only are subroutines easier to understand and write than GOTO() statements, but often you can share subroutines among macros or paste subroutines onto other macro sheets.

Subroutines are nothing more than macros that perform a specific task for the main macro. They act as efficient subcontractors who do a special and repetitive job. For example, you may have a subroutine that sets the page layout and displays dialog boxes requesting header and footer information. This same subroutine can be used by different macros. Another example is a data extract subroutine used by different databases on the same worksheet.

Subroutine macros end with RETURN(), just as normal macros do. When a subroutine macro reaches RETURN(), it returns to the macro function following the one that called the subroutine.

The best way to write macros using subroutines is to write one main macro that acts as a script. This script tells the different subroutines when to run. The main macro should do little work itself; its purpose is to coordinate which subroutines run.

To get a subroutine to run, call it by name, where *macroname* is the cell reference or name at the beginning of the macro. Use the following form:

>   =*macroname*( )

Suppose that you have a macro named Print_It, which is designed to print any selected range. You can run this macro as a subroutine from any macro with the following call:

>   =Print_It( )

If the subroutine is on another macro sheet (perhaps a sheet containing a whole library of subroutines), include an external reference to the macro. Use the following form:

>   =**worksheet!***macroname*()

or

>   =USEFUL.XLM!Print_It( )

Macros used only as subroutines can include arguments specified within the parentheses. These macros are set up in the same way that function macros are set up to use arguments. If you use a subroutine macro as a command macro, then don't set it up to accept arguments.

Repeating Operations with Loops

When you have functions you want to repeat, use a loop. There are three types of loops, each satisfying a different need.

Looping a Known Number of Times with FOR-NEXT

If you know exactly how many times you want to loop, then use a FOR() loop. The syntax for a FOR() loop is the following:

=FOR(*counter_text,start_num,end_num,step_num*)

The *counter_text* is text enclosed in quotes that becomes a name. It stores a number that counts the number of times throughout the loop. *start_num* is the starting number the first time throughout the loop. *end_num* is the number of the last time through the loop, and *step_num* is how large each increment is to the *counter_text* after each loop. When *counter_text* is larger than *end_num,* the loop stops.

All the functions between the FOR and NEXT function are executed. The following macro:

Enter.Number
=FOR("Row.Num",1,5,1)
=FORMULA(500,OFFSET(ACTIVE.CELL(),Row.Num,0))
=NEXT()
=RETURN()

repeats the FORMULA() function and enters 500 down a column as Row.Num changes each time through the loop.

Looping WHILE a Condition is TRUE

If you want to repeat a loop until some condition becomes false, then use a WHILE() loop. The syntax is the following:

=WHILE(*logical_test*)

The following is an example of a WHILE() loop is:

Loop.Til.Blank
=WHILE(NOT(ISBLANK(ACTIVE.CELL())))
=FORMAT.FONT(,,TRUE)
=SELECT("R[1]C")
=NEXT()
=RETURN()

This macro loops while the active cell is not blank. ISBLANK() returns TRUE if the active cell is blank. Because this macro should loop while the active cell is not blank, the NOT() function is used to reverse the TRUE to a FALSE. If the active cell is not blank, then the cell is formatted and the active cell moves down. When the active cell is blank, the loop ends.

Looping through the Cells in a Range

One of the most useful and easiest to use loops is the FOR.CELL()loop. It loops through every cell in the current selection or in a range you specify. The syntax is the following:

=FOR.CELL(*ref_name,area_ref,skip_blanks*)

The *ref_name* is text enclosed in quotes that becomes a name. This name stores the reference of the cell currently being worked on. The argument *area_ref* is the range of cells that will be worked on. If you do not specify an *area_ref,* then FOR.CELL() works on each cell in the current selection. If you want FOR.CELL() to skip over blank cells, then use TRUE. Omitting *skip_blanks* or using FALSE runs the loop over every cell.

The following example checks each cell in a range that you have selected before starting the macro. If a cell in the range contains a number greater than 10, then the cell is bolded.

```
Bold.It
=FOR.CELL("Cell.Check")
=IF(Cell.Check>10)
=    SELECT(Cell.Check)
=    FORMAT.FONT(,,TRUE)
=END.IF()
=NEXT()
```

Documenting Macros

Documenting macros is like backing up files on your hard disk. Many people fail to do it until they have caused themselves a great amount of work and job insecurity. Some users are tempted to create the macros, use them immediately, and leave documentation for later. Then weeks or months later, when someone must modify the macros, the user has forgotten how the macros work.

Even if you are a novice Excel user and do not understand many of the macro functions, you should put an explanation of what the macro does in the column to the right of the macro. You also can attach a note of instructions to the cell with the macro name by selecting the macro name cell and choosing Formula Note.

The sample macro in figure 28.13 shows one of the best methods for documenting macros. This method makes macros easier to read, edit, and understand. The method titles the top cells in a macro so that the macro is more organized. Borders and shading can be used for separating distinct parts.

		Microsoft Excel - CHRTMAKR.XLM	
	File Edit Formula Format Data Options Macro Window Help		
B10		=FORMAT.FONT?(0,1,FALSE,"Helv",12,TRUE,FALSE,FALSE,FALSE)	

	A	B	C
1	Ctrl+c	Chart with Input	
2		*Make chart*	
3		=NEW(2)	Open new chart (2)
4		=GALLERY.COLUMN?(6,TRUE)	Pause gallery box
5		*Title: Request and format*	
6	Title.Input	=INPUT("Enter the title",2,"Chart Title","GQC")	Request title
7		=ATTACH.TEXT(1)	Attach text title (1)
8		=IF(Title.Input=FALSE,GOTO(Legend.Create))	Check for Cancel
9		=FORMULA(Title.Input)	Enter input result
10		=FORMAT.FONT?(0,1,FALSE,"Helv",12,TRUE,FALSE,	Pause format font box
11		*Legend: Add and position*	
12	Legend.Create	=LEGEND(TRUE)	Add legend
13		=SELECT("Legend")	Select legend
14		=FORMAT.LEGEND?(1)	Pause format legend
15		=RETURN()	
16			
17			
18			
19			
20			
21			
22			

Ready   NUM

FIG. 28.13

Document your macros in two or three columns.

You can separate segments of a macro by including text and blank cells as dividers. The text and blank cells do not affect macro operation but do help to show where separate tasks begin and end within a large macro. Because Excel macros ignore text and blank cells, you can enter remarks or segment headers by typing them as text. You may want to format these remarks with italic or boldface so that they stand out.

Another way of making your macros easier to read is to use Format Border to outline the column containing macro functions or the column containing documentation. Use color formatting to format areas of a macro that are similar; for example, use blue for the first level of a FOR-NEXT() loop, and use red to mark a function you need to come back to for cross-checking or replacing.

Troubleshooting Macros

Macros save a great deal of time and work. When you customize re-corded macros by making small modifications, the macros become even more valuable. When you begin to make significant changes, or when you begin to type macros directly onto the macro sheet, however, the probability of errors increases—especially when you are learning.

This chapter includes some tips on how to troubleshoot macros and how to deal with some of the more common difficulties. One of the most important tips is to keep your macros short and simple. If you need to accomplish more than what a short and simple macro can handle, use subroutines to join small macros.

The most important technique you will learn in troubleshooting macros is the use of the STEP() function to single-step through macros as they operate. When you use the Evaluate button in the Single Step dialog box, you see the actual result returned by a function. This technique enables you to see whether the function was correctly evaluated and whether it returned an incorrect result or an error.

> Turn off screen refreshing to make your recorded macros run faster. Insert the macro function ECHO(FALSE) at the point in the macro where you want screen refreshing turned off. To turn screen refresh-ing back on in the middle of a macro, insert ECHO(TRUE). Screen re-freshing always is turned back on when the macro is finished.
>
> **T I P**

Finding Problems

Excel tries to catch errors when it runs the macros. For example, Excel warns of errors in macro syntax when you attempt to enter an incorrect function.

In addition, you can monitor the values that macro functions produce. Use the Options Display command with the Formulas option cleared or press Ctrl+` to see values on a worksheet. Most functions return a TRUE when they operate correctly. INPUT boxes, ALERT boxes, or dialog boxes return a FALSE when you choose the Cancel button. Calculations in a cell return the result of the calculation, just as a formula returns an answer. INPUT boxes return to the cell what the operator typed into the INPUT box.

A great aid in correcting macro errors is the STEP() function. You can put as many STEP() functions as you want in your macro. Whenever Excel comes across the STEP() formula, it presents a dialog box with seven options (see fig. 28.14). You also can enter Step mode by choosing **M**acro **R**un and using the **S**tep button instead of **R**un or by pressing Esc during macro operation.

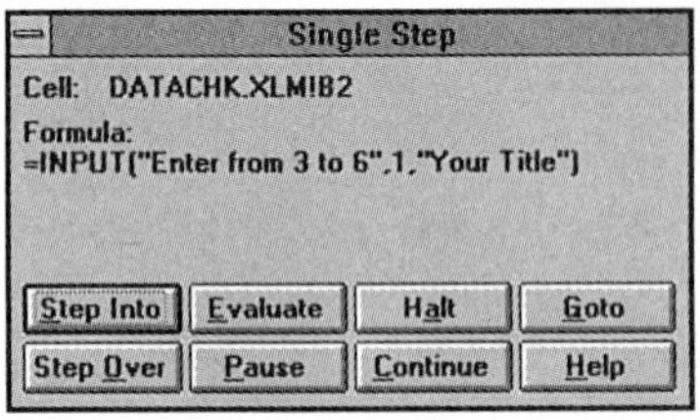

FIG. 28.14

The Single Step enables you to watch macro operation.

The following table describes the buttons in the Single Step dialog box:

Button	Description
Step Into	Runs the current macro function and then steps to the next cell in the macro. When a subroutine is reached, it steps through the subroutine.
Step **O**ver	Steps through each cell of macro but does not step through subroutine cells.
Evaluate	Calculates the smallest term within the current macro cell and displays its results in the Single Step box. Figure 28.15 shows the INPUT function from figure 28.14 after its evaluation. The number 9 was entered.
Pause	Pauses the macro to enable you to do other work. Click on the Resume macro tool to continue the macro.
Goto	Stops the macro, removes the Single Step box, displays the macro sheet, and selects the current cell the Single Step box was on; unavailable if the macro is hidden or an add-in.
H**a**lt	Exits the macro and returns to the active document.
Continue	Returns to normal macro operation until another STEP function or error is met.

Whenever you have a possible macro problem, insert a STEP() function before the suspected problem with the following procedure. The STEP() function should be entered as =STEP(). When macro operation hits the STEP() function, the macro goes into Single Step mode. At that time, you can evaluate the result of each macro function to see where the error occurred.

FIG. 28.15

Use the Evaluate
button to see the result
a function returns.

Press Esc to enter Single Step mode during normal macro operation.
Because you may not press Esc at just the right moment, however, this
procedure is less accurate than inserting STEP() in a macro.

> Excel comes with an add-in macro that helps you troubleshoot, or
> debug, your macros. This macro, named DEBUG.XLA, is located in the
> LIBRARY directory and automates such troubleshooting features as
> entering STEP() formulas, setting breakpoints, and switching the
> macro sheet between formula display and results display. This add-in
> macro is described in Chapter 15.

T I P

Troubleshooting Guide

The following tips include some of the more common problems faced
when you're running and creating macros.

Problem:

The command macro doesn't work at all.

Solution:

Choose the **Macro R**un command and see if the macro's name is displayed. If it is not visible, then you need to name the macro by using the
Formula **D**efine Name command. Make sure that you select the **Com**-
mand option button.

If you pressed a shortcut key and nothing happened, check in the Define
Name dialog box to ensure that a shortcut key was entered.

Make sure that another macro does not have the same shortcut key
name. Look in the Define Name dialog box list. Check the shortcut keys
down the left side of the list. If another shortcut key comes first, you
must rename the shortcut key or run the macro from the **Macro R**un
command.

Problem:

The command macro still doesn't work.

Solution:

Go through the following steps to filter out the most common reasons for a macro not working. Activate the macro sheet before using steps.

1. Choose Formula **D**efine Name or Formula **G**oto and verify that the top cell of the macro is named and that it is selected as a command or function type of macro (with an optional Ctrl+key combination if it is a command macro).

2. Choose **O**ptions **D**isplay and deselect the Formulas option. If you see error values displayed in macro function cells, check them out. For example, #NAME? means that the macro function cannot find one of the names used or it is interpreting a mistyped function as a name. Macro functions generally display TRUE, FALSE, or a value when they perform correctly.

3. Insert a cell with =STEP() as the first function below the macro name. Run the macro and use the Evaluate button to see how each function operates.

Problem:

The macro works, but not correctly.

Solution:

Go through the following checklist, in order:

1. Press Ctrl+` (on the ~ key) to display macro function results. If you see error values displayed in macro function cells, check them out. For example, #NAME? means that the macro function cannot find one of the cell reference names. This problem is frequently a spelling or typographic problem. Macro functions generally display a value of TRUE if the macro function performs correctly.

2. Insert STEP() functions prior to sections of the macro where you suspect a problem. Use the Evaluate button in the Single Step dialog box to see the result of each function. If a function returns an # error because the syntax or argument was wrong, or an incorrectly calculated value, you have found one of the possible functions causing the problem.

Problem:

After a reasonable amount of searching and fruitless corrections, the macro still does not work correctly.

Solution:

Try these approaches to cryptic macros:

1. Leave the problem alone for awhile and come back to it later.

2. Try breaking the macro into sections and testing the operation of each section separately. This method may isolate a section that does not work correctly. You can stop the macro temporarily at an early stage by inserting a RETURN() function where you want it to stop. Move the RETURN() down the macro as you work your way through.

3. Another method is to separate sections of the macro. When the sections work correctly, join them by pasting them or by using subroutines. Retest the operation as you add each section to the whole.

4. Start over. On difficult bugs, you may save time by starting again from scratch; but rethink, replan, and approach the macro with a different solution. Build your new macro in small sections that each can be tested independently. Link these sections together.

Problem:

A message appears from a macro problem.

Solution:

Press F1 for help in deciphering what the message means.

Problem:

The name of the function macro does not show up in the Formula Paste Function list box.

Solution:

Check the All category list in the Paste Function dialog box. If the function really is missing, then ensure that the macro sheet is open. If it is, make sure that you named the macro with Formula Define Name and that the Function option has been selected for that name.

Problem:

The macro is recorded, but the code appears at the end of another macro. When one macro runs, they both run.

Solution:

You have accidentally used the **Macro Start** Recorder command to record the second macro. This puts the second recording attached to the end of the previous recording. Instead, use the **Macro Record** command to create new macros.

You can correct the problem by copying the second set of code to a new location. End the first macro with =RETURN(). Type a name above the copied code and use the Formula Define Name command with the Command option to name the macro.

Problem:

Inexperienced operators enter values or make selections that *bomb* the macro.

Solution:

Use alert boxes that display instructions and error-trapping formulas to prevent errors by those unfamiliar with the program. The DATACHK macro examined in this chapter illustrates how to check for the Cancel button being selected and how to check for correct entry values.

Problem:

The active cell in the macro keeps jumping back to the same cell location used when the macro was recorded originally. The macro is unusable in different worksheets and different cell locations.

Solution:

This problem occurs when the macro is recorded in absolute reference mode. The macro replays exactly the same cell selections as the ones selected during recording.

Use relative addressing. Doing so enables the macro to work on cell locations that are in the same relative location to whatever cell is the active cell when the macro runs. To record with relative addressing when you are in absolute mode, choose Macro Relative Record. You can alternate between Relative Record and Absolute Record as you record the macro.

Problem:

On running Single Step with Evaluate, # error values appear as results for a function.

Solution:

If a macro function shows the error value #N/A when evaluated, the wrong type of argument has been used. For example, text that should be enclosed in quotation marks is not, or a number has been used in place of text. If #NAME! appears, you forgot to give a name to a particular cell reference, you misspelled a name, or you forgot to enclose a text value in quotation marks. If #VALUE! appears, then you probably have used an incorrect argument. Another instance where #VALUE! occurs is described in the next problem and solution.

Problem:

The macro acts as though other macros are attached to it. The first macro works; then, when the macro should end, other macros operate.

Solution:

Make sure that your first macro ends with RETURN( ) or HALT( ). A macro does not stop at a blank cell but continues down the column looking for further macro functions. If the macro runs into another macro, the second macro begins to execute.

Problem:

The hot key assigned to the macro runs the incorrect macro.

Solution:

Check the **M**acro **R**un dialog box, and note the hot keys down the left side of the list. Pressing a shortcut key operates the first macro in the list that uses that key. Run macro with the same shortcut key from the **M**acro **R**un list, or change their shortcut keys. Add-in macro shortcut keys also may take precedence, but you cannot see their shortcut keys listed.

Chapter Summary

The best thing to do at this point is to record macros and modify them. Get practice working with macros and understanding how different macro functions can be used together.

After you have some experience with the fundamental functions described in this chapter, examine and reproduce some of the sample macros in Chapter 30. Chapter 29 describes how to create custom menus and custom dialog boxes.

Adding Custom Menus and Dialog Boxes

When you build macros for yourself, often you can run macros with just the shortcut keys or from the Macro Run dialog box. When you need to create a custom application for use by others, however, you will want to create custom commands and menus for your macros.

If you are building macros that accept a great deal of input or require selections of options, you may want to create custom dialog boxes. You can draw your own custom dialog boxes in the Dialog Editor, an application that comes with Excel, and then paste the new dialog boxes into your macro sheet. With the knowledge that you acquire in this chapter, you can use the data entered or options selected in custom dialog boxes to control Excel programs that you create. You also can use Excel's custom menus and dialog boxes to create programs specific to your business or industry.

Understanding Menus and Commands

This section is an overview of the elements required to create a system of custom menus and commands. Later sections describe adding a command to a menu, adding a menu to a menu bar, or creating an entirely new menu bar.

Excel has a menu bar that holds menu names, and each of these menus pulls down to display commands. All of these menus can be customized. You can add your own menu bars, add menus to existing bars, or add commands to existing menus.

Excel has six built-in menu bars, with each menu bar defined numerically as 1 through 6. The short menu bars are available only under macro control. To these built-in menu bars, you can add up to 15 custom menu bars to display your own menus. Your custom menu bars are assigned the next available number, which is returned by the ADD.BAR( ) function that you use to add the menu bar.

The six built-in menu bars are listed here in order:

Menu Bar	Full Menu	Short Menu
Worksheet	1	5
Chart	2	6
Null (no files)	3	
Info	4	

To describe the menus and commands you want to appear on a menu bar, Excel uses a table on a macro sheet like the table shown in figure 29.1. The following description explains each column in this table. Later sections of this chapter describe the actual construction and use of this table.

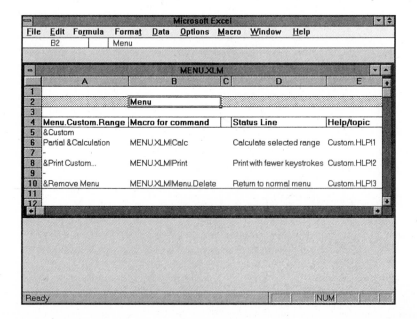

FIG. 29.1

Custom menu commands arranged in this table on the macro sheet.

The first column in the menu table (column A in fig. 29.1) contains the menu name and the commands in the order you want them to appear. Menu section lines are specified by a hyphen. An ampersand (&) precedes letters that will be the underlined (active) letters in the menu or command names. Because cell A7 contains a hyphen, for example, a line in the menu separates the commands Partial **C**alculation and **P**rint Custom. The ampersand (&) in front of the C in Custom in cell A5 indicates that the C is the active (underlined) letter for the menu name, **C**ustom. In cell A8, the & in front of the P makes the P in **P**rint Custom the active letter.

The second column in the table (column B) lists the external reference to the macro that runs when that command is chosen. Notice that the reference does not use an equals sign at the beginning. For example, if the **P**rint Custom command is chosen, the MENU.XLM! Print macro named in cell B8 will run.

The third column (column C) is blank in Excel for Windows. This column is used for shortcut keys for Excel on the Macintosh.

The fourth column (column D) contains a message that appears on the Status Bar when an operator selects the menu or command. An entry in this column is optional. When you select the command **R**emove Menu, for example, the corresponding message, Return to normal menu, appears in the Status Bar.

The fifth column (column E) indicates a custom Help file. These Help files are text files that have been compiled with the Custom Help Conversion Utility available from Microsoft. (Microsoft's phone number and address are listed in the appendix.) An entry in this column is optional.

Adding Commands to Existing Menus

Adding commands to existing menus is an easy way to make macros readily accessible to all levels of users. In fact, adding commands is a convenient way to lend a professional touch to recorded or modified macros.

Figure 29.2 shows the table needed to add a single command. This table uses five columns. In this table, the command Do**w**n Load runs the COMMAND.XLM! Down.Load macro. (The added command and macro name don't have to be the same.) The fourth and fifth columns do not need entries.

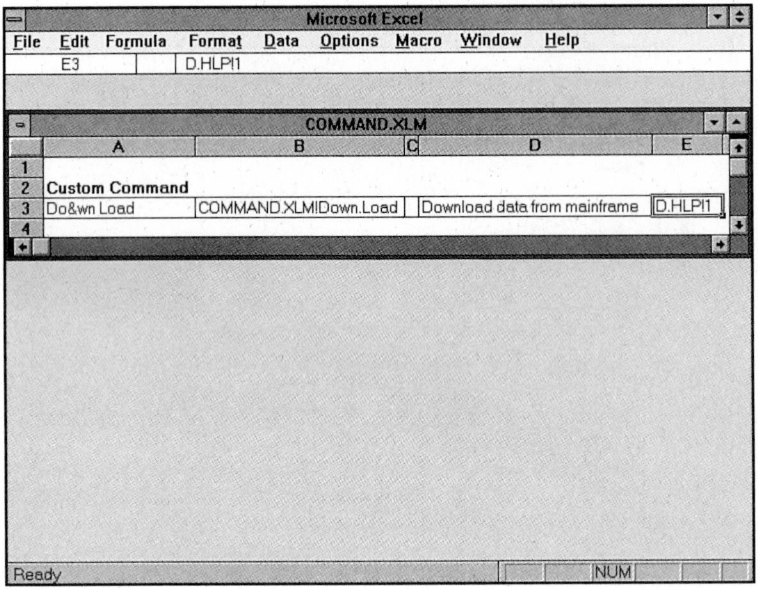

FIG. 29.2

This single-row table defines the custom command Down Load.

Figure 29.3 shows the macros needed to add the Down Load command to the bottom of the **D**ata menu. The macro functions used to add or delete commands are the following:

=ADD.COMMAND(*bar_num,menu,command_ref,position***)**

=DELETE.COMMAND(*bar_num,menu,command***)**

In figure 29.3, the macro Add.Custom.Command adds the Down Load command to the **D**ata menu. The command specifies that the predefined full worksheet menu bar will receive the command in the table whose range is A3:E3. This new command will appear under the **D**ata menu. As no position argument is specified, the Down Load command adds to the bottom of the menu.

NOTE   The name of the macro the command runs is entered in cell B3. Note that this entry is text. If you change the macro's name, you also must change the name in this cell. If you save the macro sheet to a new name, you must change the name in this cell.

The macro Delete.Custom.Command uses the name of the menu and command to delete Down Load from the **D**ata menu on the number 1 predefined full worksheet menu bar.

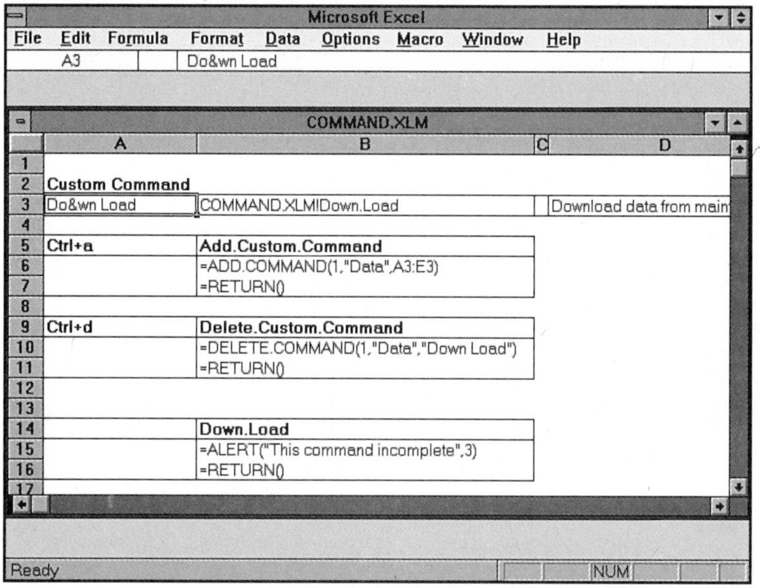

	Microsoft Excel	▼ ◆
<u>F</u>ile <u>E</u>dit Fo<u>r</u>mula For<u>m</u>at <u>D</u>ata <u>O</u>ptions <u>M</u>acro <u>W</u>indow <u>H</u>elp		
A3	Do&wn Load	

⊟	COMMAND.XLM		▼ ▲
	A	B	C	D
1				
2	Custom Command			
3	Do&wn Load	COMMAND.XLM!Down.Load		Download data from main
4				
5	Ctrl+a	Add.Custom.Command		
6		=ADD.COMMAND(1,"Data",A3:E3)		
7		=RETURN()		
8				
9	Ctrl+d	Delete.Custom.Command		
10		=DELETE.COMMAND(1,"Data","Down Load")		
11		=RETURN()		
12				
13				
14		Down.Load		
15		=ALERT("This command incomplete",3)		
16		=RETURN()		
17				

Ready | | NUM |

FIG. 29.3

Using
ADD.COMMAND
and
DELETE.COMMAND.

The macro Down.Load is a dummy macro. It displays an alert box saying that the macro is incomplete. However, this location is where you would put the macro you want the command to run.

NOTE   Remember to use the Fo**r**mula **D**efine Name command to name the top cell in manually typed macros. Macros that run from a menu table, such as the Down.Load macro (refer to fig. 29.3), do not have to be named as a command macro. The top cell in the macro, however, must be named.

Adding Menus to Existing Menu Bars

When you want to add a number of custom commands to a predefined menu bar or add commands associated with a specific task, you probably will want to add a menu to a predefined menu bar. You then can assign your new commands to this new menu. Figure 29.4 shows the Custom menu described in this section.

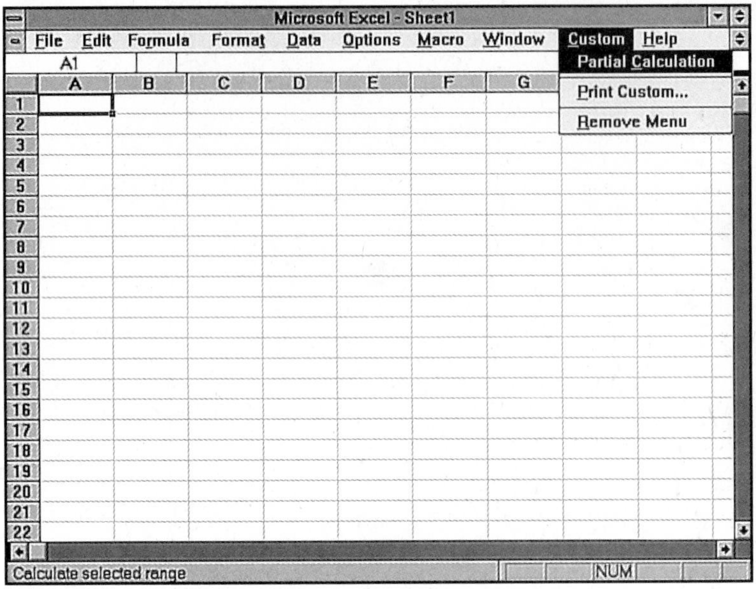

FIG. 29.4

Add your own custom
menus to a menu bar.

Figure 29.5 shows the table needed to define the new menu **Custom**. This menu name will appear to the right of the **W**indow menu on the full worksheet menu bar (1). The **Custom** menu will have these commands: Partial **C**alculation (to run the Calc macro); **P**rint Custom (to run the Print macro); and **R**emove Menu (to run the Menu.Delete macro).

The ADD.MENU( ) and DELETE.MENU( ) functions add and delete menus from a menu bar. These menus have their own sets of commands. The custom menu can be added to or deleted from built-in or custom menu bars. The syntax for the ADD.MENU( ) and DELETE.MENU( ) functions are as follows:

=**ADD.MENU(***bar_num,menu_ref,position***)**

=**DELETE.MENU(***bar_num,menu***)**

The *bar_num* argument is the number of the built-in menu bar. If you are adding to a custom bar, reference the cell containing the ADD.BAR function that added the custom menu bar. The *menu_ref* argument is the range name or cell reference of the menu table. In the example in figure 29.5, this is the range Menu.Custom.Range, with the cell reference A5:E10. The *position* argument specifies where you want the menu inserted in the menu bar. Use the quoted text name of the menu before where you want it inserted. If you omit the position argument, the added menu is placed to the right of the rightmost menu, not including the Help menu.

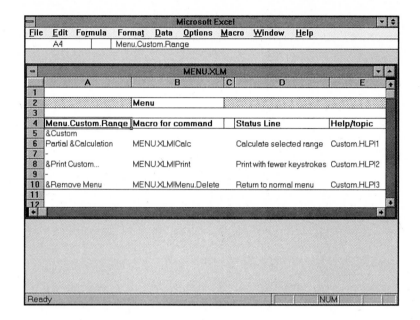

FIG. 29.5

This table defines the
Custom menu and its
own set of commands.

Figure 29.6 shows the ADD.MENU( ) and DELETE.MENU( ) functions;
these functions add and delete the menu named **Custom**. The
ADD.MENU( ) command in B19 is adding to menu bar 1 the menu
described in the table with the range name Menu.Custom.Range,
A5:E10. The DELETE.MENU( ) command deletes the menu named **Cus**-
tom from menu bar 1. The Calc and Print macros are dummy macros
that only display alert boxes.

	T I P
This menu macro used ACTVATE( ) and HIDE( ) to hide the macro sheet from the user. If you save a macro sheet as an add-in file, XLA, it will hide when opened. Chapter 27 describes creating and editing add-in macros. Run this macro with another worksheet open so that you can see the **Custom** menu between **Window** and **Help**. If no worksheet is open, the main menu bar is not displayed, and you cannot see the **Custom** command you added. Remove the menu by choosing the command **R**emove.Menu.	

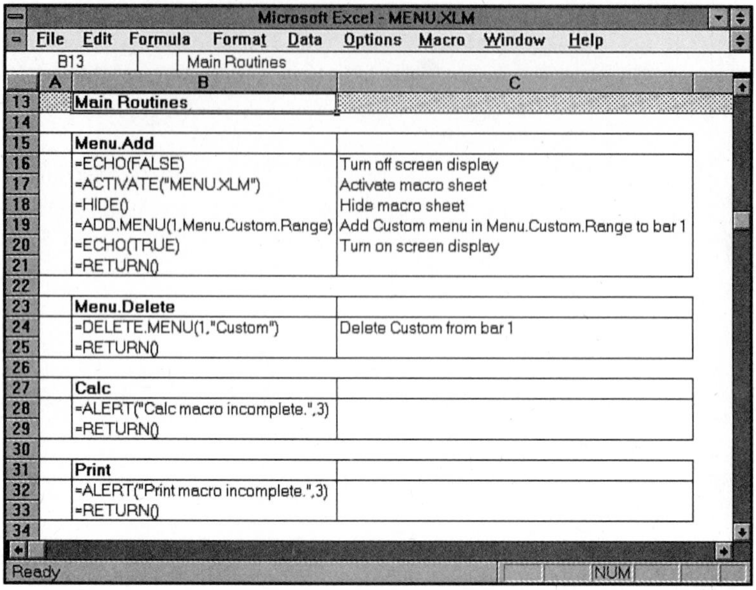

	File Edit Formula Format Data Options Macro Window Help	
	B13	Main Routines
	A	B	C
13	**Main Routines**	
14		
15	**Menu.Add**	
16	=ECHO(FALSE)	Turn off screen display
17	=ACTIVATE("MENU.XLM")	Activate macro sheet
18	=HIDE()	Hide macro sheet
19	=ADD.MENU(1,Menu.Custom.Range)	Add Custom menu in Menu.Custom.Range to bar 1
20	=ECHO(TRUE)	Turn on screen display
21	=RETURN()	
22		
23	**Menu.Delete**	
24	=DELETE.MENU(1,"Custom")	Delete Custom from bar 1
25	=RETURN()	
26		
27	**Calc**	
28	=ALERT("Calc macro incomplete.",3)	
29	=RETURN()	
30		
31	**Print**	
32	=ALERT("Print macro incomplete.",3)	
33	=RETURN()	
34		

Ready   NUM

FIG. 29.6

These commands add
and delete a menu in
the full worksheet
menu bar.

Creating Custom Menu Bars

If you have many commands to add or if you need to build an entire custom system, you can add your own menu bars. You can use 15 custom
menu bars in addition to the 6 built-in menu bars.

Menu bars require tables that define all the menus and commands in the
bar. Figure 29.7 shows the tables that define the custom menu bar; the
corresponding functions are shown in figure 29.8.

To specify, add, and show a custom menu bar, use the following order:

1. Add a custom menu bar with the ADD.BAR( ) function.

2. Add menus to this bar by referencing the bar's number and its
    menu table with the ADD.MENU( ) function.

3. When you need the bar, display it with the SHOW.BAR( ) function.

Figure 29.9 shows how this custom menu bar is added in the BAR.ADD
macro.

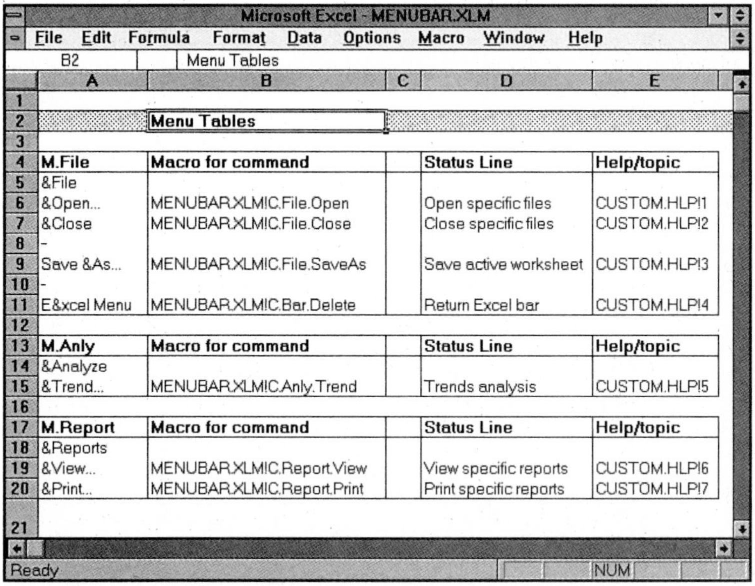

Microsoft Excel - MENUBAR.XLM

File Edit Formula Format Data Options Macro Window Help

B2 | Menu Tables

	A	B	C	D	E
1					
2		**Menu Tables**			
3					
4	**M.File**	**Macro for command**		**Status Line**	**Help/topic**
5	&File				
6	&Open...	MENUBAR.XLM!C.File.Open		Open specific files	CUSTOM.HLP!1
7	&Close	MENUBAR.XLM!C.File.Close		Close specific files	CUSTOM.HLP!2
8	-				
9	Save &As...	MENUBAR.XLM!C.File.SaveAs		Save active worksheet	CUSTOM.HLP!3
10	-				
11	E&xcel Menu	MENUBAR.XLM!C.Bar.Delete		Return Excel bar	CUSTOM.HLP!4
12					
13	**M.Anly**	**Macro for command**		**Status Line**	**Help/topic**
14	&Analyze				
15	&Trend...	MENUBAR.XLM!C.Anly.Trend		Trends analysis	CUSTOM.HLP!5
16					
17	**M.Report**	**Macro for command**		**Status Line**	**Help/topic**
18	&Reports				
19	&View...	MENUBAR.XLM!C.Report.View		View specific reports	CUSTOM.HLP!6
20	&Print...	MENUBAR.XLM!C.Report.Print		Print specific reports	CUSTOM.HLP!7
21					

Ready NUM

FIG. 29.7

Tables defining the menus used in a custom menu bar.

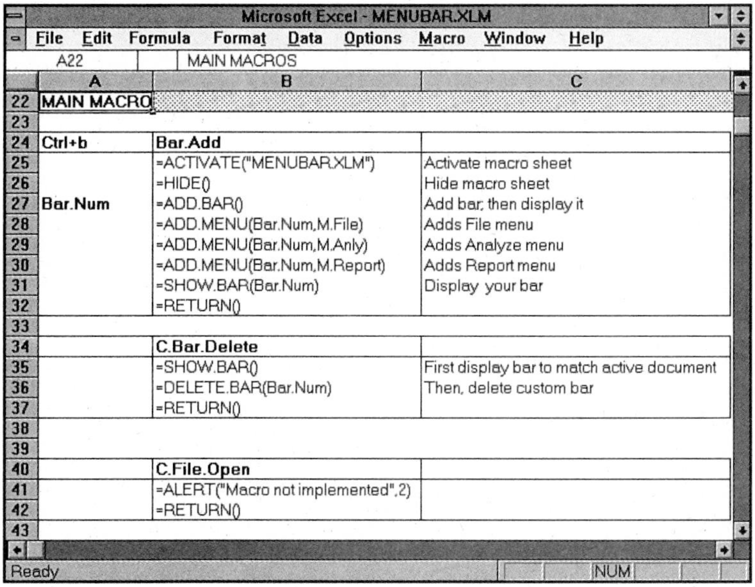

Microsoft Excel - MENUBAR.XLM

File Edit Formula Format Data Options Macro Window Help

A22 | MAIN MACROS

	A	B	C
22	MAIN MACRO		
23			
24	**Ctrl+b**	**Bar.Add**	
25		=ACTIVATE("MENUBAR.XLM")	Activate macro sheet
26		=HIDE()	Hide macro sheet
27	**Bar.Num**	=ADD.BAR()	Add bar; then display it
28		=ADD.MENU(Bar.Num,M.File)	Adds File menu
29		=ADD.MENU(Bar.Num,M.Anly)	Adds Analyze menu
30		=ADD.MENU(Bar.Num,M.Report)	Adds Report menu
31		=SHOW.BAR(Bar.Num)	Display your bar
32		=RETURN()	
33			
34		**C.Bar.Delete**	
35		=SHOW.BAR()	First display bar to match active document
36		=DELETE.BAR(Bar.Num)	Then, delete custom bar
37		=RETURN()	
38			
39			
40		**C.File.Open**	
41		=ALERT("Macro not implemented",2)	
42		=RETURN()	
43			

Ready NUM

FIG. 29.8

These functions display the menu bar defined in figure 29.7.

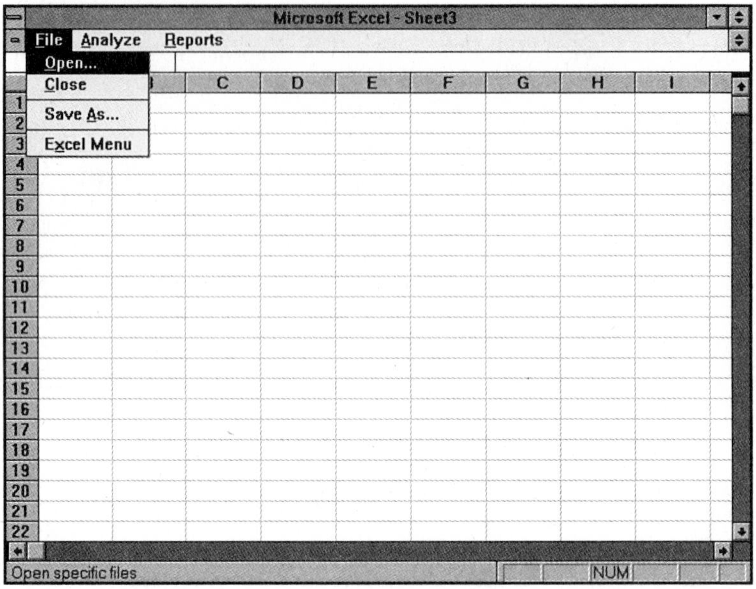

FIG. 29.9

The Bar.Add macro adds the menu bar, specifies its menus, and displays the bar.

As with menus, when you add a menu bar, the bar is assigned a number. This number is returned by the ADD.BAR( ) function. When you need the number that specifies a bar, refer to the cell containing the ADD.BAR( ) function that added the bar. In figure 29.8, for example, a bar is added with the ADD.BAR( ) function in cell B27. This cell is named BAR.NUM( ). If you press Ctrl+` to switch the display to see the result of ADD.BAR( ), you would see the number assigned to this bar.

To remove this added bar, use the DELETE.BAR( ) function in cell B36. Reference the cell containing the ADD.BAR( ) function, DELETE.BAR(BAR.NUM).

When you are ready to delete your custom menu bar, use the functions in the order shown in the BAR.A.DELETE macro. You must show another bar before you can delete your custom bar. If you leave the argument empty in the SHOW.BAR( ) function in cell B35, Excel will display the appropriate menu bar that matches the active document, worksheet, chart, and so on. In the SHOW.BAR( ) function in cell B36, Excel shows whatever bar is the default for the current mode of Excel.

FROM HERE...

For Related Information:

◄◄ "Naming Cells," p. 210.

Drawing Dialog Boxes

You may want to add a custom dialog box to macros when a command needs multiple items of information. Dialog boxes also are useful for giving an operator a choice of options that make a command operate differently. By using Excel macros, you can create custom dialog boxes that have all the features used by built-in dialog boxes. The following descriptions do not cover the most advanced features but do cover such features as groups of options, list boxes, setting defaults, and using the dialog box results to control macro operation.

Understanding a Dialog Table

To create a dialog box, you must specify the items in a dialog box and the related locations in a dialog table. You can type these tables, but a far easier method is to draw the dialog box with the Dialog Editor and paste the resulting information into a table in the macro sheet. A good understanding of the information in the table that creates dialog boxes will help you if you need to manually make minor changes.

Figure 29.10 shows the dialog box produced by the dialog table in figure 29.11. A dialog table requires seven columns of information. Figure 29.11 shows three additional columns of information on the sides of the table (columns A, I, K). A contains reference information. I contains the range names that refer left to the cells containing the results of the dialog box. K contains the contents of a scrolling list.

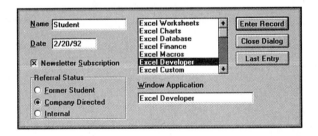

FIG. 29.10

A dialog box like this one can receive entered data and control macro operation.

	A	B	C	D	E	F	G	H	I	J	K
4	Type	Item	X	Y	Width	Height	Dlg.Text	Int/Result	Result Names		Class.List
5	blank				636	177					Excel Worksheets
6	text	5	24	14	50	18	&Name				Excel Charts
7	text edit	6	74	12	170	18		Student	Rslt.Name		Excel Database
8	text	5	24	44	90	18	&Date				Excel Finance
9	number edit	8	74	42	101	18		33654.5433912	Rslt.Date		Excel Macros
10	check box	13	24	72	220	18	Newsletter &Subscription	TRUE	Rslt.News		Excel Developer
11	group box	14	24	96	220	72	Referral Status				Excel Custom
12	radio group	11						2	Rslt.Referral		WinWord Intro
13	radio button	12	32	114	172	15	&Former Student				WinWord Adv
14	radio button	12	32	132	164	15	&Company Directed				WinWord BASIC
15	radio button	12	32	150	164	15	&Internal				Window Database
16	text	5	268	108	264	12	&Window Application				Window DB BASIC
17	text edit	6	268	126	264	18		Excel Macros	Rslt.AppText		
18	linked list box	16	268	12	207	90	Class.List	6	Rslt.AppNum		
19	default ok button	1	491	11	121	21	Enter Record				
20	cancel button	2	491	38	121	21	Close Dialog				
21	ok button	3	491	65	121	21	Last Entry				

FIG. 29.11

The dialog table and list that produces the dialog box shown in figure 29.10.

The seven columns in a dialog table control the following aspects of a dialog box:

Column	Control
B	Item number describes the item being displayed
C	X position of item's upper-left corner
D	Y position of item's upper-left corner
E	Width of item
F	Height of item
G	Text for item. Not all items have text labels.
H	Initial value when dialog box displays. Entered results from dialog box after it closes.

In figure 29.11, the seven columns are in columns B through H. For example, the TRUE/FALSE result from the Newsletter Subscription check box in cell H10 can be referenced in a macro with the name Rslt.News. Column K contains the contents of the linked list box that is specified in cell G18.

The position of items in the box, their height, and their width are specified in columns C, D, E, and F. The top-left corner of the dialog box is where X equals 0 and Y equals 0 for positioning of items in the box. The X, Y, Width, and Height measurements are in screen dots.

In the example, row 5 describes the dialog box outline. Other rows describe a specific type of item or group. The item types that correspond to each item number in column B are listed in a following table. The numbers in columns B through F are calculated by the drawing you will create in the Dialog Editor. The text for items, such as titles or option names, are also entered in the Dialog Editor. Specify the underlined active letter for options, check boxes, and text boxes by preceding a letter in the name of that item with an ampersand (&). You can draw this box in the Dialog Editor, and then modify it after you have pasted it into the macro sheet.

The results of data entered in a dialog box appear in the seventh column, H, of the dialog box range. After a dialog box displays and data is entered, your macro can use the information in column H as data for entry or to control macro settings and operations. The later section describes how to use the results from a dialog box.

> Type labels in the column to the right of the results column in a dialog box. You then can use the Formula Create Names command to assign these names to the cells to the right that contain results. In figure 29.11, the labels in column I were used to name the result cells in column H. You will find it much easier to reference to a dialog box result as `Rslt.Name` instead of the more inscrutable H7.

T I P

Text edit boxes, such as the Name edit box in row 7, place the name you enter into cell H7. The date you type in the Date edit box (a numeric edit box) in row 9 is put into cell H9. The date appears as the serial number that Excel uses to represent dates. (On the macro sheet, you should format this number as a date, but it appears as a number.) Check boxes return TRUE when selected and FALSE when cleared. The TRUE in cell H10 represents a selected check box.

Option buttons should be displayed in groups. When you insert a *Group* of option buttons by using the Dialog Editor, the grouping of these items is done for you. The first item in a group is the group box, item 14, in row 11. The group box is followed by item 11, the radio group. The option buttons, items 12, then follow. Although multiple option buttons exist, the group returns one answer, the number of which option button was selected. The number used is the order in which the option buttons are listed. For example, the second item 12 is button 2. The number of the button selected returns in cell 12, the row containing the radio group.

One of the powerful features of dialog boxes are scrolling lists. You can draw different types of scrolling lists by using the Dialog Editor. In figure 29.11, the scrolling list part of a linked list is item 16 in row 18. To define the cells containing the contents for the scrolling list, enter in the text column, *G*, the range name you have assigned to the list. In figure 29.11, the list is defined for the box by typing *Class.List* in cell G18. Class.List is the range name of cells K5:K16.

The dialog box displays a linked list containing different Windows application courses. A linked list has two parts; a scrolling list and a text edit box. If you select from the list, your selection appears in the edit box where you can edit it.

The list part of a linked list returns the row position of the selected item in the list. This number is returned to the result column for item 16, the list. The result appears in H18. You can change this number into the exact text used in the list. This method is good for restricting data-entry operators to specific entries. This method also ensures against misspellings or typing errors.

Your macro can calculate which item from this list was selected by using the number in H18 combined with the INDEX( ) function. For example, the list in the example is in cells with the range name of Class.List. The formula that returns the item from the list is the following:

=INDEX(Class.List,H18)

Because the result cell of the list has been named, you also can use the following formula:

=INDEX(Class.List,Rslt.AppNum)

For example, the preceding formulas would return Excel Developer if cell H18 contains 6, and the Class.List is the range K5:K16.

If you want to retrieve what the user has edited or typed into the edit box portion of a linked list, use the result shown in cell H17. The text edit box, item 6, that appears directly before a linked list, item 16, returns the item from the list or the edited item as text. Therefore, you can use an edited version of text from the list rather than an exact version.

The results from clicking on command buttons appear in the cell containing the DIALOG.BOX( ) function that displays the dialog box. Cancel buttons return FALSE when chosen. OK buttons return their numeric row number within the dialog box when chosen. For example, the non-default OK button that uses the label Last Entry is the sixteenth item listed in the dialog box range. If you choose this button, the cell that displayed this dialog box, containing DIALOG.BOX( ), contains the result 16.

Table 29.1 is a list of items available in dialog boxes. Take note that some items must be in a specific order. For example, an option button group must precede an option button.

Table 29.1. Items Available in Dialog Boxes

Item	Type	Description
1	OK button (default)	Closes the dialog box and returns results in the Init/Result column. Button is selected when box opens. Name of button is specified in Text column.
2	Cancel button (nondefault)	Closes the dialog box and does not return data. Name appears in Text column.
3	OK button (nondefault)	Closes the dialog box and returns results in the Init/Result column. Button is only triggered if you actually click it or tab to the button before you press Enter. Name appears in Text column.
4	Cancel button (default)	Closes the dialog box and does not return results. Button is selected when box opens. Name appears in Text column.
5	Text	Used as titles or labels.
6	Text edit box	Text column ignored; displays initial value in Init/Result column.
7	Integer edit box	Like text edit box; accepts nondecimal numbers -32765 to 32767.
8	Number edit box	Like text edit box; accepts only numbers. Decimal numbers are accepted.
9	Formula edit box	Like text edit box; accepts formulas, numbers, or text.
10	Reference edit box	Like text edit box; shows in Init/Result as text in R1C1 format.
11	Option button group	Must immediately precede a group of option buttons; text is the name of group box; Init/Result returns the number of the option in group selected.
12	Option button	Option button; text is the name of the button; number of selected button returned to Init/Result of Option button group. Groups of option buttons must be in sequence and preceded by an option button group (11).

continues

Table 29.1. Continued

Item	Type	Description
13	Check box	Text is the name of box. Init/Result is TRUE if selected; FALSE if deselected; #N/A if gray.
14	Group box	An outline box that does not affect operation. Use for appearance. It can be used to create lines or boxes and does not affect the operation of other items.
15	List box	Lists items. List referenced in text column using a range name (see fig. 29.11). Init/Result returns number of item in list selected. Use the INDEX() worksheet function to extract text item from list using this number.
16	Linked list box	Same as list box, but must be preceded in dialog table by a text edit box (6). The list item selected appears in edit box. Init/Result returns number of item, but preceding text box returns text item from list.
17	Icon	One of three (1-3) icons with buttons such as ALERT. Enter 1 to 3 in text column.
18	Linked file list box	Lists files in directory. Must follow a text edit box (6) and precede a linked drive and directory list (19).
19	Linked drive and directory list box	Lists drives and directories. If item precedes a text box (5), the text box will show the current drive and directory.
20	Directory text	Shows name of current directory.
21	Drop-down list box	Shows a list of items. List is referenced like a list box (15). Init/Result contains the number of default selection from list. The height of drop-down list is in the Height column.
22	Drop-down combination box	Like a drop-down list but it must follow a text edit box (6). The user can enter an unlisted value in the edit box.

Item	Type	Description
23	Picture buttons	This button acts like an OK button to close the dialog box and enter dialog box results in the Init/Result columns. Draw the button in the macro sheet using Excel's drawing tools. Select the object and notice its object identifier in the Reference Area— for example, Drawing 2. Type this object identifier into this item's row in the Text column. Use item number *223* to create a nonbutton graphic.

Drawing Dialog Boxes

Without the Dialog Editor, creating custom dialog boxes is an incredible chore. With the Dialog Editor, however, it can be fun—almost like drawing in a painting application.

Figure 29.12 shows a dialog box in the Dialog Editor. You can resize and move each item in the dialog box, as well as the outline of the dialog box.

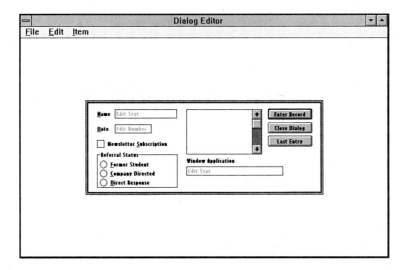

FIG. 29.12

Use the Dialog Editor to create the items you want.

Start the Dialog Editor from within Excel by selecting the Excel Control menu (press Alt, space bar) and then choosing the **R**un command. Select the **D**ialog Editor option and press Enter. The Dialog Editor will appear with a small, empty dialog box at midscreen.

Drag the corner or edge of the empty box to change it to the size you want. Add items to the box by selecting items from the Item menu. As soon as you add an item, move it into position by dragging on its center. Resize boxes or text areas by dragging on their edges. Type text labels while an item is selected. In some cases, you may need to type a blank space at the end of text for the label to show completely.

You can save time reorganizing the dialog table later if you select items in the order prescribed in table 29.1. For example, add an option group, and then add the option buttons for that group as the next items. In many cases, you can press Enter after adding an item as a shortcut to get the next appropriate item or a duplicate of the item. To delete items, select them, and then choose Edit Clear or press the Delete key.

To manually enter X,Y positions, change labels, or enter the Init/Result values, select an item, and then choose the Edit Info command; or double-click on the item. Figure 29.13 shows the Info box for an option group box.

Choose the Edit Info command to edit or align selected items precisely.

After you finish adding and arranging items, select the entire dialog box by choosing the Edit Select Dialog command. Choose the Edit Copy command. Switch to Excel by pressing Alt+Tab. Next, activate the macro sheet in which you want the table. Select the cell at the top-left corner of where you want the table, and choose the Edit Paste command. While the table is still selected, choose the Formula Define Name command and assign a name to the dialog box table. You may want to format the table as shown in figure 29.11. Make sure that items are in the correct order as described in table 29.1. If they are not listed in the correct order, insert and delete rows; then copy and paste so that items are in the correct order.

If you need to edit a dialog box, you can make minor changes within the table on the macro sheet. To make major changes, select the same area of the dialog table that was pasted into the macro sheet, copy it with **Edit Copy**, and paste it into the Dialog Editor with **Edit Paste**. When you are finished editing, copy the dialog box and paste it back into the macro sheet.

NOTE Never leave blank rows in the dialog table. A blank row in the dialog table causes the DIALOG.BOX( ) function to fail.

Using Dialog Boxes

The dialog box that you drew with the Dialog Editor appears with the single function DIALOG.BOX( ), as shown in cell B39 of figure 29.14. The function has the following syntax:

=DIALOG.BOX(CLASS.DLG.BOX)

Here, the range B5:H21 has been assigned the name CLASS.DLG.BOX. It contains the seven columns of information required by the dialog box. Notice that no blank rows occur in this range.

	A	B	C
28		Main Routines	
29			
30	Ctrl+e	Class.Enter.Data	Data entry w/Dialog
31		=ACTIVATE("CLASSDLG.XLS")	Activate database sheet
32		=ECHO(FALSE)	Turn off screen refresh for speed
33		Set defaults, start dialog box	
34	Class.Restart	=SET.VALUE(Rslt.Name,"Student")	Set Name default
35		=SET.VALUE(Rslt.Date,NOW())	Set Date as today's date
36		=SET.VALUE(Rslt.News,TRUE)	Set Newsletter as checked
37		=SET.VALUE(Rslt.Referral,2)	Select second option button
38		=SET.VALUE(Rslt.AppNum,6)	Select item 6 in list
39	Class.Dlg.Show	=DIALOG.BOX(Class.Dlg.Box)	Run dialog box
40		Check Cancel button	
41		=IF(Class.Dlg.Show=FALSE,GOTO(Class.End))	Cancel button, then End
42		Insert Row in Database	
43		=SELECT(CLASSDLG.XLS!Database)	Select database
44		=SELECT("R[2]")	Select row two down
45		=INSERT(2)	Insert a row for new data
46		Insert Data in Blank Row	
47		=FORMULA(Rslt.Name,OFFSET(ACTIVE.CELL(),0,0))	Name in active cell, offset 0
48		=FORMULA(IF(Rslt.News=TRUE,"Yes","No"),OFFSET(ACTIVE.CELL(),0,1))	News checked, then Yes, offset 1
49		=FORMULA(Rslt.Date,OFFSET(ACTIVE.CELL(),0,2))	Date, offset 2 cells right
50		=FORMULA(CHOOSE(Rslt.Referral,"Former","Company","Internal"),OFFSET(ACTIVE.CELL(),0,3))	Choice from Optn, offset 3 right
51		=FORMULA(Rslt.AppText,OFFSET(ACTIVE.CELL(),0,4))	List text; offset 4 cells right
52		Check for Done Entering button	
53		=IF(Class.Dlg.Show=16,GOTO(Class.End))	Done Entering button, then End
54		=GOTO(Class.Restart)	Otherwise, repeat
55	Class.End	=FORMULA.GOTO(!$A$1)	Move to cell A1 on active workshee
56		=ECHO(TRUE)	Turn on screen refresh
57		=RETURN()	

FIG. 29.14

The macro that displays, updates, and uses information from the dialog box shown in figure 29.10.

T I P   The names in column I of the dialog table shown in figure 29.11, refer to the cells in the Init/Result column, H. The names in column A of the macro, shown in figure 29.14, refer to the adjacent cell to the right in column B.

Using this method, your macros can use readable names to refer to the results that a dialog box or function returns. You can quickly create names, such as those in figure 29.14, by selecting the names in column A and the adjacent cells in column B and then choosing the Formula Create Names command. Select the Left column as containing the names of the macro cells in column B of figure 29.14. Press F5, select a name, and choose OK to test whether you have correctly created the names.

Setting Dialog Defaults

Initial dialog default values—the values returned by dialog entries—and selections appear in the dialog table in the Init/Result column. Initial values that a dialog box displays are those values it finds in this column. The values must be in the correct row location as specified in the table that describes each type of item. If you want a dialog box to start with specific values, use the SET.VALUE function to put a constant value in each appropriate Init/Result cell.

In figure 29.14, the cells B34:B38 set the initial values the dialog box displays on startup. For example, cell B34 places the text "Student" in cell H7, which has the name Rslt.Name. Cell B35 sets today's date serial number as the Date default. Cell H9 shows the serial date number, but if you format cell H9 as a date, the cell appears in the dialog box as a date. Cell B36 sets the Newsletter check box to selected. Cell B37 selects the second option button. Cell B38 makes the list display with the sixth item selected.

If you want the dialog box to redisplay with the values that were last entered or the options last selected, do not reset the values in the Init/Result column. If you want the dialog box to open the first time with the settings from the last time the macro was run, save the macro so that the Init/Result column is preserved when it is next opened.

Displaying the Dialog Box

Display your dialog box with a simple command, DIALOG.BOX(ref). The reference is the dialog table you created with the Dialog Editor. Make sure that you reference exactly the right range.

Retrieving Dialog Input

When you choose the OK button in a dialog box, the information entered and options selected appear in the Init/Result column next to the appropriate dialog item. If you choose the Cancel button, the Init/Result column does not change.

In the Enter Records macro, the IF( ) function in B41 checks to see if the Cancel button was chosen. If Cancel was chosen, the DIALOG.BOX( ) function returns FALSE. In this case, the IF( ) function sends the macro to B55, the cell named Class.End.

Cells B43 to B45 select the range named Database on the worksheet named CLASSDLG.XLS. The next two cells insert a new row two rows from the top of the database (see fig. 29.15).

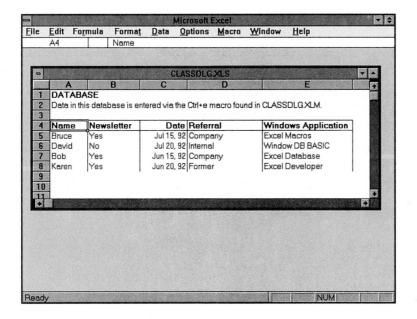

Information is taken from the dialog box and entered into the blank database row by the FORMULA( ) functions in B47:B51. The FORMULA( ) functions reference the dialog box entries by name: for example, Rslt.Name. These names are shown in column I of the dialog table. (These are not part of the table but are there for documentation.) The FORMULA( ) function then puts the named result into the worksheet cell specified by the OFFSET( ) function. Each OFFSET( ) function uses the active cell, the first cell in the blank row, as a base point and offsets the entered value by a different column position. The row argument for OFFSET( ) is zero, so data is entered in the same row as the active worksheet cell. Again, because ECHO(FALSE) was used at the beginning, you will not see this happen.

In cell B50, a CHOOSE( ) function is used to change the 1, 2, or 3 result from option buttons into a text answer stored in the database. When Rslt.Referral contains 1, for example, the choice is "Former."

Cell B53 checks to see whether the nondefault OK button, Done Entering, was selected in the dialog box. If it was selected, the macro goes to Class.End, cell B55, and the macro ends. When a nondefault OK or Cancel button is selected, its position among items in the dialog table, 16 in this case, is returned to the DIALOG.BOX( ) function. In this case, the value returned to DIALOG.BOX( ) by buttons is stored in the name Class.Dlg.Show.

When the Cancel button is chosen, cell B41 sends the macro to its end, Class.End. When the Done Entering button is chosen, cell B53 sends the macro to its end, Class.End. The final ECHO(TRUE) function refreshes the screen display so that you can see the additions to the database. If you want to see the macro as it operates, remove the ECHO (FALSE) function in B32 and rerun the macro. Notice that macro operation is slower when the screen is redrawn after each change.

FROM HERE...

For Related Information:

◄◄ "Pasting Names and Functions into Formulas," p. 191.

◄◄ "Naming Cells," p. 210.

Chapter Summary

Excel's macro language has a great deal of capability and flexibility. You can write attractive applications with extensive analytical, printing, and charting capabilities with far less planning, programming, and maintenance than if you programmed them in a language such as C.

This book does not touch on a number of advanced macro capabilities, such as controlling other Windows applications through Excel macros, linking and controlling data exchanges through Dynamic Data Exchange, or using C-language routines with Dynamic Link Libraries. Although you can do a great deal with Excel's macro language by itself, the top end is wide open.

Exploring Sample Macros

The macros examined in this section range from recordings that have been modified to manually programmed macros. Many of the command macros were created by recording a macro and then modifying it. One of the best ways to learn is through example. Use these macros as a basis for exploring. Get them to work as shown; then change them and enhance them.

Reproducing these Macros

You can create all of the macros presented in this chapter by using the same process, and you won't need to type much once you get the hang of following the steps. To reproduce the macros in this chapter, complete the following steps:

1. Open a clean macro sheet.

2. Enter the macro title in row 1. Macro functions go below the title. Leave a column on the left for labels and a column on the right for description.

3. Select the cell containing the title, and use the Formula Define Name command to name the title cell with the name you want for the macro. Select the Command or Function option depending upon the type of macro. If the macro is a command macro, enter a

shortcut key in the **K**ey edit box. Select a category if you want the macro to appear in a category within the Paste Function dialog box.

4. Select the cell in which you want to enter a macro function.

5. Choose the Formula Paste Function command, or click on the Paste Function tool.

6. Select the function you need from the scrolling list. Be certain that the Paste **A**rguments check box is on, then choose OK.

7. In the Formula Bar, double-click on any argument to select the argument. Enter the argument by typing, clicking or pointing to a reference or by using the Paste Function or Paste Name commands. (Double-clicking on an argument selects it.) Delete arguments by double-clicking on them, then pressing Del.

8. Type labels down the column to the left of the macro functions. Type descriptions of what the macro functions do down the column to the right.

9. Select the label cells and the function cells to their right, then choose the Formula **C**reate Names command. Be certain that the **L**eft Column check box is the only box selected, then choose OK.

10. Press the Goto key, F5; then select a name and determine whether the appropriate function cell is selected.

11. Save the macro sheet.

12. Open a worksheet, and run the macro as described.

Creating Command Macros

Command macros are used most frequently to increase productivity by decreasing repetitive tasks. As Chapters 27 and 28 describe, productivity macros often are built by recording a task and then modifying the command macro that was recorded. These macros have been chosen because they are useful and they demonstrate the principles described in Chapters 27 and 28.

Cross-Checking Data with IF, AND, and GOTO

The macro shown in figure 30.1 cross-checks entered data. You can use it to cross-check data being entered into a database row or into entry areas of a worksheet. One IF( ) function checks for the Cancel button selection from the input box. If Cancel was chosen, then the cell Num contains FALSE; so, the macro goes to the cell named End.

The other IF( ) function verifies that the value entered in the input box—returned to cell B2 (Num)—is greater than 2 and less than 7. The alert box shows any incorrect numeric value entered in the input box by joining together the number stored in B2 (Num) and the text. Text and numbers can be joined by using the ampersand (&). The Formula Bar shows the full ALERT( ) function.

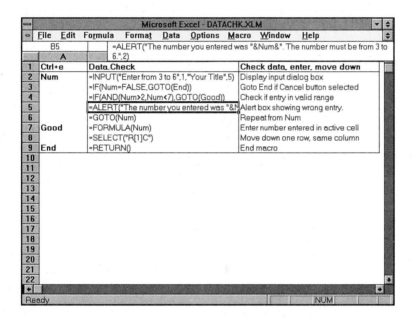

	Microsoft Excel - DATACHK.XLM	

| File | Edit | Formula | Format | Data | Options | Macro | Window | Help |

B5		=ALERT("The number you entered was "&Num&". The number must be from 3 to 6.",2)

	A		
1	Ctrl+e	Data.Check	Check data, enter, move down
2	Num	=INPUT("Enter from 3 to 6",1,"Your Title",5)	Display input dialog box
3		=IF(Num=FALSE,GOTO(End))	Goto End if Cancel button selected
4		=IF(AND(Num>2,Num<7),GOTO(Good))	Check if entry in valid range
5		=ALERT("The number you entered was "&N	Alert box showing wrong entry.
6		=GOTO(Num)	Repeat from Num
7	Good	=FORMULA(Num)	Enter number entered in active cell
8		=SELECT("R[1]C")	Move down one row, same column
9	End	=RETURN()	End macro
10			

Ready ... NUM

FIG. 30.1

Use IF() and GOTO() functions to check returned values and to change the macro's direction of operation.

Formatting Exception Reports with FOR.CELL

Before running this macro, activate a worksheet and enter numbers greater or less than 20. Select the range containing these numbers, then run the macro. The macro shown in figure 30.2 steps through each cell in the selected range and checks the value of its contents. *Shader* is the *ref_name* that holds the cell reference of the cell being examined. If less than 20, the SELECT(Shader) function selects the cell being checked. The PATTERNS( ) function then shades that cell red. (Some functions can be joined into a single statement by using the plus [+] sign, as you see in cells B3 and B4.)

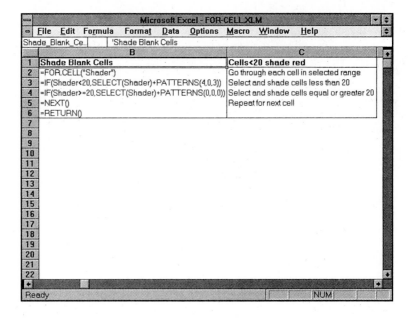

Entering Data
in a Calculated Location
with OFFSET

In the macro in figure 30.3, the FOR() and NEXT() functions step a data-entry macro through a series of cells to enter sales information for consecutive years. This procedure is the same type of stepping process used to transfer information from a worksheet form or result column in a dialog box into a blank row in a database.

Open a blank worksheet and select any cell. Then run the macro. The macro first asks for a starting year, using 1992 as the default. Then the macro asks for a sales amount. It repeats through following years, entering years and data in rows across from the active cell. Notice that by specifying a location for the data within the FORMULA() function, the active cell on the worksheet never moves. This feature makes data entry and transfer faster.

In this macro, the INPUT() cell requests a starting year. The cell is named Year so that the name can be used whenever the value that was entered is needed. The FOR() and NEXT() functions create a loop that repeats the functions between them. The first time through the loop, the number 0 is stored in Data; the second time through 1; and so on. The first FORMULA() function uses Year+Data as the value to be entered.

This string is the increasing year number. The OFFSET( ) function positions where the year is entered. The active cell is used as a base point for the offset. The data is entered in the same row (0) as the active cell, and the number of columns over is determined by the number stored in Data. The second formula works in the same way, but the data is entered one row down from the active cell.

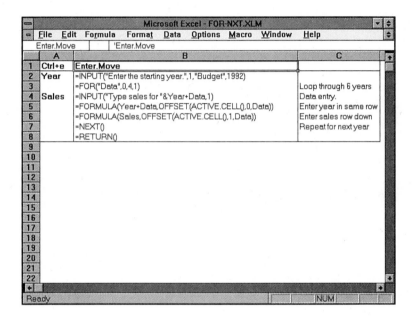

FIG. 30.3

Combine FORMULA( )
with OFFSET( ) to
rapidly enter data in
known locations.

Printing with a Macro

When you have many print jobs to perform , the macro shown in figure 30.4 cuts through the keystrokes. This macro shows how productive a recorded macro can be when it has been slightly modified. The macro uses the FORMULA.GOTO( ) function (recorded by pressing F5) to display all the named ranges on the active sheet. The rest of the macro prints the selected named range. You will be prompted for the number of copies you want to print. Choose Cancel in the Goto box to end the macro.

The PRINT( ) function in cell B4 illustrates how omitted optional arguments can still require commas as placeholders to position the other arguments. The following line contains the PRINT( ) function in B5:

    =PRINT(1,,,B4,FALSE,FALSE,1,FALSE,1)

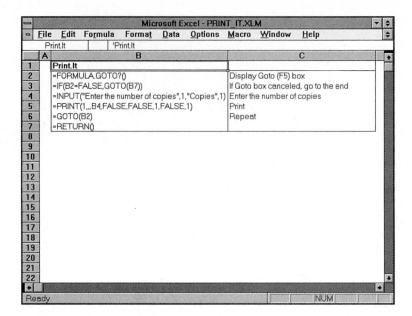

FIG. 30.4

Use this macro to print multiple named ranges or typed references.

Testing for an Open Sheet and Opening It

The macro in figure 30.5 tests whether a sheet named STUFF.XLS is open. If the sheet is open, the macro activates the sheet. If the sheet is not open, the macro displays the File Open dialog box and inserts *.* in the Name edit box so you can search through directories for STUFF.XLS or the equivalent file.

This macro uses the DOCUMENTS( ) function to find the names of all open sheets. DOCUMENTS( ) returns an array (a list) of all open sheets. If you select DOCUMENTS( )—include its parentheses—and press F9, you see the list of open sheet names.

The OR( ) function tests the name STUFF.XLS against all names in DOCU-MENTS( ). The result of the OR( ) condition is stored in the cell named Doc.Test. If there is a single match, the OR( ) function returns TRUE. If TRUE is returned, STUFF.XLS is open, so it is activated. If TRUE is not returned, an alert dialog box displays and asks the user whether he wants to open the file. If he chooses OK, the File Open box displays. You can change the quoted text used as the OPEN( ) argument string you want to search for in the File Open dialog box.

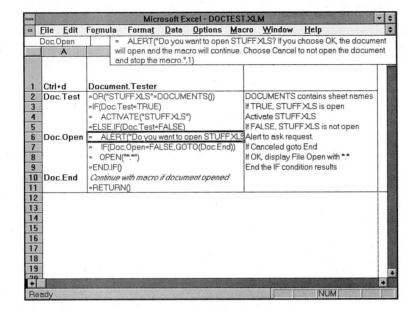

Microsoft Excel - DOCTEST.XLM

	File Edit Formula Format Data Options Macro Window Help
Doc.Open	= ALERT("Do you want to open STUFF.XLS? If you choose OK, the document will open and the macro will continue. Choose Cancel to not open the document and stop the macro.",1)

	A		
1	Ctrl+d	Document.Tester	
2	Doc.Test	=OR("STUFF.XLS"=DOCUMENTS())	DOCUMENTS contains sheet names
3		=IF(Doc.Test=TRUE)	If TRUE, STUFF.XLS is open
4		= ACTIVATE("STUFF.XLS")	Activate STUFF.XLS
5		=ELSE.IF(Doc.Test=FALSE)	If FALSE, STUFF.XLS is not open
6	Doc.Open	= ALERT("Do you want to open STUFF.XLS	Alert to ask request.
7		= IF(Doc.Open=FALSE,GOTO(Doc.End))	If Canceled goto End
8		= OPEN("*.*")	If OK, display File Open with *.*
9		=END.IF()	End the IF condition results
10	Doc.End	*Continue with macro if document opened*	
11		=RETURN()	
12			
13			
14			
15			
16			
17			
18			
19			
20			

Ready   NUM

FIG. 30.5

This macro tests whether STUFF.XLS is open; if not, the macro displays the File Open dialog box.

Creating Function Macros

As you learned in previous chapters, function macros are productive and reduce errors when you frequently use the same formulas. These examples show some methods of handling calculations where values from tables must be looked up or where one function handles more than one type of calculation.

Choosing between Multiple Solutions

In the Volume macro (see fig. 30.6), one of three solutions is calculated, depending on whether the type argument is a 1, 2, or 3. If the type is a 1, then the volume of a cylinder is found. If the type is a 2, the volume of a cone is calculated. If the type is 3, the volume of a sphere is calculated. For example, entering the following function:

=SHEET1.XLM!Volume(3,5,1)

returns the volume of a cylinder.

In this example, a slight performance increase is created by using IF( ) functions to calculate only the desired formula rather than all three. A CHOOSE( ) function then returns the result of the calculated formula. A CHOOSE( ) function uses the value of its first argument, *Type*, to select from a list of arguments that follows. For example, if Type is 1, then CHOOSE( ) returns the value in A14. If Type is 2, CHOOSE( ) returns the value in A15.

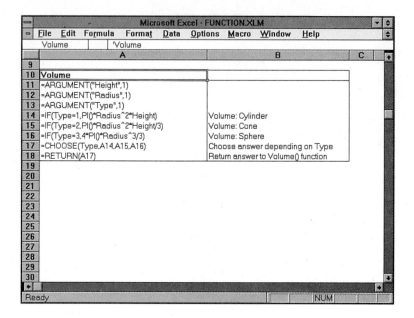

FIG. 30.6

This function macro demonstrates choosing between calculations.

Looking Up Molecular Weight

This function macro returns an element's molecular weight when given its chemical symbol. Enter the elements characters in quotes when entering the function in a worksheet, such as the following:

=SHEET1.XLM!Mole.Wt("Ca")

The molecular weight function in figure 30.7 accepts a quoted text entry or reference to a chemical element's symbol, such as Ca for calcium. This macro can be used for looking up the molecular weight for that element from a table. This lookup method uses MATCH( ) to find the row on which an exact match occurs in the range C22:C29. MATCH( ) works even when data in the range is not sorted. The INDEX( ) function then uses the row number found by MATCH( ) to find the molecular weight in D22:D29. (Check Chapter 13 on advanced worksheet techniques to learn how these methods work.)

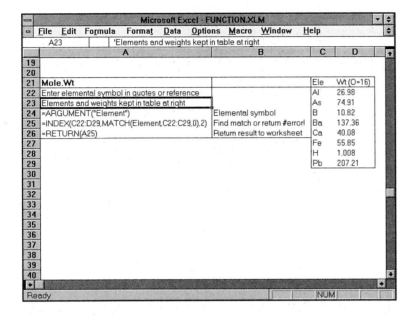

FIG. 30.7

Use MATCH() and INDEX() to look up a table and find answers from a list.

Chapter Summary

This chapter presented several basic command and function macros. If you would like to see more examples of macros, please refer to the appendix for information on the support services available for Microsoft Excel users.

Advanced Techniques

PART

VI

OUTLINE

Using Excel with Windows Applications

E xcel is part of the new generation of software taking advantage of greater processor power and the new Windows software environment. This environment has many advantages when you are working with multiple applications:

- Easy to learn: operating procedures in Windows, OS/2, and Macintosh applications are similar.

- Capability to run multiple Windows and DOS applications.

- Capability to cut and paste *static* information between Windows and DOS applications.

- Capability to create *hot links* that pass live data between Windows or Presentation Manager applications.

- Use of embedded objects that enable you to create a *compound document* composed of objects created in different Windows applications. You then can edit each object by using the application that originally created it.

In this chapter, you learn how to use some of these features to enhance and extend the capabilities of Excel. You learn how to perform the following operations:

- Link Excel charts and tables to Word for Windows documents so that you can use Excel results in your word processing documents.

■ Exchange graphics with CorelDRAW! so that you can add special graphic effects to Excel charts or use CorelDRAW! art in your Excel worksheets and charts.

■ Embed Excel worksheets and charts into PowerPoint so that you easily can update your PowerPoint presentations.

■ Copy Excel screen shots into PageMaker or Word for Windows to make instant documentation or training aids.

This chapter first presents the general concepts of how to use Excel with other Windows applications. The chapter then describes examples using specific Windows applications.

Understanding the Clipboard

For Windows applications, the Clipboard makes sharing information possible within documents in the same application and among documents in different applications. The Clipboard is a reserved part of memory in Windows—not part of any individual application—that holds one item at a time. The Clipboard holds the text, graphics, numbers, or other data that you copy or cut in the application you are using. After you store something in the Clipboard, you can move to another location in your document or switch to a document in another application and paste the information from the Clipboard into your document.

Because the Clipboard belongs to Windows rather than to an application, the information it contains can be shared among applications. Because Windows applications use similar commands—and in many cases identical commands—to move data into and out of the Clipboard, you may find that sharing data within and among applications is easy.

Data transfers within and among applications in three different ways, depending on the application and how you copy and paste the data. The first way is a simple copy and paste operation: you select and copy the data (using the **E**dit **C**opy command), switch to another location or another document, and then paste the data (using the **E**dit Pas**t**e command). In a simple copy and paste operation, the data retains no tie to its originating document.

The second and third ways to transfer data by using the Clipboard depend on a Windows technology known as *object linking and embedding*, or OLE. In this technology, the data transferred is known as an object and may be text, numbers, a graphic, or any other type of data. The object can be embedded in a document or can be linked into a document. An embedded object includes all the information necessary to update that object from within the document in which it is pasted. A linked object remains linked to its originating document and can be updated when the original document changes.

In the language of OLE, documents and applications function as *servers*, which create the data that is embedded or linked into another document, or as *clients*, which receive the data that is embedded or linked from another document or application. Some applications, including Excel, can function as a server and as a client. Excel also can handle multiple clients and multiple servers. (Chapters 9 and 12 describe other situations where linking is used in Excel.)

Data transferred by the Clipboard can assume any of several formats, which you can specify. In this way, you can control whether the data is copied and pasted or whether the data is embedded or linked.

You also can control how the data looks or behaves when pasted into another application. When you copy data from an Excel worksheet, for example, you can paste that data into a Word for Windows document as an embedded object, as linked or unlinked text that is formatted or unformatted, or as a linked or unlinked picture or bit map. These choices are described later in the section "Pasting Embedded Objects."

Copying Data between Applications

Using Excel with Windows is like having a large integrated software system, even if the applications come from different vendors. With the Windows Clipboard, you can cut or copy information from one Windows or DOS application and paste it into another. Chapter 32, "Using Excel with DOS Applications," explains the many ways to exchange Excel data and charts with common DOS applications. The Appendix lists some of the widely used Windows applications that relate to Excel and its use. A large catalog of Windows products is included in Que's *Using Windows 3.1*, Special Edition.

Copying and Pasting Text

To copy or cut text information from Excel and paste it into another Windows application such as Word for Windows (the Windows word processing application), complete the following steps:

1. Select the range of cells you want to transfer, and choose the **E**dit **C**opy or **E**dit Cu**t** command.

2. Activate the Windows application into which you want to paste the information by pressing Alt+Tab until the application appears, or by pressing Ctrl+Esc to display the Task List. Double-click the Windows application, or select the application and press Enter. If the Windows application is not running, activate the Program Manager and start the application.

3. Move the insertion point to the location in the application where you want to insert the Excel data.

4. Choose the **E**dit **P**aste command for the receiving Windows application.

The Excel data is pasted into the receiving application. The data is not linked back to Excel. Refer to "Linking Data between Applications," later in this chapter, for information on linking.

Copying and Pasting an Excel Chart

You can capture an entire Excel chart, a bitmapped picture of a worksheet range, or an image of the screen and paste it into other Windows applications, such as Aldus PageMaker (a page layout application), Word for Windows (a word processing application), or Microsoft Draw (a free graphics application that comes with some Microsoft applications).

To copy an Excel chart into another application, complete the following steps:

1. Activate the Excel chart that you want to copy.

2. Select the entire chart by clicking the chart background or by choosing the **C**hart **S**elect **C**hart command.

3. Choose the **E**dit **C**opy command.

4. Activate the other Windows application.

5. Choose that application's **E**dit **P**aste or **E**dit **P**aste **L**ink command. Applications that do not have linking capability do not have an **E**dit **P**aste **L**ink command.

Capturing a screen image (screen shot) can be valuable for technical documentation or training materials. If you do not have a Windows application for documents, such as Aldus PageMaker or Word for Windows, you can create short training or technical documents with Excel. Paste screen shots into Excel worksheets, and then use Excel text boxes or word-wrapped text in cells to create multicolumn text descriptions.

To capture an image of an entire Windows or Excel screen that you can paste into Windows applications, complete the following steps:

1. Prepare the Windows or Excel screen the way you want it to appear in the screen shot.

2. Press the Print Screen key to copy a bitmap of the screen image into the Clipboard. Alternatively, press the Alt+Print Screen key combination to copy an image or just the active window. The Print Screen key may be shown on the key cap as PrtScrn. This keystroke may not work on Toshiba portables. On older computers, pressing Print Screen may not work; use the Alt+Print Screen combination instead.

3. Activate the Windows application into which you want to paste. The application must be capable of accepting graphics from the clipboard.

4. Choose the **E**dit **P**aste command. The image now becomes an object that you can format or manipulate in the receiving program.

To copy a portion of the worksheet as a bitmapped image, complete the following steps:

1. Select the worksheet range that you want to copy.

2. Hold down the Shift key and choose the **E**dit **C**opy Picture command. This command appears on the **E**dit menu only when you hold down the Shift key as you select the menu. The Copy Picture dialog box appears.

3. Select the As Shown when **P**rinted option if you want to paste into another Windows application and preserve the highest quality.

4. Activate the other Windows application.

5. Select where you want the graphic image of the worksheet range, and then choose that application's **E**dit **P**aste command.

Linking Data between Applications

Many Windows applications can communicate with each other through linking. Through linking, a Windows application can send or receive data to other linking-capable Windows applications.

Linking takes place in two ways: linking Excel to other applications by using a remote reference formula—much as you link Excel worksheets and charts together by using external references—or by using macros to control the Dynamic Data Exchanges that produce links. You can type a remote reference formula into a cell if you know the correct syntax, or you can paste the formula into a cell by using the Edit Paste Link command.

Linking Excel to Data in Other Windows Applications

Excel can receive data from other Windows applications through *hot links* to other DDE-capable Windows applications. As data in the server application changes, the data in Excel (the client) can update automatically. Applications in which this feature is important include tracking prices in stock transactions, continuous monitoring of manufacturing line inventory, and analyzing laboratory data that is read from monitors.

Links also can update under manual control. This usually is done in most business situations if you need to update data in a worksheet or update a link between Excel and a word processor such as Word for Windows.

You can create links through the menu, through typed formulas that duplicate the external reference formula created by the menu, or through macros. Link control through the use of macros is beyond the scope of this book.

Excel can create links through its Copy and Paste Link commands if the other Windows application also has link commands available on the menu. In this case, creating links is no more difficult than linking two worksheets.

Follow these steps to link Excel as a client to another DDE-capable Windows application:

1. Open Excel and the other Windows application. Activate the Windows application that will send information—the server.

2. Select the text, cell, range, value, graphic object, or data fields that you want to link.

3. Choose the Edit Copy command.

4. Activate Excel, and select where you want the linked data to appear.

5. Choose the Edit Paste Link command or its equivalent. You may have to choose whether the linked data should update automatically or only when you manually request an update. Windows applications operate faster if you use manually updated links.

NOTE The server application may not support linking through a Paste Link command. If Excel's Edit Paste Link command is not available in the receiving application after you copy data from another Windows application, the application from which you copied does not support linking through menus; you cannot paste the link into Excel.

Turning Links On and Off

If you want Excel to use the last worksheet values it received and not request remote reference updates from other applications, choose the **O**ptions **C**alculation command and clear the Update **R**emote References option. You can put the remote reference links back in effect by selecting the Update **R**emote Reference option.

Excel can send information through DDE to other Windows applications just as it can initiate information requests. You can turn off Excel's capability to update data links to other applications by choosing the **O**ptions **W**orkspace command, and then selecting the **I**gnore Remote Requests option. To enable remote requests and allow information to pass out of Excel, deselect the **I**gnore Remote Requests option.

Embedding Data from Other Applications into Worksheets

You can embed into an Excel worksheet data from any OLE server application. After being embedded, the data is part of the Excel worksheet; if you want to edit the embedded data, you can start the server application from within Excel. (If the server is not available—as it may not be if you give the document to someone who does not have the application—Windows tries to substitute a different application that uses the same data to do the update.)

In some ways, embedding an object into an Excel worksheet is like linking an object. In both cases, you retain some connection to the server application used to create the object, enabling you to update the object in Excel by changing the original object. Embedding and linking are very different in other ways, however. Some of the advantages and disadvantages of embedding follow:

Advantages

- You don't have to maintain links to the server document. (In a link, Excel always must know where to find the server document or it cannot update the linked object.)

- You don't have to save a separate server document, because the server document becomes part of the client document.

- You can start the server application from within Excel in order to update the embedded object.

■ An embedded object updates only when you choose to update it (some links are updated automatically).

Disadvantages

■ Excel worksheets containing embedded objects are larger than documents with links, because the entire embedded object is saved with the Excel document.

■ If you update an embedded object using an application other than the server application, the resulting object may have lower resolution or lose formatting.

■ You must update each embedded object individually; whereas a single object can be linked into many Excel worksheets so that all are updated simultaneously.

Use linking when you have one server document to link to several Excel client documents; when you want to update many links at one time; or when you want instant updating when the server document changes. Use embedding when you want to keep the worksheet and data together; when you have only a single server object to embed; or when you want to control the updates manually from within Excel.

You can embed an object into an Excel document in two ways. You can insert the object by using an Insert command—actually creating the embedded object from within Excel. Alternatively, you can open an application that contains an existing object, copy the object, and paste it into Excel.

Inserting Embedded Objects

You can use two types of applications to insert embedded objects into an Excel worksheet. The first is any OLE-capable Windows server application, such as Word for Windows or Windows Paintbrush.

The second includes *applets* that come free with some Windows applications, such as Word for Windows. If you install on your computer an application that comes with free applets, the applets become available to Excel and other client applications. *Applets* are not stand-alone applications; they can be used only from within a client application such as Excel.

To insert an embedded object into an Excel worksheet, follow these steps:

1. Choose the **E**dit Insert **O**bject command. The Insert Object dialog box appears (see fig. 31.1).

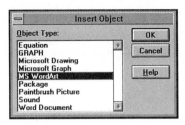

FIG. 31.1

The Insert Object
dialog box.

2. Select from the **O**bject Type list the server application you want to use to create an embedded object.

3. Choose OK or press Enter. The server application starts over the top of the Excel worksheet.

4. Create the object you want to embed or copy the object from the Clipboard. (You cannot open an existing document.)

5. In the server application, choose a command such as **F**ile **U**pdate to add the object to your Excel worksheet. You then can close the document or exit the application. As an alternative, you can choose **F**ile **E**xit (sometimes **F**ile **E**xit and Return to document) to exit the server application and update the Excel document. Respond to a dialog box asking you to confirm that you want to update the Excel document by choosing **Y**es.

Objects embedded in Excel—even if they are text objects—appear as pictures that you can resize and move.

Pasting Embedded Objects

Another way to embed objects in Excel worksheets is to open the server application containing the data you want to embed, copy the object, and paste it into Excel as an embedded object. This technique for embedding is useful if the object you want to embed already is created. You cannot use this technique with an applet, because applets can start only from within a client document.

Windows applications that are not fully OLE compliant may not appear in the Insert Object dialog box. You still may be able to use these applications to create an OLE object and embed it into your worksheet. To embed an object by using the Paste **S**pecial command, complete the following steps:

1. Start the server application in which you will create the document to be embedded.

2. Select the portion of the document you want to embed.

3. Choose the **E**dit **C**opy command.

4. Switch to Excel, activate the worksheet or macro sheet in which you want to paste the object, and select the cell where you want the object's top-left corner.

5. Choose the **E**dit Paste **S**pecial command. The Paste Special dialog box appears (see fig. 31.2).

FIG. 31.2

Use the Paste Special dialog box to paste data using different types.

6. Select from the Data Type list the data type that includes the word *Object*.

7. Choose **P**aste or press Enter.

The object appears in the worksheet or macro sheet. You can format it, size it, or move it as you would any graphic object. If the embedded object is text, it appears in your Excel document as an icon representing the server application used to create the text.

The data types that appear in the list depend on the application you are bringing information from. If you want to embed an object, select the data type that includes the word *Object*. If, for example, you copied data from the XYZ database, you would see `XYZ Database Object` in the list. Other data types in the list depend on the types of data the server application is capable of transferring. Some of the other data types you might see include the following:

Data Type	Meaning
Formatted Text (RTF)	Formatted text
Unformatted Text	Unformatted text
Picture	Graphic composed of drawing elements. Editable with Windows Draw or other major Windows drawing applications.
Bitmap	Graphic using screen dots. Editable with Windows Paintbrush.

NOTE If you do not see *Object* as one of the data types in the list, then the application you copied from is not capable of embedding OLE objects. In this case, you may be able to paste the copied information with a link; if not, you can copy it only as simple unlinked, unembedded data.

Editing Linked and Embedded Objects

The advantage to linking or embedding an object into an Excel worksheet is that you can edit the object or the linked data by using the data's original application. This technique enables you to use features designed for this specific type of data.

To edit an embedded object, double-click the object or display the shortcut menu and choose Edit Object. Either method starts the server application with the object in its document window. Make your changes and then choose a command such as File Update or File Exit—the same command you used to embed the object into the worksheet.

You can edit a linked object in one of two ways: by changing and then updating the original object or by editing the link itself.

By default, objects linked into Excel are set to update automatically; when you change the server document and save the file, the object embedded in Excel updates to reflect the change. If the embedded object is set to update manually, however (you learn how in the next few paragraphs), you can update the linked object by following these steps:

1. Select the linked object.

2. Choose the File Links command. The Links dialog box appears.

3. Choose the Update button.

   If you have additional links to update, select them in the Links list and then choose Update for each.

You also can edit the linked object directly by selecting the object, choosing File Links, and choosing the Open button to start the server application. Make and save your changes. If your link updates automatically, it will update; if it updates manually, you must update it as described earlier in this section.

To change a line from automatic to manual, select the object, choose File Links, choose the options button, and then clear the Automatic option.

You also can edit the link directly by editing the external reference in the Formula Bar. For example, you can change the document or range to which the object is linked.

FROM HERE...

For Related Information:

◀◀ "Embedding Pictures of Cells in a Worksheet," p. 331

◀◀ "Linking Worksheet Cells and Ranges," p. 453.

Examples of Transferring and Linking Data

The following examples show you how useful it can be to pass data between Windows applications or to create integrated systems.

Copying Excel Screen Shots into PageMaker

Aldus PageMaker was one of the first powerful applications written for Windows. It brought the power of extremely expensive typesetting and page-layout systems to personal computers at an affordable price. Page-Maker is designed to produce text-oriented materials that require graphic features beyond the capability of word processors. In PageMaker, you can mix text and graphics in any arrangement. The application's powers include the capability to place multicolumn formats on the same page; to insert, move, size, and crop graphics; to wrap text around graphics or text callouts; and to print to typesetting equipment.

The instructions in this section specify Aldus PageMaker; however, you can use these techniques to copy any application's screen shots into other applications. You can copy screen shots into Word for Windows, Windows Paintbrush, or an Excel worksheet, for example.

To capture the screen shot of any Windows application and paste it into Aldus PageMaker, complete the following steps:

1. Start PageMaker and open the document that will receive the screen shot.

2. Activate Excel. Display the subjects you want to capture in the screen shot.

3. Press the Print Screen key to shoot the whole screen. On some computers you may need to press Alt+Print Screen, which shoots only the active window. (These key combinations may not work on Toshiba portables.) This action copies a bit-mapped image of the screen into the clipboard.

4. Activate PageMaker by pressing Alt+Tab until the application is active or by pressing Ctrl+Esc and selecting PageMaker from the Task List.

5. Choose the **Edit P**aste command.

   PageMaker receives the image as a selected object, which you can move to any location.

Figure 31.3 shows an Excel screen shot pasted into a training document in PageMaker. After you paste the screen shot, you can move, resize, crop, or format it by using the commands available in Aldus PageMaker.

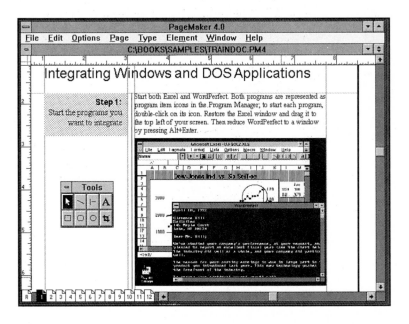

FIG. 31.3

You can take screen shots directly from within Excel and paste them into most Windows applications that accept graphics.

Linking Charts and Tables into Word for Windows

Excel and Word for Windows work side-by-side to create documents that combine the table and chart capabilities of Excel with the text-manipulation and layout features of a powerful word processor. Word for Windows' menus and commands are very similar to Excel's. Word for Windows' ribbon and ruler at the top of the screen are similar to Excel's toolbar, so you can do most of the formatting without using menu commands.

One of the advantages of using Word for Windows with Excel is the capability of Word for Windows to incorporate Excel charts and worksheets into text documents. You can paste this incorporated data as unlinked items or link the items to the original Excel documents. Linking to the Excel document enables you to update the Word document easily.

Pasting Unlinked Worksheet Data

To paste unlinked Excel worksheet data into Word for Windows and create a table, complete the following steps:

1. Select the range in the Excel worksheet that you want to transfer.

2. Choose the **Edit Copy** command in Excel.

3. Activate Word for Windows and the document you want to paste into. Move the insertion point to where you want the table to appear.

4. Choose the **Edit Paste** command in Word for Windows.

As figure 31.4 shows, the Excel range becomes a table when pasted into Word for Windows. Character, border formatting, and column widths are preserved. The information in this table is not linked to the Excel worksheet. Each cell from the worksheet becomes a cell in the Word for Windows table.

Pasting Linked Worksheet Data

To link an Excel worksheet range in a Word for Windows document, complete the following steps:

1. Select the range in the Excel worksheet.

2. Choose the **Edit Copy** command in Excel.

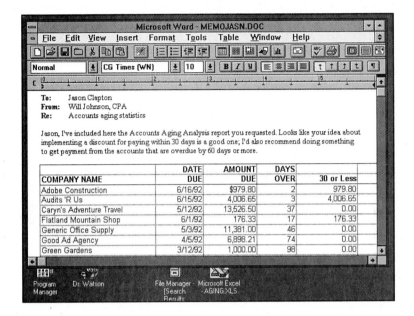

FIG. 31.4

Data pasted from
Excel into Word for
Windows becomes
a table.

3. Activate Word for Windows and the document that you want to
   paste into. Move the insertion point to where you want the data to
   appear.

4. Choose the Edit Paste Special command in Word for Windows. The
   Paste Special dialog box appears (see fig. 31.5).

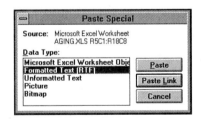

FIG. 31.5

The Paste Special
dialog box.

5. Choose the Paste Link button.

A range from Excel linked to a Word for Windows document (the one in
figure 31.4, for example) also appears in a table. This table is linked to
the Excel range.

By default, the table in the Word for Windows document updates whenever data in the worksheet changes. This form of link slows performance
and is needed only by systems requiring continuous updates. For most
business applications, change the links to manual.

When you paste the linked data into Word for Windows, you actually insert a hidden field code in the document that looks similar to the following code:

Word for Windows 2:

> {LINK ExcelWorksheet C:\\FINANCE\\ R5C2:R15C6 *
> mergeformat \r \a}

To see the code behind the table, select the entire table. Then press Shift+F9, or choose the **V**iew menu and select the Field **C**odes command.

T I P Links are easier to maintain if you edit the Excel range in Word's field code. You can change the range R5C2:R15C6, for example, to an Excel range name that defines the same cells, such as BUDGET. Using named Excel ranges in the links enables you to rearrange the Excel worksheet and still preserve the link to Word.

Including a Worksheet File

To include a disk-based worksheet file or range from a file in a Word for Windows document without opening Excel, complete the following steps:

1. Position the insertion point in the Word document.

2. Choose the **I**nsert Fi**l**e command. The File dialog box appears.

3. Change the file specification in the File **N**ame box to *.XLS.

4. Press Enter to see the worksheet names.

5. Select the worksheet file from the **F**iles list and type a range name into the **R**ange box if you are importing a range.

   If you want the Word document to maintain a permanent link to the Excel worksheet, select the **L**ink to File check box.

6. Choose OK or press Enter. The Convert File dialog box appears.

   You are asked to select from a list the type of file that you want to convert. Select the Excel Worksheet format to convert the Excel file. This command inserts an {INCLUDE} field code into the Word document that reads, converts, and imports the portion of the Excel sheet that you want. If you select the Link option, you can update the document whenever you want by selecting all the imported data and pressing the F9 key or by choosing the T**o**ols **C**alculate command.

> **T I P**
>
> If your Word for Windows conversion files are not as current as the recent version of Excel, the Excel file may not be recognized. If your Excel file is not recognized, save the Excel worksheet to a different name and select an earlier Excel file format from the Save as File Type list in the Save As dialog box. Call Microsoft to update Word for Windows conversion files. See the Appendix for Microsoft's phone number.

Pasting Excel Charts

To paste or link an Excel chart into a Word for Windows document, complete the following steps:

1. Save the Excel chart in the directory where you expect it to remain.

2. Choose the **Chart Select Chart** command.

3. Choose the **Edit Copy** command.

4. Activate the Word for Windows document, and position the insertion point where you want the chart to appear.

5. Choose the **Edit Paste** command to paste a picture of the chart. Choose the **Edit Paste Special** command, and then select Picture or Bitmap and choose Paste **Link** to paste a picture that is linked to the worksheet.

6. Use Word for Windows techniques to move, resize, and format the chart in the document. If the frame enclosing the chart is too large to select a right edge for resizing, choose the Format Picture command and set the **Height** and **Width** in the Scaling group to 50 percent. You then should be able to see and select the chart's scaling handles.

Figure 31.6 shows a linked chart in a Word for Windows document. Pasting a chart with a link into Word for Windows creates a field code that looks like the following:

Word for Windows 2:

> {LINK ExcelChart D:\\FINANCE\\FORCAST.XLC Chart *
> mergeformat \p \a}

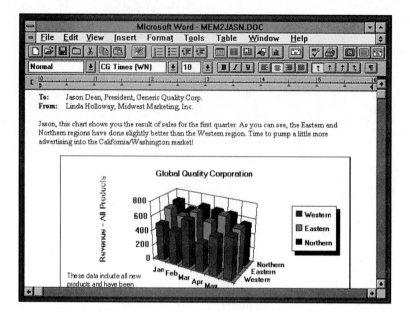

FIG. 31.6

Link Excel charts into
Word for Windows
documents.

T I P

Resizing a chart's window in Excel changes the size and cropping you
may have performed on the chart in Word for Windows. The chart in
Word changes size the next time its link is updated. To prevent this
size change, activate the chart in Excel and choose the **Chart P**rotect
Document command with the **W**indows check box selected. You do
not need to enter a password. This procedure locks the size and
position of the chart window and prevents it from changing in Excel.
This procedure prevents the linked chart in Word for Windows from
changing.

Embedding Data in a Worksheet

If you have any applets installed on your computer, you can use them to
create embedded objects in your Excel worksheet. If you have installed
Word for Windows on your computer, for example, you also received the
applets WordArt, Microsoft Draw, and Microsoft Equation for free. (You
also got Microsoft Graph, but its capabilities are a subset of Excel's
charting capabilities.) You can use any of these applets in Excel.

Embedding Drawings with Microsoft Draw

Microsoft Draw is a powerful, colorful drawing applet. You can use the applet to create complex illustrations, which you can embed in an Excel document. You also can take advantage of the library of interesting clip art that comes with Microsoft Draw.

To embed a Microsoft Draw object in an Excel document, follow these steps:

1. Choose the **E**dit Insert **O**bject command. The Insert Object dialog box appears.

2. From the **O**bject Type list, select Microsoft Drawing.

3. Choose OK or press Enter to start the Microsoft Draw applet. It appears in a window over Excel, as shown in figure 31.7.

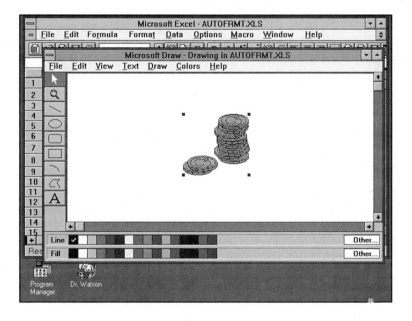

FIG. 31.7

The Microsoft Draw window, with an imported clip art image.

4. Create your drawing by using tools, lines, colors, and editing commands. To include clip art, choose the **F**ile **I**mport Picture command and switch to the CLIPART subdirectory in your WINWORD directory to locate clip art files. You can use the clip art as is, or modify it with Draw tools.

5. Choose **File Update** to add your drawing to the Excel document without closing Draw. Alternatively, you can choose **File Exit** and Return to document to exit Draw. When a dialog box asks whether you want to update the Excel document, choose **Yes**.

Your drawing appears as a movable, sizable graphic object in Excel.

To edit your Microsoft Draw object, double-click it or display the shortcut menu and select Edit Object. (You can display the shortcut menu by clicking the object with the right mouse button, or by selecting the object and pressing Shift+F10.)

Editing Excel Charts with Microsoft Draw

One way you can use Microsoft Draw is to edit an Excel chart. Although Excel has powerful chart editing capabilities, you cannot easily do some things to change a chart's appearance. You may have difficulty deleting a single column in a column chart, for example, or changing the curve of a line in a line chart. You also may want to incorporate clip art into a chart.

Although Microsoft Draw enables you to dress up a chart, be aware that after you edit a chart in Microsoft Draw, it is no longer an Excel chart; you cannot change it by changing its associated numbers or by changing the original chart.

To edit an Excel chart by using Microsoft Draw, follow these steps:

1. In your Excel worksheet, choose the **Edit Insert Object** command. The Insert Object dialog box appears.

2. From the **Object** Type list, select Microsoft Drawing (see fig. 31.8).

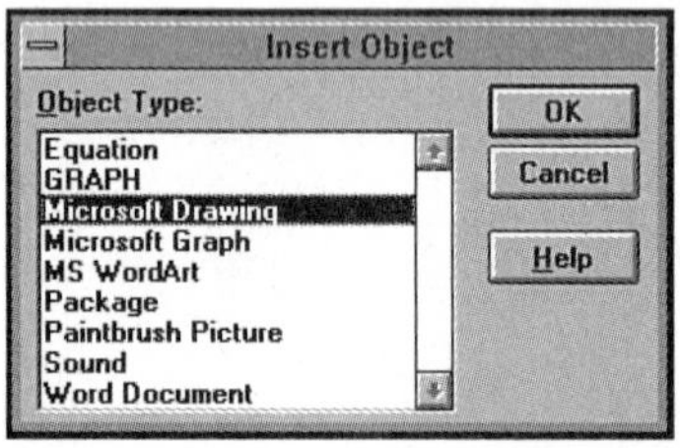

FIG. 31.8

The Insert Object dialog box with Microsoft Drawing selected.

3. Switch back to your worksheet by pressing Alt+Tab, leaving Microsoft Draw open.

4. Create and format your chart as you want it.

5. Choose **Chart Select Chart** and then choose **Edit Copy**.

6. Press Alt+Tab to switch back to Microsoft Draw, and choose **E**dit **P**aste. This action pastes the chart into Draw.

7. Edit the chart as you want.

8. Choose **F**ile **U**pdate to add your drawing to the Excel document window without closing Draw. Alternatively, choose **F**ile E**x**it and Return to document to exit Draw; when a dialog box asks whether you want to update the Excel document, choose **Y**es.

You can edit the chart as described in the section "Editing Linked and Embedded Objects" earlier in this chapter, but you cannot edit the chart as an Excel chart. It is now an embedded Microsoft Draw object.

Embedding Titles From WordArt

For creating logos and fancy titles, you cannot beat the applet WordArt that comes with Word for Windows. WordArt is a simple applet that uses its own set of graphic fonts to twist and turn words into interesting shapes. WordArt objects appear as movable, sizable graphic objects in your Excel documents.

To embed a Microsoft WordArt object in an Excel document, follow these steps:

1. Choose the **E**dit Insert **O**bject command. The Insert Object dialog box appears.

2. From the **O**bject Type list, select MS WordArt.

3. Choose OK or press Enter to start the WordArt applet, which appears in a window on over Excel (see fig. 31.9).

4. Create your logo or fancy title by typing your text in the text box at the top of the WordArt window and selecting options from the **F**ont, Si**z**e, **S**tyle, Fi**l**l, and Ali**g**n lists. You also can select the options Shado**w**, Color **B**ackground, and Stretch **V**ertical. Your logo appears in the Preview box. (If you change the text after you have selected options, however, you must choose the **A**pply button to see your change in the Preview box.)

5. Choose the Apply button to copy your logo into your Excel document and leave WordArt open. Alternatively, choose OK to copy your logo into WordArt and at the same time close WordArt.

When you use WordArt, play with the different options to see how they change your logo.

To edit your WordArt object, double-click it or display the shortcut menu and select Edit Object. (Display the shortcut menu by clicking the object with the right mouse button or by selecting the object and pressing Shift+F10.)

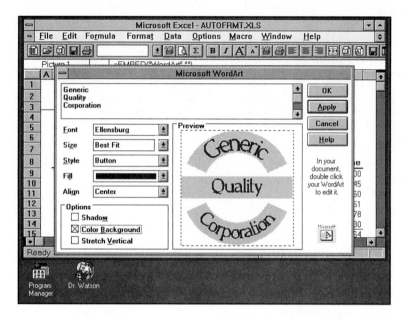

FIG. 31.9

The WordArt window.

Embedding Excel Charts and Tables into PowerPoint

Microsoft PowerPoint is designed to help you plan, compose, and create presentations. With PowerPoint, you can create and organize presentations for 35mm slides, overhead transparencies, or personal computer projectors, as well as print audience handouts and speaker's notes.

PowerPoint and Excel are the first two Windows applications to include the power of embedded objects. An *embedded object* is an object, such as an Excel chart, embedded into another application's document, such as a PowerPoint presentation. The object carries with it all the information needed so that you can open and edit the object by using the original application's menus and commands. In the following sections, you learn how to embed a chart from Excel into a PowerPoint presentation.

When you need to make a change to the chart while in PowerPoint, you need only double-click the chart in the PowerPoint slide. This action starts and activates Excel and opens the chart so that you can edit or reformat it using normal Excel procedures. After you close the chart window in Excel, you return to PowerPoint, and the updated chart appears in the slide. Excel worksheets also can be embedded in PowerPoint slides with the same process.

To embed an Excel chart into a PowerPoint slide, complete the following steps:

1. Activate Microsoft PowerPoint, open the presentation file, and move to the slide in which you want to embed an Excel chart.

2. Choose the **File Insert** Microsoft Excel Chart command; **Insert** is a cascading menu.

   Excel starts and activates. A PowerPoint chart document opens in Excel.

3. From the Excel menus, choose the **File O**pen command to open a chart or choose the **W**indow menu and activate an open chart.

4. Choose the **Chart Select Chart** command and then choose the **Edit Copy** command from the Excel menu to copy the Excel chart.

5. Activate the PowerPoint chart window in Excel by clicking it or by choosing it from the **W**indow menu.

6. Choose the **Edit Paste** command from Excel's menu to paste the Excel chart into the PowerPoint chart window.

7. Close the PowerPoint document by choosing the **File Close** command or pressing Ctrl+F4.

PowerPoint reactivates, and the chart you created appears in the PowerPoint slide. You can format, size, and move the chart as you would other objects in PowerPoint.

The embedded PowerPoint chart refers to the same worksheet from which the chart received its data. The embedded chart does not refer to the chart that was copied. If you change the worksheet, the PowerPoint chart can be updated, but if you change the chart (outside of Powerpoint), the PowerPoint chart is not updated.

You also can create a chart in the PowerPoint chart window while in Excel without using an Excel chart as an intermediate step. Open an Excel worksheet, and then select a valid worksheet range that will create a chart. Copy the range with the **Edit Copy** command, switch to the PowerPoint chart document, and choose the **Edit Paste** command. Format the new chart. Close the PowerPoint document as explained in the preceding step 7.

To edit an embedded chart or worksheet (object) in PowerPoint, complete the following steps:

1. Activate PowerPoint, and move to the slide containing the embedded object (chart or worksheet).

2. Double-click the embedded object.

Excel activates if it is open or opens and activates if it is closed. The PowerPoint chart or worksheet appears in a document window.

3. Edit the PowerPoint object by using normal Excel commands. To open a worksheet linked to the chart, choose Excel's **File Links** command, select the worksheet from the **Links** list, and press Enter or choose OK. PowerPoint's embedded object remembers where the data came from, just as Excel's charts remember.

4. Choose the **File Close** command or press Ctrl+F4 to close the PowerPoint document in Excel and return to PowerPoint.

The updated or reformatted Excel chart or worksheet appears in its slide in PowerPoint.

Chapter Summary

Two of the great powers of the Windows environment are the capability to switch between applications and to transfer data easily between applications. Another advantage of Windows applications is that their menus and operating procedures operate in the same way. In the previous examples you can see how many commands—such as **File Open**, **File Save**, **File Save As**, **Edit Undo**, **Edit Copy** and **Edit Paste**—are similar between applications. In fact, many Windows applications operate so similarly that you often can perform simple tasks without training or opening the manual.

More than 1,400 applications are designed to take advantage of Windows. To make this advantage work for you, you need to learn how to move information between Windows programs. The Appendix lists just a few of the applications designed to work with Microsoft Excel and Windows.

Using Excel with DOS Applications

I f you use DOS applications, such as dBASE II, dBASE III, Paradox, Lotus 1-2-3, Multiplan, WordPerfect, or Microsoft Word, sharing information with Excel will be easy for you. Excel also simplifies the exchange of ASCII files with mainframes.

Excel loads and saves many file formats, such as dBASE, 1-2-3, and Multiplan. Excel also loads or creates text files for information transfer with applications, such as Quicken, that do not use one of the common formats as an interchange. (Lotus 1-2-3 compatibility and data exchange are discussed in Chapter 5. For information on using Windows applications with Excel, refer to Chapter 31.)

Switching between DOS Applications

Windows enables you to load more than one DOS or Windows application simultaneously. If you are running Windows on a 386 computer with more than 2M of memory, the computer will continue to run DOS applications even when the applications are in the *background*. On a 286 computer or in Windows 3 Standard mode, DOS applications are put on hold when they are not in the *foreground*.

To switch between open applications, hold down the Alt key as you press Tab. Continue to press Tab while holding down the Alt key until you see the title bar of the application you want, and release both keys.

To see a list of the applications that are loaded and to select the application to which you want to switch, press Ctrl+Esc. The Task List that appears shows you all the applications that are loaded. Double-click on the application you want to activate; or press the up- or down-arrow keys to select an application, and then press Enter.

If you are running Windows in 386 Enhanced mode, you can run DOS applications full-screen or in a window. To switch the active DOS application between full-screen or window, press Alt+Enter.

FROM HERE...

For Related Information:

◄◄ "Manipulating Windows," p. 59.

Copying and Pasting between Applications

You can copy and paste text and numbers between DOS applications, such as those mentioned earlier, and Excel. You can perform this task with Windows in Standard or 386 Enhanced mode.

Copying and Pasting in Standard Mode

When Windows runs in Standard mode, the mode for 286 computers, DOS applications must run full-screen. Therefore, you must copy an entire screen of text from DOS applications to paste into Excel. Usually you can use more practical methods of transferring data. You can, however, paste selected data from Excel into DOS applications.

If you are running Windows with the minimum memory configuration of 1M, you may not be able to run a DOS application with Excel and copy and paste between the DOS application and Excel; you may have to add extended memory.

To copy from a full-screen DOS application when in Standard mode and paste into Excel, perform the following steps:

1. Activate the DOS application, and position the screen to show the data you want.

2. Press the Print Screen key. On PCs with older ROM BIOS, you may need to press Alt+Print Screen.

3. Switch to Excel by pressing Ctrl+Esc to display the Task List. If Excel is running, select it from the list, and then press Enter. If Excel is not running, select its icon in the Program Manager, and then press Enter so that you can start Excel.

4. Select the cell in which you want the first line from the application screen.

5. Choose the **Edit P**aste command.

Excel places each line of text or numbers into separate cells below the cell that you select in step 4. A line of data is not separated into individual cells.

Remove unwanted data by using Excel's editing or clearing techniques. Separate lines of data into individual cells by using the parsing technique described in the section "Separating (Parsing) Text" later in this chapter.

To copy selected data from Excel and paste into a DOS application, complete the following steps:

1. Select the cell or range in Excel.

2. Choose the **Edit C**opy command.

3. Switch to the DOS application.

4. Position the DOS application's typing cursor where you want to paste the Excel data.

5. Reduce the DOS application to an icon by pressing Alt+Esc.

6. With the DOS application's icon selected (press Alt+Esc to select it, if necessary), press Alt+space bar to display the icon's Control menu, and then choose the **Edit P**aste command. The application will reactivate to full screen and paste the data at the location you selected in step 4.

You must paste data into 1-2-3 one cell at a time. Pasted lines of data end with a carriage return. Therefore, when you copy multiple lines of data and paste them into 1-2-3, all lines of data are pasted into the same cell. Exporting data to 1-2-3 is easier if you save from Excel in one of three 1-2-3 file formats. Such applications as WordPerfect move the cursor to the next line when they receive a carriage return, so they accept paragraphs full of data from Excel.

Copying and Pasting in 386 Enhanced Mode

When Windows is in 386 Enhanced mode, you can run DOS applications full-screen or in a window. DOS applications in a window can be moved on-screen in the same way that true Windows applications can. DOS applications in a window operate with the same commands and display that the applications use when running under DOS. While you run DOS applications in a window, you can copy selected text or numbers from a DOS application screen and switch to another DOS or Windows application in which to paste the selected copy.

To copy from a DOS application and paste into Excel, perform the following steps:

1. If the application is running full-screen, press Alt+Enter to put it into a window. (Alt+Enter toggles the DOS application between full-screen and window.)

2. Select the data that you want copied by dragging across it with the mouse.

   If you are using a keyboard, press Alt+space bar; then select the **Edit Mark** command, press the movement keys to move to the corner of the data you want to select, and then press Shift+arrow keys to select the data. Press Alt+space bar again and select the **Edit Copy Enter** command.

   NOTE   You cannot operate a DOS application while you are in the Mark mode. To return to the document, press Esc.

3. Switch to Excel by pressing Ctrl+Esc to display the Task List. If Excel is running, select it from the list, and then press Enter. If Excel is not running, select its icon in the Program Manager and press Enter to start Excel.

4. Select the cell where you want to paste a single cell or a column of data.

5. Choose the **Edit Paste** command.

When you copy numbers from a DOS application into Excel, copy a single number or column of numbers simultaneously. The number or column pastes into a single cell or a column of cells. If you copy entire lines, the numbers do not separate for pasting into individual cells in the row. (Long lines of data can be passed into cells by using the technique described in the "Separating (Parsing) Text" section of this chapter.)

To copy data from Excel and paste it into a DOS application, complete the following steps:

1. Select the cell or range that you want to copy in Excel.

2. Choose the **Edit Copy** command.

3. Switch to the DOS application.

4. Position the application's normal cursor where you want the data located.

5. Press Alt+space bar, and select the **E**dit **P**aste command.

Data enters the DOS application as though you had typed it. Excel places a tab between each cell's contents, which makes tables of data easy to align when pasted into a word processor. All you need to do is set the tabs for the area that contains Excel data, so that the columns of data align. Use right or decimal alignment tabs for the best alignment of numbers.

For Related Information:

◀◀ "Filling or Copying Cell Contents," p. 234.

FROM HERE...

Exporting Data

Excel can share its data and charts with other applications. When you need to transfer information between Excel and a DOS application, you export data from Excel to a file that the other application can read, or you import data from the other application into a file that Excel can read. Excel reads and writes many other application file formats automatically.

Understanding File Formats

Excel imports (reads) and exports (writes) many file formats used by other DOS, Macintosh, and mainframe applications. If no specific file format is available to transfer information directly, you can create a text file format that transfers text and numbers.

The file formats that Excel can read and write are listed in table 32.1.

If you are unsure of the appearance of a CSV or text file, create an Excel worksheet and save it using CSV and text file formats. Use a word processor, such as Windows Write, to see how Excel encloses data in tabs, commas, and quotes.

If you need to export an Excel chart to an application that does not use the Windows clipboard, you can save the chart to an HPGL file (Hewlett-Packard Graphics Language). The section "Exporting Excel Charts to WordPerfect" explains this procedure.

Table 32.1. File Formats Read by Excel

File Format	File Extension	Description
Excel 2.2	XLS	Excel 2.X
Excel 3.0	XLS	Excel 3.0
Text (*variation*)	TXT	Text: tabs separate cells of data; rows end with a carriage return. ANSI text for Windows; PC-8 text for MS-DOS or OS/2; Text for Macintosh.
CSV(*variation*)	CSV	Comma Separated Values: data is separated by commas. Values are enclosed in quotation marks if the values contain a comma: "*$5,000*", for example. Numbers containing commas are enclosed in quotation marks("*number1,number2*").
		Text is enclosed in quotes only if it contains the delimiter. Remove unwanted quotes from a worksheet with the Formula Replace command.
WKS	WKS	1-2-3 Release 1, 1A, and Symphony; Microsoft Works.
WK1	WK1	1-2-3 Release 2x
WK3	WK3	1-2-3 Release 3
DIF	DIF	Data Interchange Format: common low-level worksheet format (VisiCalc).
DBF 2	DBF	dBASE II
DBF 3	DBF	dBASE III.X
DBF 4	DBF	dBASE IV.X
SYLK	SLK	Symbolic Link: Multiplan, Microsoft Works.

Saving Excel Worksheets in a Different Format

To save Excel worksheets in another format, perform the following steps:

1. Choose the File Save **As** command. The Save As dialog box, shown in figure 32.1, appears. Type the file name in the text box, but do not add a file extension. Do not press Enter.

2. From the Save File as **T**ype list, select the format in which you want to save your file.

   Table 32.1 lists these formats and their descriptions.

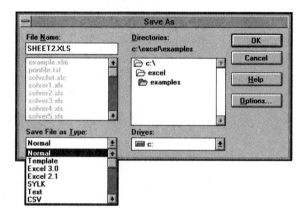

FIG. 32.1

The Save As dialog box enables you to save to different file formats.

3. If necessary, select the directory where you want to save your files in the **D**irectories list, and select the drive in the Drives list.

4. Choose OK, or press Enter.

Exporting Text

You can export data to many DOS or mainframe applications by saving the file in one of the many formats that Excel saves. Most DOS or mainframe applications can then translate from one of these formats into their own formats. You can use the formats from table 32.1 to exchange data between Excel and applications as small as Quicken's check register or as large as Cullinet mainframe accounting software.

Common file formats for exchanging data with databases or mainframes are CSV and Text. Both of these file types separate the data into worksheet cells with delimiters. Formulas are changed to results. The character set used when saving depends upon which type of CSV or Text file you select. Six different sets are defined in the list: Text, CSV, Text (Macintosh), Text (OS/2 or MS-DOS), CSV, (Macintosh), and CSV (OS/2 or MS-DOS).

Text files separate cell contents with tab characters. To see a sample Text format file, save a worksheet in Text format. Then open the worksheet by using an application, such as Word for Windows, where you can see the tab markers.

Comma Separated Value (CSV) files separate each cell's contents with a comma. Cells that contain commas are enclosed in quotes and separated by commas. Again, you can see the type of format Excel imports and exports by saving a worksheet with this format then opening it in a word processor.

T I P Use the FLATFILE.XLA macro to create column-delimited files. FLATFILE.XLA saves files by using character positioning to define field locations. The FLATFILE.XLA add-in is located in the LIBRARY directory. See Chapter 15 to learn more about add-ins.

Linking Excel Data to WordPerfect 5.1

Excel worksheets or ranges can be read directly into some programs, such as WordPerfect. Instead of using a file format as an intermediary, WordPerfect and some other word processors have the capability to read data directly from the Excel worksheet on disk. If your version of WordPerfect does not have a file converter for the current version of Excel, save your Excel document in one of the earlier Excel formats.

To import Excel data into a WordPerfect 5.1 file, complete the following steps:

1. Position the cursor in your WordPerfect file where you want the data to appear.

2. Press Ctrl+F5. Select **S**preadsheet (**5**).

3. Choose **I**mport.

4. Choose **F**ilename (**1**), and type the full path name and file name. Press Enter.

5. Choose **R**ange (**2**), and enter the range of data or range name. If you do not specify a range or a range name, the entire file is imported.

6. Choose **T**ype (**3**), and select Table (**1**) or T**e**xt (**2**). You may need to reformat fonts and columns in tables in order to fit the data on the page.

7. Choose **P**erform Import (**4**).

Exporting Excel Charts into WordPerfect

Excel can export its charts to a file that can be read and imported by many DOS applications. When you use this method, Excel charts are *printed* to disk in an HPGL format by sending the information normally sent to an HP plotter to a disk file.

Before you can perform this procedure, you must have an Excel plotter driver installed in Windows with the plotter configured to a port called File. To install an HP plotter, press Alt+space bar from Excel. Choose the **Run** command, and then select the Control **P**anel option. When the Control Panel appears, select the Printer icon, and press F1 for help on how to run the printer installation program. Install an HP plotter and connect it on the port named **File**. Choose the plotter's Setup button and clear the Draft option. When you print to this plotter, the information normally sent to the plotter will go to a file because you have connected the plotter to File and not to a printer port.

To print an Excel chart to a file on disk, perform the following steps:

1. Activate the Excel chart, choose the **F**ile Page Se**t**up command, and set the page setup with the headers, footers, and margins you want.

2. In the Page Setup dialog box, choose the Pri**n**ter Setup button. From the **P**rinter list, select the HP Plotter connected to File. Choose OK.

3. Choose the **P**rint button, and choose OK or press Enter. You will be prompted for a file name. Enter the name with a file extension you can remember, such as HGL, so that it is easy to find, and then choose OK or press Enter.

The HPGL file saves to the current Excel directory.

To import the Excel chart you saved as an HPGL file into WordPerfect 5.1, perform the following steps:

1. Position the WordPerfect cursor where you want the chart.

2. Press Alt+F9, and then choose Figure (**1**).

3. Choose Create (**1**).

4. Choose Filename (**1**), and type the full path name and file name of the chart.

5. Choose Edit (**9**) to see and rotate the chart.

WordPerfect displays the chart as a line box in the document. To see the chart as it will appear when printed, press Shift+F7, **V**iew Document (**6**) to view the document.

Exporting Files into Macintosh Excel

Newer Macintosh computers are capable of reading and writing Windows Excel files directly from an MS-DOS disk. For older Macintosh computers, you need to transfer the data between computers. Transfer between computers is performed with a null-modem serial cable (a non-normal serial cable) and a Macintosh-to-PC communication application. A number of good applications accomplish this transfer.

If you are transferring between Macintosh and Windows versions of Excel 4, you do not need to convert the file. If one computer uses Excel 3 and the other Excel 4, you need to save to the older version before transferring. If the Macintosh version is earlier than Excel 3, you need conversion software that usually comes with the file transfer software.

T I P   If the dates are four years off after importing from or exporting to the Macintosh Excel worksheet, change Excel's date system by using **O**ptions **C**alculation command, and select or clear the 1904 **D**ate System as necessary.

FROM HERE...

For Related Information:

◂◂ "Managing Files," p. 158.

Importing Data

Excel is used by many businesses to analyze data stored in other applications. If you want to automate your system or create links between Excel and the database, you should explore the use of Q+E and Excel (see Chapter 25). Many other Windows applications are designed to link Excel to network server and mainframe databases.

Many corporations download text files from their mainframes into Text or CSV format. Excel also can *parse* (separate) text lines up to 255 characters in length so that they separate into individual cells in the worksheet. Parsing is described later in this chapter.

Importing Text Files

Use text files to pass data when Excel cannot read an application's file format. Most applications can save or print data to a text file and specify how that text file will be laid out. For information on performing this task in your DOS or mainframe program, check the index of your application's manual under the headings *ASCII*, *ANSI*, *report generator*, *text file*, or *printing to disk*.

Excel imports three types of text files: CSV, text, and column-delimited. Excel automatically separates data fields from CSV and text files into cells. Each row of data reads into an Excel row. Each comma-separated or tab-separated segment of data appears in its own cell. You can specify the type of delimiter used in the text file you are importing.

To see the CSV of Text format that Excel reads automatically, create an Excel worksheet with sample data in cells. Save that worksheet by using the File Save **As** command, select the Save File as **T**ype pull-down list, and select the Text or CSV format of the character set you need (ANSI, ASCII, or Macintosh). Choose OK. Now use Windows Write or a word processor to examine that file and see how commas, quotes, or tabs are placed around data. When you create a text or CSV file, use commas, tabs, and quotes in the same way.

The third type of text file Excel reads is known as a *column-delimited* text file. Each data field is assigned to specific character locations in a line of text. For example, first names may be stored from position 1 to 12, last names from position 13 to 25, and so on. Unused positions are filled with space characters. Use the **D**ata **P**arse command to separate lines of data into cells according to each cell's range of column positions. Refer to the section "Separating (Parsing) Text" in this chapter for a description of this command.

You can see, edit, print, and save text files by opening them with the Windows Notepad. Windows Notepad saves its files back into text format.

To open a text file into Excel, perform the following steps:

1. Choose the File **O**pen command.

2. Choose the Text button to display the Text File Options dialog box (see fig. 32.2).

3. In the Column Delimiter group, select the character that separates each field of data in your file. Or enter your own delimiter in the **C**ustom option.

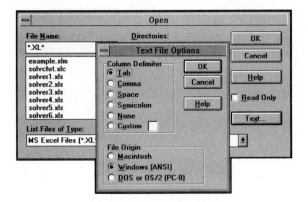

FIG. 32.2

Set the type of text file
you are opening in the
Text File Options
dialog box.

4. Select the type of application or system from which the data came. Select **M**acintosh, **W**indows (ANSI), or **D**OS or OS/2 (PC-8) to tell Excel the type of character set being used. Windows applications use ANSI; DOS and OS/2 applications use PC-8; and Macintosh applications use Macintosh.

5. Choose OK.

6. Select the file that you want to open, and choose OK or press Enter.

When Excel loads a non-Excel file, Excel remembers the format the file came from. Unless you specify otherwise, Excel saves the file back in that same format. Saving to a non-Excel format can result in the loss of formulas, functions, special features, and formatting that are unique to Excel. If you want to save the opened file in an Excel format, choose the **F**ile Save **A**s command, select the Save File as **T**ype pull-down list, and then select the Normal format. Next, enter a name, and choose OK. (Normal is the Excel 4.0 format.)

> **NOTE** If you need to read selective information from an Excel, dBASE, text or other file that is laid out in a row and column format or database table, you may want to use Q+E. By using Q+E, you can extract selective information from large files that remain on disk. Q+E is described in Chapter 25. Q+E comes free with Excel. Contact Pioneer Software, listed in the Appendix, for additional drivers that enable you to link Excel to many types of databases.

Separating (Parsing) Text

Column-delimited text files load into a new worksheet in column A. Each row of the text file enters a cell in column A. Each entire row is in a cell of column A. Data is not separated into cells. To separate these long lines into cells you must *parse*, or separate.

Before you can parse a long line of text, you need to tell Excel where to divide the text lines. Square brackets are used around data in a sample line to show Excel where data should be segmented. You can type these square brackets into a sample line yourself or let Excel guess where to put the brackets, and then edit Excel's guess as necessary. The sample line used for these brackets appears in the worksheet in figure 32.3 and in the Data Parse dialog box in figure 32.4.

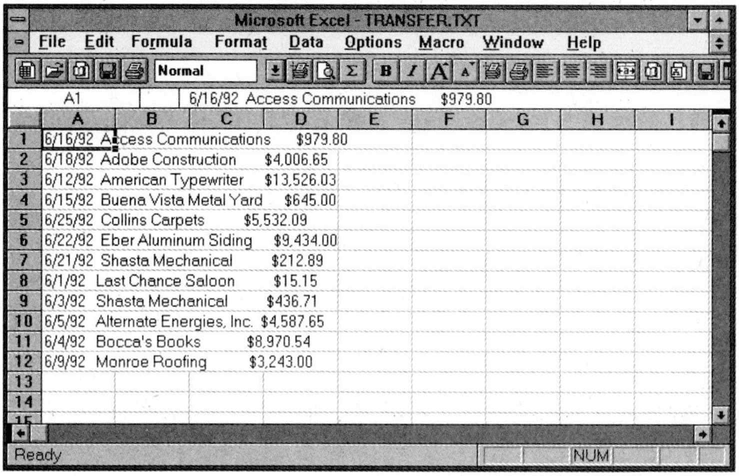

FIG. 32.3

Excel uses the active cell of text as a sample for how to parse (divide) the line into cells.

The square brackets define the left and right edges of what will be placed in separate cells. Use the left- and right-arrow keys, the left- and right-square bracket keys, Del, and Backspace to edit the **Parse** Line. Using the arrow keys, move to the extreme right in the parse box to see the full line of data. Excel beeps if you attempt to delete a character or space.

Be certain that the brackets are wide enough to include the full width of all characters in a field of data. For example, after selecting the **G**uess button, brackets appear around the first dollar amount as [$979.80]. Leaving this field with only seven characters between the brackets will leave out the leading parts of large numbers, such as $13,526.50. The brackets must be edited to allow for three more leading spaces, as shown in figure 32.4.

Figure 32.4 shows the right portion of the **P**arse Line dialog box set for a correct parse. Notice how the brackets are placed back-to-back (][) to ensure that all data is included. You can skip data by not including its character positions within brackets.

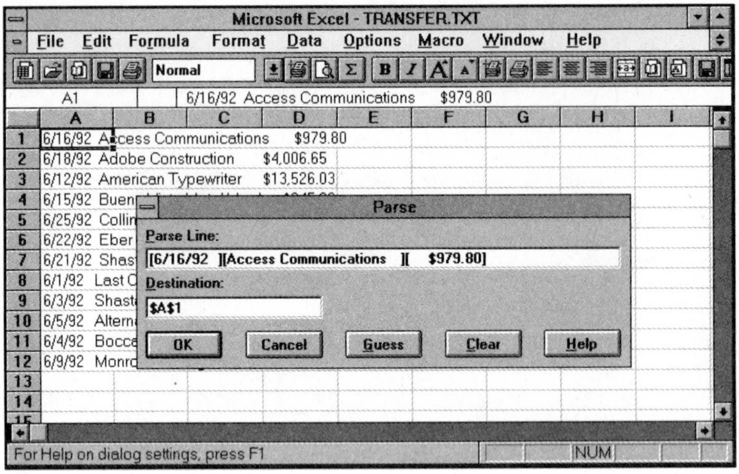

FIG. 32.4

Edit the Parse Line to show Excel how you want text lines divided into cells.

Figure 32.5 shows the results of the parse in the selected range. The data in each line has been segmented into cells. Columns have been widened after parsing to show the full cell's content.

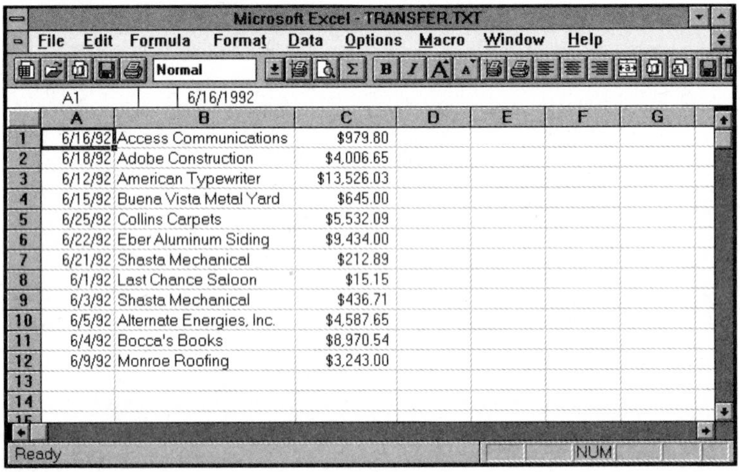

FIG. 32.5

Parsing divides a long line of text into cells.

To parse the column of text shown in figure 32.3, perform the following steps:

1. Open the text file, and then use the File Save As command with the Save File as Type list to save the file in Normal format so that it will be in Excel format.

2. Select column A and format it with a nonproportional font, such as Courier or Line Printer, to enable you to see how data aligns in columns. This step is for visual effect only and does not need to be performed for parsing.

NOTE   Be certain that sufficient blank columns exist to the right of column A to hold the data after parsing. Parsed data will overwrite cells to the right.

3. Select the cells in column A that you want to parse. Excel uses the text in the active cell you select as the sample line that determines how all selected lines will be parsed. If the column positions vary throughout the file, you may need to divide the files into rows with similarly positioned data and parse each of these groups separately.

4. Choose the **D**ata **P**arse command. The Parse dialog box displays the first selected row and shows a ruler of character positions (see fig. 32.4).

5. Choose the **G**uess button. Excel may correctly bracket data as you want it separated. If not, you can edit the sample parse line by positioning square brackets around data to be parsed. You cannot add or delete spaces or characters; you can edit the **P**arse Line by deleting brackets in one location, moving the insertion point to another location, and adding the brackets again. Data not within [ ] brackets will be ignored.

6. Select the **D**estination edit box, and enter the single cell that will be the top-left corner of where you want the parsed data. If you do not change this reference, the parsed data overwrites the existing data. You must use a single cell reference, such as $A$1; you cannot use names, ranges, or external references.

7. Choose OK, or press Enter.

If you correctly positioned the brackets, Excel separates the data into cells. If the data did not parse correctly, open the file you saved and repeat the process.

Importing Quicken Data

Quicken is a popular check register and money-manager application that runs in DOS; a Windows version also is available. Although Quicken does not save a file directly to Excel format, you can easily send any of Quicken's financial and budget reports to a text file that Excel can open and automatically separate into individual cells. You can use this same method with many DOS-based accounting programs.

To create a text file from Quicken, perform the following steps:

1. Activate Quicken, and open the account you want to work with.

2. Select the type of report that you want to print from the Main menu (3 Create Reports) or from the register (F5 Reports). Enter the requested printing data, such as titles, date range, and filter.

3. Choose F2 or Ctrl+P to print. Select the printing option for Disk (1-2-3 File). Although this option says 1-2-3 File, it is actually a CSV file.

4. When prompted for the file name, enter the path name and file name. If no path name is used, the file saves to the current Quicken directory.

To open the Quicken report into Excel, perform the following steps:

1. Choose the **File Open** command from Excel, type ***.*** in the **Name** box, and choose OK or press Enter. Change to the directory containing the Quicken CSV file. Select the file with the .PRN extension.

2. Choose the **Text** button from the File Open dialog box.

3. Select the **Comma** Column Delimiter and the **DOS** or OS/2 (PS-8) File Origin, if you have the DOS version of Quicken.

4. Choose OK twice to open the file into a new worksheet.

The Quicken report will enter into a new worksheet with data in separate cells. If necessary, widen column widths to see the data. When you save this file, be certain that you select Normal from the Save As File **Type** list.

FROM HERE...

For Related Information:

◄◄ "Managing Files," p. 158.

◄◄ "Using External Database Commands," p. 866.

Chapter Summary

Using Windows 3 and Excel with your existing DOS applications offers many advantages. Excel coexists well with character-based systems, such as WordPerfect and 1-2-3. Excel can read files from applications, such as dBASE, to perform charting and analysis tasks that are difficult in dBASE. And if dBASE files are too large to fit into a worksheet, you can link Excel to the dBASE files on disk by using Q+E, a free application that comes with Excel. (Paradox and other file drivers for Q+E are available from Pioneer Software listed in the Appendix.) Many corporations maintain corporate and division sales, marketing, and financial data on their mainframe computers, and then download the data as text files to Excel for analysis, charting, and reports.

Customizing Excel

E xcel by itself is the best computerized worksheet available. With
Windows, Excel is even more powerful and versatile. You can
customize both Excel and Windows to fit your work place and style. In
this chapter, you learn how to access Excel customization features, add
and customize toolbars, change the colors and backgrounds used by
Windows, use international character sets in your worksheets, and even
change how the mouse operates.

Using Other Customization Features

This chapter describes ways of customizing Excel that have not yet been
covered in this book. You might want to go back and explore previously
discussed topics. The following features and topics are covered in other
chapters:

- *Ten-key accounting pad.* Use the **O**ptions **W**orkspace command with
  the Fi**x**ed Decimal option so that you can type numbers on the numeric pad and have the decimal automatically entered.

- *Automatic rounding of formatted numbers.* Use the **O**ptions **C**alculation command with the **Pr**ecision as Displayed option to make
  Excel calculate with the formatted number you see on-screen.

■ *Worksheet templates.* Create templates for tasks that you perform frequently. Templates are quick to access in the **File New** box. Templates can contain worksheet formulas, formats, and display settings you want. You also can create chart templates that contain the chart type, formats, and scales for each of the chart types you use frequently. Chapter 11 describes templates.

■ *File loading on start-up.* Load worksheets, charts, and macros on start-up by storing them in the XLSTART directory. When you use the same tools and add-ins frequently, this setup enables you to get to your work quickly and easily.

■ *Add-in macros.* Create macros that are invisible when opened and act like built-in Excel features.

■ *Function macros.* Create predefined functions that act the same as built-in worksheet functions.

■ *Custom menus.* Use custom menu bars, menus, and commands to change the control system of Excel completely. You use macros to change the menu structure.

■ *Custom dialog boxes.* Use the Dialog Editor to draw custom dialog boxes; then display those boxes and retrieve information from them under macro control.

■ *Worksheet background colors.* Use the **O**ptions **D**isplay command to change gridline and heading colors.

■ *Workspace tools.* Use the **O**ptions **W**orkspace command to add or remove workspace tools, such as the Formula Bar, scrolling bars, Status Bar, and so on.

■ *Hidden elements.* Use the **W**indows **H**ide command to hide worksheets, charts, and macro sheets. Use the Forma**t C**ell Protection command to hide formulas in the Formula Bar.

■ *Protection.* Use the **O**ptions **P**rotect Document command to protect worksheets from being opened without a password. Use a Read-Only specification to protect worksheets from being written over.

Customizing Toolbars

Excel enables you to customize toolbars and create your own toolbars and tools. Specifically, you can do the following:

■ Change any of the supplied toolbars

■ Design and edit your own toolbars

■ Assign macros to custom tools

To make your work easier, you can create your own toolbars, rearrange existing toolbars, add or delete tools, and even assign macros to custom tools by using supplied icons or by drawing your own custom tool faces.

Adding Tools

The following example shows how you can add the Undo tool to the Standard toolbar. To add a new tool to any toolbar, complete the following steps:

1. Be certain that the toolbar you want to change is displayed.

2. Use the right mouse button to click the toolbar and choose Customize from the shortcut menu, or choose the Options Toolbars command.

3. When the Toolbars dialog box appears, shown in figure 33.1, choose the Customize button. You see the Customize dialog box, shown in figure 33.2. The pointer is on the Undo tool.

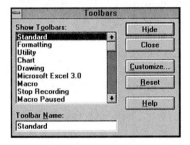

FIG. 33.1

The Toolbars dialog box.

4. Choose the category containing the tool you want to add to the toolbar. The Undo tool is in the Edit category. Chapter 2 contains a list of all the tools and their categories.

If you are unsure of a tool's function, click the tool. Look at the bottom of the Customize dialog box to see a definition of the tool's function. Release the mouse button without dragging the tool from the Customize dialog box. The same technique works on toolbars in the workspace (information appears at the bottom of the screen); however, move the pointer off the tool before releasing or you will execute the tool's command.

T   I   P

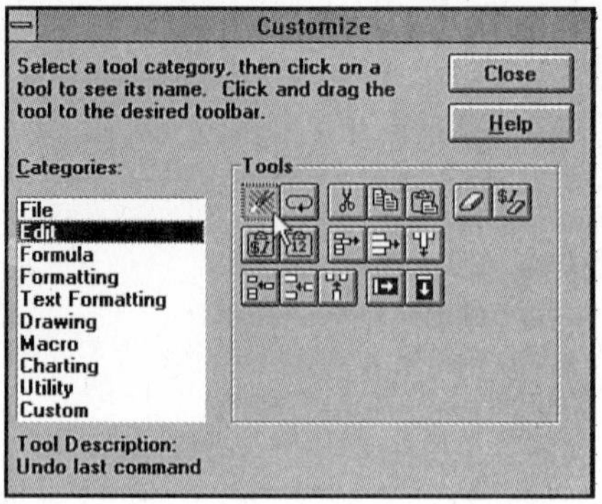

FIG. 33.2

The Customize
dialog box.

5. Drag the tool you want to add, in this case the Undo tool, so that its center is over the location on the toolbar where you want the tool to appear. The tool is added to the toolbar.

6. Release the mouse button.

At this point, the standard toolbar may appear a bit crowded, especially if you are working with a standard VGA screen. (Some tools may have vanished off the right end of the screen.) You can eliminate this crowding by removing tools, changing the spacing between tools and changing the width of a pull-down list, as described in the next section.

T I P   You also can add tools to a toolbar by moving or copying them from another toolbar. Display the Customize dialog box, and display the toolbar containing the tool you want to copy or move and the toolbar to which you want to copy or move the tool. To move a tool, drag it from one toolbar to another. To copy a tool, hold down the Ctrl key while you drag the tool from one toolbar to another.

Reorganizing Tools

When a toolbar gets crowded, you need to remove tools, resize tools so you can fit more tools on the bar, or reorganize the tools.

T I P   You can always return a predefined toolbar to its originally installed condition by selecting it in the Toolbars dialog box and choosing the **Reset** button.

To change the width of a pull-down list, like the Style tool, complete the following steps:

1. Click the right mouse button on the toolbar and choose Customize from the shortcut menu, or choose the **O**ptions T**o**olbars command and when the Toolbars dialog box appears choose the **C**ustomize button.

2. With the Customize dialog box displayed, click a pull-down tool in the toolbar, such as the Style or Font tool.

3. Move the mouse pointer to the right side of the tool. When the double-arrow appears, drag the arrow left or right (see figure 33.3) to resize the list box.

4. Choose **C**lose in the Customize dialog box.

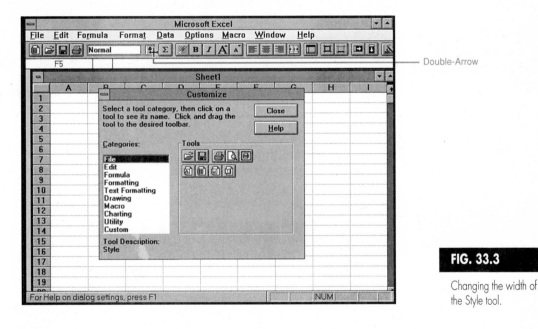

Double-Arrow

FIG. 33.3

Changing the width of the Style tool.

If you want to remove a tool, complete the following steps:

1. Click the right mouse button on the toolbar and choose Customize from the shortcut menu, or choose the **O**ptions T**o**olbars command and when the Toolbars dialog box appears, choose the **C**ustomize button.

2. With the Customize dialog box displayed, drag the tool off the toolbar.

3. Release the mouse button.

To reorganize a toolbar and move tools into new locations, complete the following steps:

1. Click the right mouse button on the toolbar and choose Customize from the shortcut menu, or choose the **O**ptions T**o**olbars command and when the Toolbars dialog box appears, choose the **C**ustomize button.

2. With the Customize dialog box displayed, drag the tool so that its center is in between the tools where you want it to be.

3. Release the mouse button.

Creating Your Own Toolbar

In addition to modifying the built-in toolbars, you also can design your own toolbar from a blank. To create your own toolbar, complete the following steps:

1. Click the right mouse button on the toolbar and choose Toolbars from the shortcut menu, or choose the **O**ptions T**o**olbars command.

2. In the Toolbar **N**ame edit box, type the name you want to give to the new toolbar (see fig. 33.4). The name can be any length and can contain spaces.

FIG. 33.4

The Toolbars dialog box.

3. Choose the **A**dd button to add the toolbar to the screen.

   The Customize dialog box is displayed. Your new toolbar will only be large enough for one tool.

4. Drag desired tools from the Customize dialog box into the new toolbar.

5. Choose **C**lose when you are finished. The new toolbar will contain the tools you copied into it (see fig. 33.5).

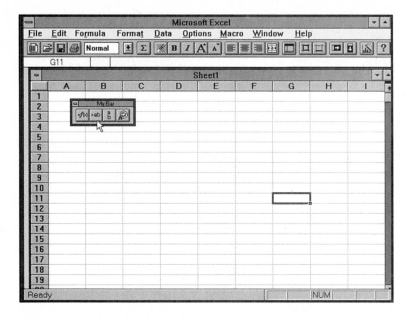

FIG. 33.5

The custom toolbar.

A quick way to create a toolbar is to display the Customize dialog box and drag one of the tools onto your worksheet. A toolbar called Toolbar1, or 2, or the next sequential number appears. You cannot re-name a toolbar. Your new toolbar's name now appears at the bottom of the list of toolbars. You can treat it like any other toolbar.

> To delete a custom toolbar, click the right mouse button on the toolbar, and choose Customize from the Shortcut menu; or choose the **O**ptions **T**oolbars command, and select your custom toolbar from the Show T**o**olbars list. Then choose the **D**elete button.
>
> **T I P**

Assigning a Macro to a Tool

In addition to providing fast access to often-used Excel commands, you also can use the toolbar to run macros. The Custom category in the Cus-tomize list contains tools that you can add your macros to. When you want to assign a macro to a tool, drag one of these custom tool faces onto a toolbar and assign your macro to it.

To assign a macro to a toolbar, perform these steps.

1. Display the toolbar that contains the tool you want to assign to a macro.

2. Click the right mouse button on the toolbar and choose Customize from the shortcut menu, or choose the **O**ptions T**o**olbars command and when the Toolbars dialog box appears, choose the **C**ustomize button.

3. With the Customize dialog box displayed, select Custom from the **C**ategories list.

4. Drag one of the custom tools onto your toolbar. The Assign to Tool dialog box appears, as shown in figure 33.6.

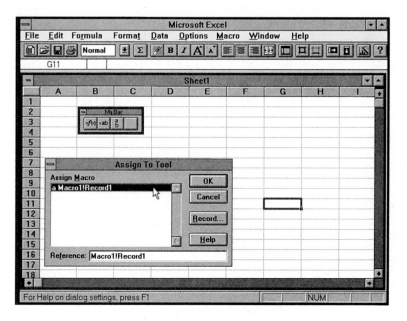

FIG. 33.6

The Assign To Tool
dialog box.

5. In the Assign **M**acro list, choose the macro you want associated with the tool and click OK, or choose **R**ecord to record a new macro.

For additional information on recording macros, see Chapters 27 through 30.

For Related Information:

◀◀ "Using the Toolbars," p. 47.

◀◀ "Building Command Macros," p. 915.

◀◀ "Assigning Macros to Macro Buttons or Graphic Objects," p. 938.

Drawing Your Own Tool Faces

To further customize a toolbar, you can draw your own tool faces by using a graphics application, such as Windows Paintbrush. You then copy the picture from the graphics application and paste it onto a tool. You will get the best results if you make the picture you draw the same size as the existing tool face; the easiest way is to copy an existing tool face into the graphics application and make your new tool face the same size.

Figure 33.7 shows a cat face tool that has been added to the Utility toolbar.

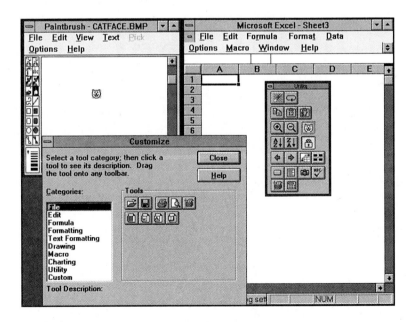

FIG. 33.7.

Draw your own tool faces.

To draw a custom a tool face, perform the following steps:

1. Click the right mouse button on the toolbar and choose Customize from the shortcut menu; or choose the **O**ptions **T**oolbars command and when the Toolbars dialog box appears, choose the **C**ustomize button.

2. In the toolbar, click the tool face you want to customize. (The Customize dialog box must be displayed, or clicking the tool face will activate the tool.)

3. Choose the **E**dit **C**opy Tool Face command.

4. Switch to your graphics application, and choose the **E**dit **P**aste command. Change the tool face as you like.

5. Select your new tool face, and choose the **E**dit **C**opy command. Be certain that you select just the tool face—not any blank space around it.

6. Switch back to Excel.

7. Choose the **E**dit **P**aste Tool Face command.

8. Choose Close to close the Customize dialog box.

As an alternative, you can use Excel's freehand tools to create a tool face. Display the Drawing toolbar, and use the tools to create a tool face. Select the drawing, and choose **E**dit **C**opy. Then display the Customize dialog box, and in a toolbar click on the tool whose face you want to customize. Choose the **E**dit **P**aste Tool Face command.

You also can copy a tool face to a different tool. Display the Customize dialog box, and click on the tool whose face you want to copy. Choose **E**dit **C**opy Tool Face. Click on the tool to which you want to copy the face, and choose **E**dit **P**aste Tool Face. Choose Close to close the Customize dialog box.

To reset a tool face back to its original appearance, display the Customize dialog box, and click with the right mouse button on the tool whose face you want to reset. From the shortcut menu, select Reset Tool Face.

Creating Your Own Colors

Excel has a palette of 16 colors available for use in worksheet and chart patterns. Although this palette is filled with a standardized set of colors when you get Excel, you can change the palette to use 16 colors that you choose. After you define a set of colors, you can copy those colors to other worksheets or save a worksheet as a template so that you can reuse the palette.

When you define a new color palette, you also are defining new default colors for chart markers. The palette also defines the colors used in 3-D surface charts. If you want to create different colors in your 3-D surface chart, you should read about the Custom Palette add-in described in Chapter 15.

If you have a monochrome video driver installed, your colors appear in color lists as color names. You are not able to edit the colors in the palette.

CAUTION: Before you change colors on the palette, consider that your changes may affect objects you have already colored. If, for example, you have created a text box with the fourth color on the palette as the background color, changing the fourth color on the palette also changes the background color of your text box.

If you want to save different sets of custom color palettes, be certain that you read about the Custom Palette add-in described in Chapter 15, "Using Excel's Add-In Macros."

T I P

To choose your own colors for the color palette, complete the following steps:

1. Open the worksheet or chart on which you want custom colors.

2. Choose the **O**ptions Color Pal**e**tte command for worksheets or **C**hart Color Pal**e**tte for charts. Figure 33.8 shows the color palette. On a color monitor, you can see the actual colors.

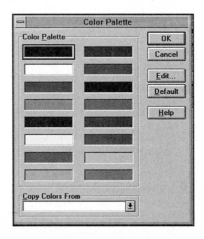

FIG. 33.8

The color palette contains 16 colors that you can change.

3. On the palette, select the color you want to change. Click that color box, or press the arrow keys to select the color.

4. Choose the **E**dit button to display the Color Picker dialog box shown in figure 33.9. The **E**dit button is unavailable if you are using a monochrome monitor; you cannot change colors on a mono-chrome screen.

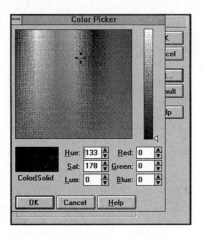

FIG. 33.9

Choose a custom color for the new color on your palette.

5. Select the new color you want for the selection you made in step 3 by performing one of the following:

    Click in the large box on the color you want. To change the luminosity, drag the pointer up or down along the right col-umn. Watch the sample color in the Color/Solid box below the large box.

    Or, choose mixtures of red, green, and blue. To mix these colors, select the **R**ed, **G**reen, and **B**lue boxes and enter a number from 0 to 255; 255 represents the greatest amount of the color. To change the hue of a color, select **H**ue and enter a number from 0 to 239; in the large box, 0 hue is the color at the left edge and 239 hue is the color at the right edge. Use the same method to change the saturation (**S**at); 0 saturation is the color at the bottom edge of the large box and 240 satura-tion is the color at the top edge. To change the luminosity (**L**um), enter a number from 0 to 240; 240 is the maximum luminosity at the top of the right column.

6. Choose OK or press Enter.

7. Choose OK or press Enter to accept your color change.

If you want to return the palette to its original set of 16 colors, choose the **O**ptions (or **C**hart) Color Pal**e**tte command. Then choose the **D**efault button.

When you copy a colored object from one document to another, the object carries with it the palette number of its color. When the object is pasted into the new document, the object uses the color assigned to that number on the palette of the new document. In other words, objects may change color when copied between documents that have different palettes.

If you want to copy the color palette from one document to another, complete the following steps:

1. Open both the document from which you want to copy and the document to which you are copying. Activate the document that should receive the new palette.

2. Choose the **O**ptions Color Pal**e**tte command or **C**hart Color Pal**e**tte for charts.

3. In the **C**opy Colors From list box, select the name of the document from which you are copying colors.

4. Choose OK or press Enter.

Colored objects in the document receiving the new palette change to reflect the new palette.

For Related Information:

◀◀ "Starting Add-Ins," p. 601

◀◀ "Changing Custom Color Palettes," p. 603

FROM HERE...

Defining a New Startup Directory

When Excel starts, it opens all files found in the XLSTART subdirectory. This feature is useful for automatically starting templates, macro-driven applications, and macro add-ins. If you want a separate start-up directory, for temporary working files or as a private start-up directory on a network, follow these steps to specify one additional start-up directory:

1. With the File Manager, create the directory you want to use as a start-up directory.

2. Activate Excel and choose the **F**ile **O**pen command.

3. Select the ALTSTART.XLA add-in macro from the LIBRARY directory. The LIBRARY directory is a subdirectory under the directory containing EXCEL.EXE.

4. In the text box, enter the path name of the directory you want as an additional start-up directory.

5. Choose OK or press Enter.

For Related Information:

◄◄ "Adding a Startup Director," p. 615.

Customizing Excel with the Control Panel

You can customize Excel's features and appearance with the Control Panel. The Control Panel runs from Excel or from the Main group of the Windows Program Manager. In the Control Panel, you can set the computer's date and time, install or delete printers and fonts, change colors used in Windows borders and backgrounds, select international date and currency formats, and more.

For information on how to use programs found in the Control Panel, activate the Control Panel window—even if you are already in a customizing program such as the Color dialog box. Press F1 or choose the **H**elp **C**ontents command. To display the topic you want information about, click the appropriate underlined name, or use the **S**earch button to search on a keyword.

To start the Control Panel from the Program Manager, complete the following steps:

1. Activate the Main group window in the Program Manager by pressing Ctrl+F6, clicking the Main group window, or double-clicking its icon. The Main window is shown in figure 33.10.

2. Choose the Control Panel icon to start the Control Panel. Double-click the icon, or press the arrow keys to select the Control Panel and press Enter. Figure 33.11 shows the open Control Panel.

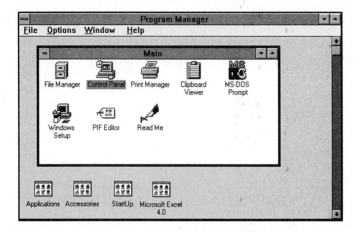

FIG. 33.10

The Main group
window contains
the Control Panel
application icon.

FIG. 33.10

The Main group
window contains
the Control Panel
application icon.

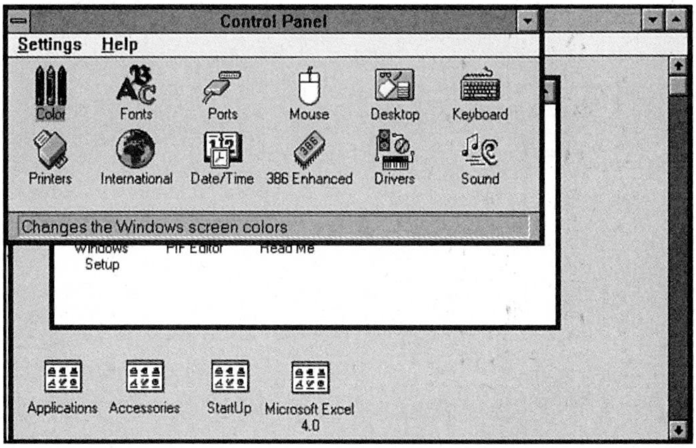

FIG. 33.11

The Control Panel
contains utilities that
customize Windows.

To start the Control Panel from within Excel, complete the following steps:

1. Activate the Excel Control menu by pressing Alt+space bar or by clicking the Excel Control menu icon to the far left of the Excel title bar.

2. Choose the **Ru**n command. The Run dialog box appears, as shown in figure 33.12.

3. Select the Control **P**anel option and choose OK or press Enter. The Control Panel window appears (refer to fig. 33.10).

FIG. 33.12

The Run dialog box enables you to run four applications from within Excel.

Changing the Screen Appearance

You can change the color or gray scale for most portions of the Excel screen. You can select from predefined color combinations or create your own color combinations for different screen parts in Windows and Windows applications. To choose from the predefined color combinations, complete the following steps:

1. Choose the Color icon from the Control Panel by double-clicking the icon or pressing the arrow keys to select the color, and then pressing Enter. Figure 33.13 shows the Color dialog box.

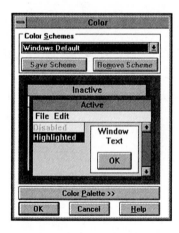

FIG. 33.13

Choose predefined or custom colors for screen elements from the Color dialog box.

2. Select Color Schemes, and select a color combination from the pull-down list.

3. Check the appearance of this color combination in the sample window in the Color dialog box. Select a different color to fit your mood or environment. Monochrome is best for monochrome screens. The default Windows color combination has the name Windows Default.

4. Choose OK or press Enter to accept the new colors.

Changing the Desktop

All Windows applications and the Program Manager reside on a desktop. You can customize Windows to show the patterns or pictures you want on this desktop. Excel comes with a number of patterns and pictures you can use; or you can draw your own desktop background pictures by using the Windows Paintbrush application that comes free with Windows.

To change the pattern or *wallpaper* (desktop background) complete the following steps:

1. Choose the Desktop icon from the Control Panel by double-clicking the icon or pressing the arrow keys to select the icon and pressing Enter. Figure 33.14 shows the Desktop dialog box that appears in Windows 3.1.

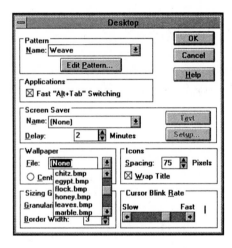

FIG. 33.14

Choose the background (wallpaper) you want from the Desktop dialog box.

2. Select **N**ame and select a pattern from the pull-down list. Patterns are two-color patterns that fill the background behind a Window.

   Or,

   Select **F**ile and select a wallpaper (picture) from the pull-down list. Wallpapers are pictures or digitized images stored in a BMP (bit-map) file. Wallpaper takes precedence over desktop patterns.

3. Choose OK or press Enter.

If the wallpaper is centered on-screen and does not fill the screen background, repeat the preceding steps and choose the Tile option. This option repeats the bit-mapped image to fill the screen. Take the time to experiment and look at some of these wallpapers and color combinations. They will keep you awake on those long dreary February workdays.

You can create your own wallpapers by drawing pictures in the Windows Paintbrush accessory and saving the picture to the Windows directory with the BMP format. Reopen the Desktop dialog box, and your drawing will be one of the listed wallpapers.

Customizing the Mouse

If you are left-handed and want to switch the left and right button functions, you can use the Control Panel to switch. You also can use the Control Panel to control the rate of motion and the click speed for the mouse. If you have an LCD display with a laptop computer (and you are using Windows 3.1) you can improve the visibility of the mouse pointer by turning on mouse trails.

To start the Mouse program, double-click the Mouse icon on the Control Panel; or press the arrow keys until the icon is selected, and then press Enter. Figure 33.15 shows the Mouse dialog box that appears.

Adjust how quickly the mouse moves across the screen by selecting the **M**ouse Tracking Speed scroll bar and dragging the scroll box to the Slow or Fast side. If you are a Windows beginner, you may want to start on the Slow side.

Adjust how quickly you must press the mouse buttons for a double-click by selecting **D**ouble Click Speed and dragging the scroll box to the Slow or Fast side. Use a slower rate if you are new to Windows. Test the double-click rate by double-clicking the TEST square. The TEST square changes color when it recognizes a double-click.

If you want to swap the active mouse button to the right side, select the **S**wap Left/Right Buttons check box. To help you find the mouse pointer on an LCD screen, you may want to turn on Mouse **T**rails.

Changing International Character Sets

When you work in Windows, you can switch among different international character sets, time and date displays, and numeric formats. The international settings you choose show up in new formatting in your Excel worksheets. For example, the Format Numbers list shows number and date/time formats for the country you have selected.

To specify the international settings you want to use, choose the International icon from the Control Panel by double-clicking the icon or by pressing the arrow keys to select the icon and pressing Enter. Figure 33.16 shows the International dialog box from which you can select country, language, date, currency, and other formats. Windows may need your original installation disks to change some settings.

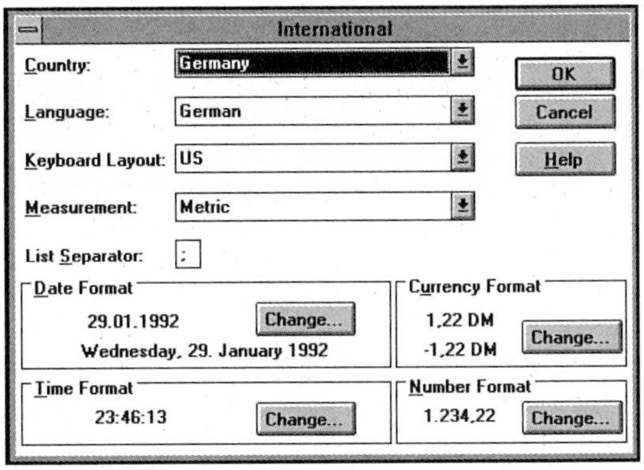

International		
Country: Germany	±	OK
Language: German	±	Cancel
Keyboard Layout: US	±	Help
Measurement: Metric	±	
List Separator: ;		

Date Format
29.01.1992   [Change...]
Wednesday, 29. January 1992

Currency Format
1,22 DM   [Change...]
-1,22 DM

Time Format
23:46:13   [Change...]

Number Format
1.234,22   [Change...]

FIG. 33.16

Select the international formatting options you need from the International dialog box.

Select from the **Country, Language, Keyboard Layout,** and **Measurement** lists the format you need to use. Review the contents of the format text boxes in the lower part of the dialog box to ensure that they show the format you want.

If you need country settings that are not in the **Country** or **Language** lists, select each formatting group, choose the Change button, and make changes to individual formats as needed. (Select Change buttons from the keyboard by pressing Tab to move to them, and then press the space bar.)

For Related Information:

◄◄ "Setting Preferences," p. 142.

◄◄ "Controlling the Worksheet Display," p. 306.

FROM HERE...

Chapter Summary

Windows and Excel are flexible work environments that make customizing your workspace easy. By changing some features, you can modify Windows and Excel to suit your needs and comfort level. You can create your own color palettes, change the screen colors and patterns, control the mouse operation and speed, change the international character set, and add start-up directories. Take advantage of Windows by setting it up the way you want it.

Support Services

This directory represents only a sampling of the products and resourcesdesigned to work with Excel. However, the directory will give you an indication of the many types of products and services available.

Resources, Consulting, and Support

Microsoft Corporation

Microsoft Corporation
One Microsoft Way
Redmond, WA 98052-6399
1-800-882-8080
206-635-7070, Excel support line
206-637-7098, Windows support line
206-454-2030, Microsoft product-support line
6AM-6PM, M-F, Pacific time

Microsoft maintains a telephone support line for technical questions concerning Windows, Excel, and Word for Windows.

CompuServe

CompuServe
5000 Arlington Centre Boulevard
P.O. Box 20212
Columbus, OH 43220
1-800-848-8199

CompuServe is a computer service available to your computer through a telephone connection. CompuServe gives you access to databases, sample files, and question-and-answer forums concerning hundreds of topics and industries. CompuServe contains an Excel forum, a trouble-shooting service, and libraries of worksheets and macros.

The Excel and Microsoft Windows services are provided by Microsoft Corporation. To access the many Windows forums and libraries, type *GO MSOFT* at any menu prompt. To directly access the Excel forums and libraries, type *GO MSEXCEL* at any menu prompt. For information on how to use CompuServe, contact CompuServe directly.

Que Corporation

Que Corporation
11711 N. College Avenue
Carmel, IN 46032
317-573-2500
1-800-428-5331, outside Indiana

Que Corporation is the world-wide leader in computer book publishing. Other books available about Windows by Ron Person or Karen Rose include *Using Windows 3.1,* Special Edition; *Windows 3.1 QuickStart*; *and Using Word for Windows 2,* Special Edition. Call Que for a free catalog. Corporate and volume discounts are available.

Ron Person & Co.

Ron Person & Co.
P.O. Box 5647
Santa Rosa, CA 95402
415-989-7508
707-539-1525

Ron Person & Co., based in San Francisco, has attained Microsoft's high-est rating for Excel consultants, as a Microsoft Consulting Partner. The firm also is a Microsoft Registered Developer for Excel and Word for

Windows. The staff members deliver high-level training in Excel for macro developers and in the areas of finance and marketing. The company provides consulting and development work for corporations in the areas of finance, marketing and executive information systems.

Windows Applications

BrainCel

Promised Land Technologies, Inc.
900 Chapel Street, Suite 300
New Haven, CT 06510
203-562-7335

BrainCel gives Excel worksheets the pattern recognition and forecasting capabilities of neural network software. BrainCel is taught by using real data and real outcomes that you enter into Excel worksheets. After being learned, BrainCel can be used to predict outcomes based on raw data entered in the worksheet. BrainCel is useful for risk analysis, stock trading, and pattern recognition of data that is too difficult to analyze by using standard statistical methods.

CICERO

Micro Modeling Associates, Inc.
395 South End Ave., Suite 17F
New York, NY 10280
212-432-4245

CICERO retrieves data from business and financial databases, such as Lotus One Source U.S. Equities, and brings the data directly into Excel for analysis and reporting. CICERO contains built-in financial models, charts, and report templates.

Heizer Software

Heizer Software
1941 Oak Park Boulevard, Suite 30
P.O. Box 232019
Pleasant Hill, CA 94523
1-800-888-7667

Heizer Software distributes hundreds of Excel worksheets, templates, and macros designed for many different purposes and industries. You can use these products as they are, as a base for customization, or you can use them to learn tricks and techniques. Stock-market data and the tax template used in this book came from Heizer Software. Call for a free catalog.

OPTIONS XL

Montgomery Investment Group
George Montgomery
P.O. Box 508
Wayne, PA 19087-0508
215-688-2508

OPTIONS enables you to calculate option theoretical values, volatilities, and sensitivities in custom spreadsheets. You can use seven models for pricing options on equities, bonds, futures, and more. OPTIONS is compatible with many real-time quote services and uses custom financial functions and models written in high performance Dynamic Link Libraries.

Q+E

Pioneer Software
5540 Centerview Drive, Suite 324
Raleigh, NC 27606
919-859-2220

A version of Q+E comes free with Excel. Q+E is one of the best tools available for linking Excel to databases. Q+E can work as a separate Windows program through which you can directly query, edit, join, or build databases. Q+E also enables Windows programs, such as Excel and Word for Windows, to integrate with databases. Q+E supports dBASE, Excel, and text files, as well as Standard Query Language and DDE links. Pioneer Software also sells a Dynamic Link Library (DLL), which performs the same functions as Q+E but with better performance. Contact Pioneer Software for information regarding the DLL and drivers for additional databases.

@RISK

Palisades Corporation
31 Decker Road
New Field, NY 14867-9988
607-277-8000

@RISK adds risk analysis capabilities to your worksheets. Input values
can be defined as probability distributions for far better analysis
through what-if or sensitivity analysis. The distribution of outputs
for up to 1,000 points in the worksheet can be analyzed for each input
distribution.

Solver

Frontline Systems, Inc.
124 University Avenue, Suite 101
Palo Alto, CA 94301
415-329-6877

Frontline Systems, Inc., developed the Solver add-in for Excel. Contact
Frontline Systems for more advanced versions of Solver and for powerful
forecasting and decision support add-ins for Excel. Frontline Systems
maintains a computer bulletin board for developers; the bulletin board
contains information on advanced uses and automation of Solver and its
other products.

C

G

H

X–Y–Z

Computer Books from Que Mean PC Performance!

Spreadsheets

?-3 Beyond the Basics	$24.95
?-3 Database Techniques	$29.95
?-3 for DOS Release 2.3 Quick Reference	$ 9.95
?-3 for DOS Release 2.3 QuickStart	$19.95
?-3 for Windows Quick Reference	$ 9.95
?-3 for Windows QuickStart	$19.95
?-3 Graphics Techniques	$24.95
?-3 Macro Library, 3rd Edition	$39.95
?-3 Release 2.2 PC Tutor	$39.95
?-3 Release 2.2 QueCards	$19.95
?-3 Release 2.2 Workbook and Disk	$29.95
?-3 Release 3 Workbook and Disk	$29.95
?-3 Release 3.1 Quick Reference	$ 8.95
?-3 Release 3.1 + QuickStart, 2nd Edition	$19.95
?el for Windows Quick Reference	$ 9.95
?attro Pro Quick Reference	$ 8.95
?attro Pro 3 QuickStart	$19.95
?ing 1-2-3/G	$29.95
?ing 1-2-3 for DOS Release 2.3, Special Edition	$29.95
?ing 1-2-3 for Windows	$29.95
?ing 1-2-3 Release 3.1, + 2nd Edition	$29.95
?ing Excel 3 for Windows, Special Edition	$29.95
?ing Quattro Pro 3, Special Edition	$24.95
?ng SuperCalc5, 2nd Edition	$29.95

Databases

?ASE III Plus Handbook, 2nd Edition	$24.95
?ASE IV PC Tutor	$29.95
?ASE IV Programming Techniques	$29.95
?ASE IV Quick Reference	$ 8.95
?ASE IV 1.1 QuickStart	$19.95
?ASE IV Workbook and Disk	$29.95
?e's Using FoxPro	$29.95
?ng Clipper, 2nd Edition	$29.95
?ng DataEase	$24.95
?ng dBASE IV	$29.95
?ng ORACLE	$29.95
?ng Paradox 3	$24.95
?ng PC-File	$24.95
?ng R:BASE	$29.95

Business Applications

?ways Quick Reference	$ 8.95
?roduction to Business Software	$14.95
?roduction to Personal Computers	$19.95
?rton Utilities Quick Reference	$ 8.95
?Tools Quick Reference, 2nd Edition	$ 8.95
?A Quick Reference	$ 8.95
?e's Computer User's Dictionary, 2nd Edition	$10.95
?e's Using Enable	$29.95
?e's Wizard Book	$12.95
?cken Quick Reference	$ 8.95
?artWare Tips, Tricks, and Traps, ?nd Edition	$26.95
?ng DacEasy, 2nd Edition	$24.95
?ng Managing Your Money, 2nd Edition	$19.95
?ng Microsoft Works: IBM Version	$22.95
?ng Norton Utilities	$24.95
?ng PC Tools Deluxe	$24.95
?ng Peachtree	$27.95
?ng PROCOMM PLUS, 2nd Edition	$24.95
?ng Q&A 4	$27.95
?ng Quicken: IBM Version, 2nd Edition	$19.95
?ng SmartWare II	$29.95
?ng Symphony, Special Edition	$29.95
?ng TimeLine	$24.95
?ng TimeSlips	$24.95

CAD

AutoCAD Quick Reference	$ 8.95
Que's Using Generic CADD	$29.95
Using AutoCAD, 3rd Edition	$29.95
Using Generic CADD	$24.95

Word Processing

Microsoft Word Quick Reference	$ 9.95
Using LetterPerfect	$22.95
Using Microsoft Word 5.5: IBM Version, 2nd Edition	$24.95
Using MultiMate	$24.95
Using PC-Write	$22.95
Using Professional Write	$22.95
Using Word for Windows	$24.95
Using WordPerfect 5	$27.95
Using WordPerfect 5.1, Special Edition	$27.95
Using WordStar, 3rd Edition	$27.95
WordPerfect PC Tutor	$39.95
WordPerfect Power Pack	$39.95
WordPerfect 5 Workbook and Disk	$29.95
WordPerfect 5.1 QueCards	$19.95
WordPerfect 5.1 Quick Reference	$ 8.95
WordPerfect 5.1 QuickStart	$19.95
WordPerfect 5.1 Tips, Tricks, and Traps	$24.95
WordPerfect 5.1 Workbook and Disk	$29.95

Hardware/Systems

DOS Tips, Tricks, and Traps	$24.95
DOS Workbook and Disk, 2nd Edition	$29.95
Fastback Quick Reference	$ 8.95
Hard Disk Quick Reference	$ 8.95
MS-DOS PC Tutor	$39.95
MS-DOS 5 Quick Reference	$ 9.95
MS-DOS 5 QuickStart, 2nd Edition	$19.95
MS-DOS 5 User's Guide, Special Edition	$29.95
Networking Personal Computers, 3rd Edition	$24.95
Understanding UNIX: A Conceptual Guide, 2nd Edition	$21.95
Upgrading and Repairing PCs	$29.95
Using Microsoft Windows 3, 2nd Edition	$24.95
Using MS-DOS 5	$24.95
Using Novell NetWare	$29.95
Using OS/2	$29.95
Using PC DOS, 3rd Edition	$27.95
Using Prodigy	$19.95
Using UNIX	$29.95
Using Your Hard Disk	$29.95
Windows 3 Quick Reference	$ 8.95

Desktop Publishing/Graphics

CorelDRAW! Quick Reference	$ 8.95
Harvard Graphics Quick Reference	$ 8.95
Que's Using Ventura Publisher	$29.95
Using Animator	$24.95
Using DrawPerfect	$24.95
Using Harvard Graphics, 2nd Edition	$24.95
Using Freelance Plus	$24.95
Using PageMaker 4 for Windows	$29.95
Using PFS: First Publisher, 2nd Edition	$24.95
Using PowerPoint	$24.95
Using Publish It!	$24.95

Macintosh/Apple II

The Big Mac Book, 2nd Edition	$29.95
The Little Mac Book	$12.95
Que's Macintosh Multimedia Handbook	$24.95
Using AppleWorks, 3rd Edition	$24.95
Using Excel 3 for the Macintosh	$24.95
Using FileMaker	$24.95
Using MacDraw	$24.95
Using MacroMind Director	$29.95
Using MacWrite	$24.95
Using Microsoft Word 4: Macintosh Version	$24.95
Using Microsoft Works: Macintosh Version, 2nd Edition	$24.95
Using PageMaker: Macintosh Version, 2nd Edition	$24.95

Programming/Technical

C Programmer'sToolkit	$39.95
DOS Programmer's Reference, 2nd Edition	$29.95
Network Programming in C	$49.95
Oracle Programmer's Guide	$29.95
QuickC Programmer's Guide	$29.95
UNIX Programmer's Quick Reference	$ 8.95
UNIX Programmer's Reference	$29.95
UNIX Shell Commands Quick Reference	$ 8.95
Using Assembly Language, 2nd Edition	$29.95
Using BASIC	$24.95
Using Borland C++	$29.95
Using C	$29.95
Using QuickBASIC 4	$24.95
Using Turbo Pascal	$29.95

For More Information, Call Toll Free!
1-800-428-5331

*All prices and titles subject to change without notice.
Non-U.S. prices may be higher. Printed in the U.S.A.*

Teach Yourself
With QuickStarts From Que!

The ideal tutorials for beginners, Que's QuickStart books use graphic illustrations and step-by-step instructions to get you up and running fast. Packed with examples, QuickStarts are the perfect beginner's guides to your favorite software applications.

1-2-3 for DOS Release 2.3 QuickStart
Release 2.3

$19.95 USA
0-88022-716-8, 500 pp., 7 3/8 x 9 1/4

1-2-3 for Windows QuickStart
1-2-3 for Windows

$19.95 USA
0-88022-723-0, 500 pp., 7 3/8 x 9 1/4

1-2-3 Release 3.1 + QuickStart, 2nd Edition
Releases 3 & 3.1

$19.95 USA
0-88022-613-7, 569 pp., 7 3/8 x 9 1/4

dBASE IV 1.1 QuickStart,
Through Version 1.1

$19.95 USA
0-88022-614-5, 400 pp., 7 3/8 x 9 1/4

Excel 3 for Windows QuickStart
Version 3 fo rWindows

$19.95 USA
0-88022-762-1, 500 pp., 7 3/8 x 9 1/4

MS-DOS QuickStart, 2nd Edition
Version 3.X & 4.X

$19.95 USA
0-88022-611-0, 420 pp., 7 3/8 x 9 1/4

Q&A 4 QuickStart
Versions 3 & 4

$19.95 USA
0-88022-653-6, 400 pp., 7 3/8 x 9 1/4

Quattro Pro 3 QuickStart
Through Version 3.0

$19.95 USA
0-88022-693-5, 450 pp., 7 3/8 x 9 1/4

WordPerfect 5.1 QuickStart
WordPerfect 5.1

$19.95 USA
0-88022-558-0, 427 pp., 7 3/8 x 9 1/4

Windows 3 QuickStart
Ron Person & Karen Rose

This graphics-based text teaches Windows beginners how to use the feature-packed Windows environment. Emphasizes such software applications as Excel, Word, and PageMaker and shows how to master Windows' mouse, menus, and screen elements.

Version 3

$19.95 USA
0-88022-610-2, 440 pp., 7 3/8 x 9 1/4

MS-DOS 5 QuickStart
Que Development Group

This is the easy-to-use graphic approach to learning MS-DOS 5. The combination of step-by-step instruction, examples, and graphics make this book ideal for all DOS beginners.

DOS 5

$19.95 USA
0-88022-681-1, 420 pp., 7 3/8 x 9 1/4

To Order, Call:
(800) 428-5331 OR (317) 573-2500

Find It Fast With Que's Quick References!

Que's Quick References are the compact, easy-to-use guides to essential application information. Written for all users, Quick References include vital command information under easy-to-find alphabetical listings. Quick References are a must for anyone who needs command information fast!

Free Catalog!

Mail us this registration form today, and we'll send you a free catalog featuring Que's complete line of best-selling books.

Name of Book _____

Name _____

Title _____

Phone (___) _____

Company _____

Address _____

City _____

State _____ ZIP _____

Please check the appropriate answers:

1. Where did you buy your Que book?
   - ☐ Bookstore (name: _____)
   - ☐ Computer store (name: _____)
   - ☐ Catalog (name: _____)
   - ☐ Direct from Que
   - ☐ Other: _____

2. How many computer books do you buy a year?
   - ☐ 1 or less
   - ☐ 2-5
   - ☐ 6-10
   - ☐ More than 10

3. How many Que books do you own?
   - ☐ 1
   - ☐ 2-5
   - ☐ 6-10
   - ☐ More than 10

4. How long have you been using this software?
   - ☐ Less than 6 months
   - ☐ 6 months to 1 year
   - ☐ 1-3 years
   - ☐ More than 3 years

5. What influenced your purchase of this Que book?
   - ☐ Personal recommendation
   - ☐ Advertisement
   - ☐ In-store display
   - ☐ Price
   - ☐ Que catalog
   - ☐ Que mailing
   - ☐ Que's reputation
   - ☐ Other: _____

6. How would you rate the overall content of the book?
   - ☐ Very good
   - ☐ Good
   - ☐ Satisfactory
   - ☐ Poor

7. What do you like *best* about this Que book?

   _____
   _____

8. What do you like *least* about this Que book?

   _____
   _____

9. Did you buy this book with your personal funds?
   - ☐ Yes   ☐ No

10. Please feel free to list any other comments you may have about this Que book.

    _____
    _____
    _____

— QUE —

Order Your Que Books Today!

Name _____

Title _____

Company _____

City _____

State _____ ZIP _____

Phone No. (___) _____

Method of Payment:

Check ☐   (Please enclose in envelope.)

Charge My: VISA ☐   MasterCard ☐

American Express ☐

Charge # _____

Expiration Date _____

Order No.	Title	Qty.	Price	Total

You can **FAX** your order to **1-317-573-2583**. Or call **1-800-428-5331, ext. ORDR** to order direct.
Please add $2.50 per title for shipping and handling.

Subtotal _____

Shipping & Handling _____

Total _____

— QUE —

BUSINESS REPLY MAIL
First Class Permit No. 9918   Indianapolis, IN

Postage will be paid by addressee

11711 N. College
Carmel, IN 46032

BUSINESS REPLY MAIL
First Class Permit No. 9918   Indianapolis, IN

Postage will be paid by addressee

11711 N. College
Carmel, IN 46032

To use this reference card, look in the left-hand column(s) for the operation or task that you want to perform. The right-hand column(s) indicate the command to execute or action to take to perform the task. On this card, as throughout this book, the functional letter to press is shown in bold. Hold down the Shift key to use symbols located on number keys. To select toolbar items, click on the tool.

Operating Guidelines

Mouse Guidelines

Action	Method
Click	Move pointer tip to item; press and release button
Double-click	Point to item; click twice rapidly
Drag	Move pointer to item; hold down button while moving pointer; release button at end of drag

Menu Guidelines

Menu Operation	Keyboard	Mouse
Activate menu	Alt or F10	Click on menu name
Select menu	Underlined letter	Click on menu name
Choose menu command	Underlined letter	Click on command name
Back out of menu	Esc	Click on menu name

Dialog Boxes

Operation	Keyboard	Mouse
Select text	Alt+letter	Click on item or list box
Open pull-down box list	Alt+letter, Alt+down arrow	Click on down arrow
Move between items next/previous	Tab/Shift+Tab	Click on item
Select/clear check box	Space bar	Click on item
Scroll in list box	Up or down arrow	Click on scroll arrows
Complete command	Enter	Click OK button
Back out of box	Esc	Click Cancel button

Help

Item	Shortcut
Help Contents window	F1
Help in dialog boxes	F1
Help when choosing a command	Shift+F1, choose command

Keyboard Shortcuts

Selecting Worksheet Areas

Item/Area Selected	Shortcut
Beginning of row	Home
Cell A1	Ctrl+Home
Last used cell	Ctrl+End
Select row	Shift+space bar
Select column	Ctrl+space bar
Entire worksheet	Shift+Ctrl+space
Show active cell	Ctrl+Backspace
Show selection corners	Ctrl+. (period)
Go to cell or reference	F5
Notes	Ctrl+?
Cells	Shift+movement
To edge of data	Shift+Ctrl+arrow
Block of data	Ctrl+*
Current array	Ctrl+/
Row differences	Ctrl+\
Column differences	Ctrl+l
Immediately dependent formulas	Ctrl+]
All dependent formulas	Ctrl+}
Immediately preceding formulas	Ctrl+[
All preceding formulas	Ctrl+{

Selecting Chart Items

Operation	Shortcut
Next/Previous chart item	Right/left arrow
Next/Previous chart class	Down/up arrow

Data and Formula Entry

Operation	Shortcut
Absolute/Relative reference	F4
Activate AutoSum button	Alt+=
Clear cell, activate Formula Bar	Backspace
Display current date	Ctrl+;
Display current time	Ctrl+:
Copy formula from cell above (without reference adjustment)	Ctrl+'
Copy value from cell above	Ctrl+"
Fill selected cells with entry	Ctrl+Enter
Fill selected cells with array	Shift+Ctrl+Enter
Insert paragraph in formula	Alt+Enter
Insert tab in formula	Ctrl+Tab

Data Edit

Operation	Shortcut
Display formulas in sheet	Ctrl+` (on ~ key)
Activate Formula Bar	F2
Repeat last action	Alt+Enter

Control Windows

Operation	Shortcut
Move window	Drag on Title Bar
Close window or application	Double-click in Control menu icon
Change row or column height	Drag on line separating headers
Maximize window	Click on up-arrow icon (top right)
Minimize to icon	Click on down-arrow icon (top right)
Restore into window	Click on two-headed arrow icon (top right)
	Double-click on Excel icon
Size window	Drag on edge or corner
Split document window	Drag black bar at end of scroll bar
Smooth scroll through window	Click on arrow in scroll bar
Scroll by page through window	Click in gray area of scroll bar
Scroll long distance	Drag square in scroll bar

Tool Bar Shortcuts

Operation	Shortcut
Display tool name	Hold click on tool in Status Bar
Display toolbar	Right-click on toolbar background shortcut menu
Add tools	Display shortcut menu, choose Customize, drag tools on or off toolbar

Function Keys

If your computer has only ten function keys, you can use the following combinations:

Alt+F1 for F11
Alt+F2 for F12

Key	Function
F1	Help
Shift+F1	Context Help
F2	**A**ctivate Formula Bar
Shift+F2	Formula **N**ote
Ctrl+F2	**W**indow **S**how Info
F3	Formula **P**aste Name
Shift+F3	Formula Paste Function
Ctrl+F3	Formula **D**efine Name
Ctrl+Shift+F3	Formula **C**reate Names
F4	Formula **R**eference
Ctrl+F4	Control **C**lose (document window)
Alt+F4	**F**ile **E**xit (close Excel)
F5	Formula **G**oto
Shift+F5	Formula **F**ind (cell contents)
Ctrl+F5	Control **R**estore (document window)
F6	Next pane
Shift+F6	Previous pane
Ctrl+F6	Next document window
Ctrl+Shift+F6	Previous document window
F7	Formula **F**ind (next)
Shift+F7	Formula **F**ind (previous)
Ctrl+F7	Control **M**ove (document window)
F8	Extend mode (on/off)
Shift+F8	Add mode (on/off)
Ctrl+F8	Control **S**ize (document window)
F9	**O**ptions Calculation, Calc **N**ow button
Shift+F9 button	**O**ptions Calculation, Calc Document
F10	Activate menu bar
Shift+F10	Activate shortcut menu
Ctrl+F10	Control Ma**x**imize (document window)
F11	**F**ile **N**ew (chart)
Shift+F11	**F**ile **N**ew (worksheet)
Ctrl+F11	**F**ile **N**ew (macro sheet)
F12	**F**ile Save **A**s
Shift+F12	**F**ile **S**ave
Ctrl+F12	**F**ile **O**pen
Ctrl+Shift+F12	**F**ile **P**rint

Mouse Shortcuts

Worksheet

Operation	Mouse Action
Display cell note	Double-click
Display linked cells	Double-click (when no notes in cell)
Select array	Shift+Ctrl+double-click
Copy cell contents	Drag fill handle
Create series	Select two cells, drag fill handle

Objects

Operation	Shortcut
Activate embedded object	Double-click
Select object	Click
Select object without macro	Ctrl+click
Move object	Drag center
Resize object	Drag black handle

Select multiple objects	Shift+click
Draw object or freehand	Click on tool, drag
Draw polygon	Click on tool, click at corners
Reshape freehand lines	Select drawing, click on Reshape tool, drag handle
Draw multiple items	Ctrl+click on tool, drag
Draw circle/square	Click on tool, Shift+drag

Chart

Operation	Shortcut
Create chart	Select data, click on ChartWizard tool
Move top of chart marker	Ctrl+click, drag marker top (line, bar, col. markers)
Activate chart in worksheet	Double-click on embedded chart
Add floating text to chart	Deselect any text, type, Enter
Format object	Double-click on object

Standard Toolbar

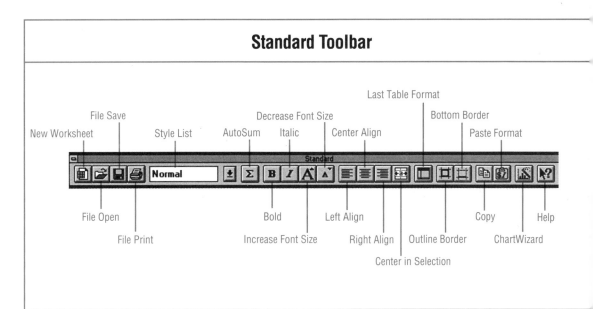

Undo last action	Ctrl+Z
Insert cells	Ctrl++
Delete cells	Ctrl+_
Insert selected row/col	Ctrl++
Delete selected row/col	Ctrl+_
Display/clear dialog box	Del
Clear only formulas	Ctrl+Del
Cut	Ctrl+X
Copy	Ctrl+C
Paste	Ctrl+V
Fill right	Ctrl+R
Fill down	Ctrl+D
Select in Formula Bar	Shift+arrow
Move by word in Formula Bar	Ctrl+arrow
Select words in Formula Bar	Shift+Ctrl+arrow
Select to end of Formula Bar	Shift+End

Formatting

Number

Format	Shortcut
General	Ctrl+~
#,##0.00	Ctrl+!
$#,##0.00_);($#,##0.00)	Ctrl+$
0%	Ctrl+%
0.00E+00	Ctrl+^
d-mmm-yy	Ctrl+#
h:mm AM/PM	Ctrl+@

Font

Font Characteristic	Shortcut
Select Style box	Ctrl+S
Normal font	Ctrl+1
Bold on/off	Ctrl+B
Italic on/off	Ctrl+I
Underline on/off	Ctrl+U
Strikeout on/off	Ctrl+S

Row Height

Operation	Shortcut
Hide rows	Ctrl+9
Unhide rows	Ctrl+Shift+9

Column Width

Operation	Shortcut
Hide columns	Ctrl+0
Unhide selected columns	Ctrl+Shift+0

Border

Operation	Shortcut
Create border outline	Ctrl+&
Remove border	Ctrl+_

Outlining

Operation	Shortcut
Promote	Alt+Shift+left arrow
Demote	Alt+Shift+right arrow
Turn outline symbols on/off	Ctrl+8

Switching Windows

Applications

Switch To	Shortcut
Next application	Alt+Tab
Task List	Ctrl+Esc

Documents

Operation	Shortcut
Activate Document Control menu	Alt+ - (hyphen)
Control Close	Ctrl+F4
Control Restore	Ctrl+F5
Control Next Window	Ctrl+F6
Control Move	Ctrl+F7
Control Size	Ctrl+F8
Control Minimize	Ctrl+F9
Control Maximize	Ctrl+F10

Workbooks

Operation	Shortcut
Next window	Alt+Page Up
Previous window	Alt+Page Down